Contents

Festivals insert following p.144

◀◀ Bondi Beach surfer mural ◀ Sydney Harbour at dusk from the north shore

Introduction to Sydney

It might seem surprising that Sydney, established in 1788, is not Australia's capital. Despite the creation of Canberra in 1927 – intended to stem the intense rivalry between Sydney and Melbourne – many Sydneysiders still view their city as the true capital of Australia, and certainly in many ways it feels like it. The city has a tangible sense of history in the old stone walls and well-worn steps in the backstreets around The Rocks, while the sandstone cliffs, rocks and caves among the bushlined harbour still contain Aboriginal rock carvings, evocative reminders of a more ancient past.

Flying into Sydney provides a thrilling close-up snapshot of the city as you swoop alongside cliffs and golden beaches, revealing toy-sized images of the Harbour Bridge and the Opera House tilting in a glittering expanse of blue water. Towards Mascot Airport the red-tiled roofs of suburban bungalows stretch ever southwards, blue squares of swimming pools shimmering from grassy back yards. The night views are as spectacular, with skyscrapers topped by colourful neon lights and the illuminated white shells of the Opera House reflecting on the dark water as ferries crisscross to Circular Quay.

Sydney has all the vigour of a **world-class city**, and a population approaching five million people; yet on the ground you'll find it still possesses a seductive, small-town, easy-going charm. The furious **development** for the 2000 Olympics, heralded as being Sydney's coming-of-age ceremony, alarmed many locals, who loved their city the way it was. But the development brought a greatly improved transport infrastructure, and the $200 million budget improved and beautified the city streets and parks and

The **Rough Guide** to

Sydney

written and researched by

Margo Daly

with additional contributions by

Neal Drinnan, Ann Mercer,
Tania Paschen and Michael Schofield

NEW YORK • LONDON • DELHI

www.roughguides.com

resulted in a rash of luxury hotels and apartments which are still multiplying, often contentiously, along the beloved harbour foreshore. The city's **setting** is one that perhaps only Rio de Janeiro can rival: the water is what makes it so special, and no introduction to Sydney would be complete without paying tribute to one of the world's great harbours: Port Jackson.

▲ Sydney Opera House

Sydney is in many ways a microcosm of Australia as a whole – if only in its ability to defy your expectations and prejudices as often as it confirms them. A thrusting, high-rise commercial centre in the **Central Business District (CBD)**, a high-profile gay community in **Darlinghurst**, inner-city deprivation of unexpected harshness, with the highest Aboriginal population of any Australian city, and the dreary traffic-fumed and flat suburban sprawl of the **western suburbs**, are as much part of the scene as the beaches, the bodies, the sparkling harbour, the booming real estate and the world-class restaurant scene. The sophistication, cosmopolitan population and exuberant nightlife of Sydney are a long way from the Outback, and yet fires are a constant threat to the bush-surrounded city.

> **The city's setting is one that perhaps only Rio de Janeiro can rival**

Sydney seems to have the best of both worlds – if it's seen at its gleaming best from the deck of a harbour ferry, especially at weekends when the harbour fills with a flotilla of small vessels, racing yachts and cabin cruisers, it's at its most varied in its **neighbourhoods**, with their lively café and restaurant scenes. Getting away from the city centre and exploring them is an essential part of Sydney's pleasures. A short ferry trip across to the leafy and affluent North Shore allows access to tracts of largely intact bushland, with bushwalking and native animals and birds right on the doorstep. In the summer the city's sweltering offices are abandoned for the remarkably unspoilt ocean and harbour **beaches** strung around the eastern and northern suburbs, and day-trips outside the city offer a taste of virtually everything you'll find in the rest of Australia.

What to see

Port Jackson, more commonly known as **Sydney Harbour**, carves Sydney in two halves, linked only by the **Sydney Harbour Bridge** and Harbour Tunnel. The south shore is the hub of activity, and it's here that you'll find the **city centre** and most of the things to see

A Saturday in Sydney

The aim is to get to the Saturday Balmain Market at least an hour or two before it closes at 4pm. Begin early with a visit to the **Fish Markets** (see p.95) at **Pyrmont** – open to the public from 7am, or come for breakfast at the *Fish Market Café* from 5am – then stroll ten minutes to the free-entry **National Maritime Museum** (see p.93) at **Darling Harbour** which opens at 9.30am. Cross Pyrmont Bridge to the brilliant **Sydney Aquarium** (see p.93), worth spending a couple of hours in, before hopping next door to King St Wharf to catch a ferry to Balmain West Wharf (Elliot St). Nearby, Elkington Park on the Parramatta River is the site of one of Sydney's most atmospheric swimming spots, **Dawn Fraser Pool** (see p.119). Wander down Darling Street and head past shops and cafés to the tree-shaded grounds of St Andrew's Church to check out the handmade, home-made and secondhand items for sale at **Balmain Market** (see p.119); don't forget to sample something from the diverse food stalls in the church hall too. Afterwards, retrace Darling Street west and along Beattie Street for a drink at the classic Balmain boozer the *Exchange Hotel*, or any of the other lively backstreet pubs on a Saturday afternoon. By nightfall, catch the #442 or #445 bus from Darling Street to Balmain East Wharf (Darling St) for the ferry to Circular Quay, which glides underneath the **Harbour Bridge**. Make sure you stand outside to make the most of the views of the lit-up city skyline and the iconic clown's face at **Luna Park** (see p.128), beside Milsons Point Wharf, where you can stop off (the amusement park closes at 11pm, the adjacent heated **North Sydney Olympic Pool** at 7pm). From Circular Quay, catch bus #380 to **Oxford Street, Darlinghurst** (see p.101) and have a drink at the lively gay bars the *Stonewall* or the *Columbian*, or head for **Victoria Street** to the ever-popular pubs at the *Green Park Hotel* or the *Darlo Bar*. Continue to Darlinghurst Road in **Kings Cross** (see p.106) to follow the traditional weekend crawl past stripclub exteriors and then down the McElhone Stairs (off Victoria St) to **Woolloomooloo** (see p.109) for more good pubs and a late-night pie at *Harry's Cafe de Wheels*.

▲ Luna Park

and do. Many of the classic images of Sydney are within sight of **Circular Quay**, making this busy waterfront area on Sydney Cove a good point to start discovering the city, with the Opera House and the expanse of the Royal Botanic Gardens to the east of Sydney Cove. It's also near the historic area of **The Rocks** to the west, and prominent museums and art galleries. From Circular Quay south as far as King Street is the **CBD**, with pedestrianized Martin Place at its centre. Just east of Martin Place, **Macquarie Street** is Sydney's civic streetscape, lined with fine colonial sandstone buildings including the New South Wales Parliament House. Beyond Macquarie Street the open space of **The Domain** stretches to the Art Gallery of New South Wales. To the south of The Domain, **Hyde Park** is very much the formal city park, overlooked by churches and the Australian Museum, and with a solemn war memorial.

Park Street divides Hyde Park into two; heading west along it you reach the ornate town hall, around which Sydney's shopping heart is focused, including the glorious **Queen Victoria Building**. Watching over it all is the Sydney Tower, with 360-degree views from the top. The city's two main thoroughfares of George and Pitt streets stretch downtown to the increasingly down-at-heel Central Station and the area known as **Haymarket**, where a vibrant Chinatown sits beside the entertainment area of **Darling Harbour**, with its major museums and attractions.

East of the city centre, following William Street uphill past Hyde Park, is **Kings Cross**, Sydney's red-light district and major travellers' centre, full of accommodation, strip joints and late-night cafés. The adjacent waterfront area of **Woolloomooloo** is home to a busy naval dockyard and some lively pubs. North and east of "the Cross" you move gradually upmarket, with the **eastern suburbs** stretching along the harbour to Watsons Bay, meeting the open sea at South Head. Running south from the head are

▲ Wooloomooloo

A walking tour of the centre

This five-kilometre walking tour from the city centre to Circular Quay takes in history, architecture, culture, nature and shopping – and there's even time for a swim. Start with a spot of window-shopping at the grand **Queen Victoria Building** (see p.84; Town Hall Station), then head up Market Street past the Art Deco State Theatre – with a possible detour into the David Jones Food Hall for gourmet supplies – into **Hyde Park** (see p.86). Check out the giant chessboard here and the Archibald Fountain, before heading out of the park past St James' Church along Macquarie Street. Spend an hour or two soaking up convict history at **Hyde Park Barracks** (see p.77), and take a free peek into **NSW Parliament House** (see p.76) and the Mitchell wing of the **State Library** (see p.76). Then stroll back along Macquarie Street to Sydney Hospital, where you can take a short cut through to The Domain and the free **Art Gallery of NSW** (see p.78). If the weather's fine, you might fancy a dip at **Andrew "Boy" Charlton pool** (Oct–April; see p.79), before continuing on to **Mrs Macquaries Chair** (see p.79) to take in the harbour views. Then take a wander through the nearby **Botanical Gardens** (see p.73) until chucking-out time at dusk, when the possums start frolicking and the fruitbats fly overhead. Afterwards, enjoy a drink and affordable meal at the outside bar at the **Sydney Opera House** (see p.69) or take in a performance or a film at the nearby Dendy Opera Quays **cinema** (see p.229). End the day by strolling along the lively Opera Quays promenade with its al fresco bars and cafés to **Circular Quay**, where you can catch a bus, train or ferry back to your hotel.

the popular and populous **eastern beaches**, from Bondi through Coogee to Maroubra ending at La Perouse and the expanse of Botany Bay. Further south brings you to surf territory at Cronulla and the **Royal National Park** across Port Hacking, and a stunning coastal drive down the south coast to Thirroul. Inland from here, the **Southern Highlands** are covered with yet more national parks, punctuated by pleasing little towns such as Bundanoon and Berrima.

From the southeast corner of Hyde Park, Oxford Street steams through the gay, restaurant, club and bar strip of **Darlinghurst**, becoming increasingly upmarket through gentrified **Paddington**, which has Centennial Park as its playground. South of Oxford Street, opposite Paddington, **Surry Hills** is another up-and-coming area, with plenty of action on Crown Street. The

▲ Wylie's Baths, Coogee

▲ Cliffs on the Bondi to Bronte walk

nearby Sydney Cricket Ground and Fox Studios are twin focal points at Moore Park. On the western side of Surry Hills lies Central Station; heading west brings you to Sydney University, surrounded by the café-packed and youthful areas of **Newtown** and **Glebe**. West of Glebe, ugly Parramatta Road heads to Italian-dominated **Leichhardt** and **Haberfield** while the nearby harbour suburb of **Balmain**, once a working-class dock area, has long gone upmarket, but its big old pubs still make for a great pub crawl. Further west, **Sydney Olympic Park** at Homebush Bay, the focus of the 2000 Olympics, is Sydney's geographical heart, and beyond the great sprawl of the western suburbs, the World Heritage-listed **Blue Mountains** offer tea rooms, scenic viewpoints and isolated bushwalking.

Sydney is in many ways a microcosm of Australia as a whole

The bushclad **North Shore** of the harbour is very much where the old money is. There are some wonderful spots to reach by ferry, from Taronga Zoo to Manly. North of Manly the **northern beaches** stretch up to glamorous **Palm Beach**, which looks across to several national parks, including **Ku-Ring-Gai Chase**. Flowing towards Pittwater and Broken Bay is the sandstone-lined **Hawkesbury River**, lined with historic colonial towns. North of here, the **Central Coast** is a weekend beach playground for Sydneysiders, while inland to the northwest is the **Hunter Valley**, Australia's oldest and possibly best-known wine-growing region, set among idyllic pastoral scenery.

When to go

Since Sydney has such wonderful beaches, the best time to come is between early October and Easter, the official swimming season, when the beaches are patrolled, and outdoor swimming pools open.

The sunny **springtime** months of September and October are when the wild flowers are in bloom, and the smell of blossoms such as jasmine fill the warming city streets. The sweltering hot **summer months** are mid-December, January and February; Christmas can often see 40°C in the shade, though it's been known to be cool and overcast; average summer temperatures are 25°C. Sydney is subtropical, with high and very oppressive humidity in summer building up to sporadic torrential rainstorms (dubbed "southerly busters" by the locals). This is party time, combining high summer with Christmas and New Year festivities, as well as the city's many other festivals and events (see "Sydney Festivals" colour section).

April, when the Royal Agricultural Show hits town, is the rainiest month. May is a contrastingly glorious time when you can bet on dry sunny weather and blue skies as Sydney heads for its mild **winter months** of June, July and August. Don't expect bare trees and grey skies – native trees are evergreen and the skies are usually just a less intense blue. Temperatures are rarely less than 10°C, but colder during the night, and decidedly chilly the further west you go, with frost on the plains heading to the Blue Mountains – where there are rare light snowfalls. Bring a coat, scarf, gloves and woolly hat if you want to go to the mountains in winter; it can get cool at night in summer too. A jumper and jacket should keep you warm enough in the city, where the cafés continue with their outdoor seating, with braziers to radiate heat.

	Jan	Feb	Mar	Apr	May	Jun	Jul	Aug	Sep	Oct	Nov	Dec
Max. temp. (°F)	78	78	76	71	66	61	60	63	67	71	74	77
Min. temp. (°F)	65	65	63	58	52	48	46	48	51	56	60	63
Max. temp. (°C)	26	26	24	22	19	19	16	17	19	22	23	25
Min. temp. (°C°)	18	18	17	14	11	9	8	9	11	13	16	17
Rainfall (inches)	3.5	4.0	5.0	5.3	5.0	4.6	4.6	3.0	2.9	2.8	2.9	2.9
Rainfall (mm)	89	102	127	135	127	117	117	76	74	71	74	74

19 things not to miss

It's not possible to see everything Sydney has to offer on a short trip – and we don't suggest you try. What follows is a selective taste of the city's highlights: outstanding museums and restaurants, beautiful beaches, exciting festivals and fantastic excursions beyond the city – all arranged in colour-coded categories to help you find the very best things to see and experience. All entries have a page reference to take you straight into the guide, where you can find out more.

01 Royal Botanical Gardens Page **73** • A picnic in the beautiful Botanical Gardens, with spectacular views of the city and harbour, is a real treat.

02 Blue Mountains Page **306** • The World Heritage-listed Blue Mountains make a great weekend break from Sydney.

03 Shopping Page **248** • From stately nineteenth-century arcades such as The Strand, to cutting-edge Australian designers like Sass & Bide (pictured) and surfwear shops at Bondi, the shopping opportunities are endless.

04 The Hawkesbury River Page **289** • Admire the magnificent sandstone cliffs of the Hawkesbury River on a leisurely cruise.

05 Taronga Zoo Page **132** • With a superb hilltop position overlooking the city, surrounded by natural bush, this is a fantastic spot to see Australian critters as well as those from further afield.

06 Paddington Page **103** • With its gorgeous colonial-style houses, Paddington is best explored on Saturday, when the famous market is in full swing.

07 Oxford Street Page **101** • Crammed with bars, clubs, restaurants, shops and cinemas, Oxford Street is worth a visit, especially at night.

08 The Rocks Page **59** • The heart of historic Sydney, The Rocks also offers great shopping and interesting pubs.

09 Climbing Sydney Harbour Bridge Page **59** • Climb the famous coathanger for great harbour views, or save your money and walk across for free.

10 Eating Page **183** • Sydney's eating scene is ever evolving but celebrity chefs such as Bill Granger, Luke Mangan, Tetsuya Wakuda, Kylie Kwong and Neil Perry deserve the gongs. From the simplicity of Granger's *bills* (pictured below) to the glamour of Perry's *Rockpool*, try them out if you can.

11 Bondi Beach Page **136** • One of the best-known beaches in the world, big, brash Bondi is synonymous with Australian beach culture.

12 Opera House performance Page **69** • Admire the stunning exterior of this Australian icon, or, better still, take in a performance.

13 Hunter Valley wineries Page **297** • One of Australia's most famous wine-growing regions.

14 Art Gallery of New South Wales Page **78** • A vast collection of Australian and European art in an imposing Neoclassical building.

15 Sydney pubs Page **206** • From ultra-chic designer bars to historic watering holes, there's a wealth of places for a great night out in Sydney.

16 Swimming in a seapool (Bronte Baths) Page **275** • If you'd rather not brave the waves, try swimming in a seaside pool instead.

17 Fish Market Page **95** • Offering an enormous variety of fish, this frenetic early-morning market is a real spectacle – with opportunities for a waterside picnic too.

18 Gay & Lesbian Mardi Gras Page **233** • The biggest celebration of gay and lesbian culture in the world.

19 Manly Page **145** • The ferry trip out to Manly, a lively beach suburb, with its unbeatable views of the harbour, is a must.

Basics

Basics

Getting there

You can fly to Sydney pretty much every day from Europe, North America and Southeast Asia. Air fares depend on the season, with the highest being the two weeks either side of Christmas, although you can get a low-season bargain if you fly on Christmas Day itself. Fares drop during the "shoulder" seasons – mid-January to March and mid-August to November – and you'll get the best prices during the low season, April to August. Because of the distance from most popular departure points, flying at weekends does not alter the price.

However, you can certainly cut costs by going through a **specialist flight agent** – either a consolidator, who buys up blocks of tickets from the airlines and sells them at a discount, or a **discount agent**, who in addition to dealing with discounted flights may also offer special student and youth fares and a range of other travel-related services such as travel insurance, rail passes, car rental, tours and the like. Some agents specialize in **charter flights**, which may be cheaper than anything available on a scheduled flight, but again departure dates are fixed and withdrawal penalties are high. One possibility is to see if you can arrange a courier flight, although you'll need a flexible schedule, and preferably be travelling alone with very little luggage. In return for shepherding a parcel through customs, you can expect to get a deeply discounted ticket. You'll probably also be restricted in the duration of your stay.

If Sydney is only one stop on a longer journey, you might want to consider buying a **Round-the-World** (RTW) ticket. Some travel agents can sell you an "off-the-shelf" ticket that will have you touching down in about half a dozen cities – Sydney is frequently part of the regular eastbound RTW loop from Europe. Figure on £850/US$1500 for a RTW ticket including Australia.

Many airlines and discount travel websites offer you the opportunity to book your tickets **online**, cutting out the costs of agents and middlemen. Good deals can often be found through discount or auction sites, as well as through the airlines' own websites.

From Britain and Ireland

The market for flights between Britain and Australia is one of the most competitive in the world and prices have remained low. Qantas, British Airways, Singapore and Malaysia Airlines all offer **direct flights** to Sydney in 21–23 hours. Other airlines may involve a change of plane for connecting flights, and potentially long waits in between, which can make the journey last up to 36 hours. However, it often costs no more to break the journey in such **stopover** points as Southeast Asia, New Zealand or North America, or even Argentina, South Africa or Japan, so that it need not be a tedious, seat-bound slog. Some airlines have great **special deals** as well that include discounted or free flights en route or in Australia itself. All direct scheduled flights to Australia depart from London's two main airports, Gatwick and Heathrow, though Singapore Airlines has daily flights from Manchester to Singapore that connect with onward flights to Sydney. There are no direct flights from Ireland.

Fares and flights

Most of the discount and specialist agents listed on p.21 can quote fares on scheduled flights. For the latest prices and special deals, check out the ads in the travel pages of the weekend newspapers, London's listing magazine *Time Out,* the free listings magazine *TNT*, but especially the **websites** of travel agents and the airlines themselves for "online specials" available via Internet auctions; also check out the discount travel websites listed on p.21.

However, **booking ahead** as far as possible is still the best way to secure the most reasonable prices, and unless it's an Internet special, it is almost invariably cheaper to buy tickets through **agents** rather than through airlines themselves.

High season differs slightly from airline to airline, but the most expensive time to travel to Sydney is always the two weeks before **Christmas** until mid-January. **Shoulder seasons** are mid-January to March and mid-August, to November, while the **low season** runs from April to the middle of August, with prices rising a little and reduced availability from the beginning of July to the middle of August, coinciding with the peak European holiday times.

Return **fares** to Sydney for a non-direct flight on one of the less prestigious airlines can start as low as £550 in the low season, with special offers occasionally dropping the price to around £450. Off-peak return fares for a direct flight on one of the better airlines such as Qantas, BA or Singapore Airlines usually start at around £800, but can drop as low as £600. In the two weeks before Christmas, all the airlines have similar rates: you can find fares for £800 but these sell fast and you would be lucky to find anything for less than £1000 return. However, if you don't mind flying on Christmas Day itself you may find a much cheaper deal. To stand a chance of getting one of the cheaper peak-season tickets, book at least six months in advance. In the shoulder seasons, you should expect to pay at least £700 (or around £950 with a prestigious airline).

Between mid-November and February, Thomsonfly offers once-weekly direct **charter flights** from London Gatwick to Sydney, with fares from £499 from mid-November to early December, rising to £899 and £999 in the two weeks before Christmas and dropping down to £649 after Christmas. The cheaper prices come with restrictions including limited departure dates and options of minimum ten-day, maximum 31-day stay. There are pricier Business Class tickets (from £1149); bookings are through Austravel (see opposite).

With Qantas you can fly from **regional airports** at Aberdeen, Belfast, Edinburgh, Glasgow, Manchester or Newcastle to connect with your international flight at Heathrow. There is no extra charge from Manchester, but you'll pay a small **supplement** from the others.

An excellent alternative to a long direct flight is a **multi-stopover ticket**, which can cost the same or just a little more than the price of an ordinary return; breaking your journey at the airline's stopover points, most commonly in Southeast Asia or in the US. Unusual routes are inevitably more expensive, but it's possible to fly **via South America** with Aerolineas Argentinas, which offers stops in Buenos Aires and Auckland – at least £925 return – or via Africa with South African Airways, which offers return fares via Johannesburg to Perth and Sydney from around £1000, with the added bonus of discounted internal flights to many other African destinations; there are also good deals **via Japan** on All Nippon Airlines and Japan Airlines.

Another option is a Round-the-World (RTW) ticket. A good agent such as Trailfinders can piece together sector fares from various airlines: providing you keep your itinerary down to three continents prices range from around £850 for a simple London–Bangkok–Sydney–LA–London deal to well over £1000 for more complicated routings.

Although most of the cheaper routings **from Ireland** involve a stopover in London and transfer to one of the airlines listed opposite, there are often good deals on Olympic Airways **from Dublin** via Greece. Singapore Airlines has flights ticketed through from Dublin, Shannon or Cork via London to Singapore and Sydney, while Malaysia Airlines also goes from all three Irish airports via Kuala Lumpur. The three airports are also served by the affiliated British Airways and Qantas; all their flights to Sydney have a Dublin–London add-on included in the price. Fares in low-season are usually around the €890 mark, €1160 in high season. For youth and student discount fares, the best first stop is Usit (see p.22).

Packages are a good option for those worried about spiralling costs or those who want to enjoy quality hotels at a cheaper price. There are plenty of more flexible tours which combine Sydney with other areas of

Australia; Travel Bag offers some good tour options, plus some action and eco-oriented trips including the Great Barrier Reef. As well as flights, the Australian expert Qantas also offers quality city packages.

Airlines

Aerolineas Argentinas ⓣ020/7290 7887, ⓦwww.aerolineas.com.ar/uk.
Air China ⓣ020/7630 0919 or 7630 7678, ⓦwww.air-china.co.uk.
Air New Zealand ⓣ0800/028 4149, ⓦwww.airnz.co.uk.
All Nippon Airways (ANA) ⓣ0870/837 8866, ⓦwww.ana.co.jp.
British Airways ⓣ0870/850 9850, Eire ⓣ 1890/626 747, ⓦwww.britishairways.com.
Emirates Airlines ⓣ0870/243 2222, ⓦwww.emirates.com.
Eva Airways ⓣ020/7380 8300, ⓦwww.evaair.com.tw.
Garuda Indonesia ⓣ020/7467 8600, ⓦwww.garuda-indonesia.co.uk.
Japan Airlines ⓣ0845/774 7700, ⓦwww.jal.com/en/.
KLM Royal Dutch Airlines ⓣ0870/243 0541, ⓦwww.klm.com.
Korean Air ⓣ0800/0656 2001, Eire ⓣ01/799 7990, ⓦwww.koreanair.uk.com.
Malaysia Airlines ⓣ0870/607 9090, Eire ⓣ 01/676 1561, ⓦwww.malaysia-airlines.com.
Olympic Airlines ⓣ0870/606 0460, Eire ⓣ 01/608 0090, ⓦwww.olympicairlines.com.
Qantas ⓣ0845/774 7767, ⓦwww.qantas.com.au.
Royal Brunei Airlines ⓣ020/7584 6660, ⓦwww.bruneiair.com.
Singapore Airlines ⓣ0870/608 8886, Eire ⓣ01/671 0722; ⓦwww.singaporeair.com.
South African Airways ⓣ020/7312 5000, ⓦwww.flysaa.com.
Thai Airways ⓣ0870/606 0911, ⓦwww.thaiair.com.
United Airlines ⓣ0845/844 4777, ⓦwww.ual.com.
Virgin Atlantic ⓣ0870/380 2007, ⓦwww.virgin-atlantic.com.

Discount travel agents

Austravel ⓣ0870/166 2020, ⓦwww.austravel.com. Specialists for flights and tours to Australia; agent for charter flights to Sydney (see opposite). Issues ETAs and traditional visas for an administration fee of £17.
Bridge the World ⓣ0870/814 4400, ⓦwww.bridgetheworld.com. Specialists in RTW tickets.
Flightbookers ⓣ0800/082 3000, ⓦwww.ebookers.com. Extensive range of low-fare scheduled flights to Sydney.
Flynow.com ⓣ0800/066 0033, ⓦwww.flynow.com. Large range of discounted tickets.
North South Travel ⓣ01245/608 291, ⓦwww.northsouthtravel.co.uk. Competitive but ethical travel agency, offering discounted fares – profits are used to support projects in the developing world, especially the promotion of sustainable tourism.
Oz Flights ⓣ0870/747 11 747, ⓦwww.ozflights.co.uk. Good deals on southeast Asian airlines.
Quest Worldwide ⓣ0870/442 3542, ⓦwww.questtravel.com. Specialists in RTW and Australian discount fares.
STA Travel ⓣ0870/1600 599, ⓦwww.statravel.co.uk. Worldwide specialists in low-cost flights and tours for students and under-26s, though other customers welcome. Also has offices in Sydney.
Trailfinders ⓣ0845/058 5858, ⓦwww.trailfinders.com. Excellent for multi-stop and RTW tickets, including some unusual routings via South Africa, the Pacific and the US – their very useful quarterly magazine is worth scrutinizing for RTW routes. Well informed and efficient – visa service available at the Kensington High Street branch. Also has a branch in Sydney.
Travel Bag ⓣ0800/082 5000, ⓦwww.travelbag.co.uk. Well-established long-haul travel agent (now part of ebookers) with a good reputation for Australian coverage.

Discount travel websites

ⓦwww.cheapflights.co.uk Flight deals, travel agents, plus links to other travel sites.
ⓦwww.dialaflight.com Useful for tracking down bargains, plus telephone sales for scheduled flights (ⓣ0870/333 4488).
ⓦwww.ebookers.com See Flightbookers, above.
ⓦwww.etn.nl/discount.htm A hub of 750 worldwide consolidator and discount agent Web links, maintained by the non-profit European Travel Network.
ⓦwww.expedia.co.uk Microsoft's venture into the Internet travel market, offering special fares and an online booking service.
ⓦwww.lastminute.com Offers good last-minute holiday package and flight-only deals.
ⓦwww.opodo.co.uk User-friendly, UK-only booking site – owned by major airlines such as BA and Air France – with good deals on flights and packages.
ⓦwww.priceline.co.uk Name-your-own-price website that has deals at around forty percent off standard fares. You cannot specify flight times (although you do specify dates) and the tickets are

Cruising to Sydney

Of course, you can still take a **boat** to Sydney from the UK and the US with P&O (@www.pocruises.com) or the Cunard Line (@www.cunardline.com) as a component of their extended "World Travel" cruises, with rates including one-way airfare at the end of the trip. P&O's *Aurora* commences a 37-night cruise to Sydney from Southampton in England in early January, sailing via the Caribbean, the Panama Canal, Mexico, San Francisco, Honolulu, Fiji and New Zealand, and costs from £4750. The 18-night component from San Francisco to Sydney costs from US$4220. Opting for the Cunard Line, the luxurious *Queen Elizabeth 2* departs from Southampton also in early January for a 43-night trip to Sydney via New York, Florida, Panama, Mexico, LA, Hawaii, Fiji, New Caledonia and New Zealand (from Southhampton from £7875; from New York 37-night cruise from US$12,000). Contact a local travel agent or the cruise companies' websites for more details and bookings.

non-refundable, non-transferable and non-changeable.

@www.travelocity.co.uk Destination guides and the best deals for car rental, accommodation and lodging as well as fares – monitors fares on over seven hundred airlines worldwide to track the best prices.

Irish flight agents and operators

Australia Travel Centre ⓣ01/804 7188, @www.australia.ie. Specialists in long-haul flights.

Trailfinders Dublin ⓣ01/677 7888, @www.trailfinders.ie. One of the best-informed and most efficient agents for independent travellers; produces a very useful quarterly magazine worth scrutinizing for RTW routes.

Usit Dublin ⓣ01/602 1600, @www.usit.ie. Student and youth specialists.

From the US and Canada

From Los Angeles it's possible to fly nonstop to Sydney in fourteen and a half hours. Qantas, United, Air Canada and Air New Zealand all operate **direct flights**. Flying on a national Asian airline will most likely involve a stop in their capital city (Singapore, Tokyo, Hong Kong etc) and if you're travelling from the West Coast of North America you'll probably find their fares on the Pacific route somewhat higher than their American or Australasian competitors.

Many of the major airlines offer deals with **stopovers** either at **Pacific Rim** destinations such as Tokyo with Japan Airlines, Honolulu with Air Canada or Kuala Lumpur with Malaysia Airlines or at a number of exotic South Pacific locations with Air New Zealand. Either there will be a flat surcharge on your ticket or they may offer you a higher-priced ticket allowing you to make several stops over a fixed period of time. But the best deal will probably be a Circle Pacific or **Round-the-World** (RTW) ticket from a discount outfit such as Airtreks.

Fares and flights

Most of the consolidators and discount agents listed opposite can quote and offer the best fares on scheduled flights, though you can go direct through airlines. It's also worth checking airline **websites** for "online specials" available via **Internet auctions**, the latest way to sell last-minute seats, or try specialist discount travel and auction websites such as Hotwire or Skyauction. If you travel a lot, **discount travel clubs** are another option – the annual membership fee may be worth the benefits, such as cut-price air tickets and car rental. Many airlines offer youth or student fares to **under-26s**.

However, **booking ahead** as far as possible is still the best way to secure the most reasonable prices. Fares vary significantly according to season – generally **high season** is December–February, **low season** April–August, and other times are **shoulder**. The highest prices are over Christmas and New Year; booking far in advance at these times is highly recommended.

Sample lowest standard **scheduled fares** for low/high seasons are: from Chicago or New York (US$1250/$1780), LA or San Francisco (US$1050/$1650), Montreal or Toronto (CDN$1500/$2500) and Vancouver (CDN$1300/$2450). To see more of the world, a sample **RTW ticket** Los Angeles–Tokyo–Kuala Lumpur–Singapore–Perth–Sydney–Los Angeles costs around US$2800.

Airlines

Air Canada ⓣ1-888/247-2262, ⓦwww.aircanada.ca.
Air New Zealand US ⓣ1-800/262-1234; Canada ⓣ1-800/663-5494; ⓦwww.airnewzealand.com, ⓦwww.ca.airnewzealand.com.
Cathay Pacific ⓣ1-800/233-2742, ⓦwww.cathay-usa.com.
Malaysia Airlines ⓣ1-800/552-9264, ⓦwww.malaysiaairlines.com.
Qantas ⓣ1-800/227-4500, ⓦwww.qantas.com.
Singapore Airlines ⓣ1-800/742-3333, Eastern Canada ⓣ800/387-0038, Western Canada ⓣ800/663-3046, ⓦwww.singaporeair.com.
United Airlines ⓣ1-800/538-2929, ⓦwww.united.com.

Discount flight agents, travel clubs and consolidators

Air Brokers International ⓣ1-800/883-3273, ⓦwww.airbrokers.com. Consolidator and specialist in RTW and Circle Pacific tickets.
Airtech ⓣ212/219-7000, ⓦwww.airtech.com. Stand-by seat broker; also deals in consolidator fares.
Airtreks.com ⓣ1-877-AIRTREKS or 415/977-7100, ⓦwww.airtreks.com. Circle Pacific and RTW tickets. The website features an interactive database that lets you build and price your own RTW itinerary.
Educational Travel Center ⓣ1-800/747-5551 or 608/256-5551, ⓦwww.edtrav.com. Student/youth discount agent.
STA Travel ⓣ1-800/781-4040, ⓦwww.sta-travel.com. Worldwide specialists in independent travel; also provide student IDs, travel insurance, car rental, etc.
Student Universe ⓣ1-800/272-9676 or 1-617/321-3100, ⓦwww.studentuniverse.com. Competitive student travel specialists, no card or membership required.
TFI Tours ⓣ1-800/745-8000 or 212/736-1140, ⓦwww.tfitours.com. Consolidator with consistent good deals on flights and accommodation.
Travel Cuts Canada ⓣ1-800/667-2887, US ⓣ1-866/246-9762, ⓦwww.travelcuts.com. Canadian student-travel organization with offices in many North American cities.
Travelers Advantage ⓣ1-877/259-2691, ⓦwww.travelersadvantage.com. Discount travel club; annual membership fee required (currently $1 for 2 months' trial).
Worldtek Travel ⓣ1-800/243-1723, ⓦwww.worldtek.com. Discount travel agency with offices in several eastern and midwestern states.

Online booking agents

ⓦwww.etn.nl/discount.htm A hub of 750 worldwide consolidator and discount agent Web links, maintained by the non-profit European Travel Network.
ⓦwww.expedia.com Discount air fares, all-airline search engine and daily deals.
ⓦwww.flyaow.com Online air travel info and reservations site.
ⓦwww.hotwire.com Bookings from the US only. Last-minute savings of up to fifty percent on regular published fares. Log-in required.
ⓦwww.priceline.com Name-your-own-price website that has deals at around forty percent off standard fares. You cannot specify flight times (although you do specify dates) and the tickets are non-refundable, non-transferable and non-changeable.
ⓦwww.skyauction.com Bookings from the US only. Auctions tickets and travel packages using a "second bid" scheme. The best strategy is to bid the maximum you're willing to pay, since if you win you'll pay just enough to beat the runner-up regardless of your maximum bid.
ⓦwww.travelocity.com Destination guides, hot Web fares and best deals for car rental, accommodation and lodging as well as fares. Monitors fares on over seven hundred airlines worldwide to track the best deals on fares for you. Provides access to the travel agent system SABRE, the most comprehensive central reservations system in the US. The Canadian version is ⓦwww.travelocity.ca.

Packages and tours

Several of the operators below, such as United Vacations, offer **city stopovers**, providing, for example, two nights' accommodation and perhaps a day-tour, starting at around US$185 on top of your ticket. Organized tours of Australia, which inevitably take in Sydney, cost from US$3500 for a typical two-week tour – such as those offered by Adventures Abroad – covering the usual cultural, historical and natural sights.

Tour operators

AAT Kings ⓣ1-800/353 4525, ⓦwww.aatkings.com.
Abercrombie and Kent ⓣ1-800/554-7016, ⓦwww.abercrombiekent.com.
Adventure Center ⓣ1-800/228-8747 or 510/654-1879, ⓦwww.adventurecenter.com.
Adventures Abroad ⓣ1-800/665-3998 or 604/303-1099, ⓦwww.adventures-abroad.com.
ATS Tours ⓣ1-800/423-2880, ⓦwww.atstours.com.

Australian Pacific Tours ⓣ1-800/290-8687 416/234-9676, ⓦwww.aptours.com.
Destination World ⓣ 1-888/345-4669, ⓦwww.destinationworld.com.
Goway Travel ⓣ1-800/387-8850, ⓦwww.goway.com.
International Gay and Lesbian Travel Association ⓣ1-800/448-8550, ⓦwww.iglta.org.
Nature Expeditions International ⓣ1-800/869-0639, ⓦwww.naturexp.com.
Qantas Vacations US ⓣ1-800/348-8145, ⓦwww.qantasvacations.com.
Swain Australia Tours ⓣ1-800/227-9246 or 610/896-9595, ⓦwww.swainaustralia.com.
United Vacations ⓣ1-888/854-3899, ⓦwww.unitedvacations.com.

From New Zealand

New Zealand–Australia routes are busy and competition is fierce, resulting in an ever-changing range of deals and special offers; your best bet is to check the latest with a specialist travel agent or the relevant airlines' websites. Flying time from Auckland to Sydney is around three and a half hours.

Ultimately, the price you pay for your flight will depend on how much flexibility you want; many of the cheapest deals are hedged with restrictions – typically a maximum stay of thirty days and a fourteen-day advance-purchase requirement. However, there are few restrictions on the web-based New Zealand airline, Freedom Air. It specializes in no-frills, low-cost trans-Tasman air travel, with flights from Auckland, Christchurch, Dunedin, Palmerston North and Wellington to Sydney. How long tickets stay open is flexible and advance purchase has little effect on ticket prices, which cost around NZ$480 return. Adding to the competition, Pacific Blue, Virgin Blue's New Zealand low-fare carrier, also with Internet-based sales, flies from Christchurch to Sydney, and from Wellington to Sydney, for around NZ$500 return.

Only Qantas, Air New Zealand, Freedom Air and Aerolineas Argentineas have tickets that stay open for one year, while Polynesian and Malaysia Airlines offer tickets open for up to six months; there are also ninety-day tickets that fall between the two extremes in price. The cheapest thirty-day return **fare from Auckland** to Sydney is usually with Aerolineas Argentineas for NZ$350–500, but flights tend to be heavily booked. Six-month return fares from Qantas, United, Emirates or Air New Zealand to Sydney are around $850–1000. Whether you fly from **Wellington** or **Christchurch** generally makes no difference to the fare.

Prices peak primarily from December to mid-January. Outside **peak season**, when the airlines often have surplus capacity, they may offer promotional fares, which can bring down prices to as low as NZ$550 for a thirty-day return from Auckland to Sydney.

There's a huge variety of **packages** to Sydney available; call or check the websites of any of the travel agents listed below. The holiday subsidiaries of airlines such as Air New Zealand and Qantas offer short **city-breaks** (flight and accommodation) and **fly-drive** deals for little more than the cost of the regular air fare.

Airlines

Aerolineas Argentinas ⓣ09/379 3675, ⓦwww.aerolineas.com.au.
Air New Zealand ⓣ0800/737 000, ⓦwww.airnewzealand.co.nz.
Freedom Air ⓣ0800/600 500, ⓦwww.freedom.co.nz.
Malaysia Airlines ⓣ09/373 2741, ⓦwww.malaysiaairlines.com.
Pacific Blue ⓣ0800/670 000, ⓦwww.flypacificblue.com.
Polynesian Airlines ⓣ09/309 5396, ⓦwww.polynesianairlines.com.
Qantas ⓣ09/661 901, ⓦwww.qantas.com.au.
Thai Airways ⓣ09/377 3886, ⓦwww.thaiair.com.

Specialist travel agents

Flight Centres 350 Queen St, Auckland ⓣ09/358 4310 or 0800/243 5444, ⓦwww.flightcentre.co.nz. Branches nationwide. Competitive discounts on air fares and a wide range of package holidays and adventure tours.
Holiday Shoppe 27–35 Victoria St West, Auckland ⓣ09/379 2099 or 0800/808 480, ⓦwww.holidayshoppe.co.nz. One of New Zealand's largest travel agencies (79 other branches around the country), good for budget air fares and accommodation packages.
STA Travel 187 and 267 Queen St, Auckland ⓣ09/366 6673 or 0508/782 872, ⓦwww.statravel.co.nz. Branches nationwide. Fare discounts for students and those under 26, as well as visas, student cards and travel insurance.

Red tape and visas

All visitors to Australia, except New Zealanders, require a visa or an Electronic Travel Authority (ETA). Visa application forms are obtained from the Australian High Commissions, embassies or consulates listed below, or can be downloaded from the embassy Internet sites (see below).

Three-month **tourist visas**, valid for multiple entry over one year, are issued free and processed over the counter, or are returned in three weeks by mail. However, the computerized system, **Electronic Travel Authority** (ETA), can speed things up for nationals of the UK, Ireland, the US, Canada, Malaysia, Singapore, Japan and most European countries. Applied for online, the ETA replaces the visa stamp in your passport (ETAs are computerized) and saves the hassle of queuing or sending off your passport. ETAs can be applied for on the Web with a credit card for A$20 (see the Australian government websites below or go directly to Ⓦwww.eta.immi.gov.au) or are available from travel agents and airlines at the same time as you book your flight. In this case an additional fee is levied on top of the cost of your ETA – in the UK around £17.

Entry requirements do change, so if in doubt, check with your nearest embassy or consulate before leaving.

Longer visas, working visas and extensions

Visits lasting from three to six months incur a fee (A$65 or the equivalent in your country). If you think you might stay more than three months, it's best to get the longer visa before departure, because once you get to Australia **visa extensions** cost A$160. If you need to extend your visa while in Sydney, contact the Department of Immigration, 26 Lee St, near Central Station (Ⓣ13 18 81). If you're visiting immediate family who live in Australia, apply for a **Sponsored Family Visitor Visa** (A$165), which has fewer restrictions. You may be asked to prove you have adequate funds to support yourself – at least A$1000 a month.

Twelve-month **working holiday visas** – with the stress on casual employment – are easily available to British, Irish, Canadian, Dutch, German, Japanese and Korean single people aged 18–30, though exceptions are made for young married couples without children. You must arrange the visa before you arrive in Australia, and several months in advance; the processing fee is A$170. Young US citizens (18–30) can join the Special Youth Program combining a four-month holiday with short-term work. Membership of the scheme costs US$550 and applications can be made through BUNAC (Ⓣ203/264-0901, Ⓦwww.bunac.com), Camp Counselors (Ⓦwww.ccusa.com) or Council/CIEE (Ⓦwww.ciee.org).

Australian embassies and consulates

You may already be living and travelling outside your own country when you decide to visit Sydney. For a full list of **Australian embassies and consulates**, consult the Australian Department of Foreign Affairs and Trade website (Ⓦwww.dfat.gov.au/missions/index.html).

Canada Australian High Commission, Suite 710, 50 O'Connor St, Ottawa, Ontario K1P 6L2 Ⓣ613/236-0841, Ⓦwww.ahc-ottawa.org.

Ireland Australian Embassy, Fitzwilton House, Wilton Terrace, Dublin 2 Ⓣ01/664 5300, Ⓦwww.australianembassy.ie.

New Zealand Australian Consulate-General, Level 7, PriceWaterhouseCoopers Tower, 186–194 Quay St, Auckland 1 Ⓣ09/921 8800; Australian High Commission, 72–78 Hobson St, Thorndon, Wellington Ⓣ04/473 6411, Ⓦwww.australia.org.nz.

UK Australian High Commission, Australia House, Strand, London WC2B 4LA Ⓣ020/7379 4334, Ⓦwww.australia.org.uk.

US Australian Embassy, 1601 Massachusetts Ave

NW, Washington, DC 20036 2273 ⓣ202/797-3000, ⓦwww.austemb.org.

Customs and quarantine

The **duty-free allowance** for alcohol and tobacco on entry is 2.25 litres of alcohol and 250 cigarettes or 250g of tobacco. Australia has strict quarantine laws that apply to fruit, vegetables, fresh and packaged food, seed and some animal products, among other things. Expect to be welcomed into the country with the ritual on-board pesticide spray.

Insurance

The national healthcare scheme in Australia, Medicare, offers a reciprocal arrangement – free essential healthcare – for citizens of the UK, Ireland, New Zealand, Italy, Malta, Finland, the Netherlands and Sweden. This free treatment is limited to public hospitals and casualty departments (though the ambulance ride to get you there isn't covered); at GPs you pay upfront (about $45 minimum) with two-thirds of your fee reimbursed by Medicare (does not apply to citizens of New Zealand and Ireland). If you are entitled to free emergency healthcare from Medicare, you may feel that the need for the health element of travel insurance is reduced. In any case, some form of travel insurance can help plug the gaps and will cover you in the event of losing your baggage, missing a plane and the like.

A typical travel insurance policy usually provides cover for the loss of baggage, tickets and – up to a certain limit – cash or cheques, as well as cancellation or curtailment of your journey. Most of them exclude **"high-risk" activities** unless an extra premium is paid: depending on the insurer, these can include water sports (especially diving), skiing or even just hiking; check carefully that any policy you are considering will cover you in case of an accident. Many policies can be chopped and changed to exclude coverage you don't need – for example, sickness and accident benefits can often be excluded or included at will. If you do take medical coverage, ascertain whether benefits will be paid as treatment proceeds or only after you return home, and whether there is a 24-hour medical emergency number. When securing baggage cover, make sure that the per-article limit – typically under £500 – will cover your most valuable possession. If you need to make a claim, you should keep receipts for medicines and medical treatment, and in the event you have anything stolen, you must obtain an official statement from the police.

Before spending money on a new policy it's worth checking whether you are already covered: some all-risks **home insurance** policies, for example, may cover your possessions against loss or theft when overseas, and many private medical schemes such as BUPA or PPP include cover when abroad, including baggage loss, cancellation or curtailment and cash replacement as well as sickness or accident. Bank and credit cards often have certain levels of medical or other insurance included and you may automatically get travel insurance if you use a major credit card to pay for your trip (check the small print on this, though, as it may not be of much use).

In Canada, provincial health plans usually provide partial cover for medical mishaps overseas, while holders of official student/teacher/youth cards in **Canada and the US** are entitled to meagre accident coverage and hospital inpatient benefits. Students will often find that their student health coverage extends during the vacations and for one term beyond the date of last enrolment.

Information, websites and maps

Information on Sydney is easy to get hold of, either from Australian Tourist Commission offices, via the Internet, or, after arrival, from any of the city's tourist offices.

If you want to do a bit of **general research** on your trip before arriving in Sydney, you should contact the Australian Tourist Commission via their website ⓦwww.australia.com (there are different versions for the UK, US, Canada, New Zealand and other countries – click on "change language or country" under "quick links") and arrange to have them post out for free their annual publication, the glossy *Australia, A Traveller's Guide*, which has a detailed section on Sydney, and a useful directory of addresses. Also check out the website for Tourism New South Wales in the list of useful websites on p.28. Once in Sydney, there's no shortage of places offering information, but the major tourist offices, the Sydney Visitor Centres, are at the international airport – grab hold of some free information booklets and maps when you arrive – and at two major tourist centres, The Rocks and Darling Harbour.

Tourist information offices

There are three **Sydney Visitor Centres** offering comprehensive information, free accommodation and tour booking facilities, and selling tourist transport tickets and sightseeing passes. At the **Sydney Visitor Centre** on the ground floor (arrivals) of the international airport terminal (daily 5am until last arrival; ⓣ02/9667 6050), staff can arrange car rental and onward travel – it's licensed to sell train and bus tickets – and book hotels (but not hostels) anywhere in Sydney and New South Wales free of charge. The **accommodation bookings** here are at stand-by rates, so it's possible to get a good deal. Most hostels advertise on an adjacent notice board; there's a free phone line for reservations. The other two branches are centrally located: at 106 George St, The

Rocks, just behind the Museum of Contemporary Art and at Darling Harbour by the IMAX cinema (both daily 9.30am–5.30pm; ⓣ02/9240 8788 or 1800 067 676, ⓦwww.sydneyvisitorcentre.com; see also p.59), offering a similar range of literature; they have a self-service budget accommodation booking board with free phones directly linked to the listed hotels. Tourism New South Wales (Tourist Information Line ⓣ13 20 77, ⓦwww.visitnsw.com.au) runs the **City Host information kiosks** (daily 9am–5pm; no phone) at Circular Quay (corner of Pitt and Alfred streets), Martin Place and Town Hall, providing brochures, maps and face-to-face information; and the **Manly Visitor Information Centre** (Mon–Fri 9am–5pm, Sat & Sun 10am–4pm; ⓣ02/9977 1088, ⓦwww.manlytourism.com.au), by the Manly Ferry Wharf, which also has lockers for valuables ($2).

National Park information

For information on Sydney Harbour National Park, the series of bush-covered foreshore and islands around the harbour, the **National Parks and Wildlife Service** (NPWS) has an information centre and bookshop at Cadman's Cottage, 110 George St, The Rocks (daily 9am–5pm; ⓣ02/9247 5033, ⓦwww.nationalparks.nsw.gov.au). They produce a very handy, detailed, free fold-out map, *Sydney Harbour National Park,* which provides excellent detail of the harbour, showing all the main sites, ferry routes and bushwalks.

For information on other national parks around Sydney, such as the Royal National Park, and camping permits, go to the National Parks Centre, nearby at 102 George St, The Rocks (ⓣ02/9253 4600). The Sydney Map Shop, part of the Surveyor-General's Department, 23–33 Bridge St, City (ⓣ02/9228 6111), sells detailed National Park, State Forest and bushwalking maps.

Publications

Ask at the tourist offices for *Sydney: The Official Guide*, a free booklet with excellent maps of Sydney and the surrounding areas, plus a CityRail and ferry plan. The *Hip Guide to Sydney* is also handy. Several free monthly **listings magazines** are worth picking up at tourist offices: the weekly *Where Magazine* is probably the best for general information, while the quarterly *This Week in Sydney* is also worth consulting. To get under the skin of Sydney, read Friday's *Sydney Morning Herald* for its "Metro" listings supplement.

TNT Magazine is the best of an array of publications aimed at **backpackers**, while **hostel notice boards** themselves act as an informal network, advertising everything from cars to camping gear; you can pick them up at travellers' centres such as Backpackers World Travel, with several offices including 234 Sussex St (ⓣ02/8268 6001, ⓦwww.backpackerstravel.net.au), 488 Pitt St near Central Station (ⓣ02/9282 9711), 91 York St (ⓣ02/8268 5000), 212 Victoria St, Kings Cross (ⓣ02/9380 2700) and 2B Grosvenor St, Bondi Junction (ⓣ02/9369 2011).

Useful websites

Though we give relevant websites throughout the guide, some general sites on Sydney are listed below. For information on Internet access in Sydney see p.43.

ⓦ**www.abc.net.au/sydney/weather** Four-day weather forecasts for Sydney and around – as far as the central coast (Gosford), the Blue Mountains, Hawkesbury River.

ⓦ**www.cityofsydney.nsw.gov.au** The City of Sydney council has useful information for visitors including a list of festivals and events under its "What's On" heading.

ⓦ**www.mardigras.org.au** The official Sydney Gay & Lesbian Mardi Gras site, with links to other gay and lesbian sites.

ⓦ**www.smh.com.au** Read selected daily news pages of the *Sydney Morning Herald*, and check the classifieds for jobs, cars, rental properties and share and holiday accommodation. Free to use, but you have to register first.

ⓦ**www.sydney.citysearch.com.au** The ultimate Sydney online guide to arts and entertainment, music, movies, eating and shopping, with links to tourist attractions and accommodation under the "Visitor Guide" section.

ⓦ**www.tourism.nsw.gov.au** The official site for Tourism New South Wales focuses on Sydney plus the surrounding state, with info on tours, events and accommodation.

ⓦ**www.viewsydney.com** Rooftop cameras in The Rocks quarter show a slice of life on Sydney Harbour in real time.

ⓦ**www.wotif.com.au** Last-minute accommodation specialists – book upmarket Sydney hotels at bargain rates.

Maps

For wandering around the centre of Sydney, the maps in this book should be sufficient, but if you crave greater detail, or are staying by the beach or in the inner or outer suburbs, or are driving, you might like to buy something more comprehensive. The best place to **buy maps** in Sydney is Map World, 380 Pitt St (Ⓣ02/9261 3601, Ⓦwww.mapworld.net.au; Mon–Wed & Fri 8.30am–5.30pm, Thurs 8.30am–6.30pm, Sat 10am–3.30pm). The two best maps to buy are HEMA's *Sydney and Region* map ($5.95; Ⓦwww.hemamaps.com) which gives an overview of the area around Sydney, showing major roads and freeways, and giving detailed coverage of the metropolitan area as well as an inset map of the CBD; UBD's Sydney Suburban Map (no. 262; $7.50; Ⓦwww.ubd-online.com) gives comprehensive street detail of the CBD and the surrounding suburbs within a 10km radius. If you've rented a car, make sure the rental company has provided a Sydney street directory before you head off. For longer stays, the best street directory to buy is the latest edition of Gregory's *Sydney Compact* street directory ($14.95; Ⓦwww.gregorys-online.com), which has all the detail but in a paperback book size that can easily fit into a handbag or daypack and at around half the price of the larger-sized directories. If you do want a car-sized directory, best to go for UBD's *Sydney & Blue Mountains Street Directory* ($39.95), which extends as far as Mt Victoria. For getting out of Sydney, a New South Wales state map doesn't provide enough detail on the areas we've included in our "Beyond Sydney" chapters, though it will show freeways and major roads. It's better to buy a copy of Gregory's *200 kilometres around Sydney* map ($5.95) for more detail and coverage of all the major tourist drives. See also opposite for details of free national park maps.

New South Wales's motoring organization, the NRMA, 74–76 King St, City (Ⓣ13 21 32, Ⓦwww.nrma.com.au), publishes **road maps** of New South Wales, and a useful map of Sydney. The maps are free to members of associated overseas motoring organizations.

Costs, money and banks

If you've stopped over from Southeast Asia you'll obviously find Sydney, with its high Western standard of living, expensive for daily purchases. Fresh from Europe or the US you'll find prices comparable and often cheaper, particularly for accommodation and eating out, and especially taking into account the very favourable exchange rate. Australia is well set up for independent travellers, and with a student, YHA or a backpackers' card (see below) you can get discounts on a wide range of travel and entertainment in Sydney.

Currency

Australia's currency is the Australian dollar, or "buck", divided into 100 cents and shown on currency tables as AU$. Colourful plastic notes with forgery-proof clear windows come in $100, $50, $20, $10 and $5 denominations, along with $2, $1, 50¢, 20¢, 10¢ and 5¢ coins. There are no longer 1¢ or 2¢ coins, but prices are regularly advertised at $1.99 etc and an irregular bill will be rounded up or down to the closest denomination, which can be confusing at first.

At the time of writing, the Australian dollar is very strong with over-the-counter rate **exchange rates** of AU$2.42 for £1; AU$1.34 for US$1; AU$1.07 for C$1 and AU$0.93 for NZ$1. For the most current exchange rates, consult the useful currency converter website Ⓦwww.oanda.com.

See Sydney & Beyond Smartvisit Card

All the Sydney Visitor Centre tourist offices sell the **See Sydney & Beyond Smartvisit Card** (ⓣ131 661 711, ⓦwww.seesydneycard.com), which comes in one-, two-, three- or seven-day versions (to be used over consecutive days), with or without a transport option (a Daytripper or Travelpass – see box on pp.38–39) and including admission to forty attractions in Sydney and the Blue Mountains – from Taronga Zoo to a guided tour of the Opera House. If an action-packed, fast-paced itinerary is your thing the card can be good value; it's certainly a convenient way to bypass the queues, and since it can be bought in advance on the Internet, a seven-day version in particular might make a good going-away present. Rates (with/without transport) are: one-day $65 (no transport component available; child $45), two-day $159/$119 (child 4–15 years $85/$65), three-day $205/$149 (child $109/$79) and seven-day $275/$209 (child $175/$139). To work out whether it's worth buying one decide what you want to see, check the entry prices in our Guide and compare the total amount to the price of a card, and work out a realistic schedule.

Costs

The absolute minimum **daily budget** for food, accommodation and transport alone is $70 if you stay in a hostel, eat in the cheapest cafés and restaurants and travel by public transport. Add on sightseeing admissions and a minimal social life and you're looking at at least $110. Staying in decent hotels, eating at moderate restaurants, and paying for tours and nightlife extend your budget to at least $160–220 per day.

Hostel **accommodation** will set you back $20–30 per person, while a double room in a moderate hotel costs $110–160. **Food**, on the whole, is good value: counter meals in hotels and cafés often start from $12; restaurant mains cost between $15 and $35 depending on the standard, and many let you BYO (bring your own) wine or beer. **Drinking** out will set you back around $3 for a small glass of draught beer, $4–6 for a bottled brew, and local wine by the glass starts at $4 for an ordinary drop but expect to pay at least $7 for something choicer. Beer is good value bought in bulk from a "bottle shop" – a "slab" of beer (24 cans) costs around $30; a decent bottle of wine will set you back from $14, with *vin ordinaire* from as little as $8.

Renting a car costs around $65 a day; the longer you rent for, the cheaper the price. Fuel, with fluctuations week to week, averages 90¢–$1.10 a litre; cheaper than in the UK, dearer than the US, but vast distances see it used up fast.

Youth and student discounts

Once obtained, various official and quasi-official **youth/student ID cards** soon pay for themselves in savings. Full-time students are eligible for the International Student ID Card (ISIC, ⓦwww.isiccard.com), which entitles the bearer to special air, rail and bus fares and discounts at museums, theatres and other attractions. For Americans there's also a health benefit, providing up to US$5000 in emergency medical coverage and US$100 a day for sixty days in hospital, plus a 24-hour hotline to call in the event of a medical, legal or financial emergency. The card costs US$22 for Americans; C$16 for Canadians; NZ$20 for New Zealanders; and £7 in the UK. If you're no longer a student, but are 26 or younger, you still qualify for the International Youth Travel Card, which costs the same price and carries the same benefits, while teachers qualify for the International Teacher Card (same price and some of the benefits). All these cards are available from your local student travel agent in the US, Canada, the UK and New Zealand, and in Australia itself, or you can download an application from the website. Once you are in Australia, purchasing either an International YHA Card or Backpacker Resorts VIP Card (ⓦwww.vipbackpackers.com) will give you discounts on not just the relevant hostel accommodation, but a host of transport, tours, services, entry fees and even meals; they're worth getting even if you're not planning to stay in hostels.

Travellers' cheques

Although they are the traditional way to carry funds, **travellers' cheques**, such as those sold by American Express and Travelex, are no longer the cheapest nor the most convenient way to bring your funds into Australia – credit or debit cards or Visa TravelMoney are more simple options (see below). However, travellers' cheques offer more security as they can be replaced if lost or stolen (remember to keep a list of the serial numbers separate from the cheques). Australian dollar travellers' cheques are ideal as theoretically they're valid as cash and so shouldn't attract exchange fees; smaller businesses may be unwilling to take them, but you can always change them for free at the local American Express or Travelex offices. Travellers' cheques in US dollars and pounds sterling are also widely accepted, and banks should be able to handle all major currencies. It's worth checking both the rate and the commission when you change your cheques (as well as when you buy them), as these can vary quite widely – many places charge a set amount for every cheque, in which case you're better off changing relatively large denominations. You'll need your passport with you to cash travellers' cheques.

The usual fee **to buy travellers' cheques** is one or two percent, though this fee may be waived if you buy the cheques through a bank where you have an account. Make sure to keep the purchase agreement and a record of cheque serial numbers safe and separate from the cheques themselves. In the event that cheques are lost or stolen, the issuing company will expect you to report the loss forthwith to their head office in Australia (for numbers, see below); most companies claim to replace lost or stolen cheques within 24 hours.

Credit and debit cards

Credit cards are a very handy source of funds, and can be used either in ATMs or over the counter. MasterCard and Visa are the most widely recognized; you can also use American Express, Bankcard and Diners Club. Remember that all cash advances are treated as loans, with interest accruing daily from the date of withdrawal; there may be a transaction fee on top of this. However, you may be able to make withdrawals from ATMs in Australia displaying the Cirrus-Maestro symbol and be able to pay for goods via EFTPOS (see p.32), using your debit card, which is not liable to interest payments, and the flat transaction fee is usually quite small – your bank will able to advise on this. Make sure you have a personal identification number (PIN) that's designed to work overseas.

Banks and foreign exchange

The major banks with branches countrywide are Westpac (Ⓦwww.westpac.com.au), ANZ (Ⓦwww.anz.com.au), the Commonwealth (Ⓦwww.commbank.com.au) and National Australia (Ⓦwww.national.com.au) banks; their head branches, all with foreign currency counters, are in the CBD, on and around Martin Place (see p.80); you can search their websites for suburban and out-of-town branch locations. **Banking hours** are Monday to Thursday 9.30am to 4pm

Visa TravelMoney

A compromise between travellers' cheques and plastic is Visa TravelMoney, a disposable prepaid debit card with a PIN which works in all ATMs that take Visa cards. You load up your account with funds before leaving home, and when they run out, you simply throw the card away. You can buy up to nine cards to access the same funds – useful for couples or families travelling together – and it's a good idea to buy at least one extra as a backup in case of loss or theft. There is also a 24-hour Australia-wide toll-free customer assistance number (Ⓣ1800 125 161). The card is available in most countries from branches of Travelex. For more information, check the Visa TravelMoney website at Ⓦinternational.visa.com/ps/products/vtravelmoney/.

and Friday 9.30am to 5pm, and some branches are now open on Saturday. Automatic Teller Machines (**ATMs**) are usually located outside banks but sometimes in front of ordinary shops in shopping strips. **Bureaux de change** are found in both the domestic and international airport terminals, and around Central Station, Darling Harbour and throughout the city centre; only a few in the city are open at the weekend, and solely the ones at the airport late at night, so try to exchange your currency during the week.

Foreign exchange offices

American Express Outlets include 105 Pitt St (Mon–Fri 9am–5pm; ⓣ1300 139 060); 296 George St (daily 8.30am–5.30pm); Shop 4, Quay Grand Hotel, Circular Quay East (Mon–Fri 9am–5pm, Sat & Sun 11am–4pm) and within the Travel Bookshop, Shop 3, 175 Liverpool St (Mon–Fri 9am–5pm, Sat 10am–1pm). Lost or stolen travellers' cheques ⓣ1800 251 902.

Travelex Domestic and international airport and several city locations including 37–49 Pitt St, near Central Station (Mon–Fri 9am–5.15pm, Sat 10am–2.45pm; ⓣ02/9241 5722, ⓦwww.travelex.com.au); Shop 64, Lower Ground Floor, Queen Victoria Building, corner of George and Market streets (Mon–Fri 9am–5.45pm, Sat 10am–3pm).

UAE Money Exchange Shop 175 Harbourside shopping centre, Darling Harbour (Mon–Fri 9.30am–9pm, Sat & Sun 10am–9pm; ⓣ02/9212 7124).

Opening and using a bank account

If you're spending some time in Sydney, and plan to work, it makes life a great deal easier if you **open a bank account**. To do this you'll need to take along every piece of ID documentation you own (a passport may not be enough, though a letter from your bank manager at home may help), but it's otherwise a fairly straightforward process. The Commonwealth Bank and Westpac are the most widespread options, and their **keycards** give you access not only to ATM machines but also anywhere that offers **EFTPOS** (Electronic Funds Transfer at Point of Sale) facilities. This includes most shops, service stations and supermarkets, where you can use your card to pay directly for goods; some of them will also give you cash (ask for "cash back"). However, bear in mind that **bank fees and charges** are exorbitant in Australia; most banks allow only a few free withdrawal transactions per month (depending on who you bank with – it's well worth shopping around before you open an account), and there are even bigger charges for using a competitor's ATM machine, as well as monthly fees.

Wiring money

Having **money wired from home** is never convenient or cheap, and should be considered a last resort. It's also possible to have money wired directly from a bank in your home country to a bank in Australia, although this is somewhat less reliable because it involves two separate institutions. If you go down this route, your home bank will need the address of the branch bank where you want to pick up the money and the address and telex number of the head office, which will act as the clearing house; money wired this way normally takes two working days to arrive, and costs around £25/US$40 per transaction. Otherwise, to have money wired from home fast, arrangements can be made with MoneyGram International (ⓦwww.moneygram.com) through Travelex foreign exchange outlets, and Western Union (ⓦwww.westernunion.com) through American Express; see outlet addresses above.

Arrival

The classic way to arrive in Sydney is, of course, by ship (see box on p.22), cruising near the great coathanger of the Harbour Bridge to tie up at the Overseas Passenger Terminal (see p.67) alongside Circular Quay. Unfortunately you're more likely to be arriving by air, train or bus, and the reality of the functional airport, train and bus stations is a good deal less romantic.

By air

Sydney's **Kingsford Smith Airport**, referred to as "Mascot" after the suburb where it's located, near Botany Bay, is 8km south of the city (international flight times ⓣ13 12 23, ⓦwww.sydneyairport.com.au). Domestic and international terminals are linked by a free shuttle bus if you're travelling with Qantas (every 30min), or you can take the KST Sydney Airport bus for $4. See box below for **buses** into the city. You can take a **train** right into the centre: the Airport Link underground railway connects the airport to the City Circle train line (15min; Mon–Fri every 10min, Sat & Sun every 15min; one-way $11; to compete with taxis,

Airport buses

State Transit

State Transit no longer offers dedicated airport buses but there is a daily commuter route heading east and west from the airport: the **Metroline #400** goes frequently to Bondi Junction via Maroubra and Randwick in one direction, and to Burwood in the other (tickets cost a maximum of $4.80).

Shuttle services – Sydney area

KST Sydney Transporter ⓣ02/9666 9988, ⓦwww.kst.com.au. Private bus service dropping off at hotels or hostels in the area bounded by Kings Cross and Darling Harbour. Service leaves when the bus is full ($9 one-way, $14 return). Bookings three hours in advance for an accommodation pick-up to the airport.

Super Shuttles ⓣ02/9311 3789, ⓦwww.supershuttle.com.au. Quick call-out minibus service to and from the city and eastern beaches – Bondi, Coogee, Randwick, Clovelly and Bronte – dropping off at all hostels, motels and hotels ($12 one-way). Book an accommodation pick-up 24hr in advance to return to airport.

Surface To Air ⓣ02/9913 9912, ⓦwww.surfacetoair.com.au. Minibus service to the city and the northern beaches – including Manly, Whale Beach and Palm Beach – dropping off at accommodation. Book in advance by phone or email giving the day, time and flight and they will designate a waiting point. Manly $28, Palm Beach $55 (cheaper rates for couples and groups).

Coach and shuttle services – central coast and south coast

Aussie Shuttles ⓣ1300 130 557, ⓦwww.ben-air.com.au. Pre-booked door-to-door service to accommodation anywhere on the central coast ($55–65, cheaper rates for couples and groups), and to Newcastle ($95).

Premier Motor Service ⓣ13 34 10, for bookings outside Australia ⓣ02/4423 5244, ⓦwww.premierms.com.au. Departs daily at 9.45am and 3.30pm, plus Monday to Friday at 7.45am from the domestic terminal, fifteen minutes later from the international terminal, to south coast towns as far as Bega ($53); the 9.45am and 3.30pm services continue on to Eden ($60). Bookings necessary.

there's a group fare for four people of $18 to Central Station, $24 to City Circle train stations; Ⓦwww.airportlink.com.au). However, as it is a suburban commuter service it can be crowded at peak hours, there is no dedicated space for luggage and it is more expensive than shuttle buses, which will drop you off near your hotel. A return Airport Link transfer is part of the **Sydney Pass** (see box on p.38), so if you're planning to buy one, make sure you purchase it on arrival at the airport's Sydney Visitor Centre (below) to get full value. A **taxi** will cost $32 to $36 from the airport to the city centre or Kings Cross.

Bureaux de change at both terminals are open daily from 5am until last arrival with rates comparable to major banks. On the ground floor (arrivals) of the international terminal, the **Sydney Visitor Centre** (daily 5am until last arrival; ⓣ02/9667 6050) can arrange car rental and onward travel – it's licensed to sell train and bus tickets – and can **book hotels** anywhere in Sydney and New South Wales free of charge and at stand-by rates. Most hostels advertise on an adjacent notice board; there's a freephone line for reservations, and many hostels will refund your bus fare; a few also do free airport pick-ups.

By train and bus

All local and interstate **trains** arrive at **Central Station** on Eddy Avenue, just south of the city centre; long-distance and interstate trains arrive at what is known as the Country Trains terminal. There are lockers by the main entrance to the country trains terminal off Pitt Street ($8/$6/$4 per 24hr depending on size) and showers at the volunteer-run **Travellers' Aid** (Mon–Sat 8am–2.30pm; shower $3, with towel $5, bed $2 per hr) on Platform 1. From Central Station and neighbouring **Railway Square** you can hop on to nearly every major bus route, and from within Central Station you can take a CityRail train to any city or suburban station (see "City transport" below).

All **buses** to Sydney arrive and depart from Eddy Avenue and Pitt Street, bordering Central Station. The area is well set up with decent cafés, a 24-hour police station and a huge YHA hostel (see p.174), as well as the **Sydney Coach Terminal** (daily 6am–10pm), which also has luggage lockers ($7–12 per 24hr, depending on size). The **Travellers' Information Service** (ⓣ02/9281 9366) in the coach terminal can make hotel **accommodation bookings** at stand-by rates while a range of hostels advertise on an adjacent notice board with free phones for direct reservations; many of them provide free pick-ups (usually from Bay 14). You can purchase coach tickets and passes from the Information Service as well as Sydney Passes (see box on p.38), and arrange harbour cruises and other tours.

City transport

Sydney's public transport network is reasonably good, though there are frequent delays with trains and, as the system relies heavily on buses, traffic jams can be a problem. As well as buses and trains, there are ferries, a light rail system and the city monorail to choose from, plus plenty of licensed taxis.

Trains stop running around midnight, as do most regular buses, though several services towards the eastern and northern beaches, such as the #380 to Bondi Beach, the #372 and #373 to Coogee and the #151 to Manly, run through the night. Otherwise a pretty good network of **Nightride buses** follow the train routes to the suburbs, departing from Town Hall Station (outside the Energy Australia Building on George Street) and stopping at train stations (where taxis wait at designated ranks); return train tickets, Railpasses and Travelpasses can be used, or buy a ticket from the driver. For stays of more than a few days, a weekly **Travelpass** is a worthwhile investment (see box on pp.38–39). For public transport information, routes and timetables contact the **Transport Infoline** ☎13 15 00 (daily 6am–10pm; Ⓦwww.131500.com.au).

Buses

Within the central area, **buses**, hailed from yellow-signed bus stops, are the most convenient, widespread mode of transport, and cover more of the city than the trains. With few exceptions buses radiate from the centre with major interchanges at Railway Square near Central Station (especially southwest routes), at Circular Quay (range of routes), from York and Carrington streets outside Wynyard Station (North Shore), and Bondi Junction Station (eastern suburbs and beaches). **Tickets** can be bought on board from the driver and cost from $1.60 for up to two distance-measured sections, rising to a maximum of $5.20 for sixteen plus sections; $2.70 (up to five sections) is the most typical fare. Substantial discounts are available with TravelTen tickets and other travel passes (see box on pp.38–39); these must be validated in the ticket reader by the front door. Bus **information** – including route maps, **timetables** and **passes** – is available from handy booths at Carrington Street, Wynyard; at Circular Quay on the corner of Loftus and Alfred streets; at the Queen Victoria Building on York Street; at Bondi Junction bus interchange; and at Manly Wharf. For detailed timetables and route maps see Sydney Buses' website Ⓦwww.sydneybuses.nsw.gov.au.

Trains

Trains, operated by **CityRail** (see colour map at back of book), will get you where you're going faster than buses, especially at rush hour and when heading out to the suburbs, but you need to transfer to a bus or ferry to get to most harbourside or beach destinations. There are six train lines, mostly overground, each of which stops at Central and Town Hall stations. Trains run from around 5am to midnight, with **tickets** starting at around $2.20 single on the City Loop and for short hops; buying off-peak returns (after 9am and all weekend) means you can save up to forty percent.

Automatic **ticket machines** (which give change) and barriers (insert magnetic tickets, otherwise show ticket at the gate) have been introduced just about everywhere. On-the-spot fines for fare evasion start from $200 and transit officers patrol trains frequently to check tickets. All platforms are painted with designated "nightsafe" waiting areas and all but two or three train carriages are closed after about 8pm, enforcing a cattle-like safety in numbers. Security guards also patrol trains at night. At other times, if the train is deserted, sit in the carriage nearest the guard, marked by a blue light.

Ferries and cruises

Sydney's distinctive green-and-yellow **ferries** are the fastest means of transport from Circular Quay to the North Shore, and indeed to most places around the harbour. Even if you don't want to go anywhere, a ferry ride is a must, a chance to get out on the water and see the city from the harbour. There's also a speedy **hydrofoil**, the JetCat, which reaches Manly in half the time the ferry takes, but with less charm. Get hold of the excellent free *Go Walkabout: easy access to Sydney's best walks* from the Sydney Ferries Information Centre, Wharf 4, Circular Quay, with details of sixteen **ferry-accessible walks** (including colour maps), from Neutral Bay to Parramatta.

There are ferries going off in various directions from the wharves at Circular Quay including cruises (see colour map at back of book). The popular **Manly Ferry service** leaves Circular Quay for Manly twice an hour, more frequently during rush hour, between about 6.30am and midnight (to 11pm Sun) and take thirty minutes. Faster JetCat **catamarans** operate in the morning and evening on weekdays (Mon–Fri 6am–9.25am & 4.20pm–8.30pm) and between 7.10am & 3.35pm on Sundays (from 6.10am Sat). Most ferry routes operate until 11.30pm from Monday to Saturday, with the exception of the Darling Harbour service which runs until 10pm, and the Parramatta River, Watsons

Bay and Taronga zoo services, which finish in the early evening. Except for the Manly Ferry, services on Sunday are greatly reduced and finish in the early evening around 6pm or 7pm. Timetables for each route are available at Circular Quay or on the Sydney Ferries website (Ⓦwww.sydneyferries.nsw.gov.au).

One-way **fares** are $4.80 ($6 for the Manly Ferry); return fares are double. The pricier JetCat to Manly and RiverCat to Parramatta are $7.90 and $7.40 respectively. Once again, the various Travelpasses and FerryTen tickets can be a good deal – see box on pp.38–39 for details.

Harbour cruises

There's a wide choice of **harbour cruises**, almost all of them leaving from Jetty 6, Circular Quay and the rest from Darling Harbour. Before you part with your cash, however, bear in mind that apart from the running commentary (which can be rather annoying), most offer nothing that you won't get on a regular harbour **ferry** for a lot less. The best of the ordinary harbour ferry trips is the thirty-minute ride to **Manly**, but there's a ferry going somewhere at almost any time throughout the day. If you really want to splash out, you could take a **water taxi** ride – Circular Quay to Watsons Bay, for example, costs $54 for the first passenger and then an additional $9 for each extra person. Pick-ups are available from any wharf if booked in advance (try Water Taxis Combined on Ⓣ02/9555 8888; Ⓦwww.harbourtaxis.com.au). One water taxi company, **Watertours**, located on Cockle Bay Wharf in Darling Harbour (Ⓣ02/9211 7730, Ⓦwww.watertours.com.au), even offers tours on its latest-model, in bright yellow taxis, which look like New York cabs on the water, from $12.50 for a speedy ten-minute one-way spin under the Harbour Bridge, past The Rocks and ending up at the Opera House (every 15min). There's also a fifty-minute cruise which takes in Fort Denison and the yacht marina in RushcuttersBay as well as some pricey waterfront real estate (every 15min; $20), and a one-hour sunset cruise (sunset nightly; $25).

The **Australian Travel Specialists** (ATS) at Jetty 6, Circular Quay and the Harbourside Shopping Centre at Darling Harbour (Ⓣ02/9211 3192, Ⓦwww.atstravel.com.au) book all cruises. Those offered by State Transit – **Harboursights Cruises** (Ⓣ13 15 00, Ⓦwww.sydneyferries.nsw.gov.au) – are the best value: choose between the Morning Harbour Cruise (daily 10.30am; 1hr; $18), the recommended Afternoon Harbour Cruise to Middle Harbour and back (Mon–Fri 1pm, Sat & Sun 12.30pm; 2hr 30min; $24) and the Evening Harbour Cruise (Mon–Sat 8pm; 1hr 30min; $22). You can buy tickets at the Sydney Ferry ticket offices at Circular Quay. The STA cruises are also included in a Sydney Pass.

Captain Cook Cruises at Jetty 6, Circular Quay (Ⓣ02/9206 1122, Ⓦwww.captaincook.com.au), the big commercial operator, offers a vast range of cruises on their very large boats, including morning and afternoon "Coffee" Cruises into Middle Harbour (daily 10am & 2.15pm; 2hr 20min; $39), a lunch cruise (daily 12.30pm; 1hr 30min; buffet $57, two- or three-course $59–69), a range of dinner cruises including the two-course Sunset Dinner (includes a drink; daily 5pm; 1hr 35min; $69) and Opera Afloat with opera singers accompanying a four-course dinner (daily 7pm; 2hr 30min; $99). Also available are a Harbour Highlights Cruise (daily 9.30am, 11am, 12.45am, 2.30pm, 4pm & 5.45pm; 1hr 15min; $20; option of getting off at Darling Harbour on the 11am, 2.30pm & 4pm trips) and a hop-on-hop-off five-stop Sydney Harbour Explorer (daily from Circular Quay 9.30am, 11.30am, 1.30pm & 3.30pm; $25; combined ticket with the zoo or the aquarium is $39) circuiting between Circular Quay, the Man O' War Jetty at the Opera House, Watsons Bay, Taronga Zoo and Darling Harbour.

Matilda Cruises, based in Darling Harbour (Aquarium Wharf, Pier 26; Ⓣ02/9264 7377, Ⓦwww.matilda.com.au), offers various smaller-scale cruises on sailing catamarans, with big foredecks providing great views. Departures are from Darling Harbour (either at the Aquarium or King Street wharves) with pick-ups from Circular Quay twenty minutes later. Morning and afternoon cruises include tea, coffee and biscuits (10am & 3.05pm from King St Wharf; 1–2hr; $27); there's a buffet on the Lunch Cruise (12.10pm; 2hr;

Whale-watching cruises

Whale watching has exploded in Sydney in the last couple of years, with an increase of around 25,000 boat-based watchers in 2004. Many operators now offer daily whale watch cruises from Darling Harbour or Circular Quay during the June–July season, when you are likely to see migratory humpback or southern right whales. The cruises head north or south depending on the whale locations at the time and day. Guidelines specify that they must keep a slow speed within 300m of whales, but can approach up to 100m (200m if a calf is present). The average trip takes 3.5hr to 4hr and costs $75–85 dollars, but will have as many as 75 passengers on board; most operators have some guarantee in place that you'll see whales or another trip will be offered. The bigger operators include True Blue Cruises (ⓣ1800 309 672, ⓦwww.sydneywhalewatching.com) and Bass and Flinders Cruises (ⓣ02/9583 1199, ⓦwww.whalewatchingsydney.net), while operators such as Sydney Eco Whale Watching (ⓣ02/9878 0300, www.austspiritsailingco.com.au) do smaller yacht trips.

$59), while the pricey Dinner Cruise allows you to dine on the foredeck (King St Wharf 7.30pm, Circular Quay 8pm; 2hr 30min; $99). They also offer the Rocket Harbour Express Cruise, a one-hour trip stopping at the Aquarium Wharf at Darling Harbour, Man O' War Jetty at the Opera House, Commissioners Steps at Circular Quay West, Taronga Zoo and Watsons Bay; you can get off at the stops and rejoin later cruises (9.30am–4.30pm; every hour; $22 includes refreshment; ticket lasts all day but for one complete circuit only). There is also a straight Matilda Ferry service, the **Rocket Express**, shuttling between Darling Harbour, the Star City Casino and Circular Quay every thirty minutes ($5.70 one-way, $10 return) and they also have a weekday Lane Cove River ferry ($5.80 one-way; see p.161) and a commuter service to Homebush Bay $5.80 one-way (see p.157).

If you're feeling romantically inclined, you might fancy a trip on an authentic old sailing ship, such as Sydney's oldest, the *James Craig*, an 1874 three-masted iron barque, which is part of the Sydney Heritage Fleet, based at Wharf 7, Pirrama Rd, Pyrmont, near Star City Casino (ⓣ02/9298 3888, ⓦwww.australianheritagefleet.com.au). The beautifully restored square rigger does cruises on Saturdays (10.30am–5pm; $193; over-12s only; morning and afternoon tea and lunch provided). A similar sailing experience is offered by Svanen Charters (ⓣ02/9698 4456, ⓦwww.svanen.com.au), moored at Campbells Cove: this sailing ship, built in 1922, offers day-sails on the harbour for $110, including morning tea and lunch, or longer overnight sails to Broken Bay, Port Hacking, Jervis Bay or Port Stephens (two nights $297, three nights $396).

With **Sydney by Sail** (ⓣ02/9280 1110, ⓦwww.sydneybysail.com), you can enjoy the harbour from on board a luxury yacht. Groups are small (from six up to twenty) and if you're interested the skipper will even show you some sailing techniques. The popular three-hour Port Jackson Explorer cruise sails Sydney Harbour and surrounding inlets (daily 1–4pm; $130). Departures are from the National Maritime Museum at Darling Harbour, with free entry to the museum thrown in on the day (so buy your ticket in the morning and check out the museum before the afternoon sail).The yachts are also available for charter (see p.273).

An alternative to the sedate cruises listed above is offered by **Ocean Extreme** (ⓣ0414 800 046 or 0418 213 145, ⓦwww.oceanextreme.com.au) on *Extreme 1*, an RIB (Rigid Inflatable Boat), with small groups of ten passengers taken on a hair-raising forty-minute "Adrenaline Tour" (daily 11am & 1pm; $90; bookings necessary) at speeds of more than 100km an hour; most of the harbour scenery is a blur but it's great fun. More thrills can be had with **Harbour Jet** (ⓣ1300 887 373, ⓦwww.harbourjet.com) on the 35-minute *Jet Blast* (daily noon, 2.15pm & 4pm; $60) that departs from the Convention Jetty, Darling Harbour; with speeds of 75km an hour, including a 270-degree spin, and accompanied by blasting music, it's not for the faint-hearted and is loathed by the locals. There are also a number of water-based cruises leaving from **Manly Wharf** (see p.146).

State Transit Authority (STA) travel passes

In addition to single-journey tickets, there's a vast array of STA **travel passes** available. The most useful for visitors are outlined below; for more **information** on the full range of tickets and timetables, phone the **Transport Infoline** or check out their website (daily 6am–10pm; ⓣ13 15 00, ⓦwww.131500.com.au).

Passes are sold at most **newsagents** and at **train stations**; the more tourist-oriented Sydney Passes and Sydney Explorer Passes can be bought on board the Explorer buses, at the airport (from the Sydney Visitor Centre and the STA booth in the international terminal and from State Transit ground staff in the domestic), at State Transit Info booths, from the Sydney Visitor Centre in The Rocks (see p.27) and at some Countrylink offices as well as at train stations.

No travel pass includes the Airport Line stations (Green Square, Mascot, Domestic Airport and International Airport). An extra Gate Pass must be purchased to exit from these two stations; however, you can purchase a Gate Pass on arrival without being fined.

Tourist passes

Sydney Explorer Pass (one-day $36, child $18, family $90) comes with a map and description of the sights, and includes free travel on any State Transit bus within the same zones as the Explorer routes. The red **Sydney Explorer** (from Circular Quay daily 8.40am–5.22pm; every 18min) takes in all the important sights in the city and inner suburbs, via 26 hop-on-hop-off stops. The blue **Bondi Explorer** (daily from Circular Quay 9.15am–4.15pm; every 30min) covers the waterside eastern suburbs (19 stops include Kings Cross, Paddington, Double Bay, Vaucluse, Bondi, Bronte, Clovelly and Coogee). A **two-day ticket** ($62, child $31, family $155) allows use of both bus services over two days in a seven-day period.

Sydney Pass (three-, five- or seven-day passes within a seven-day period; $100/$130/$150, child passes $50/$65/$75, family passes $250/ $325/$375) is valid for all buses and ferries including the above Explorer services, the ferry and JetCat to Manly, the RiverCat to Parramatta and a return trip to the airport valid for two months with the Airport Link train (buy the pass at the airport on arrival). It also includes three narrated harbour cruises, one of them in the evening, travel on trains within a central area, and discounts at many attractions.

Monorail and Light Rail

Metro Transport Sydney (ⓣ02/9285 5600, ⓦwww.metromonorail.com.au) is a privately owned company running the city's monorail and light rail system. This means STA travel-passes cannot be used on either system. However, a $28 weekly pass can be bought which includes unlimited trips on both the Monorail and the Light Rail.

Metro Monorail is essentially a tourist shuttle designed to loop around Darling Harbour every three to five minutes, connecting it with the city centre. Thundering along tracks set above the older city streets, the "monster rail" – as many locals know it – doesn't exactly blend in with its surroundings. Still, the elevated view of the city, particularly from Pyrmont Bridge, makes it worth investing $4 (day-pass $8) and the ten minutes to do the whole circuit with its eight stops (Mon–Thurs 7am–10pm, Thurs–Sat 7am–midnight, Sun 8am–10pm; frequency 3–5 minutes).

Metro Light Rail runs from Central Station to the Pyrmont Peninsula and on to Lilyfield in the inner west. There are fourteen stops on the route, which links Central Station with Chinatown, Darling Harbour, Star City Casino, the fish markets at Pyrmont, Wentworth Park's greyhound racecourse, Glebe (with stops near Pyrmont Bridge Road, at Jubilee Park and Rozelle Bay by Bicentennial Park) and Lilyfield, not far from Darling Street, Rozelle. The air-conditioned light rail vehicles can carry two hundred passengers, and are fully accessible to disabled commuters. The service operates 24 hours to the

Buses, trains and ferries

Travelpasses allow unlimited use of buses, trains and ferries and can begin on any day of the week. Most useful are the **Red Travelpass** ($32 a week), valid for the city and inner suburbs, and inner harbour ferries (not the Manly Ferry or the RiverCat beyond Meadowbank), and the **Green Travelpass** ($40), which allows use of all ordinary ferries. Passes covering a wider area cost between $44 and $54 a week, and monthly passes are also available.

DayTripper tickets ($15) are also available for unlimited travel on all services offered by CityRail, Sydney Buses and Sydney Ferries.

Buses and ferries

The **Blue Travelpass** ($29 a week) gives unlimited travel on buses in the inner-city area and on inner-harbour ferries but cannot be used for Manly or beyond Meadowbank; the **Orange Travelpass** ($36 a week) gets you further on the buses and is valid on all ferries; and the **Pittwater Travelpass** ($49 a week) gives unlimited travel on all buses and ferries. These travelpasses start with first use rather than on the day of purchase.

Buses

TravelTen tickets represent a thirty percent saving over single fares by buying ten trips at once; they can be used over a space of time and for more than one person. The tickets are colour-coded according to how many sections they cover; the Brown TravelTen ($21.30), for example, is the choice for trips from Leichhardt to the city, while the Red TravelTen ($27.90) is the one to buy if you're staying at Bondi.

Ferries

FerryTen tickets, valid for ten single trips, start at $30.30 for Inner Harbour Services, go up to $45.10 for the Manly Ferry, and peak at $65.70 for the JetCat services.

Trains

Seven Day RailPass tickets allow unlimited travel between any two nominated stations and those in between, with savings of about twenty percent on the price of five return trips. For example, a pass between Bondi Junction and Town Hall would cost $22.

casino (every 10–15min 6am–midnight; every 30min midnight–6am) with reduced hours for stops beyond to Lilyfield (Mon–Thurs & Sun 6am–11pm, Fri & Sat 6am–midnight; every 10–15min). There are two zones: zone 1 stations are Central to Convention in Darling Harbour, and zone 2 is from Pyrmont Bay to Lilyfield. Tickets can be purchased at vending machines by the stops; singles cost $3/$4.20 for zone 1/zone 2, returns $4.60/5.70; a day-pass costs $8.40 (family $20) and a weekly one $20. A TramLink ticket, available from any CityRail station, combines a rail ticket to Central Station with an MLR ticket. If you think you'll be using either the Monorail or Light Rail a lot, a METROcard can be purchased which gives six rides on either; the $18 card can then be topped up for subsequent rides at $2.50 per ride.

Taxis

Taxis are vacant if the rooftop light is on, though they are notoriously difficult to find at 3pm, when the shifts change over. The four major city cab ranks are outside the *Four Seasons Hotel* at the start of George Street, The Rocks; on Park Street outside Woolworths, opposite the Town Hall; outside David Jones department store on Market Street; and at the Pitt Street (country trains) entrance to Central Station. Drivers never expect a tip but often need directions – try to have some idea of where you're going. Check the correct tariff rate is displayed: tariff 2 (10pm–6am) is twenty percent more than tariff 1 (6am–10pm). To book a taxi, call ABC (☎13 25 22); Legion (☎13 14 51); Premier (☎13 10 17); RSL (☎13 15 81); St

Warning: The Cross City Tunnel

The A$680 million Cross City Tunnel opened in August 2005; with no toll booths, and extremely high rates for casual users, it's a nightmare for visitors to the city. Running east–west/west–east beneath the city centre between Darling Harbour and Rushcutters Bay, it links the Anzac Bridge and the Western Distributor at the western end and New South Head Road at the eastern end and has underground links with the Eastern Distributor (which heads out to the airport). The 2.1km tunnel cuts a thirty-minute traffic-jammed cross-city route to five minutes – but at a high cost. Financed and run by a private consortium, there are no subsidies here. While frequent users can use an electronic tag by opening a toll account and giving car registration details, with tolls then costing $3.49 each way (plus an annual $70 administration fee and $5.50 quarterly account print-out fees; the e-tag is also usable on all other motorways), short term visitors can apply for a one- to seven-day pass by providing credit card and registration details. Your car hire company should be able to sort it out for you, but if you're borrowing a car, you organise it online on the ⓦwww.crosscity.com.au website, or call ⓣ90 333 999. The toll fee for casual users is an extra $1.60 each way ($5.09) plus there's a pricey $4.90 registration/administration fee, forcing the one-way toll to an exorbitant $10.

George (ⓣ13 21 66); or Taxis Combined (ⓣ02/8332 8888). For harbour water taxis call Taxis Afloat (ⓣ02/9955 3222).

Driving and vehicle rental

Renting **your own vehicle** allows you to explore Sydney's more far-flung beaches and national parks and other day-trip areas.

Most foreign **licences** are valid for a year in Australia. An International Driving Permit (available from national motoring organizations) may be useful if you come from a non-English-speaking country. **Fuel prices** fluctuate from 90¢ to over $1 per litre unleaded from week to week, with diesel slightly cheaper. The **rules of the road** are similar to those in the US and UK. Most importantly, **drive on the left** (as in the UK), remember that seatbelts are compulsory for all, and that the **speed limit** in all built-up areas is 50kph (or 60kph if signposted; 40kph in school zones during school hours). Outside built-up areas, maximum limits are between 80kph and 110kph. All changes in speed limits are frequently and obviously signed. Whatever else you do in a vehicle, don't **drink alcohol** to excess; random breath tests are common even in rural areas, especially during the Christmas season and on Friday and Saturday nights. One rule that might catch you out in town is that **roadside parking** must be in the same direction as the traffic.

Vehicle rental

To **rent** a car you need a full, clean driving licence; usually, a minimum age of 21 is stipulated by the major car-rental companies, rising to 25 for 4WDs. Check on any mileage limits or other restrictions, extras and what you're covered for in an accident before signing. The multinational operators Hertz, Budget, Avis and Thrifty have offices in Sydney. **Local firms** – of which there are many – are almost always better value, and the bottom-line "rent-a-bomb" agencies go as low as $35 a day; however, these places often have restrictions on how far away from Sydney you're allowed to go. A city-based non-multinational rental agency will supply new cars for around $50 a day with unlimited kilometres.

Four-wheel drives are best used for specific areas rather than long term, as rental (and fuel) costs are steep, starting at around $120 a day. Some 4WD agents actually don't allow their vehicles to be driven off sealed roads, so check the small print first.

You can reserve a vehicle before you arrive with the businesses below, or once you're in Sydney from any of the companies listed in the "Directory".

Rental companies

Autos Abroad In the UK ☎0870/066 7788, ⓦwww.autosabroad.co.uk.
Avis In the UK ☎0870/0100 287; in Eire ☎021/428 1111; in the US ☎1-800/230-4898; in Canada ☎1-800/272-5871; in New Zealand ☎0800/655 111; ⓦwww.avis.com.
Budget In the UK ☎0800/153 9170; in Eire ☎090/662 7711; in the US ☎1-800/527-0700; in Canada ☎ 1-800/268-8900; in New Zealand ☎0800/283 438; ⓦwww.budget.com.
Hertz In the UK ☎0870/844 8844; in Eire ☎01/676 7476; in the US ☎1-800/654-3131; in Canada ☎1-800/263-0600; ⓦwww.hertz.com.
Holiday Autos In the UK ☎0870/400 0011; in Eire ☎01/872 9366; ⓦwww.holidayautos.com.
Kemwel Holiday Autos In the US ☎1-877/820-0668, ⓦwww.kemwel.com.
National In the US ☎1-800/CAR-RENT, ⓦwww.nationalcar.com.

Post, phones and email

As you might expect, Sydney has an efficient postal service, a good telephone network and plenty of places to go online and check email.

Post

Australia's national **postal service** is called Australia Post. Post offices are generally open Monday to Friday 9am to 5pm but the General Post Office (GPO) in Martin Place has longer hours (Mon–Fri 8.15am–5.30pm, Sat 9am–1pm). There are red post boxes outside post offices and on streets throughout the city. Make sure you put letters in the red box outside post offices, and not the yellow, which is for express post parcels. This guaranteed overnight express delivery service from Sydney to other major cities is handy and relatively inexpensive but ordinary mail is much less reliable: even a letter from Sydney to Katoomba in the Blue Mountains can take two days or more. **International mail** is extremely efficient, taking four to five working days to the UK, four to six to the US and five to seven to Canada. **Stamps** are sold at post offices and agencies; most newsagencies sell them for standard local letters only. A standard letter or postcard within Australia costs 50¢; printed aerogrammes for international letters anywhere in the world cost 95¢; postcards cost 1.10¢; and regular letters start at $1.80 to the US, Canada, or Europe. If you're sending anything bigger in or outside Australia, there are many different services: get some advice from the post office. Large **parcels** are reasonably cheap to send home by surface mail, but it will take up to three months for them to get there. Economy Air is a good compromise for packages that you want to see again soon (up to 20kg) – expect a fortnight to Europe. To get more information on letter and parcel postage rates, and expected delivery waits, go to ⓦwww.austpost.com.au and click on "postage calculator".

You can receive mail at any post office in or around Sydney: address the letter to **Poste Restante** followed by the town or suburb, state of NSW and postcode, but the best address to give friends before you leave is: Poste Restante, Sydney, NSW 2000, Australia. However, the address to pick up this Poste Restante mail is not at the Martin Place GPO but at the post office in the Hunter Connection shopping mall at 310 George St (Mon–Fri 8.15am–6pm), opposite Wynyard Station. You need a passport or other ID to collect mail, which is kept for a month and then returned; it's possible to get mail redirected if you change your plans – ask for a form at any post office. Some smaller post offices will allow you to phone and check if you have any mail waiting.

Most **hostels** and **hotels** will also hold mail for you if it's clearly marked, preferably with a date of arrival, or holders of Amex cards or travellers' cheques can have it sent to American Express offices.

Addresses and floor levels

The way that **addresses** are written for apartments (also more commonly known as a flats, units or home units) or offices in Australia can cause some confusion when you're trying to visit someone. What might be written in full elsewhere as, for example, Apartment 4, 6 Smith St, is always given as 4/6 Smith St; some travellers confuse this as meaning flat 6, 4 Smith St. Just remember, the apartment or office number is first, then the street address number follows. Contrary to the US system, floor levels are given as ground, first, second, third, or ground, level 1, level 2, level 3 etc. Basement levels are often called lower ground floor.

Phones, phonecards and mobile phones

The two major phone operators in Australia are the partially privatized Telstra, and Optus. As a mainly government-run organization, Telstra's coverage is wider but their daily rates are pretty similar. All public phones are Telstra-operated. Post offices (but not agencies) always have a bank of **telephones** outside; otherwise head for the nearest bar or service station. Public telephones take coins or Telstra **phonecards**, which are sold through newsagents and other stores for $5, $10, $20 or $50. You can also buy Telstra PhoneAway cards, which can be used with both private and public phones using a PIN number in $10, $20, $50 and $100 varieties. You can make **international calls** from virtually any public Telstra phones as from a private phone (though rates are much higher). Many bars, shops and restaurants have orange or blue **payphones**, but these cost more than a regular call box, and international dialling is not advised because they'll start to gobble money the moment you're connected, even if the call goes unanswered. Whatever their type, payphones do not accept incoming calls. The unattended Telstra Pay Phone Centre, 231 Elizabeth St (Mon–Fri 7am–11pm, Sat & Sun 7am–5pm) has private booths for more privacy and quiet, but bring change or a phone card with you.

Creditphones accept most major credit cards such as Amex, Visa and Diners International, and can be found at international and domestic airports, central locations in major cities, and many hotels. You can make free **reverse charge** calls using the 1800 REVERSE option.

Local calls are untimed, allowing you to talk for as long as you like; this costs 17–20¢ on a domestic phone, though Telstra public phones charge 40¢. **Rates** for STD (long-distance – over 50km) calls within Australia from a public phone box are cheapest in the evenings from 7pm to 7am, and from private phones Monday to Friday and Sunday 7pm to midnight and Saturday from 4pm to midnight. Many businesses and services operate **free-call numbers**, prefixed ☎1800, while others have six-digit numbers beginning with ☎13 or 1300 that are charged at a local-call rate no matter where you are calling from within Australia. However, you cannot call 1800 numbers from outside Australia. Numbers starting ☎1900 (and occasionally ☎0055, though these have mostly been phased out) are private information services (often recorded), from wake-up calls to weather reports, costing between 38¢ and 55¢ a minute; a message introduction will be charged at 16.5¢ (40¢ from public phones), when you'll be alerted to the exorbitant charge before being given the choice to proceed.

Phonecards can be a far cheaper way to call cross-country or abroad. Various brands are available such as Say G'day (☎1800 616 606, Ⓦwww.saygdaycallingcard.com) or Gotalk (Ⓦwww.gotalk.com.au), but all require a minimum of 25¢ to call the local centre (40¢ from a payphone), after which you key in your scratch number and telephone number. Rates are incredibly low: as little as under 5¢ a minute to the US, UK, New Zealand and Canada. Global Gossip (see "Email", opposite) offers discount-rate international calls from private phone booths and Backpackers' Travel Centres (see "Travel agents", p.283) sell their own rechargeable discount phone card.

Operators and international codes

Operator services

Local Directory Assistance ⓣ1223
Local Operator ⓣ1234
National Directory Assistance ⓣ12 455
International Operator ⓣ1234
International Directory Assistance ⓣ12455

International calls

To call Australia from overseas dial the international access code (ⓣ00 from the UK or New Zealand, ⓣ011 from the US and Canada), followed by ⓣ61, the area code minus its initial zero, and the number. To dial out of Australia it's ⓣ0011, followed by the country code, then the area code (without the zero, if there is one), followed by the number:
Ireland ⓣ0011 353
UK ⓣ0011 44
US and Canada ⓣ0011 1
New Zealand ⓣ0011 64

Country direct

Canada
Teleglobe free call ⓣ1800 881 490
Ireland
Telecom ⓣ1800 881 353
New Zealand
Clearfree call ⓣ1800 124 333
Telecom free call ⓣ1800 881 640
UK
BT operator free call ⓣ1800 881 440
BT automatic free call ⓣ1800 881 441
Mercury free call ⓣ1800 881 417
US
AT&T free call ⓣ1800 881 011
LDDS Worldcom free call ⓣ1800 881 212
MCI free call ⓣ1800 881 100
Sprint free call ⓣ1800 881 877

It's also possible to pop into Woolworths or K-Mart and buy a **prepaid mobile phone** for as little as $99 including a pay-as-you-go SIM card with $25 credit that lasts three months. Or you can just buy the prepaid SIM card alone in various denominations, which slips into your own phone – UK-sourced GSM 900 and 1800 units work fine but US systems are not compatible – to give you an instant personal number once you've registered – very handy if you need to keep in touch when trying to get a job, for example. There are six main mobile phone networks in Australia: Telstra is the main provider (ⓦwww.telstra.com.au) with the widest network coverage, while Vodafone (ⓦwww.vodafone.com.au) is a long way behind on cross coverage but may work out cheaper solely for urban use in Sydney. Other providers include Optus (ⓦwww.optus.com.au), Orange (ⓦwww.orange.net.au) and 3 (3G – the only network with live video calling; (ⓦwww.three.com.au).

Email

Public Internet access is widespread across Australia and keeping in touch via the Web is easy, fast and cheap in Sydney. **Internet cafés** are everywhere, typically charging $3–6 an hour with concessions as well as happy hours early in the morning. Many accommodation places – especially **hostels** – also provide terminals for their guests at similar rates (hotels will charge more) although some places still opt for the user-reviled coin-op booths; at some YHAs you buy a card that works like a phone card. The best machines and setups are what you'd want at home: modern, clean and fast with conventional controls and large screens. Otherwise, **local libraries** almost always provide free access, though time is generally limited to one hour and you'll have to sign up in advance on a waiting list. Some, like the State Library on Macquarie Street (see p.76), let you surf the Net for free but don't allow email access, while the Customs House Library (see "The Media", below) has free access for members and charges a reasonable $3 per hour for non-members. You can also surf the Net as part of your admission to the Australian Museum. Darlinghurst Road in Kings Cross is crammed with cut-rate Internet places, with rates as low as $3 per hour. The chain Global Gossip has seven offices ($4 for 30min–1hr; ⓣ02/9212 1466, ⓦwww.globalgossip.com), near Central Station at 790 George St, near Chinatown at 415 Pitt St (both daily 9am–11pm), in the CBD at 14 Wentworth Ave (Mon–Fri 9am–6pm), at 111 Darlinghurst Rd, Kings Cross (daily 8–1am), and at 37 Hall St, Bondi Beach (Mon–Thurs 9am–midnight, Fri–Sun 9am–11pm). *Phone.Net Cafe*, 73–75 Hall St, Bondi Beach (Mon–Fri 8am–10pm, 9pm Sat & Sun; $3.30 per hour) is a lively café haunt in its own right.

The media

There is a wide range of print media in Sydney, a rather American-influenced variety of TV channels, and a number of radio stations worth tuning in to.

The press

The Murdoch-owned *Australian* is Australia's only national daily (that is, Mon–Sat) newspaper; aimed mainly at the business community, it has good overseas coverage but local news is often built around statistics. However, its bumper weekend (Sat) edition is much more lively and interesting. The *Australian Financial Review* is the in-depth business and finance paper to buy. Each state (or, more properly, each state capital) has its own daily broadsheet, the best of which are two Fairfax-owned papers, the *Sydney Morning Herald* and Melbourne's venerable *The Age*. *The Age* is also widely available in Sydney but be warned that the two papers share similar content in their Saturday-edition weekend magazines. Sydney also has a tabloid, the Murdoch-owned *Daily Telegraph*. Both Sydney dailies have a more low-brow, advertisement-packed, multi-section Sunday version, the *Sun Herald* and the *Sunday Telegraph*. But the *Sydney Morning Herald* (*SMH*; ⓦwww.smh.com.au) is *the* paper to buy to find out what's on in Sydney and there's usually a special supplement each day: the most useful are Monday's "The Guide", a programme and review of the week's TV; Tuesday's "Good Living", which focuses on the restaurant, foodie and bar scene; and Friday's "Metro", the entertainment supplement which includes listings and film, art and music reviews. Friday's *SMH* also has "The Form", a weekly racing guide. There are employment and rental sections daily, but the big Saturday edition is the best for these.

The *Guardian Weekly* and the *International Herald Tribune* are two easy-to-buy **international papers**. The Customs House Library, on three levels of Customs House, 31 Alfred St, Circular Quay (Mon–Fri 8am–7pm, Sat 10am–4pm, Sun noon–4pm; ⓣ02/9242 8555), keeps a large selection of overseas newspapers, though nowadays it's probably easier to search for your favourite home newspaper's website and browse headlines and selected articles in a cybercafé (see "Email", p.43).

The weekly *Time Australia* and *The Bulletin* are Australia's current-affairs **magazines**. If you're interested in wildlife, pick up a copy of the quarterly *Australian Geographic* (related only in name to the US magazine) for some excellent photography and in-depth coverage of Australia's remoter corners, or the quarterly *Australian Wildlife*, a magazine published by the Wildlife Preservation Society. There are some excellent glossy Australian-focused adventure travel magazines, too, like the quarterly *Wild*. Overseas magazines are air-freighted in at exorbitant cost, but you'll find Australian versions of all the fashion mags, from *Vogue* to *Marie Claire*, plus enduring publications like the *Australian Women's Weekly* (now monthly), which is well known for its excellent recipes, while the excellent *Australian Gourmet Traveller* celebrates both fine food and travel. Gossipy magazines like *Who Weekly* feature the lowdown on the antics of international and Australian celebs. On a different note, the Australian version of *The Big Issue*, produced out of Melbourne, is called *The Big Issue Australia* and has been operating since 1996. Vendors are homeless, ex-homeless or long-term unemployed and make half of the cover price. Also speaking to Australia's conscience, the *Quarterly Essay*, published by Black Inc (Ⓦwww.quarterlyessay.com), explores political, cultural and intellectual issues of the day in a 20,000 word essay; recent essays include Robert Manne's *Sending Them Home: Refugees and the New Politics of Indifference*, Germaine Greer's *Whitefella Jump Up: The Shortest Way to Nationhood* and David Malouf's *Made in England: Australia's British Inheritance*.

TV

Australia's first **television station** opened in 1956 and the country didn't get colour television until 1974 – both much later than other Westernized countries. Australian television isn't particularly exciting unless you're into sport, of which there's plenty, and commercial stations put on frequent commercial breaks – with often annoyingly unsophisticated advertisements – throughout films. There are Australian content rulings that ensure a good amount of Australian dramas, series and soap operas, many of which go on to make it big overseas, from the Melbourne-set *Neighbours* and *The Secret Life of Us* to *Home and Away*, filmed at Sydney's Palm Beach, and the hilarious suburban send-up *Kath and Kim*. However, there's a predominance of American programmes. Australian TV is also fairly permissive in terms of sexual content compared with the programming of Britain or North America. There are three predictable commercial stations: Channel Seven; Channel Nine, which aims for an older market with more conservative programming; and Channel Ten, which tries to grab the younger market with reality TV programmes like the Australian version of *Big Brother* and some good comedy programmes including the irreverent talk show *Rove Live*. There is also the more serious ABC (Australian Broadcasting Corporation; Ⓦwww.abc.net.au) – a government-funded, national, advertisement-free station still with a British bias, showing all the best British sitcoms and mini-series, and excellent current affairs programmes such as Monday night's *Four Corners*. The lively SBS (Special Broadcasting Service), a mostly government-sponsored, multicultural station, has the best coverage of world news, as well as interesting current affairs programmes and plenty of foreign-language films, with high-quality advertisements (in between programmes only).

Pay TV was introduced into Australia in 1992. There are two pay TV stations, the Murdoch-owned Foxtel (45 channels; 100 channels on its digital service introduced in 2004) and Austar (the leading subscription provider in rural and regional Australia, though the pay-TV culture is not as firmly established yet as in other countries (a quarter of the population subscribe), and even expensive hotels often still only have terrestrial TV.

Digital broadcasting was launched in Australia in 2002 and is being slowly phased in (anaolog TV is expected to be phased out by 2008) but most people still have analog TV sets. All the free-to-air commercial broadcasters are transmitting demonstration digital television services in the capital cities, which usually include programme guides and weather, while SBS offers a World News Channel (Channel 33) broadcasting 18 hours a day, and the ABC recently launched a new digital channel, Channel 21, which shows an assorted selection of programmes. These free-to-air digital channels can also be accessed from pay TV services. You can look at channel guides on Ⓦwww.ebroadcast.com.au, with links to all the TV stations and even your favourite Aussie TV shows.

Radio

The best **radio** is on the various ABC stations, both local and national: Radio National (576 AM) offers a popular mix of arty intellectual topics; 2BL (702 AM), intelligent talk-back radio; News Radio (630 AM), 24-hour local and international news, current affairs, sports, science and finance, also using a diverse range of foreign radio networks including the BBC World Service, the US's National Public Radio (NPR) and Germany's Radio Deutsche Welle; ABC Classic FM (92.9 FM), for classical music; and 2JJJ ("Triple J"; 105.7 FM), which supports local bands and alternative rock – aimed squarely at the nation's youth. You can listen to various ABC radio stations on the Web with live or on-demand audio (Ⓦwww.abc.net.au/streaming). Koori Radio (94.5FM; Ⓦwww.gadigal.org.au) gives voice to Aboriginal and Torres Strait Island communities in Sydney; the city's only "black" radio station, it plays a great mix of indigenous Australian and World music, and other black musicians. Sydney's "underground" radio station is the university-run – though largely self-supporting – 2SER (107.3FM; Ⓦwww.2ser.com).

Opening hours and public holidays

Business and post office hours are generally Monday to Friday 9am to 5pm. Shops and services usually open Monday to Saturday 9am to 5pm and until 9pm on Thursday night. The major retailers and several shopping malls in the city and in tourist areas also open on Sunday between 11am and 5pm, and big supermarkets generally open seven days from 8am until 8 or 9pm, though some close around 4pm on Sundays but many are open until midnight. In addition, there are numerous 24-hour 7/11 convenience type stores/supermarkets in the inner city and suburbs, most often attached to petrol stations.

Tourist attractions – museums, galleries and historic monuments – are open daily, usually between 10am and 5pm. All close on Christmas Day and Good Friday but otherwise specific opening hours are given throughout the Guide.

Public holidays

When an official holiday falls at the weekend, there may be an extra day off immediately before or after. The school holiday dates, when accommodation gets booked up and prices rise, are given on p.242.

New Year's Day (Jan 1)
Australia Day (Jan 26)
Good Friday
Easter Monday
Anzac Day (April 25)
Queen's Birthday (1st Mon in June)
Bank Holiday (1st Mon in Aug)
Labour Day (1st Mon in Oct)
Christmas Day (Dec 25)
Boxing Day (Dec 26)

Travellers with disabilities

Disability needn't interfere with your sightseeing: the attitude of the management at Sydney's major tourist attractions is excellent, and staff will provide assistance where they can; most national parks have wheelchair accessible walks (including the Royal National Park, see p.328, and the Blue Mountains National Park, see p.307; also check ⓦwww.npws.nsw.gov.au). After cheerfully hosting the Paralympics in 2000, Sydney is now one of the most experienced cities at welcoming disabled travellers.

The Australian federal government provides information and various nationwide services for people with disabilities through the **National Information Communication Awareness Network** (NICAN) and the **Australian Council for the Rehabilitation of the Disabled** (ACROD) – see p.48 for contact details. The **Australian Tourist Commission** offices provide a helpline service and publish a factsheet, *Travelling in Australia for People with Disabilities*, available from its offices worldwide (see p.27 for addresses and phone numbers).

Planning a holiday

There are **organized tours and holidays** specifically for people with disabilities (including mobility, hearing, vision and intellectual restrictions). Some arrange travel only, some travel and accommodation, and others provide a complete package – travel, accommodation, meals and carer support. This last type, as well as catering fully for special needs, provides company for the trip. The contacts on p.48 will be able to put you in touch with any specialists for trips to Sydney; several are listed in the Australian Tourist Commission factsheet. If you want to be more independent, it's important to become an authority on where you must be self-reliant and where you may expect help, especially regarding transport and accommodation. It is also vital to be honest – with travel agencies, insurance companies and travel companions. Know your limitations and make sure others know them. If you do not use a **wheelchair** all the time, but your walking capabilities are limited, remember that you are likely to need to cover greater distances while travelling (often over rougher terrain and in hotter temperatures) than you are used to. If you use a wheelchair, have it serviced before you go and carry a repair kit.

Read your **travel insurance** small print carefully to make sure that people with a pre-existing medical condition are not excluded. And use your travel agent to make your journey simpler: airline or bus companies can cope better if they are expecting you, with a wheelchair provided at airports and staff primed to help. A **medical certificate** of your fitness to travel (provided by your doctor) is also extremely useful; some airlines or insurance companies may insist on it. Make sure that you have extra supplies of medication – carried with you if you fly – and a prescription including the generic name in case of emergency.

Several **books** give a good overview of accessible travel in Australia, and include: *Smooth Ride Guides: Australia and New Zealand*, *Freewheeling Made Easy* (ⓦwww.smoothrideguides.com), a UK-based guide from a charitable organization, which lists support organizations, airports and transport, specialist tour operators and places to visit and stay, though it hasn't been updated since 1994; the more up-to-date *Easy Access Australia*, by Bruce Cameron, is a comprehensive guide written by an Australian wheelchair-user for anyone with a mobility difficulty, and is available over the Internet via ⓦwww.easyaccessaustralia.com.au (A$27.45, postage extra, or available from bookshops in Australia); and there's the 1999 *A Wheelie's Handbook of Australia* by Australian-based Colin James (A$22.95 includes postage and handling within Australia; for international orders see the website Ⓦhome.vicnet.net.au/~wheelies, which has updates and links to other useful sites).

Useful contacts

Ⓦwww.wheelabout.com and **Ⓦwww.accessibility.com.au.** Both have lists of accommodation and transport in Australia for people with disabilities as well as access maps of major Australian cities. The accessibility.com.au website also has a very handy online city guide.

Ⓦwww.toiletmap.gov.au The National Public Toilet Map website details accessible toilets around Sydney and Australia.

In the UK and Ireland

Holiday Care 5th Floor, Surrey House, 4 Bedford Park, Croydon, Surrey CR0 2AP Ⓣ0845/124 9971, Minicom Ⓣ0845/124 9976, Ⓦwww.holidaycare.org.uk. Provides free lists of accessible accommodation abroad. Information on financial help for holidays available.

Irish Wheelchair Association Blackheath Drive, Clontarf, Dublin 3 Ⓣ01/833 8241, Ⓕ833 3873, Ⓔiwa@iol.ie. Useful information provided about travelling abroad with a wheelchair.

RADAR (Royal Association for Disability and Rehabilitation) 12 City Forum, 250 City Rd, London EC1V 8AF Ⓣ020/7250 3222, Minicom Ⓣ020/7250 4119, Ⓦwww.radar.org.uk.

Tripscope The Vassal Centre, Gill Avenue, Bristol BS16 2QQ, Ⓣ0845/7585 641, Ⓦwww.tripscope.org.uk.This registered charity provides a national telephone information service offering free advice on UK and international transport for those with a mobility problem.

In the US and Canada

Access-Able Ⓦwww.access-able.com. Online resource for travellers with disabilities.

Mobility International USA 451 Broadway, Eugene, OR 97401, voice and TDD Ⓣ541/343-1284, Ⓦwww.miusa.org. Information and referral services, access guides, tours and exchange programmes. Annual membership $35 (includes quarterly newsletter).

Society for Accessible Travel & Hospitality (SATH) 347 5th Ave, New York, NY 10016 Ⓣ212/447-7284, Ⓦwww.sath.org. Non-profit educational organization that has actively represented travellers with disabilities since 1976.

Travel Information Service Ⓣ215/456-9600. Telephone-only information and referral service.

Twin Peaks Press Box 129, Vancouver, WA 98661 Ⓣ360/694-2462 or 1-800/637-2256. Publisher of the *Directory of Travel Agencies for the Disabled* ($19.95), listing more than 370 agencies worldwide; *Travel for the Disabled* ($19.95); the *Directory of Accessible Van Rentals* ($12.95); and *Wheelchair Vagabond* ($19.95), loaded with personal tips.

Wheels Up! Ⓣ1-888/389-4335, Ⓦwww.wheelsup.com. Provides discounted air fare, tour and cruise prices for disabled travellers; also publishes a free monthly newsletter and has a comprehensive website.

In Australia

ACROD (Australian Council for Rehabilitation of the Disabled) NSW branch, Suite 103, 1st Floor, 1–5 Commercial Rd, Kingsgrove, NSW 2208 Ⓣ02/9554 3666, Ⓕ9554 3188, Ⓦwww.acrod.org.au. Provides lists of help organizations, accommodation, travel agencies and tour operators.

NICAN (National Information Communication Awareness Network) PO Box 407, Curtin, ACT 2605 Ⓣ02/6285 3713 or 1800 806 769, Ⓕ6285 3714, Ⓦwww.nican.com.au. A national, non-profit, free information service on recreation, sport, tourism, the arts, and much more, for people with disabilities. Has a database of 4500 organizations – such as wheelchair-accessible tourist accommodation venues, sports and recreation organizations, and rental companies who have accessible buses and vans.

People with Disability Australia 52 Pitt St, Redfern, NSW 2016 Ⓣ02/9319 6622, Ⓦwww.pwd.org.au. Rights and advocacy organisation offers rights-related info, advice and referral services.

Spinal Cord Injuries Australia PO Box 397, Matraville NSW 2036 Ⓣ02/9661 8855, Ⓦwww.spinalcordinjuries.com.au. Publishes the very useful *Access Sydney* ($10 plus postage), which can be ordered online.

Accommodation

Much of Australia's tourist accommodation is well set up for people with disabilities, because buildings tend to be built outwards rather than upwards. New buildings in Australia must comply with a legal minimum **accessibility standard**, requiring that bathrooms contain toilets at the appropriate height, proper circulation and transfer space, wheel-in showers (sometimes with fold-down seat, but if this is lacking, proprietors will provide a plastic chair), grab rails, adequate doorways, and space next to toilets and beds for transfer. There are, of course, many older hotels which may have no wheelchair access at all or perhaps just one or two rooms with full wheelchair access. Most hotels also have refrigerators for medication which needs to be kept cool.

The best place to start looking for accommodation is the *A–Z Australian Accommodation Guide* published by the Australian Automobile Association (AAA) – the umbrella organization for state- and territory-based motoring associations that rate accommodation. They also offer some specialized services, a centralized **booking service** and a repair service for motorized wheelchairs, with reciprocal rights if you are a member of an affiliated overseas motoring organization. The guide is available from the NRMA in Sydney (see p.282); NICAN also has access to its database via computer, so you can choose your accommodation over the phone. Many travel shops and bookshops have accommodation guides which detail places that have wheelchair access.

In Sydney, **accessible accommodation** is most likely found in the big chain hotels which often have rooms with wheelchair access. Some of the smaller hotels do provide accessible accommodation, and a large proportion of suburban motels will have one or two suitable rooms. In the **country** around Sydney, there are fewer specially equipped hotels, but many motels have accessible units; this is particularly true of those that belong to a chain such as Choice Hotels – get hold of one of their directories for locations or check their website (Ⓦwww.choicehotels.com.au). The newest YHA **hostels** are all accessible, and there has been an effort to improve facilities throughout; accessible hostels are detailed in the YHA *Handbook*, or check their website (Ⓦwww.yha.com.au). **Caravan parks** are also worth considering, since some have accessible cabins. Others may have accessible toilets and washing facilities. Many resorts are also fully designed and equipped for wheelchair travellers, though in all cases, it's best to check in advance what facilities are available.

Transport

Post-Olympic improvements in Sydney include many wheelchair-accessible train stations in the Central Business District. Once you get out of the city not all stations have lifts, though many have ramps, but there are plans to make more stations disabled friendly. Check "Station Facilities" on Ⓦwww.cityrail.info before setting out, or call the Transport Infoline (Ⓣ13 15 00). There are also a number of accessible bus routes throughout the city of Sydney as well as along major routes into the suburbs. See Ⓦwww.sydneybuses.nsw.gov.au/accessibility.php.

Sydney also has a fleet of **wheelchair taxis** but be prepared to wait anything from five minutes to hours for one. Call the Wheelchair Accessible Taxi Service on Ⓣ02/8332 0200. If you find a driver you like, ask for their mobile phone number and then you'll be able to access them directly during your stay.

Of the major car-rental agencies, Hertz and Avis offer **vehicles with hand controls** at no extra cost, but advance notice is required. Reserved **parking** is available for vehicles displaying the wheelchair symbol (available from local council offices). There is no formal acceptance of overseas parking permits, but states will generally accept most home-country permits as sufficient evidence to obtain a temporary permit (call NICAN for further information). With a pemit you can park on meters without paying, stay longer than the norm at some spaces and there are a number of designated parking spots in the CBD.

The City of Sydney Council has a "Disabled Access" section on their website which includes access maps (Ⓦwww.cityofsydney.nsw.gov.au/cs_disabled_services.asp). **Mobility maps**, showing accessible paths, car parking, toilets and so on, can be obtained from local councils such as Randwick Council, which will post them out (Customer Services, 30 Francis St, Randwick, NSW 2031; Ⓣ02/9399 0999, Ⓦwww.randwick.com.au). Randwick Council has installed wheelchair accessible ramps at Clovelly and Malabar **beaches**. In 2002 Spinal Cord Injuries Australia published the very useful *Access Sydney* which can be ordered online (see above). The disability information resource website has a very useful city guide to Sydney (Ⓦwww.accessibility.com.au/sydney/sydney.htm). Most **national parks** have wheelchair-accessible walks; see Ⓦwww.npws.nsw.gov.au.

Accessible Sydney – a personal view

Sydney is possibly the most beautiful city in the world, and it's my home town. It's not only a stunning harbourside haven of fabulous dining experiences, designer shopping, divine beaches, spectacular views and truly friendly locals, it's also a very accessible destination. I ride around on an electric blue scooter – no not a Vespa, unless you squint and fail to notice its three wheels and the place to carry walking sticks. I'm in my thirties and have had rheumatoid arthritis since childhood. Six joint replacements, as well as numerous other surgical procedures, has meant my life has been lived between walking sticks, crutches, wheelchairs and scooters. I've travelled the world with this disability, so I have a pretty good idea of the difficulties visitors to Sydney might face. Take a scooter or wheelchair, a mobile phone, sunscreen, hat, sunglasses and a bottle of water and you're set for an adventure around Sydney.

Stay in **accommodation** close to the Light Rail (see p.38) – it runs 24 hours and links with other accessible modes of transport throughout the city, including the Monorail, trains, buses and ferries. The Light Rail runs from Central Station through Chinatown and the tourist area of Darling Harbour, to the fish markets and then through a couple of inner city suburbs including Glebe with its cafés, restaurants and pubs. It's a great way to get around – the conductor will spot you, pull out a ramp and direct you to appropriate on-board parking.

If you bring your own wheelchair or scooter to Sydney ensure you take along some spare tubes for your tyres. And if you do get a flat then call the National Roads and Motoring Authority (NRMA; ⓣ13 11 11) and they'll come and change the tube for you.

You can **hire** everything from raised toilet seats to wheelchairs and crutches. Check out ⓦwww.accessibility.com.au, an informative site with details on everything from equipment hire and repairs to accommodation and things to do in Sydney.

My perfect Sydney day – an itinerary

You'll need to be up bright and early for the **Growers Markets at Pyrmont Park** in front of Star City Casino, foodie heaven for the Sydneysider. Held on the first Saturday of the month (7–11am, except January). Start off at Central Station on the Light Rail – alight at the Casino and follow the smell of frying bacon and hot coffee until you reach the park by the water. It's always crowded and some of the stalls are on the grass, but it's truly worth the effort and the vendors are always helpful and more than willing to ensure you get a taste of some of Sydney's finest produce: organic meats, pasta, olives, oils, cheeses and the freshest of bread, fruit, veg and strawberries dipped in delectable chocolate.

Get back on the Light Rail and head to the **Sydney Fish Markets**. It can be a bit hair-raising in the carpark as locals, tourists and taxis jostle for position but just keep your wits about you and you're in for an experience. Just about everything that swims in the sea is available fresh to take away, or to eat by the waterfront: lobster, sushi, garlic prawn skewers, plain old fish and chips or a fillet of salmon to throw on the barbecue later. There's a bottle shop with a pretty good wine selection, a deli with some fabulous Australian cheeses, and a great fruit shop. All the shops are quite accessible although sometimes you do need to wave a flag to be noticed as the pace can be quite frenetic and sales are quickly made above your head.

Jump back on the Light Rail for a quick trip to **Darling Harbour** which has loads of shops and restaurants. Follow the water around to the other side for a visit to the **Sydney Aquarium** with its Great Barrier Reef exhibition and stunning displays of sea creatures. You can access all areas easily and they have designated toilets, and wheelchairs available for hire.

Take a ferry from adjacent King Street Wharf to **Circular Quay**. Around half of Sydney ferry wharves are accessible and boarding is simple, although the gradient of the ramp does vary according to the tide. The deckhands are really eager to please which makes getting out on the harbour an easy and fun (not to mention spectacular) thing to do while in Sydney.

Have a sunset drink at the **Opera Bar at the Sydney Opera House** – the sun low in the sky behind the Harbour Bridge and the passing parade of leisure cruisers, tourist boats and government ferries make for a stunning accompaniment to the drink in your hand. Happy hour indeed. Then catch some culture inside the Opera House itself. All the theatres have accessible seating, the staff are fantastic, plus you get to use the Stage Door entrance and you never know who you might bump into! You can even do a modified version of their backstage tour at 12.15pm weekdays but it's best to check in the morning as these so called "lift tours" are sometimes restricted by rehearsals happening in different theatres.

After the Opera House, take the train from elevator-accessible Circular Quay Station back to Central. Above all bring some courage and determination with you and never hesitate to ask for help – Australians really are friendly.

Nicole Bradshaw

Crime and personal safety

You should take the same precautions in Sydney as you would in any other major city in the Western world, though the city's "heavy" areas would seem tame compared to similar areas in Europe or North America.

Drunk males may pose the usual problems on Friday and Saturday nights, though there is no sudden spill out onto the streets as closing times are variable, and you might find **restless teenagers** getting themselves into trouble in the city. CCTV cameras have been installed in city areas where there are often problems: in The Rocks, which gets very rowdy on Friday and Saturday nights, and on the George Street cinema strip, which is a popular suburban teenage hangout and, though crowded, a prime area for personal theft. Kings Cross is the **red-light district** and has a major drug problem. The main strips are crowded but there are assaults and muggings – you should be careful with your belongings here at any time and try not to walk down backstreets at night. Nearby **Woolloomooloo**, though going upmarket, has some troubled public housing, so it's wise to be careful at night, but Sydney's only no-go zone is **Eveleigh Street** in Redfern (see p.101).

You're more likely to fall victim to a fellow traveller or an opportunist crime: **theft** is not unusual in hostels and so many provide lockable boxes; if you leave valuables lying around, or on view in cars, you can expect them to be stolen. Be careful with valuables at the beach; either leave them at your accommodation if you are alone, or take turns swimming. There are lockers at Bondi Beach (see p.136) and at Manly (p.145).

Exercise caution, don't forget common-sense streetwise precautions, and you should be fine; at night stay in areas that are well lit and full of people, look like you know where you are going and don't carry excess cash or anything else you can't afford to lose.

Police stations in central and tourist areas

NSW Police Headquarters are at 14–24 College St, Darlinghurst (☎02/9339 0277). If you have any problems, or need to report a theft for insurance purposes or any other crime, you can call or drop in here or at a local police station. For **emergencies** ☎000 is a free number which summons the police, ambulance or fire service.The following stations near frequently visited areas are open 24 hours:

Balmain 368 Darling St (☎02/9556 0699).
Bondi Beach 77 Gould St, cnr Hastings Parade (☎02/9365 9699).
Broadway 3–9 Regent St, Chippendale (☎02/9219 2199).
Darling Harbour 192 Day St (☎02/9265 6499).
Glebe 1–3 Talfourd St, cnr St Johns Rd (☎02/9552 8099)
Kings Cross 1–15 Elizabeth Bay Rd (☎02/8356 0099).
Manly 3 Belgrave St (☎02/9977 9499).
Mosman 96 Bradleys Head Rd (☎02/9969 1933).
Newtown 222 Australia St (☎02/9550 8199).
North Sydney 273 Pacific Highway (☎02/9956 3199).
Paddington 16 Jersey Rd (☎02/8356 8299).
Randwick 196 Alison Rd (☎02/9697 1099).
Redfern 30 Turner St (☎02/9690 4600).
The Rocks 132 George St, cnr Argyle St (☎02/8220 6399).
Surry Hills 151 Goulburn St (☎02/9265 4144).
Town Hall 570 George St (☎02/9265 6595).

Rape and serious trouble

If the worst happens, it's best to contact the **Rape Crisis Centre** (24hr; ☎02/9819 6565, outside the Metropolitan area ☎1800 424 017) before going straight to the police. Women police officers form a large part of the force, and in general the police deal sensitively with sexual assault cases.

To **avoid** physical attack, don't get too relaxed about Australia's friendly, easy-going attitude. The usual defensive tactics apply. **Buses** are generally safer than trains – on the train, always sit next to the guard in the carriage. Pick somewhere to stay that's close to public transport so you don't have to walk far at night – an area with busy nightlife may well be safer than a dead suburban backstreet. If you're going to have to walk for long stretches at night, take a cab unless the streets are busy with traffic and people.

Police and the law

The NSW **Police** Service – all armed – were formerly notoriously corrupt and have a poor public image. Perhaps as a result they tend to keep a low profile; you should have no trouble in your dealings with them. Indeed you'll hardly see them, unless you're out on a Friday or Saturday night when they cruise in search of drink-related brawls.

Things to watch out for, most of all, are **drugs**. A lot of marijuana is grown and its use is widespread, but you'd be foolish to carry it when you travel, and crazy to carry any other illicit narcotic, especially as sniffer dogs now do random searches at Sydney train stations. Driving in general makes you more likely to have a confrontation of some kind, if only for a minor traffic infringement; **drunk driving** is regarded extremely seriously, so don't risk it – random breath tests are common around all cities and larger towns.

Lesser potential problems are **alcohol** – there are all sorts of controls on where and when you can drink in public; **smoking**, which is increasingly being banned in public places; and nude or **topless** sunbathing, which is quite acceptable in many places, but absolutely not in others – follow the locals' lead.

If for any reason you are **arrested** or need help (and you can be arrested merely on suspicion of committing an offence), you are entitled to contact a friend or lawyer before answering any questions. You could call your consulate, but don't expect much sympathy. If necessary, the police will provide a lawyer, and you can usually get legal aid to settle the bill.

The City

The City

1

Sydney Harbour Bridge and The Rocks

The Rocks, immediately beneath the **Sydney Harbour Bridge**, is the heart of historic Sydney. On this rocky outcrop between Sydney Cove and Walsh Bay, Captain Arthur Phillip proclaimed the establishment of Sydney Town in 1788, the first permanent European settlement in Australia. Within decades, however, the area had become little more than a **slum** of dingy dwellings, narrow alleys and dubious taverns and brothels. In the 1830s and 1840s, merchants began building fine stone warehouses here, but as the focus for Sydney's shipping moved to Woolloomooloo, the area again fell into decline. By the 1870s and 1880s, the notorious Rocks "pushes", gangs of "larrikins" (louts), liked to mug passers-by when they weren't beating each other up. The narrow street named Suez Canal was a favourite place for them to jump out from. Some say the name is a shortening of Sewers' Canal, and indeed the area was so filthy and rat-ridden that whole street fronts had to be torn down in 1900 to contain an outbreak of bubonic plague. In 1924, the construction of the approaches to the Sydney Harbour Bridge began, again seeing mass **demolition** in The Rocks area, as hundreds of families were displaced, uncompensated.

The Rocks remained a run-down, depressed and depressing quarter until the 1970s, when plans were made to raze the remaining cottages, terraces and warehouses to make way for office blocks. However, due to the foresight of the Builders Labourers Federation (BLF), a radical building workers' union (headed by its secretary, and now hero, Jack Mundey), which opposed the demolition, the restored and renovated **historic quarter** is now one of Sydney's major tourist attractions. Despite a passing resemblance to an historic theme park, it's worth exploring. It's the best place, apart from the airport, for tax-free shopping and many of Sydney's world class restaurants are to be found here.

There are times when the old atmosphere still seems to prevail: Friday and Saturday nights can be thoroughly drunken – so much so that there's a prominent police station and officers patrolling on horseback; CCTV has also been installed. New Year's Eve is riotously celebrated here, as fireworks explode over the harbour. The best time to come for a more relaxed drink is Sunday afternoon, when many of the pubs offer live jazz or folk music.

The Sydney Harbour Bridge

The awe-inspiring **Sydney Harbour Bridge** has spanned the water dividing north and south Sydney since the early 1930s. It's hard now to imagine the view of the harbour without the castle-like sandstone pylons anchoring the bridge to the shore and the crisscross of steel arch against the sky. At 503m, it was the longest single span arch bridge in the world when it was built; construction began in 1924 and continued to provide employment through the height of the Great Depression – sixteen workers also lost their lives to it.

As the New South Wales premier, J.T. Lang, of the Labor party, prepared to cut the ribbon to open the bridge in 1932, further excitement was provided by the dashing horseman and royalist fanatic, Francis de Groot, who galloped up like a cavalryman and cut the opening ribbon with a sabre declaring "I open this bridge in the name of the Majesty the King and all the decent citizens of New South Wales" in protest at Lang's socialist leanings.

Residents of the north of England might find the bridge familiar: the tinier Tyne Bridge in Newcastle-upon-Tyne, built in 1929, was the original model for Sydney's. Construction costs for the altogether huger Sydney project weren't paid off until 1988, but there's still a $3 toll to drive across, payable when heading south; this is now used for maintenance costs and to pay off the newer **Sydney Harbour Tunnel**, which runs below the bridge and starts south of the Opera House – the ever-increasing volume of traffic in recent years proved too much for the bridge to bear. However, you can walk or cycle the bridge for free: pedestrians should head up the steps to the bridge from Cumberland Street, reached from The Rocks via the Argyle Steps off Argyle Street, and walk on the eastern side (the western side is the preserve of cyclists).

▲ Sydney Harbour Bridge

The bridge demands full-time maintenance, protected from rust by continuous painting in trademark steel-grey. One of Australia's best-known comedians, Paul Hogan of *Crocodile Dundee* fame, worked as a rigger on "the coathanger" before being rescued by a New Faces talent quest in the 1970s. To check out the vista, you can follow a rigger's route and climb the bridge yourself (see below) – once the favoured illegal pastime of drunken uni students. If you can't stomach (or afford) the climb, there's a **lookout point** (daily 10am–5pm; $8.50; ⓦwww.pylonlookout.com.au) 5min walk from Cumberland St then 200 steps up inside the bridge's south eastern pylon where, as well as gazing out across the harbour, you can study a photo exhibition on the bridge's history.

Climbing the bridge

Bridge Climb take small, specially equipped groups (maximum twelve people) to the top of the bridge from sunrise through night-time daily, roughly every ten to twenty minutes (twilight climbs $225, Mon–Thurs day or night climbs $160, Fri–Sun day or night climbs $185; minimum age 12; ⓣ02/8274 7777, ⓦwww.bridgeclimb.com). Booking ahead is advised, particularly if you want to climb at weekends or in the summer peak period. Though the experience takes three-and-a-half hours, only two hours is spent on the bridge, gradually ascending and pausing while the guide points out landmarks and offers interesting background snippets. The hour spent checking in and getting kitted up at the "Base" at 5 Cumberland St makes you feel as if you're preparing to go into outer space, as do the grey *Star Trek*-style suits specially designed so that you blend in with the bridge – no colourful crawling ants to spoil ground-level views. It's really not as scary as it looks – there's no way you can fall off, while fully harnessed as you are into a cable system, and this fact should calm a normal fear of heights – though phobics beware.

To avoid the dangers of things accidentally being dropped on cars and passers-by, the only thing you're allowed to take up are your glasses, attached to the suit by special cords – everything from handkerchiefs to caps are provided and similarly attached. Annoyingly, as this has to be one of the world's greatest photo opportunities, this precaution also means you can't take your camera up with you. You do get one group photo – taken by the guide on top of the bridge – free with the price of the climb, but the group, of jolly strangers, arms akimbo, crowds out the panoramic background a little. To get a good shot showing yourself with the splendours of the harbour behind, you'll need to fork out $15.95 for one extra individual photo or $29.95 for two. Various other packages are offered, including $39.95 for four different small photos.

The Rocks

The best place to start your **tour** of The Rocks is the **Sailors' Home** at 106 George St (daily 9.30am–5.30pm; also see p.27), built in 1864 to provide decent lodgings for visiting sailors as an alternative to the area's brothels and inns. The building continued to house sailors until the early 1980s but is now the **Sydney Visitor Centre**, supplying tourist information about The Rocks along with a re-creation of the sailors' sleeping quarters. You can pick up a guided tour leaflet here ($2.50). Nearby, you can arrange to go on an excellent guided walking tour with the long-running **The Rocks Walking Tours**, whose office is at 23 Playfair St, Rocks Square, where the walks commence (Mon–Fri 10.30am, 12.30pm & 2.30pm; Jan 10.30am & 2.30pm only; Sat & Sun 11.30am & 2pm; $19; bookings ⓣ02/9247 6678, ⓦwww.rockswalkingtours.com.au). For a **cyber tour** of the area, the website ⓦwww.rocksvillage.com.au focuses on The Rocks precinct.

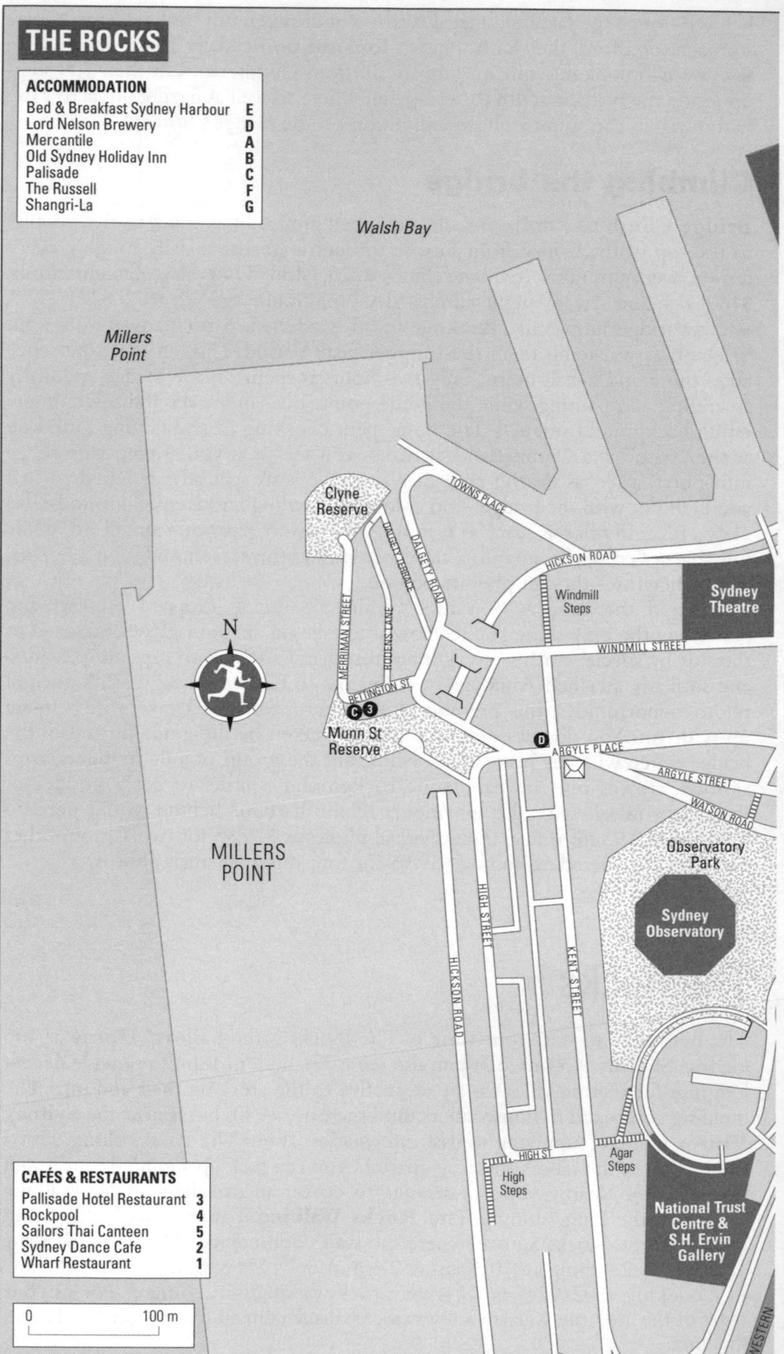
THE ROCKS
ACCOMMODATION
Bed & Breakfast Sydney Harbour E
Lord Nelson Brewery D
Mercantile A
Old Sydney Holiday Inn B
Palisade C
The Russell F
Shangri-La G
Walsh Bay
Millers Point
Clyne Reserve
TOWNS PLACE
DALGETY TERRACE
DALGETY ROAD
HICKSON ROAD
Windmill Steps
Sydney Theatre
MERRIMAN STREET
BODENS LANE
WINDMILL STREET
N
BETTINGTON ST
Munn St Reserve
ARGYLE PLACE
ARGYLE STREET
WATSON ROAD
Observatory Park
MILLERS POINT
Sydney Observatory
HIGH STREET
HICKSON ROAD
KENT STREET
HIGH ST
Agar Steps
High Steps
National Trust Centre & S.H. Ervin Gallery
WESTERN
CAFÉS & RESTAURANTS
Pallisade Hotel Restaurant 3
Rockpool 4
Sailors Thai Canteen 5
Sydney Dance Cafe 2
Wharf Restaurant 1
0 100 m

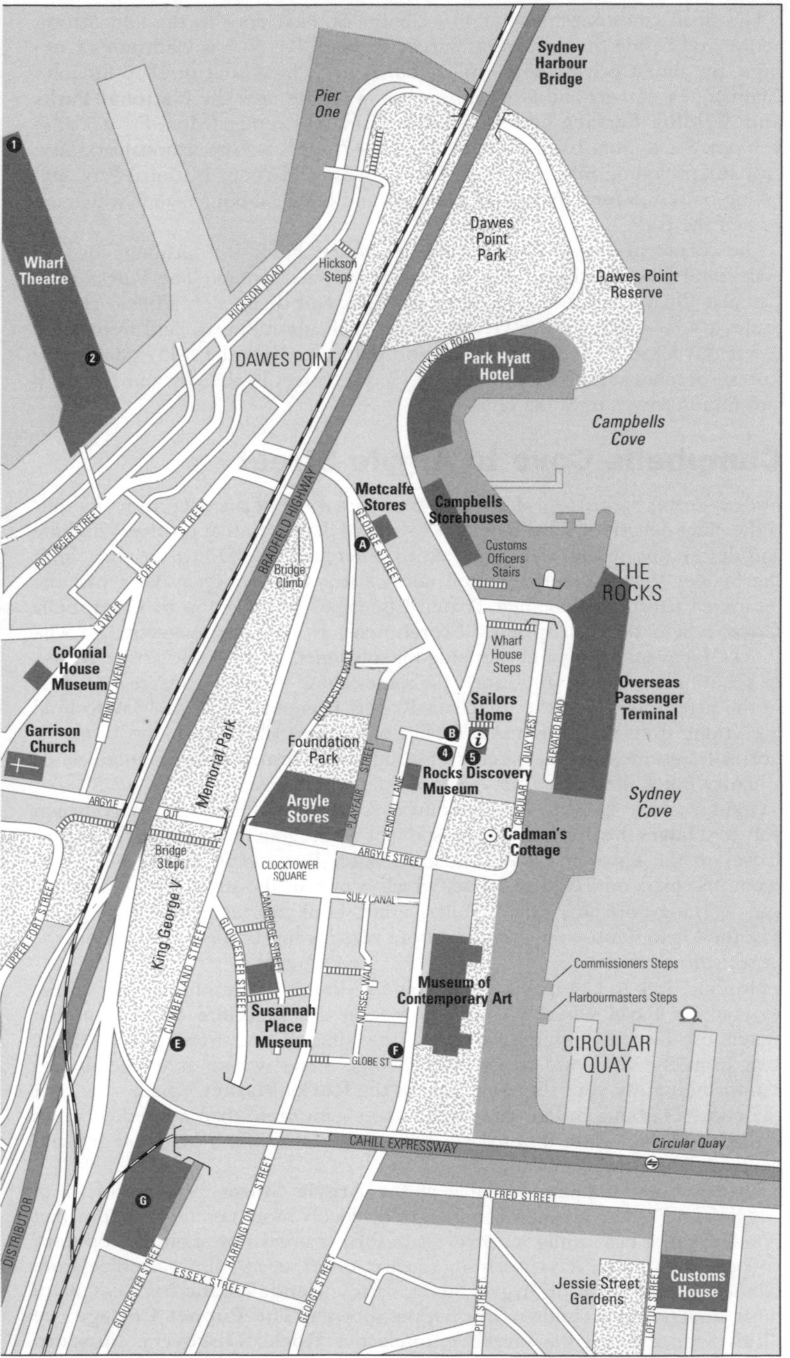
Sydney Harbour Bridge
Pier One
Dawes Point Park
Dawes Point Reserve
Wharf Theatre
Hickson Steps
HICKSON ROAD
DAWES POINT
Park Hyatt Hotel
Campbells Cove
Metcalfe Stores
Campbells Storehouses
Customs Officers Stairs
THE ROCKS
BRADFIELD HIGHWAY
Bridge Climb
GEORGE STREET
POTTINGER STREET
FORT STREET
LOWER FORT STREET
Colonial House Museum
TRINITY AVENUE
Garrison Church
Wharf House Steps
Sailors Home
Overseas Passenger Terminal
Foundation Park
GLOUCESTER WALK
PLAYFAIR STREET
KENDALL LANE
Rocks Discovery Museum
CIRCULAR QUAY WEST
ELEVATED ROAD
Memorial Park
ARGYLE CUT
Argyle Stores
Sydney Cove
Cadman's Cottage
Bridge Steps
CLOCKTOWER SQUARE
ARGYLE STREET
SUEZ CANAL
UPPER FORT STREET
King George V
CUMBERLAND STREET
GLOUCESTER STREET
CAMBRIDGE STREET
NURSES WALK
Museum of Contemporary Art
Commissioners Steps
Harbourmasters Steps
Susannah Place Museum
GLOBE ST
CIRCULAR QUAY
CAHILL EXPRESSWAY
Circular Quay
DISTRIBUTOR
HARRINGTON STREET
ALFRED STREET
ESSEX STREET
GLOUCESTER STREET
GEORGE STREET
PITT STREET
Jessie Street Gardens
LOFTUS STREET
Customs House

The small sandstone house at 110 George St, next door to the information centre and beside the tiny, grassy Barney & Bligh Reserve, is **Cadman's Cottage**, the oldest private house still standing in Sydney, built in 1816 for John Cadman, ex-convict and Government coxswain. It's now the **National Parks and Wildlife Service** bookshop and information centre (Mon–Fri 9.30am–4.30pm, Sat & Sun 10am–4.30pm; ⓣ02/9247 5033, ⓦwww.nationalparks.nsw.gov.au), providing information about the Sydney Harbour National Park, and taking bookings for trips to Fort Denison and other harbour islands which are part of the park.

The corner of Argyle and Kent streets, Millers Point, is a terminus for several useful **bus routes**, so you could aim to walk through The Rocks from Circular Quay train station or ferry terminus and then catch a bus back: bus routes #431–434 go along George Street to Railway Square and from there to various locations including Glebe and Balmain, while the #339 goes to the eastern beaches suburb of Clovelly via George Street in the city and Elizabeth and Albion streets in Surry Hills.

Campbells Cove to Argyle Street

Just exploring the narrow alleys and streets hewn out of the original rocky spur is the chief delight of **The Rocks**, a voyage of discovery that involves climbing and descending several stairs and cuts to different levels. Down the steps from the Sydney Visitor Centre, a stroll north along Circular Quay West past the revamped Overseas Passenger Terminal (see p.67), brings you to **Campbells Cove**, where the **Campbell's Storehouses** is fairly representative of The Rocks' focus on eating and shopping for souvenirs, clothing and arts and crafts in beautifully restored sandstone warehouses; these storehouses were once part of the private wharf of the merchant Robert Campbell, built in 1839 to hold everything from tea to liquor. A replica of Captain Bligh's ship, the *Bounty*, is normally moored here between cruises, adding a Disneyish atmosphere, while a luxury hotel, the *Park Hyatt*, overlooks the whole area.

Going past the hotel to Dawes Point Park under the Harbour Bridge brings you to **Dawes Point**, a favourite spot for photographers, separating Sydney Cove, on the Circular Quay side, from Walsh Bay and its several old, now-renovated piers on Hickson Road, which is part of the still mostly residential and working-port area called Millers Point. Looking out from Dawes Point, past the Opera House on a small harbour island, you can see Fort Denison, the prison-turned-fort.

Heading back to Campbells Cove, you can climb the Customs Officer's Stairs to Hickson Road where you can browse in the **Metcalfe Stores**, another warehouse-turned-shopping complex, this time dating from around 1912. Exit from the old bond stores onto George Street, where at weekends you can further satisfy your shopping urge at the **Rocks Market**, which takes over the entire Harbour Bridge end of the street with more than a hundred stores – shaded by big white umbrellas – selling souvenirs, bric-a-brac and arts and crafts with an Australian slant.

There's more shopping available at the **Argyle Stores**, on the corner of Argyle and Playfair streets, a complex of decidedly more tasteful and upmarket boutiques in a beautifully restored set of former bond stores; on the top floor you can take in great views from the bar of *bel mondo*, also accessible from Gloucester Walk. Also off Argyle Street, narrow **Kendall Lane** has a couple of great attractions for children, free puppet shows at **The Puppet Cottage** (see "Kids Sydney") and the inventive, interactive **Rocks Discovery Museum** (daily 10am–5pm; free), a great starting point for a stroll around The Rocks, providing background on Aboriginal and convict history through to the present in four permanent exhibitions.

The Argyle Cut and around

The Argyle Stores is just near the impressive **Argyle Cut**, which slices through solid stone to the more residential and working port area of **Millers Point**. The Cut took eighteen years to complete, carved first with chisel and hammer by convict chain gangs who began the work in 1843; when convict transportation ended ten years later the tunnel was still unfinished, and it took hired hands to complete it in 1859. Up the **Argyle Steps** and along the narrow brick pedestrian walkway of peaceful **Gloucester Walk** you come to the tiny **Foundation Park**. It's quite a delight to stumble across – remains of cottage foundations discovered in architectural digs have formed the basis for an arrangement of sculptural installations representing Victorian furniture. You can follow Gloucester Walk back to the northern end of George Street for a drink at *The Mercantile*, one of Sydney's best Irish watering holes. Gloucester Walk also leads to the pedestrian entrance of the Harbour Bridge on **Cumberland Street**, the location of a couple of classic old boozers, the *Glenmore* and the *Australian Hotel*. See "Drinking".

From the *Australian*, head down **Gloucester Street** to the **Susannah Place Museum** at nos. 58–64 (Jan daily 10am–5pm; Feb–Dec Sat & Sun only 10am–5pm; $7; ⓦwww.hht.net.au), a row of four brick terraces built in 1844 and continuously occupied by householders until 1990; the buildings are now a "house museum" (including a re-created 1915 corner store selling great old-fashioned sweets) that conserves the domestic history of Sydney's working class.

Millers Point

Looking west towards Darling Harbour, mostly residential **Millers Point** is a reminder of how The Rocks used to be – many of the homes are still government or housing-association-owned and there's a surprisingly real community feel so close to the tourist hype. Of course, the area has its upmarket pockets, such as the very swish *Observatory Hotel* on Kent Street, opposite Observatory Hill, and the renovated piers on **Walsh Bay**, but for the moment the traditional street-corner pubs and shabby terraced houses on the hill are reminiscent of the raffish atmosphere once typical of the whole area, and the peaceful leafy streets are a delight to wander in.

Lower Fort Street

You can reach the western side of the area through the Argyle Cut or from the end of George Street, heading onto **Lower Fort Street**. The **Colonial House Museum**, at no. 53 (daily 10am–5pm, but by arrangement only on ⓣ02/9247 6008; $1), takes up most of a residential 1883 terrace house where local character Shirley Ball has lived for over fifty years; her collection is crammed into six rooms, and includes period furnishings, hundreds of photographs of the area, etchings, artefacts and models. If you continue to wander up Lower Fort Street, don't pass up the opportunity to have a bevvy in the **Hero of Waterloo** at no. 81 (see "Drinking"), built from sandstone excavated from the Argyle Cut in 1844, then peek in at the **Garrison Church** (or Holy Trinity, as it's officially called; daily 9am–5pm), on the corner of Argyle Street, which was the place of worship for the military stationed at Dawes Point Fort from the 1840s. Next to the church, the volunteer-run **Garrison Gallery Museum** (Tues, Wed, Fri & Sat 11am–3pm, Sun noon–4pm; free) is housed in what was once the parish schoolhouse. Australia's first Prime Minister, Edmund Barton, was educated here and the collection of turn-of-the-twentieth-century photographs, complete with images of ragged barefoot children and muddy dirt roads, gives a good indication of the conditions of his tutelage. Beside the church, **Argyle Place** has some of the area's prettiest terraced houses.

Walsh Bay

You can reach the northeastern side of Millers Point from Dawes Point, where **Hickson Road** continues alongside **Walsh Bay**. Here, nearly all of the charmingly dilapidated old piers have been or are in the process of being transformed. At no. 11 Hickson Rd, the first pier has recently been taken over by a luxurious hotel, *Sebel Pier One*, while pier 4/5 has long been home to the **Wharf Theatre**, base of the prestigious Sydney Theatre Company (STC), established in 1978, and the internationally acclaimed Sydney Dance Company as well as about twenty other smaller arts organisations. From the **Wharf Restaurant** (see "Eating") and its bar, you can revel in the sublime view across Walsh Bay to Balmain, Goat Island and the North Shore, or get closer to the water (and the artists) at the cute little *Dance Cafe* (see "Eating") on the ground floor that looks across to the brand-new luxury apartments on the opposite pier. If you're keen, you can even attend a drop-in dance class at the complex. The exhibition of posters of past STC productions, featuring such luminaries as Judy Davis and Cate Blanchett, lining the hallway to the restaurant might tempt you to come back for a performance (the STC also puts on productions at the Opera House – see p.71). **Guided tours** of the theatre, including the costume department and a look at set construction, are also available (first and third Thurs of month 10.30am; 1hr; $8; bookings on ☎02/9250 1777). Sydney's literati converge on the Wharf Theatre complex in May of each year, for the wonderfully sited and mostly free **Sydney Writers Festival** (see "Festivals and events").

Observatory Park

Opposite the Garrison Church, climb up the steps on Argyle to the well-chosen spot for **Sydney Observatory**, above **Observatory Park**. The park, with its shady Moreton Bay figs, park benches and lawns, has a marvellous hilltop view over the architecture below and the whole harbour in all its aspects – glitzy Darling Harbour, the spectacularly cabled Anzac Bridge in one direction and the older Sydney Harbour Bridge in the other, gritty container terminals, ferries gliding by – and on a rainy day enjoy it from the bandstand which dominates the park. It's also easy to reach the park from the Bridge Steps off Cumberland Street by the Argyle Cut.

Sydney Observatory

The Italianate-style **Sydney Observatory** from which the park takes its name marked the beginning of an accurate time standard for the city when it opened in 1858, calculating the correct time from the stars and signalling it to ships in the harbour and Martin Place's General Post Office, by the dropping of a time ball in its tower at 1pm every day – a custom which still continues. Set among some very pretty gardens, the Observatory has had an excellent modern **museum of astronomy** since 1982 and it's well worth a visit (museum and gardens daily 10am–5pm; free; ⓦwww.sydneyobservatory.com.au).

A large section of the museum is devoted to the **Transit of Venus**, the rare astronomical event which takes place about twice every century. It was this occurrence which prompted Captain Cook's 1769 voyage of exploration, during which time he charted Australia's east coast. Venus last transited over the disk of the sun on June 8, 2004, visible from Europe, Africa, Asia and eastern parts of North America. The extensive collection of astronomical equipment, both archaic and high-tech, includes the still-working telescope installed under the copper dome to observe the 1874 Transit of Venus (the last until the transit in 2004). Another highlight, in the "Stars of the Southern Sky" section, are three animated videos of Aboriginal creation stories, retellings of how the stars came to be, from the Milky Way to Orion.

Every evening you can view the southern sky through telescopes and learn about the Southern Cross and other southern constellations; the two-hour tours include a lecture, film, the exhibitions, a guided view of the telescopes and a look at the sky, weather permitting. Otherwise, the small planetarium is used when the sky is not clear enough for observation (tour times vary seasonally; booking essential, usually up to a week in advance, on ⓣ02/9217 0485; $15).

National Trust Centre and S.H. Ervin Gallery

Also in the park, south of Sydney Observatory, is the **National Trust Centre**, located in a former military hospital dating from 1815, with a **café** (Tues–Fri 11am–3pm, Sat & Sun 1–5pm) and a specialist **bookshop** (Tues–Fri 11am–5pm, Sat & Sun noon–5pm) where you can pick up leaflets about other historic buildings and settlements in New South Wales.

The rear of the building, purpose-built as a school in 1850 in neo-Regency style, houses the **S.H. Ervin Gallery** (same hours as bookshop; free; entry to special exhibitions $6; ⓦwww.nsw.nationaltrust.org.au), the result of a 1978 million-dollar bequest by Ervin to devote it to Australian art; changing thematic exhibitions are of scholarly non-mainstream art, focusing on subjects such as Aboriginal or women artists.

2

Circular Quay and the Sydney Opera House

At the southern end of Sydney Cove, sandwiched between Sydney's first settlement, The Rocks, and its modern emblem, the Opera House, **Circular Quay** is the launching pad for harbour and river ferries and sightseeing cruises. Less attractively, it's also the terminal for buses from the eastern and southern suburbs, and a major suburban train station to boot, with the ugly 1960s Cahill Expressway also spoiling the views. However, one of the most fantastic views of the harbour can be seen from the above-ground platforms of Circular Quay train station, which has been opened up by the partial removal of a wall. A sweeping panorama of the harbour can also be enjoyed from the pedestrian walkway adjacent to the Cahill Expressway, reached by a sleek glass lift from the Quay.

It's a popular stroll from the Quay to the **Opera House** and the Royal Botanic Gardens (see p.73) just beyond, enjoying an ice cream or stopping for some oysters and a beer at a waterfront bar; all the necessities for a picnic in the Gardens, including bubbly and fresh prawns, can be purchased at the Quay.

Circular Quay and around

Always bustling with commuters during the week, "The Quay", as the locals call it, is crammed with people simply out to enjoy themselves at the weekend. Restaurants, cafés and fast-food outlets stay open until late and buskers entertain the crowds, while street vendors add to the general hubbub. For intellectual stimulation, you need only look beneath your feet as you stroll along: the inscribed bronze pavement plaques of **Writers' Walk** provide an introduction to the Australian literary canon. There are short biographies of writers ranging from Miles Franklin, author of *My Brilliant Career*, Booker Prize-winner Peter Carey and Nobel Prize-awardee Patrick White, to the feminist Germaine Greer, as well as quotations on what it means to be Australian. Notable literati who've visited Australia – including Joseph Conrad, Charles Darwin and Mark Twain – also feature.

Leading up to the Opera House is the once-controversial **Opera Quays** development, which runs the length of **East Circular Quay**. Locals and

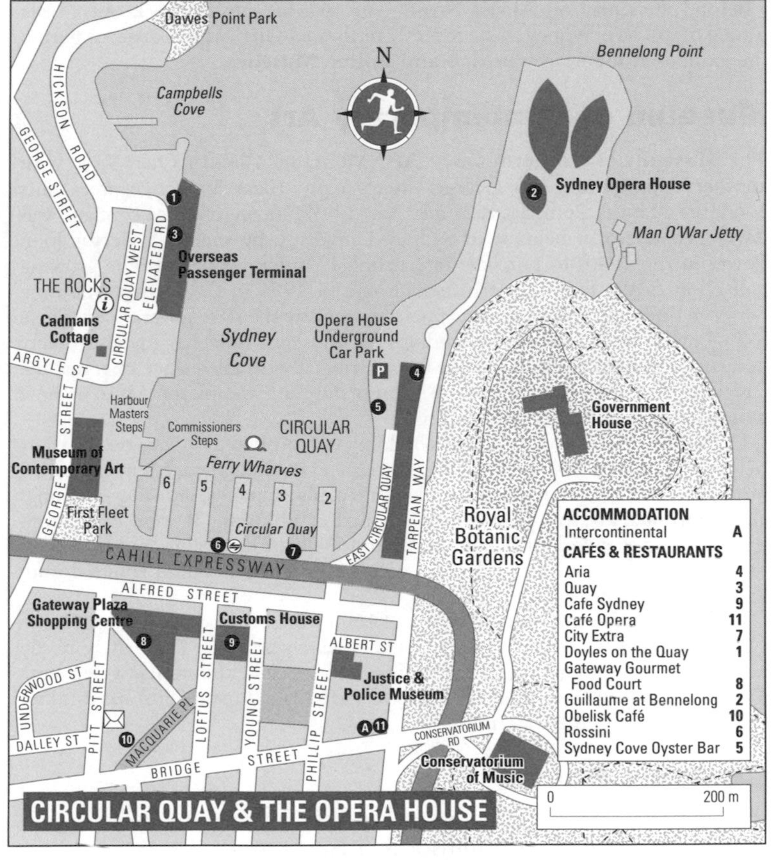

tourists flock to promenade along the pleasant colonnaded lower level with its outdoor cafés, bars and bistros, upmarket shops and Dendy Quays Cinema, all looking out to sublime harbour views. The ugly apartment building above, dubbed "The Toaster" by locals and described by Robert Hughes, the famous expat Australian art critic and historian, as "that dull brash, intrusive apartment block which now obscures the Opera House from three directions", caused massive protests, but went ahead nonetheless, opening in 1999.

Besides ferries (for a comprehensive review of the huge range of cruises starting from Circular Quay, see pp.35–37), the Quay still acts as a passenger terminal for ocean liners, though it's been a long time since the crowds waved their hankies regularly from the **Sydney Cove Passenger Terminal**, looking for all the world like the deck of a ship itself. To reach it, head in the opposite direction past the **Museum of Contemporary Art** to **Circular Quay West**; even if there's no ship, take the escalator and the flight of stairs up for excellent views of the harbour. The rest of the recently redeveloped terminal is now given over to super-trendy and expensive restaurants and bars such as *Aria* (see "**Eating**") and *Cruise Bar* (see "**Drinking**").

Behind the Quay on **Alfred Street**, you will be able to check out a scale model of modern Sydney at the recently renovated **Customs House**, or peruse the exhibits at the nearby **Justice and Police Museum**.

Museum of Contemporary Art

The **Museum of Contemporary Art** (MCA) on Circular Quay West, with another entrance on 140 George Street (daily 10am–5pm; free; free tours Mon–Fri 11am & 2pm, Sat & Sun noon & 1.30pm; ⓦwww.mca.com.au), was developed out of a bequest to Sydney University by the art collector John Power in the 1940s to purchase international contemporary art. The growing collection finally found a permanent home in 1991 in the former Maritime Services Building, provided for peppercorn rent by the state government. Since John Power left no recurrent funding, the museum now has to raise ninety percent of its own funding and has been financially troubled since opening; the free entry is courtesy of corporate sponsorship and means the MCA is now chock-a-block with locals at weekends.

The striking Art Deco-style 1950s building is dedicated to international twentieth- and twenty-first-century art, with an eclectic approach encompassing lithographs, sculpture, installations, film, video, photography, drawings, paintings and Aboriginal art, mostly shown in themed exhibitions. Recent exhibitions have featured the work of Bridget Riley and William Kentridge, looked at contemporary indigenous art, and given young Australian artists an annual forum with the Primavera exhibition series.

The museum's permanent collection of 1600 works, including pieces by Keith Haring, Bridget Riley, Jasper Johns, David Hockney and Jean Tinguely, is mostly kept in storage, though a selection is shown in special exhibitions twice a year. The museum's superbly sited, if expensive, **café** (daily 10am–5pm) has outdoor tables overlooking the waterfront.

Customs House

Immediately opposite Circular Quay, on Alfred Street, is an architectural gem, the sandstone and granite **Customs House**. First constructed in 1845 and redesigned in 1885 by the colonial architect James Barnet to achieve its current Classical Revival-style facade, the building was then neglected for many years. At the time of writing Customs House had just reopened after its second multi-million dollar refurbishment in a decade. On the ground floor of the new development is a **City Exhibition Space**, keeping pace with the development of Sydney with a continually updated 500:1 scale model of the city set into the floor under glass, accompanied by a multimedia presentation. At the front of the building a newly designed forecourt space incorporates alfresco seating for cafés and bars, while the first three floors of the building provide the new home for the City of Sydney's premier public library. On the top floor remains the only reminder of the building's previous incarnation, a pricey contemporary brasserie, *Cafe Sydney* (see "Eating"), which comes with wonderful Harbour Bridge views.

Justice and Police Museum

A block east of the Customs House, on the corner of Phillip Street, the **Justice and Police Museum** (Jan daily except Fri 10am–5pm; Feb–Dec Sat & Sun 10am–5pm; $7; ⓦwww.hht.net.au) is housed in the former Water Police station, an 1856 sandstone building whose verandah is decorated with some particularly fine ironwork.

The social history museum focuses on law, policing and crime in New South Wales with several temporary themed exhibitions throughout the year, often giving a contemporary viewpoint on crime and its part in society – past ones have delved into the art of tattooing, the effects of drugs on crime and scrutinized the relationship between the police and environmental protestors. The permanent crime displays, including some truly macabre Bushrangers' death masks, gruesome confiscated weapons (some of them murder implements) and other souvenirs of Sydney's murky past, are all shown within the context of a late-nineteenth-century police station and court mock-up. There's also an interesting display on bushrangers.

The Sydney Opera House

The **Sydney Opera House**, such an icon of Australiana that it almost seems kitsch, is just a short stroll from Circular Quay, by the water's edge on **Bennelong Point**. It's best seen in profile, when its high white roofs, simultaneously evocative of full sails and white shells, give the building an almost ethereal quality. Some say the inspiration for the distinctive design came from the simple peeling of an orange into segments, though perhaps Danish architect **Jørn Utzon**'s childhood as the son of a yacht designer had something to do with their sail-like shape – he certainly envisaged a building which would appear to "float" on water. Close-up, you can see that the shimmering effect is created by thousands of chevron-shaped white tiles.

The feat of structural engineering required to bring to life Utzon's "sculpture", which he compared to a Gothic church and a Mayan temple, made the final price tag $102 million, fourteen times the original estimates. Now almost universally loved and admired, it's hard to believe quite how controversial a project this was during its long haul from plan (as a result of an international competition in the late 1950s) to completion in 1973.

▲ Sydney Opera House at night

It's a wonder Utzon even won the competition: Eero Saarinen, architect of New York's JFK airport terminal, who was on the selection committee, vetoed the shortlist and flicked through the reject pile, pronouncing Utzon's way-out design the work of a genius. For sixteen years, construction was plagued by quarrels and scandal (the winner of the Opera House fund lottery even had his young son kidnapped for ransom and murdered, Australia's first such crime), so much so that Utzon, who won the competition in 1957, was forced to resign in 1966, calling the whole sorry situation "Malice in Blunderland". Many believe that he was hounded out of the country by politicians – the newly elected Askin New South Wales' state government disagreeing over his plans for the completion of the interior – and jealous, xenophobic local architects. Seven years and three Australian architects later, the interior, which never matched Utzon's vision, was finished: the focal Concert Hall, for instance, was completely designed by **Peter Hall** and his team.

In October 1998, the building's 25th birthday was celebrated with free concerts and the announcement of a $70 million ten-year plan to renew and modify the interior, which refocused media attention on past mistakes. In 1999 Utzon, in his mid-80s, was invited by New South Wales' Premier Bob Carr to be the principal design consultant in the preparation of a Statement of Design Principles for the building, which has become the permanent reference for its conservation and development. The invitation was both a gesture of goodwill to make up for past slights and a real attempt finally to realize his full design. Some of these ideas might be used in decades to come, but as part of the current renovation Utzon has made plans for a remodelled western exterior, and designed a huge wall tapestry, a "homage to Bach", which now hangs in the newly opened and much-acclaimed **Reception Hall**; the sound-absorbing tapestry has allowed the installation of a parquet floor with a pattern echoing the ribbed ceiling.

The Reception Hall, usually used for private functions and recitals, is occasionally open to the public: check on the Opera House website (ⓦwww.sydneyoperahouse.com) for the latest information.

Jørn Utzon is continuing his consultancy with the help of his architect and business-partner son Jan, who spent several childhood years in Sydney (Jørn's granddaughter Anna is a permanent Sydney resident). Although Jan Utzon has returned for a visit in his father's place – the pair are working from Jørn's homes in Copenhagen and Majorca – sadly Utzon senior has still never seen the finished building he designed.

Around the Opera House

"Opera House" is actually a misnomer: it's really a performing arts centre, one of the busiest in the world, with five performance venues inside its shells, plus two restaurants, several popular cafés and bars, an Aboriginal artist's gallery, and a stash of upmarket souvenir shops.

The building's initial impetus, in fact, was as a home for the **Sydney Symphony Orchestra** (SSO), the cherished dream of Sir **Eugene Goossens**, the British conductor invited in 1947 to transform the SSO into a world-class orchestra and head the Conservatorium of Sydney. By 1955, the SSO was considered to be on the world's top ten list, Goossens had been knighted by the governor-general for his sterling effort, and the Australian Broadcasting Corporation (ABC) had the whole of Australia swooning with its radio broadcasts. Before the Opera House, however, their only venue was the too-small, draughty and acoustically challenged, though splendid, Town Hall. Like Utzon, Goossens never got to see the Opera House, which was designed with the huge **Concert Hall** (seating 2690) for the SSO as the focal point. Soon after he was knighted, he left for a holiday to Europe and on his return was found to be carrying a huge haul of pornography. Australia's censorship laws were notoriously tight, its climate parochial and puritanical, and the £100 fine came with a judgement from the QC that it was "difficult to imagine a worse case … the exhibits speak for themselves …". Hundreds of prominent international and local supporters were appalled at the witchhunt and subsequent career ruination of Goossens, who resigned in disgrace and left for Europe; he died alone on a plane flight in 1962.

The smaller **Opera Theatre** (1547 seats) is used as the Sydney performance base for Opera Australia (seasons Feb–March & June–Nov), the Australian Ballet (mid-March to May & Nov–Dec) and the Sydney Dance Company (see p.227). There are three theatrical venues: the **Drama Theatre** and **The Playhouse**, both used primarily by the Sydney Theatre Company (see p.64 and p.227), and the more intimate **The Studio**. The last was added in 1999 as part of the ten-year redevelopment plan; The Studio aims to draw in a younger audience, offering cheaper tickets for innovative Australian drama, comedy, cabaret and contemporary dance, performed in an adaptable theatre-in-the-round format.

There's plenty of action outside the Opera House, too, with the use of the Mayan-temple-inspired **Forecourt** and Monumental Steps as an amphitheatre for free and ticketed concerts – rock, jazz and classical – with a capacity for around 5000 people. But Sunday is regularly the liveliest day outside, when the **Tarpeian Markets** (10am–4pm), with an emphasis on Australian crafts, are held.

There are also a number of great **places to eat and drink** at the Opera House; you could choose to dine at what is considered to be one of Sydney's best restaurants, *Guillame at Bennelong*, overlooking the city skyline (see "Eating"), or take a drink at the *Opera Bar* on the lower concourse, with wonderful views from the outside tables and an affordable all-day menu. In addition there is also a sidewalk café, a bistro and several theatre bars.

Inside the Opera House – tours and packages

If you're not content with gazing at the outside – much the building's best feature – and can't attend a performance, there are **guided tours** available (book on ⓣ02/9250 7250 or via the website, ⓦwww.sydneyoperahouse.com); the Front-of-House tour gives an overview of the site, looking at the public areas and discussing the unique architecture (daily 9am–5pm, every 30–40min; 1hr; $23). Backstage tours run each morning and include access to the scenery and docks, rehearsal rooms, technical areas, and breakfast in the Greenroom (7am; 2hr; $140). On these tours you can see the small exhibition area in the foyer of The Playhouse where two original Utzon models of the Opera House are displayed, alongside a series of small oil paintings depicting the life of **Bennelong**, the Iora tribesman who was initially kidnapped as little more than an Aboriginal "specimen" but later became a much-loved addition to Governor Arthur Phillip's household; Phillips later built a hut for him on what is now the site of the Opera House, hence the name Bennelong Point. History buffs who would like to learn more can go on a history tour, offered by arrangement on the booking number above.

The best way to appreciate the Opera House, of course, is to attend an evening **performance** (see p.226): the building is particularly stunning when floodlit and, once you're inside, the huge windows come into their own as the dark harbour waters reflect a shimmering image of the night-time city – interval drinks certainly aren't like this anywhere else in the world. **Packages** that include tours, meals, drinks and performances can be purchased on-site, over the phone or on the Internet and can be good value.

Royal Botanic Gardens to Macquarie Street

It was Governor Arthur Phillip, at the helm of the new city from 1788 to 1792, who decreed that the picturesquely sited land around the harbour, east of his newly built Government House (now the site of the Museum of Sydney) should always be in the public domain, a great park for the people to enjoy. Over two decades later Governor Lachlan Macquarie formalized his generous idea. The area remains public, but in two distinct parts: the open expanse of **The Domain**, long used for public celebrations and protests, which stretches from the stately strip of civic buildings envisaged by Governor Macquarie on the southern end of **Macquarie Street** to either side of the **Art Gallery of New South Wales** and down to the water alongside Mrs Macquaries Road; and spreading west of here, the much larger, varied expanse of the **Royal Botanic Gardens**, around 75 acres from the northern end of Macquarie Street to the Opera House and around Farm Cove.

The Royal Botanic Gardens

The **Royal Botanic Gardens** (daily 7am–sunset; free; ⓦwww.rbgsyd.gov.au) occupy a huge waterfront area between The Domain and the Opera House, around the headland on Farm Cove where the first white settlers struggled to grow vegetables for the hungry colony. Today's gardeners are much more successful, judging by the well-tended flowerbeds. While duck ponds, a romantic rose garden and fragrant herb garden strike a very English air, look out for native birds and, at dusk, the fruit bats which fly overhead as the nocturnal possums begin to stir (you can also see hundreds of the giant bats hanging by day in the Palm Grove area near the restaurant). There are examples of trees and plants from all over the world, although it's the huge, gnarled native Moreton Bay figs that stand out. The gardens provide some of the most stunning **views** of Sydney Harbour and are always crowded with workers at lunch time, picnickers on fine weekends, and lovers entwined beneath the trees.

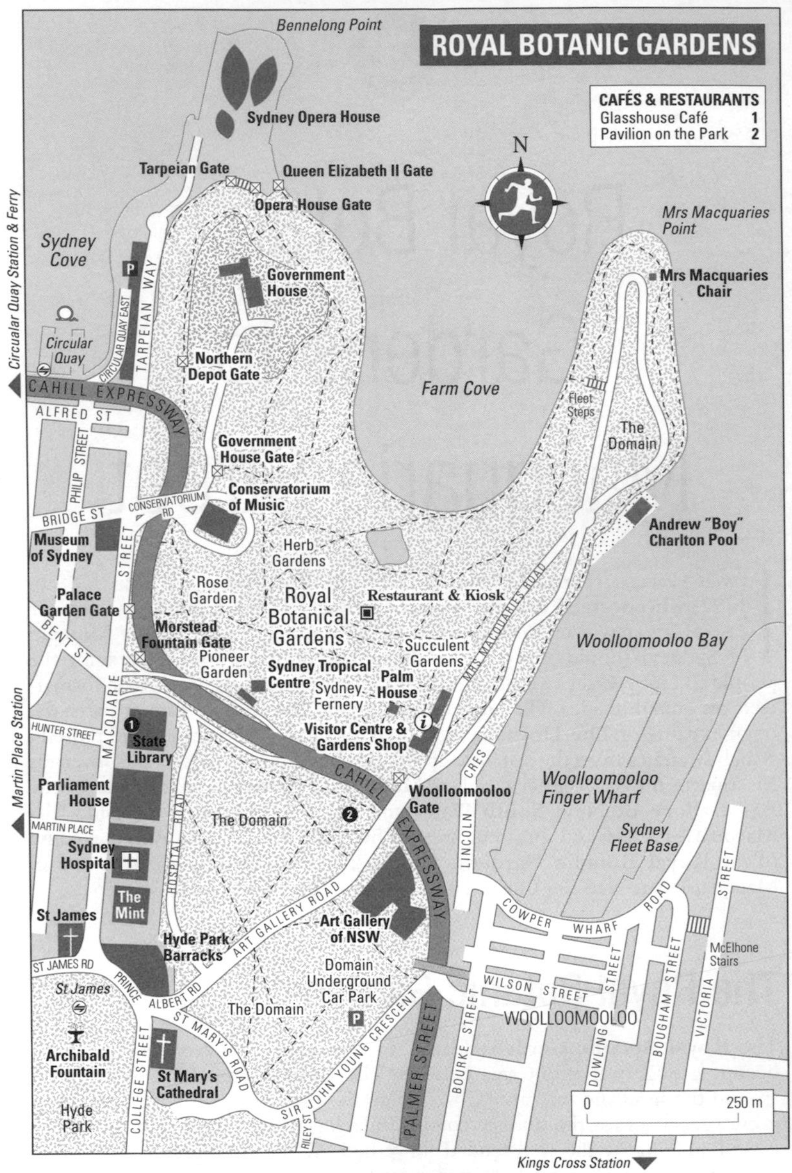

Many **paths** run through the gardens. A popular and speedy route (roughly 15min) is to start at the northern gates near the Opera House and stroll along the waterfront path to the gates which separate it from The Domain, and up the **Fleet Steps** to Mrs Macquaries Chair. Within the northern boundaries of the park, you can visit the original residence of the governor of New South Wales, and listen to lunch time recitals at the nearby Conservatorium. Below the music school, the remaining southern area of the gardens has a herb garden, a cooling palm grove established in the 1860s, a popular café/restaurant by the duck ponds, and the **Sydney Tropical Centre** (daily 10am–4pm; $2.20) – a striking glass pyramid and adjacent glass arc respectively housing native tropical plants and exotics. Nearby, the **Rare and Threatened Plants** garden has the first example of a cultivated Wollemi Pine, planted in 1998. The "dinosaur" tree, thought long-extinct, was discovered by a national park ranger in 1994; there are only 38 of these trees in the world, growing in the Blue Mountains (see p.321).

At the southeast-corner entrance, near the Art Gallery of New South Wales, off Mrs Macquaries Road, free **guided tours** of the gardens commence from the **visitor centre** (daily 9.30am–5pm; tours daily 10.30am; 1hr 30min; March–Nov Mon–Fri also 1pm; 40mins). The **Trackless Train**, which runs through the gardens about every twenty minutes, picks up from here; the main pick-up point is the entrance near the Opera House and there are also stops along the way (Mon–Fri 9.30am–5pm, Sat & Sun 9.30am–6pm; all-day hop-on-hop-off service $10, child $5).

Government House and the Conservatorium of Music

Within the northern boundaries of the Royal Botanic Gardens on Conservatorium Road, the sandstone mansion glimpsed through a garden and enclosure is the Gothic Revival-style **Government House** (built 1837–45), seat of the governor of New South Wales, and still used for official engagements by the governor, who now lives in a private residence. The stately interior has limited opening hours by free guided tour only (Fri–Sun 10am–3pm; tours half-hourly; 45min; @www.hht.net.au) but you are at liberty to roam the grounds (daily 10am–4pm).

South of Government House, just inside the gardens at the end of Bridge Street, the **Conservatorium of Music** is housed in what was intended to be the servants' quarters and stables of Government House. Public opinion in 1821, however, deemed the imposing castellated building far too grand for such a purpose and a complete conversion, including the addition of a concert hall, gave it the loftier aim of training the colony's future musicians. A two-year renovation project, finished in 2000, uncovered an earlier convict-era site which led to an archeological dig being incorporated into the final redesign. Conservatorium students have traditionally given free lunch time recitals every Tuesday and Friday at 1.10pm during term time.

Macquarie Street

Lachlan Macquarie, reformist governor of New South Wales between 1809 and 1821, gave the early settlement its first imposing public buildings, clustered on the southern half of his namesake **Macquarie Street**. He had a vision of an elegant, prosperous city, but the Imperial Office in London didn't share his enthusiasm for expensive civic projects. Refused both money and expertise, Macquarie was forced to be resourceful: many of the city's finest buildings were designed by the ex-convict **Francis Greenway** – the convicted forger who went on to be appointed civil architect and design forty buildings, eleven of which survive – and paid for with "rum-money", the proceeds of a monopoly on liquor sales.

Modern Sydney – wealthy and international – shows itself on the corner of Bent and Macquarie streets in the curved glass sails of the 41-storey **Aurora Place Tower**, designed by Italian architect Renzo Piano, co-creator of the extraordinary Georges Pompidou Centre in Paris.

State Library of New South Wales

The **State Library of New South Wales** (Mon–Fri 9am–9pm, Sat & Sun 11am–5pm, Mitchell Library closed Sun; free guided tours Tues 11am & Thurs 2pm; ⓦwww.sl.nsw.gov.au) heads the row of public architecture on the eastern side of Macquarie Street. The complex of old and new buildings includes the 1906 sandstone **Mitchell Library**, its imposing Neoclassical facade gazing across to the Botanic Gardens. Inside, an archive of old maps, illustrations and records relating to the early days of white settlement and exploration in Australia includes the **Tasman Map**, drawn by the Dutch explorer Abel Tasman in the 1640s. The floor mosaic in the foyer replicates his curious map of the continent, still without an east coast, and its northern extremity joined to Papua New Guinea.

A glass walkway links the Mitchell Library with the modern building housing the **General Reference Library**. Free exhibitions relating to Australian history, art, photography and literature are a regular feature of the Reference Library vestibules while lectures, films and video shows often take place in the **Metcalfe Auditorium** (free and ticketed events; ⓣ02/9273 1414 for details and bookings). You can refresh yourself at the glass-roofed plant-filled **Café** on level 7 (see "Eating"). The library's **bookshop** on the ground floor has the best collection of Australia-related books in Sydney.

Sydney Hospital, NSW Parliament House and the Royal Mint

Sandstone **Sydney Hospital**, the so-called "Rum Hospital", funded by liquor-trade profits, was Macquarie's first enterprise, commissioned in 1814; the two remaining convict-built original wings therefore form one of the oldest buildings in Australia. The central section was pulled down in 1879 when it began collapsing; rebuilt by 1894, the Classical Revival buildings, still functioning as a small general and eye hospital, are also impressive – peep inside at the entrance hall's flower-themed stained glass and the decorative staircase, or take an interesting short cut through the grounds to The Domain and across to the Art Gallery of New South Wales. Outside on Macquarie Street, the bronze statue of a boar, *Il Porcellino*, is a copy of one from Florence; his nose has long been rubbed shiny for luck by patients and their families.

One of the original wings of the hospital is now the **NSW Parliament House** (Mon–Fri 9am–5pm; free guided tours Mon & Fri 9.30am, 11am, 12.30pm, 2pm, 3pm & 4pm; question time Tues–Thurs 2.15pm; call ⓣ02/9230 2111 or check ⓦwww.parliament.nsw.gov.au for parliamentary recesses), where as early as 1829 local councils called by the governor started to meet, making it by some way the oldest parliament building in Australia. However, it wasn't until the May 2003 state elections that an Aboriginal Australian was elected to the NSW Parliament – Linda Burney, former head of the NSW Department of Aboriginal Affairs and now Labor member for multicultural Canterbury. You can listen in on the politicians during question time, when Parliament is sitting. Look out for the varied exhibitions in the foyer which change every fortnight or so – all represent community or public-sector interests and range from painting, craft and sculpture to particularly excellent photographic displays that often have an overt political content.

The other hospital wing was converted into a branch of the **Royal Mint** in response to the first Australian goldrush. It closed in 1927, and for some time served as a museum of gold mining; since the museum shut in 1997, the building has been taken over by NSW Historic Houses Trust offices. After an award-winning $14 million redevelopment, which combined historic restoration with contemporary architecture, in late 2004 the new head office for the Trust opened on this site. The organization has added a **café** (Mon–Fri 8am–4pm) that extends onto the verandah looking over Macquarie Street; interpretive boards detail the mint's history. Other facilities include a public auditorium created by combining the stone walls of the 1854 coining factory with a glass pavilion, and the Caroline Simpson Library and Research Collection. The most daring change though saw the demolition of the ramshackle additions where the mint site borders the Hyde Park Barracks.

The Hyde Park Barracks

Next door to the old Mint, the **Hyde Park Barracks** (daily 9.30am–5pm; $7; ⓦwww.hht.net.au), designed by convict-architect Francis Greenway, was built in 1819, again without permission from London, to house six hundred male convicts. Now a **museum** of the social and architectural history of Sydney, it's a great place to visit for a taste of convict life during the early years of the colony. Start on the top floor, where you can swing in re-creations of the prisoners' rough hammocks. Computer terminals allow you to search for information on a selection of convicts' histories and backgrounds – several of those logged were American sailors nabbed for misdeeds while in Dublin or English ports (look up poor William Pink). Later the Barracks took in single immigrant women, many of them Irish, escaping the potato famine; an exhibition looks at their lives, and there's a moving monument in the grounds erected by the local Irish community. Look out too for the excellent temporary historical exhibitions and there's also a great **café** with an outdoor courtyard.

▲ The Hyde Park Barracks

The Domain

The Domain is a large, quite plain, open space that stretches from behind the historic precinct on Macquarie Street to the waterfront, divided from the Botanic Gardens by the Cahill Expressway and Mrs Macquaries Road. Often filled with workers eating lunch under the shady Moreton Bay fig trees and people playing volleyball, or swimming in its outdoor pool, the **Andrew "Boy" Charlton**, it's a popular place for a stroll from the city across to the **Art Gallery of New South Wales** or down to the harbour for wonderful views from **Mrs Macquaries Chair**. For many more years it has been a truly public site, as Sydney's focus for anti-establishment protests. Since the 1890s, assorted cranks and soapbox revolutionaries have assembled on Sundays for the city's version of **Speakers' Corner**, and huge crowds have registered their disquiet, notably during anti-conscription rallies in 1916 and after the Whitlam Labor government's dismissal in 1975. Every January thousands of people gather on the lawns to enjoy the wonderful free open-air concerts of the Sydney Festival; in February the Tropfest short film festival takes over the grass, while December sees a night of Christmas carols and the all-Australian band line-up of the outdoor rock festival, Homebake (for details of all, see "Festivals and events"). The closest **train** stations to The Domain are Martin Place or St James CityRail, or you can take bus #441 from Market Street outside the QVB (see p.84).

Art Gallery of New South Wales

Art Gallery Road runs through The Domain to the **Art Gallery of New South Wales** (daily except Wed 10am–5pm; Wed 10am–9pm; free general tours Mon & Sat 1pm & 2pm, Tues–Fri 11am, noon, 1pm & 2pm; free except for special exhibitions; ⓦwww.artgallery.nsw.gov.au), whose collection was established in 1874. The original part of the building (1897), an imposing Neoclassical structure with a facade inscribed with the names of Renaissance artists, principally contains the large collection of European art dating from the eleventh century to the twenty-first – extensions were added in 1988 which doubled the gallery space and provided a home for mainly Australian art and in 2003 the Gallery was again expanded with a new Asian wing.

On level 1, the **Yiribana Gallery** is devoted to the art and cultural artefacts of Aboriginal and Torres Strait Islanders; the most striking exhibit is the **Pukumani Grave Posts**, carved by the Tiwi people of Melville Island. There is a highly recommended half-hour talk and performance of dance and didgeridoo by an indigenous Australian in this gallery (Tues–Sat noon), best combined with the free one-hour tour of the indigenous collection (Tues–Sun 11am).

Other highlights include some classic **Australian paintings** on level 4: Tom Roberts' romanticized shearing-shed scene *The Golden Fleece* (1894) and an altogether less idyllic look at rural Australia in Russell Drysdale's *Sofala* (1947), a depressing vision of a drought-stricken town. On level 5, the **photographic collection** includes Max Dupain's iconic *Sunbaker* (1937), an early study of Australian hedonism that looks as if it could have been taken yesterday.

A $16.4 million **extension** to the gallery opened in October 2003; on the Woolloomooloo facade, the gigantic cube of white glass, dubbed the "lightbox", is home to the gallery's Asian collection.

A particularly interesting time to visit the gallery is during "**art after hours**" on Wednesday evenings, when gallery hours are extended to 9pm. Each week from 5pm the regular and special exhibitions are accompanied by a constantly changing series of free talks, films and live performances. For details about the programme on a specific evening, check the event website (Ⓦwww.artafterhours.com.au).

In addition to the galleries, there is also an auditorium used for art lectures, an excellent bookshop, a coffee shop (level 2), and a well-regarded restaurant (level 5). Opposite the gallery, within the Domain, is the scenically sited *Pavilion in the Park* (see "Eating"), with a pricey restaurant, a café and kiosk. A pedestrian walkway behind the Art Gallery leads quickly down to Woolloomooloo and its finger wharf on Cowper Wharf Road; as well as restaurants, bars and cafés on the wharf itself, you could eat cheaply at the pie cart, *Harry's Café de Wheels*, or have some food or refreshment at the lively *Woolloomooloo Bay Hotel* (for details see "Eating").

Mrs Macquaries Chair and "The Boy"

Beyond the Art Gallery, an overpass used to give a good view of the speeding traffic of the ugly 1960s Cahill Expressway, but, largely as a result of lobbying by the Art Gallery itself, a large section has been covered over and grassed. The landscaping greatly reduces the problem of noise and fumes, and no longer disgraces the beginning of one of Sydney's most scenic routes: Mrs Macquaries Road, built in 1816 at the urging of the governor's wife, Elizabeth. The road curves down from Art Gallery Road to Mrs Macquaries Point, which separates idyllic Farm Cove from the grittier Woolloomooloo Bay and its naval base. At the end is the celebrated lookout point known as **Mrs Macquaries Chair**, a seat fashioned out of the rock, from which Elizabeth could admire her favourite view of the harbour on her daily walk from the original Government House.

On the route down to Mrs Macquaries Point, the **Andrew "Boy" Charlton Pool** (see "Sports and activities") is an open-air, saltwater swimming pool safely isolated from the harbour waters on the Woolloomooloo side of the promontory, with excellent views across to the Garden Island Naval Depot, which is fascinating to watch at work. "The Boy", as the locals fondly call it, was named after the champion swimmer, a Manly local, who turned 17 during the 1924 Paris Olympics, where he won a gold medal in the 1500-metre freestyle. He was beaten at the 400-metre event by Johnny Weissmuller, later the famous Hollywood Tarzan. The pool is a popular hangout for groovy Darlinghurst types (it's quick to get to from Kings Cross via Woolloomooloo by descending the McElhone Stairs from Victoria Street) and sun-worshipping gays. Revamped in 2002, the much-glamorized pool has its own café, pilates and yoga classes, and even a weekly biathlon.

City Centre

From Circular Quay to as far south as King Street is Sydney's **Central Business District**, often referred to as the CBD, with Martin Place as its commercial nerve centre (with its own underground train station), and the **Museum of Sydney** as its most compelling attraction. Stretching south of here to the Town Hall – with George and Pitt streets the main thoroughfares – is a shopaholics' oasis, where you'll find all the department stores and several shopping malls, including the celebrated **Queen Victoria Building**; you can walk right from the underground Town Hall train station through into the basement levels of the building. The lavish **State Theatre** and the decorative **Town Hall** are also worth a peek, and overlooking it all, with supreme views of the city, is **Sydney Tower**. Several nearby monorail stops can get you here from Darling Harbour.

The city centre's rest and recreation zone is **Hyde Park**, three blocks east of Town Hall across Elizabeth Street. It was fenced off by Governor Macquarie in 1810 to mark the outskirts of his township, and is still very much a formal city park with its war memorials and church. There are two very London Underground-like train stations at either end, opened in 1926 and well preserved (Museum Station to the south and St James Station to the north), and a peripheral natural history museum, cathedral and synagogue.

The short stretch between the Town Hall and Liverpool Street is for the most part teenage territory, a frenetic zone of multiscreen cinemas, pinball halls and fast-food joints. This stretch is trouble-prone on Friday and Saturday nights when there are pleasanter places to choose to catch a film. Things change pace at Liverpool Street, where Sydney's "**Spanish corner**" consists basically of a clutch of Spanish restaurants and a Spanish club. George Street becomes increasingly downmarket as it heads to Central Station – but along the way you'll pass Chinatown and Paddy's Market in the area known as Haymarket (see p.96).

The CBD

As you stroll from Circular Quay to the open space of Martin Place, the cramped streets of the CBD, overshadowed by high-rise office buildings, have little to offer. However, for some impression of the commerce going on here, check out the **Australian Stock Exchange**, opposite Australia Square at 20 Bond St, and join the throng gazing intently at the computerized display of stocks and shares through the glass of the ground floor. For a glimpse at how all this wealth might be spent, head over to Sydney's most upmarket shopping

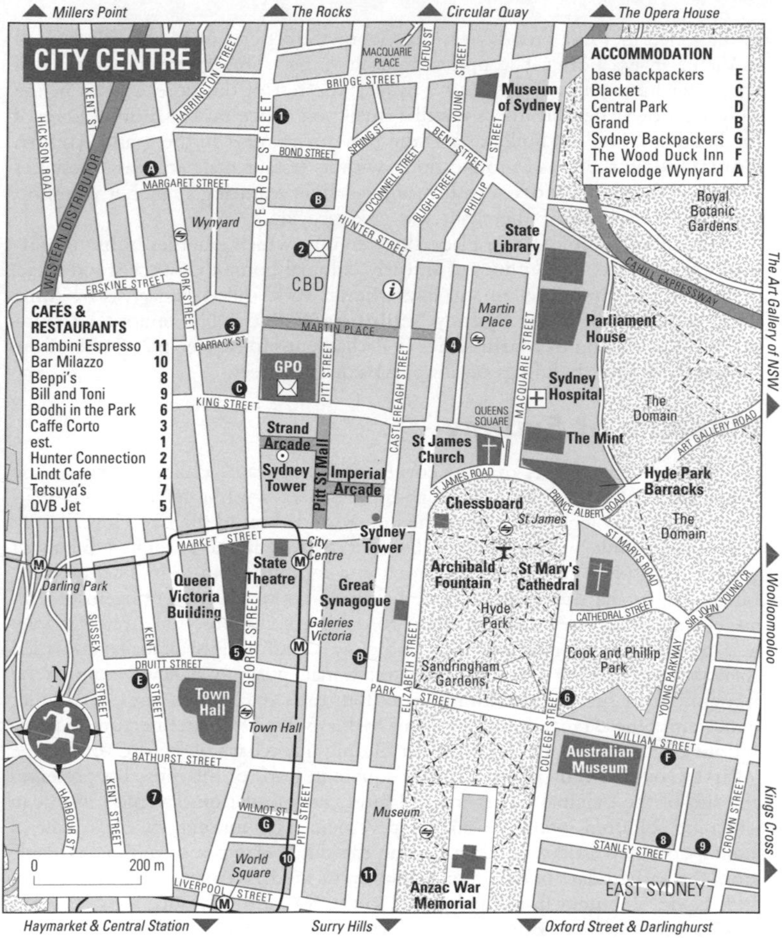

CITY CENTRE

ACCOMMODATION

- base backpackers E
- Blacket C
- Central Park D
- Grand B
- Sydney Backpackers G
- The Wood Duck Inn F
- Travelodge Wynyard A

CAFÉS & RESTAURANTS

- Bambini Espresso 11
- Bar Milazzo 10
- Beppi's 8
- Bill and Toni 9
- Bodhi in the Park 6
- Caffe Corto 3
- est. 1
- Hunter Connection 2
- Lindt Cafe 4
- Tetsuya's 7
- QVB Jet 5

centre, **Chifley Plaza**, on the corner of Hunter and Phillip streets, where you'll find Leona Edmiston, Max Mara and other exclusive labels; a huge stencil-like **sculpture** of former Australian Labor Prime Minister Ben Chifley (1945–49), by artist Simeon Nelson, stands on the pleasant palm-filled square outside.

Martin Place

Martin Place, a pedestrian mall stretching five blocks between George and Macquarie streets, with its own underground station, is lined with imposing banks and investment companies, many with splendid interiors. The mall has its less serious moments at summer lunch times, when street performances are held at the little amphitheatre, and all year round stalls of flower- and fruit-sellers add some colour. The vast Renaissance-style **General Post Office**, designed by colonial architect James Barnet (also responsible for the Customs House and Callan Park) and built between 1865 and 1887, with its landmark clock tower added in 1900, broods over the George Street end of Martin Place in all its Victorian-era pomp. The upper floors have been incorporated into part of a five-star luxury hotel, the *Westin Sydney*; the rest of the hotel resides in the 31-storey tower behind (there is still a small post office on the ground floor of the building). The old building and the new tower meet in the grand **Atrium Courtyard**, in the lower ground floor, with its restaurants, bars, classy designer stores and the **GPO Store**, a gastronome's delight featuring a butcher, fish shop, deli, cheese room, wine merchant and greengrocer.

At the other end of Martin Place, the fine mist which emerges from ground-level grilles marks the outlines of an early colonial home that once stood there, creating a ghostly house on still days; the artwork, called *Passage*, is by Anne Graham and is part of the **Sydney Sculpture Walk** (see box opposite). Opposite this eastern end of Martin Place is Parliament House (see p.76), one of the Colonial-era civic buildings on lower Macquarie Street.

Museum of Sydney

North of Martin Place, on the corner of Bridge and Phillip streets, is the **Museum of Sydney** (daily 9.30am–5pm; $7; ⓦwww.hht.net.au). From 1983 a ten-year archeological dig unearthed the foundations of the first Government House here, built by Governor Phillip in 1788 and home to eight subsequent governors of New South Wales before it was demolished in 1846. The museum, built next to the site, is totally original in its approach, presenting history in an experiential, interactive manner, through exhibitions, film, photography and multimedia; though you may come away feeling less factually informed than you might expect from a more traditional museum. A key feature of the museum is the special exhibitions, about four each year, which make for a fuller experience; these range in subject from Sydney's Art Deco architecture to exhibitions of Aboriginal art, so it's worth finding out what's on before you go.

First Government Place, a public square in front of the museum, preserves the site of the original Government House: its foundations are marked out in different coloured sandstone on the pavement. The museum itself is built of honey-coloured sandstone blocks, using the different types of tooling available from the earliest days of the colony right up to modern times; you can trace this stylistic development from the bottom to the top of the facade.

Near the entrance, **Edge of the Trees**, an emotive sculptural installation that was a collaboration between a European and an Aboriginal artist, conveys the complexity of a shared history that began in 1788. Entering the museum, you hear a dramatized dialogue between the Eora woman Patyegarang and the First Fleeter Lieutenant Dawes, giving a strong impression of the meeting and misunderstanding between the two cultures.

If you're really interested in the city's modern architecture, **Sydney Architecture Walks** offer various walking tours led by young architects leaving from the museum entrance (Wed & Sat 10.30am; 2hr; $20; bookings and further information on ⓣ02/8239 2211 or ⓦwww.sydneyarchitecture.org). If you decide to pay and enter the rest of the museum, it's best to first go upstairs to the **auditorium** on level 2 and watch the fifteen-minute video explaining the background and aims of the museum. Back on level 1 a video screen extends up through all three levels, showing images of the bush, sea and sandstone Sydney as it was before the arrival of Europeans. On level 2 again, recordings of Sydney Kooris (Aboriginal people) are combined with video images to help the viewer reflect on contemporary experience. At the dark and creepy **Bond Store** on level 3, holographic "ghosts" relate tales of old Sydney as an ocean port. On the

Sydney Sculpture Walk

The specially commissioned artworks for the **Sydney Sculpture Walk** – a City of Sydney Council initiative for the 2000 Olympics and the 2001 Centenary of Federation – form a circuit from the Royal Botanic Gardens, through The Domain, Cook and Phillip Park, the streets of the CBD, Hyde Park and East Circular Quay. One of the most striking of the ten site-specific pieces is Anne Graham's *Passage*, at the eastern end of Martin Place (see p.81). A map showing the sculpture sites is available from Sydney Town Hall (p.85) or there are details of the route on Ⓦwww.cityofsydney.nsw.gov.au.

same level, a whole area is devoted to some rather wonderful **panoramas** of Sydney Harbour with views of the harbour itself from the windows.

There is also an excellent **gift shop** with a wide range of photos, artworks and books on Sydney. Quite separate from the museum is the expensive, licensed *MOS* **café**, on First Government Place; usually filled with lawyers at lunch time, it's agreeably peaceful for a (reasonably priced) coffee at other times or a tasty weekend breakfast.

King Street to Park Street

Further south from Martin Place, the rectangle between Elizabeth, King, George and Park streets is Sydney's prime **shopping area**, with a number of beautifully restored **Victorian arcades** (the Imperial Arcade, Strand Arcade and Queen Victoria Building are all worth a look) and Sydney's two **department stores**, the very upmarket David Jones, on the corner of Market and Elizabeth streets, established over 160 years ago, and the more populist but still quality-focused Myers, on Pitt Street Mall. All are overlooked by Sydney skyline's landmark, **Sydney Tower**.

Sydney Tower and Skytour

The **Sydney Tower** (daily 9am–10.30pm, Sat until 11.30pm; viewing gallery and Skytour $22, child $13.20; Ⓦwww.sydneyskytour.com.au), long known to the locals as Centrepoint Tower, on the corner of Market and Pitt streets, is the tallest poppy in the Sydney skyline. Its observation level is the highest in the entire southern hemisphere, although the management ruefully have to admit that the height of the tower itself, at 305m, is beaten by the spire of the Sky Tower in Auckland, New Zealand, which is 23m taller. The 360-degree view from the observation level is especially fine at sunset, and on clear days you can

Sydney Tower's revolving restaurants

To see the same view, without the crowds, put the saved $20 towards a meal instead. There are a couple of **revolving restaurants** at the top of the tower; the revolution takes about one hour ten minutes and nearly all the tables are by the windows (bookings on Ⓣ02/8223 3800, Ⓦwww.sydney-tower-restaurant.com). You can choose from a $75 three-course dinner in the level 1 restaurant (Tues–Sat from 5.30pm) or a daily buffet lunch or dinner on level 2 (Mon–Sat lunch $42.50, dinner $52.50 and Sun lunch $49.50).

even see the Blue Mountains, 100km away. It can get crowded and to see the view more peacefully head downstairs to the **café**, where you can enjoy floor-to-ceiling views along with a cup of tea.

The observation level is now packaged with the **Skytour** on entry-lift level, a tacky "virtual ride" introduction to a clichéd Australia that lasts forty long minutes. The latest addition, **Skywalk** (@www.skywalk.com.au; Mon–Thurs $109, Fri–Sun $129; dusk $139; 95min) gets harnessed walkers outside on to glass-floored walkways and viewing platforms, obviously imitating the successful Harbour Bridge climb, the original and still the best thrill choice for your money.

The State Theatre

Near the Sydney Tower the restored **State Theatre**, just across from the Pitt Street Mall at 49 Market St, provides a pointed architectural contrast. Step inside and take a look at the ornate and glorious interior of this picture palace which opened in 1929 – a lavishly painted, gilded and sculpted corridor leads to the lush, red and wood-panelled foyer. To see more – decorations include crystal chandeliers in the dress circle – you'll need to attend a concert or play, or catch the Sydney Film Festival (see "Festivals"), held here annually in June. You can also go on a **guided tour** (monthly; 10.30am; 1hr 30 min; $15; @www.statetheatre.com.au) or pop into the beautiful little *Retro Cafe*, attached, for a coffee.

The Queen Victoria Building

The stately **Queen Victoria Building** (abbreviated by the locals to QVB), taking up the block bounded by Market, Druitt, George and York streets, is another of Sydney's finest. Built as a market hall in 1898, two years before Queen Victoria's death, the long-neglected building was beautifully restored and reborn in 1986 as an upmarket shopping mall with the focus on fashion: from the basement up, the four levels become progressively posher (shops Mon–Sat 9am–6pm, Thurs until 9pm, Sun 11am–5pm; cafés and restaurants open later; building open 24hr; @www.qvb.com.au; for more on the shops here see p.255). From Town Hall Station you can walk right through the basement level (mainly bustling food stalls) and continue via the Sydney Central Plaza to Myers, emerging on Pitt Street without having to go outside – very cooling on a hot day.

Stern and matronly, a huge **statue of Queen Victoria** herself sits outside the Town Hall end of the magnificent domed, Romanesque-style building. She was sourced as part of the $75 million restoration from the Irish Republic, having been wrenched in 1947 from outside the Irish Houses of Parliament in Dublin. A small bronze statue of her favourite dog, Islay, fronts the nearby wishing well.

The **interior** is magnificent, with its beautiful woodwork, mosaic-tiled floors, stained-glass windows, gallery levels, exhibits and antique lifts. A brochure listing all the shops and main features is available from the information desks on the ground level and level 2; a one-hour **guided tour** leaves from the ground-floor desk twice daily (Mon–Sat 11.30am & 2.30pm, Sun noon & 2.30pm; $8).

On **level 2** there are several exhibits including the Imperial Bridal Carriage, made from 300 tonnes of jade; a tableau of Queen Victoria's 1838 coronation, complete with copies of the Crown Jewels (the originals are in the Tower of London); a couple of pianolas constantly playing and two huge clocks hanging from the ceiling. At the south end, the five-metre-high, one-tonne mechanical

▲ The Queen Victoria Building

Royal Automata Clock shows a pageant of British royal history, every hour on the hour, including scenes of Charles I being beheaded. But in complete contrast, and outdoing it in size and weight, is the ten-metre-high, four-tonne, animated **Great Australian Clock** at the northern end, which details Australian history from the point of view of indigenous people and European settlers (animated display every half-hour).

The Town Hall

In the realm of architectural excess, however, the **Town Hall** is king – you'll find it across from the QVB on the corner of George and Druitt streets. It was built during the boom years of the 1870s and 1880s as a homage to Victorian England, and has a huge organ inside its Centennial Hall, giving it the air of a secular cathedral. Until the Opera House opened in 1973, this was Sydney's concert hall, where the Sydney Symphony Orchestra performed. Throughout the interior different styles of ornamentation compete for attention in a riot of colour and detail; the splendidly dignified toilets are a must-see.

The occasional concerts and theatre **performances** still held here set off the splendid interior perfectly, though it's more often used nowadays for public lectures (details on the City Infoline Mon–Fri 9am–6pm, ⓣ02/9265 9007, or ⓦwww.cityofsydney.nsw.gov.au).

Around Hyde Park

From the Town Hall, it's a short three-block walk east to **Hyde Park** along Park Street, which divides the park into two sections. The **Anzac War Memorial**

The Anzacs

In Australia almost every town, large or small, has a war memorial dedicated to the memory of the Anzacs, the **Australia and New Zealand Army Corps**. When war erupted in Europe in 1914, Australia was overwhelmed by a wave of pro-British sentiment. On August 5, one day after Great Britain had declared war against the German empire, the Australian prime minister summed up the feelings of his compatriots: "When the Empire is at war so Australia is at war." On November 1, a contingent of twenty thousand enthusiastic volunteers – the **Anzacs** – left from the port of Albany in Western Australia to assist the mother country in her struggle.

In Europe, Turkey had entered the war on the German side in October 1914. At the beginning of 1915, military planners in London (Winston Churchill prominent among them) came up with a plan to capture the strategically important Turkish peninsula of the Dardanelles, with a surprise attack near **Gallipoli**, thus opening the way to the Black Sea. On April 25, 1915, sixteen thousand Australian soldiers landed at dawn in a small bay flanked by steep cliffs; by nightfall, two thousand men had died in a hail of Turkish bullets from above. The plan, whose one chance of success was the element of surprise, had been signalled by troop and ship movements long in advance, thus rendering it useless. Nonetheless, Allied soldiers continued to lose their lives for another eight months without ever gaining more than a feeble foothold.

In December, London finally issued the order to **withdraw**. Eleven thousand Australians and New Zealanders had been killed, along with as many French and three times as many British troops. The Turks lost eighty-six thousand men.

Official Australian historiography continues to mythologize the battle for Gallipoli, elevating it to the level of a national legend on which Australian identity is founded. The Anzac soldiers proved themselves heroes of the new nation, their loyalty and bravery evidence of how far Australia had developed. This "birth of a nation" was at the same time a loss of innocence and a national rite of passage: never again would Australians so unquestioningly involve themselves in foreign ventures.

Today, the legend is as fiercely defended as ever and April 25, **Anzac Day**, is commemorated annually, a focal point for Australian national pride. Although it may seem like a one-battle flag-waving ceremony to outsiders, it is akin to Britain's Remembrance Day and the USA's Veterans' Day, a solemn occasion when one is asked to reflect on the sacrifices made by those who fought in all wars.

and Museum Station are in the southern half, with the **Australian Museum** just across College Street. In the northern section, the **Sandringham Memorial Gardens** are near Park Street, and just across Elizabeth Street at no. 187 is the finely wrought **Great Synagogue** (also with an entrance on parallel Castlereagh Street at no. 166; free tours Tues & Thurs noon), consecrated in 1878 and inspired by English synagogues of the time in London and Liverpool. At the far northern end, near St James Station, the **Archibald Fountain** is overlooked by **St James's Church**, across the northern boundary, and **Cook and Philip Park** and **St Mary's Cathedral**, across College Street.

Hyde Park

From Queens Square at the very south end of Macquarie Street, **St James's Church** (daily 9am–5pm; free weekday tours 2.30pm; 40min) marks the northern entry to the park. The Anglican church, completed in 1824, is Sydney's oldest existing place of worship. It was one of Macquarie's schemes, built to ex-convict Greenway's design; the architect originally planned it as a courthouse – you can see how the simple design has been converted into a graceful church. It's worth popping into the crypt to see the richly coloured **Children's Chapel** mural painted in the 1930s.

Behind St James Station, the **Archibald Fountain** commemorates the association of Australia and France during World War I and nearby is a **giant chess set** where you can challenge the locals to a match. Further south near Park Street, the **Sandringham Memorial Gardens** also commemorate Australia's military dead, but the most potent of these monuments is the famous **Anzac War Memorial** at the southern end of the park (museum daily 9am–5pm; tours 11.30am & 1.30pm; free). Fronted by the tree-lined Pool of Remembrance, the thirty-metre-high cenotaph, unveiled in 1934, is classic Art Deco right down to the detail of Raynor Hoff's stylized soldier figures solemnly decorating the exterior. Downstairs, a free, mainly photographic, exhibition looks at Australian wartime experiences. The war memorial is the Sydney focus for the solemn annual Anzac Day march and wreath-laying on April 25 (see box opposite).

The Australian Museum

Facing Hyde Park across College Street, at the junction of William Street as it heads up to Kings Cross, the **Australian Museum** (daily 9.30am–5pm; $10, extra for special exhibitions; tours 10am–3pm on the hour; 30min; ⓦwww.austmus.gov.au) is primarily a museum of natural history, with an interest in human evolution and Aboriginal culture and history. The collection was founded in 1827, but the actual building, a grand sandstone affair with a facade of Corinthian pillars, wasn't fully finished until the 1860s and was extended in the 1980s. As well as the permanent exhibitions below, there are also special exhibitions throughout the year.

The core of the old museum is the three levels of the **Long Gallery**, Australia's first exhibition gallery, opened in 1855 to a Victorian public keen to gawk at the colony's curiosities. Many of the classic displays of the following hundred years remain here, Heritage-listed, contrasting with a very modern approach in the rest of the museum.

On the **ground floor**, the impressive **Indigenous Australian** exhibition looks at the history of Australia's Aboriginal people from the Dreamtime to the more contemporary issues of the Stolen Generation and freedom rides. The ground-floor level of the Long Gallery houses the **Skeletons** exhibit, where you can see a skeletal human going through the motions of riding a bicycle, for example.

Level 1 is devoted to **minerals**, but far more exciting are the disparate collections on **level 2** – especially the Long Gallery's **Birds and Insects** exhibit, which includes chilling contextual displays of dangerous spiders such as redbacks and funnelwebs. Past this section is the **Biodiversity: Life Supporting Life** exhibition that looks at the impact of environmental change on the ecosystems of Australian animals, plants, and micro-organisms, around eighty percent of which do not naturally occur elsewhere. Beyond is **Kids' Island**, a fun play-space for under-5s (see p.242 for more on kids at the museum), while the **Tracks Through Time: Human Evolution** gallery traces the development of fossil evidence worldwide and ends with an exploration of archeological evidence of Aboriginal occupation of Australia. In the following gallery, **More Than Dinosaurs** deals with fossil skeletons of dinosaurs and giant marsupials: best of all is the model of the largest of Australia's megafauna, the wombat-like Diprotodon, which may have roamed the mainland as recently as ten thousand years ago. Finally, on level 2, **Search and Discover** is aimed at both adults and children, a flora and fauna identification centre with Internet access and books to consult.

St Mary's Cathedral and Cook and Phillip Park

North up College Street is the Catholic **St Mary's Cathedral** (Mon–Fri & Sun 6.30am–6.30pm, Sat 8am–6.30pm; tours Sun 12noon), overlooking the northeast corner of Hyde Park. The huge Gothic-style church opened in 1882, though the foundation stone was laid in 1821. In 1999 the cathedral at last gained the twin stone spires originally planned for the two southern towers by architect William Wardell in 1865, with $8 million of the project funded by state and federal governments. The cathedral also gained an impressive new forecourt – a pedestrianized terrace with fountains and pools – with the consolidation of two traffic-isolated parks into the large **Cook and Phillip Park**. The park includes a **recreation centre** with a fifty-metre swimming pool and gym (see "Sports and activities") and an excellent vegetarian restaurant, *Bodhi in the Park* (see "Eating"). The remodelling also created a green link to The Domain.

5

Darling Harbour and around

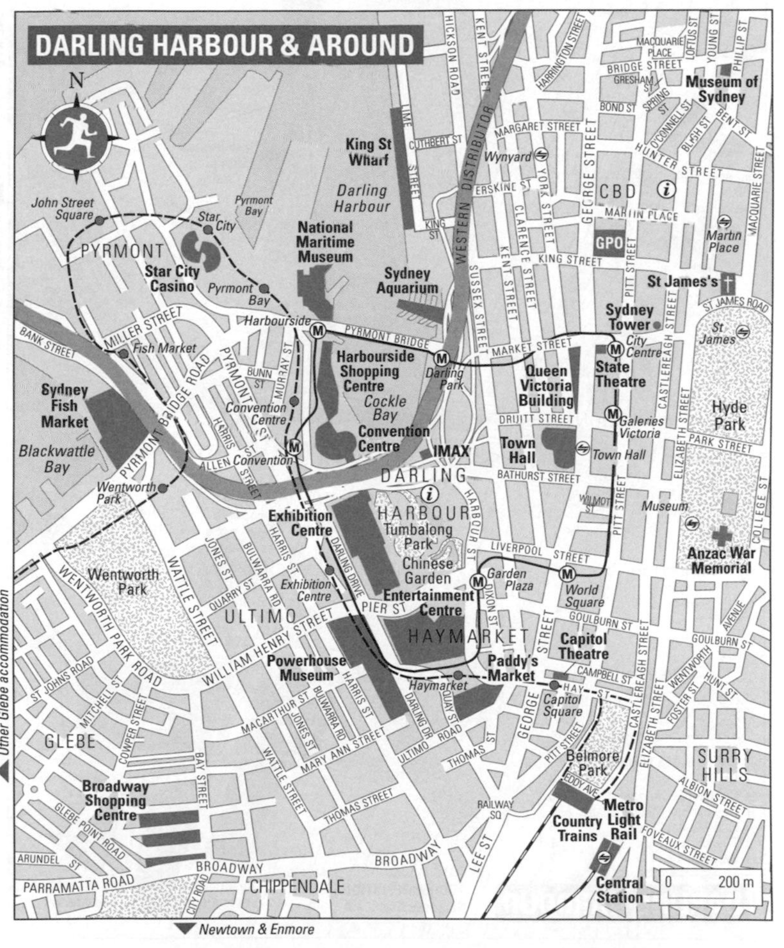

Darling Harbour

Darling Harbour, once a grimy industrial docks area, lay moribund until the 1980s, when the state government chose to pump millions of dollars into the regeneration of this prime city real estate as part of the Bicentenary Project. The huge redevelopment scheme around

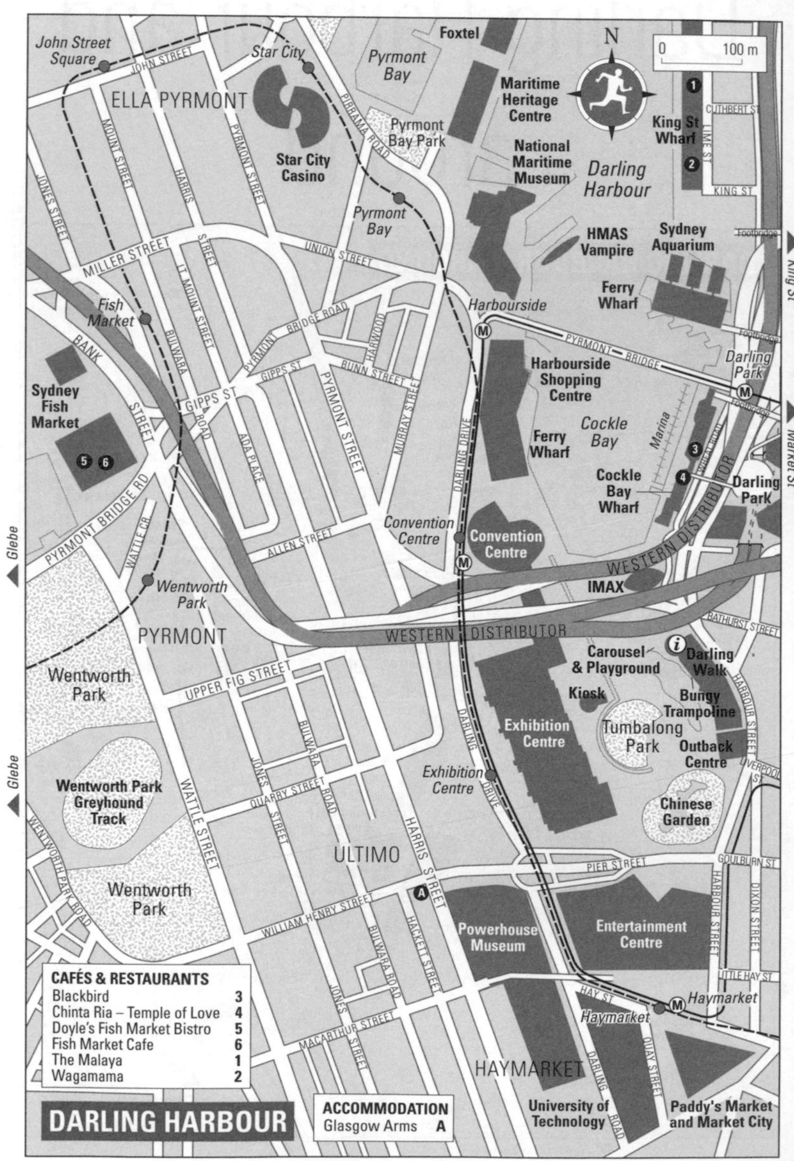

Getting to and around Darling Harbour

To **get to Darling Harbour** you could **walk** – it's only ten minutes on foot from the Town Hall; from the Queen Victoria Building, walk down Market Street and along the overhead walkway. Further south there's a pedestrian bridge from Bathurst Street or you can cut through on Liverpool Street to Tumbalong Park; both bring you out near the Chinese Garden.

Alternatively, the **monorail** (see p.38) runs from the city centre to one of six stops (Harbourside Shoping Centre, Exhibition Centre, Centrepoint Tower, Darling Park, World Square and Park Plaza) around Darling Harbour, and has the views to recommend it.

Getting there by **ferry** from Circular Quay, to the wharf outside the Sydney Aquarium, gives you a chance to see a bit of the harbour. State Transit ferries leave from Wharf 5, and stop at McMahons Point and Balmain en route. The *Matilda Ferry* runs from the Commissioners Steps, outside the Museum of Contemporary Art, and goes via the casino at Pyrmont.

Many **buses** go from Circular Quay or Central up and down George Street, where you can alight outside the QVB, or the #443 goes from Circular Quay via the QVB, Pyrmont and the casino and the #449 does a road trip between the casino, the Powerhouse Museum, the Broadway shopping centre and Glebe.

There's actually quite a bit of walking involved in getting around the large site and if you're exhausted, or just for fun, you might consider hopping on board the dinky **People Mover train** (daily: summer 10am–6pm, winter 10am–5pm; full circuit 20min; $3.50), leaving every fifteen minutes from various points around Darling Harbour.

Cockle Bay, which opened in 1988, included the building of the above-ground monorail – one of only a few in the world – as well as a massive new shopping and entertainment precinct. In many ways it's a thoroughly stylish redevelopment of the old wharves – the glistening water channels that run along Palm Avenue are a great piece of modern design – and Darling Harbour and the surrounding areas have plenty of attractions on offer, including **Sydney Aquarium**, the **National Maritime Museum**, an **IMAX cinema** and the **Chinese Garden**. Adjacent **Pyrmont** has the **Star City Casino** and the **Fish Market**, and the **Powerhouse Museum**, located just down the road in **Ultimo.** Darling Harbour's neighbouring area of **Haymarket**, heading towards Central Station, contains Sydney's **Chinatown**, as well as its oldest market. However, it's only recently that Sydneysiders themselves have embraced Darling Harbour and its environs. Sneered at for years by locals as tacky and touristy, it took the recent Cockle Bay and King Street Wharf development – an upmarket café, bar and restaurant precinct on the eastern side of the waterfront (and easily accessible from the office blocks of the city) – to finally lure locals into the much-maligned area.

Behind the development, and accessible from it, is **Darling Park**, with paths laid out in the shape of the native waratah flower. The western side of Darling Harbour is dominated by rather ugly modern chain hotels, ironically providing some of the view for the stylish Cockle Bay wharf diners, but more importantly beds for the attendees of the many conferences and trade shows held at the Exhibition Centre.

There are numerous festivals and events in and around Darling Harbour – from carols to ethnic community festivals and outdoor latin dancing bars – particularly during school holidays. To find out what's on, visit the **Darling Harbour Visitor Information Centre** (daily 9.30am–5.30pm; ⓣ02/9240 8788, ⓦwww.darlingharbour.com.au), next door to the IMAX cinema.

Tumbalong Park and the Southern Promenade

The southern half of Darling Harbour, just beyond Chinatown and the Entertainment Centre, is focused around **Tumbalong Park**, reached from the city via Liverpool Street. Backed by the Exhibition Centre, this is the "village green" of Darling Harbour – complete with water features and some interesting sculptures and public artworks – and serves as a venue for open-air concerts and free public entertainment. The area surrounding it can be Darling Harbour's most frenetic – at least on weekends and during school holidays – as most of the attractions, including a free playground and a stage for holiday concerts, are aimed at children.

The Chinese Garden

For some peace and quiet head for the adjacent **Chinese Garden** (daily 9.30am–5pm; $4.50), completed for the Bicentenary in 1988 as a gift from Sydney's sister city Guangdong; the "Garden of Friendship" is designed in the traditional southern Chinese style. Although not large, it feels remarkably calm and spacious – a great place to retreat from the commercial hubbub. The balcony of the traditional tearoom offers a bird's-eye view of the dragon wall, waterfalls, a pagoda on a hill and carp swimming in winding lakes, and does a refreshing green tea to boot.

IMAX cinema

The Southern Promenade of Darling Harbour is dominated by the **Panasonic IMAX Theatre** (films hourly from 10am; 2-D films $16, 3-D $17; ⓣ02/9281 3300, ⓦwww.imax.com.au). Its giant eight-storey-high cinema screen (the biggest in Australia) shows a constantly changing programme from an over 100-film library, with an emphasis on scenic wonders, the animal kingdom and adventure sports.

▲ Monorail

Sydney Aquarium

At the bottom of Market Street is the **Pyrmont Bridge**, a pedestrian walkway across Cockle Bay, linking the two sides of the harbour. On the eastern side is the impressive **Sydney Aquarium** (daily 9am–9pm; $25, Aquarium Pass including STA ferry from Circular Quay $29.10; ⓦwww.sydneyaquarium.com.au). If you're not going to get the chance to explore the Barrier Reef, the aquarium makes a surprisingly passable substitute.

The entry level exhibits freshwater fish from the Murray–Darling basin, Australia's biggest river system, but speed past these to get to the two underwater walkways, where you can wander in complete safety as sharks and gigantic stingrays swim overhead. Another area features exotic species from the Great Barrier Reef, including a mass of glowing, undulating Moon Jellyfish, while yet another section displays dangerous creatures like the moray eel and poisonous sea urchins. The Great Barrier Reef Oceanarium finishes with a huge floor-to-ceiling tank where you can sit and watch the underwater world while classical music plays. Alongside all the fish, there are also platypus, crocodiles, seals and fairy penguins on display.

The National Maritime Museum and around

On the western side of Pyrmont Bridge the **National Maritime Museum** (daily 9.30am–5pm, Jan until 6pm; free entry to the museum for all in-house exhibits, but a "Big Ticket" can be purchased ($20) for guided tours of the destroyer HMAS *Vampire*, the barque James Craig and HMAS *Onslow*, the submarine; ⓦwww.anmm.gov.au), with its distinctive modern architecture topped by a wave-shaped roof, highlights the history of Australia as a seafaring nation, but goes beyond maritime interests to look at how the sea has shaped Australian life, covering everything from immigration to beach culture and Aboriginal fishing methods in seven core themed exhibitions. Highlights include the "Merana Eora Nora – First People" exhibition, delving into indigenous culture, and "Navigators – Defining Australia", which focuses on the seventeenth-century Dutch explorers; major exhibits are continually being launched. Outside several vessels are moored: the navy destroyer, the *Vampire*, and a submarine, the *Onslow*, plus the beautifully restored 1874 square-rigger, the *James Craig*, are permanently on display, while a collection of historic vessels, including a 1970s Vietnamese refugee boat, are rotated. The pleasant alfresco **café** here, which you don't have to enter the museum to use, has views of the boats. The bronze **Welcome Wall** outside the museum pays honour to Australia's six million immigrants.

Included in the Big Ticket entry is a behind-the-scenes tour of the **Maritime Heritage Centre** at Wharf 7, just beyond the museum off Pirrama Road and beside Pyrmont Bay Park, where conservation and model-making work takes place and some of the collection is stored. At the wharf, the Sydney Heritage Fleet's collection of restored boats and ships is moored, the oldest of which was built in 1888. Just nearby, the two-level **Harbourside Shopping Centre** provides opportunities for souvenir shopping: don't miss the first-floor **Gavala: Aboriginal Art & Cultural Education Centre** (daily 10am–9pm), a very spacious and relaxed store selling Aboriginal art, clothing, accessories and music, and the only fully Aboriginal-owned and -run store in Sydney, with all profits going back to the artists.

Ultimo

From Tumbalong Park, a signposted walkway leads to **Ultimo** and its **Powerhouse Museum** on Harris Street. It's a lively area, with the University of Technology campus on either side of Harris Street and the headquarters of both television and radio of the national broadcaster, the ABC. Harris Street and the Powerhouse Museum can also be easily reached from Central Station via the Devonshire Street pedestrian tunnel, emerging at the northwestern end, from where it's signposted.

The Powerhouse Museum

The **Powerhouse Museum** (daily 9am–5pm; $10, $5 for children, extra for special exhibitions, free 45min tour daily 11.30am & 1.30pm; ⓦwww.phm.gov.au; monorail to Haymarket) is located, as the name suggests, in a former power station, and is arguably the best museum in Sydney. It's an exciting place with fresh ideas, combining arts and sciences, design, sociology and technology under the same roof – there's even fashion, with the much-anticipated "Fashion of the Year" display every November. There are several big temporary exhibitions on each year, with past popular themes as varied as "The Lord of the Rings" and "Audrey Hepburn, Woman of Style". The permanent displays are varied, presented with an interactive approach that means you'll need hours to investigate the five-level museum properly. The entrance level is dominated by the huge **Boulton and Watt Steam Engine**, first put to use in 1875 in a British brewery; still operational, the engine is often loudly demonstrated. The **Kings Cinema** on level 3, with its original Art Deco fittings, suitably shows the sorts of newsreels and films a Sydneysider would have watched in the 1930s. Judging by the tears at closing time, the **special children's areas** have proved a great success. On level 5, there's a licensed restaurant, with a more inexpensive courtyard cafeteria downstairs. The souvenir shop is also worth a browse for some unusual gifts.

Pyrmont

Frantic redevelopment has been taking place for the last five years at **Pyrmont**, which juts out into the water between Darling Harbour and Blackwattle Bay. The once dilapidated suburb was Sydney's answer to Ellis Island in the 1950s when thousands of immigrants disembarked at the city's main overseas passenger terminal, Pier 13. Today the former industrial suburb, which had a population of only nine hundred in 1988, is being transformed into a residential suburb of twenty thousand with A$2 billion worth of investment and groovy modern unit blocks and warehouse renovations to show for it. With the New South Wales government selling A$97 million worth of property, this has been one of the biggest concentrated sell-offs of land in Australia. The area has certainly become glitzier, with Sydney's casino, Star City, and two TV companies – Channel Ten and Foxtel – based here. Harris Street has filled up with new shops and cafés, and the area's old pubs have been given a new lease of life, attracting the young and upwardly mobile alongside the wharfies. The approach to the spectacularly cabled **Anzac Bridge** (complete with statue of an Australian and New Zealand Army Corps soldier) – Sydney's newest – cuts through Pyrmont and saves between fifteen and twenty minutes' travelling time to Sydney's inner west.

Star City Casino

Beyond the Maritime Museum, on Pyrmont Bay, palm-fronted **Star City** is the spectacularly tasteless 24-hour Sydney casino. As well as the two hundred gaming tables (from Blackjack to Pai Gow – there are heaps of Asian games, and gamblers), a big TAB lounge and sports bar, for putting bets on the horses and dogs and watching the results, and 1500 noisy poker machines, the building houses fourteen restaurants, cafés and theme bars, two theatres (see p.227), souvenir shops, a convenience store and a nightclub. It's certainly somewhere to come for late-night eats, with some quite good-value places such as *Trophies Food Court* – with everything from stir-fries to sandwiches – staying open until 6am. The casino interior itself is a riot of giant palm sculptures, prize cars spinning on rotating bases, Aboriginal painting motifs on the ceiling, Australian critters scurrying across a red desert-coloured carpet and an endless array of flashing poker machines. Dress code is smart casual. You can just wander in and have a look around or a drink, without betting.

Nearby **Pyrmont Bay Park** is a shady spot to rest, and on the first Saturday of the month it hosts an early morning **Growers Market** (7–11am). To **get to the casino** bus #449 runs in a loop to and from Broadway in the city via the QVB to the casino and the Exhibition Centre in Darling Harbour, or the #443 runs from Circular Quay via Phillip and Market streets and the QVB. The Light Rail pulls in right underneath the casino.

Sydney Fish Market

On the corner of Pyrmont Bridge Road and Bank Street, the **Sydney Fish Market** (daily 7am–4pm; Ⓦwww.sydneyfishmarket.com.au) is only a ten-minute walk via Pyrmont Bridge Road from Darling Harbour. The market is the second-largest seafood market in the world for variety of fish, after the massive Tsukiji market in Tokyo. You need to visit early to see the **auctions** (Mon–Fri only, with the biggest auction floor on Friday; buyers begin viewing the fish at 4.30am, auctions begin 5.30am, public viewing platform opens 7am); buyers log into computer terminals to register their bids.

You can take away oysters, prawns and cooked seafood and eat picnic-style on waterfront tables watching the boats come in. Everything is set up for throwing together an impromptu meal – there's a bakery, the *Blackwattle Deli*, with an extensive (and tempting) cheese selection, a bottle shop and a grocer. Alternatively, you can eat in at *Doyles*, the casual and slightly more affordable version of the famous *Doyles* fish restaurant at Watsons Bay, at the excellent sushi bar, or have dirt-cheap fish and chips or a crack-of-dawn espresso at the *Fish Market Cafe* (Mon–Fri 4am–4pm, Sat & Sun 5am–5pm). Retail shops open at 7am.

Sydney Seafood School

The **Sydney Seafood School** (Ⓣ02/9004 1111) offers seafood cookery lessons starting from $70 for a two-hour course, from Thai-style to French provincial, under the expert tuition of resident home economists as well as guest chefs drawn from the city's top restaurants. The most popular course, for which you need to book three or more months in advance, is the **Seafood Barbecue** run at weekends (4hr; $115). The school also does a two-hour early morning tour of the Fish Market's selling floor (first Thurs of month; $20, includes a coffee).

To **get to** the fish market, take the Light Rail from Central to Fish Market station on Miller Street. Take bus #443 from Circular Quay or the QVB, and it's a five-minute walk from the corner of Harris Street and Pyrmont Bridge Road.

Haymarket

Immediately west of Central Station on either side of the downmarket end of George Street is the area known as **Haymarket**. The Light Rail (see p.38) heads through here from Central Station, past Capitol Square and the **Capitol**

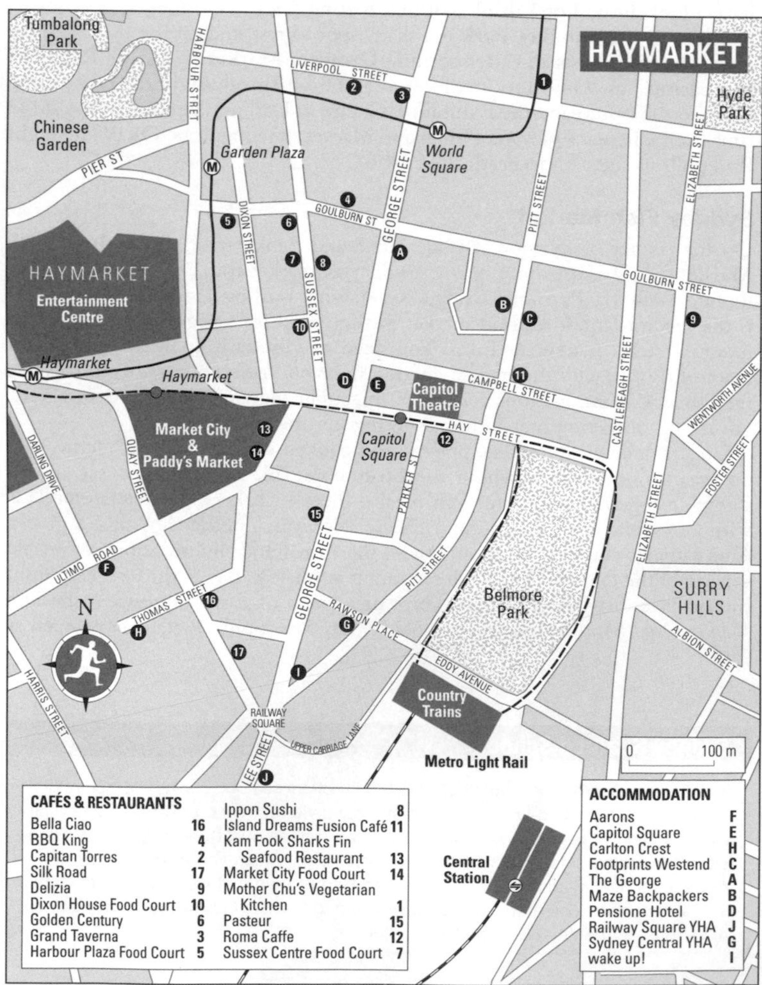

Theatre. Built as a deluxe picture palace in the 1920s, the theatre now hosts big-budget musicals and ballet under a star-studded ceiling representing the southern skies. The surrounding area is renowned for its pop culture pleasures, with the ugly concrete bunker of the **Sydney Entertainment Centre**, the city's mainstream concert venue (see p.220), on the other side of **Chinatown**.

Chinatown

Sydney's **Chinatown** is a much more full-blooded affair than "Spanish corner" on nearby Liverpool Street. No mere tourist attraction, this is a gutsy Chinese quarter, with its share of social problems. Winter 2002 saw unprecedented incidents when several restaurants were wrecked, in front of terrified diners, by rival triad gangs conducting turf wars. Chinese people first began arriving in "New Gold Mountain", as they called Australia, in the 1850s during the time of the goldrushes; after the 1880s most went back, but many stayed on and set up businesses – wholesaling and running market gardens were popular occupations and Chinatown grew up around what has been the traditional wholesale market area for over 150 years. It was only in 1980, however, that Dixon Street became Sydney's official Chinatown.

Through the colourful Chinese gates, **Dixon Street Mall** is the main drag, buzzing day and night as people crowd into numerous restaurants, pubs, cafés, cinemas, food stalls and Asian grocery stores. Towards the end of January, or in the first weeks of February, Chinese New Year is celebrated here with gusto: dragon and lion dances, food festivals and musical entertainment compete with the noise and smoke from strings of Chinese crackers. Friday nights are also a good time to visit, when a **night market** takes over Dixon and Little Hay streets (6–11pm).

Every Thursday, Friday, Saturday and Sunday, **Paddy's Market**, Sydney's oldest (1869), is conducted in its undercover home at the corner of Thomas and Hay streets, across from the Entertainment Centre (Thurs 10am–6pm, Fri, Sat & Sun 9am–4.30pm; ⓦwww.paddysmarkets.com.au). It has around one thousand stalls and is a good place to buy cheap vegetables, seafood, plants, clothes and bric-a-brac. Above the old market, the multilevel **Market City Shopping Centre** has a very Asian feel – you could easily imagine yourself in one of the air-conditioned malls of Bangkok or Kuala Lumpur; there's an excellent Asian food court (see "Eating") on the top floor next to the multiscreen cinema.

6

Inner east

To the east of the city centre **Surry Hills**, **Darlinghurst** and **Paddington** were once rather scruffy working-class suburbs, but since the 1970s they have gradually been taken over and revamped by the young, arty and upwardly mobile. **Oxford Street**, from Hyde Park to Paddington and beyond, is a major amusement strip and waiting to be discovered. Here and in the side streets is an array of nightclubs, restaurants, cafés and pubs. **Kings Cross** is home to Sydney's red-light district as well as many of its tourists, and can be reached by a series of steps from **Woolloomooloo** and the busy naval dockyards, or by walking straight up William Street from Hyde Park. Further east, "the Cross" (as locals call it) fades into the more elegant neighbourhoods of **Potts Point** and **Elizabeth Bay**, which trade on their harbour views.

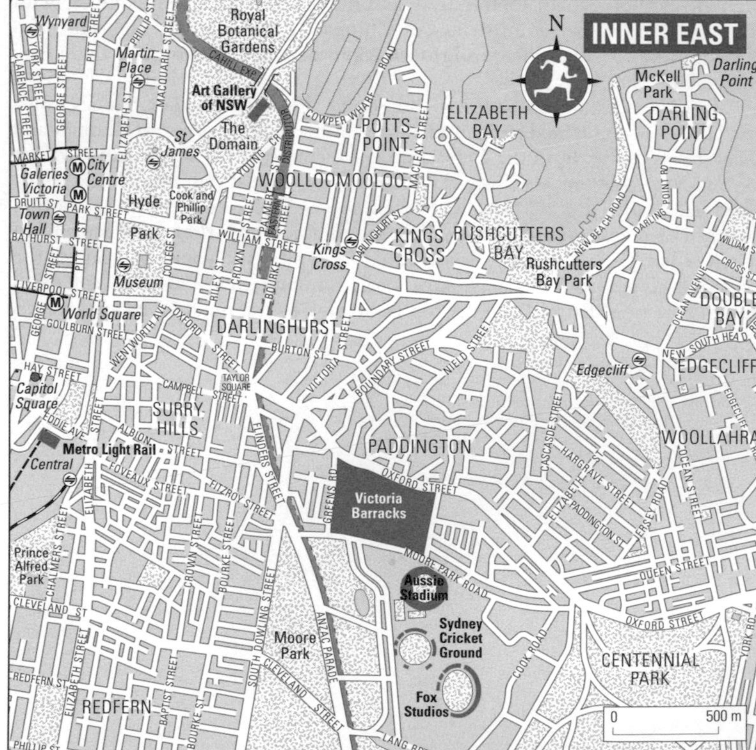

Getting to Surry Hills

Surry Hills is a short **walk** uphill from Central Station (Devonshire Street or Elizabeth Street exit): take Fouveax or Devonshire streets and you'll soon hit Crown Street, or it's an even quicker stroll from Oxford Street, Darlinghurst, heading south along Crown or Bourke streets. Several **buses** also run here from Circular Quay, including the #301 and #303, both to Crown Street.

Surry Hills

Surry Hills, directly east of Central station from Elizabeth Street, was traditionally the centre of the rag trade, which still finds its focus on Devonshire Street. Rows of tiny terraces once housed its original poor, working-class population, many of them of Irish origin. Considered a slum by the rest of Sydney, the dire and overcrowded conditions were given fictional life in Ruth Park's *The Harp in the South* trilogy (see "Books", p.360), set in the Surry Hills of the 1940s. The area became something of a cultural melting pot with European postwar immigration, and doubled as a grungy, student heartland in the 1980s, fuelled by cheap bars and cheaper rent.

By the mid-1990s, however, the slickly fashionable scene of neighbouring Darlinghurst and Paddington had finally taken over Surry Hills' twin focal points of parallel **Crown Street**, filled with cafés, swanky restaurants, funky clothes shops and designer galleries, and leafy **Bourke Street**, where a couple of Sydney's best cafés lurk among the trees. As rents have gone up, only **Cleveland Street**, running west to Redfern and east towards Moore Park and the Sydney Cricket Ground (see p.105), traffic-snarled and lined with cheap Indian, Lebanese and Turkish restaurants, retains its ethnically varied population.

A good time to visit Surry Hills is the first Saturday of the month when a lively **flea market**, complete with tempting food stalls, takes over the small Shannon Reserve, on the corner of Crown and Fouveaux streets, overlooked by the **Clock Hotel**. The hotel, which has expanded out of all recognition from its 1840s roots, is emblematic of the new Surry Hills, with its swish restaurant and bar. So too the *White Horse* across the road, which used to have a reputation for shady dealings but is now frequented by the beautiful people for cocktails and imported beers.

The Brett Whiteley Studio

The artistic side of Surry Hills can be experienced nearby at the **Brett Whiteley Studio** at 2 Raper St (Sat & Sun 10am–4pm; by appointment Thurs & Fri ⓣ02/9225 1881; $7); walk about three blocks further south from Shannon Reserve, down Crown Street, and it's off Davies Street. Whitely was one of Australia's best-known contemporary painters with an international reputation by the time he died in 1992 of a heroin overdose at the age of 53; wild self-portraits and expressive female nudes were some of his subjects, but it is his sensual paintings of Sydney Harbour for which he is best known, painted from his home in Lavender Bay. In 1986 Whitely converted this one-time factory into a studio and living space, and since his death it has become a museum and gallery showing his paintings and memorabilia, as well as an education venue for adult drawing classes and children's workshops in the holidays.

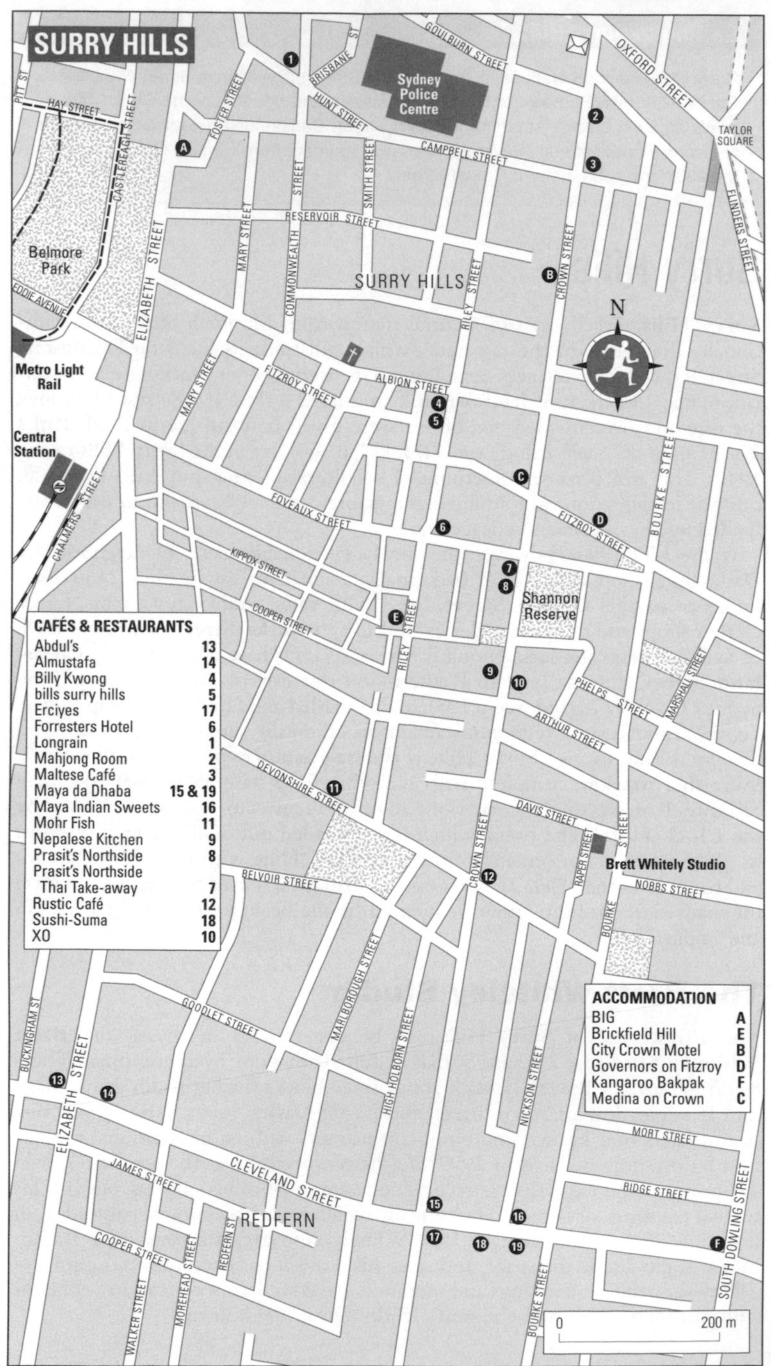

CAFÉS & RESTAURANTS

Abdul's	13
Almustafa	14
Billy Kwong	4
bills surry hills	5
Erciyes	17
Forresters Hotel	6
Longrain	1
Mahjong Room	2
Maltese Café	3
Maya da Dhaba	15 & 19
Maya Indian Sweets	16
Mohr Fish	11
Nepalese Kitchen	9
Prasit's Northside	8
Prasit's Northside Thai Take-away	7
Rustic Café	12
Sushi-Suma	18
XO	10

ACCOMMODATION

BIG	A
Brickfield Hill	E
City Crown Motel	B
Governors on Fitzroy	D
Kangaroo Bakpak	F
Medina on Crown	C

Eveleigh Street, Redfern

Just beyond Surry Hills, and only 2km from the glitter and sparkle of Darling Harbour, **Redfern** is Sydney's underbelly. Around the **Eveleigh Street** area, Australia's biggest urban Aboriginal community lives in **"the Block"**, a squalid streetscape of derelict terraced houses and rubbish-strewn streets not far from Redfern train station; this is the closest Sydney has to a no-go zone. The Aboriginal Housing Company, set up as a cooperative in 1973, has been unable to pay for repairs and renovation work, and Eveleigh Street appears in shocking contrast to Paddington's cutesy restored terraces and the harbour-view mansions of Sydney's rich and beautiful. Recently the Company began knocking down derelict houses and relocating residents, which has upset many who want to keep the community together. A full-blown street riot in 2004 was indicative of how close to the surface tensions in the area are.

Darlinghurst

Oxford Street, from Hyde Park to Paddington and beyond, is a major amusement strip. Here and in the side streets around, is an array of nightclubs, restaurants, cafés and pubs, which are also the focus of Sydney's very active **gay and lesbian** movement. Hip and bohemian, **Darlinghurst** mingles seediness with a hedonistic style: some art students and clubbers never leave the district – save for a coffee at the Cross or a swim at the "Boy" in The Domain. There's a further concentration of cafés, restaurants and fashion on Liverpool Street, heading downhill towards East Sydney, where **Stanley Street** also has a cluster of cheap Italian cafés and restaurants including the long-running *Bill and Toni* (see "Eating").

Oxford Street's shopping strip, many would argue Sydney's best for labels and funky style, starts at the corner of Victoria Rd in Darlinghurst and doesn't stop until the corner of Jersey Road in **Woollhara**. Two arthouse cinemas – the Academy Twin and the Verona (see "Performing arts and film") – always have the latest local and international alternative flicks, and late night bookshops Berkelouws (with its fabulous coffee shop upstairs) and Ariel across the street pack in students and the smart set alike till late. There's a concentration of cafés north of Oxford Street (heading towards Kings Cross) on **Victoria Street**, a classic posing spot, boasting the legendary, street-smart *Bar Coluzzi* (see "Eating").

Sydney Jewish Museum

The impressive **Sydney Jewish Museum**, at 148 Darlinghurst Rd (Mon–Thurs & Sun 10am–4pm, Fri 10am–2pm; $10; ⓦwww.sydneyjewishmuseum.com.au), is housed in the old Maccabean Hall, which has been a Jewish meeting point for over seventy years.

Sixteen Jews were among the convicts who arrived with the First Fleet, and the high-tech, interactive museum explores over two hundred years of Australian Jewish experience. An introductory fifteen-minute film discusses anti-Semitism through the ages, and the Holocaust is covered in harrowing detail with Australian survivors' videotaped testimonies.

You can pick up the pamphlet *Guide to Jewish Sydney* from the museum and there's a **kosher café** on site. You might also like to visit **the Great Synagogue** in the city opposite Hyde Park, and there is a concentration of **kosher** Jewish cafés, butchers and supermarkets on Hall Street in Bondi.

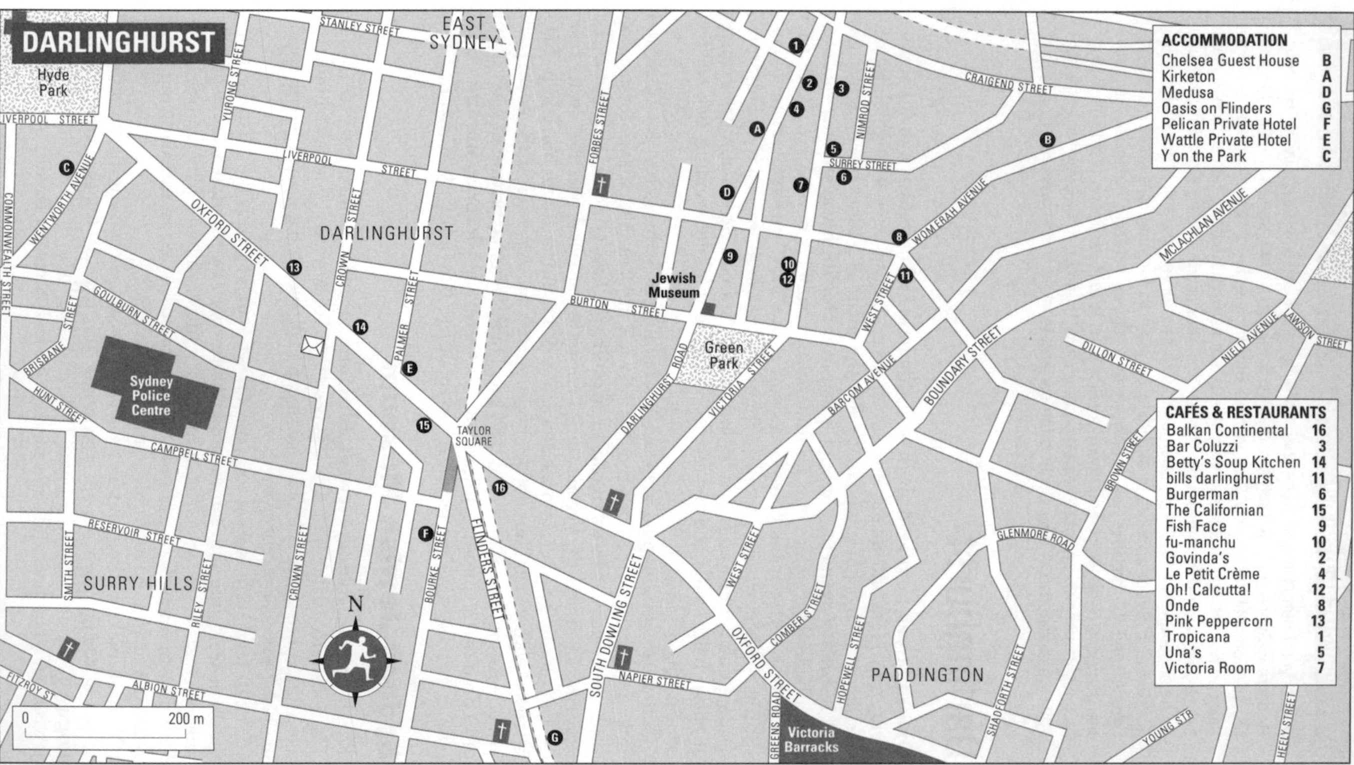
DARLINGHURST
ACCOMMODATION
Chelsea Guest House B
Kirketon A
Medusa D
Oasis on Flinders G
Pelican Private Hotel F
Wattle Private Hotel E
Y on the Park C
CAFÉS & RESTAURANTS
Balkan Continental 16
Bar Coluzzi 3
Betty's Soup Kitchen 14
bills darlinghurst 11
Burgerman 6
The Californian 15
Fish Face 9
fu-manchu 10
Govinda's 2
Le Petit Crème 4
Oh! Calcutta! 12
Onde 8
Pink Peppercorn 13
Tropicana 1
Una's 5
Victoria Room 7
Hyde Park
EAST SYDNEY
DARLINGHURST
SURRY HILLS
PADDINGTON
Jewish Museum
Green Park
Sydney Police Centre
Victoria Barracks
TAYLOR SQUARE
STANLEY STREET
YURONG STREET
LIVERPOOL STREET
WENTWORTH AVENUE
COMMONWEALTH STREET
OXFORD STREET
CROWN STREET
PALMER STREET
FORBES STREET
BURTON STREET
DARLINGHURST ROAD
VICTORIA STREET
NIMROD STREET
SURREY STREET
CRAIGEND STREET
WOMERAH AVENUE
MCLACHLAN AVENUE
WEST STREET
BARCOM AVENUE
BOUNDARY STREET
DILLON STREET
NIELD AVENUE
AWSON STREET
BROWN STREET
GLENMORE ROAD
GOULBURN STREET
BRISBANE STREET
HUNT STREET
CAMPBELL STREET
RESERVOIR STREET
SMITH STREET
RILEY STREET
BOURKE STREET
FLINDERS STREET
SOUTH DOWLING STREET
NAPIER STREET
COMBER STREET
HOPEWELL STREET
SHADFORTH STREET
GREENS ROAD
YOUNG STR
HEELY STREET
FITZROY ST
ALBION STREET
N
0
200 m

Paddington and Woollahra

From the intersection with South Dowling Street in Darlinghurst, Oxford Street strikes southeast through trendy, upmarket **Paddington** and wealthy, staid **Woollahra** to the verdant expanse of Centennial Park. **Transport** heading in this direction includes **buses** #380 and #389 from Circular Quay. The #378, from Central Station, also heads along Oxford Street.

Paddington, a slum at the turn of the twentieth century, became a popular hangout for hipsters during the late 1960s and 1970s. Since then, yuppies have taken over and turned Paddington into the smart and fashionable suburb it is today: the Victorian-era terraced houses, with their iron-lace verandahs reminiscent of New Orleans, have been beautifully restored. Many of the terraces were originally built in the 1840s to house the artisans who worked on the graceful, sandstone **Victoria Barracks** on the southern side of Oxford Street, its walls stretching seven blocks, from Greens Road to just before the Paddington Town Hall on Oatley Road. **Shadforth Street**, opposite the entrance gates, has many examples of the original artisans' homes. Though the barracks are still used by the army, there are free **guided tours** (Thurs 10am) – complete with army band – while a small **museum** is open to visitors (Sun 10am–3pm). On the other side of Oxford Street the small, winding, tree-lined streets are a pleasant place for a stroll, and offer a chance to wander into the many small art galleries or to take some liquid refreshment. Head via Underwood and Heeley streets to **Five Ways**, where you'll find cafés, speciality shops and a typically gracious old boozer, the *Royal Hotel* (see "Drinking").

▲ The Royal Hotel

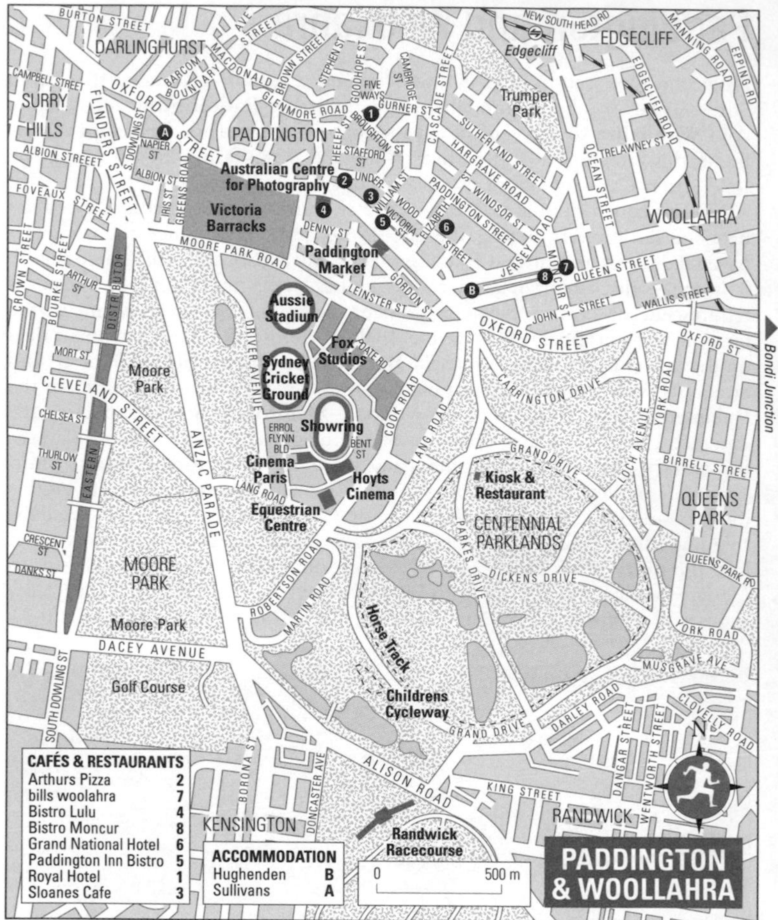

There are more shops on Elizabeth Street running off Oxford Street, but the main action is, of course, on Oxford Street itself, where stylish boutiques and arty homeware stores attract the see and be seen crowd. Always bustling, the area comes alive on Saturday from 9am to around 4pm, when everyone descends on **Paddington Markets** in the church grounds at no. 395. The markets just keep getting bigger, selling everything from funky handmade jewellery to local artwork, cheap but very fresh flowers and vintage clothes; you can even get a massage or a tarot reading between a cup of excellent coffee and an organic sandwich.

Woollahra, along Oxford Street from Paddington, is even more moneyed but contrastingly staid, with expensive **antique shops** and **art galleries** along **Queen Street** replacing the fashion and funky lifestyle stores of Paddington. Leafy Moncur Street hides *jones the grocer* (at no. 68), where Woollahra locals gather for coffee at the long central table; it sells stylishly packaged, outlandishly priced and utterly delicious groceries and gourmet treats.

Centennial Parklands

South of Paddington and Woollhara lies the great green expanse of **Centennial Park** (daily sunrise to sunset; Ⓦwww.cp.nsw.gov.au), opened to the citizens of Sydney at the Centennial Festival in 1888. With its vast lawns, rose gardens and extensive network of ponds complete with ducks it resembles an English country park, but is reclaimed at dawn and dusk by distinctly antipodean residents, including possums and flying foxes. The park is crisscrossed by walking paths and tracks for cycling, rollerblading, jogging and horse riding: you can rent a bike or rollerblades nearby or hire a horse from the adjacent equestrian centre and then recover from your exertions in the **café** with its popular outside tables (though packed and hideously slow on weekends, even for takeaways) or, in the finer months, stay on until dark and catch an outdoor film at the Moonlight Cinema (see p.231).

Adjoining **Moore Park** has facilities for tennis, golf, grass-skiing, bowling, cricket and hockey; The Parklands are also home to the Sydney Cricket Ground, Football Stadium and Fox Studios (see below). Pick up a free map from the Park Office (Mon–Fri 8.30am–5.30pm; Ⓣ02/9339 6699) near the café, and easily reached from the Paddington gates off Oxford Street (opposite Queen Street).

Fox Studios and The Entertainment Quarter

Also within Moore Park, immediately southeast of the SCG (Sydney Cricket Ground), are the Murdoch-owned **Fox Studios** (Ⓦwww.foxstudios.com.au), constructed at a cost of A$300 million within the old Showgrounds site, where the Royal Agricultural Society held its annual Royal Easter Show from 1882 until 1997; the show is now held at the Sydney Showground at the Olympic site at Homebush Bay. The **Professional Studio**, opened in May 1998, takes up over half the site and has facilities for both film and television production, with six high-tech stages and industry tenants on site providing everything from casting services to stunt professionals. Films made here include *The Matrix*, *Mission Impossible II*, Baz Luhrmann's *Moulin Rouge* and *Episode I* and *II* of the *Star Wars* saga. The **public areas** of the site known as **The Entertainment Quarter** (Ⓦwww.entertainmentquarter.com.au), focused around a state-of-the-art, twelve-screen **cinema complex**, complete with digital surround-sound and VIP lounges, and a smaller four-screen arthouse cinema; international film premieres are sometimes held here. The **theme park** area of Fox Studios, the Backlot, was a commercial failure, closing in 2001. However, there's still a lot to attract families, including the mini-golf course by the old Backlot entrance (the film-themed murals are still there) and the indoor **Lollipops Playground**, pricey but perfect for a rainy day (Mon–Thurs 9.30am–7pm, Fri 9.30am–8pm, Sat 9am–8pm, Sun 9am–7pm; under-2s $8.90, 2–9 years $12.90, adults $4 includes a coffee; Ⓣ02/9331 0811). Just outside are two free playgrounds and a carousel ($2.50).

Getting to Centennial Park

To get to the park you can take a **bus** from Central Station (#372, #393 or #395) or from in front of Museum Station on Elizabeth Street in the city (#L90, #391, #394 or #396; #394 and #396 extend to and from Circular Quay). Alternatively you could take a bus to Oxford Street, Paddington, then walk in via the Paddington gates or further along at the Woollhara gates (opposite Ocean Street). There is plenty of free parking for cars.

To get to Fox Studios catch **bus** #339, #392, #394 or #396 from Central, Wynyard or Town Hall. There's plenty of parking for cars, free for the first two hours.

The Showring

The old **Showring,** once the preserve of wood-chopping competitions and rodeo events, is now used for everything from open-air cinema and circuses, to the weekend craft market (Sat & Sun 10am–6pm), International Food Market (Fri from 6pm) and the fresh produce Farmers Market (Wed, Sat & Sun from 10am). The **Bungy Trampoline** (Wed–Sun 10am–6pm; $10) here is designed to give you the thrill of a bungy jump without the danger, and in winter an ice rink is also set up for children (and adults) to take a twirl.

Bent Street

The Showring is adjacent to the gleaming shops, cafés, restaurants and bars of pedestrianized **Bent Street**. The numerous upmarket **shops** (including a young Australian designers' store, a bookshop, record store and a bush outfitters) stay open daily until 10pm. The traditional pub atmosphere of the *Fox and Lion* – by the big **outdoor screen** which shows music-video Channel [V] – offers a quenching drink and a cheap ($7.50) Tuesday pasta night. The screen is outside the channel's live studio and there are often shows being taped both inside and out, which are free to attend; check the "What's On" page of their website ⓦwww.channelv.com.au for show times. There's a stand-up **comedy venue**, the *Comedy Store* (see "Performing arts") and a music venue, *City Live* (see "Live music"). Including bars, there are fifteen **places to eat**; an eat-in gourmet deli, wood-fired pizza, Chinese seafood, noodles and classy contemporary Australian are among the choices.

Kings Cross, Potts Point and Elizabeth Bay

The preserve of Sydney's bohemians in the 1950s, **Kings Cross** became an R&R spot for American soldiers during the Vietnam war. Now Sydney's red-light district, its streets are prowled by prostitutes, drug abusers, drunks, strippers and homeless teenagers, as well as visiting sailors from the ships docked at the bottom of the hill in Woolloomooloo. It is also a bustling centre for backpackers and other travellers, especially around leafy and quieter Victoria Street, one street back from the main drag; the two sides of "the Cross" (as locals call it) coexist with little trouble, though some of the tourists seem somewhat surprised at where they've ended up, and it can be rather intimidating for lone women. However, the constant flow of people (and police officers) makes it relatively safe, and it's always lively, with places to eat and drink that stay open all hours. A continuing programme of footpath and shopfront beautification is slowly lending a fresher air, and themed street festivals are becoming a more frequent occurrence, and bringing in a different crowd. South Sydney Council has produced a free **Kings Cross Walking Tour** map, available from the library off Fitzroy Gardens, which points out some of the Art Deco architecture the area is known for and provides some background history.

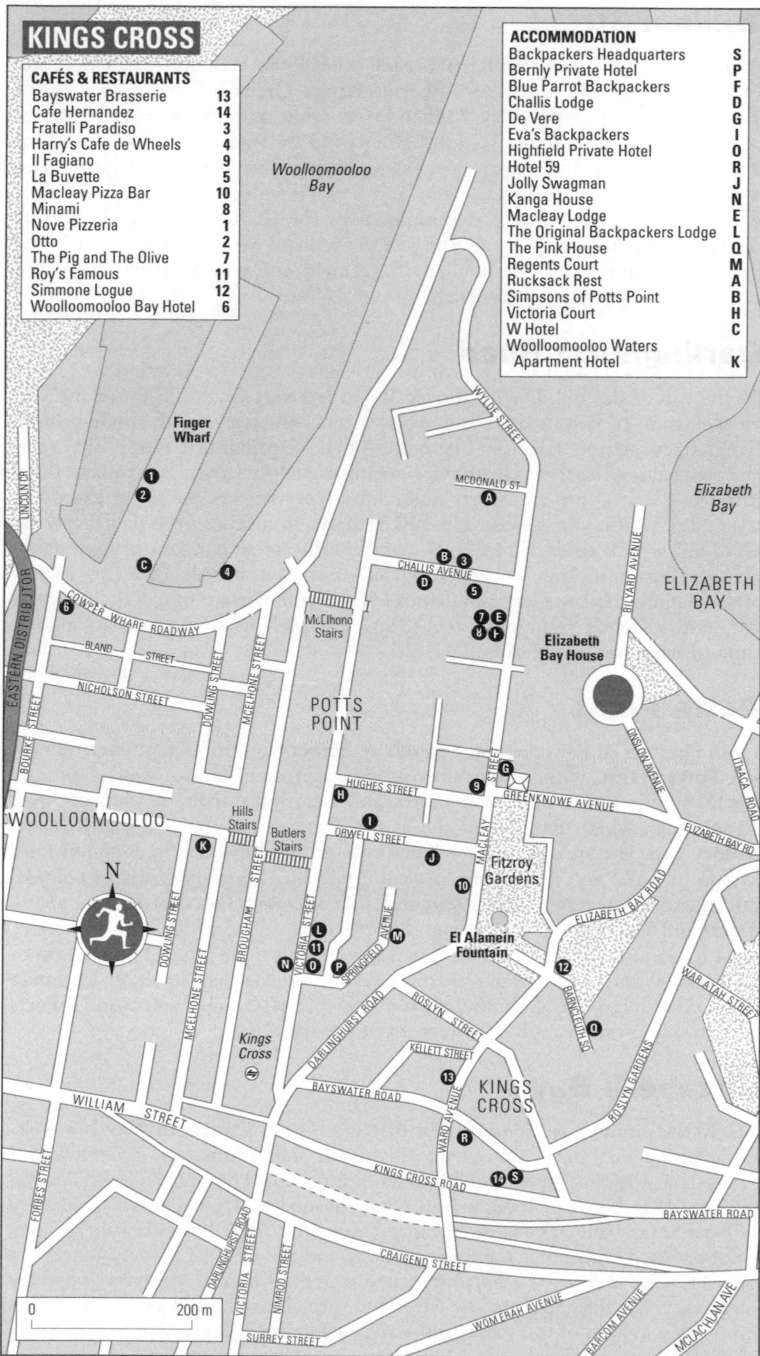

KINGS CROSS
CAFÉS & RESTAURANTS
Bayswater Brasserie 13
Cafe Hernandez 14
Fratelli Paradiso 3
Harry's Cafe de Wheels 4
Il Fagiano 9
La Buvette 5
Macleay Pizza Bar 10
Minami 8
Nove Pizzeria 1
Otto 2
The Pig and The Olive 7
Roy's Famous 11
Simmone Logue 12
Woolloomooloo Bay Hotel 6
ACCOMMODATION
Backpackers Headquarters S
Bernly Private Hotel P
Blue Parrot Backpackers F
Challis Lodge D
De Vere G
Eva's Backpackers I
Highfield Private Hotel O
Hotel 59 R
Jolly Swagman J
Kanga House N
Macleay Lodge E
The Original Backpackers Lodge L
The Pink House Q
Regents Court M
Rucksack Rest A
Simpsons of Potts Point B
Victoria Court H
W Hotel C
Woolloomooloo Waters Apartment Hotel K
Woolloomooloo Bay
Finger Wharf
Elizabeth Bay
ELIZABETH BAY
Elizabeth Bay House
POTTS POINT
WOOLLOOMOOLOO
KINGS CROSS
Kings Cross
McElhone Stairs
Hills Stairs
Butlers Stairs
Fitzroy Gardens
El Alamein Fountain
WYLDE STREET
MCDONALD ST
CHALLIS AVENUE
COWPER WHARF ROADWAY
BLAND STREET
NICHOLSON STREET
DOWLING STREET
MCELHONE STREET
LINCOLN CR
EASTERN DISTRIBUTOR
BOURKE STREET
BILYARD AVENUE
ONSLOW AVENUE
ITHACA ROAD
HUGHES STREET
GREENKNOWE AVENUE
ORWELL STREET
MACLEAY STREET
ELIZABETH BAY RD
ELIZABETH BAY ROAD
VICTORIA STREET
SPRINGFIELD AVENUE
BROUGHAM STREET
BARNCLEUTH SQ
WAR ATAH STREET
ROSLYN STREET
DARLINGHURST ROAD
KELLETT STREET
ROSLYN GARDENS
BAYSWATER ROAD
WARD AVENUE
WILLIAM STREET
KINGS CROSS ROAD
FORBES STREET
CRAIGEND STREET
NIMROD STREET
WOMERAH AVENUE
BARCOM AVENUE
MCLACHLAN AVE
SURREY STREET
N
0
200 m

6

INNER EAST

William Street

Heading up the rise of **William Street** from Hyde Park and past Cook and Phillip Park and the Australian Museum, **Kings Cross** beckons with its giant neon Coca-Cola sign. By day, William Street looks quite grotty with its stream of fast, fuming traffic heading to the eastern and western distributors and its car rental firms advertising cheap deals; at night, there are even fewer pedestrians as hardcore transvestite streetwalkers and kerb crawling patrons go about their business. However, with the development of the Cross City Tunnel, recently opened to traffic, there's a grand vision for William Street to become a European-style boulevard – tree-lined, traffic-calmed, and with wide pavements for café tables and strolling pedestrians.

Darlinghurst Road

At the top of the hill, **Darlinghurst Road** is Kings Cross's "action zone". At weekends, an endless stream of suburban voyeurs emerge from the underground Kings Cross station, near the beginning of the Darlinghurst Road "sin" strip, and trawl along the streets licking ice creams as touts try their best to haul them into tacky strip-joints and sleazy nightclubs. The strippers and sleaze extend to the end of Darlinghurst Road at the El Alamein fountain in the paved Fitzroy Gardens, which though pleasant-looking is the usual hangout of some fairly abusive drunks. It's much changed on Sundays when it's taken over by a small arts and crafts market. Generally, Kings Cross is much more subdued during the day, with a slightly "hungover" feel to it; local residents emerge and it's a good time to hang out in the cafés.

Potts Point

From Fitzroy Gardens, tree-lined **Macleay Street** runs through quieter, upmarket **Potts Point**, with its tree-lined streets, apartment blocks, classy boutique hotels, stylish restaurants, buzzy cafés and occasional harbour glimpses over wealthier Elizabeth Bay, just to the east; this is as close to European-living as Sydney gets. The area was Sydney's first suburb, developed land granted to John Wylde in 1822 and Alexander Macleay in 1826. The grand villas of colonial bureaucrats gave way in the 1920s and 1930s to **Art Deco** residential apartments and in the 1950s big, splendid hotels were added to the scene. The area is set to go more upmarket and more residential with the gradual conversion of all the large hotels into luxury apartments. Beyond Macleay Street, Wylde Street heads downhill to Woolloomooloo; you may spot white-clad sailors and officers here, strolling up through the streets from the naval base.

Elizabeth Bay

Barely five minutes' walk northwest of Kings Cross, **Elizabeth Bay** is a well-heeled residential area, centred on **Elizabeth Bay House**, at 7 Onslow Ave (Tues–Sun 10am–4.30pm; $7.50; ⓦwww.hht.net.au). The grand Greek Revival villa was built between 1835 and 1839 for Alexander Macleay, colonial secretary of New South Wales. The large Macleay family, who arrived from Britain in 1826, were obsessed with botany and entomology and the original 54-acre waterfront grounds were said to be a botanist's paradise – the Macleay Museum at Sydney University was formed from the Macleays' natural history collection. The views from the windows of the yachts and water of Elizabeth Bay are stunning.

Getting to the Kings Cross area

You can get to Kings Cross by **train** (Eastern Suburbs line) or **bus** (#311, #324 or #325 from Circular Quay; #327 from Gresham Street in the city; many others from the city to Darlinghurst Road), or it's not too far to **walk**: straight up William Street from Hyde Park. For a quieter route, you could head up from the Domain via Cowper Wharf Road in Woolloomooloo, and then up the McElhone Stairs to Victoria Street. To get to Elizabeth Bay House, take bus #311 or walk from Kings Cross Station.

Woolloomooloo

North of William Street just below Kings Cross, **Woolloomooloo** occupies the old harbourside quarter between The Domain and the grey-painted fleet of the **Garden Island Naval Depot**. Once a narrow-streeted slum, Woolloomooloo is quickly being transformed, though its upmarket apartment developments sit uneasily side by side with problematic community housing, and you should still be careful at night in the backstreets. There are some lively pubs and some more old-fashioned quiet drinking holes, as well as the legendary **Harry's Café de Wheels** on Cowper Wharf Road, a 24-hour pie-cart operating since 1945 and popular nowadays with Sydney cabbies and hungry clubbers in the small hours. Across Cowper Wharf Road, at nos. 43–51, an old stone warehouse is home to **The Gunnery Arts Centre**; its gallery (Tues–Sat 11am–6pm) shows provocative young artists with a focus on installations and new media and is worth a look.

Next door, the once picturesquely dilapidated **Woolloomooloo Finger Wharf**, dating from 1917, is now a posh complex comprising a marina, luxury residential apartments, the cool *W Hotel* (see "Accommodation") and its funky *Water Bar*, and some slick restaurants with alfresco dining – *Otto* (see "Eating"), *Manta* and *China Doll* are the swankiest. The general public are free to wander along the wharf and even go inside: there's a free exhibition space with a changing theme in the centre. Anyone can afford a cake and pastry at the Parisian-feel *Laurent Boulangerie Pâtisserie* or a pizza feed at *Nove Pizzeria*.

Getting to Woolloomooloo

Woolloomooloo is best reached **on foot** from Kings Cross by taking the McElhone Stairs or the Butlers Stairs from Victoria Street; alternatively take **bus** #311 from Kings Cross, Circular Quay or Central Station. It's also easily reached from a walkway behind the Art Gallery of New South Wales (see p.78).

7

Inner west

West of the centre, immediately beyond Darling Harbour, the inner-city areas of **Glebe** and **Newtown** surround Sydney University, their vibrant cultural mix enlivened by large student populations. On a peninsula north of Glebe and west of The Rocks, **Balmain** is a gentrified working-class dock area popular for its village atmosphere and big old pubs; up-and-coming **Rozelle** next door has both an art college and a writers' centre in the grounds of waterfront Callan Park, while, en route, **Leichhardt** and its neighbour **Haberfield** are the centre of Sydney's Italian community.

Glebe

Glebe, right by Australia's oldest university, has gradually been evolving from a café-oriented student quarter to more upmarket thirtysomething territory, with a New Age slant. Indeed, it's very much the centre of alternative culture in Sydney, with organic food stores (such as GNC *Livewell*, see "Shopping"), yoga schools and healing centres offering every kind of therapy from Chinese massage to homeopathy and floatation tanks. **Glebe Point Road**, the focus of the area, is filled with an eclectic mix of cafés with trademark leafy courtyards, restaurants, bookshops and secondhand and speciality shops as it runs uphill from **Broadway**, becoming quietly residential as it slopes down towards the water of Rozelle Bay. The side streets are fringed with renovated two-storey terraced houses with white-iron lacework verandahs. The laid-back, villagey feel makes

Getting to Glebe

Buses #431, #433 and #434 run to Glebe from Millers Point, George Street and Central Station; #431 and #434 run right down the length of Glebe Point Road to Jubilee Park, with the #434 continuing on to Balmain, while the #433 runs half-way, turning at Wigram Road, and heads on to Balmain. The #370 runs to Glebe from Coogee Beach via the University of NSW and Newtown. You can also reach Glebe via the Metro Monorail, which runs between Central Station, Pyrmont and Rozelle; the "Glebe" stop is just off Pyrmont Bridge Road (follow Allum Place and Marlborough Street to emerge on Glebe Point Road near the Valhalla Cinema), while the "Jubilee" stop is at Jubilee Park (follow Victoria Road and Cotter Lane to emerge at Glebe Point Road by the YHA). Otherwise it's a fifteen-minute **walk** from Central Station up Broadway to the beginning of Glebe Point Road.

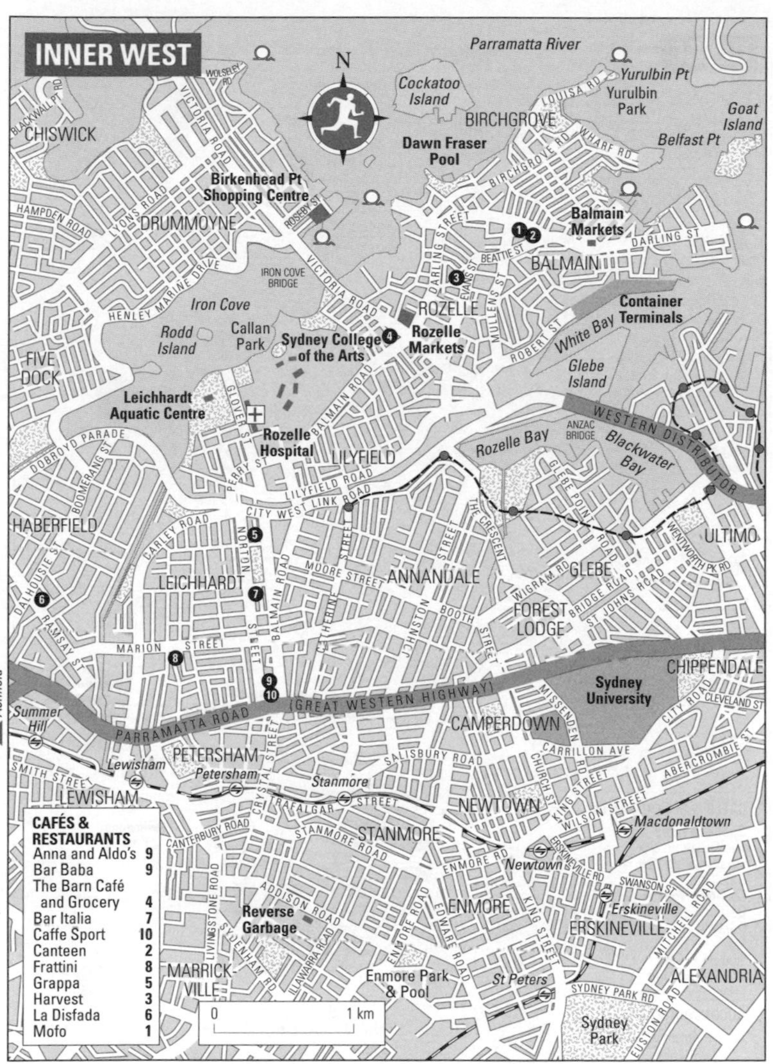

Glebe a popular **place to stay**, with some of Sydney's best hostels, as well as motels and B&Bs (see "Accommodation"); for **longer stays**, check the many café notice boards for flat shares. There's also the handy **Broadway Shopping Centre** on nearby Broadway, with supermarkets, speciality food shops, a huge food court, record, book and clothes shops and a twelve-screen cinema. It's linked to Glebe by an overhead walkway from Glebe Point Road opposite one of the street's best cafés, *Badde Manors* (see "Eating").

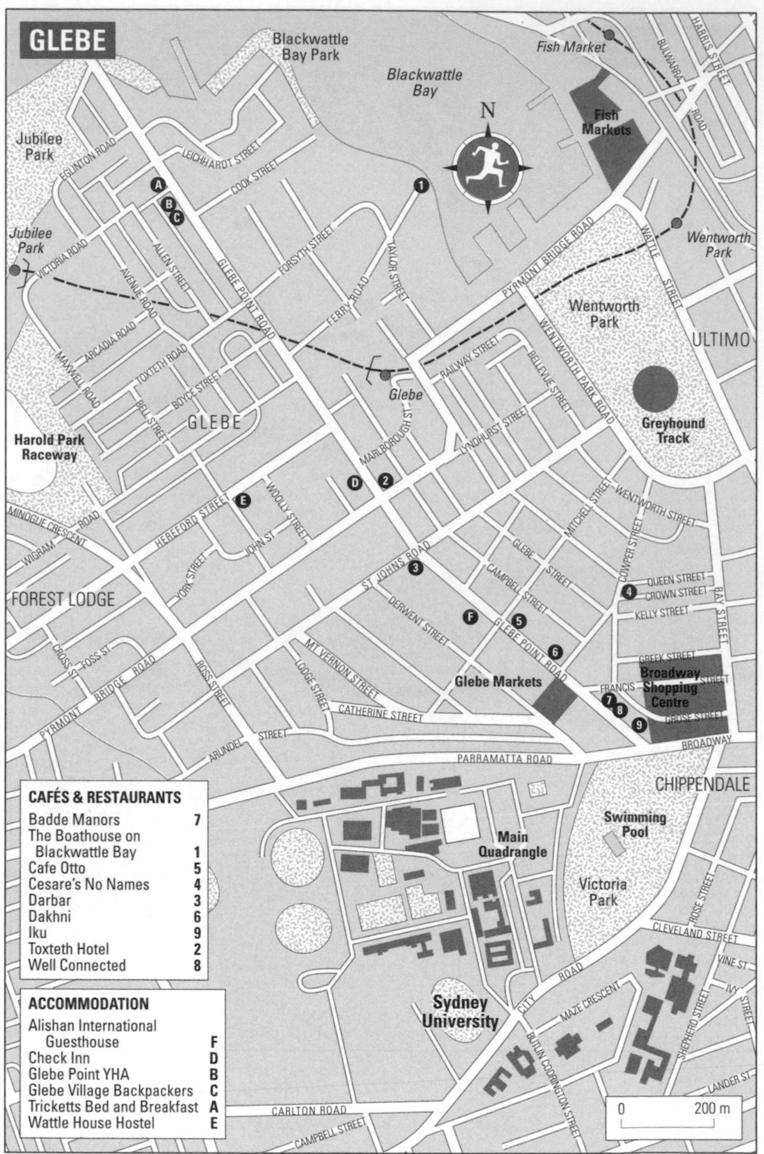

Sydney University and Victoria Park

Just before the beginning of Glebe Point Road, on Broadway, **Victoria Park** with its duck pond, huge expanse of lawn and shady trees, has a very pleasant, heated outdoor swimming pool (see "Sports and activities"), with an attached gym and sophisticated café. Leading up from the park is a path and steps into **Sydney**

University (@www.usyd.edu.au), Australia's oldest tertiary educational institution, inaugurated in 1850 and today catering to over 47,000 students. Your gaze is led from the walkway up to the Main Quadrangle and the stone clock tower, reminiscent of England's Oxford University and complete with gargoyles. The university's cedar-ceilinged, stained-glass-windowed **Great Hall** makes a glorious concert venue. You are free to walk through the gates and wander around the pleasant grounds, which take up a suburb-sized area between Parramatta Road and City Road, running up to King Street, Newtown. Famous alumni include Germaine Greer, Clive James, Jane Campion and the current prime minister, John Howard; there's a small exhibit relating to well-known former students in Fisher Library, near the Victoria Park entrance.

▲ The Old Fish Shop, Newtown

Museum collections

There are several **free museums** and galleries you can visit on weekdays. The **War Memorial Art Gallery** (Main Quadrangle; Tues–Thurs noon–4pm) holds regular temporary exhibitions, including works from the Sydney University Art Collection, gathered since 1850. The **Nicholson Museum** specializes in antiquities (Main Quadrangle; Mon–Fri 10am–4.30pm; closed Jan), while the natural history collection of the **Macleay Museum** (Mon–Fri 9am–4pm), on Science Road, was formed from that of the botany-obsessed Macleay family who built Elizabeth Bay House.

Glebe Point Road to Jubilee Park

Glebe itself is at its best on Saturdays, when **Glebe Market**, which takes place on the shady primary school playground, a couple of blocks up from Broadway, is in full swing. Just across the road, at 49 Glebe Point Rd, you'll find the excellent **Gleebooks** – one of Sydney's best-loved bookshops (see "Shopping" and "Books"). The original Gleebooks, now selling secondhand and children's books only, is worth the trek further up to 191 Glebe Point Rd, past St Johns Road and Glebe's pretty park.

A few blocks on from here, the action stops and Glebe Point Road trails off into a more residential area, petering out at **Jubilee Park**, with characterful views across the water to Rozelle Bay's container terminal. The pleasantly landscaped waterfront park, complete with huge, shady Moreton Bay fig trees and a children's playground, offers an unusual view of far-off Sydney Harbour Bridge framed within Sydney's newest, the spectacularly cabled Anzac Bridge.

Newtown and around

Newtown, separated from Glebe by Sydney University and easily reached by train (to Newtown Station), is another up-and-coming inner-city neighbourhood. What was once a working-class district – a hotchpotch of derelict factories, junkyards and cheap accommodation – has been transformed into a trendy but still offbeat area where body piercing, shaved heads and weird fashion rules. The neighbourhood is characterized by a large gay and lesbian population, a rich cultural mix and a healthy dose of students and lecturers from the nearby university. It also has an enviable number of great cafés and diverse restaurants, especially Thai.

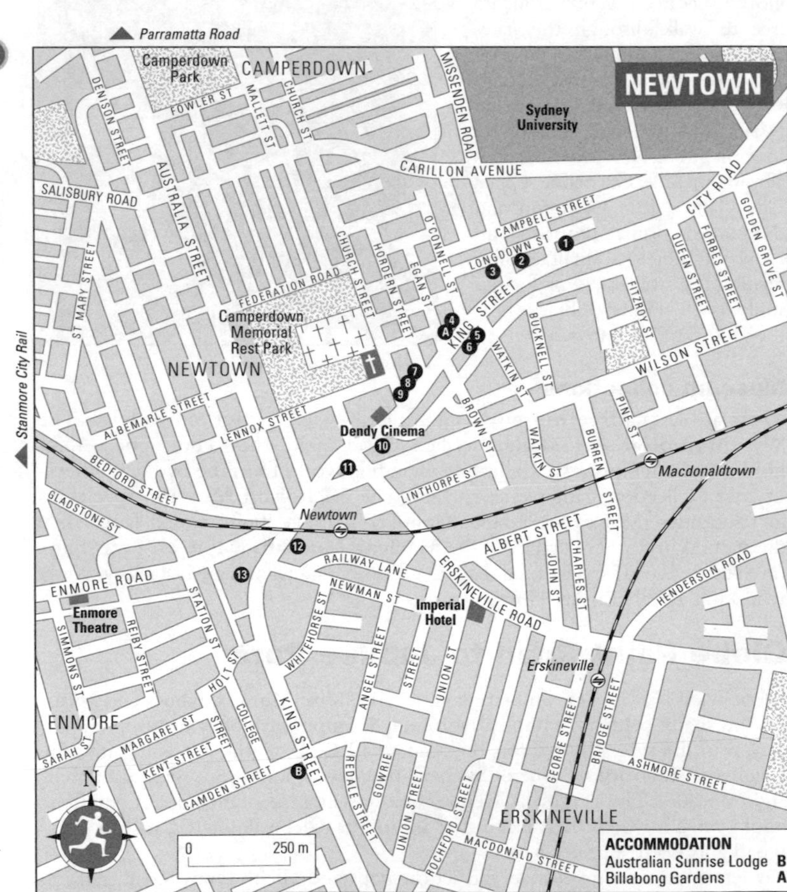

CAFÉS & RESTAURANTS							
Campos Coffee	3	Kilimanjaro	10	Steki Taverna	4	Thai Pothong	11
Citrus	7	Linda's Backstage Restaurant	5	Sumalee Thai	12	Thanh Binh	1
El Bahsa	8	The Old Fish Cafe	9	Tamana's North Indian Diner	6	Three Five Seven King	13
Green Gourmet	2						

Getting to the Newtown area

Buses #422, #423, #426 and #428 run to Newtown from Circular Quay via Castlereagh Street, Railway Square and City Road. They all go down King Street as far as Newtown Station, where the #422 continues to St Peters and the others turn off to Enmore and Marrickville. The #370 bus goes from Coogee Beach to Glebe via Newtown. You can also get to the area by **train** to Newtown, St Peters or Erskineville train stations.

King Street

Newtown's main drag, gritty, traffic-fumed and invariably pedestrian-laden **King Street**, is filled with unusual secondhand, funky fashion and speciality and homeware shops, and a slew of bookshops. The **Dendy Cinema** complex at no. 261 is a central focus, more like a cultural centre than just a film theatre; it has an attached bookshop, Better Read Than Dead, an excellent record store, Fish Records, and a street-front café, all open daily and into the night. Also check out Gould's Book Arcade (and see "Shopping"), way back near the Sydney University end of King Street at no. 32, a vast and chaotic secondhand book warehouse that is a Sydney institution, browsable until midnight.

For two weeks in June, various shop windows are taken over by young, irreverent and in-your-face art in the "Walking the Street" exhibition, but the highlight of the year is in November (second Sun) when the huge **Newtown Festival** takes over nearby Camperdown Memorial Park, with over 200 stalls and live music on three stages.

King Street becomes less crowded south of Newtown train station as it heads for a kilometre towards **St Peters** train station. It's well worth strolling down to look at the more unusual speciality shops (buttons, ribbons, vintage records, Chinese medicine among them), as well as several small art galleries and yet more retro and young new designer clothes shops. The street is also stacked with culturally diverse restaurants which range from Turkish to African, and closer to St Peter's Station are several colourful businesses aimed at the local Indian community. A couple of theatres and a High School for the Performing Arts, reputed to be one of the top-five performing-arts schools in the world, give extra energy to this end of King Street.

Enmore Road

Enmore Road, stretching west from King Street, opposite Newtown Station, is a similar mix of speciality shops and evidence of a migrant population. Look out for the African International Market at no. 2a, which sells groceries, and skin and hair products; Amera's Palace Bellydancing Boutique at no. 83; The Bead Company at no. 116; and Artwise Amazing Paper at no. 186. There's a range of **restaurants**, too, from Swedish to Thai. Enmore is generally much quieter than Newtown, except when a big-name band or comedian is playing at the Art Deco **Enmore Theatre**, at no. 130 (see "Performing arts"). When it's closed, you can play board games at the cosy booths of the *Box Office Cafe*. At the end of Enmore Road, Enmore Park hides the **Annette Kellerman Aquatic Centre** and its tiny, heated 33-metre pool (see "Sports and activities"). Combine a swim with a home-made ice cream from *Serendipity Ice Cream*, just across the road at no. 333.

Marrickville

Beyond Enmore, the very multicultural, lively but down-at-heel suburb of **Marrickville** stretches out. It has some great **places to eat**, particularly Greek and Vietnamese: two standouts are the *Corinthian Rotisserie Restaurant* at 283 Marrickville Rd and *Bay Tinh* at 318 Victoria Rd. Marrickville's other notable feature, and of great interest if you're committed to recycling, is **Reverse Garbage**, in the grounds of the Addison Road Community Centre, 8/142 Addison Rd (Mon–Sat 9am–5pm, Sun 10am–4pm; ⓣ02/9569 3132, ⓦwww.reversegarbage.org.au), which was formed as a cooperative in 1976 by a group of schoolteachers who wanted to save useful industrial discards and offcuts from landfill to use in school arts and crafts projects. The sustainable, not-for-profit business now employs around twenty people, not just on the shop floor but teaching people how to use the resources in art and craft and DIY classes; the warehouses are always being scoured by creative-looking types, from set-builders to artists, and parents with toddlers in tow. To reach Reverse Garbage, catch the #428 **bus** from Circular Quay, Railway Square or Newtown Station.

Erskineville

Erskineville Road, stretching from the southern side of King Street, marks the beginning of the adjoining suburb of **Erskineville**, a favourite gay address. The *Imperial Hotel* here at 35 Erskineville Rd (see "Gay Sydney") has long hosted popular drag shows, and is famous as the starting point of the gang in the 1994 hit film *The Adventures of Priscilla, Queen of the Desert*. The drag shows no longer include Priscilla tributes but the cocktail bar, the *Priscilla Lounge*, is lined with photos. Another good pub, *The Rose of Australia*, at 1 Swanson St (see "Live music"), focuses on live music. Just near Swanson Street, Erskineville has its own **train** station on Bridge Street.

Leichhardt and Haberfield

It's almost an hour from The Rocks to Balmain by the #440 bus, via **Leichhardt**, Sydney's "Little Italy", where the famous **Norton Street** strip of cafés and restaurants runs off ugly **Parramatta Road**. Leichhardt is full of Italian businesses and cafés; further west, on Ramsay Street in **Haberfield**, is an even more authentically Italian community, and also one of the best places to gaze at a whole suburb of charming, turn-of-the-twentieth-century federation-style houses.

Leichhardt

Leichhardt is very much up and coming – shiny, trendy, Italian cafés keep popping up all along the Norton Street strip, though its focus is the upmarket cinema complex, **The Palace**, at no. 99 (which hosts an Italian film festival in early December), with its attached record store, bookshop and Internet café (see "Performing arts"). Just opposite, at no. 70, the huge Beurkelow's new and secondhand bookstore is run by a family who've been in the antiquarian book trade since 1812; there are also CDs to browse, and two cafés (see also "Shopping"). Back on the other side of Norton Street, closer to Parramatta Road at no. 39, is an upmarket shopping and dining centre and showcase for all things Italian, the **Italian Forum**. The Forum is arranged around a central square, with two colonnaded levels surrounding it. The top level is filled with upmarket fashion shops, several featuring Italian fashion of course, while downstairs are a host of mostly Italian eateries with alfresco tables on the square; they're hugely popular for lunch on a Sunday when the whole Forum is full of Italian families. The brand-new local library branch here adds a civic note, but unfortunately the space for the Italian Cultural Centre, planned to open here for years now, still stands empty. It's also worth heading on to the lively, much-loved and enduring *Bar Italia* (see "Eating"), a fifteen-minute walk further down Norton at the extent of the tempting array of eateries; it's still the best Italian café in Leichhardt, and it was one of the first.

To get to Leichhardt you can take **bus** #436, #437, #438 or #440 from Circular Quay, George Street in the city or Railway Square.

Haberfield

The heart of Italian Sydney is in **Haberfield**; catch **bus** #436 from Leichhardt (or from Circular Quay or George Street in the city centre, or it's a twenty-minute walk from Summer Hill CityRail – take the northern exit and follow Sloane Street across Parramatta Road from where it's quite far along Ramsay Street to the shops).

Between Parramatta Road and Iron Cove on the Parramatta River, Haberfield was an entirely planned suburb. "Slum-less, Lane-less, and Pub-less" was the vision of the post-federation developers; the new nation was to have the ultimate urban environment. The style of the 1500 homes, all designed by the architect J. Spencer-Stanfield, is a classic Australian confection named **Federation Style**, which spread around the country from 1901. Eminently suited to the climate, the houses are a pleasing combination of the functional – wide verandahs that allow cooling breezes to circulate – with the fanciful, such as turrets. Stained glass is an important decorative element, often with very Australian motifs such as kookaburras and native flowers or flowing Art Nouveau designs. Elaborate chimneys, fretted woodwork, and gables and eaves are other key features. Every Spencer-Stanfield house in Haberfield is different, so you can easily spend a fascinating afternoon wandering its tranquil, leafy streets.

You still won't find a pub in Haberfield, but the many Italians who have moved to the area have opened up cafés, restaurants and delis, concentrated on Ramsay Road and Dalhousie Street. One of Sydney's best pizzerias, *La Disfida,* is here at no. 109 Ramsay Rd (see "Eating") and there are some great pasticcerias, including *A and P Sulfaro* at no. 119, where you can also sit outside and have a coffee. There are also lots of speciality shops in Haberfield – model toy cars and antiques among them.

Rozelle

From Leichhardt, the #440 bus continues to **Darling Street**, which runs from **Rozelle** right down to Balmain's waterfront. Rozelle, once very much the down-at-heel, poorer sister to Balmain, has now emerged as a fully fledged trendy area with the Sydney College of the Arts and the NSW Writers' Centre based here in the grounds of the expansive waterfront **Callan Park** on Balmain

Getting to Rozelle

To **get to Rozelle**, the #440 **bus** continues from Norton Street, Leichhardt, to Rozelle (or catch it from Circular Quay, George Street in the city or Railway Square), or you can catch the #445 from Norton Street, Leichhardt. You can also take the Metro Light Rail (see p.38) to Rozelle from Central, Pyrmont or Glebe; the "Lilyfield" stop is about 500m from Balmain Road: follow Catherine Street and Grove Street to emerge opposite the Sydney College of the Arts campus.

Road. Darling Street has a string of cafés, bookshops, speciality shops, gourmet grocers, restaurants, re-vamped pubs, and designer home-goods stores. A weekend **flea market** takes place in the grounds of Rozelle Primary School on Darling Street, Rozelle, near Victoria Road (Sat & Sun 9am–4pm). There's also the very ritzy **Rozelle Bay Super Yacht Marina** on James Craig Road; enjoy the views with a glass of wine at the bar-restaurant *Liquidity*, with its huge glass front overlooking the water. A leaflet, *Rozelle Walks* ($4.40), is available from Bray's Books in Balmain.

Callan Park

The **Callan Park** site was bought by the government for a new lunatic asylum in the 1870s, but an enlightened one for the time, under the guiding hand of the American doctor, Thomas Kirkbride, who believed that the beauty of nature could calm troubled minds. The set of Neoclassical buildings, built from sandstone quarried from the site and linked by courtyards, was designed by colonial architect James Barnet (also responsible for Customs House), and finished in 1885. They formed the core of the mental hospital, and were named after Kirkbride. The picturesque parklands sloping down to over a kilometre of waterfront were designed by the then Royal Botanic Gardens director. For as long as there has been a hospital at Callan Park, the public have freely been allowed to use the grounds as their recreation area, and attempts by the state government to sell off parcels of the land to developers have been stopped in their tracks by local opposition.

In 1996 the Kirkbride Block was taken over by Sydney College of the Arts, while the still-functioning mental institution, now called Rozelle Hospital, moved to a more ramshackle collection of buildings; the **NSW Writers' Centre** (information and bookings ⓣ02/9555 9757; ⓦwww.nswwriterscentre.org.au) has for many years occupied the Greek Revival-style Gary Owen House, an information centre and venue for readings and literary events open to the public.

Balmain and Birchgrove

Balmain, directly north of Glebe, is less than 2km from the Opera House by ferry from Circular Quay to Darling Street Wharf. But, stuck out on a spur in the harbour and kept apart from the centre by Darling Harbour and Johnston's Bay, it has a degree of separation that has helped retain its slow, villagey atmosphere and made it the favoured abode of many writers, film-makers and actors. Like better-known Paddington, Balmain was once a working-class quarter of terraced houses that has gradually been gentrified. And though the

Getting to and around Balmain and Birchgrove

For a **self-guided tour** of Balmain and Birchgrove, you can buy a *Balmain Walks* leaflet ($2.20) from Balmain Library, 370 Darling St, or the well-stocked *Bray's Bookshop*, at no.268. The most pleasurable way to **get to Balmain** is to catch a ferry from Circular Quay to Darling Street Wharf in Balmain East. From here the #442 bus waits to take you up Darling Street to Balmain proper. Buses #433 and #434 run out to Balmain via George Street, Railway Square and Glebe Point Road and down Darling Street; faster is the #442 from the QVB, which crosses Anzac Bridge and heads to Balmain Wharf. **Birchgrove** can be reached by ferry from Circular Quay or on the #441 from the QVB. You can also catch the #445 from Norton Street in Leichhardt.

docks at White Bay no longer operate, the pubs that used to fuel the dockworkers still abound: **Darling Street** and the surrounding backstreets are blessed with enough watering holes to warrant a pub crawl – two classics are the *London Hotel* on Darling Street and the *Exchange Hotel* on Beattie Street (see "Drinking" for both). Darling Street also rewards a leisurely stroll, with a bit of browsing in its speciality shops (focused on clothes and gifts), and grazing in its restaurants and cafés.

The best time to come is on Saturday, when the lively **Balmain Market** occupies the shady grounds of St Andrews Church (7.30am–4pm; see p.259), on the corner opposite the *London Hotel*.

On the Parramatta River side of Balmain, looking across to Cockatoo Island, Elkington Park contains the quaint **Dawn Fraser Swimming Pool** (March, April, Oct & Nov daily 7.15am–6.30pm, Dec–Feb daily 6.45am–7pm; $3.30), an old-fashioned harbour pool named after the famous Australian Olympic swimmer, a Balmain local. For long, stunning sunsets and wow-worthy real estate, meander from here down the backstreets towards water-surrounded **Birchgrove** on its finger of land, where Louisa Road leads to Birchgrove Wharf; from here you can catch a ferry back to Circular Quay, or stay and relax in the small park on Yurulbin Point.

8

The harbour

Loftily flanking the mouth of **Port Jackson** – Sydney Harbour's main body of water – are the rugged sandstone cliffs of North Head and South Head, providing spectacular viewing points across the calm water to the city, where the Harbour Bridge spans the sunken valley at its deepest point, 11km away. The many coves, bays, points, headlands and islands of the harbour, and their parks, bushland and swimmable beaches, are rewarding to explore. However, harbour beaches are not as clean as ocean ones, and after storms are often closed to swimmers. Finding your way by ferry is the most pleasurable method of exploring: services run to much of the **North Shore** and to the harbourfront areas of the **eastern suburbs**. The eastern shores are characterized by a certain glitziness and are the haunt of the nouveaux riches, while the leafy North Shore is very much old money. Rounding the corner of Middle Head from the main harbour, the quieter and more secluded coves of Middle Harbour beckon.

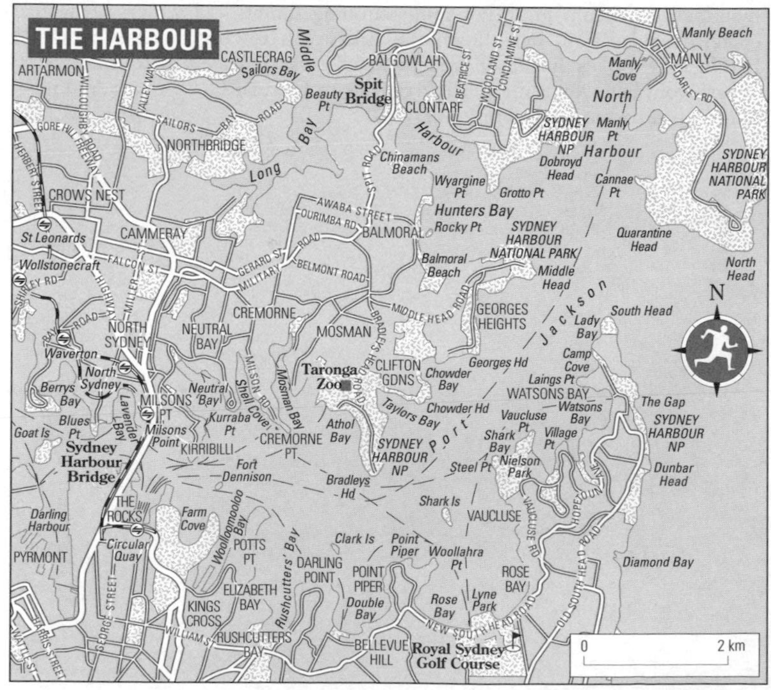

Sydney Harbour National Park and harbour islands

Both sides of the harbour have pockets of bushland which have been incorporated into **Sydney Harbour National Park**, along with five islands: Shark, Clark, Rodd, Fort Dennison and Goat. The National Parks and Wildlife Service (NPWS) publishes an excellent free map detailing the areas of the national park and its many walking tracks (ⓣ02/9337 5511, ⓦwww.nationalparks.nsw.gov.au, or visit Cadman's Cottage in The Rocks or the NPWS office in Nielson Park – see p.122 and p.125 respectively). If you're planning to visit any of the islands it's essential to book in advance (ⓣ02/9247 5033, ⓦwww.nationalparks.nsw.gov.au); prices given below include the $5 National Parks landing fee, and all tours depart from Cadman's Cottage.

Shark Island

Shark Island, located off Rose Bay, has functioned both as a quarantine area for animals and a storage depot for the Navy, but today its grassy expanse is given over to public recreation. Ringed by sandy beaches and with plenty of trees providing shade, this picturesque island makes a wonderful **picnic** spot for families. There is shelter, toilet facilities and drinking water available but visitors need to bring their own food. Matilda Cruises (see p.36) runs a weekend ferry service between Circular Quay and Shark Island (departs 10.30am, 11.45am, 1.45pm & 3.30pm, returns 12.30pm, 2.15pm, 4pm & (summer only) 5.45pm; $16 return, including the $5 National Parks landing fee). As an alternative to preparing a picnic, Matilda Cruises offers a family picnic hamper ($20; suitable for two adults & two children, pre-order when booking, collect on board).

Clark and Rodd Islands

Clark Island, located off Darling Point, contains an area of relatively untouched bushland and offers smaller groups a more intimate harbour island experience. There are toilets and drinking water available here but all food needs to be brought with visitors and rubbish removed at the end of the visit. The same rules apply to tiny **Rodd Island** in Iron Cove near Birkenhead Point, which, with its 1920s summerhouses and palm trees, is slightly reminiscent of a Victorian pleasure ground.

Access to Clark and Rodd Islands is via private vessel only. Visitor numbers are restricted by NPWS, so it is essential to book visits and pay the $5 landing fee in advance (ⓣ02/9247 5033, ⓦwww.nationalparks.nsw.gov.au). NPWS produce a list of ferry and water taxi companies approved to land on the islands.

Fort Dennison

The most visited of the harbour islands, tiny **Fort Denison** was originally used as a special prison for the tough nuts the penal colony couldn't crack; it became known as "Pinchgut" after the results the meagre rations had on the unfortunates who found themselves being punished here. During the Crimean Wars in the mid-nineteenth century, old fears of a Russian invasion were rekindled, and the fort was built as part of a defence ring around the harbour. If it's around lunchtime you'll hear the One O'Clock Gun, originally fired so sailors could accurately set their ship chronometers.

The only way to visit the island is on a NPWS **guided tour**, leaving from Cadman's Cottage (daily 11.30am and 2.30pm, other times subject to demand; 3hr; $22). If you don't want to bring a picnic, note that there's a **café** at the fort. NPWS also runs a **brunch tour** (Sat & Sun 9am; 3hr; $47).

Goat Island

Named, somewhat dubiously, for its apparent resemblance to a headless goat, **Goat Island** stands guard over Sydney's shipping channels from its prime position just across the water from Balmain East. The importance of its location was first recognized by the local Cadigal Aboriginal people, who called it Mel-Mel, meaning the eye.

The island is the site of a well-preserved sandstone **gunpowder magazine complex**, built by convicts between 1833 and 1839. Treatment of the convicts was harsh: 18-year-old Charles Anderson's refusal to work earned him over a thousand lashes and a two-year stint chained to a rock ledge, known as Anderson's Couch, which can still be seen today. The island's other architectural relics date from the twentieth century, a time when the island served as the headquarters of the Sydney Harbour Trust and later the Maritime Services Board. The original **Harbour Master's Residence** enjoys arguably the best lookout in Sydney, and its rolling lawns are perfect for picnics. You can also make out the footprint of the island's renowned 1940s **dancehall**; during its heyday revellers would row across from the mainland to fill the hall on Saturday nights. Despite the watchful eye of the dance mistress, who chaperoned the events from the doorway of the hall wielding a broomstick, local folklore credits the adjacent scrubland for the baby boom of the time.

Today Goat Island is accessible only by NPWS tour. **Heritage tours** (Wed & Sat 12.30pm; 2hr 30min; $19.80) and **picnic tours** (Sun 11.30am; 3hr; $22) run during the day, or there's a torchlit **Gruesome Tales tour** (Sat 6.45pm summer; Dec–Feb, 5.45pm rest of the year; 3hr; $24.20 including light supper; over 12s only).

Cockatoo Island

Situated at the confluence of the Lane Cove and Parramatta Rivers. **Cockatoo Island** is the largest in Sydney Harbour. Having served as a prison in the nineteenth century, the island became home to some of the most important naval and commercial dockyards in the Southern Hemisphere. Many of Australia's best-known warships were launched from the slipways here and after the fall of Singapore during World War II the island became the key ship construction and repair facility in the Pacific Ocean. Commercial use of the island's dockyards ceased more than a decade ago, and the island's dockyards and prison buildings can now be explored on a guided tour with the Sydney Harbour Federation Trust (Sat 10.30am & 1.30pm, Sun 10am & 2pm; 2hr; $25, family $75; telephone bookings essential, Mon–Fri 9am–5pm on ⓣ02/8969 2199; information ⓦwww.harbourtrust.gov.au).

Rushcutters Bay to South Head

The suburbs on the hilly southeast shores of the harbour are rich and exclusive. The area around **Darling Point**, the enviable postcode 2027, is the wealthiest in Australia, the waterfront mansions and yacht club memberships enjoyed by residents such as Nicole Kidman and Lachlan Murdoch. A couple of early nineteenth-century mansions, **Elizabeth Bay House** (see p.108) and **Vaucluse House**, are open to visitors, and give an insight into the lifestyle of the pioneering upper crust. The ferry to Rose Bay offers a good view of the pricey contemporary real estate in the area and convenient access to the beautiful Nielson Park and the surrounding part of Sydney Harbour National Park. At **South Head**, Watsons Bay was once a fishing village, and there are spectacular views from The Gap.

Buses #324 and #325 from Circular Quay via Pitt Street, Kings Cross and Edgecliff cover the places listed below, heading to Watsons Bay via New South Head Road; #325 detours at Vaucluse for Nielson Park. Bus #327 runs between Bondi Junction station and Martin Place in the city via Edgecliff station and Darling Point.

Rushcutters Bay

Only ten minutes' walk northwest from Kings Cross train station, **Rushcutters Bay Park** is set against a wonderful backdrop of the yacht- and cruiser-packed marina in the bay, revamped for the 2000 Olympics sailing competition. You can take it all in from the tables outside the very popular *Rushcutters Bay Kiosk* (good coffee and café fare). Gangs of friends book out the **tennis courts** at the Rushcutters Bay Tennis Centre (see "Sports and activities"), but if you don't have anyone to play, the friendly managers will try to provide a hitting partner

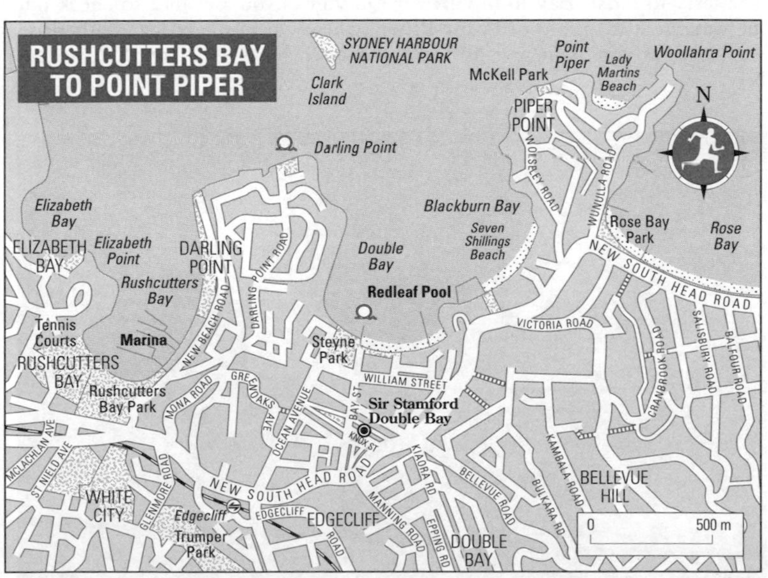

for you; there's a nice little coffee bar, too, with outdoor tables under vines and a resident squawking galah.

Woollahra Council has developed the five-and-a-half-kilometre (3hr) Rushcutters Bay to Rose Bay harbour **walk** (see box on p.126), which takes in exclusive streets, pretty parks and harbour views.

Darling Point and Double Bay

Northeast from Rushcutters Bay is **Darling Point**, Australia's wealthiest postcode zone, according to the tax office. From the point's McKell Park there are wonderful views across to Clark Island and Bradleys Head, both part of Sydney Harbour National Park; to get to the park, follow Darling Point Road (or take bus #327 from Edgecliff Station).

The next port of call is **Double Bay**, dubbed "Double Pay" for obvious reasons. The noise and traffic of New South Head Road are redeemed by several excellent antiquarian and secondhand bookshops, while in the quieter "village" are some of the most exclusive shops in Sydney, full of imported designer labels and expensive jewellery. The eastern suburbs' socialites meet on **Cross Street**, where the swanky pavement cafés are filled with well-groomed women in Armani outfits sipping coffee.

If all this sounds like a turn-off, Double Bay's real delight is **Redleaf Pool** (daily Sept–May dawn–dusk; free), a peaceful, shady harbour beach – one of the cleanest – enclosed by a wooden pier you can wander around, dive off or just laze on; there's also the excellent *Redleaf Pool Café*, famed for its fruit salad and coffee. A ferry from Circular Quay (Wharf 2) stops at both Darling Point and Double Bay; otherwise, catch bus #324 or #325, also from Circular Quay, or the #327 from Bondi Junction, Martin Place or Edgecliff stations.

Rose Bay

The ferry to **Rose Bay** from Circular Quay gives you a chance to check out the waterfront mansions of **Point Piper** (where Opera singer Joan Sutherland was born) as you skim past. You can also catch buses #324 or #325 to get here.

▲ Seaplane at Rose Bay

Rose Bay itself is quite a haven of exclusivity, with the verdant expanse of the members-only Royal Sydney Golf Course. Directly across New South Head Road from the course, waterfront **Lyne Park** provides welcome distraction in the form of a **seaplane** service, based here since the 1930s; planes can be chartered to go to Palm Beach or Berowra Waters, and there are scenic flights over Sydney, including the harbour (☎020/9388 1978). Rose Bay is also a popular **windsurfing** spot, and you can rent equipment to join in from Rose Bay Aquatic Hire (see p.273).

Woollahra Council has developed an eight-kilometre (4.5hr) harbour walk from Rose Bay to Watsons Bay via the cliffs, coves and bushland of the Sydney Harbour National Park (see "Coastal walks" box on p.126).

Nielson Park

Sydney Harbour National Park emerges onto the waterfront at Bay View Hill, where the 1.5-kilometre **Hermitage walking track** to Nielson Park begins; the starting point, BayView Hill Road, is off New South Head Road between two exclusive educational establishments, the Kambala School and the Rose Bay Convent (on bus routes #324 and #325). The walk takes about an hour, with great views of the Opera House and Harbour Bridge, some lovely little coves to swim in and a picnic ground and sandy beach at yacht-filled **Hermit Point**.

Extensive, tree-filled **Nielson Park**, on Shark Bay, is one of Sydney's delights (don't worry about Shark Bay's ominous name – it's netted), a great place for a daytime swim, a night-time skinny-dip, a picnic, or refreshment at the popular café. Within the park, the decorative Victorian-era mansion, **Greycliffe House**, built for William Wentworth's daughter in 1852, is now the headquarters of Sydney Harbour National Park; if the ranger is around (there are no regular hours) pop in for information on other waterfront walks. With views across to the city skyline, the park is a popular spot to watch the New Year's Eve fireworks display, and its position also makes it a prime spot to view the yachts racing out for the heads on Boxing Day (see "Festivals and events").

Vaucluse House and Parsley Bay

Beyond Shark Bay, Vaucluse Bay shelters the magnificent Gothic-style 1803 **Vaucluse House** and its large park-like estate on Wentworth Road (Tues–Sun 10am–4.30pm & public holiday Mondays, grounds open daily 10am–5pm; $7), with tearooms in the grounds for refreshment. The house dates from 1803, but its most famous owner was the influential Australian-born explorer and reformer **William Wentworth**, whose mother was a former convict and father a doctor with a dubious past; a major figure in the colony, William was a member of the first party to cross the Blue Mountains (see p.306). The house is restored to the middle period of the Wentworths' occupation (1829–53), and has some of the original furniture.

To get to Vaucluse House, walk from Nielson Park along Coolong Road, or take bus #325 right to the door. From Christison Park off Old South Head in Vaucluse, a one-hour coastal walk heads to Watsons Bay (see box on p.126).

Beyond Vaucluse Bay, narrow **Parsley Bay's** shady finger of a park is a popular picnic and (shark-netted) swimming spot, crossed by a picturesque pedestrian suspension bridge.

Coastal walks

Woollahra Council (☎02/9391 7000, ⓦwww.woollahra.nsw.gov.au) publishes brochures detailing three waterside walks: the five-and-a-half kilometre (3hr) Rushcutters Bay to Rose Bay harbour walk (see p.124), the eight-kilometre (4.5hr) harbour walk from Rose Bay to Watsons Bay (see p.125), and the five-kilometre (3hr) cliffside walk from Vaucluse to Watsons Bay and South Head – see p.125. The maps are downloadable or can be posted out.

On the southern, ocean side of the South Head peninsula, **Christison Park** (off Old South Head Road in Vaucluse, is the start of a magnificent coastal cliff walk heading north to the sheer drop of The Gap near Watsons Bay (2.3km) and on to South Head and the beach at Camp Cove. At the north end of Christison Park, the serenely white-painted **Macquarie Lighthouse** was the site of Australia's first, erected in 1818, and designed by convict-architect Francis Greenway who was then pardoned for his efforts. The present 1883 tower was built to the same plan.

The walk continues through **Lighthouse Reserve**; at its north end, facing out over Dunbar Head, is a **signal station** built in 1848. A watchpost was set up here from the very beginnings of the colony to alert the Sydney Town community, by use of flags, of ships arriving in the harbour. Continuing north, the rocks below the cliffs of **Signal Hill Reserve** wrecked the *Dunbar*, in 1857; the sole survivor, of 122 on board, was dragged up **Jacob's Ladder**, the jagged cleft in the cliffs here. The path heads upwards to **Gap Park**, where the *Dunbar*'s anchor is on display. Continue north along the path through the Sydney Harbour National Park to South Head (5km from Vaucluse) or cross Military Road for the settlement of Watsons Bay.

Watsons Bay

On the finger of land culminating in South Head, with an expansive sheltered harbour bay on its west side, and the treacherous cliffs of The Gap on its ocean side, **Watsons Bay** was one of the earliest settlements outside Sydney Cove. In 1790 Robert Watson was one of the first signalmen to man the clifftop flagstaffs nearby, and by 1792 the bay was the focus of a successful fishing village. The suburb has retained a villagey feel with quaint old wooden fishermen's cottages still found on the tight streets around Camp Cove. It's an appropriate location for one of Sydney's longest-running fish restaurants, *Doyles* (see "Eating"), right out on the bay by the old Fishermans Wharf (see p.202), now the ferry terminal: it's accessible by ferry from Circular Quay, or by Matilda Rocket Express (see p.37) from Darling Harbour. In fact *Doyle's* has virtually taken over the waterfront here, with two restaurants, a takeaway fish-and-chip shop, and a seafood bistro in the bayfront beergarden of the adjacent *Doyle's Watsons Bay Hotel.*

The Gap and Camp Cove

Spectacular ocean views are just a two-minute walk away from *Doyle's* through grassy Robertson Park, across Gap Road to **The Gap** (buses terminate just opposite – the #324, #325 and faster #L24 from Circular Quay, and the #L82 from Circular Quay via Bondi Beach), whose high cliffs are notorious as a place to commit suicide. You can follow a walking **track** north from here to South Head through another chunk of **Sydney Harbour National Park**, past the HMAS *Watson* Military Reserve where you can detour up the road to look at the Memorial Chapel (daily 9am–4pm) and beautifully framed water views from its picture window. The track heads back to the bay side, and onto Cliff Street which leads to **Camp Cove**, a tiny, palm-fronted, unnetted harbour beach popular with families; a small kiosk provides refreshments. Camp Cove

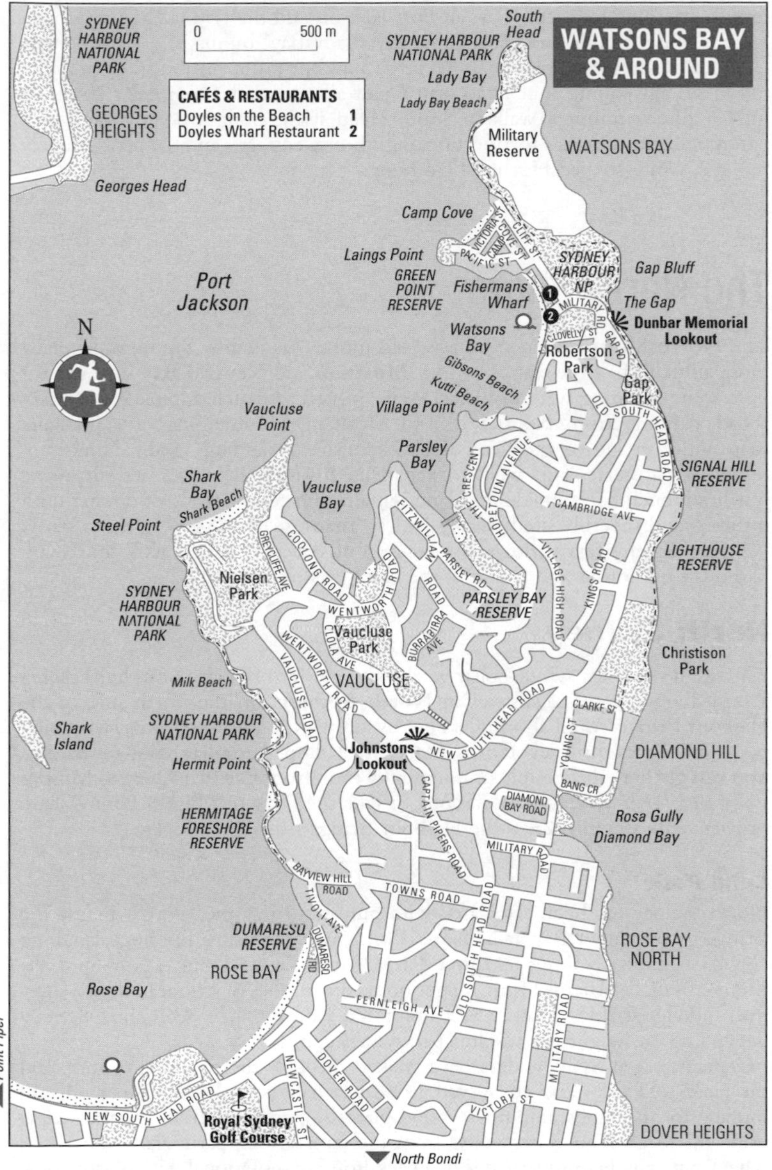

can also be reached by walking along the beach of Watsons Bay then along Pacific Street and through Green Point Reserve.

South Head

From the northern end of Camp Cove, steps lead up to a boardwalk which will take you to **South Head** (a 470m circuit), the lower jaw of the harbour mouth affording fantastic views of Port Jackson and the city, via Sydney's best-known **nude beach**, Lady Jane (officially "Lady Bay" on maps), a favourite gay hangout. It's not very private, however: a lookout point on the track provides full views and ogling tour boats cruise past all weekend. From Lady Bay, it's a further fifteen minutes' walk to South Head itself, along a boardwalked path past nineteenth-century fortifications, lighthouse cottages, and the picturesquely red-and-white-striped Hornby Lighthouse.

The North Shore

The **North Shore**, where Sydney's "old money" is mainly found, is generally more affluent than the rest of Sydney. **Mosman** and **Neutral Bay** in particular have some stunning waterfront real estate, priced to match. Upmarket Military Road, running from Neutral Bay to Mosman, is something of a gourmet strip with a string of excellent, albeit expensive, restaurants, and a number of tempting patisseries and well-stocked delis. Around the water, it's surprising just how much harbourside bushland remains intact – "leafy" just doesn't do it justice – and superbly sited among it all is **Taronga Zoo**.

A ride on any ferry allows you to gaze at beaches, bush, yachts and swish harbourfront houses and is one of the chief joys of this area.

North Sydney

Though it's easy for white-collar workers to get into the city from here, there's a busy high-rise office district in **North Sydney**, on the north side of the Harbour Bridge. You'll also find a famous fun park, a gloriously sited swimming pool, and a museum devoted to Mary MacKillop, Australia's saint-in-waiting. You can get here in a couple of minutes by train from Circular Quay to Milsons Point or North Sydney train stations, or take the ferry to Milsons Point Wharf, or even walk straight across the Harbour Bridge from The Rocks.

Luna Park

North Sydney has been associated with pure fun since the 1930s – beside the Bridge on Lavender Bay at **Milsons Point**, you can't miss the huge laughing clown's face that belongs to **Luna Park** (Mon–Thurs & Sun 11am–6pm, Fri 11am–10pm, Sat 10am–11pm, longer hours during NSW school holidays; entry free, individual ride tickets $3–5, unlimited ride day pass $39, child $18–29 depending on height; ⓦwww.lunaparksydney.com).

Generations of Sydneysiders have walked through the grinning mouth, and the park's old rides and conserved 1930s fun hall, complete with period wall murals, slot machines, silly mirrors and giant slippery dips, have great nostalgia value for locals. The water views from the park's rides, particularly the Ferris wheel, with the Harbour Bridge as a backdrop, are sensational – it's worth coming for these alone.

Getting to Luna Park can be a pleasant experience: the ferry to Milsons Point Wharf from Circular Quay or Darling Harbour pulls up right outside (or catch a train from the city to Milsons Point Station, on the North Shore Line). Beyond the park there's a boardwalk right around Lavender Bay.

North Sydney Olympic Pool

Right next door to the amusement park is Sydney's most picturesquely sited public swimming pool, with terrific views of the Harbour Bridge. The heated **North Sydney Olympic Pool**, on Alfred South Street, is open year round and was revamped in 2001, with a new indoor 25-metre pool as well as the old 50-metre outdoor pool, a gym, sauna, spa, café and an expensive, contemporary Australian restaurant, *Aqua* (⊕02/9955 2309), overlooking the pool – be prepared to be ogled by diners as you swim your laps.

Mary MacKillop Place Museum

Beyond Luna Park and the pool, is the Catholic Church-run **Mary MacKillop Place Museum**, 7 Mount St (daily 10am–4pm; $8.25; ⓦwww.marymackillopplace.org.au). Housed in a former convent, it provides a surprisingly broadminded look at the life and times of Australia's first would-be saint – MacKillop was beatified in 1995 and is entombed here – and sainthood itself. The late nun's charitable educational work began in Penola in the Coonawarra region of South Australia in the 1860s. Mary was the cofounder of the order of the Sisters of St Joseph and ran more than seventeen free Catholic schools, to encourage the education of children from poor backgrounds. The best way to get here directly is to take the train to North Sydney station and head north along Miller Street for about five minutes.

Kirribilli, Neutral Bay and Cremorne Point

Just east of the Harbour Bridge, and immediately opposite the Opera House, **Kirribilli** on Kirribilli Bay is a mainly residential area, although it hosts a great **market** on the fourth Saturday of the month in Bradfield Park (7am–3pm), the best and biggest of several rotating markets on the North Shore (see "Markets"). On Kirribilli Point, the current prime minister, native Sydneysider John Howard, lives in an official residence, **Kirribilli House**, snubbing Canberra, the usual PM's residence – a sore point with ACT locals. **Admiralty House**, next door, is the Sydney home of the governor general, and is where the British Royal family stay when they're in town.

Following the harbour around from Kirribilli is upmarket **Neutral Bay**. A five-minute walk from Neutral Bay ferry wharf via Hayes Street and Lower Wycombe Road is **Nutcote**, 5 Wallaringa Avenue (Wed–Sun 11am–3pm; $7). This was the home for 45 years of May Gibbs (1877–1969), the author and illustrator of the famous Australian children's book about two little gum nuts who come to life, *Snugglepot and Cuddlepie*, published in 1918 and an enduring classic. The highlight of North Shore **drinking** is the shady **beer garden** at Neutral Bay's *Oaks Hotel* on Military Road (see "Drinking").

Bush-covered **Cremorne Point**, which juts into the harbour here, is also worth a jaunt. Catch the ferry from Circular Quay and you'll find a quaint open-access sea pool to swim in by the wharf; from here, you can walk right around the point to Mosman Bay (just under 2km; see below), or in the other direction, past the pool, there's a very pretty walk along **Shell Cove** (1km).

Mosman Bay

Mosman Bay's seclusion was first recognized as a virtue during its early days as a whaling station, since it kept the stench of rotting whale flesh from the Sydney Cove settlement. Now the seclusion is a corollary of wealth. The ferry ride into the narrow, yacht-filled bay is a choice one – get off at Mosman Wharf,

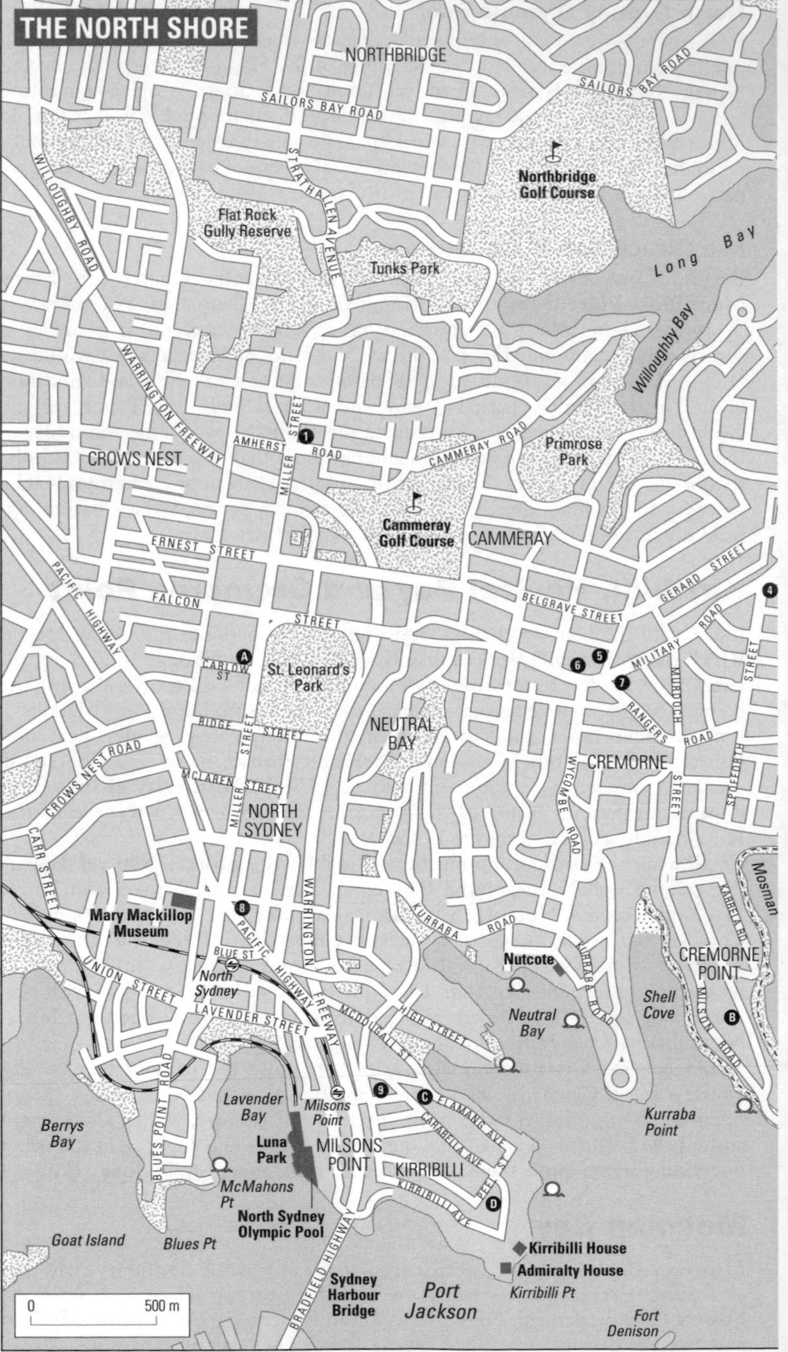
Castlecrag
THE NORTH SHORE
NORTHBRIDGE
SAILORS BAY ROAD
SAILORS BAY ROAD
Northbridge Golf Course
STRATHALLEN AVENUE
WILLOUGHBY ROAD
Flat Rock Gully Reserve
Tunks Park
Long Bay
Willoughby Bay
WARRINGTON FREEWAY
AMHERST ROAD
MILLER STREET
CAMMERAY ROAD
Primrose Park
CROWS NEST
Cammeray Golf Course
CAMMERAY
ERNEST STREET
PACIFIC HIGHWAY
FALCON STREET
BELGRAVE STREET
GERARD STREET
MILITARY ROAD
CARLOW ST
St. Leonard's Park
RIDGE STREET
NEUTRAL BAY
RANGERS ROAD
MURDOCH STREET
CREMORNE
SPOFFORTH STREET
CROWS NEST ROAD
McLAREN STREET
MILLER STREET
NORTH SYDNEY
WYCOMBE ROAD
CARR STREET
Mosman
KARRABA RD
Mary Mackillop Museum
PACIFIC HIGHWAY
WARRINGTON FREEWAY
KURRABA ROAD
BLUE ST
North Sydney
UNION STREET
Nutcote
KURRABA ROAD
CREMORNE POINT
LAVENDER STREET
McDOUGALL ST
HIGH STREET
Neutral Bay
Shell Cove
MILSON ROAD
Lavender Bay
Milsons Point
FLAMANG AVE
CARABELLA AVE
BLUES POINT ROAD
Berrys Bay
Luna Park
MILSONS POINT
KIRRIBILLI
KIRRIBILLI AVE
PEEL ST
Kurraba Point
McMahons Pt
North Sydney Olympic Pool
Goat Island
Blues Pt
BRADFIELD HIGHWAY
Kirribilli House
Admiralty House
Kirribilli Pt
Sydney Harbour Bridge
Port Jackson
Fort Denison
0
500 m
Circular Quay & Opera House

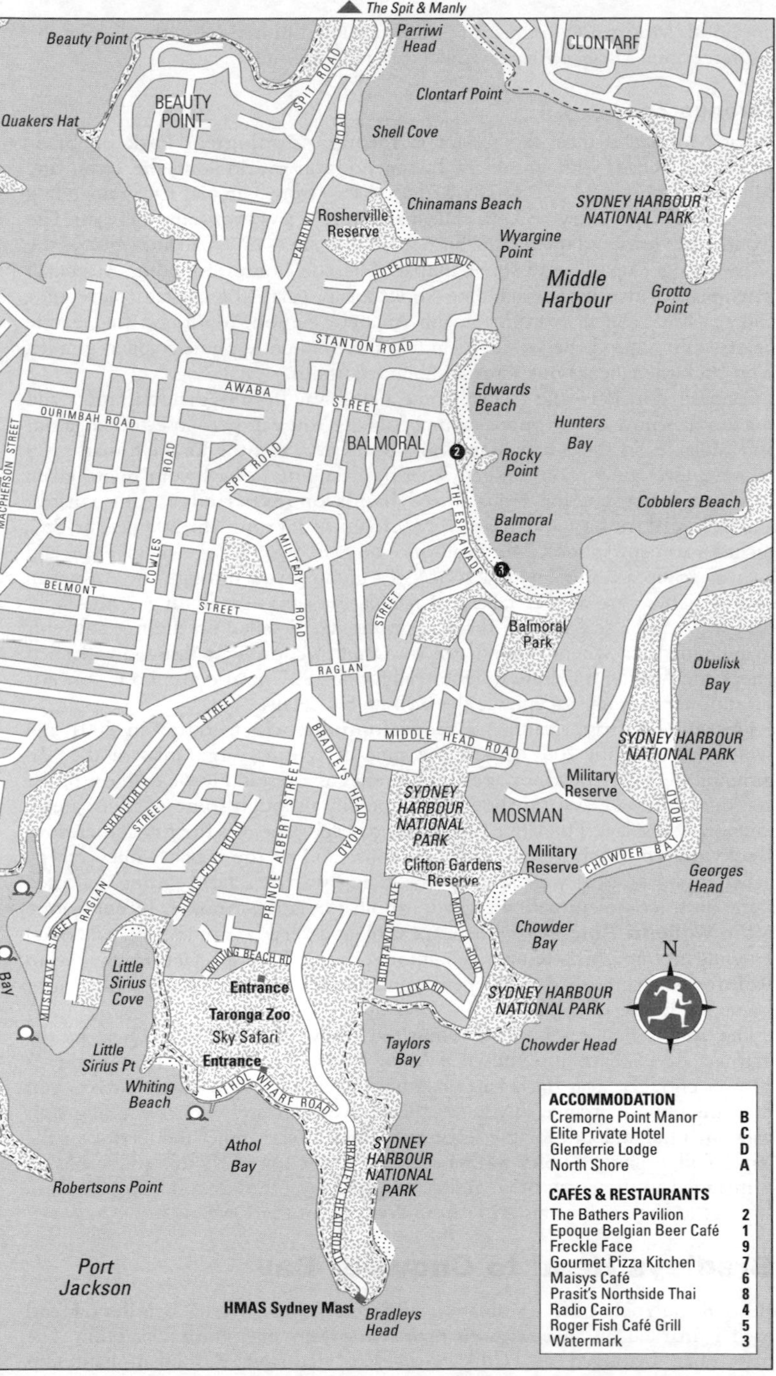
The Spit & Manly
Beauty Point
Parriwi Head
CLONTARF
Clontarf Point
BEAUTY POINT
Quakers Hat
Shell Cove
SPIT ROAD
Chinamans Beach
SYDNEY HARBOUR NATIONAL PARK
Rosherville Reserve
PARRIWI ROAD
Wyargine Point
HOPETOUN AVENUE
Middle Harbour
Grotto Point
STANTON ROAD
AWABA STREET
OURIMBAH ROAD
Edwards Beach
Hunters Bay
BALMORAL
MACPHERSON STREET
SPIT ROAD
Rocky Point
THE ESPLANADE
Cobblers Beach
Balmoral Beach
COWLES ROAD
MILITARY ROAD
Middle Head
BELMONT STREET
Balmoral Park
Obelisk Bay
RAGLAN STREET
MIDDLE HEAD ROAD
SYDNEY HARBOUR NATIONAL PARK
BRADLEYS HEAD ROAD
Military Reserve
SYDNEY HARBOUR NATIONAL PARK
MOSMAN
SHADFORTH STREET
PRINCE ALBERT STREET
SIRIUS COVE ROAD
Military Reserve
CHOWDER BAY ROAD
Clifton Gardens Reserve
Georges Head
RAGLAN STREET
BURRAWONG AVE
MORELLA ROAD
Chowder Bay
MUSGRAVE STREET
WHITING BEACH RD
N
Bay
Little Sirius Cove
Entrance
ILUKA RD
SYDNEY HARBOUR NATIONAL PARK
Taronga Zoo
Sky Safari
Taylors Bay
Chowder Head
Little Sirius Pt
Entrance
Whiting Beach
ATHOL WHARF ROAD
Athol Bay
SYDNEY HARBOUR NATIONAL PARK
BRADLEYS HEAD ROAD
Robertsons Point
Port Jackson
HMAS Sydney Mast
Bradleys Head
ACCOMMODATION
Cremorne Point Manor B
Elite Private Hotel C
Glenferrie Lodge D
North Shore A
CAFÉS & RESTAURANTS
The Bathers Pavilion 2
Epoque Belgian Beer Café 1
Freckle Face 9
Gourmet Pizza Kitchen 7
Maisys Café 6
Prasit's Northside Thai 8
Radio Cairo 4
Roger Fish Café Grill 5
Watermark 3

not South Mosman (Musgrave St) – and fittingly finished off with a beer at the unpretentious *Mosman Rowers' Club* (visitors welcome).

Taronga Zoo

What Mosman is most famous for is **Taronga Zoological Park** on Bradleys Head Road, with its superb hilltop position overlooking the city (daily 9am–5pm; $27, child $14, family $70, Zoo Pass from Circular Quay including return ferry and entry $33.50, child pass $16.10; ®www.zoo.nsw.gov.au). The wonderful views and the natural bush surrounds are as much an attraction as the chance to get up close to some animals. The zoo houses bounding Australian marsupials, native birds (including kookaburras, galahs or cockatoos), reptiles, and sea lions and seals from the sub-Antarctic region. You'll also find exotic beasts from around the world, including the frequently photographed giraffes, who stick their necks out across a sublime harbour view.

Established in 1916, the zoo has come a long way from its Victorian roots, and the animals now live in more natural habitats. You can get close to kangaroos and wallabies in the **Australian Walkabout** area, and the **koala house** gives you eye-level views; you can get closer by arranging to have your photo taken patting a koala, but for a guaranteed **hands-on experience** with a native animal, a VIP Aussie Gold Tour (daily 9.15am & 1.15pm; 1hr 30min–2hr; $57, includes zoo entry; book 24hr in advance on ⓣ02/9969 2777) will give you and a small group a session with a zookeeper, guiding you through the Australian animals. There are keeper talks and feeding sessions – including a free-flight bird show and a seal show – throughout the day, detailed on the free souvenir map handed out when you arrive; if you want to coordinate timing in advance, check the website for show times or call for details. The zoo also hosts concerts on summer evenings; again, see the website for details.

The zoo has masterplanned a **redevelopment** which started in 2001 and will continue until 2007 and at the time of writing large areas of the zoo grounds were closed off for construction ~~sites~~ as a result. However, most of the zoo's creatures are still on show to the public, although some of them are in temporary displays. The latest part of this redevelopment is the fun and creative **Backyard to Bush**. A typical urban house, full of the usual Sydney creepy crawlies and pests, is yours to explore, giving way to a farm setting and then some bush (complete with a gigantic wombat burrow). Another recent feature is the **Wollemi Pine area**, where six small and very rare pines (see p.321) are growing among warm-temperate rainforest species. The spectacular new **Asian Rainforest** exhibit is due to open soon and will include a long-awaited new home for Taronga's elephants.

The zoo is best reached by taking the **ferry** from Circular Quay to the Taronga Zoo Wharf (also known as Athol Wharf; every 30min). Though there's a lower entrance near the wharf on Athol Road, it's best to start your zoo visit from the upper entrance so you can spend several leisurely hours winding your way downhill and exit for the ferry: State Transit buses meet the ferries for the trip uphill, or take the **Sky Safari** cable car to the top of the hill (the cable car is included in the entry price and can be taken as often as you want). You can also get to the zoo on bus #247 from Wynyard or the QVB.

Bradleys Head to Chowder Bay

Beyond the zoo, at the termination of Bradleys Head Road, **Bradleys Head** itself is marked by an enormous mast that towers over the rocky point. The mast once belonged to HMAS *Sydney*, a victorious Australian battleship, long since gone to the wrecker's yard. It's a peaceful spot with a dinky lighthouse and, of course, a fabulous view back over the south shore. A colony of ringtailed possums nests here, and boisterous flocks of rainbow lorikeets visit.

▲ Bradleys Head

The headland comprises another large chunk of **Sydney Harbour National Park** and you can walk to Bradleys Head via the six-kilometre Ashton Park **walking track**, which starts near the ferry wharf, opposite the zoo entrance, and continues beyond the headland to Taylors Bay and Chowder Head, finishing at **Clifton Gardens**, where there's a jetty and sea baths on **Chowder Bay**. The defunct military reserve which separates Chowder Bay from another chunk of the National Park on Middle Head is now open to the public (see p.134) and reached by a boardwalk from the northern end of Clifton Gardens.

The NPWS offers a two-hour **Bush Food tour** of Bradleys Head on the first Sunday of the month (1.30pm; $13.20; bookings essential; ⊕02/9247 5033), departing from the rear entrance of the zoo, giving you a chance to see and taste some of the bush tucker the local Aboriginal people once survived on.

Middle Harbour

Middle Harbour is the largest inlet of Port Jackson, its two sides joined across the narrowest point at **The Spit**. The Spit Bridge opens regularly to let tall-masted yachts through – much the best way to explore its pretty, quiet coves and bays; several cruises pass by (see pp.36–37). Crossing the Spit Bridge, you can walk all the way to Manly Beach along the ten-kilometre Manly Scenic Walkway (see p.148), while buses #143 and #144 run from Spit Road to Manly Wharf, taking a scenic route uphill overlooking the Spit marina.

Middle Head

Between Clifton Gardens and Balmoral Beach, a military reserve and naval depot at **Chowder Bay** blocked coastal access to **Georges Head** and the more spectacular **Middle Head** by foot for over a century, although they could always be reached by road. However, since the military's recent withdrawal from the site, walkers can now trek all the way between Bradleys Head and Middle Head. The 1890s military settlement itself is open to visitors as a reserve, and the NPWS offers tours exploring its underground fortifications (second & fourth Sun of each month; 10.30am; 2hr; $13.20). You can reach the military reserve entrance from the northern end of Clifton Gardens or walk from Balmoral Beach, below.

Balmoral Beach and around

The bush setting provided by Middle Head helps lend **Balmoral**, on Hunters Bay, the peaceful, secluded air that makes it so popular with families. There's something very Edwardian and genteel about palm-filled, grassy Hunters Park and its rotunda (bandstand), which is still used for Sunday jazz concerts or even Shakespeare recitals in summer. The civilized air is added to by the pretty white-painted **Bathers Pavilion** at the northern end, now converted into a restaurant and café (see "Eating"). There are really two beaches at Balmoral, separated by the island-like **Rocky Point**, a noted picnicking spot. The low-key esplanade has some takeaways including an excellent fish-and-chip place, a quiet café, and a fine bottle shop – all you need for a day at the beach. South of Rocky Point, the "baths" – actually a netted bit of beach with a boardwalk and lanes for swimming laps – have been here in one form or another since 1899; you can rent sailboards and catamarans and take lessons from the nearby sailing club (see p.273). This end of the beach is great for kids – the big trees actually shade the sand and there's a popular playground and a kiosk selling ice creams.

To get to Balmoral, catch a **ferry** from Circular Quay to Athol Wharf (Taronga Zoo) and then bus #238 via Bradleys Head Road, or, after 7pm from Monday to Saturday, the ferry to South Mosman (Musgrave Street) Wharf, at nearby Mosman, then bus #233.

Cobblers and Chinamans beaches

In contrast, on the Hunters Bay side of Middle Head, tiny **Cobblers Beach** is officially a **nudist** beach, and is a much more peaceful, secluded option than the more famous Lady Jane at South Head. The hillside houses overlooking Balmoral have some of the highest price tags in Sydney; for a stroll through some prime real estate, head for **Chinamans Beach**, via Hopetoun Avenue and Rosherville Road.

Northbridge and Castlecrag

There are some architectural gems lurking around Middle Harbour: the 1889 bridge leading to **Northbridge**, from Cammeray, which Jan Morris describes rather fancifully in *Sydney* as "an enormously castellated mock-Gothic bridge, with hefty towers, arches, crests and arrow-slits, such as might have been thrown across a river in Saxe-Coburg by some quixotic nineteenth-century princeling"; and the idyllic enclave of **Castlecrag**, designed in 1924 by **Walter Burley Griffin**, the Chicago landscape architect who won the international competition in 1912 to design the nation's new capital, Canberra, which he worked on until 1920. Burley Griffin's plan for Canberra envisaged a garden city, taking into account the natural features of the landscape. His plans for Castlecrag were similar: he was intent on building an environmentally friendly suburb – free of the fences and the red-tiled roofs he hated – that would be "for ever part of the bush".

To get to Castlecrag, take **bus** #207 from Wynyard or North Sydney train station, or take bus #202 for Northbridge.

9

Ocean beaches

Sydney's beaches are among its great natural joys, key elements in the equation that makes the city special. The water and sand are remarkably clean – people actually fish in the harbour, and don't just catch old condoms and plimsolls – and at Long Reef, just north of Manly, you can find rock pools teeming with starfish, anemones, sea snails and crabs, and even a few shy moray eels. There's good **snorkelling and diving** at various spots (see "Sports and activities"), especially at the underwater nature trail at Gordons Bay. In recent years, humpback whales have begun to be regularly sighted from the Sydney headlands in June and July on their migratory path from the Antarctic to the tropical waters of Queensland, and Southern Right whales even occasionally make an exciting appearance in the harbour itself – three whales cavorting in July 2002 caused a sensation (for more information consult the Australian Museum website – Ⓦwww.livingharbour.net).

With the ocean splitting the harbour in half, the two stretches of ocean beaches on either side are deemed the **northern beaches** – which continue beyond **Manly** for 30km up to Barrenjoey Heads and Palm Beach – and the **eastern beaches**, which stretch south from **Bondi** to Maroubra.

Bondi Beach

Bondi Beach is synonymous with Australian beach culture, and indeed the mile-long curve of golden sand must be one of the best-known beaches in the world. It's the closest ocean beach to the city centre; you can take a train to Bondi Junction and then a ten-minute bus ride, or drive there in twenty minutes (parking is another story). Big, brash and action-packed, it's probably not the best place for a quiet sunbathe and swim, but the sprawling sandy crescent really is spectacular. Red-tiled houses and apartment buildings crowd in to catch the view, many of them erected in the 1920s when Bondi was a working-class suburb.

Although still residential, Bondi is now one of Sydney's trendiest suburbs, with escalating real estate and rental prices, and a thriving café and restaurant scene packed out with the young and fashionable. There's also the Saturday night "hoon" culture when suburban youngsters drive their souped-up cars up and down Campbell Parade, and it's an alternative to the city centre for weekend drinking and dining. Backpackers create another large part of the culture, drinking and otherwise, especially in summer when they turn Christmas Day into a big beach event (see "Festivals and Events").

You can reach Bondi on **bus** #380, #L82 or #389 from Circular Quay via

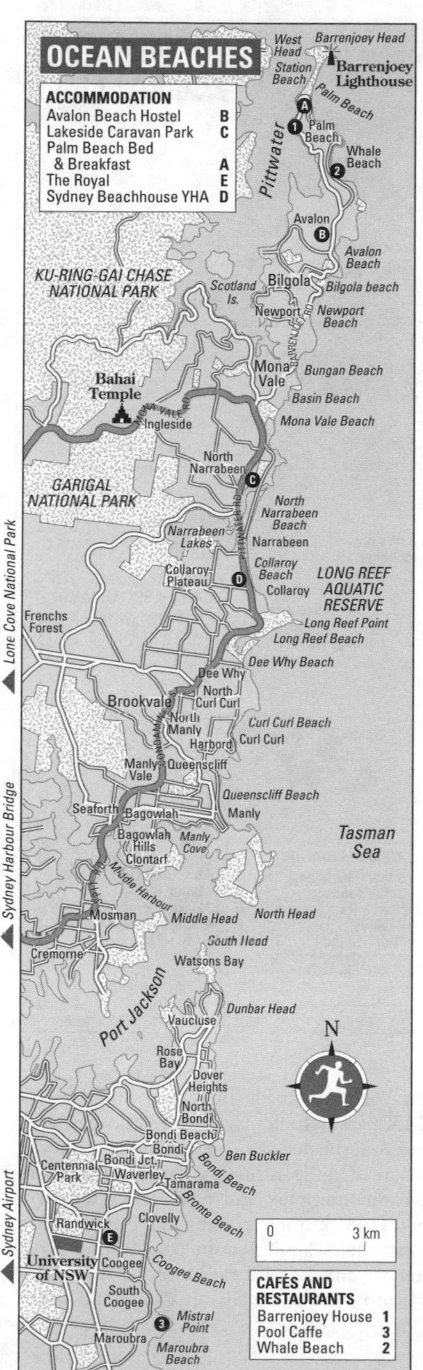

Oxford Street and Bondi Junction, or take the train directly to Bondi Junction, then transfer to these buses or to the #361, #381 and #382.

Campbell Parade and Hall Street

Beachfront **Campbell Parade** is both cosmopolitan and highly commercialized, lined with alfresco cafés, bars, restaurants, record, fashion and surfwear shops. On Sunday the **Bondi Beach markets** (10am–5pm) – in the grounds of the primary school on the corner of Campbell Parade and Warners Avenue, facing the northern end of the beach – place great emphasis on fashion and jewellery.

You'll find the locals' favourite cafés and more day-to-day shops and facilities on the calmer side streets. **Hall Street**, heading gently uphill from Campbell Parade, is Bondi Beach's real nerve centre, with a post office (and public phones), banks, bakeries, supermarkets, an assortment of kosher delis and butchers and other shops that serve the area's Jewish community, cybercafés, laundries, a health-food store with a great notice board for accommodation, bookshops (try Martin Smith's at no. 3 for new books and *Gertrude & Alice Cafe Bookstore* at no. 40 for secondhand) and some of Bondi's best cafés.

Bondi Park and the Bondi Pavilion

Between Campbell Parade and the beach, grassy (though mostly shadeless except for the few picnic group shelters) **Bondi Park** slopes down to the promenade, and is always full of sprawling bodies feasting on fish and chips

BONDI BEACH & TAMARAMA

CAFÉS & RESTAURANTS

The Bogeyhole Café	20
Bondi Social	14
Bondi Tratt	13
Brown Sugar	3
Burgerman	17
fu-manchu	9
Gelato Bar	7
Gelbison Pizzeria	11
Gertrude & Alice Cafe Bookstore	6
Gusto	8
Hugo's	12
Icebergs Dining Room and Bar	18
Lamrock Café	10
Lauries Vegetarian	16
Moorish & the North Bondi RSL	4
No Names	1
The One That Got Away	15
Sean's Panorama	2
Sejuiced	21
Speedo's	5
Swell	19
Wet Paint	22

ACCOMMODATION

Bondi Beachhouse YHA	E
Bondi Sands	B
Noah's Backpackers	D
Ravesi's	C
Swiss-Grand	A

and being mobbed by seagulls. Along the promenade there is a popular and recently built concrete **skate and BMX** park, which plays host to competitions throughout the year. For places to hire rollerblades, see "Sports and activities".

The focus of the promenade is the arcaded, Spanish-style **Bondi Pavilion**, built in 1928 as a deluxe changing-room complex and now converted to a community centre hosting an array of workshops, classes and events, from drama and comedy in the theatre and the Seagull Room (the former ballroom) to daytime dance parties, open air cinema and the outdoor short film festival "Flickerfest" in the courtyard (programme details on ⊕02/8362 3400,

Beach and sun safety

Don't be lulled into a false sense of security: the beaches do have **perils** as well as pleasures. Some beaches are protected by special shark nets, but they don't keep out stingers such as bluebottles, which can suddenly swamp an entire beach; listen for loudspeaker announcements that will summon you from the water in the event of shark sightings or other dangers.

Pacific **currents** can be very strong indeed – inexperienced swimmers and those with small children would do better sticking to the sheltered **harbour beaches** (see "The Harbour" and "Kids' Sydney") or **sea pools** at the ocean beaches. Ocean beaches are generally patrolled by **surf lifesavers** during the day between October and April (all year at Bondi): red and yellow flags (generally up from 6am until 6pm or 7pm) indicate the safe areas to swim, avoiding dangerous rips and undertows. It can't be stressed strongly enough that you must try to swim between the flags – people have drowned in strong surf. If you do get into difficulty, stay calm and raise one arm above your head as a signal to be rescued. It's hard not to be impressed as **surfers** paddle out on a seething ocean that you wouldn't dip your big toe in, but don't follow them unless you're confident you know what you're doing. Surf schools can teach you the basic skills and enlighten you on surfing etiquette and lingo: see "Sports and activities" for recommended schools. You can check daily **surf reports** on ⓦwww.realsurf.com.

The strength of the southern **sun** shouldn't be underestimated: follow the local slogan and **Slip** (on a shirt), **Slop** (on the sun block), **Slap** (on a hat). The final hazard, despite the apparent cleanliness, is **pollution**. Monitoring shows that it is nearly always safe to swim at all of Sydney's beaches – except after storms, when storm water, currents and onshore breezes wash up sewage and other rubbish onto certain beaches (though usually harbour beaches) making them – as signs will indicate – unsuitable for swimming and surfing. To check pollution levels, call the Beachwatch Bulletin on ⓣ1800 036 677 or check out ⓦwww.epa.nsw.gov.au).

A final note: topless bathing for women is accepted on many beaches but diasapproved of on others, so if in doubt, do as the locals do. There are two official **nude** beaches around the harbour (see pp.128 and 134).

ⓦwww.waverley.nsw.gov.au). Downstairs in the foyer, photos of Bondi's past are worth checking out, with some classic beach images of men in 1930s bathing suits, and there's an excellent **souvenir shop** (daily 9.30am–5.30am) which uses lots of old-fashioned Bondi imagery. There's even a community-access **art gallery** (daily 10am–5pm) featuring changing exhibitions by local artists, and some alfresco cafés and restaurants. In September, the Festival of the Winds, Australia's largest **kite festival**, takes over the beach (see "Festivals and events").

The beach

Surfing is part of the Bondi legend, the big waves ensuring that there's always a pack of damp young things hanging around, bristling with surfboards. However, the beach is carefully delineated, with surfers using its southern end, so you shouldn't have to fear catapulting surfboards. There are two sets of flags for swimmers and boogie-boarders. Families congregate at the northern end near the shallow sheltered saltwater pool (free), popular with kids, with a park with barbecues and a playground above; everybody else uses the middle flags. The beach is netted and there hasn't been a shark attack for over forty years.

Bondi's surf lifesavers

Surf lifesavers are what made Bondi famous, so naturally there's a bronze sculpture of one outside the Bondi Pavilion. The surf lifesaving movement began in 1906 with the founding of the Bondi Surf Life Bathers' Lifesaving Club in response to the drownings that accompanied the increasing popularity of swimming. From the beginning of the colony, swimming was harshly discouraged as an unsuitable bare-fleshed activity. However, by the 1890s swimming in the ocean had become the latest fad, and a Pacific Islander introduced the concept of catching waves or **bodysurfing** that was to become an enduring national craze. Although "wowsers" (teetotal puritanical types) attempted to put a stop to it, by 1903 all-day swimming was every Sydneysider's right.

The bronzed and muscled surf lifesavers in their distinctive red and yellow caps are a highly photographed, world-famous Australian image. Surf lifesavers (members of what are now called Surf Life Saving Clubs, abbreviated to **SLSC**) are volunteers who work the beach at weekends, so come then to watch their exploits – or look out for a surf carnival; **lifeguards**, on the other hand, are employed by the council and work all week during swimming season (year-round at Bondi).

If the sea is too rough, or if you want to swim laps, head for the sea-water swimming pool at the southern end of the beach under the **Bondi Icebergs Club** building entrance on Notts Avenue, with a fifty-metre lap pool, kids' pool, gym, sauna, massage service and poolside café (pool Mon–Wed & Fri 6am–8pm, Sat & Sun 6.30am–6.30pm; $3.80). The Icebergs Club has been part of the Bondi legend since 1929 – members must swim throughout the winter, and media coverage of their plunge, made truly wintry with the addition of huge chunks of ice, heralds the first day of winter. The very dilapidated club building was knocked down and rebuilt, reopening in 2002; one floor has been appropriately leased to Surf Lifesaving Australia, which has an information room with a small collection of memorabilia (Mon–Fri 10am–3pm; free). On the top floor is a posh new **restaurant**, but the club floor itself is as unpretentious as ever, with the addition of wonderful open balconies and a decent **café** (see "Drinking").

Topless bathing is condoned at Bondi – a far cry from conditions up to the late 1960s when stern beach inspectors were constantly on the lookout for indecent exposure. If you want to join in the sun and splash but don't have the gear, Beached at Bondi, below the lifeguard lookout tower, rents out everything from umbrellas, wetsuits, cozzies and towels to surfboards and body-boards. It also sells hats and sun block and has lockers for valuables.

The eastern beaches

Sydney's eastern beaches stretch from **Bondi** down to **Maroubra**. Many people find the smaller, quieter beaches to the south of Bondi more enticing, and it's a popular walk or jog right around the oceanfront and clifftop **walking track** to Bondi's smaller, less brazen but very lively cousin **Coogee** (about 2hr 30min). The track also includes a fitness circuit, so you'll see plenty of joggers and other fitness fanatics. En route you'll pass through gay favourite **Tamarama**; family-focused, café-cultured **Bronte**; narrow **Clovelly**; and a popular diving and snorkelling spot Gordons Bay (see "Sports and activities"). Randwick Council has designed the "Eastern Beaches Coast Walk" from Clovelly to Coogee and beyond to more downmarket Maroubra, with stretches of boardwalk and interpretive boards detailing environmental features. A free guide-map can be picked up from the council's Customer Service Office, 30 Francis St, Randwick (ⓣ02/9399 0999, ⓦwww.randwickcitytourism.com.au), or from Coogee at the beachfront Coogee Bay Kiosk, Goldstein Reserve, Arden Street, opposite *McDonald's*. It is now also possible to walk north all the way from Bondi to South Head along the cliffs since missing links in the pathway have been connected with bridges and boardwalks.

Tamarama

From Bondi Beach, walk past the Bondi Icebergs Club on Notts Avenue round Mackenzies Point, through Marks Park, until you reach the modest and secluded **Mackenzies Bay**. Next is **Tamarama**, a deep, narrow beach favoured by the smart set and a hedonistic gay crowd ("Glamarama" to the locals), as well as surfers. The surf here is very rough and the flags are often taken down and swimmers advised not to go into the water, hence the sun-worshipping rather than swimming crowd. Topless sunbathing is the norm for women here. Apart from the small Surf Life Saving Club, which offers drop-in yoga classes, the intimate beach has a popular café, and a small grassy park (not very shady) with picnic shelters, barbecues and a basic children's playground.

The **Sculpture by the Sea festival** turns the walk between Bondi and Tamarama into a temporary art gallery for ten days every October (see "Festivals and events"). The walk takes about fifteen minutes, or if you want to come here directly it's a 300-metre walk from the #380 bus stop on Fletcher Street (from Circular Quay or Oxford St), or hop on bus #360 or #361 from Bondi Junction.

Bronte

Walk through Tamarama's small park and follow the oceanfront road for five minutes to the next beach along, **Bronte Beach** on Nelson Bay, also easily reached on bus #378 from Central Station via Oxford Street and Bondi Junction. More of a family affair, with a large green park, a popular café strip and sea baths, the **northern end** as you arrive from Tamarama has inviting flat-rock platforms, popular as fishing and relaxation spots, and the beach here is cliff-backed, providing some shade. The **park** beyond is extensive with Norfolk Island Pines for shade; a **mini-train ride** for small children ($3 or four rides for $10) has been operating here since 1947, while further back there's an imaginative children's playground. The secluded and peaceful Bronte Gully lies to the rear where kookaburras are a common sight and loraqueets are often seen bathing in the waterfall.

At the **southern end** of the beach, palm trees lend a holiday feel as you relax at one of the outside tables on Bronte Road's cafés – there's a clutch of eight to choose from, plus a fish-and-chip shop. Back on the water at this end a natural rock enclosure, the "Bogey Hole", makes a calm area for snorkelling and kids to swim in, and there are rock ledges to lie on around the enclosed sea swimming pool known as **Bronte Baths** (open access; free), often a better option than the surf here, which can be very rough.

It's a pleasant five-minute walk past the Bronte Baths to **Waverley Cemetery**, a fantastic spot to spend eternity. Established in 1877, it contains the graves of many famous Australians, with the bush poet contingent well represented. **Henry Lawson**, described on his headstone as poet, journalist and patriot, languishes in section 3G 516, while **Dorothea Mackeller**, who penned the famous poem "I love a sunburnt country", is in section 6 832–833.

Clovelly and Gordons Bay

Beyond Waverley Cemetery – another five-minute walk – on the other side of the ominously named Shark Point, is channel-like **Clovelly Bay**, with concrete platforms on either side and several sets of steps leading into the very deep water. Rocks at the far end keep out the waves and the sheltered bay is popular with lap-swimmers – there's a free swimming pool, too – and snorkellers; you are almost certain to see one of the bay's famous blue gropers under the surface. A grassy park – Burrows Park – with several terraces extends far back and is a good spot for a picnic. There's a divinely sited **café** next to the surf club that gets packed at weekends (see "Eating"), while on Sunday afternoons and evenings the nearby *Clovelly Hotel* is a popular hangout for locals and travellers, with free live music and a great bistro. Otherwise, go for the rock-bottom-priced drinks and fab views at the Clovelly Bowling Club, also on the walk route. To get to Clovelly directly, take bus #339 from Millers Point via Central Station and Albion Street, Surry Hills; #360 from Bondi Junction; or the weekday peak-hour X39 from Wynyard.

Gordons Bay

From Clovelly you can rock-hop around to equally narrow **Gordon's Bay**, though this can be a little tricky – backed by high sandstone cliffs with some rocky tunnels to pass through – and without local knowledge you're probably better off sticking to the road route along Cliffbrook Parade. The secluded rocks are popular with locals for peaceful fishing or sunbathing, and rescuing stranded tourists tends to shatter the equilibrium. Unsupervised, undeveloped Gordons Bay itself is not a pretty beach, but another world exists beneath the sheltered water: the protected **underwater nature trail** makes it diving and snorkelling heaven (see "Sports and activities" for diving operators). From here, a walkway leads around the waterfront to Major Street and then on to **Dunningham Reserve** overlooking the northern end of Coogee Beach; the walk to Coogee proper takes about fifteen minutes in all.

▲ Wylies Baths, Coogee

Coogee

Coogee is another long-popular seaside resort, almost on a par with Manly and Bondi. Dominated by the extensive *Coogee Bay Hotel* on beachfront Arden Street, one of Sydney's best-known music venues, Coogee has had a reputation for entertaining Sydneysiders since Victorian times. At the northern end of the beach, the dome you can see over the

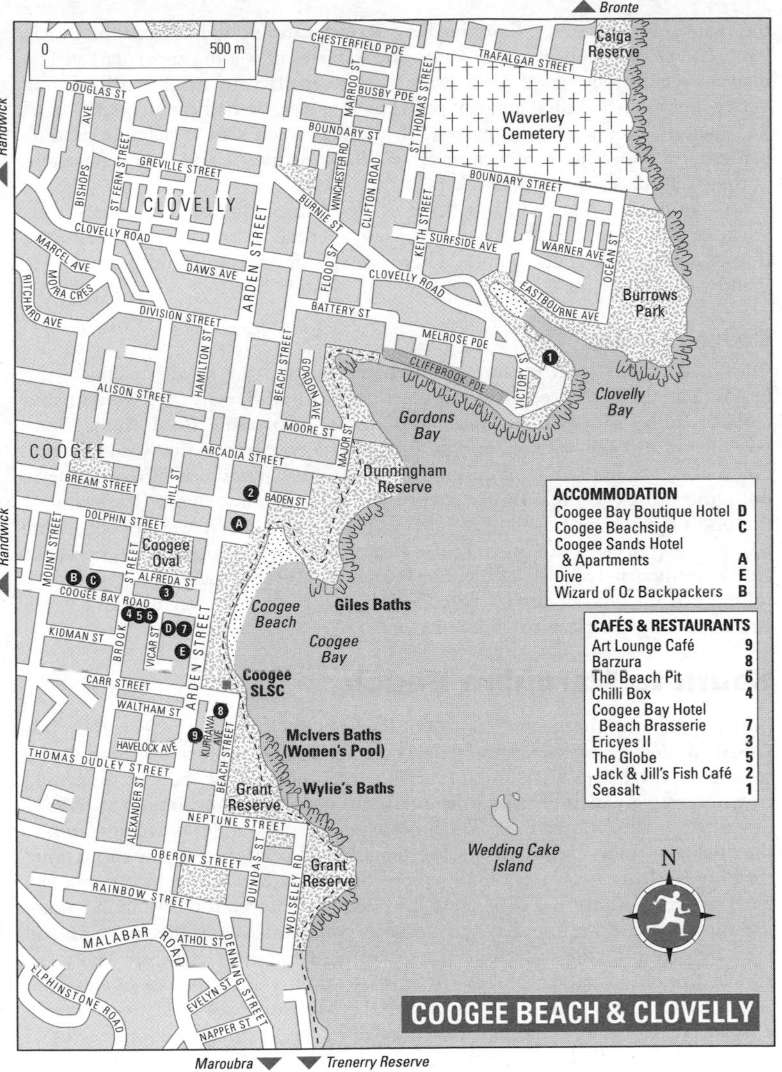

Beach Palace Hotel is an 1980s restoration of the 1887 Coogee Palace Aquarium – in its heyday a gigantic dance floor that could accommodate three thousand pleasure-seekers. Today the hotel is a popular drinking spot for backpackers, who crowd out its oceanfront balcony.

With its hilly streets of California-style houses looking onto a compact, pretty beach enclosed by headlands, Coogee has a snugness and a friendly local feel that its cousin Bondi just can't match – there's something more laid-back and community-oriented about it, and you can happily wear your old shorts to the beach. Everything is close to hand: **Arden Street** has a down-to-earth strip of cafés that compete with each other to sell the cheapest cooked breakfast, while the main shopping street, **Coogee Bay Road**, running uphill from the beach, has a choice selection of coffee spots and eateries plus a big supermarket. The imaginatively modernized promenade is a great place to stroll and hang out; between it and the beach a grassy park has free electric barbecues, picnic tables and shelters. The beach is popular with families (there's an excellent children's playground above the southern end; see "Kid's Sydney") and young travellers, as there's also a stack of backpackers' hostels here.

You can reach Coogee on **bus** #373 or #374 from Circular Quay via Randwick, or #372 from Eddy Avenue, outside Central Station; the journey time from Central is about 25 minutes. There are also buses from Bondi Junction via Randwick: #313 and #314.

Coogee's baths

One of Coogee's chief pleasures is its baths, beyond the southern end of the beach. The first, the secluded McIvers Baths, traditionally for women and children only, is known by locals as **Coogee Women's Pool** (noon–5pm; volunteer-run, entry by donation). Opposite the entrance to the women's pool, Grant Reserve has a full-on adventure playground. Just south of the women's pool, the unisex **Wylies Baths**, a saltwater pool on the edge of the sea, is at the end of Neptune Street (daily: Oct–April 7am–7pm, May–Sept 7am–5pm; $3), with big decks to lie on and solar-heated showers; its kiosk serves excellent coffee. Immediately south of Wylie's, **Trenerry Reserve** is a huge green park jutting out into the ocean; its spread of big, flat rocks offers tremendous views and makes a great place to chill out.

South to Maroubra Beach

Probably the most impressive section of Randwick Council's **Eastern Beaches Coast Walk** commences from Trenerry Reserve. The council is attempting to regenerate the native flora, and the walk, sometimes on boards, is accompanied by interpretive panels detailing the surrounding plant- and birdlife. Steps lead down to a rock platform full of small pools – you can wander down and look at the creatures there, and there's a large tear-shaped pool you can swim in, quite thrilling with the waves crashing over – but be careful of the waves and the blue-ringed octopus found here. At low tide you can continue walking along the rocks around Lurline Bay – otherwise you must follow the streets inland for a bit, rejoining the waterfront from Mermaid Avenue. Jack Vanny Memorial Park is fronted by the large rocks of Mistral Point, a great spot to sit and look at the water, and down by the sea there's the **Mahon Pool** (free; open access), a small, pleasant pool surrounded by great boulders, with an unspoilt, secluded feel. The isolated *Pool Caffe* across the road on Marine Parade makes a wonderful lunch or coffee spot.

At the southern end of the Memorial Park, the kilometre-long stretch of **Maroubra Beach** begins. With the Anzac Rifle Range at the southern end and the far-off sound of gunfire, this traditionally working-class suburb with a down-at-heel set of shops has never been a popular beach resort. However, things are changing fast, most noticeably with the opening of the phenomenally popular *Pavilion Cafe* right on the sand on Marine Parade in the former kiosk; the views are fantastic and the atmosphere and food is casual.

To get to Maroubra by public transport, take **bus** #376 or #377 from Circular Quay, Eddy Avenue at Central Station, Randwick or Coogee, or the #317 from Bondi Junction station.

Sydney **festivals**

▲ *New Year's Eve fireworks*

Sydney's huge and extravagant **New Year's Eve fireworks**, with a different theme each year and orchestrated to music, are televised around Australia and beamed via satellite to the rest of the world. Over a million people turn out on and around the harbour to watch the display live: 80,000 separate fireworks are set off around 6km of the harbour, with an astonishing midnight finale at Sydney Harbour Bridge itself (Ⓦwww.sydneynewyearseve.com.au).

▶ *Sydney Festival*

The lively, three-week-long **Sydney Festival** in **January** – Australia's most extensive cultural event – is both a celebration of the arts and of summer in the city. Many events are free and held outdoors, including the hugely popular night-time symphony and jazz concerts in The Domain. Don't miss live music and dancing on the waterfront on a hot summer's night during the vibrant Latino Festival, which runs over several evenings in Darling Harbour. A programme of international musicians, theatre companies and art exhibitions, most attracting hefty ticket prices, is also offered alongside the free stuff (ⓦwww.sydneyfestival.org.au).

▼ *Australia Day*

January 26, 1788, was the day that the First Fleet arrived to settle Sydney Cove. Celebrated as **Australia Day** nationally, it's the biggest and the best in Sydney. The whole extravaganza is free and action-packed, so be prepared to roam the city all day and into the night to make the most of it. The Rocks, Hyde Park and Darling Harbour are bursting with live entertainment; there's free museum entry, yacht and boat races on the harbour, aerial displays, a vintage car display, and 9pm fireworks at Darling Harbour (ⓦwww.australiaday.gov.au).

▶ *Tropfest*

From humble beginnings as a short film screening in the *Tropicana Cafe* in 1993, **Tropfest** has become the world's largest short film festival. The free outdoor event takes over The Domain on the **last Sunday in February**, with entertainment from mid-afternoon, and screening of the sixteen finalist films at 8pm. To ensure films are made for Tropfest, entrants must incorporate a specific item announced several months in advance (ⓦwww.tropfest.com).

▶ *Gay & Lesbian Mardi Gras*

The month-long **Sydney Gay & Lesbian Mardi Gras** runs through the hot and sweaty month of February and climaxes in **early March** in a huge, cheeky and outrageous street parade pulsating down Oxford Street. What began as a gay rights protest in 1978 is now a celebration of all things "Queer", and is even televised by the ABC. A huge percentage of straight Sydney turns out to watch the antics and cheer on the floats, which are traditionally led by the Dykes on Bikes (ⓦwww.mardigras.org.au).

▶ *Royal Easter Show*

Every **April**, cosmopolitan Sydney is invaded by visitors dressed in Akubra hats, moleskins, R.M. Williams boots and Drizabone coats: these aren't tourists overdoing "Outback" but country folk who've come to exhibit prize cows and pumpkins, and compete in rodeos and wood-chopping competitions at the **Sydney Royal Easter Show**. This agricultural festival cum fun-fair attracts around a million people over two weeks, and dates back to the establishment of the Royal Agricultural Society of NSW in 1822 (ⓦwww.eastershow.com.au).

◀ *Manly International Jazz Festival*

As spring sunshine begins to make the outdoors appealing again, five outdoor stages are set up at the legendary beachside suburb of Manly for the three-day **Manly International Jazz Festival**, held over the Labour Day long weekend in **early October**. The massive community-based festival, mostly free, has attracted hordes of Sydneysiders for over 25 years: though the water is still chilly, the combination of beach views from the oceanfront Manly Beach stage, warm sun and a live jazz soundtrack is irresistible. Well-known and upcoming Australian bands feature, as well as international acts. There's an indoor stage, a fringe programme at restaurants and bars, and a beachfront market too (ⓦwww.manly.nsw.gov.au/manlyjazz/).

▶ Sydney Food and Wine Fair

The picnic season is launched with the huge **Sydney Food and Wine Fair** which takes over Hyde Park on a Saturday in **late October**. The annual event attracts over 60,000 grazers to more than a hundred stalls representing the Sydney region's best restaurants, coffee houses, breweries and wineries, all raising funds for the AIDS Trust of Australia. Restaurants produce entree-sized portions of their signature dishes, which sell out fast after the noon start. Live music on two stages accompanies the food frenzy (ⓦwww.cityofsydney.nsw.gov.au/WhatsOn/).

◀ Sculpture by the Sea

As the weather hots up in **early November**, the stunning coastal path between Bondi and Tamarama is transformed into an outdoor sculpture park for eighteen days. More than a hundred Australian and international sculptors–reach an audience of over 400,000 during the **Sculpture by the Sea** event. The sandstone cliffs and crashing ocean create a sublime setting for often playful works encouraged to "incorporate the sun, sea, wind and rain" (ⓦwww.sculpturebythesea.com).

▼ Sydney to Hobart Yacht Race

Up there with the less frequent America's Cup and the Whitbread Around the World Race in terms of excitement and media interest, the annual **Sydney to Hobart Yacht Race** on **December 26** has been part of the festive season for over sixty years. Huge post-Christmas crowds gather at vantage points around Sydney Harbour to watch over a hundred vibrantly coloured yachts set sail through the Heads for Tasmania, 630 nautical miles and several days southwest.

For more on Sydney festivals and events see pp.263–26

Manly

Manly, just above North Head at the northern mouth of the harbour, is doubly blessed with both ocean and harbour beaches. When Captain Arthur Phillip, the commander of the First Fleet, was exploring Sydney Harbour in 1788, he saw a group of well-built Aboriginal men onshore, proclaimed them to be "manly"

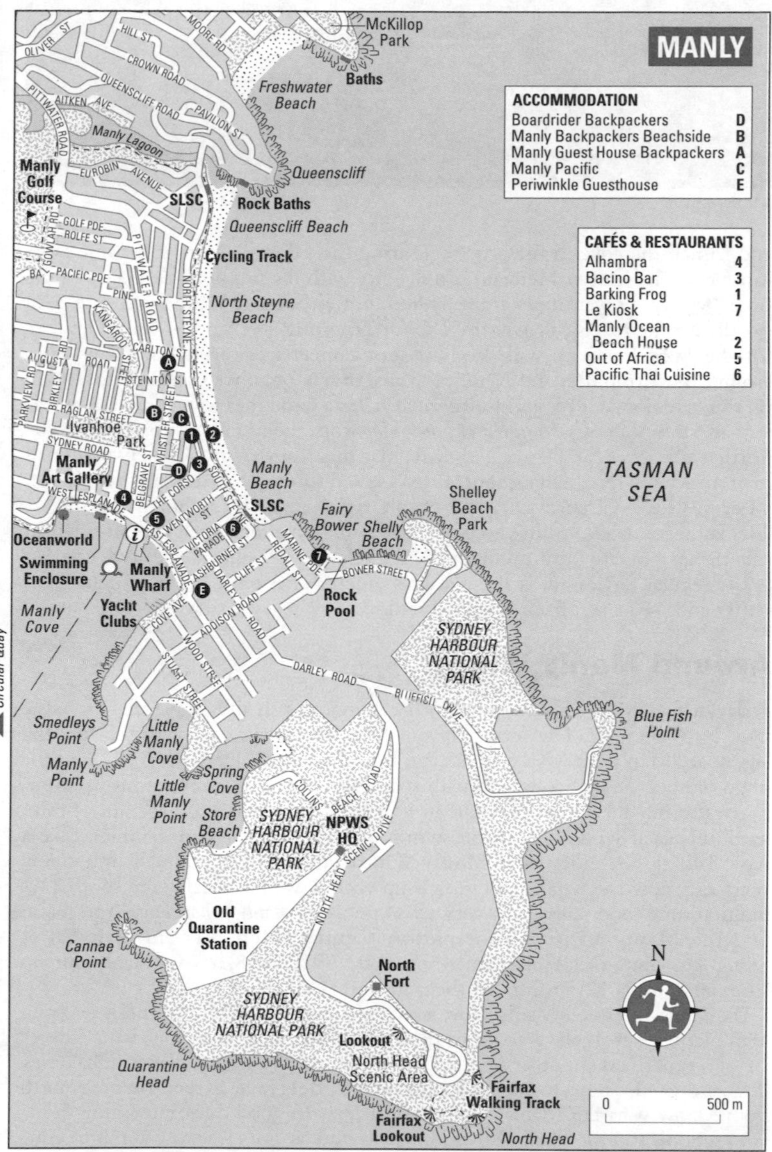

▲ Manly Beach

and named the cove in the process. During the Edwardian era it became fashionable as a recreational retreat from the city, with the promotional slogan of the time "Manly – seven miles from Sydney, but a thousand miles from care". An excellent time to visit is over the Labour Day long weekend in early October, for the **Jazz Festival**, with free outdoor concerts featuring musicians from around the world. Beyond Manly, the **northern beaches** continue for 30km up to Barrenjoey Heads and **Palm Beach**. It's a good idea to pick up the excellent and free Sydney's *Northern Beaches Map* from the Manly Visitor Centre. The northern beaches can be reached by regular **bus** from various city bus terminals or from Manly ferry wharf; routes are detailed throughout the text below.

Ferries leave Circular Quay for Manly twice an hour (30min; $4.50 single). The last ferry service from Circular Quay is at 7pm after which the faster JetCat catamarans operate until midnight. The JetCat ($7.50 single) goes twice as fast as the regular ferries but is about half as much fun. After it finishes, night buses #E69 and #E71 run from Wynyard station.

Around Manly Wharf

A day-trip to Manly, rounded off with a dinner of fish and chips, offers a classic taste of Sydney life. The ferry trip out here has always been half the fun: the legendary Manly Ferry service has run from Circular Quay since 1854, and the huge old boats come complete with snack bars selling the ubiquitous meat pie. Ferries terminate at Manly Wharf in Manly Cove, near a small section of calm harbour beach with a netted-off swimming area popular with families. Like a typical English seaside resort, **Manly Wharf** housed a tacky funfair until a few years ago; now the wharf is all grown-up with a swathe of cafés and shops, plus multicultural food stalls and a very swish pub, the *Manly Wharf Hotel*. You'll also find the **Manly Visitor Information Centre** (Mon–Fri 9am–5pm, Sat & Sun 10am–4pm; Oct–April 10am–5pm; ⓣ02/9977 1088, ⓦwww.manlytourism.com.au; lockers $2) in front of the pub.

The streets between Manly Cove and the surf beach are lively and interesting with plenty of great places to eat or find the makings of a beachside picnic. There's a Coles supermarket not far up the Corso from the Wharf and plenty of bakeries, delis and bottle shops to stock up on supplies. **Belgrave Street**, running north from Manly Wharf, is Manly's alternative strip, with good cafés, interesting shops, yoga schools and the Manly Environment Centre at no. 41, whose aim is to educate the community about local biodiversity and issues affecting it.

Water activities and cruises

Manly Wharf is a hub for adventure activity, with three **watersports** companies based here. Manly Parasailing (Ⓣ02/9977 6781, Ⓦwww.parasail.net; Oct to April only) offers the only parasailing experience in Sydney: a ten-minute "lift" costs $59 if you're on your own, but the $99 tandem is more fun; expect to be on the boat for an hour. Manly Boat & Kayak Hire (Ⓣ0412 622 662) is here daily October to April and weekends the rest of the year; single kayaks cost from $15 per hour and the five-seater motorboats start from $35 for 30 minutes. Epic Surftours (Ⓣ02/8900 1018, Ⓦwww.epicsurf.com.au) operates all year – their small-group one-hour tours ($60) through crashing surf to the cliffs of North Head are not for the faint-hearted.

Oceanworld

From the wharf, walk along West Esplanade to **Oceanworld** (daily 10am–5.30pm; $18.50; Ⓣ02/8251 7877, Ⓦwww.oceanworld.com.au), where clear acrylic walls hold back the water so you can saunter along the harbour floor, gazing at huge sharks and stingrays. Divers hand-feed sharks three times weekly (11am Mon, Wed & Fri) and there's always a new range of shows and guided tours, including the Dangerous Australians show with local (and deadly) snakes and spiders. You can also organize dives among the big grey nurse sharks with Shark Dive Extreme (qualified diver $175, refresher diver course $205 and unqualified diver $235, including all equipment, awareness lecture and 30min diving in the tank; bookings Ⓣ02/8251 7878).

Manly Waterworks and Manly Art Gallery and Museum

Opposite Oceanworld, the screams come from the three giant waterslides at **Manly Waterworks** (Oct to Easter Sat, Sun, school & public holidays 10am–5pm; 1hr $14.50, all day $19.50; must be over 120cm tall to enter). Between the slides and Oceanworld, the **Manly Art Gallery and Museum** (Tues–Sun 10am–5pm, closed Mon and public holidays; $3.60) has a collection started in the 1920s of Australian paintings, drawings, prints and etchings, and a stash of fun beach memorabilia including huge old wooden surfboards and old-fashioned swimming costumes.

The beaches

Many visitors mistake Manly Cove for the ocean beach, which in fact lies on the other side of the isthmus, 500m down **The Corso**, Manly's busy pedestrian main drag filled with surf shops, cafés, restaurants and pubs, as well as increasingly popular juice and health food bars. The ocean beach, **South Steyne**, is characterized by the stands of Norfolk pine which line the shore. Every summer, a beach-hire concession rents out just about anything to make the beach more fun, from surfboards to snorkel sets, and they also have a bag-minding service. A six-kilometre-long shared pedestrian and **cycle path** begins at South Steyne and runs north to Seaforth, past North Steyne Beach and Queenscliff. You can rent mountain bikes from Manly Cycles, a block back from the Beach at 36 Pittwater Rd (Ⓣ02/9977 1189; 1hr $12, all day $25). For a more idyllic beach, follow the footpath from the southern end of South Steyne around the headland to Cabbage Tree Bay, with two very pretty – and protected - green-backed beaches at either end: **Fairy Bower** to the west and **Shelley Beach** to the east.

Manly Scenic Walkway

The wonderful **Manly Scenic Walkway** follows the harbour shore inland from Manly Cove all the way back to Spit Bridge on Middle Harbour, where you can catch bus #180 back to Wynyard station in the city centre (20min). The wonderful eight-kilometre walk takes you through some of the area's more expensive neighbourhoods before heading into a section of **Sydney Harbour National Park**, past a number of small beaches and coves – perfect for stopping off for a dip – Aboriginal middens and some subtropical rainforest. The entire walk takes three to four hours but is broken up into six sections with obvious exit/entry points; pick up a map from the Manly Visitor Information Centre or NPWS offices.

North Head

You can take in more of the Sydney Harbour National Park at **North Head**, the harbour mouth's upper jaw, where you can follow the short circuitous Fairfax Walking Track to three lookout points, including the **Fairfax Lookout**, for splendid views. A regular #135 **bus** leaves from Manly Wharf for North Head or if you have your own car you can drop in to the NPWS office (daily 9am–4.30pm), a kilometre or so before the lookouts, to pick up free **information leaflets**. Right in the middle of this national park is a military reserve with its own **National Artillery Museum** (Wed, Sat, Sun & public holidays 11am–4pm; $8) sited in the historic **North Fort**, a curious system of tunnels built into the headland here during the Crimean Wars in the nineteenth century, as a reaction to fears of a Russian invasion. It takes up to two hours to wander through the tunnels with the obligatory guide.

The Quarantine Station

There's more history at the old **Quarantine Station**, on the harbour side of North Head, used from 1832 until 1984: arriving passengers or crew who had a contagious disease were set down at Spring Cove to serve a spell of isolation at the station, all at the shipping companies' expense. Sydney residents, too, were forced here, most memorably during the plague which broke out in The Rocks in 1900, when 1828 people were quarantined (104 plague victims are buried in the grounds). The site, its buildings still intact, is now looked after by the NPWS, which offers **guided history tours** (Tues, Thur, Sat & Sun 1.15pm; 1hr 30min–2hr; $11; booking essential on ☎02/9247 5033), giving an insight not only into Sydney's immigration history but also the evolution of medical science, often in gory detail. The tours, which co-ordinate with the #135 bus from Manly Wharf (bus fare extra), provide the only opportunity to get out to this beautiful isolated harbour spot with its views across to Balmoral Beach. The night-time **ghost tours** (Wed & Fri–Sun 7.15pm; 3hr 15min; Wed $22, Fri–Sun $27.50; light supper included) are very popular and very spooky; children under 12 have a less hair-raising, once-weekly **Kids Ghost Tour** (Fri 5.45pm; 2hr 15min; $13.20 child or adult; no supper). No public transport is available for the night-time visits.

The northern beaches

From Manly northwards it's one gorgeous stretch of sand after the next for 30km all the way up to Palm Beach along Pittwater Road – some long and open, others sheltered and secluded, and therefore more favoured by the locals. Most suburbs on the way north have a strip of shops with simple takeaways and some trendier cafés and bars, as well as the odd golf course and larger picnic areas. It's a good idea to pick up the excellent free *Sydney's Northern Beaches Map* from the Manly Visitor Centre (see p.146) or check out the associated website, Ⓦwww.sydneybeaches.com.au. **Buses** #190 and #L90 run up the peninsula

▲ Rock pools, Long Reef

from Railway Square at Central via Wynyard to Avalon, continuing to Palm Beach via the Pittwater side; change at Avalon for bus #193 to Whale Beach. Bus #L88 goes from Central and Wynyard to Avalon, and the #187 from Milsons Point in The Rocks to Newport.

Freshwater to Narrabeen

Freshwater, just beyond Manly, sits snugly between two rocky headlands on Queenscliff Bay, and is one of the most picturesque of the northern beaches. There's plenty of surf culture around the headland at **Curl Curl**, and a walking track at its northern end, commencing from Huston Parade, will take you above the rocky coastline to the curve of **Dee Why Beach**. Dee Why provides consistently good **surf**, while its sheltered lagoon makes it popular with families. Beyond the lagoon, windsurfers gather around Long Reef, where the point is surrounded by a wide rock shelf creviced with rock pools and protected as an aquatic reserve – it's well worth a wander to peek at the creatures within. Bus #136, #146, #158 from Manly Wharf, or #169 from Wynyard, or buses #151 and #178 from outside the QVB in the city, will get you to Dee Why. The long, beautiful sweep of **Collaroy Beach**, now with a popular YHA, shades into **Narrabeen Beach**, an idyllic spot backed by the extensive, swimmable and fishable **Narrabeen Lakes**, popular with anglers, kayakers and families; there's also a good campsite (see box on p.176). There are no train lines to the northern beaches, but both Collaroy and Narrabeen can be reached by bus #183 from Wynyard station and Manly Wharf or bus #190 from Central and Wynyard stations. Several other buses also go to Collaroy including the #151 from outside the QVB and from Manly Wharf, the #187 from Millers Point in The Rocks, and the #156 and #159 from Manly Wharf, and buses continue all the way up the coast with stop-off points at the more popular sites.

Mona Vale to Bilgola Beach

Beyond Narrabeen, **Mona Vale** is a long, straight stretch of beach with a large park behind and a sea pool dividing it from sheltered **Bongin Bay**, whose headland reserve, and rocks to clamber on, make it ideal for children. A short drive inland from Mona Vale at Ingleside, in the middle of the Ku-ring-gai Chase National Park, the domed **Bahá'í Temple**, in extensive gardens at 175 Mona Vale Rd (daily 9am–5pm, 9am–7pm summer; ⓦwww.bahai.org), is one of only seven in the world; the Bahá'í faith teaches the unity of religion, and Sunday services (11am) read from texts of the world's main religions. To get to the temple, catch bus #159 from Manly Wharf or the #190 from Central or Wynyard stations to Palm Beach. After Bongin Bay the Barrenjoey Peninsula begins, with calm **Pittwater** (see opposite) on its western side and ocean beaches running up its eastern side until it spears into Broken Bay. **Newport** boasts a fine stretch of ocean beach between two rocky headlands but is better known for *The Newport Arms*, a beer garden pub established in 1880 where crowds gather every afternoon to relax on the huge deck looking out over Heron Cove at Pittwater. Unassuming **Bilgola Beach**, next door to Newport and nestled at the base of a steep cliff, is one of the prettiest of the northern beaches, with its distinctive orange sand. From Bilgola Beach, a trio of Sydney's best beaches, for both surf and scenery, run up the eastern fringe of the mushroom-shaped peninsula: **Avalon** and **Whale** beaches are popular surfie territory, while the more fashionable **Palm Beach** caters to visiting celebs and the well-known Sydneysiders escaping the city.

Avalon and Whale Beach

Backed by bush-covered hills (where koalas can still be found), and reached by three kilometres of winding road, smallish **Avalon Beach** has a secluded feel, with a rock swimming pool at the southern end, and is indeed a slice of paradise on a summer's day. A pleasant set of shops and eateries runs perpendicular from the beach on Avalon Parade; *Avalon Beach Cafe* at no. 23 is a good licensed café with a very contemporary feel, moderately priced and popular with the travellers who stay nearby at the hostel (see "Accommodation").

Whale Beach, 8km further north via Barrenjoey Road and Whale Beach Road, is much less of a settlement, with the beach fronted by the inevitable Surf Life Saving Club and the classy *Whale Beach Restaurant* (24b The Strand, ☎02/9974 4009; closed Mon & Tues), which dishes up an enormous seafood platter for two for $125 alongside stunning views; it also has a much cheaper, very pleasant garden café and a kiosk with burgers and fish and chips.

Palm Beach

If you continue to follow Whale Beach Road north you'll reach **Palm Beach** which, living up to its name, is a hangout for the rich and famous, including plenty of international celebs seeking some Australian sunshine. To blend right in, you too can arrive Hollywood-style on a seaplane from Rose Bay (see p.125). The ocean beach, on the western side of the peninsula, leads a double life as "Summer Bay" in the famous, long-running Aussie soap *Home and Away*, with the picturesque **Barrenjoey Lighthouse** and bushcovered headland – part of **Ku-Ring-Gai Chase National Park** – regularly in shot. A steep walking path to the summit of **Barrenjoey Headland** from the carpark at the base takes twenty to forty minutes, rewarded by a stunning panorama of Palm Beach, Pittwater and the Hawkesbury River. The NPWS offers weekend tours of the sandstone lighthouse, which dates from 1881 (Sun every 30min from 11am–3pm; 30min; $1–2 gold coin donation).

The bulk of Ku-Ring-Gai Chase National Park is across Pittwater, and can be visited with Palm Beach and Hawkesbury River Cruises (☎02/9997 4815). The **cruises** leave from the wharf on the eastern, Pittwater side of the peninsula (11am–3.30pm, 1hr lunch break at Bobbin Head; $32); they also offer general transport to Patonga (see p.294). Alternatively, the Palm Beach Ferry Service (☎02/9918 2747) runs from Palm Beach Wharf via The Basin to Mackeral Beach, reaching picnicking and camping spots on Pittwater (departing hourly 9am–5pm weekdays, 9am–8pm Fri and 9am–6pm weekends; $10 return).

Beside the wharf, calm Snapperman Beach is fronted by yachts and a shady park, usually full of people on rugs lapping up the atmosphere. Across the road you can **eat** at *Barrenjoey House*, an upmarket guesthouse and **restaurant**, where sitting and gazing across the bay with a glass of wine in hand is almost mandatory. You can also dine well on a constantly changing menu at popular *Ancora*, but for less cash, get fish and chips from the excellent milk bar nearby and throw down your own rug on the grass. There are a few interesting **shops** to browse in on Barrenjoey Road, offering Indian clothes and accessories, funky secondhand furniture and women's clothing.

Bus #190 and #L90 run up the peninsula from Central via Wynyard to Avalon, continuing to Palm Beach via the Pittwater side; change at Avalon for bus #193 to Whale Beach; #188 and #L88 go from Central and Wynyard to Avalon, and the #187 and #L87 run from The Rocks to Newport.

10

The southern and western outskirts

Sydney's mostly unattractive **western suburbs** cover the flat plains heading to the Blue Mountains, the ultimate destination of most travellers heading westward. The city's first successful farming area, **Parramatta**, on the Parramatta River, has a cluster of historic colonial buildings not swallowed up by development and there are several **wildlife parks** out this way and in the northwestern suburbs, where the conjunction of the Lane Cove River and the Parramatta River creates gorgeous scenery at well-heeled **Woolwich** and **Hunters Hill**, and the nearby **Lane Cove National Park**. The **southern suburbs** of Sydney have pockets of beauty and interest at **La Perouse** and **Botany Bay National Park** and there's a superb surf beach at **Cronulla**.

South

The southern suburbs of Sydney, arranged around huge **Botany Bay**, are seen as the heartland of red-roofed suburbia. The popular perception of Botany Bay is coloured by its proximity to an airport, a high-security prison (Long Bay), an oil refinery, a container terminal and a sewerage outlet. Yet the surprisingly clean-looking water is fringed by quiet, sandy beaches and the marshlands shelter a profusion of birdlife. Whole areas of the waterfront, from **La Perouse** to the **Kurnell Peninsula** where Captain Cook first dropped anchor, are part of **Botany Bay National Park**, and large stretches on either side of the Georges River form a State Recreation Area. Beyond Botany Bay lies the beach surburb of **Cronulla**, and the Royal National Park (see p.328) is just across the water.

La Perouse

La Perouse, tucked into the northern shore of Botany Bay where it meets the Pacific Ocean, contains Sydney's oldest Aboriginal settlement, the legacy of a mission. The suburb took its name from the eighteenth-century French explorer, **Laperouse**, who set up camp here for six weeks, briefly and cordially meeting Captain Arthur Phillip, who was making his historic decision to forgo swampy Botany Bay and move on to Port Jackson. After leaving Botany Bay, the Laperouse expedition was never seen again.

La Perouse is at its most lively on **Sunday** (and public holidays) when, following a tradition established at the turn of the twentieth century, Aboriginal people come down from the surrounding areas to sell boomerangs and other crafts, and demonstrate snake-handling skills (from 1.30pm) and boomerang throwing. Across from **Frenchmans Bay** beach and park there are a few places to eat on Endeavour Avenue, including the popular, casual and affordable *Paris Seafood Cafe* at no. 51; you can eat in or get take-away fish and chips and have them in the grassy park opposite. More fish and chips can be had at *Danny's Seafood* at 1605 Anzac Parade.

To **get to** La Perouse, catch bus #394 or #399 from Circular Quay via Darlinghurst and Moore Park, or #393 from Railway Square via Surry Hills and Moore Park, or the #L94 express from Circular Quay.

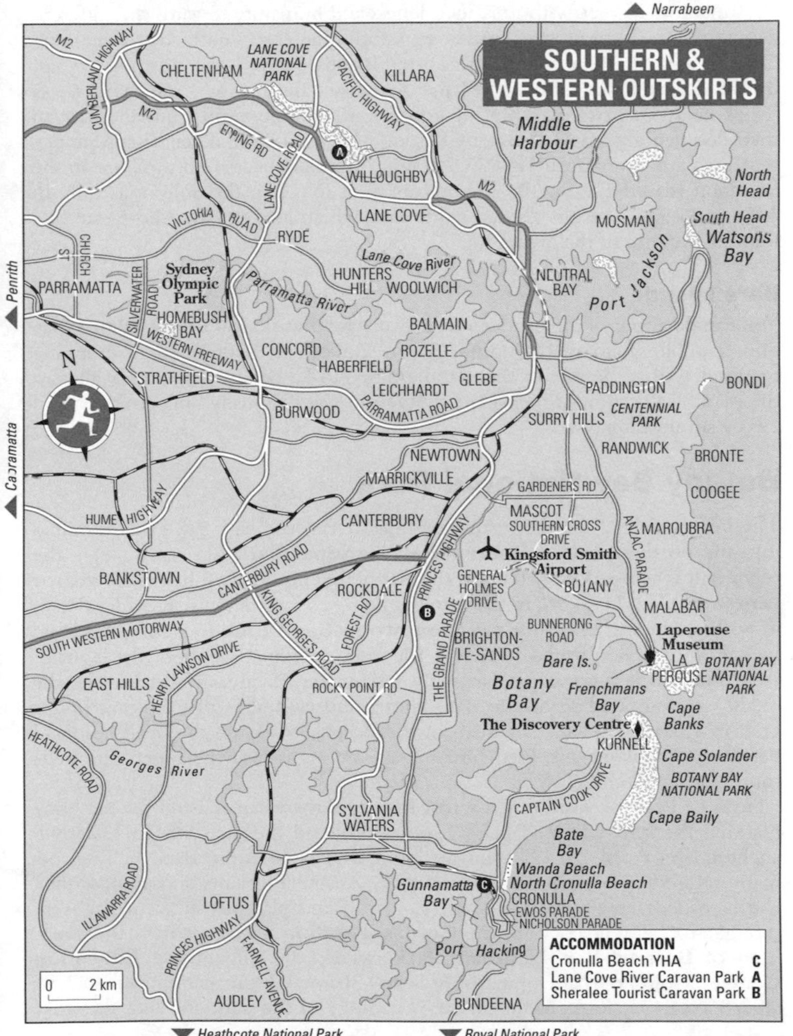

The Laperouse Museum

At least, is there any news of Monsieur de Laperouse?

Louis XVI, about to be guillotined, 1793

A monument erected in 1825 and the excellent NPWS-run **La Perouse Museum** (Wed–Sun 10am–4pm; $5.50), which sits on a grassy headland between the pretty beaches of Congwong Bay and Frenchmans Bay, tell the whole fascinating story. Tracing Laperouse's voyage in great detail, the museum displays are enlivened by relics from the wrecks, exhibits of antique French maps and copies of etchings by the naturalists on board. The voyage was commissioned by the French king Louis XVI in 1785 as a purely scientific exploration of the Pacific to rival Cook's voyages, and strict instructions were given for Laperouse to "act with great gentleness and humanity towards the different people whom he will visit". After an astonishing three-and-a-half-year journey through South America, the Easter Islands, Hawaii, the northwest coast of America, and past China and Japan to Russia, the *Astrolobe* and the *Boussole* struck disaster – first encountering hostility in the Solomon Islands and then in their doomed departure of Botany Bay, on March 10, 1788. Their disappearance remained a mystery until 1828, when relics were discovered on Vanikoro in the Solomon Islands; the wrecks themselves were found in the Solomons only in 1958 and 1964. There is also an exhibition which looks at the Aboriginal history and culture of the area.

Bare Island

You can do a tour of the nineteenth-century fortifications on **Bare Island** (Sat, Sun & public holidays 12.30pm, 1.30pm, 2.30pm & 3.30pm; $5; no booking required, wait at the gate to the island), joined to La Perouse by a thin walkway; the island featured in *Mission Impossible II* and was originally built amid fears of a Russian invasion.

Botany Bay National Park

The headlands and foreshore surrounding La Perouse have been incorporated into the northern half of **Botany Bay National Park** (no entry fee) – the other half is across Botany Bay on the Kurnell Peninsula (see below). A **visitor centre** (☎02/9311 3379), in the same building as the museum, provides details of walks including a fine one past **Congwong Bay Beach** to Henry Head and its lighthouse (5km round trip). Ask for more information about the "whale" Aboriginal rock carving. Also worth a visit is the Macquarie Watchtower, the oldest existing building on the Bay's shores and Australia's first customs house, built in 1820. The idyllic verandah of the *Boatshed Cafe*, on the small headland between Congwong and Frenchmans Bays, sits right over the water with pelicans floating about below.

From La Perouse, you can see across Botany Bay to Kurnell and the red buoy marking the spot where Captain James Cook and the crew of the *Endeavour* anchored on April 29, 1770, for an eight-day exploration. Back in England, many refused to believe that the uniquely Australian plants and animals they had recorded actually existed – the kangaroo and platypus in particular were thought to be a hoax. **Captain Cook's Landing Place** is now the south head of **Botany Bay National Park**, where the informative **Education Centre** (Mon–Fri 10am–4pm, Sat & Sun 9.30am–4.30pm; car entry fee $7.50; ☎02/9668 8431) looks at the wetlands ecology of the park and tells the story

Whale watching

Humpback whales and southern right whales are now regularly sighted from Sydney headlands and surf beaches in June and July on their migratory path north from the Antarctic to breeding grounds in the tropical waters of Queensland. Whales even occasionally make an appearance in Sydney Harbour itself – three southern right whales frolicking under the Harbour Bridge in July 2002 caused a sensation as city offices emptied out and sightseers flocked to the shores. The whales swim close to shore on their trip north and can be spotted without binoculars; while they do head back the same way south during the summer months, they are much further from shore.

The best and most popular whale watching spot is **Cape Solander** in the southern Kurnell half of Botany Bay National Park. This is where the official whale count is taken – in 2003, just over 500 humpbacks were counted which was doubled in 2004. Essentially Cape Solander is the most southern point of Sydney before the Royal National Park extends southwards, and the first obvious place to site the whales as they head north. From here, it could take two and a half hours for the same whale to be seen at Bondi Beach, and another three hours or so for it to be spotted along the northern beaches at the popular whale watching site of Long Reef – but any headland or beach with a good ocean view is fine (there are several superb lookout points on North Head and South Head).

Whale spotting from land takes patience. You might have to sit for at least three hours before your first "blow" (humpbacks spout a rounded vapour, while the southern right whales' is v-shaped), though the more commonly seen, lunge-feeding humpback is very energetic and spouting might be followed by dives, the waving of fins and arcing through the water. Since it can be windy and cold, make sure you bring a beanie hat and a warm jacket, food supplies and something to sit on. To get the most out of the experience, get hold of a pair of decent binoculars to guarantee a close-up view.

For more information, check out the IFAW (International Fund for Animal Welfare) website at Ⓦwww.ifaw.org. For details of whale-watching cruises, see "Basics", p.37.

▲ Whale watching in Botany Bay

of Cook's visit and its implications for Aboriginal people. Indeed the political sensitivity of the spot, which effectively marks the beginning of the decline of an ancient culture, has led to the planned renaming of the park to Kamay-Botany Bay National Park, "Kamay" being the original Dharawal people's name for the bay. Set aside as a public recreation area in 1899, the heath and woodland is unspoilt and there are some secluded beaches for swimming; you may even spot some parrots and honeyeaters. However, one of the main attractions in this half of Botany Bay National Park is whale watching from **Cape Solander** in June and July (see box on p.157). To get here, take the train to Cronulla and then Kurnell Bus Services route #987 (☎02/9524 8977).

Cronulla

On the other side of the Kurnell Peninsula sits **Cronulla**, Sydney's most southern beach suburb and the only beach accessible by train. The locals call it "God's country" and Cronulla does have the atmosphere of a holiday village rather than a community only a half-hour by car from the CBD. Steeped in surfer culture, everything about the suburb centres on water sports and a laid-back beach lifestyle, from the multitude of surf gear shops and outdoor cafés on the beachfront to the surfrider clubs and boating facilities on the bay. Once the haven of panel vans and all night campfire parties, in the last decade Cronulla has become increasingly trendy and upmarket – restaurants are serving more than fish and chips and pizza, the rundown red-brick beach houses are disappearing and the prime beachfront real estate is fast being bought up and built on. Townhouses and multistorey mansions with million-dollar price tags have done nothing to change the relaxed beach vibe of the area, though, with walkers and joggers out every morning on the sand and the standard cluster of surfers still gathering on the point to check out the swell.

Cronulla is set on a peninsula with the ocean on one side and the calmer **Gunnamatta Bay** on the other, the outcrop forming one side of the heads at the entrance to the Port Hacking River. The long arch of Bate Bay is Sydney's longest beach at 4.8km. There are four **patrolled beaches** at the south of this strip – **North Cronulla**, **Elouera** and **Wanda** on the main arc of sand, and the smaller and more protected **South Cronulla** beach in its own inlet to the south. Each beach has a **surf club** with facilities and canteens, and **car parking** extends right along this stretch of coast. **South Cronulla** is the only Sydney beach directly accessible by train (40min from Central Station on the Sutherland line), and as such can become quite crowded. It's also protected from the wind and most tidal rips so many families bring their children here to swim. The beach is 300m from Cronulla **train station**, located at the southern end of the main shopping strip, Cronulla Street, which becomes a pedestrianized mall further down and houses a handful of hip young **café-bars**, including *Nulla Nulla*, at no. 75, which has Internet access. Emerging from the station and crossing the road, a small alleyway leads straight down through a park and onto the sand. Facing the sea, on the right is the Cronulla Sports Complex, which houses a heated indoor pool and gym (☎02 9544 1234). *Cronulla Kiosk*, next to the complex and practically in the ocean, is good for an unpretentious "Big Beach Breakfast" or lunch and the nearby *Cronulla RSL Memorial Club*, where floor to ceiling windows expose the coastline and the city skyline in the distance, does a good line in cheap counter meals and drinks.

Around Cronulla

Heading south is a well-trodden **footpath**, **The Esplanade**, following the coastline around to Bass and Flinders Point and beyond to Salmon Haul Bay and Hungry Point. Across the mouth of the Hacking River lies the small artist community of **Bundeena**, nestled on the edge of the **Royal National Park**. Cronulla National Park Ferry Services runs ferries to Bundeena from Cronulla Marina on Tonkin Street, behind the train station (see p.329).

Past **Bass and Flinders Point**, at low tide the path can be followed right around the headland, down the back of the promontory and across the sand to **Gunnamatta Park**. The large park is a popular and sheltered **BBQ spot** with a sizeable amphitheatre, which in summer hosts Shakespeare in the Park performances. The calmer inlet is filled with yachts and run-about dinghies and is a good place to paddle a surfski, kayak, or swim in the netted-off ocean pool.

West

For over fifty years, Sydney has been sliding ever westwards in a monotonous sprawl of shopping centres, brick-veneer homes and fast-food chains, along the way swallowing up towns and villages, some of which date back to colonial times. The first settlers to explore inland found well-watered, fertile river flats, and quickly established agricultural outposts to support the fledgling colony. **Parramatta**, **Liverpool**, **Penrith** and **Campbelltown**, once separate communities, have now become satellite towns inside Sydney's commuter belt. Yet, despite Sydney's advance, bushwalkers will find there's still plenty of wild west to explore. Three wildlife parks keep suburbia at bay, and the beauty of the **Blue Mountains** (see p.306) is a far cry from the modernity of Sydney. Heading west, however, now starts for many travellers with a visit to the Olympic site at **Homebush Bay**.

Sydney Olympic Park at Homebush Bay

The main focus of the 2000 Olympic events was **Sydney Olympic Park** at **Homebush Bay**, a down-at-heel working-class area in the city's west, far removed from the glamour of Sydney's harbour. Virtually the geographical heart of a city that sprawls westwards, Homebush Bay already had some heavy-duty sporting facilities – the State Sports Centre and the Aquatic Centre – in place. The **Sydney Olympic Park Authority (SOPA)** is in the process of turning Sydney Olympic Park into an entertainment and sporting complex for family-oriented recreation, with events such as free outdoor movies, multicultural festivals, school holiday and weekend children's activities and Sydney Festival-related events. For details call ⊕02/9714 7888 or check ⊛www.sydneyolympicpark.nsw.gov.au.

The most pleasant way to get out to Olympic Park is to take a ferry up the Parramatta River: the **RiverCat** from Circular Quay ($6 one-way to Homebush Bay) stops off frequently en route to Parramatta. The second best option is the direct **train** from Central to Olympic Park station (on Dawn Fraser Avenue, a few minutes' walk to the Telstra Stadium on Olympic Boulevard), which runs four times daily on weekdays (at weekends change at Lidcombe station from where trains depart every 10min) to the Homebush Bay Olympic Centre, the State Sports Centre and the Athletic Centre via Strathfield station and Olympic

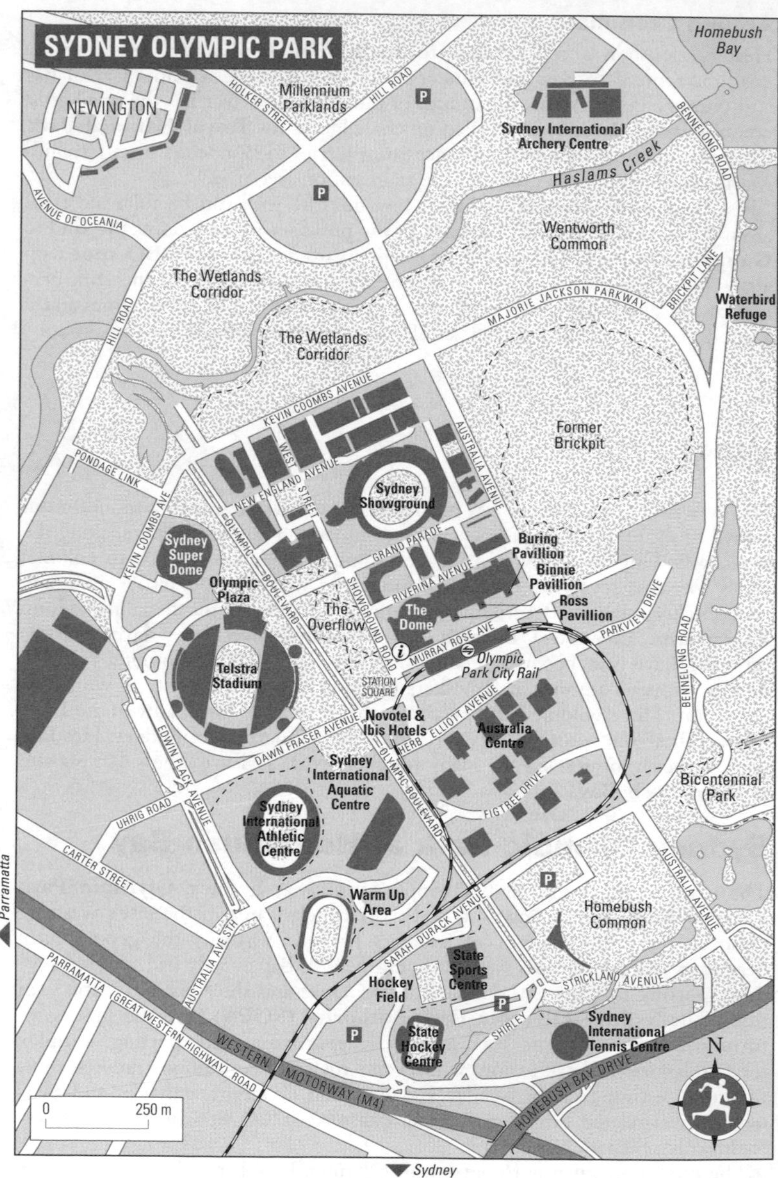

Park ferry wharf. To get around the extensive site (there are 35km of **cycleways**, including those in Bicentennial Park), on the weekend you can **hire bikes** from the visitor centre (see below; from $12 per hour, $22 half-day).

Information is available from the **Sydney Olympic Park Visitor Gateway**, right next to Olympic Park station on the corner of Showground Rd and Murray Rose Avenue (daily 9am–5pm; ☎02/9714 7888). The **Games Trail Tour**

▲ Homebush Olympic Park

is a walking tour exploring the sites and stories of the 2000 Olympics; it leaves from outside the centre (daily noon, 1.30pm & 3pm; no bookings necessary; $20; 1hr).

To get an overview of the site, there is an **observation centre** on the 17th floor of the *Novotel Hotel* (daily 10am–4pm; $4; ⓦwww.sydneyolympicparkhotels.com.au), on Olympic Boulevard between Telstra Stadium and the Aquatic Centre. The *Novotel* is the social focus of the Olympic Park, with several places to eat and drink including the popular *Homebush Bay Brewery*.

Visiting the sporting venues

The A$470-million Olympic site was centred around the 110,000-seat **Telstra Stadium**, the venue for the opening and closing ceremonies, track and field events, and marathon and soccer finals. Since then, an A$68-million overhaul has reduced the number of seats to 83,500 – a more realistic number for its use as an Australian Rules football, cricket, rugby league, rugby union, soccer and concert venue, though it's still Sydney's largest stadium. Tours of the stadium, with commentary, are available daily in one-hour or half-hour versions (hourly 10.30am–3.30pm; 30min tour $15, 1hr $26; turn up at Gate C but check it's a non-event day first by contacting ⓣ02/8765 2360 or checking ⓦwww.telstrastadium.com.au).

Just south of the stadium is the **State Sports Centre** (daily 9am–5pm; ⓣ02/9763 0111, ⓦwww.sscbay.nsw.gov.au), where you can visit the **NSW Hall of Champions**, devoted to the state's sporting heroes (same hours; free; the Hall of Champions is closed when events are being held at the State Sports Centre, so call the latter before setting out); and the **Sydney International Aquatic Centre** (April–Oct Mon–Fri 5am–8.45pm, Sat & Sun 6am–6.45pm; Nov–March Mon–Fri 5am–8.45pm, Sat & Sun closes 7.45pm; swim & spa $6; ⓣ02/9752 3666, ⓦwww.sydneyaquaticcentre.com.au; also see p.275 for more detail).

On the south side of the site, you can watch tennis tournaments (the big one is the Medibank International, held during the second week of January) or

Cuddly Koalas: wildlife parks around Sydney

It is no longer legal to pick up and hold a koala in New South Wales' wildlife parks but photo-opportunity "patting" sessions are still on offer. Several hands-on wildlife experiences on the outskirts of Sydney are listed on pp.243–244. Also see Taronga Zoo (p.132) and the Australian Reptile Park (pp.293).

About 10km northwest of Parramatta at **Featherdale Wildlife Park** located 30km west of Sydney's city centre off the M4 Motorway between Parramatta and Penrith (217 Kildare Rd, Doonside; daily 9am–5pm; $17.50; Ⓦwww.featherdale.com.au), patting koalas is the special all-day attraction. To get there by public transport, take the train from Central to Blacktown station then bus #725.

The **Koala Park Sanctuary** (daily 9am–5pm; $18; Ⓦwww.koalaparksanctuary.com.au) was established as a safe haven for koalas in 1935 and has since opened its gates to wombats, possums, kangaroos and native birds of all kinds. Koala-feeding sessions (daily 10.20am, 11.45am, 2pm & 3pm) are the patting and photo-opportunity times. The sanctuary is situated 25km north of Sydney, not far from the Pacific Highway on Castle Hill Road, West Pennant Hills; or take the train from Central to Pennant Hills station then bus #651 or #655 towards Glenorie (Mon–Sat).

hire a court at the **Sydney International Tennis Centre** (Ⓣ02/8746 0777, Ⓦwww.sydneytennis.com.au), while on the north side, the **Sydney Superdome** (tours Mon–Fri 11am & 3pm; 45min; $15.40; Ⓣ02/8765 4321, Ⓦwww.superdome.com.au), which hosted the basketball, rhythmic gymnastics and paralympic basketball, is Sydney's basketball stadium.

Bicentennial Park and around

Opposite the Olympic site is the huge **Bicentennial Park**, opened in 1988; more than half of the expanse is conservation wetlands – a boardwalk explores the mangroves and there's a bird hide from which you can observe a profusion of native birds. There are around 8km of cycling and walking tracks (and bike hire available from the Sydney Olympic Park Visitor Gateway, see p.158), and the Parklands Express Shuttle tours the wetlands on Sundays (12.30pm, 1.15pm, 2.15pm, 3pm & 3.45pm; 45min; $4.40), with four stops where you can hop off and on.

Further north, the site of the green-friendly **Athletes' Village** consisted mostly of modular dwellings, which have been moved and reused elsewhere; the village is now incorporated into a new solar-powered suburb, **Newington**.

Parramatta

Situated on the Parramatta River, a little over 20km upstream from the harbour mouth, **PARRAMATTA** was the first of Sydney's rural satellites – the first farm settlement in Australia, in fact. The fertile soil of "Rosehill", as it was originally called, saved the fledgling colony from starvation with its first wheat crop of 1789. It's hard to believe today but dotted here and there among the malls and busy roads are a few eighteenth-century public buildings and original settlers' dwellings that warrant a visit if you're interested in Australian history. Today Parramatta is the headquarters of many government agencies and has a multicultural community and a lively **restaurant scene** on its main drag, Church Street.

You can **stop off** in Parramatta on your way west out of Sydney – a rather depressing drive along the ugly and congested Parramatta Road – or endure the

Lane Cove River

Some of Sydney's prettiest suburbs lie on the **Lane Cove River**, which runs into the Parramatta River a few kilometres west of the city centre. Exclusive Hunters Hill and Woolwich are found on a peninsula, with the Parramatta River on its southern side and the Lane Cove River on its northern side. As Lane Cove River meanders north from Hunters Hill, a valley of bushland between North Ryde and Chatswood forms the Lane Cove National Park.

Hunters Hill and Woolwich

The impressive houses in **Hunters Hill** and **Woolwich** with beautiful gardens and views over both rivers provide the setting for an elegant stroll. A great way to explore the area is to take a ferry from Circular Quay to Woolwich's Valentia Street Wharf, then bus #538 up the hill from here to Hunters Hill, and then wander back down Woolwich Road, Gale Street and The Point Road to the wharf. Turn right off Woolwich Road at Elgin Street and follow it down into Clarke Road for Clarke Point Reserve with its lookout. On a Sunday afternoon, you might also like to drop in to look at an example of early Sydney domestic architecture – the tiny, National Trust-owned four-room Vienna Cottage (38 Alexandra St, Hunters Hill; second & fourth Sun 2–4pm; $4; ⓦwww.nationaltrust.org.au), built in 1871 with an adjoining park and orchard. At the end of Gale Street, the recently renovated *Woolwich Pier Hotel* is a terrific place to stop for a drink or a simple pub meal (lots of seafood and steaks), with fantastic water views. A walking track runs opposite the hotel through parkland to Woolwich Dock, carved into the sandstone cliff, taking you beyond to Clarkes Point Reserve.

Lane Cove National Park

Lane Cove National Park (ⓣ02/9412 1811; Chatswood CityRail, then bus #550 or #551) offers riverside walking tracks, a wildlife shelter and boat rental. You can camp or stay in en-suite cabins at an adjoining caravan park (see box on p.176). If you're driving, the park is accessed by Delhi Road, Lane Cove Road or Lady Game Drive.

dreary thirty-minute suburban train ride from Central Station. But much the most enjoyable way to get here is on the sleek RiverCat **ferry** from Circular Quay up the Parramatta River (1hr; $7 one-way). The wharf at Parramatta is on Phillip Street, a couple of blocks away from the helpful visitor centre within the **Parramatta Heritage Centre**, on the corner of Church and Market streets (daily 9am–5pm; ⓣ02/8839 3300, ⓦwww.visitsydney.org/parramatta/), by the convict-built Lennox Bridge. The Heritage Centre details the area's Aboriginal and colonial history, and hands out free **walking route maps** to help you find the historical attractions detailed below. From the ferry wharf, you can walk to the centre in around ten minutes along the colourful paved Riverside Walk, decorated with Aboriginal motifs and interpretative plaques which aim to tell the story of the Burramatagal people.

One block south of the visitor centre, the area around the corner of Church and Phillip streets has become something of an "**eat street**" with around twenty cafés and restaurants, from Filipino through Chinese and Malaysian to Japanese, reflecting Parramatta's multicultural mix.

Historic buildings

Parramatta's most important historic feature is the National Trust-owned **Old Government House** (Mon–Fri 10am–4pm, Sat & Sun 10.30am–4pm; $7) in **Parramatta Park** by the river. To get there turn left onto Marsden Street from the visitors' centre, cross the river, then go right onto George Street. Entered through the 1885 gatehouse on O'Connell Street, the park – filled with native trees – rises up to the gracious old Georgian-style building, the oldest remaining public edifice in Australia. It was built between 1799 and 1816 and used as the Viceregal residence until 1855; one wing has been converted into a pleasant teahouse.

The three other main historic attractions are close together: from Parramatta Park, follow Macquarie Street and turn right at its end onto Harris Street. Running off here is Ruse Street, where the aptly named **Experiment Farm Cottage** at 9 Ruse St (Tues–Fri 10.30am–3.30pm, Sat & Sun 11am–3.30pm; $5.50), another National Trust property, was built on the site of the first land grant, given in 1790 to reformed convict James Ruse. On parallel Alice Street, at no. 70, **Elizabeth Farm** (daily 10am–5pm; $7) dates from 1793 and claims to be the oldest surviving home in the country. The farm was built and run by the Macarthurs, who bred the first of the merino sheep that made Australian wealth "ride on a sheep's back"; a small **café** here serves refreshments. Nearby **Hambledon Cottage**, 63 Hassel St (Wed, Thurs, Sat & Sun 11am–4pm; $4), built in 1824, was part of the Macarthur estate.

Listings

Listings

Accommodation

There are a tremendous number of places to stay in Sydney, and fierce competition helps keep prices down. Finding a bed for the night is only a problem during peak holiday periods from Christmas to the end of January, during Mardi Gras in late February/early March and over Easter: at these times you'll definitely need to **book ahead**.

Many places offer a discount for **weekly bookings**, and may also reduce prices considerably during the **low season** (roughly May–Oct, school holidays excepted). Rates are inflated during the peak holiday season from Christmas and through January and other school holiday periods (see box on p.242 for school vacation times); our prices are given in Australian dollars and indicate the price for a double room in high season, excluding these peak times. We've divided our accommodation listings into the following categories: hotels and motels; B&Bs and guesthouses; pubs; and hostels.

All accommodation is marked on the relevant chapter maps throughout the Guide.

Where to stay

The listings below are arranged by area. For short visits, you'll want to stay in the **city centre** or the immediate vicinity: The Rocks, the CBD and Darling Harbour have the greatest concentration of expensive hotels but also several backpackers' hostels, while the area around Central Station and Chinatown, known as Haymarket, has some cheaper, more downmarket places and an ever greater concentration of megahostels including two huge YHAs. **Kings Cross** is still hanging on as a travellers' centre, with more backpackers' accommodation and cheaper hotels than elsewhere, but it's falling out of favour as travellers head for the new establishments in town to avoid the sleaze and all-night partying. In its favour, Kings Cross makes a convenient base as it's only a ten-minute walk from the city and has its own train station. The adjacent suburbs of **Woolloomooloo** and **Potts Point** are moving gradually upmarket, and what little you lose in terms of accessibility, you gain in peace and quiet. To the west, leafy and more peaceful **Glebe** is another slice of prime backpackers' territory, featuring a large YHA hostel, as well as several other backpackers' places and a number of small guesthouses.

If you're staying longer, consider somewhere further out, on the **North Shore**, for example, where you'll get more for your money and more of a resident's feel for Sydney as a city. **Kirribilli**, **Neutral Bay** or **Cremorne Point** offer some serenity and maybe an affordable water view as well: they're only a short ferry ride from Circular Quay. Large old private hotels (as opposed to pubs, which are also called hotels and often offer rooms) out this way are increasingly being converted into guesthouses. **Manly**, tucked away in the northeast corner of the harbour, is a seaside suburb with ocean and harbour beaches and a concentration of hostels as well as more upmarket accommodation, just thirty minutes from Circular Quay by ferry. The **eastern suburbs** also have a couple of great beachside locations close to the city – **Bondi** and **Coogee** – both with hostels and budget accommodation.

Hotels and motels

The term "**hotel**" does not necessarily mean the same in Australia as it does elsewhere in the world – traditionally, an Australian hotel was a pub, a place to drink which also always had rooms above. Some budget places use the name **private hotel**, to distinguish themselves from licensed establishments. The city's larger **international hotels** are concentrated in The Rocks and the CBD, and charge around $150 to $250 for a double room, and from $260 to $400 for the best five-star establishments. Rates in Kings Cross and nearby Potts Point and Woolloomooloo are much less expensive, with budget hotels charging around $60 to $100 (cheaper rooms share bathrooms), and three- or four-star hotels from $90 to $160. **Motels**, such as ones we've listed in Glebe and Surry Hills, charge around $100 a night. **Holiday apartments** can be very good value for a group, and are perfect for families, but are generally heavily booked; we have listed serviced apartment hotels which have overnight rates in the general listings below and holiday apartments which give weekly rates only and are mostly unserviced in the box on p.171.

The Rocks

Old Sydney Holiday Inn 55 George St ⓣ02/9252 0524, ⓦwww.sydney.holiday-inn.com. Circular Quay CityRail/ferry. In a great location right in the heart of The Rocks, this four-and-a-half-star hotel has eight impressively designed levels of rooms around a central atrium, which creates a remarkable feeling of space. The best rooms have harbour views but the rooftop swimming pool (plus spa and sauna) also gives fantastic vistas. 24hr room service. Rooms from $260 including breakfast.

Shangri-La 176 Cumberland St ⓣ02/9250 6000, ⓦwww.shangri-la.com. Circular Quay CityRail/ferry. Luxurious five-star hotel on 36 floors with over five hundred rooms – all with fantastic harbour views from huge windows. The best panorama, however, is from the top floor *Horizons Bar* (see "Drinking"). Facilities include a gym, indoor pool, spa, sauna and several restaurants and bars. Hefty prices start at $400 per night (but cheaper packages are often available, particularly on weekends.

Circular Quay

Intercontinental 117 Macquarie St ⓣ02/9230 0200, ⓦwww.intercontinental.com. Circular Quay CityRail/ferry. The old sandstone Treasury building forms the lower floors of this 31-storey five-star property, with stunning views of the Botanic Gardens, Opera House and harbour. The café/bar is the perfect place for everything from champagne to afternoon tea, and there are three other eateries, a cigar divan, and a pool and gym on the top floor. Rooms cost from $290 for city view and $345 harbour view. Parking is $25 per night.

City centre

Blacket 70 King St ⓣ02/9279 3030, ⓦwww.blackethotel.com.au. Town Hall or Wynyard CityRail. Totally stylish four-and-a-half-star small hotel (42 rooms) in a converted nineteenth-century bank, with original features such as the 1850s staircase contrasting with the minimalist modern interiors in muted charcoals, blues and off-whites. Many of the rooms are studios, with designer kitchenettes complete with washing machines and there are also loft suites, two-bedroom apartments and a suite with its own terrace. Rates start from $210 and go up to $410 for the terrace suite. The basement bar, *Minc Lounge*, is very trendy, and there's a smart on-site restaurant where breakfast (included) is served.

Central Park **185 Castlereagh St ⓣ02/9283 5000, ⓦwww.centralpark.com.au. Town Hall CityRail.** A small chic three-and-a-half star hotel in a great position amid the city bustle (right near the Town Hall and Hyde Park) though rooms remain quiet. Larger rooms have king-size beds and smart and spacious bathrooms with big bathtub and shower. Standard rooms, while smaller, are still spacious but minus the tub; all come with sofa, desk, air-con, kitchenette with sink, toaster, kettle, coffee plunger, crockery, fridge and iron. The small lobby café runs daytime only, but there's a 24hr reception. Light breakfast included. $135–145.

Travelodge Wynyard **7–9 York St ⓣ02/9274 1222, ⓦwww.travelodge.citysearch.com.au. Wynyard CityRail.** Central position for both the CBD and The Rocks. This 22-storey three-and-a-half-star hotel has the usual motel-style rooms but excels with its spacious studios, which come with kitchen area, CD player, voicemail and a safe. Small gym; 24hr room service; pleasant café-brasserie. Cheaper weekend packages available. Rooms $147, studios $193.

Darling Harbour and around

See map on p.96 for locations.

Aarons **37 Ultimo Rd, Haymarket ⓣ02/9281 5555, ⓦwww.aaronshotel.com.au. Central CityRail.** Large, three-star hotel right in the heart of Chinatown, with its own modern café downstairs (which does room service too). Some colourful feature walls add a splash to comfortable en suites rooms, all with TV, air-con and fridge. The least expensive are internal, small and box-like, with skylight only, while the pricier courtyard rooms have their own balconies. Parking (around the corner) is $16 extra. $135–165.

Capitol Square **Capitol Square, cnr Campbell and George streets, Haymarket ⓣ02/9211 8633, ⓦwww.capitalsquare.com.au. Central CityRail.** A more affordable four-star hotel in a National Heritage-listed building right next to the Capitol Theatre and cafés and across from Chinatown. Small enough not to feel impersonal and run by international chain Rydges so decor in the rooms is modern if a little chintzy. In-house restaurant serves Asian and European food. Buffet breakfast. Parking $18. Rooms from $198.

Carlton Crest **169–179 Thomas St, Haymarket ⓣ02/9281 6888, ⓦwww.carltonhotels.com.au. Central CityRail.** Architecturally interesting, this modern eighteen-storey tower is fronted by the charming nineteenth-century facade of the site's former hospital. In a quiet street but right near Central station, Chinatown and the fringes of Darling Harbour. Modern decor plain enough to suit all tastes. Heated outdoor swimming pool and spa; terrace garden with BBQ area; 24hr room service. The city's most affordable four-and-a-half star hotel. $164–199.

The George **700A George St, Haymarket ⓣ02/9211 1800 or 1800 67 96 06, ⓦwww.georgehotel.com.au. Central CityRail.** Budget private hotel on three floors opposite Chinatown with four girl's dorms available too. Bargain-priced rooms – all but two sharing bathrooms – have air-con, are clean and acceptable, though staff are unhelpful. Facilities include a small share kitchen/TV room and a laundry. Dorms $25–28, single $52, double $64, with en suite $90.

Pensione Hotel **631–635 George St, Haymarket ⓣ02/9265 8888, ⓦwww.pensione.com.au.** Stylish new budget private hotel opposite Chinatown that couldn't be more centrally located. The building has some well-preserved nineteenth-century features but the style overall is minimalist. Cheaper rooms are smaller, but come with cable TV and a funky bathroom. Facilities include a guest kitchen and laundry, and Internet access. Rooms for around $100.

Woolloomooloo

See Kings Cross map on p.107 for locations.

W Hotel **6 Cowper Wharf Rd ⓣ02/9331 9000, ⓦwww.whotels.com. Bus #311 from Circular Quay CityRail.** This luxury boutique hotel, with bags of colourful contemporary style and fantastic service and facilities, is Sydney's hippest. On the redeveloped finger wharf, it couldn't be any closer to the water and is a dream choice for a splurge. One end of the wharf is an apartment complex and a marina, and along its length are restaurants and cafés, includ-

▼ W Hotel

ing some of Sydney's best. *W Hotel's* lobby is spacious and striking in design, often host to art exhibitions, and its lush *Water Bar* is one of Sydney's trendiest watering holes (see "Drinking"). The rooms have everything including a CD player (with a CD library to choose from), big-screen TV with Internet, cordless phone, writing desk and coffee-maker; loft rooms have a lounge or work area downstairs and bedroom and bathroom upstairs. 24hr room service; day spa, indoor heated pool and gym. Rooms start at $345 for a rafter room (no view), to $480 for a loft room and upwards.

Woolloomooloo Waters Apartment Hotel 88 Dowling St ⓣ02/9358 3100, ⓦwoolloomooloo-waldorf-apartments.com.au. Kings Cross CityRail. Serviced studio, one- two- and three-bedroom apartments with balcony views over Woolloomooloo Bay or the city. Pool, spa and sauna. Light breakfast in the ground-floor *Waldorf Lounge* included. Cheaper weekly rates available. One-bedroom apartment from $170, two-bedroom from $270.

Surry Hills

BIG 212 Elizabeth St ⓣ02/9281 6030, ⓦwww.bigonelizabeth.com. Central CityRail. Stylish 140-bed part-boutique hotel, part-hostel. Lousy location opposite the railway line but a five- to ten-minute walk to surrounding locations – Central Station, Chinatown and Oxford Street. Sunny rooms have extra-thick glass, good curtains and contemporary decor in natural colours; all are air-con with TV and video but lack lamps and telephones. The ground-floor lobby, with designer lounges and Internet terminals, doubles as the common area with a high-tech guest kitchen to the side. An organic café serves breakfast through dinner (plus $5 specials). Four-, six- and eight-bed dorms; rates include linen, towels and breakfast (pancakes, fresh scones, juice). Roof-terrace BBQ area. Guest laundry. Dorm $24.50, room $80, en suite $100.

City Crown Motel 289 Crown St, cnr Reservoir Street ⓣ02/9331 2433, ⓦwww.citycrownmotel.com.au. Bus #301–303 from Circular Quay CityRail or Castlereagh Street. A fairly typical motel but in a great location. The en-suite units are air-con with free in-house movies and the added bonus of a large balcony looking onto Crown Street. One self-catering unit, sleeping six, is available. Some parking space (extra $15 and only if pre-booked): enter on Reservoir St. $110–140.

Medina on Crown 359 Crown St ⓣ02/9360 6666, ⓦwww.medinaapartments.com.au. Bus #301–303 from Circular Quay CityRail or Castlereagh St, City. Tastefully decorated one- or two-bedroom serviced apartments, with well-equipped kitchen, laundry and balcony, air-con, lounge suite, dining area, TV, video and telephone. There's also an on-site café, gym, sauna, swimming pool and rooftop tennis court. 24hr reception and free covered parking. *Medina* also has a range of apartments around Sydney – see box p.171. Rooms $238, private apartments $485.

Darlinghurst

Kirketon 229–231 Darlinghurst Rd ⓣ02/9332 2011, ⓦwww.kirketon.com.au. Kings Cross CityRail. Location, location, and top in the fashion stakes, thanks to the big name Australian designers who created the swish but very understated interiors. New owners have taken away little of the style but recently dropped the price. A swish bar and restaurant beckon on the ground level, while the forty rooms boast luxuries such as toiletries by Aveda. Beautiful staff, slick service. Free parking; room service. Standard room $169–189.

Medusa 267 Darlinghurst Rd, Darlinghurst ⓣ02/9331 1000, ⓦwww.medusa.com.au. Kings Cross CityRail. This grand Victorian-era terrace houses one of Sydney's swankiest boutique hotels, close to Oxford Street and very popular with gay guests. Interiors were designed by architect Scott Western, known for his innovative use of colour, and the furnishings and fixtures are cutting-edge dramatic. The seventeen guest rooms all have a balcony plus luxurious marble bathrooms, sleek kitchenettes, stereos and VCRs (with plenty of CDs and videos to choose from). De luxe rooms come with chaise longues and access to the stunning interior courtyard. Rooms $270 to $385; specials available.

Paddington

Sullivans 21 Oxford St ⓣ02/9361 0211, ⓦwww.sullivans.com.au. Bus #378 from Central CityRail; #380 from Circular Quay CityRail. Medium-sized contemporary-style private hotel in a trendy location, run by staff tuned into the local scene. Comfortable, modern en-suite rooms with TV and telephones. Free (but limited) parking, garden courtyard and swimming pool, in-house movies, free Internet access, free guest bicycles, fitness centre, laundry, 24hr reception, tour-booking service, and a café open for a huge and yummy breakfast. Rooms $120–135, family rooms $150. Free guided walking tour of Paddington included.

Kings Cross and Potts Point

Bernly Private Hotel 15 Springfield Ave, Kings Cross ⓣ02/9358 3122, ⓦwww.bernlyprivatehotel.com.au. Kings Cross CityRail. This clean budget hotel, which also has a few dorms, is one street back from the seedy heart of the Cross but has good security, 24hr reception, and courteous staff. Private rooms have air-con, TV, sink and fridge and are either en suite or have shared bathroom. There's a tidy kitchen, TV lounge and big sunroof with deck chairs and fantastic views across the Harbour to the Bridge and Opera House. Good single rates. Dorms $22–25, rooms $66, en suite $99, family rooms $121.

Challis Lodge 21–23 Challis Ave, Potts Point ⓣ02/9358 5422, ⓦwww.budgethotelssydney.com. Kings Cross CityRail. Budget hotel in a wonderful old mansion with polished timber floors throughout. In a great location on a quiet, tree-filled street a short walk from Woolloomooloo and Kings Cross, it's also a step away from some of the areas coolest cafés and a couple of trendy restaurants. All rooms have TV, fridge and sink; laundry but no kitchen. Rooms $65, en suite $70, $100 with balcony.

De Vere 44–46 Macleay St, Potts Point ⓣ9358 1211, ⓦwww.devere.com.au. Kings Cross CityRail. Comfortable three-and-a-half star hotel in a great position, close to cafés, restaurants and transport. Third- and fourth-floor rooms have stunning views of Elizabeth Bay; rooms with kitchenette are also available, and there is a suite with a spa. Some rooms have balconies and all have air-con. There is also a breakfast room (buffet-style), guest laundry and 24hr reception. Standard room $139, with kitchenette $225, spa suite $260.

Highfield Private Hotel 166 Victoria St, Kings Cross ⓣ02/9326 9539, ⓦwww.highfieldhotel.com. Kings Cross CityRail. Swedish-run, very clean, modern and secure budget hotel well located in between the hostels on leafy Victoria Street. Rooms are well equipped with fans, heating and sinks but a little dark. Three-bed dorms also available. Tiny kitchen/common room with TV, microwave, kettle and toaster; no laundry but there's one a few doors down. Dorms $23, rooms $60.

Hotel 59 59 Bayswater Rd, Kings Cross ⓣ02/9360 5900, ⓦwww.hotel59.com.au. Kings Cross CityRail. Small hotel (just eight rooms), reminiscent of a pleasant European *pension*, with a friendly owner and small but tastefully decorated air-con rooms. Situated in a quiet leafy location, but close to the action, and with a downstairs café where delicious cooked breakfasts are served (included in the room rate). Very popular, so book in advance. One family room (sleeps four) has a small kitchenette. Outdoor courtyard. $88–121, family room $132.

Macleay Lodge 71 Macleay St, Potts Point ⓣ02/9368 0660, ⓦwww.budgethotelssydney.com. Kings Cross CityRail. Don't expect anything fancy from this budget option, but it's perfectly fine and in a fab spot in the midst of Potts Point's café and restaurant scene. All rooms (bar one) share bathrooms and come with sink, plates, cutlery, kettle, fridge, cheap furniture and TV. Best ones have access to the balcony. Single room $50, double $65.

Glebe

Check Inn 146 Glebe Point Rd ⓣ02/9660 7777, ⓔcheckinnglebe@pubboy.com.au. Bus #431, #433 & #434 from Central CityRail. Reasonably priced motel right in the heart of Glebe. On three floors (no lift), it has very light, spacious and clean air-con rooms with plain, recently updated decor. Most have a double and a single bed. There's a rooftop courtyard with city views, BBQ and an L-shaped pool. 24hr reception. Parking included. $88–92.

Newtown

Australian Sunrise Lodge 485 King St ⓣ02/9550 4999, ⓦwww.australiansunriselodge.com. Newtown CityRail. Inexpensive and well-managed small, private hotel with guest kitchen, well positioned for King Street action but with good security. Single and double rooms, shared bathroom or en suite, come with TV, fridge and toaster. Ground floor rooms are darker, smaller and cheaper – a better option are the sunny rooms on the top two floors, all with cute balconies. En-suite family rooms also available. Rooms $68, en suite $89.

The North Shore

Elite Private Hotel 133 Carabella St, Kirribilli ⓣ02/9929 6365, ⓦwww.elitehotel.com.au. Milsons Point CityRail or ferry to Kirribilli Wharf. Bright place surrounded by plants offering good rooms with sink, TV, fridge and kettle; some dearer ones have a harbour view and most share bathrooms. Small communal cooking facility but no laundry; garden courtyard. Cheaper weekly rates. Rooms $66–88.

North Shore 310 Miller St, North Sydney ⓣ02/9955 1012, ⓦwww.smallanduniquehotels.com. Bus #207 & #208 from Clarence Street, City and North Sydney City Rail. Two-storey mansion with balconies in a quiet location opposite St Leonards Park but within walking distance (10–15min) of the cafés and restaurants of North Sydney, or a bus runs from outside. En-suite rooms or family studios sleeping four, all with air-con, TV, fridge, hot drinks and telephone. Shared kitchen and laundry facilities; breakfast available. $85–115.

Sir Stamford Double Bay 22 Knox St, Double Bay ⓣ02/9363 0100, ⓦwww.stamford.com.au. Ferry to Double Bay Wharf. See map on p.123. Mid-sized (73-room) hotel in a great spot among the wealthy village atmosphere of Double Bay, surrounded by posh fashion shops, sidewalk cafés and restaurants. Rooms are either romantic with four poster beds or urban New York-loft style. Pool, spa and sauna. Breakfast included. $190–770.

Bondi

Bondi Sands 252 Campbell Parade, Bondi Beach ⓣ02/9365 3703 or 1800 026 634, ⓦwww.bondisands.com. Bus #380 & #389 from Bondi Junction CityRail. This budget hotel, straight across from the northern end of the beach, has fantastic views from its oceanfront rooms, and also from its best feature, the rooftop common area, which has a BBQ, and a handy kitchen and laundry. Rooms all share bathrooms but come with sinks; the pricier oceanfront ones have more furniture and queen-size beds, while the cheaper rooms have tri-bunks (single over a double). There are dorms with a maximum of four beds. Often booked up in advance. Dorms from $24, rooms $60.

Bondi Serviced Apartments 212 Bondi Rd, Bondi ⓣ02/9387 1122, ⓦwww.bondi-serviced-apartments.com.au. Bus #380 from Bondi Junction CityRail. Good-value serviced motel studio apartments halfway between Bondi Junction and Bondi Beach – a ten-minute walk to either but in the thick of the local shops and on bus routes. Air-conditioned units all have clean modern furniture, TV, telephone, kitchen and a balcony with sea view. There are more stylish recently decorated rooms, and some older-style apartments without views which are cheaper. The rooftop pool has far-off ocean views. Nightly rates from $105; cheaper rates if you stay a week or more. Parking included.

Swiss-Grand Cnr Campbell Parade and Bondi Road, Bondi Beach ⓣ02/9365 5666, ⓦwww.swissgrand.com.au. Bus #380 from Bondi Junction CityRail. Four-and-half-star hotel on five floors opposite the beach, which suffers from tacky-looking architectural design from the outside (it looks like a big wedding cake) but which is suitably luxurious within. All rooms have fab ocean views. Health club, gym, rooftop and indoor pools, two bars and restaurants, free parking. From $308 per night (though cheaper packages are available from $165).

Coogee

Coogee Bay Boutique Hotel 9 Vicar St, Coogee ⓣ02/9665 0000, ⓦwww.coogeebayhotel.com.au. Bus #372 from Central CityRail & #373, #374 & #376 from Circular Quay CityRail. New

Holiday apartments

The following places rent out **apartments**, generally for a minimum of a week. Expect to pay between $350 and $600 per week, depending on the size and the season; all are completely furnished and equipped – though occasionally you're expected to provide linen and towels: check first. Those listed below are only serviced if stated. Many **hotels** (some called "apartment hotels") have serviced apartments or self-catering studios available at a nightly rate, which are listed under "Hotels" – see *Bondi Serviced Apartments* (opposite), *Coogee Sands Hotel & Apartments* (p.172), *Travelodge* (p.167), *City Crown Motel* (p.168), *De Vere* (p.169), *Hotel 59* (p.169), *Regents Court* (p.172) and *Y on the Park* (p.179). All **hostels** also have communal self-catering facilities – see pp.177–182 for details – and on-site vans and cabins at caravan parks are another affordable option (see box on p.176).

Enochs Holiday Flats ⓣ02/9388 1477, ⓕ9371 0439. Bus #380 & #389 from Bondi Junction CityRail. One-, two- or three-bedroom apartments, all close to Bondi Beach, sleeping four to six people. $500–2000 weekly, depending on the size and season.

Manly National 22 Central Ave, Manly ⓣ02/9977 6469, ⓕ9977 3760. Ferry to Manly Wharf. One- and two-bedroom apartments accommodate up to four people; swimming pool; linen not supplied. One-bedroom $580–700 weekly, two-bedroom $980.

Medina Executive Apartments Head office, Level 1, 155 Crown St, Surry Hills, ⓣ02/9360 1699 or 1300 300 232, ⓦwww.medinaapartments.com.au. Upmarket studio or one-, two- and three-bedroom serviced apartments with resident managers and reception in salubrious locales. Various locations include Lee Street near Central station, Kent Street and Martin Place in the CBD, King Street Wharf at Darling Harbour; inner-city and eastern suburbs include Chippendale, Surry Hills, Paddington, Double Bay and Coogee; on the lower North Shore at Crows Nest, and at North Ryde. All include undercover parking. From $750 weekly upwards.

The Park Agency 190 Arden St, Coogee ⓣ02/9315 7777, ⓦwww.parkagency.com.au. Bus #372 from Central CityRail & #373, #374 & #376 from Circular Quay CityRail. Several spacious, well-set-up studio and one-, two- and three-bedroom apartments near the beach from $800 per week for the smaller units, and $800–1200 per week for the larger properties. Cheaper quarterly leases also available. All fully furnished including washing machine and linen.

Raine and Horne 255 Miller St, North Sydney ⓣ02/9959 5906, ⓦwww.accommodationinsydney.com. Modern executive fully furnished apartments fitted out by interior designers, on the leafy North Shore: North Sydney, Kirribilli, Milsons Point and McMahons Point. Studios from $550, one-bed from $675, two-bed from $800, three-bed from $1500 per week. All have TV, video, CD player, telephone; several have spas, pools or gyms. Rates are much cheaper if you stay for at least a month but the one-off cleaning fee is pricey: $120 for studios and one-bedders, $220–320 for larger apartments.

Sydney City Centre Serviced Apartments 7 Elizabeth St, Martin Place ⓣ02/9233 6677, ⓦwww.accommodationsydneycity.com.au. Martin Place CityRail. Fully equipped open-plan studio apartments sleeping up to three; kitchenette, laundry, TV, video and fans; basic, but in an excellent location. A good choice for long-stayers, as they rent out for a minimum of thirteen weeks. $250–350 weekly.

hotel attached to the rear of a pub, the older, sprawling *Coogee Bay Hotel*. Rooms – all with balconies, half with ocean views – look like something from *Vogue Interior*; luxurious touches include marble floors in the bathrooms, minibars, in-room safes and data ports; expect to pay $220, or $240 for an ocean view. Cheaper "heritage wing" rooms ($130) in the old hotel are noisy at weekends but just as stylish; several offer splendid water views Parking included. 24hr reception. The pub has an excellent brasserie, several bars and a nightclub.

Coogee Sands Hotel & Apartments 161 Dolphin St, Coogee ⓣ02/9665 8588, ⓦwww.coogeesands.com.au. Bus #372 from Central CityRail & #373, #374 & #376 from Circular Quay CityRail. Very pleasant one-, two- and three-bedroom beachside apartments (from $275) with all mod cons plus spacious, well-set-up self-catering studios, some with beach views.

Manly

Manly Pacific Sydney 55 North Steyne, Manly ⓣ02/9977 7666, ⓦwww.accorhotels.com. Ferry to Manly Wharf. Beachfront, multistorey, four-star hotel with 24hr reception, room service, spa, sauna, gym and heated rooftop pool. You pay for it all, and more for an ocean view, which is spectacular. Rooms $189 to $660 for a suite.

B&Bs and guesthouses

We have included places that label themselves **boutique hotels** in this section. Generally small and upmarket, they offer more personal service; you'll pay around $125 to $220 for a double en-suite room. **Guesthouses** and **B&Bs**, which are usually cheaper, are often pleasant, renovated old houses; some have shared bathrooms (and possibly kitchen facilities), with prices from around $100 per room up to about $175.

The Rocks

Bed & Breakfast Sydney Harbour 140–142 Cumberland St, The Rocks ⓣ02/9247 1130, ⓦwww.bedandbreakfastsydney.com. Circular Quay CityRail. This charming brick building close to the start of the Harbour Bridge began life as a boarding house in 1901 and original features include its cedar doors and staircase. The friendly, local-family-run, nine-bedroom B&B has been furnished in period style from Australian hardwood timber recycled from a colonial courthouse. Every room is different; one has a kitchenette and all have top-of-the-range mattresses. The gorgeous garden courtyard is a peaceful haven and although the cooked breakfast can be eaten in the guest sitting room, most people prefer to hang out here – braziers keep it warm in winter. Thick walls and double insulated windows keep out bridge-traffic noise. $155–260.

The Russell 143A George St ⓣ02/9241 3543, ⓦwww.therussell.com.au. Circular Quay CityRail/ferry. Charming, small National Trust-listed hotel. Rooms have Colonial-style decor; some are en suite but the small shared bathroom options are very popular – and at $140 are a great price for the area. Other rooms range from $195 to $290, the best with views of the Quay. Sunny central courtyard and a rooftop garden, sitting room and bar, and downstairs restaurant for continental breakfast. $140–280.

Woollahra

Hughenden 14 Queen St ⓣ02/9363 4863, ⓦwww.hughendenhotel.com.au. Bus #378 from Central CityRail; #380 from Circular Quay CityRail. See map on p.104. Old-fashioned Victorian-era guesthouse, built in 1876, decorated to retain its nineteenth-century charm, including features such as servants' bells and black marble fireplaces. Situated opposite Centennial Park and close to both the Paddington shops and sports stadiums. Expensive en-suite singles and doubles with rates ranging from $128 to $288, depending on size of room. Hot breakfast included.

Kings Cross and Potts Point

Regents Court 18 Springfield Ave, Kings Cross ⓣ02/9358 1533, ⓦwww.regentscourt.com.au. Kings Cross CityRail. Small hotel raved about by international style mags – for its fab fit-out, this place is a little piece of glam without an outrageous pricetag. Classic designer furniture, and each studio-style room has a sleek kitchen area, air-con and TV/video. Instead of a bar downstairs, you'll find a well-chosen wine list (at bottle-shop prices), and you can help yourself to coffee and biscotti. A small kitchen and BBQ area is located on the rooftop, among potted citrus trees. A breakfast of home-made muesli, just-squeezed juice and other goodies costs extra. Rooms $220–253.

Simpsons of Potts Point 8 Challis Ave, Potts Point ⓣ02/9356 2199, ⓦwww.simpsonspottspoint.com.au. Kings Cross CityRail. Small personal hotel, designed in 1892 for a parliamentarian, and beautifully restored. Carpeted and quiet, the three floors of comfortable rooms, all en suite, are furnished with antiques (the guest sitting-room even has a piano); breakfast (included in price) is served in a sunny conservatory. $195, spa suite $330.

Victoria Court 122 Victoria St, Kings Cross ⓣ02/9357 3200, ⓦwww.victoriacourt.com.au. Kings Cross CityRail. Boutique hotel in two interlinked Victorian terraced houses; very tasteful and quiet though décor is overly floral. En-suite rooms with all mod cons, some with balconies; buffet breakfast included and served in the conservatory. Secure parking a bonus. Rooms from $150, deluxe $200.

Glebe

Alishan International Guesthouse 100 Glebe Point Rd ⓣ02/9566 4040, ⓦwww.alishan.com.au. Bus #431, #433 & #434 from Central CityRail. Restored Victorian-era mansion in a handy spot at the bottom of Glebe Point Road. Rather bland but very clean en-suite, motel-style rooms plus one furnished in Japanese fashion (minus an actual futon), and some four- and six-bed dorms. Facilities include a kitchen, spa, airy common room, garden patio and BBQ area. Internet access available. There's a very spacious family room sleeping six, cots are available and children are most welcome. Though there are dorms, this is a peaceful, not party, option. Dorms $25–33, rooms $99–115.

Tricketts Bed and Breakfast 270 Glebe Point Rd ⓣ02/9552 1141, ⓦwww.tricketts.com.au. Bus #431, #433 & #434 from Central CityRail. Luxury B&B in an 1880s mansion. Rooms – en suite – are furnished with antiques and Persian rugs, and the lounge, complete with a billiard table and leather armchairs, was originally a small ballroom. There's also a fully self-contained one-bedroom garden apartment with its own verandah. Delicious, generous and sociable breakfast. $176–198.

The North Shore

Cremorne Point Manor 6 Cremorne Rd, Cremorne Point ⓣ02/9953 7899, ⓦwww.cremornepointmanor.com.au. Ferry to Cremorne Point Wharf. Huge restored federation-style villa run by a friendly couple, offering very cheap singles (from $52) and good-value doubles. Nearly all rooms are en suite – except for a few singles which do, however, have their own toilet and sink – with TV, fridge, kettle and a fan. Pricier rooms have harbour views as does the guest balcony. One family room has its own kitchen, but there's also a communal kitchen and a laundry. Rate includes continental breakfast. Reception sells bus and ferry passes and books tours. $99–200.

Glenferrie Lodge 12A Carabella St, Kirribilli ⓣ02/9955 1685, ⓦwww.glenferrielodge.com. Milsons Point CityRail or ferry to Kirribilli Wharf. A made-over Kirribilli mansion, clean, light and secure with 24hr reception. Rates include a continental breakfast whether you're in a three-share dorm, single, double or family room (all share bathrooms). Some pricier rooms have their own balcony and harbour glimpses but guests can also hang out in the garden and on the guest verandahs. Facilities include a TV lounge, laundry and dining room with free tea and coffee and buffet-style $7 dinner. Dorms $35, rooms $95–125.

Bondi

Ravesi's Cnr Campbell Parade and Hall St ⓣ02/9365 4422, ⓦwww.ravesis.com.au. Bus #380 & #389 from Bondi Junction CityRail. The first-floor restaurant and most rooms at this boutique hotel have glorious ocean views. The facade is pure 1914, but interiors are totally modern; well-thought-out rooms (sixteen in all) have minimalist Asian-style decor and ceiling fans (in addition to air-con). Most of the second-floor rooms have French windows opening onto small balconies; split-level and penthouse suites

Gay and lesbian accommodation

Gay men and lesbians won't encounter any problems booking into a regular hotel, but here are several places that are particularly gay-friendly or close to Oxford Street in Darlinghurst. Some other particularly welcoming places in our general listings include *BIG* (p.168), *Coogee Sands Hotel and Apartments* (p.172), *De Vere* (p.169), *Kirketon* (p.168), *Medusa* (p.169), *Sullivans* (p.169) and *Victoria Court* (p.173). For **flat shares** check the community press and café notice boards.

Brickfield Hill Bed & Breakfast Inn 403 Riley St, Surry Hills ⓣ02/9211 4886, ⓦwww.brickfieldhill.com.au. Central CityRail or bus #301 from Circular Quay CityRail. See map on p.100. In a terraced house, five minutes' walk from Oxford Street and convenient for Surry Hills' diverse cafés, restaurants and bars, this gay-owned and -operated ornate four-story terrace recalls a bygone Victorian era, with antique-style furnished rooms, window drapes, chandelier lights and four poster beds. Popular with both a gay and lesbian clientele. Cheaper rooms share bathrooms. Wireless Internet in the communal area. Breakfast optional $10 extra. Cheaper single rates available. Rooms $105, en suite $125.

Chelsea Guest House 49 Womerah Ave, Darlinghurst ⓣ02/9380 5994, ⓦwww.chelsea.citysearch.com.au. Kings Cross CityRail. See map on p.102. In a tastefully decorated terraced house in the leafy residential backstreets of Darlinghurst, this gay-owned guesthouse is in a quiet location but not far from the action. Doubles are en suite, mostly with queen-sized beds, but there are some de luxe rooms with king-sized beds, including a couple of suites ($185–195); singles ($93) share bathrooms but have sinks. All rooms have fridge, kettle and TV and the price includes a light breakfast which is served in the courtyard. Standard double $143, deluxe $155.

Governors on Fitzroy 64 Fitzroy St, Surry Hills ⓣ02/9331 4652, ⓦwww.governors.com.au. Bus #378 from Central CityRail; #380 from Circular Quay CityRail. See map on p.100. Long-established gay B&B in a restored Victorian terrace just a few blocks from Oxford Street. The six guest rooms share two bathrooms but have their own sinks. The rooms are big, well appointed and each has its own style. A full cooked breakfast is served in the dining room or the garden courtyard. Guests – mostly men – can also meet and mingle in the spa. B&B $120.

Oasis on Flinders 106 Flinders St, Darlinghurst ⓣ02/9331 8791, ⓦwww.oasisonflinders.com.au. Bus #397–399 from Circular Quay CityRail. See map on p.102. Small men-only nudist B&B retreat in a three-storey terraced house. Two of the guest rooms share a bathroom, the other is en suite; all have ceiling fans, TV and video. Spa and sundeck in the courtyard. Continental help-yourself-breakfast included. Very civilised noon check-out time. Room $120, en suite $150.

Pelican Private Hotel 411 Bourke St, Darlinghurst ⓣ02/9331 5344, ⓦwww.pelicanprivatehotel.iwarp.com. Bus #378 from Central CityRail; #380 from Circular Quay CityRail. See map on p.102. Comfortable budget accommodation in one of Sydney's oldest gay guesthouses, a short walk from Oxford Street. The mid-nineteenth-century sandstone building's wonderful tree-filled garden is like an inner-city oasis and the communal kitchen and laundry out here make it even more of a sociable hangout. Appealing, good-sized, well-furnished rooms have fans, TV and fridge, but share bathroom facilities. Back rooms overlook the garden; front rooms are much bigger. Rate includes help-yourself continental breakfast from the kitchen, or pay $5 extra for a cooked breakfast in the hotel's street-front café. Rooms $75.

Wattle Private Hotel 108 Oxford St, cnr Palmer Street, Darlinghurst ⓣ02/9332 4118, ⓦwww.sydneywattle.com. Bus #378 from Central CityRail; #380 from Circular Quay CityRail. See map on p.102. Long-running gay-friendly hotel, right in the thick of the Oxford Street action – with all this so close, there's no need for a bar or breakfast facilities. The décor in the spacious, well-appointed, air-con, en-suite rooms has recently been modernised; new in-room facilities include VCRs and DVDs with an extensive library to choose from. There are also more de luxe spa rooms, including a pricey King Spa Suite ($389), or ask for the room on the roof, which opens out to the rooftop garden with spectacular city and harbour views. Rooms $100–389.

have spacious ones. Smaller standard rooms don't have views, but offer great value. Large, popular bar at ground level. Standard $125, beachfront $295.

Coogee

Dive 234 Arden St, Coogee Beach ⓣ02/9665 5538, ⓦwww.divehotel.com.au. Bus #372 from Central CityRail & #373, #374 & #376 from Circular Quay CityRail. Far from living down to its name, this is a wonderful small hotel in a renovated former boarding house opposite the beach. The hall features Art Deco tiling and high, decorative-plaster ceilings and there's a pleasant, bamboo-fringed courtyard (with BBQ and discreet guest laundry) that opens out from a spacious breakfast room for buffet style breakfasts. Two larger rooms at the front have splendid ocean views; one at the back has its own balcony. All have funky little bathrooms, CD players, cable TV, queen-size beds and a handy kitchenette with microwave and crockery. Free Internet access. Standard $165, ocean view $240.

▼Dive

Manly

Periwinkle Guesthouse 18–19 East Esplanade ⓣ02/9977 4668, ⓦwww.periwinklemanlycove.com.au. Ferry to Manly Wharf. Pleasant B&B in a charming, restored 1895 villa on Manly Cove. Close to the ferry, shops and harbour and a perfect base for swimming, sailing or just watching the lorikeets. Rooms, furnished in Colonial style, have fridge and fans. Single rooms ($110) share bathroom, doublesare en suite ($180), with big bathtubs to soak in; larger family rooms are available. Guest kitchen, laundry, courtyard with BBQ and car park. Light breakfast included.

Northern beaches

Palm Beach Bed and Breakfast 122 Pacific Palm Rd, Palm Beach ⓣ 02/9974 4220, ⓦwww.palmbeachbandb.com.au. Bus #L90 from Central CityRail or Wynyard CityRail. **See map on p.137.** Incredibly friendly and slightly quirky B&B (antique cars are scattered about the front lawn), perched on a hilltop in one of Sydney's most sought-after streets. All rooms have balconies and water views of either Pittwater or the Pacific Ocean and the emphasis is on relaxing and unwinding. Four rooms with French themes have either private en suite or shared bathroom. From $165–245.

Pubs

Plenty of **pubs** have cleaned up their act and offer pleasant old-fashioned rooms, usually sharing bathrooms. The main drawback can be the noise from the bar; ask for a room well away from the action. Rates average $100.

City centre

Grand 30 Hunter St ⓣ02/9232 3755, ⓕ9232 1073. Wynyard CityRail. Very well-located budget accommodation occupying several floors above one of Sydney's oldest, but not necessarily nicest, pubs (open until 3am Thurs–Sat). Pub and hotel have quite separate entrances and rooms (all sharing bathrooms) are brightly painted, with colourful bed covers, fridge, kettle, TV, heating and ceiling fans. Rooms from $100.

The Rocks

Lord Nelson Brewery Cnr Argyle and Kent streets ⓣ02/9251 4044, ⓦwww.lordnelson .com.au. Circular Quay CityRail/ferry. B&B in a historic pub (see p.208). The ten very smart Colonial-style rooms are mostly en suite and come with all mod cons. Price varies according to size and position ($120–180): best is the corner room with views of Argyle Street. Meals served in the upmarket brasserie. Breakfast included.

Mercantile 25 George St, The Rocks ⓣ02/9247 3570, ⓔmerc@tpg.com.au. Circular Quay CityRail/ferry. Sydney's best-known Irish pub (see p.208), right on the edge of The Rocks near the Harbour Bridge, has a stash of fab rooms upstairs which are always booked out – get in early. Original features include huge fireplaces in several rooms, all furnished in Colonial style. Several have bathrooms complete with spa baths. Cooked breakfast included. Rooms $110, en suite $140.

Palisade 35 Bettington St, Millers Point ⓣ02/9247 2272, ⓦwww.palisadehotel.com. Circular Quay CityRail/ferry. Magnificent tiled pub standing like an observatory over Millers Point; plenty of old-world charm about its bar (no pokies) and simple, clean and bright shared-bathrooms, some of which have fantastic views over the inner harbour and Harbour Bridge. Also has a stylish, contemporary restaurant (see p.194). Rooms $118–128.

Darling Harbour

Glasgow Arms 527 Harris St, Ultimo ⓣ9211 2354, ⓕ9281 9439. Central CityRail. Handy for Darling Harbour, and opposite the Powerhouse Museum, this pleasant pub with courtyard dining has good value accommodation upstairs. Double-glazed windows are handy now the bar closes as late as 3am. The high-ceilinged rooms – nicely decorated down to the polished floorboards – are air-con with en suite, TV and radio. Light breakfast included. $135.

Randwick

The Royal 2 Perouse Rd, cnr Cuthill St, Randwick ⓣ02/9399 3006 or 9399 5659, ⓦwww .royalhotel-sydney.com. Bus #372, #374 & #376 from Central CityRail; bus #373 & #377 from Circular Quay CityRail or Oxford Street. See map on p.137. Big, historic, stylish pub (listed by the

Campsites around Sydney

It's possible to camp or stay in a self-catering on-site van or cabin in one of several well-equipped **caravan parks** around Sydney, though your own bed linen is usually required for the latter two options. The three listed below are the closest sites to the centre. Camping rates rise in the peak season, costing from $25–30 for two people in an unpowered site to $30–36 for a powered site; expect to pay $5 less out of season.

Lakeside Caravan Park Lake Park Road, Narrabeen, 26km north of the city ⓣ02/9913 7845, ⓦwww.sydneylakeside.com.au. Bus #L90 from Wynyard CityRail and then a 10min walk. See map on p.137. Great spot by Narrabeen Lakes on Sydney's northern beaches. Free gas BBQs, camp kitchen and a nearby shop. Unpowered site $28, powered site $33. Minimum two-night stay in a range of modern two-bedroom villas ($180–220) and cheaper cabins ($145); all are en suite and linen is included.

Lane Cove River Tourist Park Plassey Road, North Ryde, 14km northwest of the city ⓣ02/9888 9133, ⓦwww .lanecoverivertouristpark.com.com. Bus #550 & #551 from Chatswood CityRail. See map on p.153. Wonderful bush location beside Lane Cove National Park, right on the river, in Sydney's northern suburbs. Great facilities include a bush kitchen (with fridge), TV room and swimming pool. Unpowered site $30, powered $36. En-suite cabins $130–145.

Sheralee Tourist Caravan Park 88 Bryant St, Rockdale 13km south of the city ⓣ02/9567 7161. Rockdale CityRail, then a 10min walk. See map on p.153. This small park with camp kitchen is the cheapest and closest camping option. Only one on-site van – not usually available. Unpowered site $25, powered $30.

National Trust), with fairly upmarket rooms – TV, fridge, fan, telephone, kettle – but all sharing bathrooms. The pub is a very popular drinking hole (open until late nightly, but there are no live bands to disturb sleepers) and has a traditional Italian restaurant. Good transport to the city and beaches. Shared bathroom $88, en suite $100.

Hostels

All **hostels** have a laundry, kitchen, and common room with TV unless stated otherwise. Most include linen but sometimes not blankets, which makes it a good idea to travel with a sleeping bag. Office hours are generally restricted, typically 8am–noon and 4.30–6pm, so it's best to call and arrange an arrival time. The **Kings Cross** area, which includes Potts Point and Woolloomooloo, has a heavy concentration of hostels. Avoid the dodgy places that spring up overnight on Darlinghurst Road; nearby leafy Victoria Street and the backstreets of Potts Point offer a more pleasant atmosphere. **Glebe** is a laid-back, inner-city locale, and the beachside hostels at **Bondi**, **Coogee** and **Manly** are popular. Private rooms cost between $50 and $85 for a shared bathroom option (average price $65) or $80–100 for an en suite, while dorm beds usually cost $25, though rates can range from $20 to $34. *Alishan Guesthouse* (p.173), *Bernly Private Hotel* (p.169), *BIG* (p.168), *Glenferrie Lodge* (p.173) and *Highfield Private Hotel* (p.169) also offer dorm beds.

City centre

base backpackers 477 Kent St ⓣ02/9267 7718, ⓦwww.basebackpackers.com. Town Hall CityRail. This huge, modern 360-bed hostel is in a good location near the Town Hall. Having recently undergone a name change and a complete refurbishment, this hostel is well set up with two TV rooms, laundry and Internet facilities, a newly renovated kitchen and a solarium (for that all year tan). Globetrotting single gals can enjoy their "Sanctuary" concept, a women-only section of the hostel featuring all the comforts of home, including hairdryers in the bathrooms, free AVEDA hair care products and feather pillows. Well-furnished rooms and dorms, (four-, six-, eight- and ten-bed), all have air-con with shared bathrooms. Dorms $26–34, rooms $89.

Sydney Backpackers Victoria House, 7 Wilmot St ⓣ02/9267 7772 or 1800 88 77 66, ⓦwww.sydneybackpackers.com. Town Hall CityRail. Very central choice off the George Street cinema strip. Clean and spacious, although lacking a little in atmosphere, staff encourage sociability and there's a comfortable, colourful common room with cable TV, books and Internet access. Small but clean kitchen. Four-, eight-, ten- and twelve-bed dorms – one en-suite dorm on every floor – and spacious doubles and twins; all have air-con, cable TV, fridges and lockers. Modern but cramped bathrooms. Dorms $27–34, rooms $80.

The Wood Duck Inn 49 William St, East Sydney ⓣ02/9358 5856 or 1800 110 025, ⓦwww.woodduckinn.com.au. Hostel run by two switched-on brothers in a great spot right near the Australian Museum and Hyde Park and at the safer city end of William Street. The dingy and seemingly endless flights of concrete steps are off-putting, but you emerge onto a sunny rooftop, the nerve centre of the hostel, with fantastic park and city views. Here you'll find the all-day reception-cum-bar, BBQ, a small but functional kitchen (plenty of fridge space), laundry and a TV/dining room with quirky surfboard tabletops. Accommodation is on the floors below; expect polished wood floors, citrus-coloured walls, high ceilings, and fresh flowers. Spacious, clean dorms (mostly four- and six-bed; one en suite for women) have fans, good mattresses and cage lockers under the bunks. Lots of activities, including free lifts to the beach. Dorms $22.

Haymarket

See map on p.96 for locations.

Footprints Westend 412 Pitt St, Haymarket ⓣ02/9211 4588 or 1800 013 186, ⓦwww.footprintswestend.com.au. Central CityRail. Bright and contemporary hostel in a large renovated hotel close to Central Station and

Chinatown. Common areas are spick-and-span with funky furniture and there's a big modern kitchen and dining area, and a pool table. The young staff are local, clued-up and organize nights out and tours. Some rooms have TV and/or minifridge while dorms (four- and six-bed) come with lockers; all are en suite with nice bedding. Many rooms have air-con: request these in summer, as there are no fans. Travel centre and small café with Internet downstairs. 24hr reception. Dorms $28–30, rooms $69, en suites, including breakfast, $85.

Maze Backpackers 417 Pitt St, Haymarket ⓣ02/9211 5115, ⓦwww.nomadsworld.com. Central CityRail. With charming original 1908 features, this huge hostel is a good choice if you're after a single room ($50); there are sixty of them, although they're tiny, cubicle-like and dim. The atmosphere is sociable and all rooms and dorms (four- to six-bed) have ceiling fans, but stark fluoro lighting and shared bathrooms. Doubles have a wardrobe, chair and bedside table. The kitchens are small and lacking in facilities. Yoga classes every Friday. 24hr reception. Dorms $22–24, rooms $55–62.

Railway Square YHA 8–10 Lee St, cnr Upper Carriage Lane ⓣ02/9281 9666, ⓔwww.railway@yhansw.org.au. Central CityRail. It's all about location, and this brand new architect-designed hostel in a historic 1905 industrial building is literally next to the tracks of Central Station – some of the dorm rooms are in actual train carriages and can look out over the early-morning commuters. A swimming pool/spa, Internet café and kiosk serving light meals, travel centre, excellent noticeboards and planned activities, funky indoor and outdoor common areas and heated floors in the bathrooms make this a very comfortable hostel to stay in. Dorms $27–33, rooms $78, en suite $88.

▼ Railway Square YHA

Sydney Central YHA Cnr Pitt St and Rawson Place, opposite Central Station ⓣ02/9281 9111, ⓔsydcentral@yhansw.org.au. Central CityRail. Very successful YHA in a centrally located listed building transformed into a huge and snazzy hostel with over 550 beds, which are almost always full. Hotel-like facilities but very sociable. Spacious four- and six-bed dorms and twins sharing bathrooms or en-suite twins and doubles. Wide range of amenities, including employment desk, travel agency, rooftop pool, sauna and BBQ area. 24hr reception. Licensed bistro plus a cute, popular basement bar, *Scu Bar* (see p.211). Some parking available. Maximum stay fourteen days. For longer stays, the YHA also has a "working holidaymaker hostel" at Dulwich Hill (ⓣ02/9550 0054). Dorms $28–33, rooms $82, en suites $94.

wake up! 509 Pitt St, opposite Railway Square ⓣ02/9264 4121, ⓦwww.wakeup.com.au. Central CityRail. The catchy name goes perfectly with the oh so trendy atmosphere of this mega-backpackers' complex (over 500 beds). The vibrant interior sits inside a character, turn-of-the-twentieth-century corner building, Highly styled – right down to the black-clad staff in the huge intimidating foyer with its banks of Internet terminals it could be anywhere in the world. Rooms, which aren't as stylish as you'd expect, are light-filled and well furnished; only nine doubles are en suite. Dorms (four-, six-, eight- and ten-bed) have lockers. Facilities include a streetside café and an underground late-opening bar and eatery. The best feature is the huge modern kitchen, on a corner with gigantic windows overlooking busy Railway Square. Dorms $24–33, rooms $88, en suite $98.

Surry Hills

Kangaroo Bakpak 665 South Dowling St, Surry Hills ⓣ02/9319 5915, ⓦwww.kangaroobakpak.com.au. Bus #372, #393 & #395 from Central CityRail. Small, clean and very friendly family-run backpackers' hostel in a terraced house on a major traffic artery – though it's surprisingly calm inside. Spacious dorms (three-, four- or six-bed) are well furnished and most have lockers. There's a BBQ in a green area out back. The owners also run *Gracelands Budget Accommodation* on nearby Cleveland Street, which is aimed more at long-stayers (weekly rates only), with more twins and doubles; rooms are brightly painted and there's a great common room downstairs. Dorms $22–26, rooms $60.

Darlinghurst

Y on the Park 5–11 Wentworth Ave ⓣ9264 2451, ⓦwww.ywca-sydney.com.au. Museum CityRail. Surprisingly stylish and very comfortable YWCA (both sexes welcome) in a great location just off Oxford Street and near Hyde Park. The huge range of rooms cater to all levels of traveller – "corporate" (single $118 and twin $136) have Internet connections and "deluxe" ($130) come with a pamper pack and plunger coffee. Regular rooms have all you'd expect in a good hotel, and come in en-suite, shared-bathroom or self-catering studio varieties ($134). There are good-value singles ($74), as well as single rates in larger rooms, and four-bed dorms (made-up beds with towel, no bunks). There's no common kitchen, but facilities include a café (open 7am–8pm) and a laundry. Rates include a light breakfast. Dorms $33, rooms $88, standard en suite $130.

Kings Cross and Potts Point

Backpackers Headquarters 79 Bayswater Rd, Kings Cross ⓣ02/9331 6180, ⓦwww.backpackershqhostel.com.au. Kings Cross CityRail. In a quieter position close to Rushcutters Bay, this modern hostel is well run but showing some cracks around the edges. Large, bright, partitioned dorms for six or ten people, with firm mattresses, fans, heaters and mirrors; only two doubles. Usual amenities plus big-screen TV in the lounge area, sun deck and BBQ area on the rooftop. Excellent security. Dorms $22, rooms $64.

Blue Parrot Backpackers 87 Macleay St, Potts Point ⓣ02/9356 4888, ⓦwww.blueparrot.com.au. Kings Cross CityRail. In a great position in the trendy (and quieter) part of Potts Point, and with helpful staff, this converted mansion is sunny, airy, brightly painted and tastefully furnished. One of its best features is the huge courtyard garden out back with wooden furniture and big shady trees, looking onto a heritage building but 8.30pm curfews been introduced to give the neighbours a break). Mostly six- and eight-bed dorms; one four-bed dorm but no doubles or twins. Common room has cable TV, gas fire and free Internet. Dorms $25–27.

Eva's Backpackers 6–8 Orwell St, Potts Point ⓣ02/9358 2185, ⓦwww.evasbackpackers.com.au. Kings Cross CityRail. Recommended family-run hostel away from Darlinghurst Road's clamour. Colourful and clean rooms and common areas. Four-, six-, eight- and ten-bed dorms; four-beds are en suite. Peaceful rooftop garden with table umbrellas, greenery, BBQ area and fantastic views over The Domain. The guest kitchen/dining room, positioned at street level, feels like a café and is conducive to socializing, though this isn't a "party" hostel. Dorms $22–26, rooms $60–70.

Jolly Swagman 27 Orwell St, Kings Cross ⓣ02/9358 6400, ⓦwww.jollyswagman.com.au. Kings Cross CityRail. Vibrant, long-established hostel geared towards the louder, liveller backpacker. Organized social events range from sports to pub crawls; in-house travel centre, good notice boards and work connections. Along with the usual communal facilities, every room has its own fridge and lockers; there are also four- to six-bed dorms. Cheap licensed café with Internet access out front. 24hr reception. Dorms $24, rooms $65.

Kanga House 141 Victoria St, Kings Cross ⓣ02/9357 7897, ⓦwww.kangahouse.com.au. Kings Cross CityRail. On leafy Victoria Street, this terraced-house hostel may have fairly ordinary-to-rundown facilities – though it's regularly repainted – but the city views are tremendous from the back rooms, taking in the bridge and Opera House. Staff are friendly, the atmosphere is laid-back and it's still one of the cheapest hostels in the Cross. Dorms are four-, six- and eight-bed and doubles have sink, TV, microwave and fridge. The sunny courtyard is used for regular BBQs. Dorms $22, rooms $50–65.

The Original Backpackers Lodge 160–162 Victoria St, Kings Cross ⓣ02 9356 3232 or 1800 807 130, ⓦwww.originalbackpackers.com.au. Kings Cross CityRail. In a spacious Victorian mansion with gorgeous ornate ceilings, chandeliers and artwork throughout, this hostel tends to have a quieter clientele. A large kitchen and sunny, café-style courtyard back onto clean lounge and common areas with comfy chairs, internet and cable TV. All rooms have a TV and fridge and security lockers and a laundry are available at the 24hr reception. Dorms (six-, eight- or ten-bed) $24–25, rooms $65.

The Pink House 6–8 Barncleuth Square, Kings Cross ⓣ02/9358 1689 or 1800 806 385, ⓦwww.pinkhouse.com.au. Kings Cross CityRail. Attractive Art Deco mansion with big dorms – up to eight-bed – and a few doubles, some with en suite sink and shower but none with toilet. All the expected amenities plus cable TV in the common room and garden courtyards with BBQ. Friendly and very peaceful but also close to the action on the other side of the strip. Dorms $24, rooms $80, en suite $100.

Rucksack Rest 9 McDonald St, Potts Point ⓣ02/9358 2348. Kings Cross CityRail. Small (thirty-bed), well-run private hostel in a lovely old terraced house, exuding a shabby charm. Very friendly atmosphere, quiet leafy location and on-site local owner-manager. Facilities include a BBQ area and an outdoor kitchen perfect for summer. Three-bed dorms and doubles. Not a party hostel. Dorms $20, rooms from $50.

Glebe

Glebe Point YHA 262 Glebe Point Rd ⓣ02/9692 8418, ⓔglebe@yhansw.org.au. Bus #431, #433 & #434 from Central CityRail. Reliable YHA standard with helpful staff who organize lots of activities. The hostel sleeps just over 150 in a mix of private rooms – no en suites – as well as four- and five-bed dorms. All the usual facilities plus a pool table, luggage storage and roof terrace with city views. Dorms $24–28, rooms $68.

Glebe Village Backpackers 256 Glebe Point Rd ⓣ02/9660 8133 or 1800 801 983, ⓦwww.glebevillage.com Bus #431, #433 & #434 from Central CityRail. Three large old houses with a mellow, sociable atmosphere, more akin to that of a guesthouse than a hostel – the generally laid-back guests socialize in the leafy streetside fairy-lit garden. Staffed by young locals who know what's going on around town. Doubles and twins plus four-, six-, ten- or twelve-bed dorms. Dorms $26–30, rooms $75.

Wattle House Hostel 44 Hereford St ⓣ02/9552 4997, ⓦwww.wattlehouse.com.au. Bus #431, #433 & #434 from Central CityRail. Top-class small, cosy and clean privately owned hostel in a restored terraced house on a quiet street. Four-bed dorms and well-furnished doubles (no en suites). Pretty gardens and an outdoor eating area make staying here extra pleasant, and there's even a library room. Rates include linen and towels. Very popular, so book in advance. Dorms $27, rooms $75–85.

Newtown

Billabong Gardens 5–11 Egan St, off King St ⓣ02/9550 3236, ⓦwww.billabonggardens.com.au. Newtown CityRail. In a quiet street but close to the action, this long-running purpose-built hostel is arranged around a peaceful inner courtyard with swimming pool and, though there's now some competition, is still the best hostel in Newtown, with excellent communal facilities. It offers clean dorms (four- to six-bed; some en suite), single ($49), twin and double rooms and motel-style en suites. Parking is limited and metered in Newtown, so there's a daily charge for the popular undercover car park. Dorms $23–25, rooms $66, en suite $88.

Bondi

Bondi Beachhouse YHA 63 Fletcher St, cnr Dellview Street ⓣ02/9365 2088, ⓔbondi@intercoast.com.au. Bus #380 from Bondi Junction CityRail. The YHA's latest beach hostel, a former student boarding house, is actually closer to Tamarama Beach than its namesake Bondi but benefits from being slightly removed from the latter's often overly frenetic atmosphere, and the cafés, restaurants and shops of Bondi Road are close by. International students still form a large slice of its guests, hence the availability of buffet-style breakfasts and dinners at cut-rate prices in the big dining room; there's also a small but very well-equipped guest kitchen and regular free surfing talks. Brightly painted with a sunny internal courtyard with BBQ, and a rooftop deck with fabulous ocean views. Spacious high-ceilinged dorms (four-, six- and eight-bed, with lockers) and rooms – some en suite, with fridges and kettles – all have ceiling fans. Bag a beach-view room which go for the same price. Dorms $27, rooms $70, en suite $80.

Noah's Backpackers 2 Campbell Parade, Bondi Beach ⓣ02/9365 7100 or 1800 226 662, ⓦwww.noahsbondibeach.com. Bus #380 from Bondi Junction CityRail. Huge hostel right opposite the beach. Fantastic ocean views from the rooftop deck with a BBQ area and kitchen conveniently on hand. Beach-view rooms with sink, TV, fridge, fan, chair and lockable cupboard. Four-, six- and eight-bed dorms have sinks, lockers, table and chairs. Clean and well run but with cramped bathrooms. On-site bar, TV room and pool table; greasy-spoon food available. Excellent security. Dorms $24, rooms $55, beach-view $65.

Coogee

Coogee Beachside 178 Coogee Bay Rd, Coogee ⓣ02/9315 8511, ⓦwww.sydneybeachside .com.au. Bus #372 from Central CityRail & #373, #374 & #376 from Circular Quay CityRail. Airy old two-storey house, pleasantly renovated, with wooden floors. All rooms and dorms (four- and six-bed) come with TV, in-house videos and fans but share bathrooms. Doubles and family rooms also have fridge. Small well-equipped kitchen but no common room – everyone hangs out in the big, sunny back garden. Up the hill from the beach but handy for shops and the supermarket. Dorms $22, rooms $65.

Wizard of Oz Backpackers 172 Coogee Bay Rd, Coogee ⓣ02/9315 7876, ⓦwww .wizardofoz.com.au. Bus #372 from Central CityRail & #373, #374 & #376 from Circular Quay CityRail. Top-class hostel run by a friendly local couple in a big and beautiful Californian-style house with a huge verandah and polished wooden floors. Spacious, vibrantly painted dorms with ceiling fans, and some well-set-up doubles. TV/video room, dining area, modern kitchen, good showers and big pleasant backyard with BBQ. The owners also rent out furnished one-bedroom apartments (sleeping up to four) with linen supplied at nearby *Coogee Beachside Budget Accomodation*, 178 Coogee Bay Rd ($120 per night, min three nights, or from $490 per week). Dorms $22–25, rooms $55–99.

Manly

Boardrider Backpackers 63 The Corso, Manly ⓣ02/9977 6077, ⓦwww.boardrider.com.au. Ferry to Manly Wharf. Clean hostel in a great spot on the Corso (entry round the back) only metres from the surf beach and even closer to the just-renovated *New Brighton Hotel*. Several rooms and dorms have balconies, some with ocean views, but the constant pub and club action at street level can make it noisy at night. Modern facilities include a large, well-equipped kitchen and dining area, big common room and lockers in the bedrooms and good security; some en suites. Rooftop terrace with BBQ. Dorms $25, rooms $69, en suite $79.

Manly Backpackers Beachside 28 Raglan St, Manly ⓣ02/9977 3411, ⓦwww .manlybackpackers.com.au. Ferry to Manly Wharf. Under new management, this "hostel with lifestyle" is a modern and purpose-built two-storey building one block from the surf. One of the few hostels that manages to be both clean and fun, this place has free Internet access, a spacious well-equipped kitchen and outside terrace with BBQ and offers group movie discounts at the local cinema. Attracts long-stayers. Twin and double rooms – all share bathroom – plus small three-bed dorms (six-bed is largest). Best dorm is at the front with a balcony. Dorms $22, rooms $62.

Manly Guest House Backpackers 6 Steinton St, Manly ⓣ02/9977 0884, Ferry to Manly Wharf. A little further from the action on the Corso but still only a few steps to the beach, this place feels a little shabbier, though quieter, than the other hostels around. Big common area and kitchen, and clean linen supplied. Single $40, double $50; all share bathrooms; triple rooms available. Small dorms $25, rooms $69.

Northern beaches

See map on p.137 for locations.

Avalon Beach Hostel 59 Avalon Parade, Avalon ⓣ02/9918 9709, ⓔgunilla@avalonbeach.com .au. Bus #L88 & #L90 from Central CityRail or Wynyard CityRail. This hostel, at one of Sydney's best – and most beautiful – surf beaches, has seen better days, but its location and atmosphere still make it worth considering. Built mainly of timber, it has an airy beachhouse feel with breezy balconies, warming open fires in winter, and plenty of greenery and rainbow lorikeets to gaze at. The hostel could be cleaner, and bathroom facilities are stretched at peak times, though are apparently undergoing renovations.

Dorms (four- and six-bed) and rooms have storage area and fans. Boat trips can be organized; surfboard rental available. Excellent local work contacts. Dorms $20–22, rooms $55.

Sydney Beachhouse YHA 4 Collaroy St, Collaroy Beach ⓣ02/9981 1177, ⓦwww.sydneybeachouse.com.au. Bus from Manly Ferry Wharf: #151, #155 & #156; bus from Central CityRail and Wynyard CityRail: #L88 & #L90. Purpose-built beachside YHA hostel with a casual, relaxed attitude. Heated outdoor swimming pool, sun deck, BBQs, open fireplaces, video lounge and games and pool rooms. Four- to six-bed dorms plus several doubles (some en suite) and family rooms. Too far out for your entire Sydney stay (45min bus ride from the city), it's a good base for kicking back on the sand or exploring the northern beaches – bikes are free for guests – and kayaking and sailing can be organized. Free use of boogie- and surfboards with surfing lessons for weekly guests and didgeridoo lessons on offer. Internet available. Free parking. Dorms $20–26, rooms $64, en suite $84.

Cronulla

See map on p.153 for location.

Cronulla Beach YHA 40 Kingsway, Cronulla ⓣ9527 7772, ⓦwww.cronullabeachyha.com.au. Cronulla CityRail. No fuss, friendly hostel in this unpretentious, surf-side suburb, two minutes from the sand and even less to the shops and restaurants in Cronulla Mall. Well situated for day-trips to the Royal National Park; the friendly live-in manager offers surf trips. Surfboards, kayaks and bicycles for rent but free use of boogie boards. Private rooms are en suite and there are four- and six-bed dorms, all with fans and lockers, plus Internet, pool table and TV/video room. It's so popular that plans for expansion are underway. Dorms $21–26, rooms $55.

Staying longer

If you're staying for any length of time, you might want to consider a **flat-share** as an alternative to hotels or hostels. The best place to look is in Saturday's real-estate section of the *Sydney Morning Herald* or on café notice boards, especially in King Street in Newtown, Glebe Point Road in Glebe and Hall Street in Bondi Beach (the window of the health-food store at 29 Hall St is crammed with house-share notices aimed at travellers). The average room price in a shared house in these areas is $150 a week (rent is usually two weeks in advance, plus a deposit, called a "bond", of four weeks' rent, and you'll normally need to provide at least your own bedroom furniture and linen). Sleeping With The Enemy, 373 Bulwara Rd, Ultimo (ⓣ02/9211 8878, ⓦwww.sleepingwiththeenemy.com) organizes travellers' house-shares in inner-city terraced houses; homes are fully equipped, but expect to share a room with up to five others (from $120 per week for a one-month stay, cheaper for longer stays).

Eating

Sydney has blossomed into one of the great **restaurant** capitals of the world, and offers a fantastic range of cosmopolitan eateries, covering every imaginable cuisine. Quality is uniformly high, with the freshest produce, meat and seafood always on hand, and a culinary culture of discerning, well-informed diners. The places we've listed below barely scratch the surface of what's available and, as the restaurant scene is highly fashionable, businesses rise in favour, fall in popularity and close down or change names and style at an astonishing rate. For a comprehensive guide, consider investing in the latest edition of *Cheap Eats in Sydney* or the *Sydney Morning Herald Good Food Guide*, both of which try to keep track of the best places in town.

Sydney has several great eat streets, each with a glut of cafés and restaurants: **Victoria Street** and **Oxford Street** in Darlinghurst; **Macleay Street** in Potts Point; **Crown Street** in Surry Hills; **King Street** in Newtown; **Glebe Point Road** in Glebe; the **Darling Street strip** running from Rozelle to Balmain; and on the North Shore, **Military Road**, running from Neutral Bay to Mosman and **Miller Street**, from North Sydney to Cammeray. By the sea, **Bondi Beach**, **Coogee** and **Manly** all have countless café and dining options. All New South Wales's restaurants are nonsmoking, except for at reception areas and outside tables.

Cafés, snacks and light meals

The city boasts a thriving café scene, and a selection of the best can be found along **Victoria Street** in Darlinghurst; **Challis Avenue** in Potts Point; **Glebe Point Road** in Glebe; **King Street** in Newtown; and in the beachside neighbourhoods of **Bondi**, **Bronte** and **Coogee**. Sydney can thank its sizeable Italian population for having elevated **coffee-drinking** to the status of a serious pastime: in the local coffee lingo, a flat white is a cappuccino without the froth; a cafe latte is a milkier version served in a glass; a long black is a regular black coffee; and a short black is an espresso (transformed by a splash of milk into a *macchiato*). Any of these will cost $2.80–3.50 and, except for in the most traditional Italian joints, are also available with soya milk. Most cafés are open for breakfast, particularly those in the beach areas, and some stay open until the small hours. All those listed are inexpensive, many serving main courses for $14 or less.

The Rocks

There isn't really a café culture in **The Rocks** and it's hard to find a decent cup of coffee or a reasonably priced light meal or snack. Pubs rule supreme, and many of those in The Rocks serve great light meals and bar snacks at lunchtime; see pp.207–208 of the "Drinking" chapter, where we've mentioned the kind of meals served. It's also only a hop, skip and jump from Circular Quay, where there's a much wider choice.

Sydney Dance Cafe Pier 4, Hickson Rd, Millers Point. Circular Quay CityRail/ferry. On the ground level of the Wharf Theatre complex, home to the Sydney Dance Company and several other dance, theatre and arts organizations, this is a relaxing spot for a coffee or a light meal with water views and an interesting, arty crew of fellow customers. Mains $6.50–12.50. Mon–Sat 7.30am–7.30pm.

Circular Quay and the Opera House

In addition to these listings, there's a wide choice of snacks and light meals at the Gateway Gourmet Food Court (see "Food courts" box on p.188).

City Extra East Podium, Circular Quay. Circular Quay CityRail/ferry. Licensed 24hr coffee shop with a stop-the-press theme – and, of course, newspapers for customers to read. Breakfast is served round the clock plus burgers, pasta, steaks and desserts. Quayside seating, too. Mains $13–27.

Obelisk Café Shop 1, 7 Macquarie Place. Circular Quay CityRail/ferry. Stylish outdoor café close to Circular Quay. Fab spot on a historic square with big shady trees, or you can

Ethnic eats

Sydney features many diverse enclaves, often in far-flung suburbs, where you can sample authentic cuisines from around the world and buy imported goods from local shops and delis. Where the areas are detailed in the text, we've given page references; where they are not, we have provided transport details to point you in the right direction.

African On King Street, Newtown (see p.115).

Chinese In the Chinatown section of Haymarket (see p.97) and in Ashfield (Ashfield CityRail).

Indian On Elizabeth Street and Cleveland Street in Surry Hills (p.99) and on King Street, St Peters (p.115).

Indonesian On Anzac Parade, Kingsford and Kensington (bus #393 or #395 from Central CityRail).

Italian On Stanley Street in East Sydney (p.101), Norton Street in Leichhardt (p.116), Ramsay Street in Haberfield (p.117) and Great North Road, Five Dock (bus #438 from Central CityRail).

Japanese There's a concentration at Bondi Junction (Bondi Junction CityRail), Neutral Bay (see p.129) and Crows Nest (bus #273 from WynyardCityRail).

Jewish On and around Hall Street, Bondi (p.137).

Korean In Campsie (Campsie CityRail).

Lebanese On Elizabeth Street and Cleveland Street in Surry Hills; in Punchbowl (Punchbowl CityRail) and Lakemba (Lakemba CityRail).

Portuguese At New Canterbury Rd, Petersham (Petersham CityRail); Greek at Marrickville (see p.116), Earlwood (bus #409 from Ashfield CityRail), and Brighton Le Sands (bus #302 or #303 from Circular Quay CityRail).

Spanish On Liverpool Street in the city (p.80).

Turkish On Elizabeth Street and Cleveland Street in Surry Hills (p.99).

Vietnamese Concentrated in Cabramatta, far to the west of the CBD (fourteen stops from Central CityRail); there are some superb restaurants clustered along Park Road and John Street, just west of Cabramatta Station.

sit inside on stools and listen to jazzy music on a wet day. Attracts a working crowd who plunge in for great coffee, pizzetta, Turkish bread sandwiches and salads. Breakfast $3.50–12, lunch $8.50–13.50. Mon–Fri 6am–5pm, Sat & Sun 9am–1pm.

Rossini Between wharves 5 and 6, Circular Quay. Circular Quay CityRail/ferry. Eat quality Italian fast food alfresco while you're waiting for a ferry. Panzerotto – big, cinnamon-flavoured and ricotta-filled doughnuts – are a speciality. Pricey but excellent coffee. Mains $7–13. Licensed. Daily 7am–11pm.

Sydney Cove Oyster Bar Circular Quay East. Circular Quay CityRail/ferry. It's hard not to be lured into this place on a stroll to the Opera House. The quaint little building housing the bar and kitchen was once a public toilet, but don't let that put you off. Outdoor tables provide a magical location to sample Sydney Rock Pacific oysters (from $17.50 for half a dozen). There's other seafood as well, or just come for coffee, cake and the view. Mains generally $29–37 and up to $129 for their "Ultimate Indulgence" seafood platter. Daily 11am–11pm.

Royal Botanical Gardens to Macquarie Street

There are also great cafés in this area at the Hyde Park Barracks (see p.77), the old Mint building (see p.77), and within the Botanical Gardens (see p.73) and the Art Gallery of NSW (see p.78).

Glasshouse Café Level 7, State Library, Macquarie St. Martin Place CityRail. Airy and with masses of plants, this glass-roofed space at the State Library is a relaxing spot for lunch (Mon–Fri, mains $22–27) or just coffee and cake in the adjacent Cafe Trim (Mon–Fri 8.30am–4.30pm, Sat & Sun 11am–4pm).

Pavilion on the Park 1 Art Gallery Rd. Martin Place or St James CityRail. Right opposite the Art Gallery of New South Wales and just by the Botanical Gardens entrance, this is a great place to take a break from sightseeing – there's an outdoor kiosk, a café section and an upmarket restaurant (bookings ⓣ02/9232 1322), rated for its expensive modern Australian cuisine and great views of the city. Restaurant mains $28–32. Licensed. Café daily 9am–5pm; restaurant lunch daily, dinner Sat.

City centre

Nearly all of the **city centre** pubs and bars serve great light meals and bar snacks at lunchtime; see the listings on pp.209–210. There are also several cosmopolitan food courts which are a great source of cheap and tasty snacks and light meals (see "Food courts" box on p.188), and loads of great little Italian espresso bars (see box "City coffee hits" on p.187). You can also get scrummy snacks and light meals from the wonderful David Jones Food Hall (see "Shopping", p.254).

Bill and Toni 74 Stanley St, East Sydney. Museum CityRail. This atmospheric, cheap Italian restaurant (mains $8.50–15) with balcony tables is an institution, and there's generally a queue snaking up the stairs to get in. Once you're finally seated beneath the Italian landscape murals, huge servings of simple home-made pasta and sauces hit the spot. The café downstairs is a popular Stanley Street local (daily 7am–midnight) and serves tasty Italian sandwiches. BYO. Dinner daily.

Bodhi in the Park Cook and Phillip Park, College St, East Sydney. Museum CityRail (another branch at Capitol Square, 730–742 George St, Haymarket). Top-notch Chinese vegetarian and vegan food, with the focus on delicious *yum cha* which is served daily until 5pm (mains $9–18). Organic and biodynamic produce is used. A good option if you've just been for a swim in the adjacent park pool, or for a visit to the nearby Australian Museum. Licensed. Daily 11am–11pm.

Lindt Café 53 Martin Place, East Sydney. Martin Place Cityrail. In somewhat of a coup for Sydney, the world's first Lindt Café opened its doors in the CBD in mid-2004 and brought the world-renowned Swiss Chocolatier's temptations to a sit-down audience. A surprisingly creative and tasty range of gourmet sandwiches are on offer at lunchtime ($6–12.50) but the stars of the show are the to-die-for desserts ($2.80–13) and the dark iced chocolate drinks. You can even come here early for breakfast ($2.50–10.50). Chocaholics beware, this experience is definitely not for the calorie-shy. Mon–Fri 7am–6pm, Sat 10am–3pm.

QVB Jet Cnr York and Druitt streets. Town Hall CityRail. On the corner of the QVB building looking across to the Town Hall, with big windows and outdoor seating providing people-watching opportunities, this is a very lively Italian café/bar. The coffee is predictably excellent, and the menu is big on breakfast. The rest of the day choose from pasta and risotto (mains $15–21) plus soups, salads and sandwiches. Licensed. Mon–Fri 8am–10pm, Sat 9am–10pm.

Darling Harbour and around

Also check out the "Food courts" box for several great Asian-style food courts around Chinatown.

Fish Market Cafe Sydney Fish Markets, Pyrmont. Fish Market Light Rail. Come and watch the early morning fish-market action (or just head here after a very late night out) and grab breakfast and an excellent coffee at this Italian-run café. You can eat inexpensive fresh fish and chips later in the day. Mon–Fri 4am–4pm, Sat & Sun 5am–5pm.

wagamama 10/45 Lime St, King St Wharf. Town Hall CityRail (also on Bridge St, City and Crown St, Surry Hills). Huge high-tech Japanese noodle bar based on the London model: young trendy staff equipped with a computerized ordering system, communal tables and no bookings (which can mean long queues), though service and turnover is fast. No desserts. Average main $13. Licensed but a basic drinks list, which includes sake. Daily from noon to 10pm Mon–Wed & Sun, 11pm Thurs, midnight Fri & Sat.

Haymarket

Bella Ciao Shop 5, 187 Thomas St, cnr Quay St, Haymarket. Central CityRail. A café culture spot in Chinatown is a find: colourful 1950s fish-shop feel, huge windows and funky music. Breakfast until 2pm – blueberry bagels with fresh ricotta and Hank's legendary jam go well with the excellent Italian coffee. Lunch on woodfired bread sandwiches, soups and salads; very reasonable prices. Mon–Fri 7am–6pm, Sat 8.30am–2pm. Moderate.

Delizia 148 Elizabeth St, City. Museum CityRail. A high-ceilinged Italian deli-café bustling with black-clad staff: the gleaming glass counters groan with pasta dishes and the shelves are stacked with gourmet goods. It looks pricey, but there's nothing much over $10 on the menu. With a secondhand literary bookshop tucked out the back, *Gertrude and Alice* (an offshoot of the popular Bondi bookstore-café), there's nothing else like it in the city. The tables and lounge chairs among the bookshelves create a private haven. Weekend breakfasts here are popular – most other city cafés are closed then. Mon–Fri 7am–6pm, Sat & Sun 8am–4pm.

Ippon Sushi 404 Sussex St, Haymarket. Central CityRail. Fun, inexpensive Japanese sushi train downstairs, with a revolving choice of delectable dishes from $2 to $5.50 (depending on plate colour) and a proper menu upstairs. Licensed and BYO. Daily 11am–11pm.

Island Dreams Fusion Café 40–50 Campbell St, Haymarket. Central CityRail. For something completely different, try the halal fare from the tiny Cocos and Christmas islands (situated in the Indian Ocean near Indonesia and Malaysia). The place itself is a little oasis in the city. Daily specials complement hearty regulars like the *nasi goring* (spicy tomato rice with shrimp, a choice of meat and a runny fried egg) and delicious home-made *roti* paired with the *ayam panggang* (BBQ chicken in chilli sauce). No alcohol. Mon–Thu 8am–9pm, Fri 8am–9.30pm, Sat 9.30am–9.30pm, Sun 9.30am–9pm.

Pasteur 709 George St, Haymarket. They mysteriously dropped "pho" from the name, but *pho* (Vietnamese rice noodle soup, served with fresh herbs, lemon, bean sprouts and meat) is exactly what you get at this popular though simple eatery. Most noodles (mainly pork, chicken and beef) are $9, and there's nothing over $12. Refreshing pot of jasmine tea included. BYO. Daily 10am–9pm.

Roma Caffe 191 Hay St, Haymarket. The veteran *Roma* offers fabulous coffee, great breakfasts and a huge gleaming display of wicked Italian desserts, plus delicious focaccia with every imaginable topping and fresh pasta – try the home-made pumpkin tortellini. Inexpensive. Mon–Sat 7.30am–5.30pm.

Silk Road Chinese Restaurant 8 Quay St. Scrumptious and very fresh dumplings and noodles, northwest Chinese halal style, and some unusual regional salads, in this modest but friendly little eatery in a lively, student-filled spot near the University of Technology's library. Very cheap. BYO. Daily 10.30am–9pm.

City coffee hits

Italian **espresso bars** are all over the CBD, many with outside seating for sunny days (and smokers...), and braziers for the winter. We've listed three of the best below. See map on p.81 for locations.

Bambini Espresso 299 Elizabeth St. Museum or Town Hall CityRail. Mon–Fri 7am–6pm.

Bar Milazzo 379 Pitt St. Museum or Town Hall CityRail. Mon–Fri 7am–6pm.

Caffe Corto 10 Barrack St. Martin Place CityRail. Mon–Fri 7am–4.30pm.

Inner east

The **inner east** has probably the greatest concentration of cafés and also several late-night and all-night options (see box "Eating around the clock", on p.190). Its equally vast range of pubs and bars also serve up great light meals: see pp.211–214 of "Drinking".

Surry Hills

Abdul's 563 Elizabeth St, cnr Cleveland St. Bus #393, #395 from Central CityRail. This cheap Lebanese place is a late-night, post-pub institution. Eat in or take away; belly-dancing Fri & Sat nights. BYO. Daily 10am–midnight (Thurs–Sat until 2am).

Maltese Cafe 310 Crown St, Surry Hills. Bus #378 from Central CityRail; bus #380 from Circular Quay CityRail. Established in the early 1940s, this café is known for its delicious (and ridiculously cheap at $0.80) Maltese *pastizzi* – flaky pastry pockets of ricotta cheese, plain or with meat, spinach or peas – to eat in or take away. Also enormous servings of fresh lasagne and other pastas ($6.50). No alcohol. Mon 10am–8pm & Sun, Tues, Wed 8am–8pm, Thur–Sat 8am–10pm.

Maya Indian Sweets, 470 Cleveland St, Surry Hills. Bus #393, #395 from Central CityRail. A recent expansion means this very cheap, authentic South Indian cafeteria-style restaurant (you pay at the counter) can now fit in even more people to enjoy its exquisite vegetarian food, including dosas, *chaat* salads, *paneer kulcha*, thalis and more. Very popular with local Indian families, especially at weekends for the delicious snack menu. A vast display of very sickly Indian sweets too. BYO. Daily 10am–10.30pm.

Rustic Café 560 Crown St, Surry Hills. Bus #378 from Central CityRail; #380 from Circular Quay CityRail. This bright yellow corner building has been a Sydney fixture for years and, with its combination of good-value comfort food – any of the breads are great – and enjoyable atmosphere, it's a good bet for a hearty breakfast or a late night munch. There's an outdoor area too. Moderate. Licensed and BYO. Tues–Sat 7.30am–11pm, Sun 9am–9pm.

Darlinghurst

Darlinghurst also boasts a branch of the gourmet burger joint, *Burgerman* (see p.192), and you can get cheap but fresh noodles nearby at *Noodle King*.

Bar Coluzzi 322 Victoria St, Darlinghurst. Kings Cross CityRail. "45 years and still going strong" announces the sign over this famous Italian café; it is tiny but always packed with a diverse crew of regulars spilling out onto wooden stools on the pavement and partaking of the standard menu of foccacias, muffins, open bagels and of course coffee. You can watch from a safe distance at the trendier, though equally tiny and very popular *Latteria* next door. Daily from 5am–6pm.

Betty's Soup Kitchen 84 Oxford St, Darlinghurst. Bus #378 from Central CityRail, bus #380 from Circular Quay CityRail. As the name suggests, soup is the speciality and with continually changing specials makes for a cheap but filling meal, served with damper bread (an Australian campfire staple). There's also a range of very simple but cheerful mains like thicker stews, sausages or fish fingers with mash, pasta and salads. Yummy home-made ginger beer or lemonade and desserts available. Nothing over $15. BYO. Daily noon–10.30pm, Fri & Sat to 11.30pm.

bills 433 Liverpool St, Darlinghurst. Kings Cross CityRail. Owned by celebrity chef Bill Granger, this sunny corner café–restaurant in the quieter, terraced house-filled

Food courts

Some of the best cheap eats in Sydney, with hot dishes at $6–10, are to be found in the multitude of cosmopolitan **food courts** in city shopping malls, mainly along the Pitt Street Mall. Those around Chinatown are also particularly good, serving everything from Japanese to Vietnamese, and of course Chinese food.

Dixon House Food Court Off Dixon St, basement level, corner of Little Hay and Dixon streets. Central CityRail. Chinese noodles, Vietnamese, Thai, Indonesian, Malaysian, Japanese and Korean plus a bar. Daily 10.30am–8.30pm. See map on p.96.

Gateway Gourmet Quayside Shopping Centre, ground floor, bounded by Alfred St, Reiby Pl and Loftus St, Circular Quay. Circular Quay Cityrail/ferry. Pizza, pasta, seafood, patisserie, healthy sandwiches and Asian food. Business hours. See map on p.67.

Harbour Plaza Corner Factory and Dixon streets, Haymarket. Central CityRail. Food court in basement. More lacklustre than other Chinatown food courts. Malaysian, Japanese, Korean, Indonesian, and Vietnamese. Licensed bar. Daily 10am–10pm. See map on p.96.

Hunter Connection 310 George St, City. Wynyard CityRail. Fantastic and frenetically busy food court on the first floor with a small supermarket, sushi bar, fresh juice shop, sandwiches, noodles, seafood, pasta, Asian buffet, plus Mexican, Filipino, Malaysian and Chinese food. Business hours. See map on p.81.

Market City Food Court Level 3, Market City Shopping Centre, corner Quay and Thomas streets, Haymarket. Central CityRail. Apart from one Italian place they are all Asian – Vietnamese, Chinese, Japanese, Thai and Singaporean. The best stall is *McLuksa* – the spicy coconut noodle soups which give it its name are delicious. Daily 8am–10pm. See map on p.96.

Sussex Centre 401 Sussex St, Haymarket. Central CityRail. Food court on first floor. Vietnamese, Japanese, several Chinese. Delicious natural ice cream. Daily 10am–9pm. See map on p.96.

Sydney Central 450 George St, City. Town Hall CityRail. Buzzing basement food court beneath Myer department store. Enter from Pitt St Mall or via the QVB. Mon–Wed 7am–7pm, Thurs 7am–10pm, Sat 8am–7pm, Sun 10am–6pm. See map on p.81.

▼ bills

backstreets of Darlinghurst is one of Sydney's favourite breakfast spots, with a mix-match of people gathering around the big central table and spending hours lingering over ricotta hotcakes with honeycomb butter and banana, muffins and newspapers. Breakfast isn't cheap ($15 for hotcakes), but is definitely worth it. The modern Australian lunches start at about $15. BYO. Mon–Sat 7.30am–3pm, Sun 8.30am–3pm. The bistro-style *bills surry hills*, 359 Crown St, is just as trendy and also does dinner (Mon–Fri 7am–3pm, Mon–Sat dinner 6–10pm). No bookings; *bills woollahra* has also recently opened at 118 Queen St (daily 8am–5pm; breakfast till midday, lunch till 5pm, no dinner).

Le Petit Crème 116 Darlinghurst Rd, Darlinghurst. Kings Cross CityRail. Aim for a verandah table for breakfast at this friendly and thriving French café as it's always crammed inside. Renowned for their huge, good-value filled baguettes, also on offer is steak and *frites*, omelettes, home-made paté, *pain au chocolat* and big bowls of *café au lait*. Bread and pastries are baked on the premises and can be smelt down the road. Mon–Sat 7am–3pm, Sun 8am–3pm.

Tropicana Cafe 227B Victoria St, Darlinghurst. Kings Cross CityRail. The birthplace of the Tropfest film festival (see box on p.230) this hugely popular café has recently moved to bigger digs just across the road, and is still packing in the trendies, junkies and everyone in between. Don't come for the decor, which is clinical, but for the choose your own sandwich fillings and pasta toppings, plus hearty daily specials. Licensed. Daily 5am–11pm, Fri & Sat until midnight.

Una's Coffee Lounge 340 Victoria St, Darlinghurst. Kings Cross CityRail. Cosy two-roomed open café that's been here for years dishing up schnitzel, dumplings, sauerkraut and other almost authentic German dishes that are cheap, plentiful and tasty. The big breakfasts are very popular and served til 2.30pm. BYO. Mon–Sat 6.30am–11pm, Sun 8am–11pm. Also at 133–135 Broadway, Ultimo (7.30am–10.30pm) and at 372 New South Head Rd, Double Bay (same hours).

Paddington and Woollahra

See pp.256–257 of "Shopping" for details of Woollahra's foodie focus, jones the grocer, which has a small eat-in café section.

Arthurs Pizza 260 Oxford St, Paddington. Bus #378 from Central CityRail; bus #380 from Circular Quay CityRail. Paddington pizza institution recognized by its upside down sign out front – queuing to get in is mandatory (no bookings), though once inside and seated at the crammed tables, the takeaway option seems appealing. Pizzas here are the thin kind, with a huge range of toppings (from around $14 for a small), though the fresh pasta is a very worthy alternative, BYO. Mon–Fri 5pm–midnight, Sat & Sun noon–midnight.

Sloanes Cafe 312 Oxford St, Paddington. Bus #378 from Central CityRail; bus #380 from Circular Quay CityRail. The emphasis in this veteran café is on good, unusual vegetarian food, moderately priced, but some meatier dishes have slipped onto the menu, including a BLT with guacamole to die for; the fresh juice bar has always been phenomenal. The stone-floored dining room opens onto the street for views of the Saturday market action, or for more peace eat out back under vines in the delightful courtyard. Breakfast and lunch served all day. BYO. Mon–Wed 7am–5pm, Thur–Sat 7am–10pm, Sun 7am–5pm.

Kings Cross and around

Cafe Hernandez 60 Kings Cross Rd, Kings Cross. Kings Cross CityRail. Veteran Argentinian-run 24hr coffee shop, open daily. Relaxed and friendly with a dark, old-fashioned ambience, you can dawdle here for ages and no one will make you feel unwelcome. Popular with taxi drivers and a mixed clientele of locals who don't mind looking out onto the busy road. Spanish food is served – *churros*, tortilla, *empanadas* and good pastries – but the coffee is the focus.

Harry's Café de Wheels Cnr Cowper Wharf Rd and Brougham St, Woolloomooloo. Kings Cross CityRail. Sometimes there's nothing like a good old-fashioned pie and this little cart has been serving them up to the famous and ordinary alike for over sixty years now. Some gourmet and vegetarian options have made it onto the menu but the standard meat pie with mashed peas and gravy is still the favourite, at any time of the day or night.

Il Fagiano 95 Macleay St, Potts Point. Kings Cross CityRail. Light and airy Italian café with a huge selection of fresh breads and deli items, including daily salads and antipasto as well as mini cakes and slices to go with the excellent coffee. Enormous breakfasts with the works attract the locals, who stay on for hours. Daily 7.30am–10pm.

La Buvette 35 Challis Ave, Potts Point. Kings Cross CityRail. Hole in the wall coffee stop right next door to the *Spring Espresso Bar*. Sidewalk seating is almost interchangeable and both are packed with mid-morning caffeine seekers. *La Buvette* features some unusual bite-sized French delicacies on top of the usual but yummy whiteboard menu. Daily 6am–11pm, closes 7pm on Mon.

Macleay Pizza Bar 101 Macleay St, Potts Point. Kings Cross CityRail. Unassuming pizza bar: great prices and great pizzas. Daily noon–2.30am except Fri & Sat until 4.30am.

Minami 87C Macleay St, Potts Point. Kings Cross CityRail. Blink and you'll miss this tiny,

Eating around the clock

Loads of places in Sydney cater to hungry night owls, or those in need of a late-night caffeine fix, and some are open **24 hours**. At Circular Quay, *City Extra* (p.184) is a 24-hour licensed coffee shop. There's a **late-night food court** at the Star City Casino in Pyrmont (see p.228); nearby at the **Sydney Fish Market** you can start the day at 4am at the Italian-run *Fish Market Café* (see p.186). Several late-night options can be found in **Chinatown**, such as *BBQ King* (p.196) and *Golden Century* (p.197). In **Kings Cross**, there's the 24-hour *Café Hernandez* (see p.189) and late-opening *Macleay's Pizza Bar* (see p.189). At nearby **Woolloomooloo**, *Harry's Café de Wheels* (see p.189) has dished up pies through the night for nearly sixty years. On the **North Shore** you'll find *Maisys Cafe* (p.194), open 24hr.

authentic Japanese noodle bar, where you'll find both Japanese residents and visitors squeezed around one large counter; popular choices include *ramen*, *yakisoba* and *kushikatsu*. BYO. Mon–Sat noon–1am, Sun noon–midnight.

Roy's Famous 176 Victoria St, Potts Point. Kings Cross CityRail. It's all about the meal deal at this backstreet backpacker hangout, with Sunday Roast for two people with a bottle of wine at $33 (from 6pm) and the Wednesday Pasta night, with garlic bread and glass of wine for $14.50. (from 6pm). Hearty regular menu and a friendly atmosphere. Daily 7am–10pm.

Simmone Logue 21 Elizabeth Bay Rd, Elizabeth Bay. Kings Cross CityRail. Combination deli and café, this new addition to the Simmone Logue franchise (others can be found in Balmain, Bondi Junction and Double Bay) offers a delicious range of home-made and very fresh salads, quiches and pasties, out-of-the-oven bread and desserts. The cheesecakes are especially divine with the great coffee. Sit along the sunny windowsill or take away to nearby Rushcutters Bay Park. Daily 7am–10pm.

Inner west

The **inner west**, stretching from Newtown and Glebe west to the very Italian Leichhardt and Haberfield, and harbourside Balmain, has a well-established café culture and plenty of casual eateries. The area's pubs also usually serve up bar snacks and light meals; for more options, see pp.214–215 of "Drinking".

Glebe

Badde Manors 37 Glebe Point Rd. Bus #431, #433 & #434 from Central CityRail. Veteran vegetarian corner café with a wonderful light-and-airy ambience, eclectic decor and laid-back staff; always packed, especially for weekend brunch. One of the best cafés on this strip, with yummy cakes and ice cream, and inexpensive and generous servings – nothing over $12.50. Mon–Fri 8am until midnight, Sat 8am–1am, Sun 9am–midnight.

Cafe Otto 79 Glebe Point Rd, Glebe. Bus #431, #433 & #434 from Central CityRail. With its pleasant shaded street-front courtyard, this is a good choice for a drink, a sandwich or a full meal. The varied, eclectic menu extends from Indonesian *gado gado* through to Mexican and sandwiches (from $8.50), pasta, pizza, and meaty pub-style mains including roasts for around $17. Licensed. Mon 11am–11pm, Tues–Fri 9am–11pm, Sat & Sun 9am–midnight.

Iku 25A Glebe Point Rd. Bus #431, #433 & #434 from Central CityRail. (Also at 612a Darling St, Rozelle; 168 Military Rd, Neutral Bay; 279 Bronte Rd, Waverly; and 62 Oxford St, Darlinghurst). The original *Iku* at Glebe proved so popular it keeps branching out. Healthy but delicious macrobiotic meals and snacks, all vegetarian or vegan, plus organic, pesticide-free coffee. Meditative interior and outdoor dining area. Mon–Fri 11am–9pm, Sat 11am–7pm, Sun noon–7.30pm.

Toxteth Hotel 345 Glebe Point Rd. Bus #431, #433 & #434 from Central CityRail. Done-up pub with a wonderful courtyard dining area complete with murals, mosaics and greenery, plus braziers to keep you warm in winter. Inside tables look on to the courtyard through folding glass doors. The

Italian- and French-run bistro has a small, simple menu of pub food – steaks ($19–21), salads (nicoise to calamari, around $14), and burgers – as well as classier European dishes, from marinated sardines to duck à la orange.

Well Connected 35 Glebe Point Rd. Bus #431, #433 & #434 from Central CityRail. A popular Glebe hangout: choose from pavement tables, sofas or balcony seats upstairs in this colourful, funky café. With breakfast served until 6pm, when dinner starts, people blow in and out all day. Simple good-value menu – Turkish-bread sandwiches, lasagne, soups and salads – with loads for vegetarians; generous servings. Daily 7am to midnight.

Newtown

Campos Coffee 193 Missenden Road, just off King St. Newtown CityRail. Superb coffee (among the best in Sydney) is the thing here – roasted, blended and ground in-house and served up to perfection by trained baristas. The only nibbles on offer are a few delicious biscuits and morsel-sized pastries. Mon–Fri 7am–4pm, Sat 8am–5pm.

Citrus 227 King St. Newtown CityRail. A Newtown café favourite: vibrant coloured walls, friendly service, huge servings of delicious food – the Mediterranean-inspired chicken-breast burger and the steak sandwich are stand-outs – with nothing much over $12. Big fold-back windows bring in light and views of Newtown's unconventional inhabitants, while retaining a bit of a distance from the fumes and throng. BYO. Mon–Thurs & Sun 8am–10pm, Fri & Sat 8am–midnight.

El Bahsa 233 King St. Newtown CityRail. Updated Lebanese coffee lounge – with dark purple walls and a modern airy ambience – offering a range of traditional sweets, all home-made. Meals – international and Lebanese – are good-value, especially the breakfast grills on Turkish bread (between $6.50 and $12). Mon–Thurs & Sun 9am–10pm, Fri & Sat 9am–11pm.

The Old Fish Cafe 239 King St. Newtown CityRail. This little corner place, decorated with strands of dried garlic and chilli, is pure Newtown: lots of shaven heads, body piercings, tattoos and bizarre fashions. Food is simple – mainly focaccia and mini-pizzas – and the excellent raisin loaf goes well with a coffee. Daily 6am–7pm, later in summer.

Tamana's North Indian Diner 196 King St. Newtown CityRail. Very cheap, absolutely delicious fast meals to eat in or take away. Licensed and BYO.

Leichhardt

Bar Baba 31 Norton St, Leichhardt. Bus #438 & #440 from Central CityRail. This gleaming but relaxed veteran family-run Italian place is open all day. Great desserts include baked ricotta cheesecake and tiramisu. On two levels; there's a courtyard and balcony too. Mon–Sat 8.30am–11.30pm, Sun 9am–11.30pm.

Bar Italia 169 Norton St, Leichhardt. Bus #438 or #440 from Central CityRail. Like a community centre with the day-long comings and goings of Leichhardt locals, and positively packed at night. The focaccia, served during the day, comes big and tasty, and coffee is spot-on. Some of the best gelato in Sydney; pasta costs from $9.50, and the night-time menu includes more substantial meat dishes. Don't overlook the shady courtyard out the back when you hunt for a table. BYO. Mon & Sun 10am–midnight, Tues–Thurs 9am–midnight, Fri 9am–1am, Sat 10am–1am.

Caffe Sport 2A Norton St, Leichhardt. Bus #438 & #440 from Central CityRail. One of the original Norton Street cafés, decorated with Italian sporting paraphernalia. Very casual, very Italian and very friendly. Cheap prices and generous helpings of focaccia. Daily 7am (Sun 8am) to 6pm.

Balmain and Rozelle

The Barn Café and Grocery 731–735 Darling St, Rozelle. Bus #440 from Central CityRail. This appealing huge and high-ceilinged gourmet grocery store cooks up the ingredients for sale in the courtyard café out back – and they'll even give you the recipe. With its fruit trees and fresh herbs, it's a delightful space for the popular all-day breakfast (delicious field mushrooms feature) and lunch dishes from a meze plate ($16.50) to Moroccan spiced lamb ($22.50). For something simpler – coffee, pastries and sandwiches – there's a separate espresso bar out front (daily 7am–3pm). Café daily 8am–5.30pm, store until 7.30pm.

Canteen 332 Darling St, Balmain. Bus #432, #433 & #434 from Central CityRail. Airy, high-ceilinged café with whitewashed walls, inside the old Working Men's Institute. Simple fare: generous baguettes, burgers and salads, and big cooked breakfasts particularly popular at weekends when customers spill onto the sunny outside tables. Order and pay at the counter. Mon–Fri & Sun 7am–5pm, Sat 6am–5pm.

Mofo 354 Darling St, Balmain. Bus #432, #433 & #434 from Central CityRail. Funky, laidback vegetarian café with a sunny front courtyard and outdoor seating area, and just a tiny cushioned area inside. Breakfast is served until 3pm and there's a simple lunch menu, from lentil burgers to a daily selection of salads. Good-value, with nothing much over $12. Mon–Fri daily 7am–4pm.

Ocean beaches

From Bondi south to Maroubra, and from Manly north to Palm Beach, the **ocean beaches** have a stash of great cafés and relaxed eating places: early breakfasts are a beachside speciality. The beaches' pubs also usually offer bar snacks and light meals, see pp.217–218 of "Drinking" for more options. There's also a branch of the noodle eatery *fu-manchu* (see p.199) at Bondi, with great ocean views from its balcony.

Bondi and Bronte

Brown Sugar 100 Brighton Boulevarde, North Bondi. Bus #389 from Bondi Junction CityRail. A stroll from the northern end of the beach, this little café is tucked in a quiet residential street around the corner from the North Bondi shops. The decor is funky distressed and the staff – cooking at the open kitchen – are suitably sweet and the atmosphere comfortable and relaxed. Locals straggle in for the very good breakfast menu; they have an interesting way with eggs, from green eggs (with pesto) to dill salmon eggs, and the pancakes come with a week's supply of fruit. Lunch on toasted Turkish sandwiches, salad and pasta. $14 is the most expensive item. Daily 7.30am–4.30pm.

The Bogeyhole Café 473 Bronte Rd, Bronte. Bus #378 from Central/Bondi Junction CityRail. Long-established café offering breakfast until 3pm and a variety of lunch specials from $9. Top-notch iced coffee beneath an excellent example of a pressed metal ornate ceiling, so don't forget to look up. Daily 7am–5pm.

Burgerman 249 Bondi Rd, Bondi. Bus #380 from Bondi Junction CityRail. Gourmet burgers to slaver over, starting at $6.80. Vegetarian options too. Busy takeaway service and small eat-in area. Daily noon–10pm. There's another branch at 116 Surrey St, off Victoria St, Darlinghurst. See map on p.102.

Gelato Bar 140 Campbell Parade, Bondi Beach. Bus #380 from Bondi Junction CityRail. A gleaming window display of indulgent creamy continental cakes and strudels lure beachgoers to this Hungarian-run place. For over thirty years it has been serving up Eastern European dishes, huge portions of cake and gelato (though the best is at *Pompei's*, round the corner on Roscoe St). Old-fashioned coffee-lounge decor. Daily 8am–midnight.

Gertrude & Alice Cafe Bookstore 40 Hall St, cnr Consett Ave, Bondi Beach. Bus #380 & #389 from Bondi Junction CityRail. It's hard to decide if *Gertrude & Alice's* is a café or a secondhand bookshop. With small tables crammed into every available space, a big communal table and a comfy couch to lounge on, it can be hard for browsers to get to the books at busy café times. Expect generous, affordable servings of Greek and Mediterranean food, great cakes, coffee and a genial hubbub of conversation. Open daily from 7.30am until late at night.

Gusto 16 Hall St, Bondi Beach. Bus #380 & #389 from Bondi Junction CityRail. Deli-café which creates quite a Bondi scene, with its cosmopolitan crew of regulars and travellers blocking the pavement outside. Excellent coffee, delicious edibles piled high on platters and a separate deli counter too. There's just enough room for a few more people to perch on stools inside and along the front. Good notice board. Daily 6.15am–7.30pm.

Lamrock Cafe 72 Campbell Parade, cnr Lamrock Ave, Bondi Beach. Bus #380 from Bondi Junction CityRail. Stalwart lively Bondi café. The unpretentious local crowd come for magnificent ocean views, uncomplicated food – *panini*, salads, pasta, burgers and fish and chips – and breakfasts. You can even have a cocktail with your brunch. Umbrella-covered tables outside, cushions inside. Licensed. Daily 7am–midnight.

Lauries Vegetarian 286 Bondi Rd, Bondi. Bus #380 from Bondi Junction CityRail. Excellent veggie takeaway with a couple of eat-in tables. Daily 11am–10pm.

The One That Got Away 163 Bondi Rd, Bondi. Bus #380 from Bondi Junction CityRail. Award-winning fish shop which even sells kosher fish plus sushi; also BBQ grills and fish and chips. There's a small eat-in section where salads and unusual yam chips are served. Daily 10am–9pm.

Sejuiced 487 Bronte Rd, Bronte. Bus #378 from Central CityRail. Delicious fresh juices, smoothies and frappés, combined with ocean and palm-tree views, make this tiny place a beauty to kick-start a summer's day. Salads, soups and pasta are terrific too. If it's full, choose from several other great options on this wonderful café strip. Daily 6.30am–6pm.

Speedo's 126 Ramsgate Ave, North Bondi. Bus #380 & #389 from Bondi Junction CityRail. Totally casual café bang opposite the north end of the beach, where the locals and their kids and dogs hang out, with no busy road between you and the view. The inexpensive breakfast specials are very popular; expect long waits for your order. Daily 6am–6pm.

Eastern beaches: Clovelly, Coogee and Maroubra

See map on p.143.

Art Lounge Café 275 Arden St, Coogee. Bus #372 from Central Cityrail, #374 & #376 from Circular Quay Cityrail. *Art Lounge* is worth the short walk up the hill, just south of the beach. Sink into a soft chair, lose yourself gazing at the paintings, bring yourself round with a coffee, and restore your energy with an all-day breakfast or gourmet burger that won't break the bank. Wed–Sun 8am–4pm.

Barzura 62 Carr St, Coogee. Bus #372 from Central CityRail & #373, #374 & #376 from Circular Quay CityRail. Fantastic spot with ocean views, this popular café–restaurant serves a wholesome breakfast until 1pm, snacks until 7pm, and restaurant meals – from seafood spaghetti to grilled kangaroo rump – at lunch and dinner. Unpretentious though stylish service encourages a local crowd and it's always packed. Lunch and dinner mains $13–26, pasta deals available 5–7pm. Licensed and BYO. Daily 7am–11pm.

Ericyes II 240 Coogee Bay Rd, Coogee. Bus #372 from Central CityRail & #373, #374, #376 from Circular Quay CityRail. This casual eat-in or takeaway place has delicious *pide* – Turkish-style pizzas – and just-baked bread and tasty dips that are perfect for a beach picnic. BYO. Daily 10am–midnight.

The Globe 203 Coogee Bay Rd, Coogee. Bus #372 from Central CityRail & #373, #374 & #376 from Circular Quay CityRail. This relaxed local daytime hangout has good coffee and interesting, healthy food, from gourmet sandwiches to Mediterranean-slanted mains. Daily 8am–5pm.

The Pool Caffe 94 Marine Parade, Maroubra ⓣ02/9314 0364. Bus #376 & #377 from Circular Quay CityRail. In a quiet residential spot opposite the Mahon sea pool on the Coogee–Maroubra coastal walk, this café has a relaxed holiday feel. Breakfast on organic porridge and fresh-fruit plates, have a coffee with fresh muffins, biscuits and cakes, or tuck into more expensive restaurant-style meaty modern food, often with an Indian flavour (bookings recommended weekends). Mains from $16. Breakfast and lunch daily 8am–6pm, except Mon & Tues to 3pm; dinner Wed–Sat. See map on p.137.

Seasalt 1 Donnellan Circuit, Clovelly. Bus #339 from Circular Quay and Central CityRail. Open-fronted, with fantastic views over the beach to cliffs, greenery and houses, this renovated kiosk is now a smart contemporary café–restaurant, but it's still the sort of place you can come into in your cossie and covered in sand and have a casual coffee or even a full meal. The cuisine is fresh and modern, often with seafood; lunch mains from $16 to $27, and summer-only dinner (when fully clothed and groomed is more the norm) starts from $19. The sophisticated, extensive breakfast – dishes like goat's ricotta and fresh herb omelette – packs the punters in at the weekends. Arrive early to be sure of a seat – or get a takeaway from the small kiosk section. Licensed. Mon–Fri 9am–3.30pm, Sat & Sun 8.30am–4pm, dinner 6pm until late: Tues–Sat in summer, Fri & Sat only rest of year.

Manly and the northern beaches

Bacino Bar 1a The Corso, Manly (also at cnr The Strand & Howard Ave, Dee Why Beach, and 83 Mount St, North Sydney). All-day café with a wide range of mainly Italian food, including standard lasagne ($6.50), though there are some Australian favourites too. Upstairs is a lounge area and communal tables, which add to the beachside vibe. Licensed and BYO. Mon–Sat 6am–5pm, Sun 7am–5pm.

Barking Frog 48 North Steyne, Manly. Ferry to Manly Wharf. One of Manly's most popular surf-front breakfast spots, though it has a proper bistro upstairs and becomes a bar/lounge on Thurs and Sun evenings when a DJ cranks out some relaxing tunes. The fave breakfast is their version of eggs hollandaise ("Barking Frog's eggs") and the huge pancakes are delicious and inexpensive. Lunch fare includes packed-full baguettes. Mon & Tues noon–midnight, Wed–Sun 8am–midnight.

The harbour

Several pubs around the **harbour** – in Neutral Bay, Watsons Bay and North Sydney – serve good snacks and light meals and all have great beer gardens. See the box "Legendary Beer Gardens" on p.216 and the *Greenwood Hotel* (p.216). To locate these places, see the map on pp.130–131.

Freckle Face 32 Burton St, Kirribilli. Milsons Point CityRail or ferry to Kirribilli Wharf. This café is a good place to recharge after walking over the Harbour Bridge or wandering through Kirribilli Markets. It's near the north side of the bridge at Milsons Point. Coffee is good and comes with a special Freckle chocolate. Healthy fare includes fresh juices, smoothies, salads and sandwiches (lunch mains $8–15). Mon–Sat 7am–5pm, Sun 8am–5pm.

Maisys Cafe 164 Military Rd, Neutral Bay. Bus #247 from Clarence St, City. Cool hangout on a hot day or night (open 24hr), with funky interior and music. Good for breakfast – from croissants to bacon and eggs – or delicious Maltese *pastizzi* plus soups, burgers, pasta and cakes. Not cheap (mains $8.50–16.50), but servings are generous. BYO.

Restaurants

You're likely to come across the term "**contemporary Australian**", "modern Australian" or "Pacific Rim" in various restaurant descriptions. This refers to an adventurous blend of influences from around the world – mostly Asian and Mediterranean – combined with fresh local produce (including kangaroo, emu and crocodile); the result is a dynamic, eclectic and very healthy cuisine.

An average Sydney restaurant main is about $18; top dollar at the city's finest is around $40. Many places allow you to **BYO** (Bring Your Own) wine or beer, but will probably add a corkage charge ($1–2 per person). Several **pubs** have well-regarded restaurants; pub meals rarely cost more than $16, with huge steaks likely to be at the top of the menu.

The Rocks

Palisade Hotel Restaurant 35–37 Bettington St, Millers Point ☎02/9251 7225. Circular Quay CityRail/ferry, bus #431–434. On the first floor of a classic tiled pub, which stands sentinel-like over Millers Point, the intimate dining room provides absorbing water and city views. Cuisine is expensive modern Australian (mains $24–30) and service is friendly. Have a drink downstairs first in the wonderfully unspoilt pub. Licensed. Closed Sat lunch and all Sun.

Rockpool 107 George St, The Rocks ☎02/9252 1888. Circular Quay CityRail/ferry. Owned by top chef Neil Perry, the raved-about seafood – blue swimmer crab omelette, mud crab ravioli – and other contemporary creations make this one of Sydney's best dining spots. With mains ranging from $54 to $65, however, it's definitely splurge material. Licensed. Closed Sat lunch & Sun. A less expensive Perry restaurant, inspired by Asian cuisines, is *XO*, 490 Crown St, Surry Hills (☎02/9360 7007).

Sailors Thai Canteen 106 George St, The Rocks. Circular Quay CityRail/ferry. The cheaper version of the much-praised, pricey downstairs restaurant (☎02/9251 2466 for bookings), housed in the restored Sailors' Home. The ground-level canteen with a long stainless-steel communal table looks onto an open kitchen, where the chefs chop away to produce simple one-bowl meals. Come early for dinner in the canteen. Mains $15.50–26.50. Licensed. Mon–Sat noon–8pm.

Sydney's star chefs

Sydney's top restaurants have long had a great reputation internationally, mastering the east-meets-west fusion that contemporary Australian cuisine is so well known for, using the freshest local ingredients, and with interiors straight out of the latest style mags. The city's top **chefs** are regularly poached to work overseas and many of them have become TV stars or publishing legends, endorsing products or producing their own commercial food range. For the moment, the stars of Sydney's restaurant scene are: Luke Mangan, with a couple of new restaurant projects planned at the time of writing; Neil Perry at *Rockpool* (opposite); Tetsuya Wakuda at *Tetsuya's* (p.196); Bill Granger at *bills* (p.187); Guillaume Brahimi at *Guillaume at Bennelong* (see p.196); Matthew Moran at *Aria* (see below); Kylie Kwong at *Billy Kwong* (p.197); Martin Boetz at *Longrain* (see p.198); Peter Doyle at *est*; (p.196); Peter Gilmore at *Quay* (p.196); Damien Pignolet at *Bistro Moncur* (p.200); Sean Moran at *Sean's Panaroma* (p.204); and Serge Dansereau at *Bathers Pavilion* (p.202).

Wharf Restaurant Pier 4, Hickson Rd, Millers Point ⓣ02/9250 1761, next to the Wharf Theatre. Circular Quay CityRail/ferry. Enterprising modern food (lots of seafood), served up in an old dock building with heaps of raw charm and a harbour vista; bag the outside tables for the best views. Cocktail bar open from noon until end of evening performance. Mains $26.50–32. Closed Sun.

Circular Quay and the Opera House

Aria 1 Macquarie St, East Circular Quay ⓣ02/9252 2555 Circular Quay CityRail/ferry. On the first floor of the Opera Quays building (aka the much-maligned "Toaster" – see p.67), the 200-seater *Aria* has knock-out harbour views, one of Sydney's best chefs, Matthew Moran (dishing up modern Australian fare), and wonderful service to recommend it. The interiors are also pretty slick. All this comes at a price, but there are more affordable set lunch menus and pre-theatre dinners (5.30–7.30pm; one/two/three courses $36/$58/$72). Mains cost $42 to $49. Closed lunch Sat & Sun.

Café Opera Intercontinental 117 Macquarie St ⓣ02/9240 1260. Circular Quay CityRail/ferry. The five-star *Intercontinental* (see p.166) has long been a hit with the locals, not just tourists, and the buffet offered by its *Café Opera*, groaning under the display of seafood, is legendary. You can stuff yourself silly for $42 at lunchtime ($59 Sun, with live jazz), $48 at dinner ($54 Fri & Sat, $52 Sun) or $28.50 at supper from 10pm on Friday and Saturday. Licensed.

Cafe Sydney Level 5, Customs House, 31 Alfred St, Circular Quay ⓣ02/9251 8683. Circular Quay CityRail/ferry. Though the overpriced food here has never been that highly rated (wide-ranging, from a tandoor oven to French- and Greek-inspired dishes), the views of the Harbour Bridge and Opera House from the balcony are jaw-dropping – so *Cafe Sydney* is firmly on the tourist agenda. Service is great and the atmosphere is fun, especially with the live jazz accompaniment on Fri nights. Mains $24–38. A drink at the bar is the affordable option. Lunch daily, dinner Mon–Sat.

Doyles on the Quay Overseas Passenger Terminal, Circular Quay West ⓣ02/9252 3400. Circular Quay CityRail/ferry. Downtown branch of the Watsons Bay seafood institution (see p.202; branch at Sydney Fish Market p.197); pricey but excellent, with great harbour views from the outdoor waterfront tables. You'll probably need to book. Licensed. Mains $28–60.

Vegetarian Sydney

Veggies are well catered for on just about every café menu, and most contemporary restaurant menus too. The following are specifically or virtually all **vegetarian**: *Badde Manors* (p.190), *Bodhi in the Park* (p.185), *Green Gourmet* (p.201), *Harvest* (p.202), *Iku* (p.190), *Maya Indian Sweets* (p.187), *Mofo* (p.192), *Mother Chu's Vegetarian Kitchen* (p.197) and *Sloanes* (p.189).

Guillaume at Bennelong Sydney Opera House, Bennelong Point ⓣ02/9241 1999. Circular Quay CityRail/ferry. French chef Guillaime Brahimi has fused his name with the enduring *Bennelong*, the Opera House's top-notch restaurant. If you want to have one splash-out romantic meal in Sydney, come here. The restaurant fills one of the iconic building's smaller shells, with dramatic rib-vaulted ceilings, huge windows providing stunning harbour views, and sensuous lighting. With mains at around $35, this is not the priciest in town, but if you can't afford it, you could opt for a drink at the bar. Pre-theatre meals are available (two-courses $55, three courses $65). Lunch Thurs & Fri, dinner Mon–Sat.

Quay Upper Level, Overseas Passenger Terminal, Circular Quay West ⓣ02/9251 5600. Circular Quay CityRail/ferry. The breathtaking views of the Sydney icons, the bridge and the Opera House, accompany the exquisite modern Australian food on offer here, from one of the ciy's most talented chefs, Peter Gilmore. Vying for the crown of Sydney's best restaurant, and understandably very expensive, with mains from $38. Licensed. Closed Mon lunch.

City centre

est. Level 1, Establishment Hotel, 252 George St, City ⓣ02/9240 3010. Wynyard CityRail. Above one of Sydney's most deluxe bars (see p.209), this top-notch restaurant, one of Sydney's best, has a dramatic classical but contemporary interior. The food, by renowned chef Peter Doyle, is contemporary Australian but with a French slant. Very expensive (mains from $39). Licensed. Closed Sat lunch and all Sun.

Tetsuya's 529 Kent St ⓣ02/9267 2900, ⓕ9799 7099. Town Hall CityRail. Stylish premises – a Japanese timber interior and a beautiful Japanese garden outside – and the internationally renowned chef Tetsuya Wakuda creating exquisite Japanese/French-style fare. As Sydneysiders will attest, an evening here is a once-in-a-lifetime culinary experience and the month long waiting list (you can fax your booking ahead) is worth it to sample the twelve-course *dégustation* menu ($175); wine teamed with each course starts from $60. Licensed and BYO. Lunch Fri & Sat, dinner Tues–Sat.

Darling Harbour and around

BBQ King 18 Goulburn St, Haymarket ⓣ02/9267 2433. Central CityRail. Late night hangout of rock stars and students alike, this unprepossessing but always packed Chinese restaurant does a mean meat dish, as indicated by the name and the BBQ ducks hanging in the window. A big vegetarian list on the menu caters to the crowds scattered across various rooms and communal tables. Daily 11.30am–2am (last orders 1.30am). Licensed.

Blackbird Cockle Bay Wharf, Darling Harbour ⓣ02/9283 7835. Town Hall CityRail. Bar-restaurant with the feel of a funky American diner; sit on stools at the bar or couches out the back, or enjoy the water views from the terrace. Generous, good-value meals to suit all cravings – from dahl to spaghetti, T-bone steaks, noodles, salads, pizzas from a hot-stone oven, and breakfast until 4pm. Licensed. Daily 7am–1am.

Capitan Torres 73 Liverpool St ⓣ02/9264 5574. Town Hall CityRail. Atmospheric and enduring Spanish place with old country charm – white walls and wrought iron – specializing in seafood. A fresh display of the catch of the day helps you choose, but old favourites from the inexpensive tapas menu are hard to pass up, including chorizo and garlic prawns, plus authentic paella. Sit downstairs at the bar or upstairs in the restaurant. Licensed.

▼ Sashimi at Tetsuya's

Chinta Ria – Temple of Love Roof Terrace, 201 Sussex St, Cockle Bay Wharf, Darling Harbour ☎02/9264 3211. Town Hall CityRail. People still queue to get in here (bookings lunch only) years after opening, as much for the fun atmosphere – a blues and jazz soundtrack and decor which mixes a giant Buddha, a lotus pond and fifties-style furniture – as for the yummy moderately priced Malaysian food. Any of the curries will satisfy, though ask for extra chilli if you want a real kick. Quick, helpful service, including a mobile phone call-back system for busy nights, when patrons are sent to the bars elsewhere in the Darling Harbour restaurant complex. Licensed and BYO.

Doyles Fish Market Bistro Sydney Fish Market, Pyrmont ☎02/9552 4339. Metro Light Rail to Fish Market. A very casual and more affordable version of the famous *Doyles* fish restaurant in Watsons Bay; you sit at plastic tables and order at the counter. Daily specials from the best fish market offers served all day. BYO. Mon–Thurs 11am–3pm, Fri & Sat 11am–9pm, Sun 11am–5pm.

Golden Century 393 Sussex St, City ☎02/9281 1598. Central CityRail. Seafood is the thing here, and it's very fresh – you can watch your potential dinner swimming around in the tanks. Be adventurous – try the oysters sitting on black moss ($15), or the raved-about Pipis in XO sauce ($18). And you can eat as dawn approaches – this one's open very late. Keep an eye out for visiting rock stars – it's also a favourite after-show haunt. Licensed and BYO. Daily noon–4am.

Grand Taverna Sir John Young Hotel, 557 George St, cnr Liverpool St, Haymarket ☎02/9267 3608. Town Hall CityRail. Spanish food, including moderately priced tapas, in the heart of the Spanish quarter. No frills but loud, slightly raucous setting for some of the best paella and sangria (by the jugfull) in town. A remarkably large selection of seafood, including a hearty platter for the indecisive. Licensed.

Kam Fook Sharks Fin Seafood Restaurant Level 3, Market City complex, cnr Quay and Haymarket streets, Haymarket ☎02/9211 8988. Central CityRail. The long name matches the size of this Cantonese establishment, officially Australia's largest restaurant, seating 800. It's always a good indicator when the locals are lining up; you can eat some of the best *yum cha* in Sydney here, though you'll have to queue if you haven't booked, despite the size of the place. Licensed. *Yum cha* Mon–Fri 10am–5.30pm, Sat & Sun 9am–5.30pm; dinner nightly.

The Malaya 39 Lime St, King Street Wharf, Darling Harbour ☎02/9279 1170. Town Hall CityRail. Popular, veteran Chinese–Malaysian place now in swish water surrounds, serving some of the best and spiciest laksa in town (chicken or vegetable *laksa* $18, king prawn version $22). Seafood dishes are definitely worth a try. Licensed.

Mother Chu's Vegetarian Kitchen 367 Pitt St. ☎02/9283 2828. Central CityRail. Gaining a reputation fast, this Taiwanese Buddhist restaurant is set in suitably plain surroundings and, true to its name, is family-run. Though traditionally onion and garlic aren't used the inexpensive eats here aren't bland and it's a perfect option for vegetarians. Don't try to BYO – there's a no-alcohol policy. Closed Sun.

Inner east

The **inner east** has the biggest concentration of places to eat in Sydney, and some of its best restaurants.

Surry Hills

Almustafa 276 Cleveland St, Surry Hills ☎02/9319 5632. Bus #393 & #395 from Central CityRail. Very homey Lebanese place and one of the stalwarts of the area; a recent revamp hasn't changed the traditional look of low couches and cushions. Tasty, inexpensive food with all the favourites – falafel, *baba ganouj*, *kefta* – you can sample a wide range with a shareable mezze platter and on the weekends head upstairs for some bellydancing. BYO. Closed lunch Mon–Wed, open until 12.30am Fri & Sat.

Billy Kwong 355 Crown St, Surry Hills ☎02/9332 3300. Bus #301–303 from Circular Quay CityRail or Castlereagh St, City. It's a fight for a table but worth the wait when traditional Chinese cooking gets a stylish new slant at this restaurant of contrasts. The space itself – all dark polished wood and Chinese antiques but brightly lit and with contemporary fittings – complements the often adventurous combination of dishes and flavours. Scallops, jellyfish, prawn wontons, plus wagyu beef, all with unusual sauces, are highlights. Mains start from $22. No bookings. Licensed and BYO. Dinner daily.

Erciyes 409 Cleveland St, Surry Hills ☎02/9319 1309. Bus #393 & #395 from Central CityRail. Among the offerings of this busy, inexpensive, family-run Turkish restaurant is delicious *pide* – a bit like pizza – available with 22 different toppings, many vegetarian. There are also cabbage rolls, stuffed eggplant and various other cheap and tasty options, including delicious dips. A takeout section caters to those who didn't book. Belly dancing Fri & Sat nights. BYO. Daily 10am–midnight.

Forresters Hotel 336 Riley St, Surry Hills ☎02/9211 2095. Central CityRail. The Forresters' Sun–Wed steak and chicken lunchtime specials (available until 6pm on Sat) have become a legend: a 300g scotch fillet or T-bone steak or a chargrilled chicken breast with mash and Asian greens (and a different sauce each day) for $5 all day. There's not much of a catch – you must buy a drink, which is fine with wine by the glass and cocktails $5 Thursday to Sunday. There are of course other menu options, including mussels and squid, but the steaks taste great and the three-levelled pub itself is very pleasant, with an unpretentious crowd. Licensed.

Longrain 85 Commonwealth St, Surry Hills ☎02/280 2888. Central CityRail. This popular bar-restaurant is all warm, sensuous woods – big communal tables made of jarrah, black Japanese-style floorboards and pine walls. Superb Thai food, among the best in Sydney, and a hip clientele. Closed Mon & lunch Sat & Sun.

Mahjong Room 312 Crown St, Surry Hills ☎02/9361 3985. Not a mahjong game in sight, but the other Chinese restaurant on Crown Street offers a cheaper alternative to *Billy Kwong* and has a few more staples, like fresh tiger prawns and snow peas in XO sauce, and bang bang chicken, to entice patrons. The three rooms are usually teeming but the atmosphere is casual. Licensed and BYO. Dinner daily.

Maya da Dhaba 431 Cleveland St, Surry Hills ☎02/8399 3785. Bus #393 & #395 from Central CityRail. The more upmarket, non-vegetarian version of the phenomenally popular veggie *Maya Indian Sweets* (see p.187) across the road. This one is also noisy and crowded but it's much comfier, and decor extends to craft-covered walls. The tender goat curry and the Goan fish curry in particular are superb, and prices are low (nothing over $15). Lunch Fri–Sun, dinner daily.

Mohr Fish 202 Devonshire St, Surry Hills. This tiny but stylish and convivial fish-and-chip bar, with stools and tiled walls, packs in the customers and provides fresh, well-priced, well-prepared and sometimes distinctive seafood options. Pop into the pub next door and they'll come and fetch you when a table is free – you can even bring your drink in with you. BYO. Daily 10am–10pm.

Nepalese Kitchen 481 Crown St, Surry Hills ☎02/9319 4264. Bus #301–303 from Circular Quay CityRail or Castlereagh St, City. It's peaceful just walking into this staple of the Surry Hill scene – all cosy wooden furniture, religious wall hangings and traditional music. The inexpensive specialities here include goat curry, served with freshly cooked relishes which traditionally accompany these mild Nepalese dishes, and the simple but delicious *momos* (handmade dumplings stuffed with spicy chicken and vegetables or cheese and spinach). There's a whole range of vegetarian options and a lovely courtyard for warmer nights. BYO. Dinner nightly.

Prasit's Northside Thai Take-away 395 Crown St, and Prasit's Northside on Crown, 415 Crown St, Surry Hills ☎02/9319 0748. Also 77 Mount St, North Sydney ☎02/9957 2271, see map on pp.130–131. Bus #301–303 from Circular Quay CityRail or Castlereagh St, City. Be prepared for some inexpensive spicy Thai taste sensations among the bold purple colour scheme. Since entrees are available cheaply by the portion, you can attempt to work your way through their delicious repertoire; plenty of vegetarian options too. The takeaway branch can squeeze diners out front on stools, with a few more places upstairs, though it's often a fairly rushed affair. Both BYO. Both closed Mon.

Sushi-Suma 421 Cleveland St, Surry Hills ☎02/9698 8873. Bus #393 & #395 from Central CityRail. That this small, noisy Japanese restaurant is extremely popular with Japanese locals and visitors says it all, and being able to watch the chef prepare is no greater indicator of freshness. Book a table to avoid disappointment. BYO. Closed Mon & Sun lunch.

Darlinghurst

Balkan Continental Restaurant 209 Oxford St, Darlinghurst ☎02/9360 4970. Bus #378 from Central CityRail, bus #380 from Circular Quay CityRail. For almost 40 years this bustling Croatian place has been chargrilling inside the front window and luring Sydneysiders in with good-value traditional continental favourites like schnitzels and mixed grills with potato, onion and cabbage salad, plus an extensive range of excellent fish and seafood. Balkan specialities such as *cevapci* (spicy skinless sausages) are worth a try but save room for dessert. Lunch and dinner Mon & Wed–Sun. Licensed and BYO. There's another Balkan Seafood restaurant at Bent St, Fox Studios, Moore Park ⓣ02/9360 0097.

Beppi's Cnr Yurong & Stanley Sts, East Sydney. ⓣ02/9360 4558 Kings Cross CityRail. Old-fashioned service and cosy surrounds, especially if you get a seat in the wine cellar and dine among the floor-to-ceiling bottles of often very expensive wine, have ensured this restaurant has stayed open since 1956. Solid Italian food, including veal scaloppini and various pastas, make it a first-class night out. Closed Sat lunch & Sun. Expensive. See map on p.102.

Fish Face 132 Darlinghurst Rd, Darlinghurst ⓣ02/9332 4803, takeaway ⓣ9332 4809. Kings Cross CityRail. This is one place where size doesn't matter, and where the excellent range of pricey seafood and sushi speak for themselves. Everything is the freshest of fresh in this tiny place and fish 'n' chips served in a paper cone, pea soup with yabby tails, or any of the sushi prepared before your eyes, will make you forget you're in the city and not near the sea at all. Licensed and BYO. Dinner Mon–Sat.

fu-manchu 249 Victoria St, Darlinghurst. Kings Cross CityRail. Perch yourself on red stools at stainless-steel counters and enjoy stylish but inexpensive Chinese and Malaysian noodles and noodle soups in this small, popular diner. Seasonal specials add variety to a standard but tasty menu, organic chicken and many vegetarian options. BYO. Closed Sun lunch, dinner daily. Also a branch with fabulous ocean views at Level 1, 80 Campbell Parade, Bondi Beach.

Govinda's 112 Darlinghurst Rd, Darlinghurst ⓣ02/9380 5155. Kings Cross CityRail. Legendary among in-the-know locals, this Hari-Krishna run restaurant-cum-cinema offers excellent, cheap mostly Indian all-you-can-eat vegetarian buffet for a bargain $15.90. Soup, lentils, pasta and curry, and for an extra $4 a new release or classic movie thrown in at the attached cinema with huge comfy couches (see p.231). Dinner nightly from 6pm and two screenings at 7.30 or 9.30pm.

Oh! Calcutta! 252 Victoria St, Darlinghurst ⓣ02/9360 3650. Kings Cross CityRail. Certainly not your average neighbourhood Indian: the interior was fitted out by a star interior designer and *Oh! Calcutta!* keeps getting suitably exclamatory reviews for its authentic – and occasionally inventive – well-priced food. Dishes like quail and goat regularly appear beside the more mainstream but renowned butter chicken, and the option of wholemeal naan and chapatti is a welcome twist. Try for a balcony table upstairs. Licensed and BYO. Lunch Fri only, dinner Mon–Sat.

Onde 346 Liverpool St, Darlinghurst. ⓣ02/9331 8749. Kings Cross CityRail. Thankfully there's a great bar and cushions for waiting on the ledge at the front end of this French-owned restaurant down a Darlinghurst side street, as regulars keep returning and there are no bookings. Everyone wants to try the outstanding and very authentic bistro-style food, starting with soups and patés and moving through to mains such as steak and *frites* or confit of duck, and always a special fish dish. Portions are generous and moderately priced, service is excellent and desserts decadent. Licensed, and all wine is available by the glass. Dinner nightly.

Pink Peppercorn 122 Oxford St, Darlinghurst. ⓣ02/9360 9922. Town Hall or Museum CityRail. This place keeps springing up on critics' lists of favourite eating holes. It might have something to do with the unusual Laotian-inspired cooking – which ranges from spicy chicken with yoghurt dressing to the signature stir-fried king prawns with veggies and pink peppercorns, and speciality lamb dishes – or the hip layout complete with pictures of traditional monks on the back wall. Whatever it is, it's fast gaining a reputation, and a deserved one at that. Licensed and BYO. Dinner daily.

Victoria Room Level 1, 235 Victoria St, Darlinghurst ⓣ02/9357 4488. Kings Cross CityRail. Dark, moody and fashioned in the style of the British Raj, this bar-restaurant, with its patterned wallpaper and mismatched but comfortable antique furniture, is a successful addition to an already crowded restaurant strip. The space is separated into a slick bar area where deep-cushioned couches and a couple of long tables keep the beautiful crowd back from the diners in the homely restaurant, where imaginative tapas-style morsels are served. Chorizo sausage with lentils and wilted spinach and sautéed scallops on a pea mash are inspired mains from $18, plus there's a huge mezze plate. On Sunday afternoons (2–4pm) a High Tea is also served ($25, $35 with champagne). Licensed. Tues–Sat 6pm–midnight (Fri 5pm–midnight) and Sun 2–10pm.

Paddington and Woollahra

Bistro LuLu 257 Oxford St, Paddington ☎02/9380 6888. Bus #378 from Central CityRail, #380 from Circular Quay CityRail. Attached to the Australian Centre for Photography (see p.259), this good-value French-style bistro is sleekly modern with huge fold-back windows and views of street action. With a chef trained by some of the city's finest, the food here is heavenly but it's not all fancy – the old French favourite, *steak frites*, is on the menu. Licensed. Lunch Thurs–Sat, dinner nightly.

Bistro Moncur Woollahra Hotel, 116 Queen St, Woollahra ☎02/9363 2519. Bus #378 from Central CityRail, #380 from Circular Quay CityRail. Stalwart of the Sydney fine-dining scene, this classic, though pricey, French bistro is fighting back the competition with the superb cooking of chef Damien Pignolet. No bookings. Licensed. Closed Mon lunch.

Grand National Hotel 161 Underwood St, cnr of Elizabeth St, Paddington ☎02/9963 4557. Bus #378 from Central CityRail, bus #380 from Circular Quay CityRail. Another grand pub-restaurant that has moved with the times and is now dishing up imaginative, filling but expensive fare, with old-fashioned attentive service. Bookings essential on weekends, Sunday lunch being a peak time for locals recovering from the night before. Lunch Tues–Sun, dinner Tues–Sat.

Paddington Inn Bistro 338 Oxford St, Paddington ☎02/9380 5913. Bus #378 from Central CityRail, bus #380 from Circular Quay CityRail. Busy upmarket pub-bistro with a tasty tapas menu as well as more substantial meals, from risotto to imaginative salads. The decor of textured glass, cushioned booths, polished concrete floors and fabric-lined walls is dark but comfortable and perfect for a few long hours spent over drinks, dinner and dessert. Packed on Saturdays, as it's opposite the market, but a good crowd can be found there most nights making the most of the pool tables upstairs.

Royal Hotel Restaurant Royal Hotel, 237 Glenmore Rd, off Five Ways, Paddington ☎02/9331 5055. Bus #389 from Circular Quay CityRail. Grand old triple-storey pub-restaurant serving some of the most mouth-watering steaks in Sydney, nonstop from noon to 11pm (9pm Sun). Antiques and classic cornicing downstairs and a slick cocktail lounge *Elephant Bar* upstairs (from 4.30pm daily) make it an enjoyable place to wait for a seat, since they don't take bookings and tables fill fast. Eating on the verandah is a real treat, with views over the art gallery and Five Ways action below.

Kings Cross and Woolloomooloo

Bayswater Brasserie 32 Bayswater Rd, Kings Cross ☎02/9357 2177. Kings Cross CityRail. Busy, lively, upmarket brasserie consistently rated for its interesting modern food (constantly changing seasonal menu) – it's a long-time hangout for Sydney's media types. Licensed. Lunch Fri only, dinner Mon–Sat.

Fratelli Paradiso 12–16 Challis Ave ☎02/9357 1744. Kings Cross CityRail. This place has got everything, from gorgeous wallpaper and a dark furniture fit-out, to flirty waiters and a diverse wine list. There's even an adjoining bakery which runs out of stock before lunchtime most days. And the food's amazing and well priced too – calamari, veal, pizza and pastries – with a blackboard menu that changes daily offering variety from the great standard menu. Licensed. Breakfast and lunch daily, dinner Mon–Fri.

Nove Pizzeria The Wharf, 6 Cowper Rd, Woolloomooloo ☎02/9368 7488. Kings Cross CityRail. Considering Nove's position right next door to some of Sydney's more expensive restaurants, you can tuck into excellent thin-base pizza for an incredibly reasonable price. There's also an appetizing array of fresh pasta with some unusual ingredients, and of course seafood options to complement the stunning view. Closed Mon. Licensed.

Otto The Wharf, 6 Cowper Wharf Rd, Woolloomooloo ☎02/9368 7488. Kings Cross CityRail. Otto is the sort of restaurant where agents take actors and models out to lunch, and a well-known politician could be dining at the next table. Trendy and glamorous, with a location not just by the water but on the water (the boats are bobbing within arms reach), the exquisite though expensive Italian cuisine – very fresh seafood and top-of-the-range everything else – coupled with friendly service and a lively atmosphere, is what keeps them coming back. Licensed. Lunch & dinner daily.

The Pig and The Olive 71A Macleay St, Potts Point ☎02/9357 3745. Kings Cross CityRail. Gourmet pizza bar with wild toppings like marinated lamb with feta. Also check out the small menu of contemporary dishes, which includes grilled polenta and spicy rack of lamb. Licensed and BYO. Dinner nightly.

Woolloomooloo Bay Hotel 2 Bourke St, Woolloomooloo ☎02/9357 1177. Kings Cross CityRail. Big old pub popular for its bistro food, particularly the enormous $40 seafood platters. Usual pub steaks and pasta also on offer, with mains under $20. Views across to the wharf and marina and over the bay from the outside tables on the footpath – Kingsley's Alehouse (see "Drinking") has taken over the space upstairs, including the verandah.

Inner west

Though the **inner west** is heavy on café culture, it also has some great, often multicultural, restaurants and pub bistros.

Glebe

The Boathouse on Blackwattle Bay End of Ferry Rd, Glebe ☎02/9518 9011. Bus #431, #433 & #434 from Central CityRail. Atmospheric restaurant located in a former boatshed, with fantastic views across the bay to Anzac Bridge and the fishmarkets opposite. Fittingly, seafood is the thing here, from the six different kinds of oysters to the raved-about snapper pie. One of the best fish restaurants in Sydney; very expensive but worth it. Licensed. Closed Mon.

Cesare's No Names Friend in Hand Hotel, 58 Cowper St, Glebe ☎02/9660 2326. Bus #431, #433 & #434 from Central CityRail. Excellent, cheap Italian restaurant in the gazebo and beer garden of the characterful backstreet pub (see p.214). Generous pasta meals from $10 and pricier meaty main courses like schnitzels. Restaurant closed Sun lunch.

Dakhni 65 Glebe Point Rd ☎02/9660 4887. Bus #431, #433 & #434 from Central CityRail. With its cream walls hung with Indian art and white tablecloths, this Indian looks upmarket, but with mains from $12.90 and averaging $15, it's good-value. The dishes span tandoori to delicious South Indian vegetarian *masala dosai* (filled pancakes), or try a range in a meat or vegetarian *thali* ($19.50). A popular spot, so book ahead. BYO. Closed Mon lunch.

Darbar 134 Glebe Point Rd ☎02/9660 5666. Bus #431, #433 & #434 from Central CityRail. An old sandstone building with a leafy courtyard provides a gorgeous setting for a surprisingly inexpensive – but superb – Indian meal. Mains average $14–16. Licensed and BYO. Closed Mon lunch

Newtown

Green Gourmet 115–117 King St ☎02/9519 5330. Newtown CityRail. Loud, busy and cheap Chinese vegan eatery, which always has plenty of Asian customers, including the odd Buddhist monk. The devoted-Buddhist owner's creativity is particularly reflected in the divine tofu variations on offer. To get a taste of everything, there's a nightly buffet or *yum cha* at weekend lunches, or you can order off the menu at lunch and dinner (mains around $14). The same people run the excellent Vegan's Choice Grocery next door.

Kilimanjaro 280 King St ☎02/9557 4565. Newtown CityRail. Newtown is the focus of a small African community, with the African International Market providing supplies at 2a Enmore Rd, just around the corner. This long-running Senegalese-owned place serves authentic and simple dishes that span Africa – from West African marinated chicken to North African couscous. Inexpensive, casual and friendly atmosphere, with African art and craft adorning the walls. BYO.

Steki Taverna 2 O'Connell St, off King St ☎02/9516 2191. Newtown CityRail. Atmospheric and moderately priced Greek taverna, with live music and dancing at weekends – when you'll need to book. Courtyard dining is also an option. Licensed. Dinner Wed–Sun.

Sumalee Courtyard of the Bank Hotel, 324 King St ☎02/9565 1730. Newtown CityRail. Great Thai restaurant which takes over the fairy-lit leafy beer garden of the pub. Charmingly reminiscent of an al fresco restaurant in Bangkok or Chiang Mai. Moderate to expensive. Licensed.

Thai Pothong 294 King St ☎02/9550 6277. Newtown CityRail. King Street's best Thai; excellent service and inexpensive to moderate prices (mains average $16.90). Essential to book at the weekend. Licensed and BYO. Closed Mon lunch.

Thanh Binh **111 King St ☎02/9557 1175. Newtown CityRail.** With a celebrated original in Cabramatta (see box on p.184), the Vietnamese food at this Newtown offspring is just as fresh, delicious and inexpensive. The roll-your-own rice paper rolls are sensational (and fun). Licensed and BYO. Closed lunch Mon–Wed.

Three Five Seven King **357 King St ☎02/9519 7930. Newtown CityRail.** Hidden at the quirkier end of King St as it heads to St Peters, *Three Five Seven King*, with its white tablecloths, stylish interior, ambient lighting, lovely service and fresh modern Australian cuisine, appears like a fine-dining mirage. What's also amazing is the value, with a set menu (entrée and main) available for $24. The small menu is constantly changing, but the melt-in-your-mouth duck, whether done French style or with Asian greens, is one to look out for. Tasting plates for the delicious entrées and divine desserts are also available. Licensed and BYO. Dinner Tues–Sat.

Leichhardt, Haberfield and Rozelle

See map on p.111 for locations.

Anna and Aldo's **9 Norton St, Leichhardt ☎02/9550 9760. Bus #438 & #440 from Central CityRail.** Enduringly popular and very traditional inexpensive Italian trattoria. Licensed and BYO. Closed Sun.

Frattini **122 Marion St, Leichhardt ☎02/9569 2997. Bus #438 & #440 from Central CityRail.** One of the best Italian restaurants in Little Italy, run by a genial family. Modern, airy space, old-fashioned service and moderately priced food. The fish is recommended, especially the whitebait fritters. BYO. Closed Sat lunch and all Sun.

Grappa **267 Norton St, Leichhardt ☎02/9560 6090. Bus #438 & #440 from Central CityRail.** One of the liveliest restaurants in Little Italy, with a busy open kitchen, a huge dining area and gregarious staff. The wood-fired oven takes pride of place and turns out tasty Italian sausage, pizza and pasta, plus there are more sophisticated and expensive mains ($20–35), including the signature slow-roasted duck. An extensive wine list – Italian and local – includes a section devoted to the namesake digestive liqueur. Licensed and BYO. Closed Sat lunch and all Sun.

Harvest **71 Evans St, Rozelle ☎02/9818 4201. Bus #440 from Central CityRail.** Established in the 1970s, this vegan and vegetarian restaurant has kept up with the times, dipping into Vietnamese, Japanese, Italian and a whole range of cuisines. The moderately priced food is delicious, desserts decadent and the coffee gets the thumbs up. Licensed and BYO. Dinner Tues–Sat.

La Disfada **109 Ramsay St, Haberfied ☎02/9798 8299.** A little off the beaten track in Sydney's true Italian heartland, but reckoned to serve the best wood-fired pizza in town; no bookings so you might have to queue as it's so popular. The pasta ($11.50) is also delicious. Al fresco dining too. BYO. Dinner Wed–Sun.

The harbour

See maps on pp.130-131

The Bathers Pavilion **4 The Esplanade, Balmoral Beach ☎02/9969 5050. Bus #230 or #247 from North Sydney CityRail to Mosman Junction then #257.** Indulgent beach-house-style dining in the former (1930s) changing rooms on Balmoral Beach, now a very pricey restaurant and café double-act, presided over by one of Sydney's top chefs, Serge Dansereau. The fixed-price dinner menu in the restaurant starts from $90 for two courses (from $60 lunch-time). Weekend breakfast in the café is a North Shore ritual – expect to queue to get in (the resto has Sun breakfast only, for which you can book) – while the wood-fired pizzas are popular later in the day. Expensive to very expensive. Licensed. Café daily 7am–midnight, restaurant lunch and dinner daily.

Doyles on the Beach **11 Marine Parade, Watsons Bay ☎02/9337 1350; also Doyles Wharf Restaurant ☎02/9337 1572 next door. Ferry to Watsons Bay Wharf.** The original of the long-running Sydney fish-restaurant institution is the first of these, but both serve great, if overpriced, seafood and have views of the city across the water. They have also taken over the adjacent pub, which serves pub meals in its beer garden. A water taxi can transport you from Circular Quay to Watsons Bay. Mains $20–40. Licensed. Daily lunch and dinner.

Epoque Belgian Beer Café **429 Miller St, Cammeray ☎02/9954 3811. Bus #202, #207 &**

#208 from Wynyard CityRail. With a Belgian owner and original wood panelling and fittings, this is a slice of Belgium in Sydney. Draught beer taps dispense Hoegaarden, Leffe Blonde and Brune and Stella Artois, and there are 24 other beers by the bottle. There's only room for eighteen people at the bar, so best to book a table and come to eat. Mussels, of course, are the thing, served with *frites* and mayo, or try the satisfying *andouillettes* (sausage) and mashed potato, all moderately priced. Mains $18.50–26.50. Licensed.

Gourmet Pizza Kitchen 199 Military Rd, Neutral Bay ☎02/9953 9000. Bus #247 or #230 from North Sydney CityRail. Spacious, busy place that's especially popular with families – how many other pizza joints provide dough for the kids to play with? Traditional pizzas from $14, gourmet $17–20. Licensed.

Radio Cairo Cafe 83 Spofforth St, Cremorne ☎02/9908 2649. Bus #247 or #230 from North Sydney CityRail. A spectacular view of the city. This funky café features a creative and varied menu with a strong emphasis on African tastes. It's in a great location for cinema goers on their way to the nearby Hayden Orpheum Picture Palace. Sharing a selection of dishes with companions and taking advantage of the early-bird special (finish before 7pm to get 20 percent off the bill) makes it even better value. Mains $16–25. Licensed and BYO. Dinner daily.

Roger Fish Café Grill Shop 6, 2A Waters Rd, Neutral Bay ☎02/9953 6242. Bus #247 or #230 from North Sydney Cityrail. An interactive fresh seafood experience, where you choose not only your preferred catch of the day (from a changing menu of up to 26 choices), but also the style in which it is cooked, its flavouring and even the thickness of the fillet. A great way to have personalized, yet still reasonably priced, fish and chips. Mains $16–23. Licensed and BYO.

Watermark 2A The Esplanade, Balmoral Beach ☎02/9968 3433. Bus #247 or #230 from North Sydney CityRail to Mosman Junction, then #257 or #238 from Taronga Zoo Wharf, or after 7pm bus #233 from Mosman South (Musgrave St) Wharf. For a memorable Sydney meal, both for location and food, you can't go wrong here. Chef Kenneth Leung is well known for his fusion of Eastern and Western cooking styles and ingredients, plus there are views right across the water, a terrace to dine on under the sun or stars (or sit by the fireplace in winter), a stylish interior and fabulous service (mains $31–42). Licensed.

Bondi

Bondi Social 1st Floor, 38 Campbell Parade, Bondi Beach ☎02/9365 4303. Bus #380 from Bondi Junction Cityrail. You could easily miss the sandwich board sign which leads you to this hidden gem, but once found a million-dollar balcony view of the beach awaits the diner who wants to escape the melee of the Campbell Parade pavement. The interior is wood rich and dim lit at night; the mood promises romance and an interesting dining experience with worldwide influence. Mains at dinner $21–26. Licensed. Dinner daily, also Sat & Sun 9am–3.30pm for brunch.

Bondi Tratt 34B Campbell Parade, Bondi Beach ☎02/9365 4303. Bus #380 from Bondi Junction CityRail. Considering the setting, with outdoor seating overlooking the beach, *Bondi Tratt* is not at all expensive. Come here to take in the view and the invariably buzzing atmosphere over breakfast, lunch and dinner, or even a coffee. Serves contemporary Australian and Italian food. Cheap pasta deals 5–7pm. Daily 7am–10.30pm. Licensed and BYO.

Gelbison Pizzeria 10 Lamrock Ave, Bondi Beach ☎02/9130 4022. Bus #380 from Bondi Junction CityRail. Popular 'breezy' pizza restaurant with sea views from a couple of pavement tables. The pizzas get the critical thumbs up and range from traditional to inspired – their potato and garlic pizza is surprisingly yummy. Big range of pasta, too, from $12. Worth booking later in the week as fills up fast. BYO. Daily 5–10.30pm, until 10pm Sun.

Hugo's 70 Campbell Parade, Bondi Beach ☎02/9300 0900. Bus #380 from Bondi Junction CityRail. Set smack among the parade of posers, surfers and travellers, this is contemporary Bondi – part café, part bar, part fine dining – with a fun, young and friendly feel. At weekends it opens for all-day brunch (Sat & Sun 9am–4pm; no bookings), while from 7pm to 11pm every night white tablecloths and softly glowing lamps appear. Service is wonderful and honed for your comfort, including blankets for the chilly sea breeze if you sit outside. Generous, if expensive, portions of modern Asian and

Mediterranean-slanted creations; mains cost $30–39. Licensed.

Icebergs Dining Room and Bar 1 Notts Ave, Bondi Beach ☎02/9365 9000. Bus #380 from Bondi Junction CityRail. In the renovated *Icebergs Club* building, this restaurant has got it all – the views, the sharp surrounds, the celebs and some of the best cuisine Sydney has to offer. Don't expect all that to come cheap though; the Mediterranean-style mains are $32–44, but, hey, you only live once. Closed Mon.

Moorish & the North Bondi RSL 120 Ramsgate Ave, North Bondi. Bus #380 & #389 from Bondi Junction CityRail. Luke Mangan of *Salt* restaurant fame has taken over the dining room of the once downmarket North Bondi RSL and has installed a protégé as chef. Huge windows look right over the north end of the beach, and the modern Australian food is sensational (mains $18–30). The once near deserted RSL club upstairs has also seen a surge in popularity since being renovated and has an excellent and affordable bar menu. Licensed. Breakfast Sat & Sun 10am–noon, lunch & dinner daily.

No Names Beach Road Hotel, 71 Beach Rd, cnr Glenayr Ave, Bondi ☎02/9130 7247. Bus #389 from Bondi Junction CityRail. This is the choice for a big, filling, cheap and tasty Italian feast after a day at the beach. Eat in the sunny beer garden. Pasta $10, mains such as veal in tomato sauce, $14. Licensed.

Sean's Panaroma 270 Campbell Parade, Bondi Beach ☎02/9365 4924. Bus #380 & #389 from Bondi Junction CityRail. A funky, relaxed little restaurant across from the north end of the beach. Sean Moran's food is considered to be some of the best and most inventive in Sydney – the blackboard menu reflects the latest inspirations, though Mediterranean is the touchstone. Mains $36–42. BYO. Lunch Sat & Sun, dinner Wed–Sat.

Bronte and Coogee

The Beach Pit 211 Coogee Bay Rd, Coogee ☎02/9665 0068. Bus #372 from Central CityRail & #373, #374 & #376 from Circular Quay CityRail. Really enjoyable café-restaurant with Coogee's trademark informality and friendliness. Small but succulent menu has European and Asian influences and plenty of fish and seafood on offer; dishes are generous, well priced (mains $13–21) and well presented. You can breakfast here at the weekend too. BYO. Closed Tues & Wed.

Chilli Box 205 Coogee Bay Rd, Coogee. Bus #372 from Central CityRail & #373, #374 & #376 from Circular Quay CityRail. Follows the current trend for Thai food – choose your noodles, choose your flavours. Good fresh ingredients, the clatter of woks, and plenty of other diners make this a great place for a cheap feed. $12–17. BYO. Daily 11.30am–10pm.

Coogee Bay Hotel Beach Brasserie 212 Arden St, Coogee ☎02/9665 0000. Bus #372 from Central CityRail & #373, #374 & #376 from Circular Quay CityRail. Very reasonably priced pub food, with an interesting menu, but traditionalists can cook their own steaks on the barbie, and breakfast is available. Licensed. Daily 7am–9.30pm.

Jack & Jill's Fish Café 98 Beach St, Coogee ☎02/9665 8429. Bus #372 from Central CityRail & #373, #374 & #376 from Circular Quay CityRail. This down-to-earth fish restaurant is a local legend. Come here to enjoy beautifully cooked fish from the basic battered variety to tasty tandoori perch. Mains cost $13–20. BYO. Tues–Sat from 5pm, Sun from noon.

Swell Restaurant 465 Bronte Rd, Bronte ☎02/9386 5001. Bus #378 from Central CityRail or Bond Junction CityRail. One of three Bronte café-restaurants to open in the evening down at the beach. Sit inside for the latest in sharp interiors, or out on the pavement for the million-dollar Bronte Beach view. There's plenty of competition here so prices are very reasonable for what you're getting. Dinner mains all $28. Licensed. Daily 7am–10pm.

Wet Paint 50 Macpherson St, Waverley ☎02/9369 4634. Bus #378 from Central CityRail or Bondi Junction CityRail. Everything about this off-the-beaten-track place says it's an old faithful. The menu never changes much, the decor has a frayed homeliness and the delicious Cajun-slanted cooking is all done within a few metres of your seat. Very reasonable at $17–24 for mains. Licensed. Tues–Sat 6–10pm.

Manly and the northern beaches

Alhambra 54 West Esplanade, Manly ☎02/9976 2975. Ferry to Manly Wharf. Opposite the wharf, you can't miss this place when you get off the ferry. The owner is from Spanish Morocco, and the food is both authentic North African and Spanish – tapas, paella, *merguez* sausage, lamb and fish tagines, seven vegetable couscous, and a chicken version of *b'stilla* all feature and are well priced. There are even flamenco dancers some nights (Thurs–Sun) and a classical Spanish guitarist on Tues evenings. Licensed and BYO.

Le Kiosk 1 Marine Parade, Shelly Beach ☎02/9977 4122. Ferry to Manly Wharf. The coastal walk from Manly Wharf to secluded Shelly Beach is a delight in itself, and *Le Kiosk* has just the right laid-back beach-house feel. If you can't afford the generous but expensive contemporary fare, fish and chips from the attached kiosk is an excellent alternative. Licensed. Dinner Mon–Sat.

Manly Ocean Beach House Ocean Promenade, South Steyne, Manly ☎02/9977 0566. Housed in the old Tourism Information office just metres from the waves at Manly Beach, this very chic restaurant packs them in for costly breakfast, lunch and ever-so elegant dinner daily. The windows open wide and let in the ocean breeze, the perfect accompaniment for mains including kangaroo, mash, mushrooms and port, or breakfasts with any kind of egg and delectable champagne cocktails. Licensed. Daily 7am–10pm.

Out of Africa 43–45 East Esplanade, Manly, opposite Manly Wharf ☎02/9977 0055. The zebra skin seat covers and tribal spears, masks and colourful photos on the walls put you in the mood for the "Couscous Royale" (for two people), dips of the day and other African speciality dishes, prepared traditionally, moderately priced and oozing with unusual flavours like harissa. Thursday nights from 7.30pm there's live acoustic funk jazz and world music. BYO. Lunch Thurs–Sun, dinner daily.

Pacific Thai Cuisine 2nd Floor, 48 Victoria Parade, cnr South Steyne, Manly ☎02/9977 7220. Crisp decor and fantastic views of the beach from its upstairs location, this inexpensive Thai restaurant offers a variety of fresh favourites as well as some Chef's Specials, like Chu Chi Curry (red curry with kaffir lime leaves) and spicy seafood dishes. There are vegetarian options too. Licensed and BYO. Lunch Tues–Sun, dinner daily.

13

Drinking

Australians have a reputation for enjoying a drink or two, and hotels – more commonly known as **pubs** – are where this mostly takes place. After many years in the serviceable though mainly bland pub wilderness, Sydneysiders woke up one day to find a fashionable, renovated bar on almost every corner, serving interesting food and offering everything from poetry readings and art classes to groovy Sunday afternoon jazz or DJ sessions. Which means the choice of a drinking hole is big and you can be assured of finding one to suit any mood and taste. Traditional old **hotels** are no longer being outdone by the groovy bars and cocktail lounges and the more recent craze for wine bars, and have upped the ante themselves by employing renowned chefs and putting on food a cut above the old pub grub fare. In Sydney the *mixologist* – bar tenders with a knack for a good cocktail – are fast becoming king, and imported beers are more common than not. Sydney has many Art Deco pubs and we've mentioned some of the best below. Also, keep an eye out for RSL and Tradesmen's clubs, where the drinks remain ridiculously cheap, the food is honest and conversation with the regulars always a treat.

Typically, pubs have at least one public bar (traditionally rowdier) and a lounge bar (more sedate), a pool table, and in some cases a beer garden. Many offer meals, either in a restaurant or bistro setting, or served up informally at the bar. Ten percent of the world's **poker machines** are found in New South Wales, however, and the noisy, money-eating things have taken over many Sydney pubs. We have chosen places where these monsters are absent, or at least few and unobtrusive.

Some pubs and bars have 24-hour licences, though few actually stay open continuously (we have indicated those that have them, and their normal hours of operation). Standard **opening hours** are Monday to Saturday 11am–11pm/midnight and Sunday 11am–10pm, but many places stay open until at least 2am or later, particularly on Friday and Saturday nights. **Smoking** at bar or service counters has been banned in New South Wales and a designated non-smoking area must be provided within at least one bar area.

Draught **beer** is served in a ten-ounce (half-pint) glass known as a **middy** (around $2.80) or a fifteen-ounce **schooner** (around $3.80). Imports such as Guinness and Stella cost a bit more. Three local beers readily available on tap are Toohey's New, a pretty standard lager; Toohey's Old, a darker, more bitter brew; and Reschs, a tastier, Pilsner-style beer. Upmarket places may only serve beer in bottles, costing from $5. Wine by the glass is available at many places, usually from $5, but expect to pay at least $7 for something choicer. Cocktail bars are very popular, and happy hour (times given in reviews) at one of these can be a great chance to catch the sunset over cheap drinks; outside these times a cocktail will set you back $8.50–14.50.

We have divided our drinking account into areas, starting from The Rocks and ending with Bondi. A few **CBD** bars are closed on Saturday and most also close Sunday (the big nights out downtown are Thursday and Friday). **The Rocks**, with its huge range of lively watering holes, is a fair option on any night, though it does attract a pretty boisterous, beery crowd. A better choice for a cool, gay or arty scene is **Darlinghurst**, or nearby **Paddington** and **Surry Hills**. You can get a drink any time, day or night, in **Kings Cross**; there's a burgeoning gay and lesbian pub scene in inner-city **Newtown**, and the old neighbourhood pubs of **Balmain** make for a great pub crawl. The best seaside drinking spots are **Bondi**, **Coogee**, **Watsons Bay**, **Manly** and **Newport**. Some pubs serve such good food that we have listed them separately in the "Eating" chapter. Likewise, some pubs listed in the "Live music and clubs" chapter are also among the city's best watering holes.

The Rocks

Australian Hotel 100 Cumberland St, The Rocks. Circular Quay CityRail/ferry. Convivial corner hotel seemingly always full of Brits. The crowded outside tables face a sports centre under the Harbour Bridge, but the verandah upstairs gives sweeping vistas of Circular Quay and the Opera House. Inside, original fittings lend a lovely old-pub feel. Known and loved for its Bavarian-style draught beer brewed in Picton, plus delicious gourmet pizzas with toppings which extend to native animals – emu, kangaroo and crocodile.

Blu Horizons Bar 36th Floor, Shangri La Hotel, 176 Cumberland St, The Rocks. Circular Quay CityRail/ferry. Top-floor cocktail bar of the five-star Shangri-La Hotel. Often overlooked but very cosmopolitan, this mega-expensive lounge is worth it for the 270-degree view of the Opera House, Darling Harbour and on towards the Blue Mountains. Dress smartly to get in, and make a night of it sipping cocktails and mixing with the jet set. Closes 1am Mon–Thurs, 2am Fri–Sat, midnight Sun.

▼ Blu Horizons Bar

Firefly Pier 7 17 Hickson Rd, Dawes Point. Circular Quay CityRail/ferry. It may be small but that's the beauty of this little gem located out of the crowded city and down near the revamped Sydney Theatre. It has harbour views to go with the 22 wines by the glass, creative cocktails and micro-brewed beers, plus some funky tapas snacks. Open late but closes sunset Sun.

Glenmore Hotel 96 Cumberland St, The Rocks. Circular Quay CityRail/ferry. Unpretentious, inexpensive breezy pub perched over The Rocks, with great views from large windows in the public bar and spectacular ones from the rooftop beer garden, where large groups gather every night. A handy refresher before or after the Harbour Bridge walk – it's opposite the pedestrian walkway entrance – and serving up reasonably priced and unfussy pub grub.

Harbour View Hotel 18 Lower Fort St, The Rocks. Circular Quay CityRail/ferry. Sibling to the stately *Exchange Hotel* in Balmain, this three-storey renovated gem puts you right under the bridge – and close enough from the top balcony cocktail bar to raise a glass to the Bridgeclimbers making their way back from the summit. Function rooms and a pricey but exceptional restaurant above the classy bar downstairs; the crowd is mixed, and better for it.

Heritage Belgian Beer Café 135 Harrington St, The Rocks. Circular Quay CityRail/ferry. It's so authentic and continental you'll forget you're in Sydney in this former school hall in the middle of a heritage-listed building. There are 35 draught and bottled varieties of beer, plus mussels and other hearty European food. The whole atmosphere is conducive to a long session with good mates. Closes 1am Mon–Sun daily.

Hero of Waterloo 81 Lower Fort St, Millers Point, The Rocks. Circular Quay CityRail/ferry. One of Sydney's oldest pubs, built in 1843 from sandstone dug out from the Argyle Cut (see p.63), this place has plenty of atmosphere and feels steeped in history. Open fireplaces make it a good choice for a winter drink, and it serves simple meals.

Lord Nelson Brewery Hotel 19 Kent Street (cnr of Argyle St), Millers Point, Circular Quay Cityrail/ferry. As the only pub in the Rocks that has been brewing six of its own beers since 1987, this pub is a beer lover's paradise and as such attracts a unique crowd. The 3 Sheets and the Old Admiral are recommended. Mon–Sat 11am–11pm, Sun noon–10pm.

Lowenbrau Keller Argyle St (corner of Playfair St), The Rocks. Circular Quay CityRail/ferry. It's Oktoberfest all year round in this Bavarian beer hall in an historic Rocks courtyard. This is the only place in Australia that serves Löwenbräu Original and Franziskaner Weissbier on tap, and you can also eat Bavarian food for breakfast, lunch and dinner. If you like it rowdy, this is for you. Mon–Thurs till midnight, Fri, Sat & Sun to 2am.

Mercantile Hotel 25 George St, The Rocks. Circular Quay CityRail/ferry. High-spirited Irish pub with Sydney's best-poured Guinness on offer to accompany the filling bistro meals. Outdoor tables are a fine spot to watch the weekend market crowds.

Circular Quay and Sydney Opera House

Sydney Opera House has several bars, including the very swish one at its top-notch restaurant, *Guillaume at Bennelong*. But there are plenty of other bars to distract you on your walk around the concourse.

Aqua Luna Bar Building 2, Shop 18, Opera Quays, Circular Quay East. Circular Quay CityRail/ferry. Be lured by the blue light into this slick ground-floor bar near the Opera House. Fantastic views of the harbour from the terrace and a restaurant upstairs. A speciality is infused vodka, with over 60 flavours to choose from. Plans to make this into an ice bar are well under way.

Bridge Bar Level 10, 1 Macquarie St, City. Circular Quay CityRail/ferry. The harbour and its attractions are everywhere you look in this tenth floor bar near the infamous "Toaster" building at Circular Quay. Despite the plush surrounds, the crowd's not as exclusive as you'd expect and the addictive speciality drinks like the apple and cinnamon mojito are a perfect accompaniment to a Sydney sunset. Mon–Fri till late, Sat to 2am, closed Sun.

Cruise Bar Level 2, Overseas Passenger Terminal, Circular Quay West. Circular Quay CityRail/ferry. With glass walls providing an uninterrupted view of the harbour, the location of this fun and bright bar has ensured it's a popular destination for the young and urbane. You'll need to dress well, but drink prices aren't exorbitant, and cocktail classes are offered for the keen mixer. Open till 2am Fri & Sat.

Customs House Bar 19 Macquarie Place, off Bridge St. Circular Quay CityRail/ferry. This ground-floor bar is in an attractive building (circa 1826) fronting onto a city square near Circular Quay (but not at Customs House itself). A suited crowd spills out of the doors and schmoozes among the palm trees and statues. Cheap bar lunches. Upstairs on Level 5 the *Havana Bar* (open Mon–Sat 5pm–late) is a little slicker, but has

Bars with views

There are some wonderful harbour and beach **views** from several of Sydney's pubs and bars. The best are at the *Blu Horizons Bar* at the *Shangri-La* (see p.207) and at the *Glenmore Hotel* (p.207), both in The Rocks; *Bridge Bar* (see above), *Cruise Bar* (above) and *Posh* (opposite) around Circular Quay; the *Opera Bar* (see opposite) at the Opera House; *Orbit Bar* in the Australia Square tower in the city centre (p.210); and by the beach at *Bondi Icebergs Club* (p.217) and *Coogee Bay Hotel* (p.171).

great views over the Cahill expressway to the Bridge and Opera House. Closed Sat.

Opera Bar Lower Concourse Level, Sydney Opera House, Circular Quay CityRail/ferry. In summer you can't move for the people, but that's half the fun of this stunningly located bar. Concert goers mingle with tourists and office workers who have come across from the city to catch the sea breeze, watch the ferries come in and drink next to one of the world's great buildings. There's Jazz on Sunday afternoons and a bar snack menu available from the two bars – one inside and one on the concourse itself. Not to be confused with the *Oyster Bar* (1 Circular Quay East), which has an equally gorgeous setting but the added benefit of serving the finest oyster shooters around.

Posh Level 3, Overseas Passenger Terminal, Circular Quay West. Circular Quay CityRail/ferry. On the top floor above *Cruise Bar* (see above), *Posh* is also a level up in class: views are even better, and decor is seriously sultry – expect steep drink prices to go with the sophisticated martinis and daiquiris. Closed Sun.

City centre

Art House Hotel 275 Pitt St. Town Hall CityRail. A grand nineteenth-century School of Arts Building in the middle of the CBD, this high-ceilinged space does more than just sell drinks. The main bar, *The Verge*, is a converted chapel which makes for a dramatic setting. The polished wooden floorboards and beautiful Victorian-era design extend through four ever-changing rooms, which feature new and sometimes famous artworks. *Art House* lives up to its name with free life-drawing classes in the library, art exhibitions, short-film screenings and guest DJs. Both bar and restaurant food are moderately priced and taste great. Closed Sun.

Brooklyn Hotel 225 George St, cnr Grosvenor St. Wynyard or Circular Quay CityRail. Rather posh, the *Brooklyn* has a well regarded, pricey restaurant (specializing in prime beef from the chargrill), magenta walls and gleaming wood floors. Stools run along the length of the big glass windows from where you can watch the city crowds. Popular with cashed-up traders from the nearby Sydney Futures Exchange but also now attracting a younger crowd for the Fri and Sat night DJs. Upmarket eclectic bar food includes $5 steaks. Open till 2am Fri & Sat, closed Sun.

CBD 75 York St, cnr King St. Wynyard CityRail. Clamorous and swanky ground-floor bar in a renovated Art Deco bank, popular with an after-work crowd. The hotel covers four floors, which include an award-winning modern Australian restaurant and two other bars. Closed Sun.

Establishment 252 George St. Circular Quay CityRail. The huge main room boasts an extraordinarily long marble bar, white pillars, high decorative ceilings, and an atrium and fountain at the back. Despite the size, it gets jam-packed, particularly on Thursday nights (when it's free champagne for ladies before 7pm) and Fridays, when the door policy is very strict. On level 4 is Hemmesphere, a sophisticated Moroccan-themed bar room with cushions and lavish couches, and a drinks list to match. On-site ballroom, a world-class restaurant est (with top chef Peter Doyle), Tank nightclub (p.223) and thirty-odd luxurious hotel rooms complete the de luxe options. Open late every night.

Forbes Hotel Cnr King and York streets. Wynyard CityRail. Atmospheric, turn-of-the-twentieth-century corner hotel with a lively downstairs bar; resolutely untrendy. Upstairs is more sedate, with a pool table and plenty of window seating – the best spot is the tiny cast-iron balcony, with just enough room for two. Very popular Thurs & Fri nights. Open till 3am Fri & Sat.

Industrie Bar 107 Pitt St. Martin Place CityRail. The theme is "south of France" yet the biggest point of difference from the proliferation of cocktail bars springing up in the city is *Industrie's* intimacy. Located in the Pitt Street corporate precinct, it's an ideal spot to shift down a gear from the hustle and bustle of the world outside in a dark and decidedly sexy interior. Baguettes and omelettes make up the all-day brasserie-style menu and there's live jazz on Thursday nights till late. Thur–Sat till 2am. Closed Sun.

Marble Bar 259 Pitt St. Town Hall CityRail. A sightseeing stop as well as a great place for a drink: this was the original 1893 basement bar of the *Tattersalls Hotel*, and the stunningly ornate Victorian interior features Italian marble. It was preserved when the *Hilton Hotel* was built in 1973 and the *Marble Bar* was encased in concrete while major renovations went in 2005, emerging more splendid than ever. On the fourth floor, the glamourous *Zeta Bar* is also worth checking out and there's the traditionally staid *George Adams Bar* on Pitt Street. *Marble Bar* drinks start from a reasonable $6 for a glass of wine, and $8 for a cocktail; there's a sound system with DJ sessions – eclectic rock and jazz – at 7pm and again at 10pm. The Marble Bar is open Mon–Thurs 5pm–3am, Fri & Sat 4pm–3am.

Orbit Lounge Level 47, Australia Square, 264 George St. Wynyard CityRail. Australia's first Manhattan-style skyscraper, designed by perhaps Sydney's best-known architect Harry Seidler, was built in 1968, and the fifty-storey building was Sydney's tallest for many years. The views from the revolving bar are best when darkness falls and the city is dramatically lit up. It's much easier to get in here than into the crowded *Blu Horizons Bar* (see p.207); dress code is smart casual. The drinks list is very James Bond and there's bar food if you're peckish.

Roof Bar Roof Level Skygarden, 77 Castlereagh St, Sydney. Town Hall CityRail. After a hard day shopping in the Pitt St Mall and surrounding centres, this Balinese-inspired rooftop bar is a breath of fresh air, literally, as you sit among the highrises and look down at the bustling streets below. Very zen-like water features and a wooden sundeck make it relaxing and the drinks are reasonable too. Sat & Sun private functions only.

Senate Bar Lower ground floor, 1 Martin Place. Martin Place CityRail. Elegant, stylish bar below the old GPO, where lawyers and bankers come to sip on imported beers. Sandstone walls and funky ottomans provide a sophisticated feel. Good-value $10 curry-of-the-day lunch includes a drink, and draws them in during the day. Closed Sun.

Slip Inn 111 Sussex St, cnr King St. Town Hall CityRail. Now infamous as the place where Mary Donaldson met her Prince Frederick of Denmark, this huge three-level complex has several bars, a bistro and a nightclub, the *Chinese Laundry*, overlooking Darling Harbour. A young style-conscious crowd still comes here, but it's dropped some of its past pretension. Front bars have a pool room, while downstairs a boisterous beer garden fills up on sultry nights, with the quieter, more sophisticated *Sand Bar* beside it. Excellent wine list, with lots available by the glass and bar food including Thai and pizzas. Fri & Sat club opens till 4am. Closed Sun.

Verandah Bar 60 Castlereagh St. Town Hall CityRail. Lively after-work crowd packs out the *Verandah* on Fridays, when it's impossible to appreciate the wonderful spacious, white and shiny glass interior. You'll need to get in early for a prime position on the verandah overlooking Pitt Street or one of the great booths. If you're after a quiet chat, this isn't for you. Fri till 1am. Closed Sat & Sun.

Darling Harbour and around

As well as those places that we cover below you can also drink 24 hours in **Darling Harbour** at the Star City Casino (see p.228) and at *Home* nightclub (p.223), which has its own waterfront bar. The *Glasgow Arms Hotel* (see p.176), opposite the Powerhouse Museum, is a pleasant spot for a drink, too.

Cargo Bar 52–60 The Promenade, King Street Wharf, Sydney. Town Hall CityRail. Multi-level bar with plenty of outdoor seating at long tables downstairs and a cool crowd on sofas and stools upstairs. Views across to the casino and hotels of Darling Harbour are dazzling at night when the lights are glittering off the water. Drinks aren't cheap, and some standard beers are missing from the fridge, but yummy pizzas are satisfying. Just down the Wharf is *Bungalow 8* (8 The Promenade, King Street Wharf), which is much the same as far as views, beverages and clientele goes, but has a glossy bamboo and rattan interior making it feel like a tropical island hideaway. Mon–Wed & Sun noon–midnight, Thurs–Sat noon–2am. *The Loft* (3 Lime Street, King Street Wharf), another too cool for school bar, is also along this strip.

Civic Hotel **388 Pitt St, cnr Goulburn St ⓣ02/8267 3186. Town Hall CityRail.** Beautiful 1940s Deco-style pub, its original features perfectly preserved. Upstairs, there's a glamorous dining room and cocktail bar and owners have declared their mission to nurture young artistic talent by offering a unique creative performance space. A handy meeting point for Chinatown and George Steet cinema forays. Closed Sun.

Pontoon **Cockle Bay Wharf, Darling Harbour. Town Hall CityRail.** This open-fronted bar with outdoor tables feels like one big lively beer garden, right on the water opposite the marina. Big umbrellas shade you from the sun during the daytime, and there are pool tables inside. Attracts a young casual crowd, despite the upmarket restaurants surrounding it, and is a great place to wait for a table at *Chinta Ria* (on the level above). 24hr licence.

Scruffy Murphy's **43 Goulburn St. Central CityRail.** Rowdy, late-opening Irish pub with Guinness on tap, naturally; phenomenally popular, particularly with travellers and expats, who come for some hearty home-cooking too. Just around the corner from Central Station. Closes around 4.30am most nights.

Scu Bar Basement **4 Rawson Place, off Pitt St. Central CityRail.** This is the bar of the adjacent YHA but it's open to all-comers. Not surprisingly, it's most popular with the many backpackers staying in the area. There's crab racing on Mon nights, and a summer-party theme Thurs. Affordable pub prices and a casual atmosphere.

Inner East

The **inner east** of Sydney has the biggest concentration of places to drink, from fun pubs where you can play pool to some of the city's hippest bars, with a huge concentration in Darlinghurst. Many gay bars (see pp.236–237) are also worth checking out: the legendary *Taxi Club* (p.238) is a weird and wonderful place to end a big night out.

Surry Hills

Surry Hills is packed with great pubs, and a couple listed in the "Live music and clubs" and "Eating" chapters are also fun drinking spots: check out the lively *Hopetoun Hotel* (p.221) and the sprawling cheap-eats venue the *Forresters Hotel* (p.198).The nearest station to the suburb is "City".

Bar Cleveland **Cnr Cleveland and Bourke streets. Bus #372, #393 & #395 from Central CityRail.** Huge plate-glass windows open onto the busy, gritty street, and punters come in for an authentic urban brew. There's a pool table in the main bar, or head for the cosier rear bar. Trivia Nights and bar games such as "Toss the Boss" (when the barman could end up paying for your drinks) bring in an assortment of colourful locals. 24hr licence.

The Clock Hotel **470 Crown St, Surry Hills. Central CityRail or bus #301–303 from Circular Quay CityRail or Castlereagh St.** Much has been said about the transformation from dive to classy establishment The Clock underwent seven years ago, but it was a change that paid off, as the fashionable clientele will attest to. The chocolate-coloured lounge bar upstairs is big enough for large groups, and the booths and tables downstairs fill up quickly with local business people after work. The restaurant has really excelled, with prime position seating on the verandah and a satisfying menu with plenty of swish touches; tapas is available too.

Cricketers Arms **106 Fitzroy St, Surry Hills. CityRail or bus #301–303 from Circular Quay CityRail or Castlereagh St, City.** Just down the road from the live music scene at the *Hopetoun* (see p.221), the *Cricketers* has an equally dedicated clientele. A young, offbeat crowd – plenty of piercings and shaved heads – cram in and fall about the bar, pool room and tiny beer garden, and yell at each other over a funky soundtrack. Hearty bar snacks and a bistro. Closed Mon.

Dolphin Hotel **412 Crown St. Central CityRail or bus #301–303 from Circular Quay CityRail or Castlereagh St, City.** Fashionably renovated pub; the lounge bar doubles as a café, while the public bar is as down-to-earth as ever. The tiny upstairs bar, overlooking the stunning architecture of the *Dolphin's* restaurant, is a good spot for a chat and a glass of wine.

Mars Lounge 16 Wentworth Ave, Surry Hills. High ceilings, red-and-black dominated decor, moody lighting, heaps of seating – from booths to stools – *Mars* is both comfortable and stylish. DJ choices are eclectic and there's a different emphasis each night, from funky, retro-flavoured jazz, world grooves, latin, Seventies funk and uplifting house through to electronica. Mediterranean menu, including lots of shareable platters. Closed Mon.

White Horse 381–385 Crown St, Surry Hills. Central CityRail or bus #301–303 from Circular Quay CityRail or Castlereagh St, City. The newest kid on the block but off to a flying start, this well-appointed two-storey bar, with open fires and ottomans, has enough space to take the crowds and an open, light balcony which sets it apart from other bars in the area. The bar staff really know their stuff and can whip up a delicious cocktail to go with the swanky menu, or the cheaper bar food which is also available.

Darlinghurst

Several restaurants in **Darlinghurst** also have their own separate bars, including the dark and moody *The Victoria Room* (see p.199).

Burdekin 2 Oxford St, Darlinghurst. Museum CityRail. This well-preserved Art Deco pub near Hyde Park has several trendy bars on four levels. The basement *Dug Out Bar* (from 5pm) is tiny and beautifully tiled, and has table service and generous cocktails, while the spacious, ground-level *Main Bar* sports dramatic columns and a huge round bar. *Main Bar* Mon–Thurs noon–1am, Fri noon–4 or 5am, Sat 3.30pm–4 or 5am; *Dug Out Bar* Tues–Thurs 5pm–midnight, Fri 5pm–2am, Sat 6pm–3am. Closed Sun.

Darlo Bar Royal Sovereign Hotel, cnr Darlinghurst Rd and Liverpool St, Darlinghurst. Kings Cross CityRail. Popular Darlinghurst meeting place, with a lounge-room atmosphere. Comfy colourful chairs and sofas have a 1950s feel but there aren't enough to accommodate the mixed and unaffected crowd who are there to play pool or just curl up under the lamps and chat. Drinks, including the house wines, aren't expensive. At night you can order from the menus of local eateries, like *Burgerman* and *Fish Face*, and they'll fetch the food for you.

East Village Hotel 234 Palmer St, cnr Liverpool St, Darlinghurst. Kings Cross CityRail. Downhill from the main Darlinghurst bar and café action, this beautifully tiled corner pub, built in 1917, sits alone in a grittier sleazy backstreet area – tables on the street provide a glimpse of the street life. The bar is self-consciously stylish, with wooden floors and Sixties-style white swivel chairs – and they won't serve anything as downmarket as a schooner; fellow drinkers include young arts professionals.

Fix Kirketon Hotel, 229 Darlinghurst Rd, Darlinghurst. Kings Cross CityRail. This intimate little bar, with lacquered red walls and moody lighting, is very sexy and upmarket. The long communal table with its leather bar stools heightens the intimacy, putting the almost-too-cool customers in close proximity. Drinkers are quite often celebs or from the fashion set, who come here for a pre-dinner drink before dining at the adjacent restaurant *Salt*. Very expensive. Closed Sun.

Green Park Hotel 360 Victoria St, Darlinghurst. Kings Cross CityRail. A Darlinghurst stalwart, partly because of the stash of pool tables in the back room and TVs over the doors, but mainly because of the unpretentious vibe. There's nothing decorating the walls, the bar couldn't be more unassuming and humble bar tables with stools and a few lounge chairs accommodate the regular arty crowd.

Judgement Bar Courthouse Hotel, 189 Oxford St, Darlinghurst. Bus #378 from Central CityRail, #380 from Circular Quay CityRail. Overlooking Taylor Square, the upstairs bar of this pub is often open 24hr. Totally undiscriminating – you may find yourself here in the wee hours among an assortment of young clubbers and old drunks – and with cheap drinks. Wakes up around 1am. Mon–Thurs till 3am, Fri & Sat 24hr.

Middle Bar 1st floor, Kinsela's, 383 Bourke St, Darlinghurst. Bus #378 from Central CityRail, #380 from Circular Quay CityRail. Once a de luxe Art Deco funeral parlour, *Kinsela's* has long been transformed into a lively drinking and dancing spot. The *Middle Bar* is seriously sexy, from its lush decor and sunken seating area to the young good-looking crowd who drink here. You can gaze at the action in Taylor Square from the open-air balcony. In contrast, the unglamorous ground-floor bar is full of noisy poker machines. Open Tues, Wed & Sun till 1am, Thurs till 3am, Fri & Sat till 4am; ground-floor bar 24hr.

Palace Hotel 122 Flinders St, cnr South Dowling St, Darlinghurst. Bus #397–399 from Circular Quay CityRail. Classic Art Deco tiled corner pub, fashionably done-up. The noisy boho and student hangout is downstairs, where tiny eating area services the recommended Thai kitchen (student discount on Tues nights); eat meals where you can find a spot. Star attraction are the rooms of pool tables upstairs.

Paddington and Woollahra

Two lively drinking spots reviewed in the "Eating" chapter, the *Paddington Inn* (and the *Grand National Hotel*) shouldn't be overlooked.

Elephant Bar Royal Hotel, 237 Glenmore Rd, Paddington. Bus #389 from Circular Quay CityRail. The top-floor bar of this beautifully renovated, Victorian-era hotel has knockout views of the city, best appreciated at sunset (happy hour 6–7pm). The small interior is great, too, with fireplaces, paintings and elephant prints. As it gets crowded later on, people cram onto the stairwell and it feels like a party.

Lord Dudley 236 Jersey Rd, Woollahra. Bus #389 from Circular Quay CityRail. Sydney's most British looking pub, complete with fireplaces, fox-hunting pictures, dark wood furniture – and a dartboard. Thirty-six beers on tap including Newcastle Brown Ale. The bistro serves up hearty British fare and on winter afternoons you can while away the hours playing scrabble or backgammon in the comfy overstuffed chairs.

Kings Cross and Woolloomooloo

There are several pubs and bars in **Kings Cross**, many of them backpackers' hangouts, which we've listed in the "Live music and clubs" chapter, as the emphasis is on DJs and dancing – the bars reviewed below are the more sophisticated options. There are several boisterous pubs in **Woolloomooloo** opposite the naval base including the *Woolloomooloo Bay Hotel* (see p.201).

The Bourbon 24 Darlinghurst Rd, Kings Cross. Kings Cross CityRail. Infamous 24hr Kings Cross drinking hole recently given a swish new upgrade, which unfortunately hasn't done much to deter some of the colourful regulars. The place first opened in 1968 to attract US soldiers on R&R, and has become notorious with late night "incidents", often including well-known sporting and media personalities. The addition of a terrace section upstairs (Plan B) and a lounge bar at the back, the opening up of the front section onto the street, plus the dropping of "Beefsteak" from the original name, means more people are stopping off for a meal and to take in the still slightly low-rent ambience. Bands every night (usually cover bands) and DJs play retro four nights a week. May be a cover charge at weekends. Open 24hr.

Hugo's Lounge 33 Bayswater Rd, Kings Cross. Kings Cross CityRail. The same people who run the very successful *Hugo's* restaurant opposite Bondi Beach have opened this very cool bar and restaurant. The beautiful bar, complete with ottomans to loll on, has a very decadent Oriental feel and attracts a beautiful crowd – it can be hard to get into. Expensive drinks. Tues–Sat till 1am.

Kingsleys Alehouse Level 1, The Woolloomooloo Bay Hotel, cnr Bourke St and Cowper Wharf Rd, Woolloomooloo ⓣ02/8353 1333. Kings Cross CityRail. Upstairs from the *Wolloomooloo Bay Hotel* and commandeering the verandah with its gorgeous marina and harbour views, this sister to *Kingsleys Steak and Crabhouse* (ⓣ02/9331 7788) across the road prides itself on its impressive beer selection and is set up inside like a beerhall, with long communal tables. There are plenty of options, including international favourites like Tiger from Singapore and Trumer Pilsner from Austria, and a great selection of ales like St Arnou from Australia. Girls love the Beez Neez, a sweet wheat beer with honey tones. Closed Mon.

Lotus 22 Challis Ave, Potts Point. Kings Cross CityRail. Style and substance combine in the back room of the *Lotus Bistro*, and the padded snakeskin walls and retro wallpaper will put you in the mood for love, or at least a famous Lotus martini. Cocktails are a speciality, and there's an extensive list – enough to keep you happy all night, if you can afford it. Closed Mon.

Peppermint Lounge 281 Victoria St, Kings Cross. Kings Cross CityRail. Decor is sexy and plush in this European-style bar, with plenty of couches and private booths to relax in. A young funky crowd enjoy the live world music. Open Wed & Thurs till 4am, Fri & Sat till 5am, Sun till 3am.

Soho Bar & Lounge Piccadilly Hotel, 171 Victoria St, Kings Cross. Kings Cross CityRail. Trendy Art Deco pub on leafy Victoria Street, looking better than ever after yet another refurbishment. The ground-floor *Gold Room Bar* is the most fancy, but locals head to the upstairs *Leopard Lounge Bar* (Tues–Sun nights only) to hang out on the back balcony, play pool and sample the seasonally updated cocktail menu. The attached nightclub, *Yu*, runs on Fri and Sat nights from 10pm to sunrise, though DJs play every night.

Tilbury Hotel Cnr Forbes St and Nicholson St. Kings Cross CityRail. The beer garden isn't huge, but it's good looking, opening up from the polished wood and leather furniture café/restaurant area behind the bar. A smoke-free policy hasn't deterred customers, who come not only for the hip atmosphere, but for the food. Serving fruity breakfasts and lunches Mon to Sat 8am–4pm and Sun 10am–noon, there are also end of week BBQs for a very cheap $6, and Sunday Sessions in summer, including live jazz and soul and some surprise big-name artists.

Water Bar W Hotel, Cowper Wharf Rd, Woolloomooloo. Kings Cross CityRail. The bar of Sydney's hippest hotel (see p.167), this place is fabulously located in a dramatically renovated old iron and timber finger wharf. The sense of space is sensational, the lighting lush, and the sofas gorgeously designed and comfortable. A favourite with local celebrities, the pricey drinks (cocktails from $16) and the extortionate cost of the snacks (nuts from $8) are just worth it for the architecture and ambience.

Inner West

The areas around the Sydney University – **Glebe**, **Chippendale** and **Newtown** – have always had plenty of lively pubs. Further west, **Leichhardt** and **Balmain** also have some great boozers and the latter is a good place for a bar crawl.

Glebe

Ancient Briton 225 Glebe Point Road, cnr Bridge Rd, Glebe. Bus #431, #433 & #434 from Central CityRail. This lively pub is popular with the area's travellers, helped by claims of the coldest beer in Sydney, plus free Internet access (15min) for every drink bought, and cheap drink deals (happy hour daily 4.30–7.30pm). There's inexpensive Asian noodles on offer, and a stash of cheap pool tables upstairs, as well as a cosier cocktail bar.

Friend in Hand 58 Cowper St, cnr Queen St. Bus #431, #433 & #434 from Central CityRail. This characterful pub in the leafy backstreets of Glebe, with all manner of curious objects dangling from the walls and ceilings of the public bar, is a popular haunt for backpackers. Diverse entertainment in the upstairs bar (where you can also play pool) includes script-reading (Mon), poetry nights (Tues) and quizzes (Thurs). In the public bar, crab racing takes over Wed nights, and there's a piano player on Sat nights. There's also a cheap Italian restaurant, *Cesare's No Names* (see p.201) on site.

Nag's Head 162 St Johns Rd, off Glebe Point Rd. Bus #470 from Central CityRail. Calling itself a "posh pub", this is a good place for a quiet drink – definitely no pokies. Decor and atmosphere is very much that of a British boozer: several imported beers on tap – Guinness, Boddingtons, Stella and Becks – and pints or half-pints available. Its bistro dishes up excellent steaks and other grills, and there's an extensive bar menu. For more action, there's a loft area upstairs with pool tables.

Chippendale and Newtown

In addition to the watering holes included here, the *Lansdowne Hotel* in **Chippendale** opposite Victoria Park (see p.112) has a great little cocktail bar upstairs and popular pool tables downstairs, while the *Sandringham Hotel* ("Sando") in **Newtown** (see p.114) has long been one of the area's favourite places to drink.

Bank Hotel 324 King St, next to Newtown Station. Newtown CityRail. Smart-looking pub that's always packed and open late. Pool table out front, cocktail bar out back and a big beer garden downstairs (with Thai restaurant). 24hr licence.

Kellys on King 285 King St, Newtown. Newtown CityRail. Celtic mysticism meets Outback charm in this quaint Irish pub in the middle of Newtown. Colourful locals drink with students and backpackers in a relaxed setting. A good selection of Irish beers on tap. Open Mon–Thurs till 2am, Fri to 3am, Sat to 4am, Sun closes midnight.

Kuleto's 157 King St, Newtown. Newtown CityRail. Small but lively and unpretentious cocktail bar, packed with inner-city types for the two-for-one cocktails during happy hour (Mon–Sat 6–7.30pm & bonus happy hour Thurs 9.30–10.30pm). Ideal meeting point before a King Street dinner.

Marlborough Hotel 145 King St, Newtown. Newtown CityRail. A local favourito for a pre-dinner drink and a hangout for students from nearby Sydney University, the "Marly" is benefiting from almost a decade of major structural work. The spacious pub, with several bars and a great beer garden, also has a popular, good-value restaurant, *Bar Prego*, serving a diverse assortment of meals with an Italian slant. Cover bands Tues & Sat and a funk band on Sun, trivia nights Wed and DJs Thurs. 24hr licence.

The Rose 54 Cleveland St, Chippendale. Bus #423, #424, #426 & #428 from Central CityRail. This funkily decorated pub near Victoria Park is a real treasure, despite the unpromising location at the traffic-laden end of Cleveland Street. A mock-Renaissance ceiling mural overlooks a popular pool table, while a bizarrely decorated rocking horse is suspended over the partly covered beer garden out back (doubling as a modern Australian eatery with a huge blackboard menu). Good wine list, available by the glass.

Balmain and Leichhardt

Exchange Hotel Cnr Beattie and Mullens St, Balmain. Bus #442 from Darling Street Wharf or the QVB. This popular Balmain drinking spot has had a trendy makeover: the legendary *Safari Bar* has been replaced by the wood-themed *Martini Bar* and the old Library restaurant is now the swankier *Zetalli*. Known for its range of nightly events (live music, comedy and theatre), the *Exchange's* four bars cater to all tastes. The sweeping heritage verandah is still the best place to sit, and a perfect location to sample the $7 martini specials on a Thurs night – the lychee, ginger and chocolate martinis are especially good.

Leichhardt Hotel 95 Norton St, Leichhardt. Bus #438 & #440 from Central CityRail. With a courtyard opening onto the busy Italian restaurant strip and a first-floor balcony also providing a vantage point, the newly incarnated *Leichhardt Hotel* is a very slick designer pub. The dramatic contemporary interior includes a huge Caravaggio-style mural, a modern Italian restaurant (bar snacks also available) and a good selection of Italian bottled beers. Open Mon–Wed till midnight, Thurs–Sat till 3am, closed Sun.

London Hotel 234 Darling St, Balmain. Bus #442 from Darling Street Wharf or the QVB. Convivial British-style pub, with a high verandah overlooking the Saturday market. Attracts a typically mixed Balmain crowd.

Monkey Bar 255 Darling St, Balmain. Bus #442 from Darling Street wharf or the QVB. Stylish, crowded bar with an atrium restaurant, the *MB Bistro*. There's a small stage for the loud, free live music – blues, soul, jazz or acoustic rock (Tues & Sun). Inexpensive bar menu and a big selection of wines by the glass.

Vanilla Room 153 Norton St, Leichhardt. Bus #438 & #440 from Central CityRail. Norton Street is known for its Italian restaurants and pizza joints, not its swish bars, but this newly decked-out space fits right in with the surrounding trattorias. Red ceilings, dark floorboards and dim lanterns lend an air of mystery to the extensive rows of exciting wine bottles glinting behind the bar. There are cheap pizzettas on offer too. Closed Mon.

Legendary beer gardens

Many Sydney pubs have an outdoor drinking area, perfect for enjoying the sunny weather – the five listed below, however, are outright legends.

The Coogee Bay Hotel Arden Street, Coogee. Bus #374 from Central Station. Loud, rowdy and packed with backpackers from the nearby hostels, this enormous beer garden across from the beach is legendary in the eastern suburbs and open in winter, too, when they crank up the heaters. One of six bars in the *Coogee Bay Hotel,* including a big screen sports bar for all international sporting events, revellers can buy jugs of beer and cook their own meat in the garden from 9.30am till late. Events include Miss International Backpacker.

Doyles Palace Hotel 10 Marine Parade, Watsons Bay. Ferry to Watsons Bay Wharf or bus #324 & #325 from Edgecliff CityRail. Watson's Bay is Sydney's not-so-well-kept secret, and the *Doyles Palace Hotel* (still known to locals as the *Watson's Bay Hotel*) is the best place to experience the laid-back lifestyle – a seat in the sun with a cool beer, fresh fish and chips from the renowned *Doyles* kitchen or a steak from the BBQ and uninterrupted views across the harbour. The hours will just disappear.

The Mean Fiddler Cnr Commercial and Windsor roads, Rouse Hill. No public transport. About an hour's drive from Sydney's CBD, the *Fiddler* is off the beaten track; you'll need your own transport but a day out here is not misspent. Join the huge crowds at the 170-year-old Irish pub and sample the range of attractions – small, intimate rooms, open fires, live televised sport in the sports bar, and one of the best beer gardens in Sydney – a big courtyard with cook-your-own-steaks and help-yourself salad bar by day and live entertainment at night.

Newport Arms Hotel 2 Kalinya St, Newport. Bus #190 from Wynyard CityRail. A famous beer garden pub, established in 1880, where crowds gather every afternoon to relax on the huge deck looking out over Heron Cove at Pittwater. Good for families, with a children's play area, the bistro has also upgraded its fare – Asian-themed salads and standard but large seafood servings match an expanded wine list.

▼ Newport Arms Hotel

The Oaks Hotel 118 Military Rd, Neutral Bay. Bus #247 & #263 from Wynyard CityRail. The North Shore's most popular pub where generations of locals have spent Friday and Saturday nights crowded out back under the giant oak tree which shades the large beer garden. Cook your own (expensive) steak, or order a gourmet pizza from the restaurant inside.

The harbour

Three of the best places to drink around the harbour, **Watsons Bay**, **Newport** and **Neutral Bay**, are listed in the "Legendary beer gardens" box above.

Greenwood Hotel 36 Blue St, North Sydney. North Sydney CityRail. A former school, this gorgeous old sandstone building has been turned into a very pleasant, extensive pub, with the big courtyard serving as a haven from the corporate bustle of the North

Shore's high-rise business district. There are four bars, one of which includes a restaurant area serving lunch Mon–Fri (modern Australian with mains at around $20); you can also eat outside and bar snacks are available in the evenings. From Thurs to Sun there is much more of a party atmosphere here; the best time to come is on Sun, when around 1500 trendy young people flock to the day club, which takes over the whole pub; between twelve and fifteen DJs in three different areas, including the courtyard, play everything from funky house to hip hop ($15). There's a free student night, also with DJs, on Thurs (7pm–3am). Mon–Wed 11pm, Thurs & Sat till 3am, Fri 1.30am, Sun 10pm.

Ocean beaches

Whether for a casual afternoon of drinking and watching the surf roll in, or a an evening of dancing and partying beside the sea, Sydney's beachside pubs have the location and the facilities to ensure a good time will be had by all.

Bondi and the eastern beaches

In addition to the places listed below, the *North Bondi RSL* is also a lively drinking hole (see p.204).

Beach Palace Hotel 169 Dolphin St, Coogee. Bus #372 & #373 from Central CityRail. Home to a young and drunken crowd, made up of locals, beach babes and backpackers. Features seven bars, two restaurants and a great view of the beach from the balcony under the distinctive dome. There are DJs on the middle level Wed–Sat (Wed & Thurs 8pm–1am, Fri & Sat 10pm–3am) and on the top floor Thur & Fri (8pm–midnight), entrance for which is free except on Sat after 10pm when it's $5.

Beach Road Hotel 71 Beach Rd, Bondi Beach. Bus #389 from Bondi Junction CityRail. Huge, stylishly decorated pub with a bewildering range of bars on two levels and a beer garden. Popular with both travellers and locals for its good vibe. Entertainment, mostly free, comes from rock bands, DJs and a jazz supper club. The hotel also has a cheap Italian bistro, *No Names* (see p.201), and an upmarket contemporary Australian restaurant.

Bondi Hotel 178 Campbell Parade, Bondi Beach. Bus #380 from Bondi Junction CityRail. Huge pub dating from the 1920s, with many of its original features intact. Sedate during the day but at night an over-the-top, late-night backpackers' hangout. Mon–Sat till 4am.

Bondi Icebergs Club 1 Notts Ave, Bondi Beach. Bus #380 from Bondi Junction CityRail. Famous for its winter swimming club (see p.140), the *Icebergs* is a fantastic place to soak up the views and atmosphere of Bondi Beach. The clubhouse was recently rebuilt at a cost of $10 million, and it fast became the place to be seen. Sunday afternoons are an especially big time to dress up and mingle with the beautiful, bronzed people sampling the 37 types of champagne on the terrace. The *Sundeck Café* within the club offers Mediterranean-style light meals all day, but the seafood-inspired menu in the upstairs restaurant is expensive. Cover bands usually play Wed and Fri–Sun and there are trivia competitions on Mon. To guarantee entry, bring your passport or other ID to show you're an out-of-towner.

Bondi Social Level 1, 38 Campbell Parade, Bondi Beach. Bus #380 from Bondi Junction CityRail. It's one floor up from the busy Bondi strip, and a world away from the bikini shops and bikini-clad locals. Recycled timber interiors add a warm, cutting-edge flavour – not a bad place to kick back with a cocktail or beer and take in the unrivalled view out to sea.

Clovelly Hotel 381 Clovelly Rd, Clovelly. Bus #360 from Bondi Junction CityRail. Known to the locals as the "Cloey", this huge hotel perched slightly away from the beach has four bars and a fantastic, very popular bistro complete with a great terrace eating area with views over the water. Come on a Sunday, when there's a free DJ in the bar upstairs (from 7pm), or you can relax at the pool tables and upstairs deck.

Ravesi's Campbell Parade, cnr Hall St, Bondi Beach. Bus #380 from Bondi Junction CityRail. This corner spot looking across to the beach now houses a very popular and stylish bar attached to the boutique hotel above (see p.173). Huge windows ensure full people- and ocean-watching opportunities. There's a dress policy in the evening but you can get away with beach gear by day. There's beer on tap, but it's pricier than elsewhere. Wine by the glass starts from $7. There is also a basement bar open Thurs–Sun and a bistro-style restaurant upstairs, with more great views from its balcony tables.

Manly and the northern beaches

Ceruti's Street Bar 15 Sydney Road, Manly. Ferry to Manly Wharf. The music by resident and visiting DJs is cool and low, perfectly matched to the narrow bar and general vibe of this surprisingly sophisticated place near the beach. *Ceruti's* has the best collection of spirits in Manly, and there's an Italian restaurant attached. Outside seating comes with a view. Tues–Sun till 3am.

Ivanhoe Hotel 27 The Corso, Manly. Ferry to Manly Wharf. This huge Corso pub combines several bars with a nightclub and brasserie over four floors and includes a terrace and balcony where you can take in some sun. Locals and backpackers crowd the place out, from the oldtimers in the public bar, to the smartly dressed 20-somethings in the lounge bar. The weekend two-for-one cocktail deals (before 11pm Fri & Sat, before 9pm Sun) ensure a merry atmosphere, and there's various live music and also DJs Wed–Sat nights (free or $5–10). 24hr licence but generally Mon–Wed till midnight, Thurs till 1am, Fri & Sat till 5am, Sun till midnight.

Old Manly Boatshed 40 The Corso, Manly. Ferry to Manly Wharf ⓣ 02/9977 4443, ⓦ www.manlyboatshed.com.au. Characterful and relaxed basement bar overflowing with Manly Surf Club paraphernalia, popular with both backpackers and a crew of local regulars. There's a long-running comedy night on Mon (see p.229) and live music the rest of the week (Tues–Thurs & Sun 8.30pm; Fri & Sat 9.30pm; usually free, occasionally big-name bands attract a $5–15 cover charge); Thurs is the night for emerging songwriters. Food is served until midnight – the bistro-style menu includes good-value steaks ($15) and the Boatshed's legendary steak sandwich ($12). Mon–Sat 6pm–3am, Sun to midnight.

Live music and clubs

It's easy enough to find out exactly what's going on in the Sydney music and club scene. You'll find **listings** of music events in the "Metro" supplement in Friday's *Sydney Morning Herald* and "Time Out", a weekly entertainment lift-out in Sunday's *Sun-Herald*, but the best listings are in the "Sydney Live Magazine" in the *Daily Telegraph* every Wednesday, aimed squarely at the 18–30 market; there's also a more general what's on pull-out, "Seven Days", in Thursday's *Daily Telegraph*. A plethora of **free magazines** with information on more alternative goings-on – clubbing, fashion and the like – and band interviews and reviews can be found in the cafés, record shops and boutiques of Surry Hills, Darlinghurst, Glebe and Newtown; well-written *Drum Media* (with an online gig guide at Ⓦwww.drummedia.com.au) and *The Brag* have weekly listings and informed reviews, and *TNT* magazine has a new listings section, too; *3D World* and *Beat* cover the clubbing scene. **Radio** station 2 MMM (FM 104.9MHz) details music gigs around town daily on the hour between 2 and 6pm. There's also a handy Web-based gig guide prepared by ABC Radio's youth station Triple J (Ⓦwww.abc.net.au/triplej/gigs). Also check the useful **website** Ⓦwww.sydney.citysearch.com.au, a kind of listings mag on the Net, with plenty on the music and club scene.

Live music

Australia in general, and Sydney in particular, has a well-deserved reputation for producing quality **live bands**: the thriving pub scene of the late 1970s and early 1980s produced a spectrum of great acts, from indie stars Nick Cave, The

Buying tickets

Ticketek is the main **booking agency**, with branches located throughout Sydney, including 195 Elizabeth St (corner Park St) and at the State Theatre (see p.220) and the Theatre Royal (bookings Ⓣ02/9266 4800, Ⓦwww.ticketek.com.au). There's also Ticketmaster7, at the Capitol Theatre, 13 Campbell St, Haymarket, or the Entertainment Centre (bookings Ⓣ13 61 00, Ⓦwww.ticketmaster7.com). Fish Records sells tickets to selected gigs in-store (see "Shopping" for locations or Ⓦwww.fishrecords.com.au) or over the phone on Fish Tix (Ⓣ02/9410 1444), Central Station Records (see p.261), Red Eye Records (see p.261), Electric Monkeys (78 Gould St, Bondi) and Moshtix, a newer ticket agent (Ⓦwww.moshtix.com.au or Ⓣ02/9209 4614). It's best always to check the gig guides as the venues often sell tickets independently, depending on the size and scope of the show.

Church and the Triffids, to globe-straddling stadium-shakers like INXS. Sadly, the live music scene in Sydney has passed its boom time, and pub venues keep closing down to make way for the dreaded poker machines.

However, there are still enough venues to nourish a steady stream of local, interstate and overseas acts passing through each month, peaking in summer with several huge open-air festivals (see box on p.222).

Besides the big concert halls, Sydney's live music action still centres around pub venues. Pub bands are often free, especially if you arrive early (bands generally go on stage around 9.30–10.30pm, earlier on Sundays); otherwise, $5–8 is a standard entry fee for local bands, $12–15 for the latest interstate sensation and upwards of $20 for smaller international acts. Late Sunday afternoon and early evenings are notably laid-back – an excellent time to catch some funk or mellow jazz bands, which are usually free.

Concert venues

Capitol Theatre 13 Campbell St, Haymarket ⓣ02/9266 4800. Central CityRail. Refurbished, older theatre with balcony seating and room for around 2000 people. The Capitol hosts musicals and even ballet, but crooners and mellow pop groups occasionally appear here (see also p.227).

Enmore Theatre 118–132 Enmore Rd, Enmore ⓣ02/9550 3666, ⓦwww.enmoretheatre.com.au. Newtown CityRail. A pleasingly intimate, old-world Art Deco theatre venue for 1500 people – dingier than the Capitol, a fact which sits comfortably with its location, near to inner-city Newtown. Bands like Elvis Costello, the Pogues, Kraftwerk and the Cranberries are among notables to have played here but they often have well-known comedians too.

Hordern Pavilion Driver Ave, Fox Studios ⓣ02/9383 4063. Big enough without lacking in atmosphere (capacity of 5500), the Hordern has hosted everyone from Moby to Destinys Child to Justin Timberlake. No seating means it's perfect for dancing too; after Mardi Gras the dance party is held here every year.

Metro Theatre 624 George St ⓣ02/9264 2666, ⓦwww.metrotheatre.com.au. Town Hall CityRail. Purpose-designed to handle everything from musicals to bands and dance parties, the Metro is exceptionally well laid out and has an excellent sound system; holds up to 1200 people.

State Theatre 49 Market St ⓣ02/9373 6655, ⓦwww.statetheatre.com.au. Town Hall CityRail. This 2000-seat theatre is decked out perhaps a bit too opulently in marble and statuary, but performers who insist on a bit of grandeur play here. No dancing on the top balcony.

Sydney Entertainment Centre Haymarket, beside Darling Harbour ⓣ02/9266 4800, ⓦwww.sydentcent.com.au. Central CityRail. Soulless, 12,000-seat arena with video screens and a good sound system – Sydney's most popular indoor venue, for big international acts.

Sydney Superdome Olympic Boulevard, Sydney Olympic Park ⓣ02/8765 4321, ⓦwww.superdome.com.au. Homebush CityRail. Sydney's biggest venue, holding up to 21,000 people, the Superdome is at the Sydney Olympic site at Homebush and has hosted everything from the KISS and the Rolling Stones to Supercross Masters motorcycle extravaganzas. Because of its location there is not much to do after a show and it's a bit of a trek from the city, but for the big shows there is nowhere better.

Pub venues

As well as the places listed below, which are well known as live music venues, many of the **pubs and bars** reviewed in the "Drinking" chapter also have regular music or dance nights: see the *Opera Bar* at the Opera House (p.209), the *Civic Hotel* in the city (p.211), the *Marlborough Hotel* in Newtown (p.215), the *Monkey Bar* in Balmain (p.215), in Bondi the *Beach Road Hotel* (p.217) and the *Bondi Icebergs Club* (p.217), in Manly the *Ivanhoe Hotel* (p.218) and the *Old Manly Boatshed* (p.218), and the *Newport Arms Hotel* (p.216) in Newport.

Annandale Hotel Cnr Nelson St and Parramatta Rd, Annandale, ⓣ02/9550 1078. Bus #438 & #440 from Central CityRail. A showcase for indie bands, from up-and-comers to headline international acts, through rock, funk, metal and groove, with a capacity of 450. Music Tues–Sat nights (door $5–12).

The Basement 29 Reiby Place, Circular Quay ⓣ02/9251 2797. Circular Quay CityRail. This dark and moody venue is an institution that attracts the great and rising names in jazz, acoustic and world music as well as a roster of the world's most renowned blues performers. The best way to take in a show is to book a table and dine in front of the low stage, otherwise you'll have to stand all night at the bar at the back. They also record shows and broadcast live on the net live (ⓦwww.thebasement.com.au).

Brass Monkey 115a Cronulla St, Cronulla ⓣ02/9544 3844. Cronulla CityRail. This small jazz and music club attracts some big names, who often play *The Basement* and then head south for a more intimate show here. Cover charge depending on act, but food, beer and good wine is reasonable.

Bridge Hotel 135 Victoria Rd, Rozelle ⓣ02/9810 1260. Bus #501 from Central CityRail. Legendary inner-west venue specializing in blues and pub rock, with some international but mostly local acts. Also good pub theatre and comedy nights.

Excelsior Hotel 64 Foveaux St, Surry Hills ⓣ02/9211 4945. Central CityRail. Something of a muso's pub; jazz four nights a week, with residencies covering every style, from swing to avant garde (Mon–Wed 8pm; $5). Sun evening from 6pm is usually a jamming session. Bistro. Bar until 3am Fri & Sat.

The Gaelic Theatre Club 64 Devonshire St, Surry Hills ⓣ02/9211 1687. Central CityRail. Anything and everything plays at the *Gaelic Club* – one night there's DJs and dance music, the next some heavy metal or hard core punk – which makes it one of Sydney's more interesting live venues, and recently fully licensed too. Only open when there's a show but can go on until 5am.

Hopetoun Hotel 416 Bourke St, cnr of Fitzroy St, Surry Hills ⓣ02/9361 5257. Central CityRail. One of Sydney's best venues for the indie band scene, everyone wants to play at "The Hoey", and the new, young bands get to mix it up with local, interstate and international acts all playing in the small and inevitably packed front bar Mon to Sat (from 7.30pm; cover charge depends on the act, though sometimes free), and on Sun there are DJs (5–10pm; $5). Popular pool room, a drinking pit in the basement, and an inexpensive little restaurant upstairs (meals $5–10). Closes midnight.

@ Newtown Petersham RSL Club, 52 Enmore Rd, Newtown ⓣ02/9550 3666. Another multi-level venue with diverse line-ups. Level 1 is free and includes karaoke nights in between local DJs and rock bands, but this level is also becoming known for its new talent (alongside a few older acts that still pull the crowds). Open daily, gigs various times.

Rose of Australia Hotel 1 Swanson St, Erskineville ⓣ02/9565 1441. Erskineville CityRail, Trendy inner-city types mix with Goths, locals and gays to sample some favourites of the pub circuit. Line-up changes regularly, with bands on Fri and Sun in rotation, so you can catch anything from an original rock act, through to a country and western cover band. Music starts from 8.30pm (from 6.30pm Sun) and is always free. The bistro is cheap (from $7) and popular, with hundreds of thousands of Rose Burgers sold.

Sandringham Hotel 387 King St, Newtown ⓣ02/9557 1254. Newtown CityRail. "The Sando" features local and interstate indie bands, who are no longer squeezed beside the bar but play on a new stage upstairs (Thurs–Sat 8.30pm–midnight, Sun 7pm–10pm; usually $5–8, more well-known bands $12–15).

Soup Plus 1 Margaret St, cnr Clarence St, Sydney ⓣ02/9299 7728. Wynyard CityRail. After more than thirty years at its old basement location, *Soup Plus* has upgraded and turned into a much larger music and dining venue. Still serving up live jazz with its bowls of $5 soup, the menu and the acts have expanded accordingly. Music Mon–Sat 7–11.30pm. Mon–Thurs $8 cover charge, $10 for big bands, Fri & Sat cover charge $35 including a two-course meal. Open for lunch midday to 3pm.

The Vanguard 42 King St, Newtown ⓣ02/9557 7992. Billed as bringing jazz, blues and roots to Newtown (and therefore Sydney), this venue, with restaurant attached, attracts some big name acts, plus some excellent raw local talent. It's incredibly relaxed, and very cool. There are 2 for 1 cocktails 4–8pm every Wed–Sun, with a special weekly cocktail. Most acts play till 11.30pm.

Outdoor music festivals

There are now several big outdoor rock concerts in Sydney, throughout spring and summer, but the **Big Day Out** in late January is the original and the best (around $100 plus booking fee; ⓦwww.bigdayout.com). Held at the showground at the Sydney Olympic Park at Homebush Bay (see p.157), it features big international names such as the Foo Fighters and PJ Harvey, as well as local talent, and attracts crowds of over 50,000. One of the latest additions to the rock circuit is **Livid**, the one-day Brisbane music festival which was held in Moore Park for the first time in late October 2002, with 43 acts from internationals such as Oasis, to locals Machine Gun Fellatio (around $90 plus booking fee; ⓦwww.livid.com.au). **Homebake** (around $70 plus booking fee; ⓦwww.homebake.com.au) is a huge annual open-air festival in The Domain (see p.78) in early December, with food and market stalls, rides and a line-up of over fifty famous and underground Australian bands from Powderfinger to Grinspoon.

The big outdoor dance music festival is **Vibes on a Summers Day**, a sweltering day of sultry beats, trip-hop, reggae flavours and excruciatingly beautiful bodies at the end of January, either in and around the Bondi Pavilion at Bondi or at the Arthur Byrne Reserve at Maroubra Beach (around $90; ⓦwww.vibes.net.au); past guests have included the Afro Celt Sound System and Jazzanova.

Across the Easter long weekend music lovers head north to the **Blues and Roots Festival** at Byron Bay, but Sydney also has its own **Easter music festival** on Cockatoo Island in the middle of the harbour. This includes camping on the island, a film festival, stalls and rides and some great local and international acts.

Tickets for all of the above festivals are available from Fish Records (see p.261) and also Ticketek.

The **Manly International Jazz Festival** runs over the Labour Day long weekend in early October. Free outdoor stages include one on the scenic harbourfront and one on the oceanfront; there are also a number of indoor concert venues charging admission. The wide-ranging guests of previous years have included a Slovenian band playing Gypsy swing, a Japanese jazz orchestra and an Italian trio, plus well-known local, US and UK acts. You can get advance details from Manly Council (ⓦ www.manly.nsw.gov.au). For other musical events through the year, see the "Festivals and events" chapter.

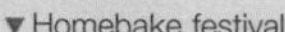
▼ Homebake festival

Clubs

Many of Sydney's best clubs are at **gay** or **lesbian** venues, and although we've listed these separately on pp.237–238, the divisions are not always clear – many places have specific gay, lesbian and straight nights scheduled each week. A long strip of thriving clubs stretches from Kings Cross to Oxford Street and down towards Hyde Park. There are also clubs attached to several of the pubs we've listed – see *Slip Inn* for the *Chinese Laundry* and *Soho Bar* for *Yu* – and some pubs actually transform into clubs, such as the hugely popular Sunday day club that takes over the entire *Greenwood Hotel* in North Sydney (see p.216), even the beer garden. Most other pubs and bars don't push things quite so far, but DJs are fast taking over from the live music scene and you'll find people dancing at least one night a week in the city at the *Art House Hotel* (p.209) and *Brooklyn Hotel* (p.209), in Newtown at the *Marlborough Hotel* (p.215) and by the beaches at the *Clovelly Hotel* (p.217), the *Beach Palace Hotel* in Coogee (p.217) and *Beach Road Hotel* in Bondi. Many of the clubs listed below are open to different promoters, so have different styles on different nights. Check the gig guides and listings, and look out for posters on the streets.

The **club scene** can be pretty snobby, with door gorillas frequently vetting your style. **Admission** ranges from $5 to $30, depending on the club and DJ; many stay open until 5am Saturday morning and until 6am Sunday morning.

Candy's Apartment 22 Bayswater Rd, Kings Cross ⓣ02/9380 5600. Kings Cross CityRail. It's gone through many incarnations (most recently Zen and China White) but this is the freshest and coolest of them all. Resident and visiting DJs crank out a constantly changing music mix in the main and back rooms, and it's a good option after checking out the Kings Cross strip. Wed–Sun 8pm–late. $10–18.

Cave Nightclub Star City Casino, Pirrama Rd, Pyrmont ⓣ02/9566 4755. Town Hall CityRail, then monorail. There are two bar areas, and "Substance" every Sat night is the most popular evening, with some of Sydney's more well-known R&B DJs on rotation. Fri–Sun 8pm–5am; $20 Fri & Sat, $12 Sun.

Gas 467 Pitt St, Haymarket ⓣ02/9211 3088. Central CityRail. One huge cutting-edge room downstairs where international DJs appear about once a month, and a mezzanine level which acts as a viewing area over the dance floor, with chill-out lounges attached to get away from the hard edge house and trance which pervades most nights. Three bar areas. Thurs–Sun 10pm–6am, $15, $20 Fri & Sat.

Globe Disco Lounge and Cocktail Bar 60 Park St, City ⓣ02/9264 4944. Wynyard CityRail. Globe's cocktail-bar lounge is open 24 hours,Thurs to Sat from 10pm it's linked to a downstairs club section – you'll have to dress way cool to get past the door. Great place for soul, energetic house and hip-hop sounds. Thurs–Sat $10–15.

Home Cockle Bay Wharf, Darling Harbour ⓣ02/9266 0600, Town Hall CityRail. The first really big club venture in Sydney, the lavish *Home* can cram 2000 punters into its cool, cavernous interior, which also features a mezzanine, a chill-out room, and outdoor balconies. Decks are often manned by famous DJs, drinks are expensive, and staff beautiful. The place gets packed with a younger crowd on Fri for its flagship night "Sublime", with four musical styles across four levels. On Sat, "Together at Home" plays progressive and funky house. Fri & Sat 11pm–late. $25.

Le Panic 20 Bayswater Rd, Kings Cross ⓣ02/9368 0763. Kings Cross CityRail. The old site of nightclub *Sugareef*, an extreme makeover has *Le Panic* aiming to be a one-stop-shop for late-night partying, with the sizeable dance floor still open for boogying but now surrounded by a bar and comfy booths with food on offer. A private and exclusive lounge off to the side acts as a chill-out room. Thurs–Sun 7pm–late. $15.

Rogues Cnr Oxford St and Riley St, Darlinghurst ⓣ02/9380 9244. Museum CityRail. For the straight crowd with a bit of cash to burn ($15 cocktails on top of steep cover charge), *Rogues* is a two-level club that's dark'n'dirty downstairs with its stone arches and murky corners, and chilled and relaxed at street level. Something for everyone, especially Eighties funk on Wed nights. Special events at least once a month. Wed, Fri & Sat 9.30pm–6am. $15–25.

Tank 3 Bridge Lane, off George St, City ⓣ02/9240 3094, ⓦwww.tankclub.com.au. Wynyard CityRail. This is for the glamorous industry crowd – fashion, music and film aficionados. If you don't belong, the style police will spot you a mile away. All very "funky" – from the house music played by regular or guest DJs to the mirrors and wash basins in the toilets. Three amazing bars and a VIP section. Attire is smart casual to street wear, but attitude and good looks override the dress code. Fri & Sat 10pm–6am. $15–20.

Tantra 169 Oxford St, Darlinghurst ⓣ02/9331 7729, ⓦwww.tantrabar.com.au. Bus #378 from Central CityRail or #380 from Circular Quay CityRail. Rotating resident DJs and live musicians/percussionists ensure that there's always something new happening. The younger crowd comes on Fri for the high-octane beats, while Sat is predominantly for 25–30-year-olds. Fri & Sat 10pm–6am. $10–30.

The World 24 Bayswater Rd, Kings Cross ⓣ02/9357 7700. Kings Cross CityRail. With cheap drinks on Fri and Sat nights and a relatively relaxed door policy, *The World* is popular with a fun, party-loving crowd of travellers, who jive to a pleasing mix of funk and house grooves in a pleasant Victorian-era building with a big front balcony. The atmosphere throughout is lively, if a little beery in the front bar. Fri & Sat noon–6am, Sun–Thurs noon–4am. Free.

15

Performing arts and film

From Shakespeare to gay film festivals, Sydney's arts scene takes itself seriously while managing never to lose its sense of fun. Free summertime outdoor performances, such as the Sydney Festival's **Symphony in The Domain** (see p.263), are among the year's highlights, as Sydneysiders turn out in their thousands to picnic and share in the atmosphere.

For **listings** of **what's on** at the venues below, check the *Sydney Morning Herald*'s Friday supplement "Metro", the *Daily Telegraph*'s Thursday pull-out "Seven Days" or any of the diary-style magazines available at the tourist office (see "Information, p.27). To buy tickets for performing arts events, either contact the venues direct or book through Ticketek, the main **booking agency**, or Ticketmaster7; details of both can be found in the box on p.219.

Classical music, opera and ballet

The **Sydney Opera House** is the centre of high culture in Sydney, and while it's not necessary to don tie-and-tails or an evening dress when attending a performance, it's still about the only place you're likely to see locals in formal attire.

Sydney's five most prestigious performing arts companies, the Australian Ballet, Opera Australia, the Sydney Symphony Orchestra, the Sydney Theatre Company (see p.228) and the Sydney Dance Company (see box on p.227) all have Opera House seasons. The **Australian Ballet**, which features contemporary as well as classical dance (tickets from $67; information Ⓦwww.australianballet.com.au), shifts between Sydney and Melbourne – it's based in the latter, but performs at the Opera House from mid-March to early May, and November through December, and sometimes at the Capitol Theatre. **Opera Australia** (tickets from $96; information Ⓦwww.opera-australia.org.au) also alternates between the two cities, with Opera House seasons in either the Concert Hall or the Opera Theatre from June to November and during February and March; it also performs at the Capitol Theatre. The **Sydney Symphony Orchestra** (tickets from $50; information and bookings Ⓦwww.sso.com.au) performs at the Sydney Opera House Concert Hall and the City Recital Hall.

▲State Theatre

City Recital Hall **Angel Place, between George and Pitt streets. Martin Place CityRail. On-site box office ⓣ02/8256 2222, ⓦwww.cityrecitalhall.com.** Opened in 1999, this classical music venue right next to Martin Place was specifically designed for chamber music, and is the major concert venue for the renowned Australian Brandenburg Orchestra (ⓦwww.brandenburgorchestra.org.au; tickets from $55), who use seventeenth-century period instruments and original scores in their baroque and classical concerts. The hall seats 1238, but on three levels, giving it an intimate atmosphere.

Conservatorium of Music **Off Macquarie St, in the Botanic Gardens ⓣ02/9351 1263, ⓦwww.usyd.edu.au/su/conmusic. Circular Quay CityRail/ferry.** Students at the "Con", a prestigious branch of Sydney University, give free lunchtime recitals every Wed at 1.10pm during term time in Recital Hall West. Other concerts, both free and ticketed (anywhere from $10 up to around $35) involve students and staff here and at venues around town; a programme is available from the concert department or check the website. Also see p.75.

Eugene Goossens Hall **ABC Centre, Harris St, Ultimo ⓣ02/9333 1500, ⓦwww.abc.net.au/classic. Central CityRail.** Auditorium (320-seater) with state-of-the-art acoustics within the radio headquarters of the ABC, used for very reasonably priced ABC Classic FM Recital Series and sometimes free lunchtime concerts; check the website for event details. Named after the British conductor who brought the Sydney Symphony Orchestra to world-class standards in the 1940s and 1950s.

St James' Church **King St, beside Hyde Park ⓣ02/9232 3022, ⓦwww.stjameschurchsydney.org.au. St James or Town Hall CityRail.** This beautiful little Anglican church has long been associated with fine music. It has its own director of music and a highly acclaimed semi-professional chamber choir, whose repertoire extends from Gregorian chants to more contemporary pieces. The choir can be heard every Sun morning at 11am and on the last Sun of the month at 4pm. St James' music programme also includes a series of free lunchtime concerts (Wed 1.15pm; 30min).

Sydney Opera House **Bennelong Point ⓣ02/9250 7777, ⓦwww.sydneyoperahouse.com. Circular Quay CityRail/ferry.** The Opera House is Sydney's prestige venue for opera, classical music and ballet. Forget quibbles about acoustics or ticket prices – it's worth going just to say you've been. The huge Concert Hall, seating 2690, is home to the Sydney Symphony Orchestra and also hosts opera; the smaller Opera

Contemporary dance companies

NAISDA Dance College, 3 Cumberland St, The Rocks ⓣ02/9252 0199, ⓦwww.naisda.com.au. Established in 1976, this famous training company for young Aboriginal and Islander dancers, based in The Rocks, puts on mid-year and end of year performances at the NAISDA Studios at the college; call or check the website for times.

Bangarra Dance Theatre Pier 4, Hickson Rd, Millers Point ⓣ02/9251 5333, ⓦwww.bangarra.com.au. Formed in 1989, Bangarra's innovative style fuses contemporary movement with the traditional dances and culture of the Yirrkala Community in Arnhemland. They are based at the same pier as the Wharf Theatre but perform at other venues in Sydney and tour nationally and internationally – call or check their website for the latest details.

Sydney Dance Company ⓣ02/9221 4811, ⓦwww.sydneydance.com.au. Graeme Murphy, Australia's doyen of dance, has been at the helm of the Sydney Dance Company since 1976, and continues to set the standard with ambitious sets and beautifully designed costumes. The company is based at the Wharf Theatre, with Opera House seasons April–May and Sept–Oct.

Theatre (1547 seats) hosts opera, ballet and contemporary dance. See p.228 for details of performances at the Opera House's three theatrical venues. See also p.69.

Town Hall Cnr Druitt and George streets ⓣ02/9265 9007, ⓦwww.cityofsydney.nsw.gov.au. Town Hall CityRail. Centrally located concert hall (seats 2000) with a splendid high-Victorian interior – hosts everything from chamber orchestras to bush dances and public lectures. See also p.85.

Theatre

Prices for mainstream theatre performances are fairly high, from $25 to $70 for the best seat at a Sydney Theatre Company performance; tickets in smaller, fringe venues cost from around $25.

Major venues

Capitol Theatre 13 Campbell St, Haymarket ⓣ02/9320 5000. Central CityRail. Built as a de luxe picture theatre in the 1920s, the Capitol was saved from demolition and beautifully restored in the mid-1990s. The 2000-seater now hosts big-budget musicals, ballet and opera, which you watch from beneath its best feature, the deep blue ceiling spangled with the stars of the southern skies.

Seymour Theatre Centre Corner City Rd and Cleveland St, Chippendale ⓣ02/9351 7940. Bus #422, #423, #426 & #428 from Central CityRail. Opened in 1975 and refurbished in 2000, this three-theatre multi-purpose performing arts venue was a businessman's bequest to Sydney University for a venue for musical and dramatic arts. From lectures by eminent writers to plays from the Sydney University Dramatic Society, and off-beat comical musicals, the Seymour's range is varied and often interesting. The main stage, the 788-seat York Theatre, hosts everything from serious imported theatre such as Steven Berkoff's *Shakespeare's Villians* to international piano competitions and the Sydney Peace Prize lecture. The smaller Everest Theatre's acoustics are designed for musical events, from classical pianists to contemporary dance (seats 419–605), while the Downstairs Theatre is the informal studio space (seats 150–200). The new 120-seater cabaret room, Sound Lounge, hosts Cafe Carnivale, featuring World Music, on Thurs nights (from 8.15pm; $17), and improvised jazz from SIMA (Sydney Improvised Music Association) on Fri and Sat nights (9pm to midnight; same price); light meals and drinks are offered during performances. Belvoir Street Theatre's Company B will stage productions at the Seymour Centre while the Surry Hills' theatre is being redeveloped (see below).

Star City Casino 20–80 Pyrmont St, Pyrmont ⓣ02/9657 9657, ⓦwww.starcity.com.au. Star

City Light Rail. Sydney's Vegas-style casino has two theatres catering to popular tastes. The technically advanced Lyric Theatre, seating 2000, stages big musical extravaganzas imported from the West End and Broadway such as *Saturday Night Fever*, while the smaller Star City Showroom puts on more off-beat musicals – such as the *Rocky Horror Picture Show* – and comedy.
Theatre Royal MLC Centre, King St, City ⓣ02/9266 4800. Martin Place CityRail. Imported musicals and blockbuster plays in a Harry Seidler-designed building opened in 1976; seats 1180.

Drama and performance

Belvoir St Theatre 25 Belvoir St, Surry Hills ⓣ02/9699 3444, ⓦwww.belvoir.com.au. Central CityRail. Highly regarded two-stage venue for a wide range of contemporary Australian and international theatre. Company B, the resident theatre company, is one of Australia's most innovative and productive tour nationally and abroad. The theatre is being redeveloped from July 2005 until around September 2006 – in the meantime Company B productions will be held at the Seymour Centre (p.227).
Ensemble Theatre 78 McDougall St, Milsons Point ⓣ02/9929 0644, ⓦwww.ensemble.com.au. Milsons Point CityRail. Australian contemporary and classical plays.
Sydney Opera House Bennelong Point ⓣ02/9250 7777, ⓦwww.sydneyoperahouse.com. Circular Quay CityRail/ferry. The Opera House has three theatrical venues; the Playhouse and the Drama Theatre show modern and traditional Australian and international plays mostly put on by the Sydney Theatre Company, while The Studio, the Opera House's smallest venue (with the most affordable ticket prices), is flexible in design with a theatre-in-the-round format. It offers an innovative and wide-ranging programme of contemporary performance – theatre, cabaret, dance, comedy and hybrid works.
Wharf Theatre Pier 4, Hickson Rd, Millers Point ⓣ02/9250 1777, ⓦwww.sydneytheatre.com.au. Circular Quay CityRail/ferry. Home to the highly regarded Sydney Theatre Company (STC) – which produces Shakespeare and modern pieces and has two theatres here – and to the Sydney Dance Company (SDC, see box on p.227). Atmospheric waterfront location, and a well-regarded restaurant, bar and café. See also p.195. The brand-new 850-seater Sydney Theatre, diagonally opposite, also puts on STC and SDC performances (for more details see ⓦwww.sydneytheatre.org.au).

Fringe and repertory

New Theatre 542 King St, Newtown ⓣ02/9519 8958, ⓦwww.ramin.com.au/online/newtheatre. Newtown or St Peters CityRail. Formed in 1932. Professional and amateur actors (all unpaid) perform contemporary dramas with socially relevant themes.
NIDA 215 Anzac Parade, Kensington ⓣ02/9697 7613, ⓦwww.nida.unsw.edu.au. Bus #390–394 from Central CityRail. Australia's premier dramatic training ground – the National Institute of Dramatic Art – where the likes of Mel Gibson and Judy Davis started out. Student productions (tickets around $25) in a new auditorium, are open to the public as well as talent-spotters.
The Performance Space 199 Cleveland St, Redfern ⓣ02/9319 5091, ⓦwww.performancespace.com.au. Central CityRail. Stages experimental performances.
Stables Theatre 10 Nimrod St, Darlinghurst ⓣ02/9361 3817, ⓦwww.griffintheatre.com.au. Kings Cross CityRail. Home to the Griffin Theatre Company whose mission is to develop and foster new Australian playwrights.

Comedy and cabaret

As well as the listings below, the **drag shows** at the *Imperial Hotel* in Erskineville (see p.236) are also great fun. There's also occasional comedy at the *Bridge Hotel* in Rozelle (see p.221) and the *Exchange Hotel* in Balmain (see p.215).

Bailey's Bar Clarence Hotel, 450 Parramatta Rd, Petersham ⓣ02/9560 0400, ⓦscriptless.improaustralia.com.au. Bus #338 or #440 from Central CityRail. Every Friday at 8pm (entry $5), Impro Australia hosts the Theatresports night "Scared Scriptless". Theatresports is the intellectual's answer to footy – pure performance improvisation on-the-run; there are occasionally other big events such as Celebrity Theatresports.

Old Manly Boatshed 40 The Corso, Manly ⓣ02/9977 4443 ⓦwww.manlyboatshed.com.au. Ferry to Manly Wharf. Characterful and relaxed basement bar with Mon night stand-up comedy (8.30pm; $7) and a pub bistro-style menu (also see p.218).

Sydney Comedy Store Fox Studios, Driver Ave, Moore Park ⓣ02/9357 1419, ⓦwww.comedystore.com.au. Bus #339 from Central CityRail. International (often American) and Australian stand-up comics Thurs to Sat; open mic nights Tues and new comics Wed. Bar open from 7pm, show 8.30pm. Meals aren't available, but the lively Dog Gone Bar on Bent Street (see p.106) offers meal discounts for Comedy Store ticket holders. Bookings recommended for Thurs–Sat. Entry Tues & Wed $15, Thurs $20, Fri & Sat $27.50.

Cinema

Sydneysiders love going to **the pictures**, and in recent years Hollywood itself has come to town in the shape of the Fox Studios site (see p.105), which offers superb facilities and filming locations in the heart of the city, plus sixteen cinema screens. During the summer you can watch films **outdoors**, either at one of Sydney's open-air cinemas (see box on p.231), or at one of the city's lively film festivals (see box on p.230).

Main venues

The commercial movie centre of Sydney is two blocks south of the Town Hall at 505–525 George Street, where you'll find the two big **chains** – Hoyts (ⓣ02/9273 7431, ⓦwww.hoyts.com.au) and Greater Union (ⓣ02/9267 8666, ⓦwww.greaterunion.com.au) – under one roof. This is mainstream, fast-food, teenager territory and there are much nicer places to watch a film. Other more pleasantly located Hoyts can be found at the Broadway Shopping Centre, on Broadway near Glebe (ⓣ02/9211 1911), and at Fox Studios, and there's a Greater Union in the Westfield Shopping Centre in Bondi Junction (Level 6, 500 Oxford St, ⓣ02/9300 1555). Standard tickets cost around $15, but Tuesdays are reduced-price (around $9.50–10.50) at all Hoyts and Greater Union/Village cinemas and their suburban outlets, and Monday or Tuesday at the arthouse and local cinemas listed below.

Cinema Paris Driver Ave, off Lang Rd, Moore Park ⓣ02/9332 1633, ⓦwww.hoyts.com.au. Bus #339 from Central CityRail. Hoyts' "arthouse" option; a pleasant four-screen cinema which also offers Sun double features and mini film festivals (Spanish, Mexican) and events throughout the year.

The Dendy 261 King St, Newtown ⓣ02/9550 5699, ⓦwww.dendy.com.au. Newtown CityRail. Trendy four-screen cinema complex with attached café, bar and bookshop, showing prestige new-release films. Discount day is Mon but if you're staying in Sydney longer, and will be living or working nearby, it's worth investing in a Club Dendy card ($15 for twelve months) which discount's tickets to $9.50 each for two people. The newer three-screen Dendy Quays is superbly sited at 2 East Circular Quay (ⓣ02/9247 3800).

Hoyts at Fox Studios Driver Ave, off Lang Rd, Moore Park ⓣ02/9332 1300, ⓦwww.hoyts.com.au. Bus #339 from Central CityRail. Twelve-screen multiplex showing mainstream new releases. Five of the screens have a special deluxe section, La Premiere, aimed at couples (bookings ⓣ02/9332 1300, ext. 5), where custom-made sofa seats for two have wine holders and tables for food – you can buy bottles of wine and cheese plates; soft drinks and popcorn are all included in the ticket price; prices start at $25, rising to $30 on Sat night.

IMAX Theatre Southern Promenade, Darling Harbour ⓣ02/9281 3300, ⓦwww.imax.com

Film festivals

The great variety of **film festivals** in Sydney provides opportunities to catch a movie in one of a number of attractive settings, some of them outdoors.

Sydney Film Festival

The **Sydney Film Festival**, held annually over two weeks in **early June**, is an exciting programme of features, shorts, documentaries and retrospective screenings from Australia and around the world. Founded at Sydney University in 1954, the festival struggled with prudish censors until freedom from censorship for festival films was introduced in 1971. From the early, relaxed atmosphere of picnics on the lawns between screenings, it has gradually moved off-campus, to find a home from 1974 in the magnificent State Theatre (see p.84). Films are also shown at the wonderfully located three-screen Dendy Quays on Circular Quay East (see p.229).

The festival was once mainly sold on subscription, but subscriptions now only apply to screenings at the State Theatre; the more provocative line-up of films at the Dendy Quays aims to attract a new, under-35 audience to the festival on a single or packaged ticket basis. Single **tickets** cost around $15, selected film packages of five to ten $12.50, eleven or more $11 each or, if you can't decide, there are ten or twenty film Flexi Passes for $120/$200; **subscriptions** for the State Theatre programme start from $170 for one week's daytime unreserved stalls seating, and go up to $290 for two week's reserved dress circle night-time screenings. For more information and a programme, call or drop in to the festival office at Level 5, 414–418 Elizabeth St, Surry Hills (Mon–Fri 9am–5pm; ⓣ02/9280 0511, bookings ⓣ02/9280 0611 or via ⓦwww.sydneyfilmfestival.org).

Flickerfest and Tropfest

There are also two short-film festivals in Sydney, both of which echo the young and irreverent attitude that once fuelled the Sydney Film Festival. Stars above and the sound of waves accompany the week-long **Flickerfest International Short Film Festival** (ⓣ02/9365 6888, ⓦwww.flickerfest.com.au; single ticket $4, season pass $120), held in early January in the amphitheatre of the Bondi Pavilion; foreign and Australian productions are screened, including documentaries.

The **Tropfest** (ⓣ9368 0434, ⓦwww.tropfest.com.au) is a competition festival for short films held annually on the last Sunday of February. Its name comes from the *Tropicana Café* on Victoria Street, Darlinghurst, where the festival began almost by chance in 1993 when young actor John Polsen persuaded his local coffee spot to show the short film he had made. He pushed other filmmakers to follow suit, and the next year a huge crowd packed themselves into the café. Nowadays the entire street is closed to traffic to enable an outdoor screening, while cafés along the strip screen films on TVs inside, but the festival has grown enormously over the years and the focus of the event has now moved to The Domain, with live entertainment from 3pm and huge crowds turning up to picnic on the grass and watch the free 8pm screening of sixteen finalist films from around seven hundred entries. Each state capital also screens the event simultaneously in venues ranging from cafés to parks. The films (maximum seven minutes) must be specifically produced for the festival, and to this end an item which must feature in the shorts is announced a few months in advance of the entry date; in 2005 it was "umbrella" – however you wanted to interpret it. The judges, who turn up for the screenings, are often famous international actors, which adds some excitement, and Polsen himself, still the festival's director, made it as a Hollywood director in 2002 (and you can see him acting in *Mission Impossible II* alongside Tom Cruise).

Other film festivals

Other film festivals include the **World of Women (WOW) Film Festival** (ⓦwww.FutureTrain.com.au/wift/wow), held over three days in late October at the Chauvel Cinema, Paddington. There is also a **Gay and Lesbian Film Festival** in late February as part of the Sydney Gay & Lesbian Mardi Gras (see p.233), and French, Italian, Spanish and Greek film festivals at the Palace Cinemas – look out for ads and see opposite.

.au. Town Hall CityRail. State-of-the-art giant eight-storey-high cinema screen showing a choice of four films designed to thrill your senses, for $16 for 2-D version, $17–20 for 3-D. Films hourly 10am–10pm.

Palace Academy 3A Oxford St, cnr South Dowling St, Paddington ☎02/9361 4453, ⓦwww.palacecinemas.com.au. Bus #378 from Central CityRail & #380 from Circular Quay CityRail. One of a chain of three inner-city cinemas (see "Norton" and "Verona" below) showing foreign-language, arthouse and new releases, with discounts on Mon. If you're going to be in Sydney for a while, and staying or working near one of these cinemas, it's worth buying a Palace Card ($16.50 for twelve months), which gives you discount-price ($9.50) tickets anytime for yourself and a friend; it doesn't take long to recoup the membership price.

Palace Norton 99 Norton St, Leichhardt ☎02/9550 0122, ⓦwww.palacecinemas.com.au. Bus #438 & #440 from Central CityRail. Has a bookshop and cybercafé and hosts an Italian film festival in early Dec as well as French, Spanish and Greek film festivals. For baby-restricted parents, there are popular "Babes in Arms" sessions weekly (Thurs 11am), similar to those at the Randwick Ritz (see p.232).

Palace Verona 17 Oxford St, cnr Verona St, Paddington ☎02/9360 6099, ⓦwww.palacecinemas.com.au. Bus #378 from Central CityRail & #380 from Circular Quay CityRail. Arthouse and foreign-language fare, plus new releases. Also has a trendy first-floor bar.

Reading Cinema Level 3, Market City Shopping Centre, Haymarket ☎02/9280 1202, ⓦwww.readingcinemas.com.au. Central CityRail. Mainstream five-screen multiplex in a great spot in the heart of Chinatown and close to Central Station. Adjacent Asian food court and bar handy for quick pre- or post-movie meals. Cheap day Tues plus discounted tickets daily before 6pm.

Locals and independents

Chauvel Theatre Paddington Town Hall, cnr Oatley Rd and Oxford St, Paddington ☎02/9361 5398, ⓦwww.chauvelcinema.com.au. Bus #378 from Central CityRail or #380 from Circular Quay or Bondi Junction CityRail. A Sydney cinema institution, the arthouse Chauvel, with its varied programme of Australian and foreign films plus classics, has been operating in the Paddington Town Hall since 1977, but closed its doors in 2005. However, it is set to reopen as part of the Palace cinema chain, with its status as a unique arthouse film centre intact. For more details check the Palace website.

Cremorne Orpheum 380 Military Rd, Cremorne ☎02/9908 4344, ⓦwww.orpheum.com.au. Bus #243 from Wynyard CityRail or #246 & #247 from Clarence St. Charming Heritage-listed six-screen cinema built in 1935 with a splendid Art Deco interior. The main cinema keeps up a tradition of Wurlitzer organ recitals preceding the Sat evening and Sun afternoon films. Mainstream and foreign new releases. Discount day Tues.

Govinda's Movie Room 112 Darlinghurst Rd, Darlinghurst ☎02/9380 5162, ⓦwww.govindas.com.au. Kings Cross CityRail. Run by the Hare Krishnas (but definitely no indoctrination), Govinda's shows two films every night from a range of classics and recent releases in a pleasantly unorthodox cushion-room atmosphere (you're encouraged to take off your shoes if you lie on the cushions so choose unsmelly footwear). The movie and dinner deal (all-you-can-eat vegetarian buffet) is popular – $15.90 for the meal and then an

Outdoor cinema

In the summer, two open-air cinemas set up shop. From November to the end of March, the **Moonlight Cinema**, in the Centennial Park Amphitheatre on Oxford Street (Woollahra entrance; Tues–Sun, films start 8.45pm, tickets from 7pm or bookings on ☎1300 551 908; $14.50; ⓦwww.moonlight.com.au; bus #378 from Central CityRail or #380 from Bondi Junction CityRail), shows classic, arthouse and cult films. Throughout January and February, the **Open Air Cinema** is erected at Mrs Macquaries Point in the Royal Botanic Gardens (tickets from 6.30pm or bookings on ☎13 61 00; $19), screening mainly mainstream recent releases and some classics. Other opportunities to watch films under the stars are detailed in the "Film festivals" box opposite.

extra $4 to see the movie. Buy your film ticket after you've ordered your meal, or you may miss out on busy nights; you can see a film only for $10.90 but diners are always given preference.

Randwick Ritz 45 St Paul St, Randwick ⓣ02/9611 4811, ⓦwww.ritzcinema.com.au. Bus #339 from Central CityRail or #372, #373, #374 & #377 from Circular Quay CityRail. Characterful old cinema handy if you're staying in Coogee, with five screens showing mainstream new releases and always at discount prices ($10, though all sessions on Tues are just $5). "Bubs Clubs" child-friendly sessions for parents every Mon morning (10.30am) are also offered. The area around the cinema known to the locals as "the Spot" has a big concentration of cafés and culturally diverse restaurants to eat at before or afterwards.

16

Gay Sydney

Sydney is indisputably one of the world's great gay cities – indeed, many people think it capable of snatching San Francisco's crown as the Queen of them all. A big draw is the **Sydney Gay & Lesbian Mardi Gras**; the festival lasts for four weeks, starting the first week of February, kicking off with a launch in Hyde Park followed two weeks later by a Fair Day in Victoria Park and culminating in the parade and party on the last weekend of February or the first weekend of March.

Don't despair if you can't be here for Mardi Gras or the Sleaze Ball (the annual Mardi Gras fundraiser in late September/early October). The city has much more to offer. **Oxford Street** is Sydney's official "pink strip" of gay restaurants, coffee shops, bookshops and bars, and here you'll find countless pairs of tight-T-shirted guys strolling hand-in-hand, or checking out the passing talent from hip, streetside cafés. However, the gay–straight divide in Sydney has less relevance for a new generation, perhaps ironically a result of Mardi Gras' mainstream success. Several of the long-running gay venues on and around Oxford Street have closed down and many of the remaining ones attract older customers, as younger gays and lesbians embrace inclusiveness and party with their straight friends and peers or choose to meet new friends via gaydar.com instead. **King Street** in Newtown and nearby **Erskineville** are other centres of gay culture, while lesbian communities have carved out territory of their own in **Leichhardt** (known affectionately as "Dykehart") and **Marrickville**. The bar and club listings below have not been split into separate gay and lesbian listings, as the scene thankfully doesn't split so neatly into "them and us".

A good starting point for **information** is The Bookshop, 207 Oxford St, Darlinghurst (Ⓣ02/9331 1103, Ⓦwww.thebookshop.com.au), which has a full stock of gay- and lesbian-related books, cards and magazines, including the free gay and lesbian weeklies, *Sydney Star Observer* (Ⓦwww.sssonet.com.au) and *SX* (Ⓦwww.sxnews.com.au), which both come out on Thursdays and include weekly event listings; the free lesbian-specific monthly *LOTL* (*Lesbians on the Loose*, Ⓦwww.lotl.com); and the monthly nationally distributed *DNA* (Ⓦwww.dnamagazine.com.au), an upmarket lifestyle glossy for gay men ($7.60), and *REFRESH Magazine* ($9.95; Ⓦwww.refreshmag.com.au), a slightly more in-depth but similarly glossy commentary on gay male life in Australia. The websites of all these magazines are also worth checking out before you leave home.

The Mardi Gras and Sleaze

The first parade was held in 1978 as a gay-rights protest, and today it's the biggest celebration of gay and lesbian culture in the world. In 1992, an unprecedented crowd of four hundred thousand, including a broad spectrum of straight society, turned up to watch the parade and two years later it began to be broadcast nationally on television. By 1999, the combined festival, parade and party was making the local economy $100 million dollars richer and the increasing commercialization of Mardi Gras was drawing criticism from the gay and lesbian community. Its bubble burst in 2002, after financial mismanagement saw the Mardi Gras organization in the red to the tune of $500,000. Instead of throwing in the towel, the fundraising organization was rebuilt as the "New Mardi Gras"; although less cash-rich, New Mardi Gras is drawing on the resources and creativity of its talented community along with the desire to keep the festival going in order to revive the old Mardi Gras spirit.

The festival and parade

Four weeks of exhibitions, performances and other events – including the ten-day **Mardi Gras Film Festival** in mid-February at the Palace Academy cinema (see p.231 and Ⓦwww.queerscreen.com.au) – represent the largest lesbian and gay arts festival in the world. This paves the way for the main event, an exuberant night-time **parade** down Oxford Street, when up to half-a-million gays and straights jostle for the best viewing positions, before the Dykes on Bikes, traditional leaders of the parade since 1988 (though the boys on bikes, The Roadrunners, made their debut in 2003), roar into view.

Participants devote months to the preparation of outlandish floats and outrageous costumes at Mardi Gras workshops, and even more time is devoted to the preparation of beautiful bodies in Sydney's packed gyms. The parade begins at 7.30pm (finishing around 10.30pm), but people line the barricades along Oxford Street from mid-morning (brandishing stolen milk crates to get a better view). If you can't get to Oxford Street until late afternoon, your best chance of finding a spot is along Flinders Street near Moore Park Road, where the parade ends. Otherwise, AIDS charity The Bobby Goldsmith Foundation (Ⓣ02/9283 8666, Ⓦwww.bgf.org.au) has around 9000 grandstand seats on Flinders Street, at $65 each.

The post-parade, wild-and-sexy **dance party** is one of the hottest tickets in Sydney. Over twenty thousand people sashay and strut through several differently themed dance spaces at Fox Studios, Moore Park (including a women's space, *G-Spot*). The two biggest are the Hordern Pavilion and the Royal Hall of Industries, where past performers have included Kylie Minogue, Boy George and Grace Jones. You may have to plan ahead if you want to get a **ticket**: ($125 for pre-bought tickets or $140 at the gates) – they sometimes sell out by the end of January. The purchase of tickets used to be restricted to "Mardi

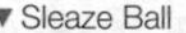
▼ Sleaze Ball

Gay and lesbian contacts

AIDS Council of NSW (ACON) 9 Commonwealth St, Surry Hills ⓣ02/9206 2000, ⓦwww.acon.org.au.

Albion Street Centre 150–154 Albion St, Surry Hills ⓣ02/9332 1090. Counselling, testing clinic, information and library.

ALSO Foundation ⓦwww.also.org.au. Based in Victoria, they have a good website with an excellent nationwide business and community directory.

Anti-Discrimination Board ⓣ02/9268 5544.

Gay & Lesbian Counselling Service ⓣ02/8594 9596 (daily 4pm–midnight).

GALTA (Gay and Lesbian Tourism Australia) ⓣ02/8379 7498, ⓦwww.galta.com.au. A non-profit organization set up to promote the gay and lesbian tourism industry. Its website has links to accommodation, travel agents and tour operators, and gay and lesbian printed and online guides.

Pinkboard ⓦwww.pinkboard.com.au. A popular, long-running Australian website featuring personal ads and classifieds sections with everything from houseshares, party tickets, employment and a help and advice section. It's free to run your own personal or classified ads.

The Pink Directory ⓦwww.thepinkdirectory.com.au. Launched in 2001, this is an online and print directory of gay and lesbian businesses and community information.

Qbeds ⓦwww.qbeds.com.au. Handy general guide giving information on where to stay Australia-wide.

redOyster.com ATS Pacific Pty, Level 10, 130 Elizabeth St, Sydney ⓣ02/9268 2188, ⓦwww.redOyster.com. A gay- and lesbian-branded tour operator that can arrange packages for Mardi Gras, and other festivals and destinations.

Gras members" to keep the event Queer, with special provisions for visitors from interstate and overseas, but as the New Mardi Gras is rebuilding the old memberships and procedures have all but disappeared. It's best to book through Ticketek on ⓣ02/9266 4800 (ⓦwww.ticketek.com.au) or for general enquiries contact the **New Mardi Gras office** (ⓣ02/9568 8600, ⓦwww.mardigras.org.au). Your local gay-friendly travel agent can also organize tickets. The **Sydney Gay & Lesbian Mardi Gras Guide**, available from mid-December, can be picked up from bookshops, cafés and restaurants around Oxford Street or viewed online at ⓦwww.mardigras.org.au.

The Sleaze Ball and PRIDE

Sydney just can't wait all year for Mardi Gras, so the **Sleaze Ball** is a very welcome stopgap in early October. It was set up in 1982 as a fundraiser for the first Mardi Gras Party, and has since become an annual fixture. There's not quite the same frenzied build-up as for Mardi Gras, but it's just as wild and can be every bit as much fun. It's held the first Saturday night in October, also at the old showground site at Moore Park, and is attended by up to 15,000 people. Prebought tickets cost around $100 ($125 if you buy them at the gates) and are available through New Mardi Gras (see above).

The community centre **PRIDE** (ⓣ02/9331 1333, ⓦwww.pridecentre.com.au) also arranges a similarly priced and over-the-top **New Year's Eve party**, usually at Fox Studios; contact them for details.

Cafés and restaurants

Below we've listed a few gay favourites on Oxford Street and in Newtown. See maps of Darlinghurst and Newtown for locations.

Battuta 137 Oxford St, Darlinghurst ⓣ02/9331 3229. Popular and central, this Oxford St favourite serves reliably good Italian style food and coffee in a location which ensures you'll miss none of the street life. Mon–Wed, 6am–noon, Thurs–Sat & Sun open 24hr.

The Californian 177 Oxford St, Darlinghurst ⓣ02/9331 5587. Bus #378 from Central CityRail, bus #380 from Circular Quay CityRail. Marilyn gazes down at you from the front counter in provocative pose, while Fifties rock blasts from the jukebox. The all-day *Californian* breakfast ($14) is fuel for the boys streaming in from the clubs at 5am. Mon–Wed 8am–midnight/1am, Thurs–Sun 24hr.

Food Game 185 Campbell St, Surry Hills. Eat in or take away their wide range of tasty pre-prepared dishes and good coffee. Popular spot off Oxford St to watch the world go by and a very handy place to pick up good food to take back to your hotel. Mon–Sun 10am–10pm.

Grumpy Baker 151 Oxford St. For coffees, breads, pies and pastries there's no ignoring this popular street café in the heart of it all. 6am until late, open 24hr on weekends.

Linda's Backstage Restaurant Newtown Hotel 174 King St, cnr Watkin St, Newtown ⓣ02/9550 6015. Newtown CityRail. At the rear of Newtown's popular gay hangout, well-regarded *Linda's* serves up delicious, very reasonably priced modern Australian fare. Dinner Tues–Sat.

Una's 340 Victoria St, Darlinghurst. This hearty European schnitzel joint has served up delicious and very filling fare for years. Always a popular gay refuelling stop and another great window on the gay world. Mon–Sat 8am–11pm. Also see p.189.

Pubs and bars

A few of the **bars** listed here have dance-floor-type areas, open at weekends; most have regular DJs, and could easily be included in the club listings opposite.

Bank Hotel 324 King St, Newtown ⓣ02/9557 1692. Newtown CityRail. This stylish bar is a dyke favourite on Wednesday nights, when the long-running women's pool competition (8pm) draws large crowds to socialize and maybe even compete. 24hr licence: Mon & Tues noon–12.30am, Wed & Thurs noon–1.30/2am, Fri & Sat noon–4am, Sun noon–midnight.

The Colombian 117–123 Oxford St, cnr Crown St, Darlinghurst ⓣ02/9360 2151, ⓦwww.colombian.com.au. Bus #378 from Central CityRail or #380 from Circular Quay CityRail. The fun and funky faux South American-style interior – which includes a giant red tribal mask in the ground-floor public bar – was designed by Andrew Parr, who was responsible for *Middle Bar* (p.212) and *Establishment* (p.209). Upstairs, there's a more intimate cocktail bar. There are different DJs and musical styles every night, from R&B to funky house and drag-cum-variety nights Wed & Thurs. Hip but not pretentious. Mon & Tues 10am–3pm, Wed–Sun 9am–5am.

Flinders Bar 63–65 Flinders St Darlinghurst ⓣ02/9356 3622, ⓦwww.barflinders.com.au. Recently reopened, revamped and welcoming a very mixed crowd, this hotel offers a funky, sleek modern environment to drink or dance with friends. Once very popular with younger gays and their admirers, this bar is now a much more mixed after work drinks place and late-night groove lounge. It also boasts a Thai restaurant upstairs that serves meals from $7. Tues–Sun 3pm until late.

Imperial Hotel 35 Erskineville Rd, Erskineville ⓣ02/9519 9899, ⓦwww.theimperial.com.au. Erskineville CityRail. A notorious late-night gay and lesbian venue, with four bars including a popular hot and sweaty dance floor in the basement (progressive, commercial, high energy; Fri & Sat 11pm–6am; $5), and a riotous drag-show line-up in the Cabaret Room. This is where *Priscilla, Queen of the Desert* both started and ended. It was the *Imperial's* finest hour, and the memories are kept alive in the cocktail bar, the *Priscilla Lounge*, with photos from the movie lining its walls. The drag shows here are hilarious, inventive and constantly changing: expect anything from the gay-version of *Survivor* ("Ten queens, ten weeks, one winner") to the *Rocky Horror Drag Show* (Wed 9.30pm, 10.30pm & 11.30pm; Thurs–Sat 10pm, 11pm, midnight & 1am; free). There's also cabaret in the cocktail bar on Fri and Sat nights from 10.30pm; to escape the live entertainment you can play pool (free all day Mon), watch music videos and talk in the public bar. "Go Girl" on Thursday nights in the cellar bar is a girls' only club night from 10pm (free). Mon–Thurs 3pm–2/3am, Fri & Sat 3pm–7am, Sun 3pm–midnight.

Manacle Rear lane of the Taylor Square Hotel, cnr Bourke & Flinders streets, Surry Hills (enter from Patterson Lane) ⓣ02/9698 1908. Currently Gay Sydney's only regular hardcore, day recovery spot. When most of the other clubs have shut their doors at 7am on Saturday, Sunday or Monday, all those who don't want to go home scurry underground to this club and dance the rest of the day away. The crowd is a good mixture of seasoned partygoers of every persuasion – gay, lesbian, straight and including drag queens. Admission is $5. By night the same place serves as a popular leather and Levis bar and is the last remaining men-only bar in the neighbourhood offering pool tables and very dim lighting as well as free nuts. The night bar opens from 7pm Thurs–Sun and closes at 3am.

Newtown Hotel 174 King St, cnr Watkin St, Newtown ⓣ02/9557 1329, ⓦwww.newtownhotel.com.au. Newtown CityRail. A stalwart of the Sydney scene. Laid-back mix of Newtown lesbians and gays (though predominantly male), drag shows (Tues–Sat 10pm & 11pm, Sun 8.30pm & 9.15pm) and pool tables (free on Mon nights). There's also a tiny dance floor and nightly DJs. At the rear, the well-regarded *Linda's Backstage Restaurant* (Mon–Sat from 6pm) serves up delicious, very reasonably priced modern Australian fare. Upstairs, but with a separate entrance, Bar 2 is a quiet, intimate space – no entertainment, but a couple of pool tables to amuse. Mon–Sat 11am–midnight, Sun 11am–10pm; Bar 2 Wed–Sun 6pm–midnight.

Oxford Hotel 134 Oxford St, Darlinghurst. The ground-floor bar, open 24hr, once the macho pillar of the gay community, has now expanded offering an open-to-the-street bar and café that is comfortably mixed as well as its traditional darker space, with dim lights, pool table, hard and handbag house and a regular clientele. On the first floor, *Gilligans* (daily 5pm–3am) is a very different scene, a popular cocktail bar which attracts a mixed crowd of gay boys, lesbians and the straight party set; happy hour 5–7pm. On the second floor, *Gingers* (Thurs–Sat from 6pm) is a quieter, more elegant bar – decor is plush, and several small cosy rooms provide intimacy.

Stonewall Hotel 175 Oxford St, Darlinghurst ⓣ02/9360 1963, ⓦwww.stonewallhotel.com.au. Bus #378 from Central CityRail, bus #380 from Circular Quay CityRail. Extending over three action-packed levels, this pub is a big hit with young gays and lesbians and their straight friends. You can expect theme nights like karaoke, celebrity drag, or Mailbox (a dating game), and there are DJs in the various different bars Wed–Sat. The downstairs bar plays commercial dance music, the cocktail bar on the next level accelerates on uplifting house, while the top-floor, weekend-only VIP Bar gets off on campy, "handbag" sounds (Fri & Sat 11pm–6am; free). There's natural light and outside tables downstairs, where you can also order in a meal from the neighbouring café, *The Californian* (see opposite). Tues–Sun noon–5am.

Clubs

The scene is rapidly changing, and bars and **clubs** have recently been closing down at an alarming rate: try and check recent listings magazines before going out of your way for a big night. Entry is free unless otherwise indicated.

Arq 16 Flinders St, cnr Taylor Square, Darlinghurst ⓦwww.arqsydney.com.au. Huge nine-hundred-person capacity, state-of-the-art club with everything from DJs and drag shows to pool competitions. Two levels, each with a very different scene:

the Arena, on the top floor, is mostly gay, while the ground-floor Vortex is a quieter, less crowded mix of gay and straights, with pool tables. Chill-out booths, laser lighting, viewing decks and fishtanks add to the fun, friendly atmosphere. Sunday is the big night. Thurs–Sun from 9pm; Thurs free, Fri $10, Sat $20, Sun $5. Check out the website for specific events.

Exchange Hotel 34 Oxford St, Darlinghurst. In the downstairs Phoenix bar, Saturday night's Crash underground "alternative" dance club is mostly gay men dancing en-masse and shirtless, but on Sunday nights there's a happy mix of gays and dykes. After midnight it's at its peak and a more raunchy, bacchanalian crowd you won't find anywhere else on the strip. Sat & Sun from 10pm; Sat $10, Sun $5.

Midnight Shift 85 Oxford St, Darlinghurst ⓣ02/9360 4319, ⓦwww.midnightshift.com.au. Bus #378 from Central CityRail, bus #380 from Circular Quay CityRail. Commonly known as "The Shift", this veteran of the Oxford Street scene has now been running for over twenty years. On the ground floor, the Shift Video Bar is a large drinking and cruising space to a music-video backdrop, with pool tables out the back. Upstairs, the weekend-only club has been revamped; the massive place is now rather splendid, with everything from a waterfall to a cutting-edge laser light show. The club hosts drag shows (usually Fri nights), DJs and events, with a cover charge of $5 and upwards, depending on the event. Mainly men. Bar daily noon–6am, club Fri & Sat 11pm–7am.

Taxi Club 40 Flinders St, Darlinghurst. Last stop. It's a Sydney legend and famous (or notorious) for being the only place you can buy a drink on Good Friday or Christmas Day, but don't bother before 2 or 3am, and you'll need to be suitably intoxicated to appreciate it fully. There's a strange blend of drag queens, taxi drivers, lesbians and boys (straight and gay) to observe, and the cheapest drinks in gay Sydney. An upstairs dance club (free) operates Fri and Sat from 1am. 24hr except for daily cleaning from 6am to 9am. Bring ID to show you're from out of town: draconian liquor licensing laws do allow clubs to serve alcohol to those "visiting from afar", so it could come in handy.

Gyms

The prices below are for a casual pass, which can last all day if you want it to, and includes any fitness classes on offer. Many **gyms** have a one-week free introductory offer, which is a cheeky way for travellers to do the rounds and get a buff bod for nothing.

Bayswater Fitness 33 Bayswater Rd, Kings Cross ⓣ02/9356 2555, ⓦwww.bayswaterfitness.com.au. Kings Cross CityRail. Clientele of mostly gay men, although lesbians are also welcome. Weights, circuit-fitness and aerobics classes. Mon–Thurs 6am–midnight, Fri 6am–11pm, Sat 7am–10pm, Sun 7am–9pm; $15.

City Gym 107–113 Crown St, East Sydney ⓣ02/9360 6247, ⓦwww.citygym.com.au. Museum CityRail. Unbelievably popular (at all hours) among gay men, lesbians and straights. There are plenty of weights, aerobics, body combat and yoga classes and a sauna – which can be cruisey. 24hr Mon–Sat 7am–10pm, Sun 8am–10pm; $13.50.

Gold's Gym 23 Pelican Street, Surry Hills, ⓣ02/9264 4496, ⓦwww.goldsgymsydney.com. Possibly the most popular gay gym in Sydney. Located virtually on Oxford St, it offers a huge range of equipment and classes as well as a ladies only training area. From 5.30am until 11pm weekdays and from 8am until 9pm weekends.

Newtown Gym Level 1, 294 King St, Newtown ⓣ020/9519 6969. Newtown CityRail. Large lesbian membership. Step, stretch and yoga classes, weight training, solarium and sauna. Free childcare facilities (Mon–Sat 9am–noon). Mon–Fri 6am–10pm, Sat & Sun 8am–8pm; $13.

Beaches and swimming pools

During Sydney's hot summer, a popular choice among the gay set is **Tamarama** (known locally as Glamarama, see p.141), a fifteen-minute walk from the southern end of Bondi Beach. But if showing off is not your thing, **Bondi** (p.136) or nearby **Bronte** (p.141) may suit you better. The calm harbour waters of **Redleaf** at Double Bay (p.124) also lure a big gay crowd and, if you want to get your gear off, try **Lady Jane Beach** at Watsons Bay (p.128).

Pools of choice are Redleaf harbour pool at Double Bay and the appropriately named Andrew "Boy" Charlton pool in The Domain (pp.124 & p.275). The Coogee Women's Baths, at the southern end of Coogee Beach (p.144), is popular with lesbians.

17

Kids' Sydney

With its sunny climate, fabulous beaches and wide open spaces, Sydney is a great place to holiday with kids. There are lots of parks, playgrounds, sheltered bays and public pools for safe swimming, and a range of indoor options for rainy days. Museums are mostly child-friendly, in particular the **Powerhouse Museum** and the **Australian Museum**, both of which have exhibits and activities designed to entertain as well as educate, and most offer a range of special school-holiday programmes. Three areas, **The Rocks**, **Darling Harbour** and **Fox Studios** have much to keep children amused and all offer lots of free activities during the school holidays; check these websites for the latest goings on: Ⓦwww.rocksvillage.com.au, Ⓦwww.darlingharbour.com.au and Ⓦwww.foxstudios.com.au.

Also see "Sports and activities" for details on the many options for children, from renting bikes or rollerblades to the free pony rides and jumping castle at Canterbury Racetrack (p.271). And check out the "Festivals" chapter where everything from Sydney's kite festival at Bondi to the balmy evening Christmas carols in The Domain will keep the kids happy. Out of town, rail-enthusiast kids will love the Zig Zag Railway (p.325) near Lithgow, the Toy and Railway Museum at Leura (p.315) and the Sydney Tramway Museum and tram rides at the Royal National Park (see p.328); fire-engine-mad children should experience the Museum of Fire at Penrith (p.311).

Costs and access

Children under 5 get **entry into museums** for free, while those aged from 5 to 15 have a half-price or reduced rate (teenagers 16 or older should bring a student card or get hold of an ISIC card – see p.30); discounted family tickets, usually based on two adults and two children, are also offered in most places. We give the child and family entry prices in this chapter and while we don't list these rates in the rest of the Guide, assume they are available.

Children under 4 travel on **public transport** for free, while children from 4 to 15 travel at a fifty percent discount. There are also "family fares" – when one fare-paying adult travels with their children, the first child travels at half-price and the rest are free. Special family discounts are also available on the Sydney Pass, Sydney Explorer and Bondi Explorer services, ferry cruises and the Aquarium Pass.

The "Travellers with disabilities" section in Basics, which gives information about accessible transport and even bushwalks, is all relevant to pram-pushers as well.

Public toilets and parents' rooms

Sydney is well serviced with free **public toilets** (see p.282), and those in shopping malls and department stores invariably have a quite separate unisex **parents' room** attached, where you can change nappies. There's often even

▲ Bronte beach

a microwave to heat bottles or baby food, and curtained booths with vaguely comfy chairs for breastfeeding. However, it's your legal right to breastfeed in public and on the whole most people are pretty unfazed, given the amount of flesh routinely bared on Sydney's beaches.

Information and childminding

Sydney's Child is an excellent free monthly magazine with intelligent articles, detailed listings of **what's on**, and adverts for a range of services including **babysitting**; pick up a copy at libraries, major museums and many kid-oriented shops and services, or check out Ⓦwww.sydneyschild.com.au.

Two popular books detailing activities for kids in Sydney are also available at bookshops, and are reviewed in "Contexts" (see p.362).

Some hotels, usually the most expensive variety, offer in-house babysitting; enquire when you're booking. There are casual **childminding services** at many gyms (see Newtown Gym, p.238) and swimming pools (see Leichhardt Park Aquatic Centre, p.275 and Victoria Park Pool, p.276), usually with a limit of up to two hours.

Museums and galleries

The dynamic **Historic Houses Trust of New South Wales**, including the Justice and Police Museum (p.68), the Museum of Sydney (p.82), Hyde Park Barracks (p.77), Susannah Place Museum (p.63), Elizabeth Bay House (p.108), Vaucluse House (p.125), Government House (p.75), and Elizabeth Farm in Parramatta (p.162) and Rouse Hill estate, offer a huge range of school-holiday programmes for children aged 6 to 12 (2hr; $7–12; Ⓣ02/8239 2211, Ⓦwww.hht.net.au), from theatrical performances exploring pioneering history at Elizabeth Farm and feeding the farm animals at Rouse Hill estate to drawing classes at Vaucluse House.

Art Gallery of New South Wales The Domain Ⓦwww.artgallery.nsw.gov.au. Martin Place or St James CityRail. The gallery's free "Fun-days at the Gallery" Sunday performances (11.30pm & 1.45pm) for families – art appreciation, drama, storytelling, dance and mime – run most of the year and also daily except Sat during school holidays. Kids will be mesmerized by the Aboriginal dance and didgeridoo performances which are held Tues–Sat at noon. There are also kids' practical art workshops during the vacation periods (1hr 30min–2hr; $20; 5–8 years & 9–13 years; booking essential on Ⓣ02/9225 1740). Daily 10am–5pm. Entry free (except special exhibitions). Also see p.78.

Australian Museum Cnr College and William streets, East Sydney Ⓦwww.austmus.gov.au. Museum or Town Hall CityRail. The people here clearly know a thing or two about the special relationship kids have with dinosaurs – their dino exhibition is aimed squarely at 5–12 year olds. The museum's biodiversity section has a Search and Dis-

New South Wales' school holidays

Summer, six weeks, beginning roughly ten days before Christmas, to last week in January; **autumn**, two weeks coinciding with Easter (normally early to mid-April); **winter**, two weeks, beginning the second week of July; **spring**, two weeks, beginning the last week of September. Check the public schools section of the New South Wales Department of Education website for exact dates: Ⓦwww.schools.nsw.edu.au/calendar.

cover room, complete with microscopes, specimens (and books to help with identifying them), and a child-size kitchen where kids can learn about being environmentally friendly. Kids Island is for under-5s; it has a shipwreck boat and all sorts of crawling pits and cubby houses to explore, plus a baby change area. Every Thursday during term time is "Family Day", with organized activities for under 5s (10.30–11.30am; no bookings), while there are occasional weekend scientific workshops for 5–8 year olds and over-9s (in term time) and school holiday scientific and craft programmes ($1–15; bookings on ⓣ02/9320 6326). Daily 9.30am–5pm; entry $10, child $5, family $25.

Australian National Maritime Museum Darling Harbour ⓦwww.anmm.gov.au. Harbourside Monorail. This modern museum now has free entry, which makes it even more inviting for families. Activity trail sheets related to exhibitions and aimed at 7–12 year olds are available from the entry desk anytime, but Sunday is the big family day, when free films are shown in the theatrette at 2.30pm and the Kids Deck activity area is in full swing (10am–4pm; $5); activities include exhibition-related stories, games and craft activities. There's also an imaginative school holiday programme in Kids Deck ($7 per session), which could include a session pretending to be an eighteenth-century sailor or something involving stories, drawings, dress-ups and games. Information and bookings ⓣ02/9298 3655. Daily 9.30am–5pm, to 6pm in Jan. Also see p.93.

Powerhouse Museum 500 Harris St, Ultimo ⓦwww.powerhousemuseum.com. Central CityRail. Each level of this science and technology museum has a noisy and colourful corner aimed at small children, with hands-on exhibits exploring machines and movement, domestic activities, music, film and television. The general exhibits, from the huge steam engine to the chiming Strasbourg clock, will interest older kids. On weekends kids can get creative musically at "Soundhouse openhouse" (noon–1pm), a music and multimedia lab on level 3, and listen to a fifteen-minute grand piano performance (4.15pm) on level 2; there are also organized kids activities between 11am and noon, from craft activities and science experiments to historical dress-ups. These weekend activities are extended to daily sessions during the school holidays – information and bookings on ⓣ02/9217 0111. The Powerhouse Shop in the foyer is crammed with quirky and educational toys. Daily 10am–5pm; $10, child $5, family $25. Also see p.94. The Powerhouse also runs the Sydney Observatory (see p.64), where the 3-D Space Theatre and the animated Aboriginal dreamtime stories are a big hit with kids; The Observatory also has a big school holiday programme, from making and launching rockets and electronic workshops to star- and planet-related fun days (activities cost $10–35).

Parks and wildlife

Sydney and the surrounding area provide plenty of opportunities to see – and in some cases touch – native wildlife. The kids can pat koalas at Taronga Zoo (see p.132), and at **Featherdale Wildlife Park** (p.160) and the **Koala Park Sanctuary** (p.160). They can also meet Eric the giant crocodile and watch snakes and spiders being milked at the **Australian Reptile Park** on the Central Coast (p.293). Children also love observing the sea creatures, seals and fairy penguins, and dipping their hands into the touch-and-feel rockpool at **Sydney Aquarium** (see p.93), and seeing the scary sharks at Manly's **Oceanworld** (see p.147). And if you're visiting during June or July, be sure to take the kids on a **whale-watching cruise** (see p.37).

Centennial Park Cnr Oxford St and Lang Rd, Paddington ⓦwww.cp.nsw.gov.au. Bus #378 from Central CityRail or #380 from Circular Quay CityRail. Offering typical park pleasures such as feeding ducks and climbing trees, you'll also find bike paths (and a learners' cycleway) and bridleways here. You can rent kids' bikes and rollerblades nearby (see p.277) and the Equestrian Centre offers horse and pony rides. If children are over

5, they can go on an escorted horse ride around the park, while younger ones (older than 3) can go on an escorted pony ride in the grounds of the centre, offered by Centennial Stables, in Pavilion B (ⓣ02/9360 5650; $55 for 30min which can be shared between a couple of children). Also see p.277 for more on horse riding. If you can't afford a ride, it's great fun and perfectly fine for kids to wander through the Equestrian Centre and see the different horses in their stables. Back in the park, during the school holidays the park itself offers shorter pony rides ($9.50 for 10min), ranger-led dusk "Spotlight Prowls" searching for wildlife ($9.50 per adult or child; bookings essential on ⓣ02/9339 6699) and other ranger-led nature-based activities, aimed at varying age groups from 2 years up ($9.50–10.50). The child-friendly café (with a courtyard fountain kids love to play in) even serves up "babyccinos" (hot frothy milk). Daily 8am–6pm, to 8pm during Daylight Saving.

Cumberland State Forest 95 Castle Hill Rd, West Pennant Hills ⓣ02/9871 3377, ⓦwww.forest.nsw.gov.au/cumberland. Pennant Hills CityRail, then bus #631–635. Australia's only metropolitan state forest is in Sydney's northwestern suburbs with over half a century of native forest growth. The Information Centre (Mon–Fri 9am–4.30pm, Sat & Sun 10am–4.30pm) has displays and videos on the park and a great range of wooden toys among its Forest Shop stock, and an attached café. There are bushwalking trails, a native plant nursery and family activities at weekends, from an introduction to bushtucker (1hr; $4.40, family $15), dusk wildlife-spotting walks (2hr; 6 years and over; $8.80 or $30 per family) and birdwatching bush breakfasts (over 10s only; 2hr; $8.80, $30 family). The school-holiday programme includes activities such as making an animal mask or kids' bushtucker classes (most are for kids 6–12 and over but some "mini-ranger" activities for kids aged 3–6), which usually last an hour and cost $4.40 (bookings necessary). Free barbecue and picnic areas.

Sydney Harbour National Park National Parks and Wildlife Service, Cadman's Cottage, 110 George St, The Rocks ⓣ02/9247 5033, ⓦwww.nationalparks.nsw.gov.au. The NPWS offers special ranger-led walks for families in the school holidays (from $9.90 per child or adult) and special activities for kids, detailed on their website; they also lead a Kid's Ghost Tour of the Quarantine Station near Manly on Fri nights (2hr; $13.20 child or adult; see p.148).

Taronga Zoo Bradleys Head, Mosman Bay ⓦwww.zoo.nsw.gov.au. Ferry to Taronga Zoo (Athol) Wharf. Taronga Zoo occupies an enviable position high over the harbour, and the ferry ride there plus the cable car up the hill are half the fun. Favourites with the kids are the lumbering Kodiak bears, playful gorillas, poised meerkats, the native animal walkabout enclosure and aviaries where you wander among birds. There's also a petting zoo with domestic animals (milking show 11am, farm feed 2pm), a nocturnal animal house, seal training show (1.30pm), a free-flight bird show (noon & 3pm), a chance to be photographed with a koala (11am–3pm) plus keeper talks and feedings throughout the day. Daily: Jan 9am–9pm; Feb–Dec 9am–5pm. Entry $27, child (4–15) $14, family $70.

Shops

Suburban K-Mart, Target, Best and Less and Pumpkin Patch stores sell affordable kidswear, and the department stores in the city centre stock a full range of quality clothes and toys. The huge Toys "R" Us stores are found at various suburban locations. More interesting shops are detailed below. A delightful selection of kids' books set in Sydney are reviewed in "Contexts" on p.362 and are available at the bookshops listed in "Shopping" on pp.249–250 as well as the specialist Gleebooks store below.

ABC Shop Level 1, Albert Walk, QVB ⓦwww.shop.abc.net.au. Town Hall CityRail. ABC (and BBC) television's merchandising outlet – books, audio, video, toys, clothing and accessories – sells all the Australian favourites, from Bananas in Pyjamas to The Wiggles. Mon–Fri 9am–5.30pm (Thurs to 8pm), Sat 9am–5pm, Sun 11am–5pm.

Gleebooks Children's Books 191 Glebe Point Rd, Glebe ⓦwww.gleebooks.com.au. Bus #431–434 from Central CityRail. Children's bookshop, attached to the well-respected Gleebooks secondhand store (see p.250). Mon–Wed & Sun 10am–8pm, Thurs & Fri 10am–9pm, Sat 9am–9pm.

Hobbyco Top floor, MidCity Centre, 197 Pitt St Mall ⓦwww.hobbyco.com.au. Town Hall CityRail. Established as a business in 1935, this huge hobby shop has everything from dolls' houses to kites, Meccano sets, trains and slot cars. The working model railway is a major attraction. Mon–Sat 9am–6pm (Thurs to 9pm), Sun 11am–5pm.

The Kids Room 83 Paddington St, Paddington ⓦwww.thekidsroom.com.au. Bus #378 from Central CityRail or #380 from Circular Quay or Bondi Junction CityRail. Quality clothes and shoes, for babies through to early teens. Stocks Australian brands like Fred Bare and Gumboots. Mon–Fri 10.30am–5.30pm, Sat 10am–5.30pm, Sun 12.30–4.30pm.

Play House Toy Shop 152 Clarence St ⓣ02/9299 5498. Town Hall CityRail. Catering for younger children, from babies up to about 9 years. Playhouses, lots of handmade wooden toys, and attentive service and advice. Mon–Fri 9am–5.30pm, Sat 9am–4pm.

Swimming and water sports

Beware Sydney's **strong surf** – young children are safer swimming at sheltered harbour beaches or ocean pools. Public swimming pools (typically outdoor and unheated) generally have a toddlers' **paddling pool**. For year-round swimming there's a heated pool at North Sydney (p.275), right beside Luna Park, or at the indoor Sydney International Aquatic Centre (p.275), which has a rapid water ride and slides. The Cook and Phillip Park Aquatic and Leisure Centre (p.275) is another good place to take kids, while the Leichhardt Park Aquatic Centre (p.275) and Victoria Park Pool (p.276) have creche facilities. If you're going to be in Sydney for a while and your children can't swim, or are weak swimmers (or you're envisaging a future Olympic career for them), the NSW Department of Sport and Recreation conducts excellent inexpensive small-group **Swimsafe courses** at local swimming pools, held over nine consecutive days (information and bookings ⓣ13 13 02, ⓦwww.dsr.nsw.gov.au; pre-schoolers from 18 months, 30min per day, $36.45; school-age, 40min per day, $48.60; shorter courses available). Bondi's Lets Go Surfing (ⓣ02/9365 1800, ⓦwww.letsgosurfing.com.au) offers Saturday group lessons in **board-riding** and **surf safety** for kids aged 7–11 and 12–16 (2hr; $35), including longer surf camps in school holidays (4 days; 2hr per day; $199), and individual and family lessons. On the northern beaches, Manly Surf School (ⓣ02/9977 6977, ⓦwww.manlysurfschool.com) offers small-group surfing classes (6–17 years; 1hr; $40) and school holiday surfing classes at Manly, Collaroy and Palm beaches (2hr per day over 4 days; $120). Balmoral Windsurfing, Sailing and Kayaking School at Balmoral Beach has a **learn to sail** camp during summer and Easter holidays (ages 6–13; 5 days;

Sun protection

A broad-spectrum, water-resistant **sunscreen** (with a minimum SPF of 20) is a must, and colourful zinc cream on nose and cheeks is a good extra protectant when swimming. Most local kids wear UV-resistant lycra **swim tops** or wetsuit-style all-in-ones to the beach, and schoolchildren wear **hats** in the playground – the legionnaire-style ones are especially popular, as they shade the face and the back of the neck. All these items can be purchased at surfwear shops, department stores, or at the NSW Cancer Council Shop in the Westfield Centrepoint shopping centre, Castlereagh St entrance (ⓦwww.nswcc.org.au; Town Hall CityRail).

9.30am–3pm; $348; ⓣ02/9960 5344, ⓦwww.sailingschool.com.au). Northside Sailing School, Spit Bridge, Mosman (ⓣ02/9969 3972, ⓦwww.northsidesailing.com.au) specializes in weekend dinghy sailing courses on Middle Harbour during the sailing season (Sept–April) and also has lessons for kids (7–15 years; 2hr lesson for two children $80) and holiday camp programmes (4- or 5-day programmes; $305/350) during all school holidays except the winter break.

Beaches

Balmoral Beach On the north side of the harbour, around the corner from Taronga Zoo, this is the pick of the family beaches for its wide sandy bays, sheltered from the wind and waves. Much of the sand is shaded by big trees, and there's a great children's playground right next to the beach kiosk where you can buy ice creams and takeaway coffee (there's fish and chips across the road). See p.134.

Bronte Beach The most popular of the eastern beaches for families, fronted by an extensive and shady park with picnic shelters and barbecues (plus a stash of good alfresco cafés across the road), a mini-train ride ($3 per ride, $10 for 4 rides) and an imaginative children's playground. A natural rock enclosure provides a calm area for swimming. See p.141.

Coogee Coogee Bay is popular with families, with a grassy park with picnic shelters and barbecues. Past the southern end of the beach, Coogee Women's Pool (see p.144) is for women and children only (boys are welcome up to age 12). There's a big adventure playground in Grant Reserve opposite the pool. See p.142.

Manly On the north side of the harbour, tucked in beside Manly Wharf, Manly Cove has a small harbour beach with a netted-off swimming area and, on the ocean side of Manly, there are sheltered beaches on Cabbage Tree Bay, Fower Bower (with a rock pool) and Shelly Beach (fronted by a big park). The ferry ride over is lots of fun, and there are plenty of attractions for kids in the area, including an aquarium and a water slide. You can rent bikes or rollerblades and get onto the Manly bike path, which is shared with pedestrians. See p.145.

North Bondi The northern end of Bondi Beach has a shallow enclosed seapool for children. It's backed by a grassy park rising up the hill with electric barbecues and a children's playground on the next level up the steps. Consequently this is the child-overrun "family" end of the beach; an ice-cream van takes advantage of the situation, and there are a couple of beachfront cafés across the street. See p.136.

Northern beaches Stretching from Manly, the northern beaches also have some good family choices – Dee Why Beach is backed by a sheltered lagoon, Long Reef's creature-filled rockpools provide wonderful exploration opportunities, while Narrabeen Beach fronts extensive, swimmable lakes. Beyond Narrabeen, sheltered Bongin Bongin Bay, with a headland reserve and rocks to clamber on, is ideal for children. See p.149–p.151.

Theatre

Marian Street Theatre for Young People 2 Marian St, Killara bookings ⓣ02/9645 1611. Killara CityRail. Bookings are essential for the popular matinees for kids aged 3–10, often involving audience participation (Sat 1pm; school holidays: Mon–Fri 10.30am & 1pm; $15, child $12).

Sydney Opera House Bennelong Point, Circular Quay ⓣ02/9250 7770, ⓦwww.sydneyoperahouse.com. Circular Quay CityRail/ferry. The popular Kids At The House programme includes "Babies Proms" for 2–5 year olds to learn about orchestral music (1hr; $15 child or adult) and Holidays @ the House, a series of school holiday theatre performances aimed at school-age children ($22). The Australian Ballet holds twice yearly "Introduction to the Ballet" sessions for children aged 5 and upwards and adults (May & Nov; 1hr 30min; $15–20).

Theme parks, playgrounds and activities

Sydney's first theme park, harbourfront **Luna Park**, opened in the 1930s but has been shutting down and reopening since the 1980s and is currently open (see p.128). You can head south to **Jamberoo Recreation Park** (below), or, if you're in town around April, to Homebush Bay for the biggest annual funfair at the **Royal Easter Show** (see p.265).

Darling Harbour (see p.90) is never short of kids' amusements and is big on family festivals. The area along **Darling Walk** is particularly child-focused – there's a watery playground with fountains to race among, colourful stationary bikes spouting water, **paddleboats** on the small lake (Mon–Fri 11am–5pm, Sat & Sun 10am–6pm; $12 for 15min), a **mini-golf** course under the blue cone (Mon–Fri 11am–5pm, Sat & Sun 10am–6pm; one player $7 per round, two players $12, three to four players $15), plus naughty sweetshops and the inevitable *McDonald's*. Also on Darling Walk, Pacific Fly Motion is a **bungy trampoline** which whizzes participants as high as two storeys – even small kids can participate, as the lowest weight limit is 10kg (daily 10.30am to dusk; $10 for 4 min) and nearby there are free **didgeridoo performances** at the rather incongruous Outback Centre (daily 1pm, 3pm & 5pm plus 2pm Sat & Sun). During school holidays, events are held on the floating stage on Darling Walk's lake. West of the lake, there's a colourful children's playground area and a charming nineteenth-century **carousel** right next door.

At **Fox Studios** (see p.105) there's plenty on tap for little kids to teenagers: a big choice of movies at its cinemas, an outdoor music screen, lots of shops to browse in, including a huge bookshop and a kids' dress-up store, a mini-golf course (Mon–Thurs & Sun 10am–8.30pm, Fri & Sat 10am–10pm; $10, child $7.50, family pass $28), a winter ice-skating rink (p.277), a bungee-jumping trampoline (p.277), ten-pin bowling at Strike Bowling Bar, two outdoor adventure playgrounds and, beside them, a carousel ($2.50 per ride) and a (pricey) indoor playground, Lollipops (see below), that's perfect for rainy days.

Jamberoo Recreation Park Jamberoo Rd, Jamberoo, 7km from Kiama (see p.343) ⓦwww.jamberoo.net. Running from Sept to April on weekends and during school holidays, this is a water-themed fun park with a mix of thrilling and gentle water-rides and -slides and an artificial lagoon to swim in. There are non-watery attractions, too: a chairlift, toboggan rides, a park train, racing cars and a mini-golf course. A picnic area has coin-operated barbecues plus there are several fast-food outlets and a sit-down licensed eatery, *The Loft*, serving healthier food. Entry 4–12 year olds $25, over-12s & adults $30. Special bus service from Albion Park CityRail departs 10.15am, returns Jamberoo at 5.30pm; $32 (child or adult) includes park entry.

Lollipops Playground Fox Studios, Driver Ave, Moore Park ⓦwww.lollipopsplayland.com.au. Bus #339 from Central CityRail. This indoor playground is aimed at children aged 1–9, and is guaranteed to physically exhaust them, with a jungle gym, giant mazes, tunnels, jumping castle and everything from a ball pool to a tea-cup merry-go-round ride, books, toys, dress-ups and games as well as organized activities. Socks are obligatory. There are also two free playgrounds, and a carousel outside. Mon–Thurs 9.30am–7pm, Fri 9.30am–8pm, Sat 9am–8pm, Sun 9am–7pm; Mon–Fri 1–2 year olds $9, 2–9 year olds $12, adults $5 includes a coffee from the well-stocked café; Sat & Sun all children over 1 $14.

Sydney Learning Adventures ⓦwww.sydneylearningadventures.com.au. Interactive activities for kids aged 5 to 10 during school holidays in The Rocks and Chinese Gardens run by a mix of educators, archeologists and theatre practitioners who bring the area's history alive: kids might get to experience anything from what life was like in the 1900s in The Rocks, to a fun day at the Chinese Gardens or learning about Chinese horoscopes and paper folding. Bookings and further information ⓣ02/9240 8552; $11–14.

Shopping and galleries

The rectangle bounded by Elizabeth, King, York and Park streets is Sydney's prime shopping area, with a number of beautifully restored **Victorian arcades** and the main **department stores**. The city also has plenty of sparkling shopping complexes where you can hunt for fashion and accessories without raising a sweat. The Rocks is packed with Australiana and **souvenir shops**, where you can satisfy the urge to buy boomerangs, didgeridoos and stuffed toy koalas, and it's also the best place for duty- and GST-free shopping.

Paddington's Oxford Street is best for stylish one-stop shopping, with its enticing array of designer shops, funky fashion, some of the city's most appealing bookshops – and the best **weekend market** in town. The more avant-garde **Darlinghurst** and **Surry Hills** (notably the stretch of Crown Street between Devonshire and Oxford streets) have become a focus for retro-influenced interior design and clothes shops. In the inner west, **Balmain** has chic shops and gourmet delis to supplement its Saturday market, while cheerfully offbeat **Newtown** and neighbouring St Peters are great for secondhand fashions and quirky speciality stores. Down at the beach, **Bondi Pavilion** has an excellent souvenir shop, and the Campbell Parade strip offers lots of beachwear and surf shops.

The main **sales** take place immediately after Christmas and into January, and in June and into July; there are also stock clearances throughout the year, often around public holidays.

Finally, if you've run out of time to buy presents and souvenirs, note that **Sydney Airport** has one of the biggest shopping malls in Sydney, with outlets for everything from surfwear to R.M.Williams bushoutfitters, at the same prices as downtown stores; see box below.

Duty-free shopping

If you have an air ticket out of Australia, you may be able to save around thirty percent on goods such as perfume, jewellery, imported clothing, cameras and electronic equipment. One of the main outlets is DFS Galleria, with a major store on four floors at 155 George Street in The Rocks (Mon–Fri 11am–8pm, Sat & Sun 10am–8pm; ⓦ www.dfsgalleria.com).

Opening hours

Most stores are open Monday to Saturday from 9am or 10am until 5.30pm or 6pm, with late-night shopping on Thursdays until 9pm. Many of the larger shops and department stores are also open on Sunday from 10am or noon until 4 or 5pm, as are most malls and shopping centres at tourist hotspots such as Darling Harbour and The Rocks. We've given the opening hours for the shops listed below when they are open earlier or later than these general hours, and indicated if they are closed on Sundays.

Books

In addition to the small selection of places listed below, there is a concentration of **secondhand bookshops** on King Street in Newtown and Glebe Point Road in Glebe, and good **secondhand stalls** at Glebe, Balmain, Paddington and Bondi markets (see "Markets", pp.259–260). *Gertrude & Alice Cafe Bookstore* at Bondi (see p.137) and *Delizia* in the city (see p.186) also sell secondhand books. The Bookshop, a specialist **gay and lesbian** bookshop in Darlinghurst, is detailed on p.233.

The worldwide book **superstores** also have a presence in Sydney – there's Borders at the Skygarden shopping centre (see p.256) and a Books Kinokuniya at The Galeries Victoria (see p.250), but the Australia-owned Collins, near Glebe, was the first and is still the best in terms of high-comfort-level browsing – and this has prompted many bookshops to offer added value, in terms of in-store coffee shops, Internet terminals, discounted bestsellers and author talks. For extended opening hours and knowledgeable staff, though, you'll still do better with the independents.

The bookshop at the State Library (see p.76) has one of the best collections of **Australian-related books** in Sydney, while if you're interested in Australian art, the Art Gallery of New South Wales (p.78) has an extensive bookshop. The shop at the Museum of Sydney (see p.82) has plenty on the city and there's a National Trust bookshop at the S.H. Ervin Gallery (p.65). If you're after Australian **first editions**, seek out Nicholas Pounder, who now only operates online (Ⓦ www.nicholaspounder.com); for **antiquarian books**, check out Berkelouw (below) and Hordern House (p.259).

Abbey's 131 York St Ⓦ www.abbeys.com.au. Town Hall CityRail. This big academic and general bookstore, established in 1968 and still mostly family-run, is one of Sydney's best-known independent booksellers – great at ordering in books – and in a prime spot opposite the QVB. The Language Book Centre on the first floor is the place to buy foreign-language books in Sydney. Abbey's also runs Sydney's science fiction, fantasy and horror bookshop, Galaxy, which is two doors up at no. 143. Mon–Fri 8.30am–7pm (Thurs to 9pm), Sat 8.30am–6pm, Sun 10am–5pm.

Ariel 42 Oxford St, Paddington Ⓣ 02/9332 4581, Ⓦ www.arielbooks.com.au. Bus #378 from Central CityRail or #380 from Circular Quay CityRail. Not too large, lively and very hip, Ariel is especially good for design books and cutting-edge fiction. It's a great place to browse in the evening after a movie (the Palace cinemas Verona and Academy are just across the road; see p.231) and often has author readings and book launches. The branch at 103 George St (Circular Quay CityRail) also offers respite from the stuffed-koala overdose that frequently afflicts shoppers in The Rocks. Both daily 9am–midnight.

Berkelouw Books 19 Oxford St, Paddington Ⓦ www.berkelouw.com.au. Bus #378 from Central CityRail or #380 from Circular Quay CityRail. Catering to collectors as well as casual browsers, Berkelouw has been dealing in antiquarian books since 1812.

New books are downstairs, and their upstairs coffee shop, with huge windows overlooking the busy Oxford Street strip, is a popular pre- and post-movie meeting place (the Palace Verona is just next door); daily 9.30am–midnight. Also Berkelouw Books and Music at 70 Norton St, Leichhardt, for new and secondhand books and CDs (including a big range of World Music), an Aboriginal art gallery (Walkabout; see p.258) and two in-store cafés, the streetfront *Berkelouw Cafe* and the second floor *Booklounge Cafe*, which hosts fortnightly Philo Cafe philosophy discussions (first & third Tues; 8pm; $5 includes coffee) and monthly poetry readings (last Thurs month; $5 includes glass of wine or a coffee) and even a performance space; Mon–Thurs & Sun 9am–11pm, Fri & Sat 9am–midnight (bus #438 & #440 from Central CityRail). Berkelouw Discovery Bookstore in Gowings' Market Street store (see p.254) stocks travel-related books and maps.

Books Kinokuniya The Galeries Victoria, 500 George St, cnr Park St ⓦwww.kinokuniya.com. Town Hall CityRail. Now Sydney's biggest book superstore, the Japanese-owned Kinokuniya has seventy percent of its estimated 300,000 titles in English. A range of books in Japanese and Chinese make up the rest, and it also stocks the city's best stash of magazines, both local and imported. As you'd expect, there's a good range of comics, including *Manga*. The art and design section is also impressive and there's an antiquarian books section, an art gallery, a selection of world globes for sale, a fossil collection and the now-obligatory bookstore café. Mon–Sat 10am–7pm (Thurs to 9pm), Sun 11am–7pm.

Collins Superstore Level 2, Broadway Shopping Centre, Broadway, near Glebe ⓦwww.collinsbooks.com.au. Buses #431–434, #438 & #440 from Central CityRail. Vast bookstore – Sydney's first book superstore and Australian-owned – with curving bookshelves, soft lighting and comfy sofas and window seats in the arched windows where you can easily lose yourself for an afternoon. When it's time to face the real world again, make for the in-store coffee shop to ease the transition. Mon–Fri 9am–6pm (Thurs to 9pm) Sat 9am–7pm, Sun 10am–6pm.

Dymocks 424 George St ⓦwww.dymocks.com.au. Town Hall CityRail. Sprawled across several floors, Dymocks has a particularly impressive Australian selection, and an upstairs café where you can slurp generous smoothies; Mon–Fri 9am–6.30pm (Thurs to 9pm), Sat 9am–6pm, Sun 10am–5pm. Another city branch with longer hours and in-store espresso bar is at Level 2, Harbourside Shopping Centre, Darling Harbour (daily 10am–9pm; Harbourside Monorail).

Gleebooks 49 Glebe Point Rd, Glebe, ⓦwww.gleebooks.com.au. Bus #431–434 from Central CityRail. Legendary independent Sydney literary bookshop specializing in academic and alternative books, philosophy and cultural studies, contemporary Australian and international literature, plus author appearances and book-signings upstairs; daily 10am–9pm except Sat 9am–9pm. Further up the hill is Gleebooks Secondhand and Children's Books, at 191 Glebe Point Rd.

Gould's Book Arcade 32–38 King St, Newtown ⓣ02/9519 8947. Newtown CityRail. Chaotic piles of books greet you in this near legendary secondhand bookstore run by Bob Gould. The incredible range of non-fiction includes a whole host of leftie political tomes; you'd never find anything specific here unless you were incredibly lucky but it's great for browsing. Daily 7am–midnight.

Lesley McKay's Bookshop 118 Queen St, Woollahra ⓣ02/9327 1354. Bus #378 from Central CityRail or #380 from Circular Quay CityRail. Excellent range and knowledgeable staff, and a big children's section; Mon–Sat 9am–6pm, Sun 9.30am–4.30pm. There's also an equally good store, with a big photography, design and architecture section and longer hours at 14 Macleay St, Potts Point (Mon–Sat 9am–9pm, Sun 10am–6pm; Kings Cross CityRail).

Macleay Bookshop 103 Macleay St, Potts Point ⓦwww.macleaybookshop.com.au. Kings Cross CityRail. When you're sick of all the bigger stores, this tiny, independent and very literary bookstore is a peaceful choice for browsing, with a well-chosen selection. It also stocks books by local Kings Cross writers. Daily 10am–9pm.

The Travel Bookshop Shop 3, 175 Liverpool St ⓦwww.travelbooks.com.au. Museum CityRail. The place for maps, guides, phrasebooks and travelogues, plus a good selection of Australiana and specialist walking and cycling books, as well as travel accessories. Also a good range of secondhand travel literature. There's a handy American Express branch in store. Mon–Fri 9am–6pm, Sat 10am–5pm.

Clothes and accessories

For interesting **fashion** to suit a range of budgets, Oxford Street in Paddington is the place, along with the glitzy Sydney Central Mall in the city. With more time to explore, take a stroll down Crown Street, near the junction with Oxford Street, where there are great stores stuffed with Hawaiian shirts, frocks from the Fifties and cool clubbing gear. Or check out the **secondhand stores** on Newtown's King Street – though you'll probably find that prices are higher than for similar stuff in the UK or US. If you want to peek at expensive Australian **designer fashion**, head for David Jones Department Store (see p.254) or the shops of the designers themselves, mostly on Oxford Street in Paddington or the Strand Arcade in the city centre – see p.252.

High street fashion

Country Road 142–144 Pitt St ⓦwww.countryroad.com.au. Town Hall CityRail. Classic but stylish (if a little preppy) Australian-designed clothes for men and women, plus a high-quality range of shoes and accessories. Several other stores include one on the ground level of the QVB (see p.255) and others at 255 Oxford St, Paddington, the Harbourside Shopping Centre, Darling Harbour, and 213 Oxford St, Bondi Junction. There is also a clearance outlet at Birkenhead Point, Drummoyne (see "Factory outlets" box on p.253). Store hours, Mon–Fri 9am–5.30pm (Thurs to 9pm), Sat 9am–5pm, Sun 11am–5pm. Other locations include Shop 205, Harbourside Shopping Centre, Darling Harbour; 213 Oxford St, Bondi Junction.

Dangerfield 84 Oxford St, Paddington ⓦwww.dangerfield.com.au. Bus #378 from Central CityRail or #380 from Circular Quay. Offers edgy street fashion, "from punk to funk", for both sexes. Also at 268 King St, Newtown, and Market City, Hay St, Haymarket.

Mambo 17 Oxford St, Paddington ⓦwww.mambo.com.au. Bus #378 from Central CityRail or #380 from Circular Quay. Influenced by comic-strip and graffiti art, Reg Mombassa's designs are now emblazoned on T-shirts, surf gear, beach towels, watches and wallets around the world, promoting his tongue-in-cheek philosophy of "salvation through shopping". Also at Market City, Hay St, Haymarket, 80 Campbell Parade, Bondi Beach, and 80 The Corso, Manly.

Marcs Shop 228, Mid-City Centre, Pitt St Mall ⓦwww.marcs.com.au. Town Hall CityRail. The place to buy great shirts for men and women. Also stocks a selection of hip European and US lines such as Diesel. Several other locations including 280 Oxford St, Paddington, and 118 Campbell Parade, Bondi Beach.

Mooks Clothing Co Shop 2, The Galeries Victoria, cnr George and Park streets ⓦwww.mooks.com. Town Hall CityRail. Now known internationally, Mooks' trendy streetwear originated in Melbourne; clothing and footwear.

Sarah Jane 94 Oxford St, Paddington ⓦwww.sarah-jane.com. Bus #378 from Central CityRail or #380 from Circular Quay CityRail. Gorgeous, highly feminine frocks, from silky slip dresses to ethereal, floaty chiffon numbers, embroidered velvet coats and appliquéd tops, all with a vintage feel. Prices are mid-range, somewhere between chain store and designer levels, with substantial reductions during summer and winter clearances. Also at 134 King St, Newtown and 340 Darling St, Balmain.

▼ Mambo store

Surf Dive N Ski 462 George St ⓦwww.sds.com.au. Town Hall CityRail. Chain of surf wear shops stocking all the major labels. As well as casual clothes, swimming and surfing gear and shoes, there are great accessories – sunglasses, jewellery and watches, hats, beach towels and bags to stash it all in.

Zomp Shoez Shop 303, Mid-City Centre, Pitt St Mall, City ⓣ02/9221 4027. Town Hall CityRail. A shoe fetishist's heaven, with styles (and prices) that run the gamut from sensible to extravagant; women's shoes only. Other locations include 255 & 468 Oxford St, Paddington.

Designer fashion

Australian Fashion Week (ⓦwww.afw.com.au) is held annually in May, with around sixty designers from Australia and the Asia-Pacific region showing their collections. Since Fashion Week's inception in the mid-1990s, there's been a stronger focus both at home and abroad on Australian designers, many of whom, such as **Collette Dinnigan**, have made a name for themselves internationally. We have listed designers with their own outlets below, all on (or just off) Oxford Street in Paddington and Woollahra and in the Strand Arcade. Some designers don't have their own shops, but **David Jones** department store stocks a big range of home-grown designers. You can combine a visit to Paddington's boutiques with a visit to Saturday's Paddington Market (see p.260), where you'll find original fashion, but expect big crowds. The "Fashion of the Year" display in November at the Powerhouse Museum (see p.94) is also worth a look. All the stores below are open daily. To get to Oxford Street (Queen St is just off it), Paddington and Woollahra, take bus #378 from Central CityRail or #380 from Circular Quay or Bondi Junction CityRail; the nearest train station to the Strand Arcade in the city is Town Hall CityRail.

The Akira Boutique 12A Queen St, Woollahra ⓦwww.akira.com.au. Japanese-born designer Akira Isogawa has been living in Sydney since the mid-1980s. His ethereal, Japanese-influenced designs, which also include clothes for men, have found favour overseas, with stockists including Barney's in New York and Browns in London.

Alannah Hill 118–120 Oxford St, Paddington ⓣ02/9380 9147; Level 1, The Strand Arcade. Over-the-top, vintage-look, feminine clothing in rich fabrics; boudoir-like stores.

Bettina Liano 440 Oxford St, Paddington; Shop 74–78, Level 1, The Strand Arcade ⓦwww.bettinaliano.com. Well-cut designer jeans for women.

Brave/Wayne Cooper 302 Oxford St, Paddington ⓦwww.waynecooper.com.au. Wayne Cooper makes hip but practical clothes for men and women in the latest high-tech fabrics; even the store feels futuristic. There's also a Wayne Cooper store at Level 1, The Strand Arcade.

Colette Dinnigan 33 William St, Paddington; also stocked in David Jones Department Store ⓦwww.collettedinnigan.com. Australia's most internationally recognized designer has her own shop in London and her designs stocked in Harrods and Liberty in the UK and Barneys in the US. Dinnigan is known for her very feminine, finely made clothes for women – lots of beading and embroidery.

Lisa Ho Shop 2A–6A Queen St, Woollahra; Level 1, The Strand Arcade ⓦwww.lisaho.com. Girly frocks; lots of evening wear.

Morrissey 372 Oxford St, Paddington ⓣ02/9380 7422. Peter Morrissey designs sexy clothes with an edge, for men and women; also accessories. Other locations include Sydney Central Plaza and Direct Factory Outlets, Homebush (see "Factory outlets" box opposite).

Saba Sydney Central Plaza, 450 George St (women: Shop 6; men: Shop 23) ⓦwww.saba.com.au. Town Hall CityRail. Understated, urbane range of clothing for men and women (in separate stores) by veteran designer Joe Saba. Other locations include a men's store at 270 Oxford St, Paddington.

sass & bide 132 Oxford St, Paddington ⓦwww.sassandbide.com. The hot Australian designer duo, Heidi Middleton and Sarah-Jane Clarke, who burst onto the world fashion scene in early 2000 with their low-slung jeans, have finally opened their own store. This Oxford Street flagship features their entire collection.

Scanlan & Theodore 122 Oxford St, Paddington

Factory outlets

If you like **designer labels** and fashion but not the price tags, there are several **factory outlets** in Sydney you can check out. The best is out in the 'burbs at the vast **Direct Factory Outlets** (DFO) on the corner of Homebush Bay Drive and Underwood Rd, Homebush (daily 10am–6pm; ⓦwww.dfo.com.au; Strathfield CityRail then bus #525 to Underwood St) where there are eighty clearance outlets of big fashion brands – men's, women's and children's wear and underwear, jewellery, shoes, handbags and luggage – including Esprit, Jigsaw, Laura Ashley, Polo Ralph Lauren, Portmans, Colorado and Rivers; surfwear outlets Billabong Mambo and Ripcurl; Pumpkin Patch for kids; and Australian designer fashion at Country Road, Marcs, Charlie Brown, Morrissey and Lisa Ho (see above); there are also two food courts to choose from. A more pleasant spot for samples and seconds hunting is the competing **Birkenhead Point Outlet Centre** (ⓦwww.birkenheadsc.com.au), Roseby Street, Drummoyne. It can be reached on a very pleasant ferry trip from Circular Quay to Birkenhead Ferry Wharf (Mon–Fri only; alternatively any #500–508, #510, #515, #518, #520 bus departing from George St in the city and alighting at Victoria St) and you can enjoy more waterviews from the alfresco cafés; fashion and accessory outlets include Oroton, French Connection, Country Road, Esprit, Marcs, Mambo, Sunglass Hut and David Jones bargain warehouse, Shoes n Sox Wharehouse for kid's shoes, and outdoor/climbing/bushwalking gear at Kathmandu and Mountain Designs, sportwear at Insport; Australian designer outlets are Alannah Hill and Morrisey.

If you don't want to stray from the city, **Market City shopping centre** in Chinatown (see p.255) has dropped most of the designer seconds shops lately, but has a good selection of mainstream fashion factory outlets which include mixed fashions at Calvin Klein Jeans, Esprit (separate men's, women's and children's stores) and women's fashion chains Bracewell, Seduce, Sisco and Supre. For more detail on the best places to head for discounts, shopaholics should get hold of the excellent *Bargain Shoppers Guide to Sydney*, sold at newsagents.

ⓦwww.scanlanandtheodore.com.au. Original, stylish clothes for women; great cuts and fabrics.

Wheels & Doll Baby 259 Crown St, Darlinghurst ⓦwww.wheelsanddollbaby.com. This quirky store with its own label has been here – just off Oxford Street – since the late 1980s but the Australian designer rock-chick cum French bordello fashion by Melanie Greensmith (with own rock star husband of Divinyl fame) is just starting to take off in the UK.

Zimmermann Wear 387 Oxford St, Paddington and 24 Oxford St, Woollahra; Level 1, The Strand Arcade ⓦwww.zimmermannwear.com. Simone Zimmermann is known for her trendy women's swimwear.

Secondhand

The Look 230 King St, Newtown ⓣ02/9550 2455. Newtown CityRail. A stylish variant on the charity shop, run by the Wesley Mission and worth a look for bargain buys. Mon–Thurs 10am–6pm, Fri–Sat 10am–10pm.

Pretty Dog 1 Brown St, Newtown, just off King St ⓣ02/9519 7839. Newtown CityRail. A good range of retro secondhand gear and over-the-top club and streetwear.

Route 66 257 Crown St, Darlinghurst ⓣ02/9331 6686. Bus #378 from Central CityRail or #380 from Circular Quay CityRail. Taking its inspiration from America's legendary highway (Route 66) to the Wild West, this is where you'll find US vintage gear, and cowgirl-chic leather boots just made for line-dancing.

The Vintage Clothing Shop 147 Castlereagh St, City ⓣ02/9267 7135. Town Hall CityRail. This is Sydney's (and probably Australia's) premier vintage clothing store, established in 1976. It has a fabulous range from the 1890s to the 1970s, including an incredible collection of beaded and sequinned tops and dresses from the 1960s. Closed Sun.

Zoo Emporium 332 Crown St, Surry Hills ⓣ02/9380 5990. Bus #378 from Central CityRail or #380 from Circular Quay CityRail. The very best in Seventies disco gear, from a world where day-glo never died.

Outdoor and workwear

Gowings 45 Market St, cnr George St ⓦwww.gowings.com. Town Hall CityRail. The place to go for Australian workwear is this delightfully old-fashioned men's department store, which has become a beloved Sydney institution since it was established in 1868. It has everything a bloke could want (or in some cases sheilas too), from Bonds T-shirts and Speedo swimwear, to Blundstone boots and a range of Akubra hats – all at the best prices in town. With a floor devoted to outdoor pursuits, it's also a useful pitstop for basic camping equipment and there's a travel bookstore and cheap haircuts available at the barber's upstairs too. Their very amusing catalogue is worth keeping as a souvenir. Other central branches are located at 319 George St, Wynyard, and 82 Oxford St, Darlinghurst.

R.M. Williams 71 George St, The Rocks (Circular Quay CityRail) ⓦwww.rmwilliams.com.au. This quality bush outfitters is great for moleskin pants and shirts, Drizabone coats and superb leather riding and dress boots. Also at **389 George St near Central and** the airport.

Strand Hatters The Strand Arcade, 412 George St (through to Pitt St) ⓦwww.strandhatters.com.au. Town Hall CityRail. For the widest range of Akubra hats and other Australian classics, this old-fashioned store is the place.

Accessories and jewellery

In addition to the following shops, it's worth checking out the markets (see pp.259–260), museum shops (especially the MCA, see p.68, the Powerhouse Museum, see p.94, and, the Art Gallery of New South Wales, see p.78) for unusual treasures and trinkets, as well as the smaller, private galleries (see pp.257–259).

Dinosaur Designs Shop 77, The Strand Arcade, 412 George St (through to Pitt St) ⓦwww.dinosaurdesigns.com.au. Town Hall CityRail. Dinosaur's trademark chunky resin and silver jewellery, and beautifully tactile tableware in muted shades of amber and earth, are terribly hard to resist. Closed Sun. Also at 339 Oxford St, Paddington.

Love and Hatred Level 1, The Strand Arcade, 412 George St (through to Pitt St) ⓣ02/9233 3441. Town Hall CityRail. Funky Australian jewellery incorporating Gothic and medieval imagery. They will also make commissioned pieces here.

Department stores and shopping malls

Australia has followed the American trend in shopping and you're bound to find yourself in mall-land at some stage. Although lacking in neighbourhood character, big city and suburban malls and department stores are handy for familiarizing yourself with prices and variety, especially if time is short. Mall air-conditioning, too, can be a big plus on hot, sticky days.

Department stores

David Jones Cnr Elizabeth and Castlereagh streets ⓦwww.davidjones.com.au. St James or Town Hall CityRail. Straddling Market Street, David Jones' flagship store is an utterly civilized shopping experience: the ground floor of this flagship store is graced with seasonal floral displays and a coiffured pianist playing tasteful tunes. There's a fantastic gourmet food hall and lots of Australian and International designer labels in stock. A less salubrious version is located at 229 Oxford St, Bondi Junction (Bondi Junction CityRail), and there's a warehouse outlet at Birkenhead Point (see box on p.253).

Myer 436 George St ⓦwww.myer.com.au. Town Hall CityRail. The more workaday of Sydney's two main department stores, the Myer store, at the heart of the Sydney Central Plaza mall, nevertheless has several gleaming floors of fashion and a tranquil Wellness Spa flanked by elegant minimalist homewares.

Shopping malls

Broadway Shopping Centre Cnr Broadway and Bay streets, Broadway ⓦwww.broadway-centre.com.au. Bus #431–434, #438 & #440 from Central CityRail. On Broadway, between Central Station and Glebe, this

The face of Australia

In recent years, Aussie skincare companies have wowed the world with their minimalist approach to packaging, lavish use of essential oils and vibrant lippy colours – not to mention some savvy marketing. All the following are available at David Jones and/or Myer, or their own stores detailed below.

Aesop Ⓦwww.aesop.net.au. Divine skin balms and haircare products packed in pharmaceutical-grade brown glass, which rely on essential oils for their beneficial properties and fragrance, and eschew the usual exaggerated claims and hype.

Bliss Ⓦwww.blissaromatherapy.com. Aromatherapy range of pure essential oils, massage oils and incense.

Bloom Ⓦwww.bloomcosmetics.com. Whimsically packaged cosmetics, candles and body range, including hugely popular fruity lip balms and lipsticks, from young entrepreneur Natalie Bloom. Available at Blooms The Chemist, 202 Coogee Bay Rd, Coogee.

Jurlique Ⓦwww.jurlique.com.au. Pure, hypoallergenic skin and haircare based on essential oils produced from herbs grown organically in South Australia. Not tested on animals. Jurlique has its own stores, including the flagship Jurlique Day Spa, Shop 33, Ground Floor, 193 Pitt St Mall Ⓣ02/9231 0626.

Napoleon Perdis Ⓦwww.napoleoncosmetics.com. Individually colour-matched cosmetics to suit all types and shades of skin, as you might expect from a company that also runs a school for make-up artists. Napoleon has a chain of its own stores, including one on Level 2 of the Skygarden shopping centre (see p.256) and on the fashionista strip, Oxford Street, at no. 74.

mall benefits from its proximity to Sydney University and the arty enclave of Glebe, with a less run-of-the-mill mix of street fashion and chain stores. A Hoyts multiplex cinema shows art-house and mainstream movies (see p.229); for books there's Collins Superstore, plus there's a big Rebel Sport store, a vast K-Mart, a great Harris Farm Markets for fresh fruit and vegetables and an extensive Asian section in the Coles supermarket. If you have a car, the three-hour free parking is handy, as Glebe Point Road's street parking is all metered.

The Galeries Victoria 500 George St, cnr Park St Ⓦwww.tgv.com.au. Town Hall CityRail. Diagonally opposite the Town Hall, this upmarket shopping mall has a great sense of space provided by its central glass-roofed piazza and a series of arcades throughout. The fashion stores are virtually all mixed clothing or menswear – including funky Mooks Clothing Co and Polo Jeans Co. Its main drawcard, however, is the city's biggest book superstore, Kinokuniya (see "Books" section). There are lots of cafés, patisseries, sandwich bars, a sushi shop and an ice-cream parlour on the lower ground floor. You can enter the contrastingly heritage *Art House Hotel* (see p.209) from one end of the ground floor, where there are also cheap eats by day.

Market City 9–13 Hay St, Haymarket Ⓦwww.marketcity.com.au. Central CityRail. This cavernous mall above Paddy's Market houses two food courts, the multiplex Reading Cinema (see p.231) and a bar. The shopping centre has a distinctly Asian feel, with Chinese lanterns hanging from the ceiling and resident shiatsu masseurs. There are Asian supermarkets, factory outlets for big-name stores like Esprit, and smaller boutiques selling cute street and club wear imported from Asia (think smaller sizes).

QVB (Queen Victoria Building) 455 George St, City Ⓦwww.qvb.com.au. Town Hall CityRail. This splendid Victorian arcade is a sight in its own right, attracting more visitors than either the Harbour Bridge or the Opera House. The interior is magnificent, with beautiful woodwork, elevated walkways and antique lifts. Brave the weekend hordes for a wistful look at the designer shop fronts upstairs and a wander around the ubiquitous Esprit, Jigsaw or the Body Shop at ground level. Or come just for a coffee fix in *Bar Cupola* or *Jet* (see p.186), both at street level. From Town Hall Station you can walk right through the basement level (mainly bustling food stalls) and continue via the Sydney Central Plaza to Myer, emerging on the Pitt St Mall.

Skygarden 77 Castlereagh St and off Pitt St Mall ⓦwww.skygarden.com.au. Town Hall CityRail. Stylish shopping centre with lots of fashion for men and women, and the Borders book superstore. Level 2 is virtually devoted to homewares, plus there's a Napoleon Perdis Cosmetics (see box p.255). There are also several places to eat including a stylish Chinese restaurant, serving a big range of *yum cha*.

The Strand Arcade 412 George St (through to Pitt St) ⓦwww.strandarcade.com.au. Town Hall CityRail. Built in 1892, this elegant arcade with its wrought-iron balustrades houses tiny fashion boutiques including outlets of several of Australia's top designers on level 1, jewellers including Dinosaur Designs and Love and Hatred, an outlet of Jurlique (see box on p.255), plus gourmet coffee shops and tea rooms.

Sydney Central Plaza 450 George St, City ⓣ02/9261 2266. Town Hall CityRail. Sprawling from George Street through to Pitt St Mall, this maze of shops and fast-food outlets takes in Myer and a whole host of mostly clothing and fashion stores, not to mention a stage where variable, but free, entertainers perform for the munching masses.

Westfield Centrepoint Cnr Pitt St Mall and Market St, City ⓦwww.westfield.com/centrepoint. Town Hall CityRail. At the base of the landmark Sydney Tower, Westfield Centrepoint has over 130 speciality stores, 60 of them focusing on fashion and accessories, though nothing terribly exciting. There's an excellent basement food court, and the Australian Geographic Shop (p.261) and the Wilderness Society Shop (p.262) here are both good for quality souvenirs.

Food and drink

The handiest **supermarkets** for the city centre are Woolworths Metro, opposite the Town Hall (Mon–Fri 6.30am–midnight, Sat & Sun 8am–midnight), and the three small Coles supermarkets in the Wynyard Station complex, and at 388 and 580 George St (all daily 6am–midnight). The larger Coles in Kings Cross, at 88 Darlinghurst Rd, is also handy for travellers (same hours), as is the one in the Broadway Centre near Glebe (see p.254). The Asian supermarkets on Sussex and Burlington streets in Chinatown and in the Market City complex offer more exotic alternatives, and for deli items and impromptu picnic supplies head for the splendid food hall at David Jones (see p.254), or one of the gourmet stores listed below. In the suburbs, the big supermarkets such as Coles now stay open until midnight, and there are plenty of (overpriced) 24-hour convenience stores in the inner city and suburbs, often attached to petrol stations.

There are also several **food markets**: Paddy's Market in Chinatown (see p.97) has been selling fruit and vegetables since the nineteenth century, and there's a bigger version at far-flung Flemington beside the city's wholesale markets (Fri 10am–4pm & Sun 9am–4.30pm; Flemington CityRail). Rural growers and producers of gourmet goods also distribute direct to Sydney's regular **produce markets**: at Pyrmont Bay Park in front of the Star City Casino on the first Saturday of the month (7–11am); at the Showring at Fox Studio's every Wednesday and Saturday (10am–4pm); and at the Northside Produce Market at the Civic Centre, Miller Street, North Sydney, between Ridge and McClaren streets, on the third Saturday of the month (8am–noon). There's a hugely popular, quite festive **organic market** every Saturday morning (8am–1pm) within the grounds of the Orange Grove Public School, at the corner of Perry Street and Balmain Road, in Leichhardt.

Australian Wine Centre Shop 3, Goldfields House, 1 Alfred St, cnr George St, Circular Quay ⓦwww.australianwinecentre.com. Circular Quay CityRail/ferry. Basement store stocking more than a thousand wines from over 300 wineries around Australia. It holds regular tastings, or you can just buy a test-drive glass of wine at its in-house wine bar during the week (open till 7pm Fri, closed Sat & Sun). They also ship overseas.

GNC LiveWell 53–55 Glebe Point Rd, Glebe ⓦwww.gnclivewell.com.au Bus #431–433 from Central CityRail. International chain offering a vast range of wholefoods, organic fruit and vegetables, speciality foods and supplements.

Infinity Sourdough 225 Victoria St, Darlinghurst ⓣ02/9380 4320. Kings Cross CityRail. A great place for breakfasts on the hoof, and for the sheer pleasure of wonderful bread baked on the premises – from sourdough and wholemeal to the more exotic Guinness beer rye bread and oatmeal polenta loaves. Daily 6am–7pm or later.

jones the grocer 68 Moncur St, Woollahra ⓦwww.jonesthegrocer.com.au. Bus #389 from Circular Quay CityRail. Stylishly packaged, outlandishly priced and utterly delicious groceries and gourmet treats to eat in or take away; includes a cheese room. Also at Shop 45, The Grove, 166 Military Rd, Neutral Bay.

Simon Johnson 181 Harris St, Pyrmont ⓦwww.simonjohnson.com.au. Pyrmont Light Rail. When only the best will do, try Simon Johnson's superb cheeses (kept in a dedicated conditioning room), teas and coffees, top-of-the-range pastas, oils and vinegars, as supplied to discriminating restaurateurs. Also at 55 Queen St, Woollahra and Quadrangle Shopping Village, 100 Edinburgh Rd, Castlecrag.

Sydney Fish Markets Pyrmont Bay, Pyrmont ⓦwww.sydneyfishmarket.com.au. Fish Market Light Rail. Sydney's seafood comes straight off the fishing boats here, from where it's sold to retailers at the fish market auction and then goes on to the several fishmonger outlets. There's also excellent fruit and veg, flowers, a reliable deli, a bottle shop, plus takeaway (and eat-in) sushi and fish and chips for the picnic tables by the water's edge. Daily 7am–4pm. Also see p.95.

Galleries

Sydney's diverse arts scene is reflected in a myriad of **small art galleries**, which are concentrated in Paddington and Surry Hills, with a new gallery precinct developing on the southwestern fringes of Surry Hills at Banks Street, Waterloo (bus #343 from central CityRail). The useful *Artfind Guide* to selected Sydney art galleries and antique dealers is published by the Josef Lebovic Galleries (see p.259); its website has links to the galleries selected in their guide and includes maps (ⓦwww.artfind.com.au). Alternatively, you can buy a copy of *Art & Australia* magazine (ⓦwww.artaustralia.com), Australia's authoritative national art journal which has major exhibition reviews and listings. It's published quarterly and available at bookshops and newsagents. The Citysearch Sydney website, ⓦwww.sydney.citysearch.com.au, has comprehensive listings of art galleries and current exhibitions, while Friday's "Metro" section of the *Sydney Morning Herald* offers reviews of recently opened shows. For shops attached to Sydney's major galleries and museums see the individual reviews in the main Guide section.

If you're interested in buying **Aboriginal art and crafts**, try some of the galleries that direct profits back to Aboriginal communities, rather than settling for the standard tourist tat.

Aboriginal art and craft

For background on Aboriginal art styles and communities, visit the Art Gallery of New South Wales (see p.78) or check out the excellent Aboriginal Art Online website, ⓦwww.aboriginalartonline.com.

Boomalli Aboriginal Artists Co-operative 55–59 Flood St, Leichhardt ⓦwww.boomalli.org.au. Bus #438 & #440 from Central CityRail. Boomalli, initiated by ten indigenous artists in the late 1980s, is still wholly Aboriginal-operated and now has a membership of seventy. Unlike many other Aboriginal galleries, it prioritizes the work of New South Wales urban and rural Aboriginal artists: expect controversial, cutting-edge contemporary art including photography and mixed media. Tues–Sat 10am–4pm.

The Boomerang School **224 William St, Kings Cross ⓣ02/9358 2370. Kings Cross CityRail.** Boomerangs sold here are mostly authentic, made by Aboriginal artisans from around Australia. The owner, Duncan MacLennon, has been running his store for over forty years, and though insurance now precludes Duncan from his free boomerang-throwing lessons once held in a nearby park, he still promises to provide crucial in-store tips. Mon–Sat 9am–6.30pm, Sun 2–6pm.

Gavala Aboriginal Art and Cultural Centre **Level 2, Harbourside Shopping Centre, Darling Harbour ⓦwww.gavala.com.au. Town Hall CityRail.** Highly credible Aboriginal-owned and -run arts and crafts store – all profits go to the artists and their communities, and the centre aims to raise awareness of indigenous cultures through education programmes. Also music, books, clothes, jewellery and souvenirs. Daily 10am–7pm.

▼ Gavala Centre didgeridoos

Hogarth Galleries Aboriginal Art Centre **7 Walker Lane (off Brown St), Paddington ⓦwww.aboriginalartcentres.com. Bus #378 from Central CityRail or #380 from Circular Quay CityRail.** This long-established gallery has a sound reputation for its support of contemporary Aboriginal artists, and its broader commitment to reconciliation. Extensive collection of work by contemporary Aboriginal artists, both tribal and urban, and special exhibitions. Tues–Sat 10am–5pm.

Walkabout Art **Berkelouw Books, 70 Norton St, Leichhardt, ⓦwww.worldvision.com.au/walkaboutart. Bus #438 & #440 from Central CityRail.** This Aboriginal art gallery is a World Vision Australia project; as well as providing a source of income for individual artists, any profits fund education and health programmes in indigenous communities. Work is exhibited from communities all over Australia, with a focus on the Western Desert, and Utopia and Pintupi. Mon–Sat 10am–5pm, Sun 11am–4pm.

Contemporary painting and sculpture

Art House Gallery **66 McLachlan Ave, Rushcutters Bay ⓣ02/9332 1019. Kings Cross CityRail.** This cavernous gallery showcases Australian artists and always has interesting exhibits, as well as pieces for sale. Tues–Fri 11am–5pm, Sat 10am–4pm.

Australian Galleries: Painting & Sculpture **15 Roylston St, Paddington ⓣ02/9360 5177. Edgecliff CityRail.** Serene gallery exhibiting and selling contemporary Australian art, including works by Gary Shead, Jeffrey Smart and John Coburn. Tues–Sat 10am–6pm.

Ray Hughes Gallery **270 Devonshire St, Surry Hills. Central CityRail. ⓦwww.rayhughesgallery.com.** Influential dealer with a stable of high-profile contemporary Australian and New Zealand artists. Tues–Sat 10am–6pm.

Sherman Galleries **16–20 Goodhope St, Paddington ⓣ02/9331 1112, ⓦwww.shermangalleries.com.au. Bus #389 from Circular Quay or Bondi Junction CityRail.** Influential Australian and international painters and artists feature at this cutting-edge gallery, whose huge interior is echoed in the 350-square-metre outdoor sculpture garden. Tues–Sat 11am–6pm.

Experimental, multimedia and installation

Artspace **The Gunnery Arts Centre, 43–51 Cowper Wharf Rd, Woolloomooloo ⓦwww.artspace.org.au. Kings Cross CityRail.** In a wonderful location, showing provocative young artists with a focus on performance, installations and new media. Tues–Sat 11am–5pm.

Ivan Dougherty Gallery **Cnr Albion Ave and Selwyn St, Paddington ⓦwww.cofa.unsw**

.edu. Bus #378 from Central CityRail or #380 from Circular Quay CityRail. This is the exhibition space for the College of Fine Arts (COFA), University of New South Wales. The ten shows per year focus on international contemporary art with accompanying forums, lectures and performances. Mon–Sat 10am–5pm.

The Performance Space 199 Cleveland St, Redfern, opposite Prince Alfred Park ⓦwww.performancespace.com.au. Redfern or Central CityRail. Experimental multimedia and plastic arts, installations, sculpture, photography and painting. Wed–Fri noon–6pm.

Roslyn Oxley9 Gallery 8 Soudan Lane, off Hampden St, Paddington ⓦwww.roslynoxley9.com.au. Edgecliff CityRail. Avant-garde videos and installations among the Australian and international offerings. Tues–Fri 10am–6pm, Sat 11am–6pm.

Photography, drawing and prints

Australian Centre for Photography 257 Oxford St, Paddington ⓣ02/9332 1455, ⓦwww.acp.au.com. Bus #378 from Central CityRail or #380 from Circular Quay CityRail. This non-profit organization is part-funded by various government agencies. Exhibitions of photo-based art from established and new international and Australian artists in two galleries. Emerging photographers are showcased on the Project Wall, and it's something of a developing (and visiting) photographers' Mecca, with basic and specialist courses and a darkroom available for use (daily noon–6pm). There's also a specialist bookshop plus the French-style *Bistro Lulu* (see p.200). Tues–Sun 11am–6pm.

Australian Galleries: Works on Paper 24 Glenmore Rd, Paddington ⓣ02/9380 8744. Bus #378 from Central CityRail or #380 from Circular Quay CityRail. Works for sale here include drawings by William Robinson, Brett Whiteley and Arthur Boyd, as well as prints and sketches by young Australian artists. Tues–Sat 10am–6pm, Sun noon–5pm.

Hordern House 77 Victoria St, Potts Point ⓦwww.hordern.com. Kings Cross CityRail. Eminent antique dealer, trading in colonial art including antiquarian prints and maps, rare books and manuscripts. Tues–Fri 9am–5pm.

Josef Lebovic 34 Paddington St, Paddington ⓦwww.joseflebovicgallery.com.au. Bus #378 from Central CityRail, #380 from Circular Quay CityRail. Renowned print and graphic gallery specializing in Australian and international prints from the nineteenth, twentieth and twenty-first centuries, as well as vintage photography. Wed–Fri 1–6pm, Sat 11am–5pm.

Stills Gallery 36 Gosbell St, Paddington ⓦwww.stillsgallery.com.au. Kings Cross CityRail. One of the most high-profile Sydney photography galleries; exhibits contemporary Australian and international work. Wed–Sat 11am–6pm.

Markets

Weekend **markets** have become a feature of the leisurely lives of Sydneysiders, so be prepared for crowds. The best for general browsing are the trendy Paddington Bazaar, the more arty Balmain market and the relaxed market on Glebe Point Road. Apart from the markets listed below, there is a Sunday art and craft market in Kings Cross (see p.106); a Sunday craft market on the Opera House forecourt (see p.71); a monthly flea market in Shannon Reserve, on the corner of Crown and Foveaux streets, Surry Hills (see p.99); a weekend flea market in the grounds of Rozelle Primary School on Darling Street, Rozelle, near Victoria Rd (see p.118); and a Sunday Aboriginal craft market at La Perouse (see p.152).

In addition, a series of alternating Saturday markets takes place on the **North Shore**, the most well known being Kirribilli market (see p.260); call North Sydney Council ⓣ02/9936 8100 for details of the others. There are also several produce markets, detailed on p.256, including Sydney's oldest, Paddy's Market, where you can also buy cheap and cheerful clothes and souvenirs.

Balmain Markets St Andrews Church, cnr Darling St and Curtis Rd, Balmain. Bus #433 from Central CityRail or #442 from the QVB. An assortment of books, handmade jewellery, clothing and ceramics, antiques, home-made chocolates, cakes and gourmet foods and organic produce are sold. The highlight is an eclectic array of food stalls in the church hall where you can snack your way from the Himalayas to South India. Sat 7.30am–4pm.

Bondi Beach Markets Bondi Primary School, cnr Campbell Parade and Warners Avenue. Bus #380 & #389 from Bondi Junction CityRail. In the grounds of a lucky beach-facing primary school, these relaxed Sunday markets place great emphasis on hip fashion – both new and secondhand – and jewellery. Sun 10am–4pm, to 6pm Dec–Feb.

Glebe Market Glebe Primary School, 38 Glebe Point Rd. Bus #431–434 from Central CityRail. The market is shady, relaxed and quietly sociable, like Glebe itself. A mixture of funky new and secondhand clothes and accessories, including beach dresses, handbags, jewellery – plus plants, records and CDs, and the inevitable New Age knick-knacks and secondhand books. Chinese masseurs ply their trade, but the small range of food stalls are disappointing; there is, however, a strip of great cafés opposite, including *Badde Manors*, *Iku*, and *Well Connected* (see pp.190–191). Sat 9am–4.30pm.

Kirribilli Markets Bradfield Park, cnr Alfred and Burton streets, Kirribilli. Milsons Point CityRail or ferry from Circular Quay to Milsons Point wharf. Fantastically sited market just across the North Shore and practically under the Harbour Bridge. Nearly 200 stalls – lots of food stalls, secondhand clothes and bric a brac plus plants, jewellery and arts and crafts. There are typically lots of small stalls, many where locals are selling off unwanted gear – however, given the North Shore's wealth, the pickings are good. The atmosphere is festive, with live music throughout the day. Fourth Sat every month 7am–3pm.

▾ Paddington Markets

Paddington Markets 395 Oxford St, Paddington. Bus #378 from Central CityRail or #380 from Circular Quay or Bondi Junction CityRail. As well as being a great location for people-watching in the shady church grounds, these markets offer contemporary Australian crafts – particularly leather goods and jewellery – plus original fashion, both old and new. Even if you're just here to browse, the atmosphere, music and buskers come free, and it's all conveniently located in the middle of an excellent shopping and grazing strip. Sat 10am–4pm.

The Rocks Market George St, The Rocks. Circular Quay CityRail/ferry. Completely taking over The Rocks end of George Street, this collection of more than a hundred stalls offers jewellery, antiques and art and crafts, mostly with an Australiana/souvenir slant and shaded from the sun by big white umbrellas. The excellent remaindered book stall is great for coffee-table books on Sydney. Sheltered from the sun and rain by huge canvas sails. Sat & Sun 10am–5pm.

Music

Tyranny of distance has traditionally kept many big-name bands from including Sydney on their world tours. As a result, perhaps, there is fierce loyalty here to home-grown music. In addition to specialist **Australian music** shops, you'll find a smattering of places catering for **jazz** and **folk** aficionados, as well as the usual megastores.

Australian Music Centre Shop Level 4, The Arts Exchange, 10 Hickson Rd, The Rocks ⓦwww.amcoz.com.au. Circular Quay CityRail/ferry. Specialist Australian music store of the Australian Music Centre, set up in 1974 to provide information, publications and scores relating to Australian music. The retail outlet covers genres from classical through jazz and folk to traditional Aboriginal music and experimental sounds. With its relaxed, listen-before-you-buy policy and knowledgeable staff, this is a great place to get a taste for antipodean music; you are also welcome to visit the centre's resource library, which has listening facilities (Mon–Thurs 10am–5pm). Mon–Fri 9am–5pm.

Birdland Records Mezzanine Level, City Centre Building, 231–247 Pitt St ⓦwww.birdland.com.au. Wynyard or Martin Place CityRail. This is arguably Sydney's premier jazz and blues store (the dedicated Australian section aims to stock everything available), helped along by some soul and a big world music section. CDs and vinyl available.

Central Station Records 46 Oxford St, Darlinghurst ⓦwww.centralstationrec.com. Museum CityRail. Sydney's dance music specialist, stocking the latest imported and local sounds on vinyl and CD. At the heart of the gay scene in Darlinghurst, they also put together and sell the official Mardi Gras compilations.

Fish Records 261 King St, Newtown ⓦwww.fishrecords.com.au. Newtown CityRail. Australia's largest independent music chain but catering to eclectic tastes – indie, top 40, dance, jazz, soundtracks and some classical. Also Fishtix, in-store (and online) ticket sales for the best gigs. Mon–Sat 9am–11.30pm, Sun 10am–9.30pm. Also at 47 Glebe Point Rd, Glebe; 289 Darling St, Balmain; 472 Oxford St Mall, Bondi Junction; and Norton Plaza Shopping Centre, Norton St, Leichhardt. Fish Fine Music at 350 George St specializes in classical and jazz (Town Hall or Martin Place CityRail).

Folkways 282 Oxford St, Paddington ⓦwww.folkways.com.au. Bus #378 from Central CityRail or #380 from Circular Quay CityRail. Long catering to Sydney's folk-music devotees; there's a comprehensive selection of folk recordings, plus some world music.

HMV Mid-City Centre, Pitt St Mall ⓦwww.hmv.com.au. Martin Place or Town Hall CityRail. The most conspicuous of the city-centre music shops, this megastore stocks just about everything, including extensive classical and world music selections, and often has in-store events.

Red Eye Records 66 King St, City ⓦwww.redeye.com.au. Martin Place CityRail. Sydney's biggest independent record store is the place to track down your favourite Australian bands on hard-to-find independent labels, plus rare, out-of-print and collectable items. The ground floor is all new, with everything from alternative to jazz; upstairs there's a huge range of secondhand vinyls, CDs and memorabilia. This is also where you can plug into the live music scene, with heaps of flyers available. They also ship overseas. Their shop at 370 Pitt St (Central CityRail) offers a larger secondhand range.

Souvenirs

Also see the "Outdoor and workwear" section on p.254 and "Aboriginal art and craft" on p.257. For toys see "Kids' Sydney" pp.244–245.

Aussie Koala Shop Shop 8, The Rocks Centre, 10–26 Playfair St, The Rocks ⓣ02/9247 6388. Circular Quay CityRail. The place for those kitsch souvenirs: lots of furry koalas, of course, snowdomes featuring the Harbour Bridge and the Opera House, and even mini-boomerangs. Daily 9am–6pm.

Australian Geographic Shop International Airport ⓦwww.australiangeographic.com.au. Linked to the *Australian Geographic*

Buy before you fly...

If you forget that vital present for your pet-minder or plant-waterer, your conscience can be salved at the international terminal of the airport, where there are enough surfwear shops, branches of Australian Geographic (above), R. M. Williams (see p.254), Virgin Music and WH Smith, plus Australian wine and craft shops, to cover most eventualities. And, if you've trawled Sydney for the height of kitsch without success, this is your chance to buy a Sydney Opera House snowdome or a set of shot glasses adorned with paintings of koalas in incongruous primary colours – your mantelpiece will thank you. A full list and details of all the airport stores can be checked out at ⓦwww.sydneyairport.com.au.

magazine, this is the place for quality souvenirs including portable indigenous art, coffee-table and travel books, and quirky novelty items. Perfect for last-minute shopping. Daily 6am–10pm. Also at Darling Harbour Harbourside Shopping Centre and Westfield Centrepoint in the city.

Done Art and Design 123 George St, The Rocks ⓦ www.done.com.au. Circular Quay CityRail/ ferry. Love the stuff or loathe it, there's no doubt that Ken Done's loud and colourful knitwear, T-shirts and other design oddments are as identifiably Sydney as the Harbour Bridge. Appropriately, the bridge, Opera House and harbour scenery feature prominently in his artwork, which graces items from duvet covers to swimwear. Daily 10am–6pm. Also at 1 Hickson Rd, The Rocks (daily 10am–5.30pm); 595 Military Rd, Mosman (Mon–Sat 10am–6pm, Sun 11am–3pm); and at the International departure terminal at Sydney Airport (daily 6am–10pm). There's a factory outlet at level 2 of the Market City shopping centre in Chinatown, too (see p.255).

Wilderness Society Shop Westfield Centrepoint, Castlereagh St, City ⓦ www.wildshop.com.au. Town Hall CityRail. The shop of Australia's national community environmental campaigning group, the Wilderness Society, is an oasis in a very commercial district, with friendly young staff and information about current campaigns. It's great for quality souvenirs, including a great range of cards, calendars and books, children's and adults' T-shirts (the one with the "Treehugger" caption is one of their bestsellers), children's picture books and games, native bush-scented candles and must-have chocolate bilby babies. Mon–Fri 9am–6pm (Thurs to 8pm), Sat 9am–5pm, Sun 11am–4pm.

Festivals and events

The Sydney year is interspersed with festivals, both sporting and cultural, with summer being the peak time for big events. The **Sydney to Hobart Yacht Race** starts on Boxing Day (December 26); then there's the **New Year's Eve fireworks**, eclipsed by the big extravaganza of the **Australia Day** celebrations (January 26). Running throughout January is the **Sydney Festival** whose highlights are the free outdoor concerts in The Domain. The summer winds up in a whirl of feathers and sequins at the **Sydney Gay & Lesbian Mardi Gras**, held in late February/early March. An entirely different side of Sydney life is on view at the impressive summer **surf carnivals**, staged regularly by surf life-saving clubs; for details contact Surf Life Saving NSW (Ⓣ02/9984 7188, Ⓦwww.surflifesaving.com.au) or check newspapers. For details of other sporting events, see "Sports and activities". The "What's on" section of the City of Sydney Council's website (Ⓦwww.cityofsydney.nsw.gov.au) has details of festivals and events including a rundown of the Sydney Festival. For more on Sydney's festivals, see the "Sydney festivals" colour section.

January

New Year Sydney sees in the New Year with a spectacular multimillion-dollar fireworks display on Sydney Harbour. The more family- focused part of the proceedings begins at 9pm at Darling Harbour, with lots on for kids (for more information check Ⓦwww.darlingharbour.com.au), followed by the main event at midnight, when themed fireworks are set off from the Harbour Bridge itself, synchronized to music. People crowd out vantage points including North Head, South Head, The Rocks, Cremorne Point, Blues Point and Neutral Bay – anywhere with the Bridge in sight is good – and many bag their spots from early morning; more information can be found at Ⓦwww.cityofsydney.nsw.gov.au. Thousands of vessels also anchor on the water to take in the views; contact any of the ferry cruise companies listed under "Ferries and cruises" on pp.35–36, as well as Sydney Ferries (Ⓦwww.sydneyferries.nsw.gov.au) and, if you can sail yourself, the boat and yacht charters on p.273 of "Sports and activities" to organize getting out on the water.

Sydney Festival After the New Year celebrations, there's a week's hiatus before the start of the Sydney Festival around January 8 (Ⓣ02/8248 6500, Ⓦwww.sydneyfestival.org.au), an exhaustive (and exhausting) arts event that lasts until a few days after the Australia Day celebrations (Jan 26), and ranges from concerts, plays and outdoor art installations to circus performances. About fifty percent of the events are free and based around urban public spaces, focusing on Circular Quay, The Domain, Darling Harbour and Sydney Olympic Park; the remainder – mostly a fantastic roster of international performances – can cost a packet. Highlights of the free outdoor programme are the Jazz in the Park and Symphony in the Park concerts in The Domain, and the lively Bacardi Latino Festival at Darling Harbour. A dynamic bar is set up in the grounds of the Hyde Park Barracks. The general programme is usually printed in the *Sydney Morning Herald* in October

▲ Sony Tropfest

or November, while a full eighty-plus-page (free) programme is available nearer the time from the Town Hall. A weekly listing of events appears in the *Sydney Morning Herald* during the festival. Darling Harbour also hosts its own festival (Dec 26–Jan 31); apart from the Bacardi Latino Festival, with its live music and dancing in the streets on the balmy summer nights, most attractions are aimed at children (more information on Ⓦwww.darlingharbour.com.au).

Flickerfest International Short Film Festival Week-long film festival, held mostly outdoors in the amphitheatre of the Bondi Pavilion in early January; some films in the auditorium. More details on Ⓦwww.flickerfest.com.au; see also box on p.230.

Sydney Fringe Festival Headquartered by the beach at the Bondi Pavilion), the Sydney Fringe Festival (Ⓣ02/9130 3325, Ⓦwww.waverly.nsw.gov.au) runs for two weeks from mid-January, and encompasses performance, music, visual art, workshops, kids' shows and some very unusual, irreverent sporting events, from the very camp Drag Race Meet to the Nude Night Surfing competition. The lively Festival Club, with DJs and performances, and ABC Triple J radio broadcasts, takes place nightly in the pavilion's balcony bar.

Australia Day January 26 is the anniversary of the arrival of the First Fleet in Sydney Harbour in 1788, and Australia Day activities are focused on the harbour (Australia Day Council of NSW; Ⓦwww.australiaday.com). Sydney's passenger ferries race from Fort Denison to the Harbour Bridge, and there's a Tall Ships Race from Bradleys Head to the Harbour Bridge, a 21-gun salute fired from the Man O'War steps at the Opera House and a thrilling military air show over the harbour. The Australia Day Regatta takes place in the afternoon, with hundreds of yachts racing all over the water, from Botany Bay to the Parramatta River. There are also free events, entertainment and activities in The Rocks, Hyde Park (including a Food and Wine Fair, a concert stage and a vintage car display) and at Darling Harbour, where there's a 9pm fireworks display to rival the New Year's Eve extravaganza. In addition, many Sydney museums have free entry all day. Besides all this, there are at least two outdoor rock concerts to choose from: **Yabun** (formerly "Survival"), organized by the National Indigenous Arts Advocacy Association, celebrates Aboriginal culture and acts as an antidote to the mainstream white Australia Day festivities. It is held at Redfern Oval and you can expect to see some of Australia's best Aboriginal bands and performers (contact Koori Radio on Ⓣ02/9564 5904 or check out Ⓦwww.gadigal.org.au for the latest details; free; no alcohol allowed);

the **Big Day Out** is usually held the same day at the Showground at Homebush Bay, featuring around sixty local and international bands and DJs; more details on Ⓦwww.bigdayout.com and box on p.222.

February

Chinese New Year Towards the end of January or in the first weeks of February, Chinese New Year is celebrated in Chinatown – firecrackers, dragon and lion dances, food stalls and music. More details on Ⓦwww.cityofsydney.nsw.gov.au.

Tropfest Hugely popular competition festival for short films, taking place at the end of February, with an outdoor screening in The Domain. More details on Ⓦwww.tropfest.com.au; see also box on p.230.

Sydney Gay & Lesbian Mardi Gras The festival runs through February, and features films, theatre and exhibitions that range from cheeky to outrageous. It all culminates in one of the world's biggest street parades, when up to a million people line the streets on the last Sat in February or first Sat in March. More details on Ⓦwww.mardigras.com.au; see also pp.233–235.

March–April

Greek Festival of Sydney This month-long celebration kicks off with the all-day Greek Fest at Darling Harbour in late March, featuring food and wine stalls, plus live entertainment, including traditional dance (and dance workshops). More information on Ⓦwww.greekfestivalofsydney.com.au.

Royal Easter Show The Royal Easter Show, an agricultural and garden show, moved in 1998 to the Sydney Showground at the Olympic site at Homebush Bay. For fourteen consecutive days in late March/early April (the Easter weekend is neatly sandwiched in between) the country comes to the city with parades of prized animals and various farm/agriculture related displays, plus a frantic array of amusement-park rides, and frenzied consumerism in the Showbag Pavilion. At night, in the main arena there's a celebration of Australian bush heritage, stunt shows, a rodeo and fireworks displays; by day, there are usually horse-related events, judging of show animals, and the traditional, and very popular, woodchopping competitions. Open 9.30am–10pm, last admission 8.30pm. Tickets include public transport to the show from anywhere in the greater Sydney area; $27, child $17.50, half-price tickets after 5pm; rides extra; Show Infoline Ⓣ02/9704 1000, Ⓦwww.eastershow.com.au.

May–July

Kings Cross Food & Wine Festival On a Sunday at the beginning of May, Fitzroy Gardens, Kings Cross, is host to a one-day food fair with local restaurateurs (around twenty stalls) and NSW wineries (around sixteen) showing their wares, plus entertainment and community stalls. Sponsored by the City of Sydney Council, more information can be found on Ⓦwww.cityofsydney.nsw.gov.au and Ⓦwww.kingscrossonline.com.au.

Sydney Writers Festival Week-long high-profile mid-May event with readings, workshops and discussions, mostly free; Australian and international writers. There are events in and around town, but most of the action takes place in a very scenic location at the Wharf Theatre, Hickson Rd, Millers Point. More details on Ⓦwww.swf.org.au.

Sydney Italian Festival Street festival in early June (11am–5pm) celebrating Sydney's strong Italian community, along the Stanley Street strip of cafés and restaurants. An Italian produce market, motorcycle and scooter display and entertainment feature. More details on Ⓦwww.cityofsydney.nsw.gov.au or Ⓦwww.sydneyitalianfestival.com.au.

Biennale of Sydney Every alternate (even-numbered) year, this international contemporary art festival takes place over six weeks from early June until mid-August, featuring artists from every continent. Provocative contemporary exhibitions and events at various venues and outdoor spaces around town, including the Art Gallery of New South Wales, the Opera House, Customs House and the Museum of Contemporary Art. Usually free. More details on Ⓦwww.biennaleofsydney.com.au.

Sydney Film Festival Takes over several of the city's screens for two weeks from early June. More details at Ⓦwww.sydneyfilmfestival.org; see also box on p.230.

August

Sun Herald City-to-Surf Race A newspaper-sponsored fourteen-kilometre fun run from Park Street in the city to Bondi, held on the second Sun of August. Over 60,000 participants raced in 2005. Entry forms are in the

Sun Herald from June 1 or entry is available online; entry costs $30, $20 for children up to 18. More details from the official website Ⓦcity2surf.sunherald.com.au or Ⓦwww.coolrunning.com.au/citytosurf.

September–October

Festival of the Winds In September, as the skies get bluer, Australia's largest kite festival takes over Bondi Beach. More details on Ⓦwww.waverley.nsw.gov.au.

Manly International Jazz Festival Taking place over the Labour Day weekend in early October, this festival consists of mostly free outdoor, waterfront events with some indoor concerts charging entry for some of the bigger Australian and international acts. As Sydney gets into the swim of summer, and the beaches officially open for the year, this jazz-fest by the sea is a wonderful way to enjoy the warming weather. More details on Ⓦwww.manly.nsw.gov.au or Ⓦwww.manlytourism.com.au; also see p.146.

Blessing of the Fleet Labour Day weekend (early October) sees revellers dressed in traditional fancy dress for the blessing of brightly decorated fishing boats for their life at sea. Most of Sydney's fishing industry workers come from the Italian community, hence this very Italian festival at Darling Harbour. More details on Ⓦwww.darlingharbour.com.au.

World on Women (WOW) Film Festival Held over three days in late October at the Chauvel Cinema, Paddington. More details on Ⓦwww.FutureTrain.com.au/wift/wow; see also box p.230.

Sydney Food and Wine Fair Part of the *Sydney Morning Herald* sponsored Good Food Month. On a Saturday in late October, Hyde Park is taken over for a day by around one hundred stalls representing restaurants, wineries, cheese-makers and the like, plus live entertainment from the concert stage. The usually sunny event, co-hosted by the City of Sydney Council, attracts around 60,000 visitors and is an important fundraiser for the AIDS Trust of Australia. More details on Ⓦwww.cityofsydney.nsw.gov.au and Ⓦwww.smh.com.au.

November

Sculpture By the Sea The coastal walk between Bondi and Tamarama becomes crowded during this eighteen-day installation (in early November) of around a hundred wonderfully playful and provocative sculptures by Australian and international artists, many designed to be site-specific. More details on Ⓣ02/9357 1457, Ⓦwww.sculpturebythesea.com.

Newtown Festival Organized by the Newtown Neighbourhood Centre, Town Hall, 1 Bedford St, Newtown (Ⓣ02/9516 4755, Ⓦwww.newtowncentre.org), this is one of Sydney's biggest community festivals, held on the second Sun in November, when nearby Camperdown Memorial Park is overtaken by a bazaar with food, community and market stalls (over 200 stalls) and live music on three stages. For more festival details drop into the Centre or check the website.

Glebe Street Fair Second to last Sun in November. Thousands flock to one of Sydney's great eat-streets, Glebe Point Road, for a vibrant street festival – notably fabulous food for sale, representing the local restaurants and cafés, plus lots of arts and crafts. More details on Ⓦwww.cityofsydney.nsw.gov.au.

December

Homebake Australian (and New Zealand) music is celebrated in The Domain with a line-up of bands from around the country. More details on Ⓦwww.homebake.com.au; also see box on p.222.

Sydney to Hobart Yacht Race It seems like almost half of Sydney turns out at around 1pm on December 26 to cheer the start of this classic regatta, and watch the colourful spectacle of a hundred or so yachts setting sail on their 630-nautical-mile slog. The toughest bit is the crossing of Bass Strait, which is swept by the "Roaring Forties" (conditions were so rough in 1999 that six sailors tragically died and many crews abandoned the race). Good vantage points include South Head, Lady Bay and Nielson Park on the eastern shores, or Georges Head, Middle Head, Chowder Bay, North Head and Bradleys Head on the North Shore. For more background information, check out the Cruising Yacht Club of Australia's website Ⓦwww.cyca.com.au, or the dedicated website they produce: Ⓦwww.rolexsydneyhobart.com.

Carols in the Domain Mid-December; a balmy night of Christmas carols under the stars. More details on Ⓦwww.cityofsydney.nsw.gov.au.

Christmas Day on Bondi Beach

For years, backpackers and Bondi Beach on **Christmas Day** were synonymous. The beach was transformed into a drunken party scene, as those from colder climates lived out their fantasy of spending Christmas on the beach under a scorching sun. The behaviour and litter had been getting out of control over several years, and after riots in 1995, and a rubbish-strewn beach to clean up, the local council began strictly controlling the whole performance – but with the idea of trying to keep a spirit of goodwill towards the travellers, and also tempting local families back to the beach on what is regarded as a family day. Nowadays alcohol is banned from the beach on Christmas Day, and police enforce the rule with on-the-spot confiscations – even locals can't enjoy a bottle of beachfront bubbly.

However, a big **beach party** is organized in the Bondi Pavilion (see p.138) and outdoors in its grounds, with a bar, DJs, food and entertainment running from 11am to 8pm. Around three thousand revellers cram into the Pavilion, while thousands of others – including a greater proportion of the desired family groups – enjoy the alcohol-free beach outside. In 2004, tickets for what is now known as **Sunbeats** were $55 in advance from record stores or from Ticketek (Ⓣ02/9266 4800, Ⓦwww.ticketek.com.au).

20

Sports and activities

Sydneysiders are sports mad, especially for the ostensibly passive spectator sports of Rugby League, Aussie Rules football, cricket, tennis and horse racing. No matter what it is, from surf life-saving competitions to yacht races, it'll draw a crowd. They're keen participants, too, whether it's a game of tennis or the latest infatuation with yoga, but getting into (or onto) the water is their greatest joy. The *Sydney Morning Herald*'s Friday listings supplement, "Metro", has a Sport and Leisure section, with details of the best events around town. Most seats can be booked through Ticketek (Ⓣ02/9266 4800, Ⓦwww.ticketek.com.au).

See the "Festivals and events" chapter for details of the annual City-to-Surf race, a fourteen-kilometre fun run.

Rugby League

Rugby League is *the* football code in Sydney, and was for many years a bastion of working-class culture. Formerly run by the Australian Rugby League (ARL), the game was split down the middle in 1996, when Rupert Murdoch launched Super League in an attempt to gain ratings for his Foxtel TV station. It quickly became obvious, however, that the game could not support two separate competitions, and in 1997 they united to form the National Rugby League (NRL; Ⓣ02/9339 8500, Ⓦwww.nrl.com.au). There are now fifteen clubs in the NRL, the majority of them Sydney-based. The Sydney teams are the Canterbury Bulldogs, Manly Sea Eagles, Parramatta Eels, Penrith Panthers, Sydney Roosters, Cronulla Sharks and South Sydney Rabbitohs, St George Illawarra Dragons and West Tigers, all with associated "leagues clubs" where you can drink, eat, be entertained and above all gamble on the "pokies" (see Penrith Panthers, p.311). The other NRL clubs are Brisbane Broncos, Canberra Raiders, New Zealand Warriors, Newcastle Knights, Melbourne Storm and North Queensland Cowboys. The western-suburbs clubs Canterbury Bulldogs, Parramatta Eels and Penrith Panthers have the most loyal and most boisterous supporters – expect any of their matches to be well attended. The NRL dropped the South Sydney Rabbitohs in 1999, but their large, still strongly working-class supporter base organized huge street rallies in protest, which were attended by up to 150,000 people, and the NRL bowed to pressure and allowed the Rabbitohs back into the premiership in 2001.

The season starts in early March, and the **Grand Final** is played at the end of September, when huge crowds pack out the Aussie Stadium next to the Sydney Cricket Ground (SCG) at Moore Park (tours of the SCG also take in

Sydney Olympics 2000

Sydney proudly beat Beijing and Manchester in the chase for the **Olympics** in the year 2000, but no one would have guessed that Juan Antonio Samaranch, Olympic Chairman, IOC President at the time, would pronounce it the "best games ever". Unseasonably fine spring weather, a public transport system that held up to the job, cheerful volunteers who gave it their all and a public who at the last minute pulled out the stops to buy tickets (91 percent of seats were sold) and party hard in the Live Sites dotted around town all added up to a hitch-free three-week sporting fiesta. Cries of "Aussie Aussie Aussie Oi Oi Oi" filled the air as Australia won its biggest pile of gold medals ever, 16 in all (plus 25 silver and 17 bronze), putting it fourth on the list (behind the US, Russia and China), an amazing achievement for its population size. Cathy Freeman's lighting of the Olympic flame, and then her gold medal run in the women's 400m, became symbolic of the hopes for reconciliation between Aboriginal and white Australia. It was all over too soon as far as Sydney was concerned, though the 11th summer **Paralympics**, a few weeks later, extended the excitement somewhat as tickets sales far outran expectations, and tested the city's disabled access.

The **Sydney Olympic Park Authority** came into existence on January 1, 2001, tasked with turning Sydney Olympic Park into an entertainment and sporting complex with family-oriented recreation in mind (see "The southern and western outskirts" chapter, p.157, for information on visiting the former Olympic site and facilities).

this stadium – see p.270) or the Telstra Stadium (formerly Stadium Australia) at Sydney Olympic Park.

The **State of Origin** series, where Queensland and New South Wales battle for state supremacy over three matches (at least one of which is held in Sydney), is incredibly hard-fought, and coverage of these matches consistently produces the highest ratings on Australian television.

Australian Rules

Victoria has traditionally been the home of **Australian Rules** ("Aussie Rules") football, and Victorian sides are still expected to win the AFL Flag – decided at the Grand Final in Melbourne in September – as a matter of course. However, the enormously popular **Sydney Swans** (Ⓦwww.sydneyswans.com.au), New South Wales' contribution to the AFL, have ensured Aussie Rules a place in the city, helped along by legendary goal-kicker Tony "Plugger" Lockett. During the 1999 season, Plugger finally broke the game's all-time goal-scoring record, which had stood for 62 years. The game itself is a no-holds-barred, eighteen-a-side brawl, closely related to Gaelic football, and known dismissively north of the Victorian border as "aerial ping pong". The ball can be propelled by any means necessary, and the fact that players aren't sent off for misconduct ensures a lively, skilful and, above all, gladiatorial confrontation. Aussie Rules stars have delightful sobriquets such as "Tugger" and "Crackers", and their macho garb consists of tiny butt-hugging shorts and bicep-revealing tank tops. The game is mostly played on cricket grounds, with a ball similar to that used in rugby or American football. The aim is to get the ball through the central uprights for a goal (six points). There are four 25-minute quarters, plus lots of time added on for injury. Crowds tend to be very well behaved; you'll be surrounded by boisterous fans, but perfectly safe, if you go to watch the Swans at their home base at the Sydney Cricket Ground (see p.270). See the website of the Australian Football League, Ⓦwww.afl.com.au, for more details.

Rugby union

Rugby union, in spite of the huge success of the national team (the Wallabies, who play at Telstra Stadium), still lags behind Rugby League in popularity. However, the introduction of the Super 14 competition (Ⓦwww.super14.com), which runs from the end of February to the end of May, and involves regional teams from Australia, New Zealand and South Africa, has generated broader interest in what has traditionally been an elitist game. The state's contribution to the Super 14 is the NSW Waratahs, who play at the Aussie Stadium about six times per season. For more details and the latest rugby info check out the Australian Rugby Union (ARU) website at Ⓦwww.rugby.com.au.

Soccer

Soccer is still a minority sport in Australia. Around half of twelve clubs of the former National Soccer League, disbanded in 2004, evolved from communities of postwar immigrants – mainly Italians, Greeks and Yugoslavs. In the mid-1990s, a ban on clubs with these nation's flags in their team logos won considerable support, but also came in for accusations of "ethnic cleansing". The new Hyundai A-League competition (Aug–Feb) has eight teams from Australia and New Zealand: Adelaide, Brisbane, Melbourne, Perth, Sydney, Gosford, Newcastle and Auckland. However, the best players invariably head off to play overseas, such as Harry Kewell, who plays in the English Premiership and cost Liverpool £5m when he transferred there in 2003. Details of matches and grounds can be obtained from **Football Federation Australia** on Ⓣ02/8354 5590 or at Ⓦwww.footballaustralia.com.au. Australia's national team, the **Socceroos**, competes in the Oceania group against teams such as Fiji and Western Samoa, for World Cup selection. Their home matches at the Aussie Stadium still generate only limited interest.

Cricket

Cricket is the most popular summer spectator sport in Australia. Sydney's cricket season runs from October to March, and offers some of the year's best sporting days out (locals go for the atmosphere, the sunshine and the beer as much as the game). The **Sydney Cricket Ground** (SCG) is the venue for most four-day, interstate Sheffield Shield matches (not much interest for spectators, but a breeding ground for Australia's Test cricketers); five-day international **Test matches**; and the colourful, crowd-pleasing **one-day internationals**. The venerated institution of the SCG earned its place in cricketing history for Don Bradman's score of 452 not out in 1929, and for the controversy over England's bodyline bowling techniques in 1932. Ideally, you would observe today's proceedings from the Members Stand while sipping an icy gin and tonic – but unless you're invited by a member, you'll end up elsewhere, drinking beer from a plastic cup. Cricket spectators aren't a sedate lot in Sydney, and the noisiest barrackers come from "the Hill" near the Doug Walters stand. Still the cheapest spot to sit, the now concreted area was once a grassy hill, where rowdy supporters threw beer cans at players and each other. The Bill O'Reilly Stand gives comfortable viewing (until the afternoon, when you'll be blinded by the sun), whereas the Brewongle Stand provides a consistently good vantage. Best of all is the Bradman Stand, with a view from directly behind the bowler's arm. For information, scores, prices and times, call the Sydney Cricket Trust on ⓣ02/9360 6601 or check out ⓦwww.sydneycricketground.com.au. You can buy **tickets** in advance, or at the gates on the day (subject to availability), or purchase them in advance from Ticketek (ⓣ02/9266 4800, ⓦwww.ticketek.com.au). Cricket fans can take a **tour** of the SCG on non-match days (Mon–Fri 10am & 1pm; 1hr 30min; bookings ⓣ02/9380 0383, ⓦwww.scgt.nsw.gov.au; $19.50).

Tennis and squash

Sydney's major tennis event is the **Medibank International**, held during the second week of January as a lead-up to the Australian Open in Melbourne; it's played at the 10,500-seat centre court of the **Sydney International Tennis Centre** (ⓣ02/8746 0777, ⓦwww.sydneytennis.com.au), at Sydney Olympic Park in Homebush Bay (see p.157). Tickets are available from September. You can play tennis on one of the fifteen outdoor courts (off-peak Mon–Fri 8am–6pm; $17 per hour; peak Mon–Fri 6–10pm, Sat & Sun 8am–6pm; $20 per hour; bookings ⓣ02/8746 0444). Another place to play is **Rushcutters Bay Tennis Centre**, Rushcutters Bay Park, New South Head Road (daily 8am–11pm; ⓣ02/9357 1675; $20 per hour, $24 after 4pm and Sat & Sun; racket hire $3). The clay courts are in a picturesque park by the marina; use Kings Cross CityRail.

A central place to play **squash** is Hiscoe's Fitness Centre, 525 Crown St, Surry Hills (Mon–Fri 6am–10pm, Sat 8am–8pm, Sun 9am–1pm & 4–8pm; squash bookings essential on ⓣ02/9699 3233; $24–27 per 45min; racket hire $4.50; gym casual visit $17).

Racetracks

Australians lose approximately $1000 a head each year succumbing to the temptation of a flutter. This eagerness to bet, coupled with relaxed **gambling** laws, has tax-collectors rubbing their hands as the revenue rolls in. Sydney offers plenty of opportunities for any punter heading for the fast lane to millionaire's row – or the slippery slope to the poorhouse. Every Friday the *Sydney Morning Herald* publishes its racing guide, "The Form". Bets are placed at TAB (Totalisator Agency Board) shops; these are scattered throughout the city, and most pubs also have TAB access, as does Star City Casino (see p.228).

There are **horse-racing** meetings on Wednesday, Saturday and most public holidays. This is due mainly to the accessibility of courses, the high quality of racing, the presence of bookmakers and cheap admission prices ($10, $15–20 for carnivals). The venues are well maintained and peopled with colourful racing characters and often massive crowds. Best times to hit the track are during the spring and autumn carnivals (Aug–Sept and March–April respectively), when prize money rockets, and the quality of racing rivals the best in the world. The principal racecourses are: **Royal Randwick**, Alison Road, Randwick (ⓣ02/9663 8400), which featured in *Mission Impossible II*; **Rosehill Gardens**, James Ruse Drive, Rosehill (ⓣ02/9930 4070; Rosehill Gardens CityRail), which also has loads of free kids' entertainment including a bouncy castle and pony rides (entry for children is also free); and **Canterbury Park** (King St, Canterbury ⓣ02/9930 4000; Canterbury CityRail), which has midweek racing, and floodlit night racing from September to March. For further information, contact the Sydney Turf

Club (Ⓣ02/9930 4019, Ⓦwww.stc.com.au). There are also plenty of picturesque country venues to choose from; contact the Australian Jockey Club for more details on Ⓣ02/9663 8400 or at Ⓦwww.ajc.org.au.

If the chariot scenes of *Ben Hur* are more to your taste, a trip to the trots might be the ticket. **Harness racing** occurs at **Harold Park Paceway**, Ross Street, Glebe (Ⓣ02/9660 3688; $8), on Tuesday afternoons (1–6pm) and Friday evenings (7–11pm), though Tuesdays are best avoided unless you need to escape human contact for a few hours. There is more of a buzz on Friday nights, the excitement reaching its peak on the last Friday of November when the Miracle Mile is run. For some, watching horses lope around the fibres and course is too sedate, but just around the corner, money is thrown away at greater speed as the **greyhounds** hurtle around **Wentworth Park** (Ⓣ02/9660 4308; $5.50) each Monday and Saturday night – gates open at 5.30pm and races are run between 7.30pm and 10.30pm.

Surfing and surf carnivals

One peculiarly Australian institution is the **surf carnival**, where teams of volunteer life-savers demonstrate their athletic skills in mostly inflatable life-saving boats, usually on summer weekends, which makes for a great day out at the beach. Community surf life-saving organizations began forming across Australia in 1905, and the Surf Life Saving Association was established in 1907. Women have been allowed to join since 1980, and now make up about forty percent of members (also see box on p.140). Contact Surf Life Saving NSW for details of the current season's carnivals (Ⓣ02/9984 7188, Ⓦwww.surflifesaving.com.au). **Surfing** competitions are good opportunities to catch some hot wave-riding action. Check the Surfing NSW website for details (Ⓦwww.surfingaustralia.com).

Surf schools can teach you the basic skills, and enlighten you on surfing etiquette and lingo. The best two in Sydney, offering both individual and group lessons, are Lets Go Surfing (Ⓣ02/9365 1800, Ⓦwww.letsgosurfing.com.au), which also has its own surf store renting and selling boards at 28 Ramsgate Ave, North Bondi (daily 9am–6pm); and Manly Surf School (Ⓣ02/9977 6977, Ⓦwww.manlysurfschool.com), which covers the northern beaches. Let's Go charges $65 for a two-hour group lesson, including boards and wet suit, and private lessons for singles, pairs or families are also available (1hr; $95 one person, $49 each extra person). Manly Surf School charges $50, with cheaper deals if you have more than one lesson (private lessons $80 per hour). You can **rent boards** from surfshops for $25 half-day to $40 full-day, usually including a wet suit (otherwise $5 extra). Try Lets Go Surfing at Bondi (see above) or Aloha Surf, 44 Pittwater Rd, Manly (Ⓣ02/9977 3777, Ⓦwww.alohasurfboards.com.au). You can check daily **surf reports** on Ⓦwww.realsurf.com. Also see the box "Beach and sun safety" on p.139.

Canoeing, kayaking, sailboarding and sailing

The sailing season and best time to sail in Sydney is from April to September, and some sail schools only offer lessons and rental during these months. For other sailing courses and yacht rental check out the NSW Yachting Association's website Ⓦwww.nsw.yachting.org.au, or phone them on Ⓣ02/9660 1266. If you want to try rafting, you can take a thrilling white-water rafting circuit at the

Penrith Whitewater Stadium, a former Olympic venue at the foothills of the Blue Mountains (see p.312).

Balmoral Windsurfing, Sailing and Kayaking School Balmoral Boatshed, southern end of the Esplanade, Balmoral Beach ⓣ02/9960 5344, ⓦwww.sailingschool.com.au. Bus #257 from Wynyard CityRail. Rents sailboards and Hobiecat dinghies as well as giving lessons. There are windsurfing courses for beginners (4hr over 2 days; $245) and for improving technique (6hr over 2 days; $245), plus Hobiecat sailing courses (beginners' course 4hr over 2 days; $245). For classes for children, see p.245. Sailboard hire $40 per hour; Hobiecat hire $50 per hour. Open Oct–April.

Natural Wanders ⓣ02/9899 1001, ⓦwww.kayaksydney.com. Guided sea-kayaking in the harbour: the most popular trip is the Bridge Paddle (4hr; suitable for beginners; $90), which starts from Lavender Bay near Luna Park, goes under the Harbour Bridge and explores the bush-clad, yacht-filled North Shore, with a picnic brunch included on a beach near Taronga Zoo.

Northside Sailing School Middle Harbour Skiff Club Spit Bridge, Mosman ⓣ02/9969 3972, ⓦwww.northsidesailing.com.au. Bus #169, #175, #178, #L80 & #180 from Wynyard CityRail. Specializes in weekend dinghy sailing courses on Middle Harbour (Sept–April); tuition is one-on-one and costs $130 per 3hr lesson (four lessons are equal to an Australian Yachting Federation beginners' course). Also runs lessons for kids (see p.246).

Rose Bay Aquatic Hire 1 Vickery Ave, Rose Bay ⓣ02/9371 7036. Rose Bay Wharf; bus #323, #324 & #325 from Edgecliff CityRail. Rents out catamarans ($40 first hour, $30 thereafter), kayaks ($20 per hour) and motorboats (weekends $60 for the first two hours, $15 for each subsequent hour, plus charge for petrol). No boat licence required, only a drivers' licence.

Sydney by Sail Based at the National Maritime Museum, Darling Harbour ⓣ02/9280 1110, ⓦwww.sydneybysail.com.au. Town Hall CityRail. Learn To Sail programmes for yacht sailing throughout the year for all levels, from a Level 1 Introductory Course (12hr course over 2 days; $425) to a Level 4 Inshore Skipper Course (3-day, 2-night live-aboard course; $695 includes all meals). Experienced sailors can also charter the yachts from $400 half-day to $995 for a weekend.

Diving and snorkelling

Visibility in the waters around Sydney is good – and divers can expect to see to a distance of 10–15m. One of the best places to dive is at **Gordon's Bay** in Clovelly, where there is easy access to Sydney's only underwater nature trail – a sort of beneath-the-sea bushwalking track, marked by a series of chains connected to concrete drums. The trail includes typical Sydney shoreline life: sponges, sea jellies, anemones, shrimps and crabs, molluscs, cuttlefish, octopus, sea stars and sea squirts. The seven-hundred-metre trail takes around 35–40 minutes to cover, and has a maximum depth of 14m. It is one of Sydney's most dived locations; diving off North and South heads is also popular. All of the operators below also offer diving courses.

Aquatic Explorers 40 Kingsway, under Cronulla Beach YHA, Cronulla ⓣ02/9523 1518, ⓦwww.aquaticexplorers.com.au. Cronulla CityRail. Local coordinated shore dives on the weekend (free but gear rental costs $50–75 per day) dives including Shiprock and the Botany Bay National Park on the Kurnell Peninsula. Also organizes boat dives, night dives and weekends away up and down the New South Wales coast.

Deep 6 Diving 351–355 Clovelly Rd, cnr Beach St, Clovelly ⓣ02/9665 7427, ⓦwww.deep6diving.com.au. Bus #339 from Central CityRail. Closest dive shop to Gordons Bay, so naturally they run lots of trips there, though their rates are high if you don't become a member, low if you do (membership $100 for one year). Sunday shore dives meet at the store between 8.45am and 9.30am; single $90, double $115; also single and double boat dives. If you just want to hire equipment it's $88 per 24hr and snorkelling sets are $10 per day (fins extra $10). With an associated Deep 6 at Jervis Bay on the south coast, they often do weekend trips down there.

Dive Centre Bondi 192 Bondi Rd ⓣ02/9369 3855, ⓦwww.divesydney.com. Bus #380 from Bondi Junction CityRail. Shore dives at Camp Cove (Watsons Bay) and Ben Buckler at North Bondi (double dive $95) and boat dives to South Head and Maroubra where there's a chance to see sharks.

Dive Centre Manly 10 Belgrave St, Manly ⓣ02/9977 4355, ⓦwww.divesydney.com. Ferry to Manly Wharf. Offers shore dives to Shelley Beach, Fairlight, and Little Manly plus Harbord if conditions are good, and boat dives off North and South Head and Long Reef (boat dives Fri–Sun 9am, 11am, 1pm & 3pm; single boat dive $90, double $145; shore dives daily 9am & noon; single shore dive $75, double $90; rates include full gear).

Prodive Coogee 27 Alfreda St, Coogee ⓣ02/9665 6333, ⓦwww.prodive.com.au. Bus #373 & #374 from Circular Quay CityRail. Offers equipped boat and shore dives anywhere between Camp Cove (Watsons Bay) and La Perouse (4hr double boat dive $169 weekend, $125 mid-week, double shore dive $105), plus dives all over Sydney.

▲ North Sydney Olympic Pool

Swimming pools

Most public, council-run pool complexes are outdoors and have a fifty-metre pool, a smaller children's pool and a wading pool, all usually unheated. The **swimming season** is generally the warmer months, from the long weekend in October until Easter. Many pools are closed to the public for several days in February when school swimming carnivals traditionally take place. There are over seventy public pools, as well as 74 enclosed sea pools at beaches and on the harbour; several of the latter are detailed in the text, including the Dawn Fraser Swimming Pool in Balmain (p.119), Women's Pool (p.144) and Wylie's Baths (p.144), both in Coogee; the pool at the Bondi Icebergs (p.140); and the Mahon Pool at Maroubra (p.144). The following are a selection of favourites in popular areas; check "Swiming pools" in the *Yellow Pages* for a full list.

Andrew "Boy" Charlton The Domain ⓣ02/9358 6686. Martin Place CityRail. Revamped in 2002, the much-glamorized pool now has its own café-restaurant and yoga, pilates and kickboxing classes, plus a regular Thursday night biathlon (running and swimming) open to all competitors. Oct–April daily 6am–8pm; $5.

Annette Kellerman Aquatic Centre Enmore Pool, Enmore Park off Enmore Rd, Enmore ⓣ02/9565 1906. Bus #423, #426 & #428 from Central CityRail. Not far from Newtown, and known to the locals simply as Enmore Pool, the heated 33m pool stays open all year. Mon–Sat 5.30am–8.30pm, Sun 8am–6pm; $3.80.

Cook and Phillip Park Aquatic and Leisure Centre Cnr William and College streets ⓣ02/9326 0444, ⓦwww.cookandphillip.com.au. Museum CityRail. State-of-the-art undercover complex with a 50m heated indoor pool for laps, a 25m leisure pool with a wave-making machine at weekends and during school holidays, a bubbling "river run" feature and toddlers area with its own beach, a hydrotherapy pool with disabled access and a gym. There's access to an outdoor courtyard and café, plus two external restaurants, one of which is the vegetarian *Bodhi in the Park* (see p.185). Mon–Fri 6am–10pm, Sat & Sun 7am–8pm. Swim $5.50, swim and gym $16.

Cronulla Sports Complex The Esplanade, Cronulla ⓣ02/9523 5842. Cronulla CityRail. Beachfront complex with heated indoor pools and a gym. Mon–Fri 7am–3.45pm, Sat 7am–4.45pm, Sun 8am–4.45pm. Swim $3.30, swim and gym $13.

Leichhardt Park Aquatic Centre Mary St Leichhardt ⓣ02/9555 8344, ⓦwww.lmc.nsw.gov.au. Bus #440 from Central CityRail. A great spot for a swimming centre, on an extensive park on Iron Cove, an inlet of the Parramatta River. The pool grounds themselves are green and spacious. The heated outdoor 50m pool is a great place to swim in winter and there's also a diving pool. Alternatively, you can stay inside in the smaller 25m heated pool (with an indoor toddlers' pool and spa beside it). Just outside there's a popular, landscaped, gate-surrounded toddlers' pool. The gym has aerobics, aqua aerobics and yoga classes in its programme. There's a handy weekday childminding service, too (Mon–Fri 9am–1.30pm; max 2hr; bookings essential; $3.40 per hour). The café is mediocre and the Norton St ones are quite a long haul away. Daily 5.30am–8pm. Swim $5.40, swim and gym $14.50.

North Sydney Olympic Pool Alfred St South, Milsons Point ⓣ02/9955 2309. Milsons Point CityRail. The heated 50m outdoor pool here is open all year (covered in winter); situated by the water in the shadow of the harbour bridge, it's one of Sydney's best. Revamped in 2001, it has a new indoor 25m pool, a gym, sauna, spa and café, and the slick restaurant *Aqua*, overlooking the swimmers. Mon–Fri 5.30am–9pm, Sat & Sun 7am–7pm; $4.70.

Sydney International Aquatic Centre Olympic Boulevard, Sydney Olympic Park, Homebush Bay ⓣ02/9752 3666, ⓦwww.sydneyaquaticcentre.com.au. Olympic Park CityRail. As well as being a great place to swim laps in the competition pools, there are landscaped leisure pools with amusements such as the rapid river-ride, as well as water slides. Also spas, steam rooms and saunas, a gym and fitness classes. Nov–March Mon–Fri 5am–8.45pm, Sat & Sun 6am–7.45pm; April–Oct Mon–Fri 5am–8.45pm, Sat & Sun 6am–6.45pm. Swim and spa $6, child $4.90 ($12 includes steam rooms and sauna; also including gym and fitness classes $18). A crèche is available (max 2hr; book in advance; $6.50).

Victoria Park Pool Cnr City Rd and Broadway ⓣ02/9660 4181. Bus #431, #433, #434, #438 & #440 from Central CityRail. Heated outdoor pool next to Sydney University and close to Glebe Point Road, in a landscaped park, and a shaded toddlers' wading pool. Great café (daily 7.30am–3pm), plus a good-value gym and crèche (Mon, Wed & Fri 9am–2pm; book in advance; $2 for 45min). Mon–Fri 6am–7.15pm, Sat & Sun 7am–5.45pm; $3, swim and gym $7.

Cycling

The narrow maze of streets in Sydney's CBD, combined with traffic congestion, means that **cycling** has never been too popular. Bicycles can be carried free on trains (outside peak hours of Mon–Fri 6–9am & 3.30–7.30pm), and on ferries at all times if there is room in the bicycle racks. It is a legal requirement that you wear a helmet – police issue fines for non-compliance. The Roads and Traffic Authority (RTA; ⓣ1800 060 607, ⓦwww.rta.nsw.gov.au) produces a handy fold-out map, *Sydney Cycleways*, showing both off-road paths and suggested bicycle routes, which they will post out. The best source of information, however, is the very helpful advocacy organization Bicycle NSW, based at Level 5, 822 George St (Mon–Fri 9am–5.30pm; ⓣ02/9281 4099, ⓦwww.bicyclensw.org.au). Two useful publications available here are *Bike It Sydney* ($13), which has backstreet inner-city bike routes, and *Cycling Around Sydney* ($25), which details 25 of the best rides. They also hand out free council and RTA bike route maps.

For leisure cycling, head for **Centennial Park** or the **cycleway at Manly**. **Critical Mass** is an activist group "reclaiming the streets for cycling" which began in San Francisco and now has groups all over the world, including one in Sydney. The Sydney movement organizes a cycling event on the last Friday of the month; meet at the Archibald Fountain in Hyde Park for an hour-long ride through the city leaving at 6pm (or you can skate, jog, rollerblade; even runners turn up, too).

Recommended central **bicycle shops** for sales and repairs include Clarence Street Cyclery, 104 Clarence St (ⓣ02/9299 4962, ⓦwww.cyclery.com.au); Woolys Wheels, 82 Oxford St, Paddington (ⓣ02/9331 2671, ⓦwww.woolyswheels.com); and Inner City Cycles, 151 Glebe Point Rd, Glebe (ⓣ02/9660 6605, ⓦwww.innercitycycles.com.au). The cheapest **bike rental** is at Cheeky Monkey Cycle Co, 456 Pitt St, near Central Station (ⓣ02/9212 4460, ⓦwww.cheekymonkey.com.au; closed Sun); mountain bikes cost $25 per day, $100 per week, and they also sell bikes and rent out and sell cycle-touring equipment. Clarence Street Cyclery also rents out mountain bikes ($65 per day, $100 per weekend), as do Inner City Cycles ($33 per 24hr, $55 per weekend). For a leisurely ride in the park head for Centennial Park Cycles, 50 Clovelly Rd, Randwick (ⓣ02/9398 5027, ⓦwww.cyclehire.com.au; mountain bikes $12 per hour, $32 per day; bikes for kids $10 per hour, $27 per day; tandems $18 hour, $50 day); it also rents out pedal cars ($25–35 hour). To get onto Manly's bike path, you can rent bikes from Manly Cycles, a block back from the beach at 36 Pittwater Rd (ⓣ02/9977 1189, ⓦwww.manlycycles.com.au; mountain bikes $12 per hour, $25 per day).

Rollerblading, skateboarding and ice-skating

Rollerblading is banned in the CBD. The most popular areas for bladers are along the bike track at Manly; along the Luna Park concourse and Lavender

Bay walkway at Milsons Point (which you can reach by rollerblading across the Sydney Harbour Bridge along the cycle path on the western side); in Centennial Park; and along the Esplanade at Bondi Beach – teenagers also use the skateboarding ramp at Bondi. **Rental places** charge $15 for the first hour for either inline skates or skateboards, inclusive of protective gear, then up to around $25–30 for the day: try Total Skate, corner of Oxford and Queen streets, Woollahra (ⓣ02/9380 6356, ⓦwww.totalskate.com.au), handy for Centennial Park and also offering lessons; and Manly Blades & Skates, 49 North Steyne (ⓣ02/9976 3833, ⓦwww.manlyblades.com.au), close to Manly's bike track. Centennial Park Cycles (see above) also hire's out rollerblades.

During the colder months, from mid-June to the September, an outdoor ice-skating rink operates on the Showring at Fox Studios, Moore Park near Paddington (hours and entry fee information varies each season; for details call ⓣ02/9383 4333; bus #339 from Central CityRail). There are also a few permanent ice-skating rinks out in the suburbs, including one at leafy North Ryde, 16km northwest of the centre at the big shopping mall Macquarie Centre, on the corner of Waterloo and Herring roads (ⓣ02/9888 1100, ⓦwww.macquarieicerink.com.au; Epping CityRail then bus #288, #289 or #294; $17 for a 2hr session includes skate hire; hours and session times vary daily and during school holidays).

Horse riding

The vast expanse of **Centennial Park** has extensive horse-riding tracks, and people stable their horses at the Centennial Parklands Equestrian Centre at the southeast corner of the Fox Studios site, on the junction of Cook and Lang roads just through the Showground gate to Centennial Park. Several stables offer **horse riding**; you can just wander into the centre and enquire, or book in advance with one, such as Centennial Stables in Pavilion B (ⓣ02/9360 5650, ⓦwww.centennialstables.com.au; 1hr escorted rides $60; 1hr lesson $85). There's more scenic horse riding in the Blue Mountains' Megalong Valley and in the Hunter Valley; for operators see p.313.

Abseiling, canyoning, climbing and bungee jumping

For **thrill sports**, from rap jumping to skydiving and aerobatic flights, contact the Adrenalin Club (ⓣ02/8456 7777, ⓦwww.adrenalin.com.au). A popular spot for **hang-gliding** is Stanwell Park just south of the Royal National Park; the Sydney Hang Gliding Centre (ⓣ02/4294 4294, ⓦwww.hanggliding.com.au) offers tandem flights with an instructor for $180 during the week, $195 at weekends or courses from $195 per day. The **Bungy Trampoline** at the Showring at Fox Studios (Wed–Sun 11am–6pm; $10 for 4min, see p.106) and at Darling Harbour (see p.247) is an ordinary trampoline with several bungee cords, designed to give you the thrill of a bungee jump but without the danger.

See "The Blue Mountains" chapter for information on operators offering abseiling and canyoning trips. Sydney's best **indoor climbing centre** is near Newton: Sydney Indoor Climbing Gym, 4C Unwins Bridge Rd, St Peters (Mon–Wed & Fri 9.30am–10pm, Thurs 9.30am–11pm, Sat & Sun 9.30am–9pm; ⓣ02/9716 6949, ⓦwww.indoorclimbing.com.au; St Peters CityRail; casual entry $15, harness, shoes and chalk bag rental $10).

Gyms

Most **gyms** charge between $15 and $17 for a casual visit, which applies all day, and includes access to aerobics and even yoga classes. In their quest for new members, many gyms have a no-obligation one-week free introductory offer, which provides a cheeky way for travellers to do the rounds and get fit for free. Several gyms are reviewed in the "Gay Sydney" chapter, with the (nearly) 24-hour City Gym (see p.238) recommended. Many of the city's swimming pools also have gyms, and with a swim usually thrown in, the rates are much more reasonable (see p.275). Also see Hiscoe's Fitness Centre (p.271), where a casual gym visit costs $17.

Yoga

Yoga is very popular in Sydney, and we've included three specific **yoga schools** allowing casual visits and offering different styles of yoga. Most gyms also organize yoga classes – see above, p.275 and box on pp.312–313.

Bikram's Yoga College of India Level 1, 256 Crown St, Darlinghurst ⓣ02/9356 4999 (Museum CityRail) and 713 Darling St, Rozelle ⓣ02/9810 3146 (bus #440 from Central CityRail), ⓦwww.bikramyogaaustralia.com.au. The latest yoga craze, Bikram yoga consists of 26 set postures done in sequence in a very hot room (37°C), allowing your body to sweat out toxins. It's very exhausting but many people feel exhilarated afterwards. There's an introductory offer of $17 for the first ten days – they recommend coming three to five times – which is a bargain for a Sydney visitor wanting to try something different. Casual drop-in class $18 (1hr 30min).

Bondi Beach Iyengar Yoga Institute Suite 10, 78 Campbell Parade, Bondi Beach ⓣ02/9130 1295, ⓦwww.bondibeachyoga.com. Bus #380 from Central CityRail. All classes are Hatha yoga taught in the Iyengar method; 1hr 30min beginners and general classes $17.

Yoga Synergy 115 Bronte Rd, Bondi Junction (Bondi Junction CityRail), 196 Australia St, Newtown (Newtown CityRail) and Market Lane, off The Corso, Manly (ferry from Circular Quay) ⓣ02/9389 7399, ⓦwww.yogasynergy.com.au. The directors here are also physiotherapists: the yoga taught is a synthesis between Hatha yoga and modern medical science. More strenuous Ashtanga yoga is also practised. Classes 1hr 30min, beginners to advanced; $17.

Dance classes

The prestigious Sydney Dance Company, Wharf 4–5, Hickson Rd, Millers Point (ⓣ02/9221 4811, ⓦwww.sydneydancecompany.com; Circular Quay

The Ginseng Bathhouse

After you've got all sweaty, try a traditional ginseng bath and skin-scrub treatment at the wonderful Korean-style **Ginseng Bathhouse**, *Crest Hotel*, 1st floor, 111 Darlinghurst Rd, Kings Cross (ⓣ02/9358 2755, ⓦwww.ginsengbathhouse.com.au; Kings Cross CityRail). There are separate bathhouses for men and women – everyone must take off all their clothes – but robes are provided for the unisex refreshment room where you can make yourself a herbal tea and read a magazine. The men's bathhouse can get a little cruisey. All-day bath access costs $25; extras include a 15-minute exfoliation scrub for $53 and Korean or shiatsu massage at $69 for 30min. Mon–Fri 9.30am–9.30pm, Sat & Sun 9am–9.30pm.

CityRail), holds day and evening open **dance** classes at their waterfront studios on an atmospheric converted wharf – ranging from funk and jazz, through contemporary to ballet. You can just turn up for a $16 casual class.

21

Directory

Airlines (domestic) Aeropelican ⓣ13 13 00, ⓦwww.aeropelican.com.au; Air Link ⓣ 02/6884 2435, ⓦwww.airlinkairlines.com.au; Big Sky Express ⓣ1800 008 759, ⓦwww.bigskyexpress.com.au; Jetstar ⓣ13 15 38, ⓦwww.jetstar.com.au; Qantas ⓣ13 13 13, ⓦwww.qantas.com.au; Regional Express (REX) ⓣ13 17 13, ⓦwww.regional-express.com.au; Sydney Harbour Seaplanes ⓣ02/9388 1978, ⓦwww.sydneyseaplane.com.au; Virgin Blue ⓣ13 67 89, ⓦwww.virginblue.com.au.

Airlines (international) Aeroflot, 44 Market St ⓣ02/9262 2233; Aerolineas Argentinas, Level 3, 64 Clarence St ⓣ1300 131 744; Air Canada, Level 18, Australia Square, 264 George St ⓣ1300 655 767; Air New Zealand, Level 4, 10 Barrack St ⓣ13 24 76; Alitalia, 64 York St ⓣ02/9244 2400; British Airways, Level 19, AAP Centre, 259 George St ⓣ1300 767 177; Cathay Pacific ⓣ13 17 47; Continental, 64 York St ⓣ02/9244 2242; Delta, Level 9, 189 Kent St ⓣ02/9251 3211; Emirates, Level 10, 1 York St ⓣ1300/303 777; Eva Airways ⓣ02/9313 5199; Finnair, 64 York St ⓣ02/9244 2299; Freedom Air ⓣ1800 122 000; Garuda, 55 Hunter St ⓣ1300 365 330; Gulf Air 12/403 George St ⓣ02/9244 2149; Japan Airlines, Level 14, 201 Sussex St ⓣ02/9272 1111; KLM, 13th floor, 115 Pitt St ⓣ1300 303 747; Korean Air, Level 4, 333 George St ⓣ02/9262 6000; Lauda Air, Level 2, 1 York St ⓣ02/9251 6155; Malaysia Airlines, 16 Spring St ⓣ13 26 27; Olympic, 3rd floor, 37–49 Pitt St ⓣ02/9251 1047; Pacific Blue ⓣ13 16 45; Polynesian Airlines, Level 9, 99 York St ⓣ02/9299 1733; Qantas, 70 Hunter St ⓣ13 13 13; Royal Brunei, Level 4, BT Tower, 1 Market St ⓣ02/8267 5300; Scandinavian Airlines, Level 15, 31 Market St ⓣ1300 727 707; Singapore Airlines, 17–19 Bridge St ⓣ13 10 11; South African Airways, Level 1, 117 York St ⓣ02/9286 8960; Swiss International, Level 3, 117 York St ⓣ1300 724 666; Thai Airways, 75 Pitt St ⓣ1300 651 960; United, Level 6, 10 Barrack St ⓣ13 17 77; Virgin Atlantic, Level 8, 403 George St ⓣ02/9244 2747. For airline websites see "Getting there" p.19.

Banks and foreign exchange See "Costs, money and banks" p.29.

Bike rental See p.276 in "Sports and activities".

Bus companies Interstate services: Firefly Express (ⓣ1300 730 740); Greyhound Pioneer (ticket office at Eddy Ave, Central Station; ⓣ13 14 99); Murray's (ⓣ13 22 51); Pioneer Motor Service (ⓣ13 34 10). Services within NSW: Kean's (ⓣ02/6543 1322), daily Sydney to Hunter Valley; Premier Motor Service (ⓣ13 34 10), daily to the south coast; Prior's Scenic Express (ⓣ02/4472 4040 or 1800 816 234), daily except Sat from Parramatta, Liverpool and Campbelltown train stations to the Southern Highlands including Kangaroo Valley; Rover Coaches (ⓣ4990 1699 or 1800 801 012), daily to Cessnock and Hunter Valley resorts from Sydney Airport, Eddy Ave and Circular Quay; Selwoods (ⓣ02/6362 7963), daily to Orange via the Blue Mountains, Lithgow and Bathurst.

Bus terminal Sydney Coach Terminal, cnr Eddy Ave and Pitt St, next to Central Station (daily 6am–10pm; ⓣ02/9281 9366).

Bus tickets Make bookings at the Traveller's Information Service at the bus terminal (ⓣ02/9281 9366), at Backpackers World Travel outlets listed under "Travel agents" p.283, or direct with the bus companies listed above.

Campervans and 4WD rental All Seasons Campervans, 77 Planthurst Rd, South

Hurstville (☎02/9547 0100, ⓦwww.camper.com.au) has a wide range of campervans, motorhomes, four-door sedans plus camping equipment; prices include linen, sleeping bags and free delivery to CBD accommodation. Other options include, Australian Outback 4 Wheel Drive Hire Co, 184 Elizabeth St, City ☎02/9281 9676; Britz Campervan Rentals, 653 Gardeners Rd, Mascot (☎02/9667 0402 or 1800 331 454, ⓦwww.britz.com), for campervans, 4WDs and camping gear; Hertz Campervans, 1084–1088 Botany Rd, Botany ☎02/9316 4188); Travel Car Centre, 26 Orchard Rd, Brookvale (☎02/9938 1129 or 1800 440 300, ⓦwww.travelcar.com.au), which has been established for nearly 20 years and has hatchbacks, stationwagons, campervans and 4WDs available for long- or short-term rental; Travellers Auto Barn, 177 William St, Kings Cross (☎02/9360 1500; ⓦwww.travellers-autobarn.com.au) who offer budget campervan rental.

Camping equipment and rental Kent Street in the city behind the Town Hall is nicknamed "adventure alley" for its plethora of outdoor equipment stores; the best known is the high-quality Paddy Pallin at no. 507 (☎02/9264 2685, ⓦwww.paddypallin.com.au). Cheaper options include disposal stores at the downtown ends of George and Pitt streets near Central Station – and suburban K-Mart stores (closest stores to the city are at Spring St, Bondi Junction and at the Broadway shopping centre, Bay St) or hostel notice boards. Only a few places rent out gear, mostly based in the suburbs: try Alpsport, 1045 Victoria Rd, West Ryde (☎02/9858 5844), with weekend rent of a backpack for around $32, sleeping bag from $27, and tent from $30.

Car rental and sales Most car-rental firms have a branch in William Street, Kings Cross; the big four, with new-model cars, are also at the airport. Average daily charge is $50–70 for a small manual, with much cheaper rates for 5- to 7-day and longer rentals. Avis, airport ☎02/8374 2847 and 220 William St ☎02/9357 2000, ⓦwww.avis.com.au; Budget, airport ☎13 27 27 and 93 William St ☎02/8255 9600, ⓦwww.budget.com.au; Hertz, airport and elsewhere including cnr William and Riley streets ☎13 30 39, ⓦwww.hertz.com; Thrifty, 75 William St ☎1300 367 227, ⓦwww.thrifty.com.au. There are cheaper deals with: Bayswater, 180 William St, Kings Cross (☎02/9360 3622, ⓦwww.bayswatercarrental.com.au), which has low rates but limited kilometres; Daytona Rentals, 164 Parramatta Rd, Ashfield (☎02/9716 8777), which has slightly older cars at very good rates for weekly rentals all inclusive of insurance; and Rent-a-Ruffy, 29 Pittwater Rd, Manly (☎02/9977 5777), which has new model cars and cheap, older-model cars – both have limited kilometres. Travellers Auto Barn, 177 William St, Kings Cross (☎02/9360 1500, ⓦwww.travellers-autobarn.com.au), does cheap long-term rentals and sells station wagons and combivans with buy-back deals; travellers can also easily buy a car at the Kings Cross Car Market, Kings Cross Car Park, Level 2, Ward Ave, Kings Cross (daily 9am–6pm; ☎02/9358 5000, ⓦwww.carmarket.com.au).

Coach terminal Sydney Coach Terminal, cnr Eddy Ave and Pitt St, next to Central station (daily 6am–10pm; ☎02/9281 9366). You can make coach ticket bookings here or at Backpackers Travel Centres (see "Travel agents", p.283).

Consulates Canada, Level 5, 111 Harrington St ☎02/9364 3000; New Zealand, Level 10, 55 Hunter St ☎02/8256 2000; UK, Level 16, Gateway Building, 1 Macquarie Place ☎02/9247 7521; US, Level 59, MLC Centre, 19–29 Martin Place ☎02/9373 9200. For visas for onward travel, consult "Consulates and Legations" in the Yellow Pages.

Electricity Australia's electrical current is 240/250v, 50Hz AC. British appliances will work with an adaptor; American and Canadian 110v appliances need a transformer.

Emergency ☎000 for fire, police or ambulance.

GST (Goods and Services Tax) A GST of ten percent was introduced in 2000, and caused a general across-the-board price hike, though fresh foods are not included. Under the Tourist Refund Scheme, visitors can claim GST refunds for goods purchased in Australia as they clear customs, providing that individual receipts exceed $300 (from one supplier, not over $300 from various suppliers) and the claim is made within thirty days of purchase. Many stores in The Rocks and the airport have a "sealed bag" system which lets you buy goods without paying GST, and the minimum of $300 is waived.

Hospitals (with emergency departments) St Vincents Hospital, cnr Victoria and Burton streets, Darlinghurst ☎02/8382 1111; Royal

Prince Alfred, Missenden Rd, Camperdown ⓣ02/9515 6111; Prince of Wales, Barker St, Randwick ⓣ02/9382 2222.

Immigration Department of Immigration, 26 Lee St, near Central Station, Haymarket ⓣ13 18 81.

Laundries Virtually all accommodation will have a coin-operated laundry and dryer and possibly even a clothesline outside. If not, there are always a few laundromats in busy tourist and residential areas; a load of washing costs about $3 do-it-yourself at any of these (plus extra for powder and drying) or about a reasonable $9 per load to have it washed, dried and folded for you.

Left luggage There are serve-yourself lockers at Central Station inside the country trains terminal; make sure you have $1 and $2 coins as there's no longer a change machine (daily 6.30am–9.30pm; $8, $6 or $4 per 24hr depending on size). Also lockers at the airport and the Sydney Coach Terminal ($7–12 per 24hr).

Libraries City of Sydney Public Library, Customs House, 31 Alfred St, Circular Quay ⓣ02/9242 8555, ⓦwww.cityofsydney.gov.au; Mon–Fri 8am–7pm, Sat 10am–4pm, Sun noon–4pm. State Library of NSW, Macquarie St ⓣ02/9273 1414, ⓦwww.sl.nsw.gov.au; Mon–Fri 9am–9pm, Sat & Sun 11am–5pm.

Medical centres and clinics See "Medical Centres" in the Yellow Pages for the closest clinic to where you're staying. Broadway Medical Centre, 185–211 Broadway, near Glebe ⓣ02/9281 5085: general practitioners open Mon–Fri 9am–7pm, Sat & Sun 11am–5pm, no appointment necessary. Skin Cancer Centre, ground floor, 403 George St ⓣ02/9262 4877; Sydney Sexual Health Centre, Nightingale Wing, Sydney Hospital, Macquarie St ⓣ02/9382 7440; The Travel Doctor, 7th floor, 428 George St ⓣ02/9221 7133, ⓦwww.traveldoctor.com.au.

Motorbike rental and sales Wentworth Ave in the city has a concentration of motorbike salerooms for new models. For secondhand motorbikes and rental, there's Bikescape, Unit 17, 566 Gardeners Rd, Alexandria (ⓣ1300 736 869, ⓦwww.bikescape.com.au), with scooters from $75 per day and motorbikes from $115; cheaper weekend and longer term rates available.

Motoring organizations The New South Wales' motoring organization, the NRMA, is at 74–76 King St, City (ⓣ13 21 32, ⓦwww.nrma.com.au), and is handy if you belong to a motoring organization back home, as the maps are free to associated members. They provide road maps of New South Wales and a useful map of Sydney; lots more information is also available and there's an accommodation booking service.

Pharmacy (late-night) Crest Hotel Pharmacy, 60A Darlinghurst Rd, Kings Cross (daily 8.30am–midnight; ⓣ02/9358 1822).

Police Headquarters at 14–24 College St, Darlinghurst (ⓣ02/9339 0277; emergency ⓣ000). Also see box p.52.

Post office The General Post Office (GPO) is in Martin Place (Mon–Fri 8.15am–5.30pm, Sat 9am–1pm). Poste restante is located at the post office in the Hunter Connection shopping mall at 310 George St (Mon–Fri 8.15am–6pm), opposite Wynyard Station. The address to write to is: Poste Restante, Sydney, NSW 2000, Australia.

Public toilets Free public toilets are found at beaches, in parks, shopping arcades, train stations and department stores.

Seasons Don't forget that in the southern hemisphere the seasons are reversed. Summer lasts from December through February, winter from June through August.

Time Sydney follows Australian Eastern Standard Time (AEST), half an hour ahead of South Australia and the Northern Territory, two hours ahead of Western Australia, ten hours ahead of Greenwich Mean Time (GMT) and fifteen ahead of US Eastern Standard Time. Clocks are put forward one hour in November and back again in March for daylight saving.

Tips Apart from in restaurants, tipping is not customary in Australia, and cab drivers, bar staff (and hairdressers) don't generally expect anything. In fact, cab drivers often round the fare down rather than bother with change. In cafés and cheap-eat restaurants you might leave the change, but most Australians tip in better restaurants, around ten percent, but only if the service has been good.

Tours Recommended small-group return tours from Sydney to the areas outside the city are covered in chapters 22–25. In addition, the coach tour company AAT Kings (ⓣ02/9518 6095, ⓦwww.aatkings.com/au), one of the largest operators, offers big-group, sedentary bus tours covering city sights, wildlife parks, the Blue

Mountains, Jenolan Caves, the Hawkesbury River and the Hunter Valley; admissions and hotel pick-ups and drop-offs are included in their prices. CityRail (ⓣ13 15 00, see Transport Infoline on ⓦwww.131500.com.au) offers package day-trips by rail, which can be very good value, generally covering all transport and entry fees – trips include the Blue Mountains, and the Hawkesbury River (which includes a cruise); details and tickets from CityRail at Circular Quay or Central Station. Also see "Tourist passes" in the box on pp.38–39 for information on the Sydney Explorer and Bondi Explorer hop-on-hop-off bus tours, and p.36 for cruises.

Trains All out-of-town trains depart from the country trains terminal of Central Station, with its entrance on Pitt Street. Information and booking 6.30am–10pm ⓣ13 22 32.

Travel agents STA Travel does international and domestic flights, tours and accommodation. Numerous branches include 841 George St ⓣ02/9212 1255; Shop 205, Broadway Shopping Centre, Bay St, Broadway ⓣ02/9211 2563; 308 King St, Newtown ⓣ02/9557 7396; 404 Oxford St, Paddington ⓣ02/9360 1822; and Shop 6, 127–139 Macleay St, Kings Cross ⓣ02/9368 1111, ⓦwww.statravel.com.au. The British travel agency Trailfinders has a branch in Sydney at 8 Spring St ⓣ02/9247 7666, ⓦwww.trailfinders.com. Flight Centre, 52 Martin Place (ⓣ02/9235 0166), also at several other locations, offers cheap domestic and international air tickets. YHA Travel, 422 Kent St, City (ⓣ02/9261 1111, ⓦwww.yha.com.au), provides domestic and international travel services: transport, tours and accommodation as well as an excellent selection of day-trips around Sydney (branch at Sydney Central YHA, 11 Rawson Place off Eddy Ave ⓣ02/9281 9444). Backpackers World Travel, 234 Sussex St (ⓣ02/8268 6001, ⓦwww.backpackerstravel.net.au), does everything from international flights to bus passes; offices also 91 York St (ⓣ02/8268 5000), at 488 Pitt St near Central Station (ⓣ02/9282 9711), 212 Victoria St, Kings Cross (ⓣ02/9380 2700) and 2b Grosvenor St, Bondi Junction (ⓣ02/9369 2011). For details of day tours from Sydney, see p.308, and the day-trip chapters themselves.

Weights and measures Australia has been fully metric since the early 1970s and is thoroughly adapted to kilometres, kilograms, litres and degrees Celsius. Shoe sizes (at least for women) are unique to Australia; for example, Australian women's size 7.5 is roughly equal to a European size 39 and may be up to half a size different from the US/Canadian 7.5. Men's shoe sizes in Australia are the same as UK sizes – if you're from the US or Canada, ask for one size up from your usual fitting to be safe; dress sizes are the same as in the UK (but a US 8 is equivalent to an Australian 10).

Women The big events are around International Women's Day in March. Contact the Women's Information and Referral Service (Mon–Fri 9am–5pm; ⓣ1800 817 227) for information on this and women's organizations, services and referrals. The Women's Library, 8–10 Brown St, Newtown (Tues, Wed & Fri 11am–5pm, Thurs 11am–8pm, Sat & Sun noon–4pm; ⓣ02/9557 7060), lends feminist and lesbian literature. Jesse Street National Women's Library, housed in the Town Hall, 456 Kent St (Mon–Fri 10am–2pm; ⓣ02/9265 9486), is an archive collecting literature detailing Australian women's history and writing. The Feminist Bookshop is in Orange Grove Plaza on Balmain Rd, Lilyfield ⓣ02/9810 2666.

Work If you have a working holiday visa, you shouldn't have too much trouble finding some sort of work, particularly in hospitality or retail. Offices of the government-run Centrelink (ⓣ13 28 50) have a database of jobs; the most central of their offices are at 140 Redfern St, cnr of George St, Redfern; 151 Crown St, Darlinghurst; and 231 Oxford St, Bondi Junction. Centrelink also refers jobseekers to several private "Job Network" agencies, including Employment National (ⓣ13 34 44). The private agency Troy's, Level 11, 89 York St (ⓣ02/9290 2955, ⓦwww.troys.com.au), specializes in the hospitality industry. If you have some office or professional skills, there are plenty of temp agencies that are more than keen to take on travellers: flick through "Employment Services" in the Yellow Pages. For a whole range of work, from unskilled to professional, the multinational Manpower (ⓣ13 25 02, ⓦwww.manpower.com.au), is a good bet. Also check out Australia-wide job seeking networks on the Internet; one of the most popular is ⓦwww.seek.com.au. Otherwise, scour hostel notice boards and the *Sydney Morning Herald's* employment pages

– Saturday's bumper edition is best.

YHA NSW 422 Kent St, City ⓣ02/9261 1111, ⓦwww.yha.com.au. Youth Hostel Association membership and travel centre. Mon–Fri 9am–5pm (Thurs to 6pm), Sat 10am–2pm.

Out of the City

Out of the City

22

The Hawkesbury River and the Central Coast

North of Sydney the Hawkesbury River widens and slows as it approaches the South Pacific, joining **Berowra Creek**, Cowan Creek, Pittwater and Brisbane Water in the system of flooded valleys that form the jagged jaws of the aptly named **Broken Bay**. The bay and its surrounding inlets are a haven for anglers, sailors and windsurfers, while the entire area is surrounded by bush, with the huge spaces of the **Ku-Ring-Gai Chase National Park** in the south and the **Brisbane Waters National Park** in the north. Beyond Broken Bay, the **Central Coast** between Gosford and Newcastle is an ideal spot for fishing, sailing and lazing around.

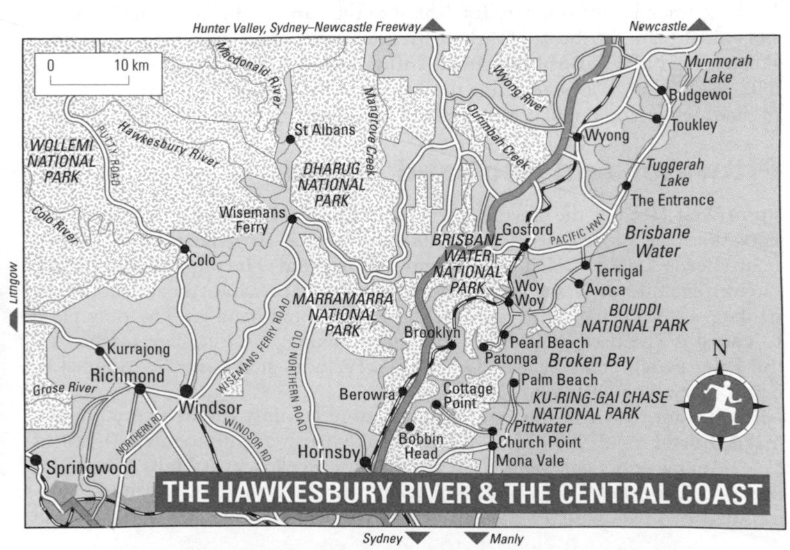

The **Pacific Highway** up here, partly supplanted by the **Sydney–Newcastle Freeway**, is fast and efficient, though not particularly attractive until you approach Ku-Ring-Gai Chase; if you want to detour into the park or towards Brooklyn on the Hawkesbury River, don't take the freeway. The **rail** lines follow the road almost as far as Broken Bay, before they take a scenic diversion through Brooklyn and Brisbane Waters to Woy Woy and Gosford.

Ku-Ring-Gai Chase National Park

Ku-Ring-Gai Chase is much the best known of New South Wales' national parks and, with the Pacific Highway running all the way up one side, is also the easiest to get to. The bushland scenery is crisscrossed by walking tracks, which you can explore to seek out Aboriginal rock paintings, or just to get away from it all and see the forest and its wildlife. Only 24km from the city centre, the huge park's unspoilt beauty is enhanced by the presence of water on three sides: the Hawkesbury, its inlet Cowan Creek, and the expanse of **Pittwater**, an inlet of Broken Bay.

From Palm Beach you can take a **boat cruise** with the Palm Beach Ferry Service (see p.151) across Pittwater to the park's Bobbin Head. There are four **road entrances** to the park and an $11 entrance fee for cars. Alternatively, take a **train** to Turramurra CityRail Station and then Hornsby Bus #577 (☎02/9457 8888 for times) to the Bobbin Head Road entrance; some buses continue down to Bobbin Head itself.

Bobbin Head

Ku-Ring-Gai Chase National Park's most popular picnic spot is at **Bobbin Head**, with its colourful marina on Cowan Creek. At the **Kalkari Visitor Centre** (daily 9am–5pm), on the Ku-Ring-Gai Chase Road, you can watch videos about the area's Aboriginal heritage and the wildlife you might encounter, pick up information about walks in the park or take a guided walk. The Birrawanna Walking Track leads from here for 1.5km to the park headquarters in the *Bobbin Inn*, which can also be approached by car further along Ku-Ring-Gai Chase Road. The NPWS **Bobbin Head Information Centre** (daily 10am–4pm; ☎02/9472 8949) is located inside the Art Deco *Bobbin Inn*, which also has a very pleasant restaurant, popular for weekend breakfasts and Sunday afternoon jazz.

Pittwater and Scotland Island

From West Head at the northeastern corner of Ku-Ring-Gai Chase National Park there are superb views across Pittwater to the Barrenjoey Lighthouse at Palm Beach (see p.151). The **Garigal Aboriginal Heritage Walk** (3.5km circuit) heads from West Head Road to the most accessible Aboriginal art site in the park, featuring Aboriginal rock engravings and hand art. The only place to **camp** is The Basin (☎02/9974 1011 for bookings) on Pittwater, reached via the Palm Beach Ferry Service (see p.151). Facilities at the site are minimal so bring everything with you.

If you want to stay in the park in rather more comfort, there's a very popular **YHA hostel** (☎02/9999 5748, ©pittwater@yhansw.org.au; rooms $60, dorms $23; bookings essential and well in advance for weekends) at **Halls Wharf**. It's one of New South Wales' most scenically sited – a rambling old house surrounded by bush, with a verandah where you can feed rainbow lorikeets and look down onto the water; sailing lessons can also be arranged. You must bring everything with you – the last food (and bottle) shop is at Church Point where the **ferry** departs to Halls Wharf (last departure Mon–Fri 7pm, Sat & Sun 6.30pm; $7.50 return; call ☎02/9999 3492 for times).

Two direct **buses** run from Sydney to Church Point: #E86 from Central Station or #156 from Manly Wharf; it's then a ten-minute uphill walk. Alternatively a 24-hour **water-taxi** service operates from Newport (Pink Water Taxi ☎02/9634 4791); bus #190 from Wynyard runs up the coast to Newport.

The Church Point–Halls Wharf ferry service can also get you to and from **Scotland Island** at the southern end of Pittwater, where it stops on the forty-minute round trip from Church Point. The bush-clad island is residential only, with no sealed roads or shops, just a school, a kindergarten and a bush-fire brigade, and makes for an interesting wander.

The Hawkesbury River

One of New South Wales' prettiest rivers, with bush covering its banks for much of its course, and some interesting old settlements alongside, the **Hawkesbury River** has its source in the Great Dividing Range and flows out to sea at Broken Bay. For information about the many national parks along the river, contact the NPWS in Sydney (see p.28) or at 370 Windsor Rd in Richmond (☎02/4588 5247). Short of chartering your own boat, the best way to explore the river system is to take a cruise (see box on p.290); the River Boat Mail Run is the most interesting.

Upstream: Wisemans Ferry and around

The first ferry across the Hawkesbury River was opened by ex-convict Solomon Wiseman in 1827, ten years after he was granted 200 acres of river frontage at the spot now known as **WISEMANS FERRY**. The crossing forged an inland connection between Sydney and the Hunter Valley via the convict-built Great North Road. Unfortunately, travellers on this isolated route were easy prey for marauding bushrangers and it was largely abandoned for the longer but safer coastal route. Today it's a popular recreational spot for day-trippers – just a little over an hour from Sydney by car, and with access to the **Dharug National Park** over the river by a free 24-hour car ferry. Dharug's rugged sandstone cliffs and gullies shelter Aboriginal rock engravings which can be visited only on ranger-led trips during school holidays; there's a camping area at Mill Creek (contact Gosford NPWS on ☎02/4320 4203 for details of walks and camping; bookings for both are essential at weekends and during holiday periods). Open to walkers, cyclists and horse-riders but not vehicles, the **Old Great North Road** was literally carved out of the rock by hundreds of convicts from 1829; you can camp en route at the Ten Mile Hollow camping area.

Taking the ferry across the river from Wisemans Ferry, it's a scenic nineteen-kilometre river drive north along Settlers Road, another convict-built route, to **ST ALBANS**, where you can partake of a cooling brew (or stay a while) at a pub built in 1836, the sandstone hewn *Settlers Arms Inn* (☎02/4568 2111, ⓕ4568 2046; en-suite rooms $130 mid-week, $150 weekends). The pub is set on two-and-a-half acres and many of the vegetables and herbs for the delicious home-cooked food are organically grown on site (lunch daily, dinner Fri–Sun).

Exploring the Hawkesbury River system

Brooklyn, just above the western mass of Ku-Ring-Gai Chase National Park, and reached directly by train from Central Station (Country Trains), is the base for Hawkesbury River Ferries (Ⓣ02/9985 7566), whose River Boat Mail Run still takes letters, as well as tourists, up and down the river. Departures are from Brooklyn Wharf on Dangar Road (Mon–Fri 9.30am excluding public holidays, connecting with trains from Sydney's Central Station and from Gosford; 4hr; $35 including morning tea; booking essential). They also run two-hour coffee cruises towards the mouth of the river (Mon–Thurs 1.30pm; $20), which can be used as transport to Patonga (see p.294; $10 one-way).

Gosford's Public Wharf is the starting point for the MV *Lady Kendall* (Ⓣ02/4323 1655, Ⓦwww.starshipcruises.com.au), which cruises both Brisbane Water and Broken Bay (Mon–Wed, Sat & Sun, daily during school & public holidays, 10.15am & 1pm; 2hr 30min; $22; bookings essential; licensed kiosk on board).

Windsor is the base for the *Hawkesbury Paddlewheeler* (Ⓣ02/4575 1171, Ⓦwww.paddlewheeler.com.au), which has a good-value Sunday afternoon Jazz Cruise: live jazz and a BBQ lunch for $28 (12.30–3pm; advance bookings essential).

Woy Woy is a port of call for the MV *Lady Kendall* (see above) at 10.40am and 12.10pm.

Boat and houseboat rentals

Barrenjoey Boating Services at Governor Phillip Park, Palm Beach (Ⓣ02/9974 4229), hires out **boats** which comfortably seat six people (from $40 2hr, $55 4hr, $90 8hr) and are perfect for fishing expeditions around the mouth of the Hawkesbury or Dangar Island. The centre has a fishing shop and sells bait supplies; you'll need to buy rather than hire rods here though. If you're keen to **fish** on the Hawkesbury and can get four people together, you can charter a boat, all the gear and bait, plus a skipper who knows exactly where to go for $150 a head – Fishabout Tours runs trips lasting 7hr and has a good reputation (Ⓣ02/9451 5420, Ⓦwww.fishnet.com.au/fishabout). **Houseboats** can be good value if you can get a group together, with prices starting from $530 a weekend and $960 a week for four people. The Sydney Visitor Centre in Sydney (Ⓣ02/9667 6050) has details of operators, or try Able Hawkesbury River Houseboats, on River Road in Wisemans Ferry (Ⓣ/1800 024 979, Ⓦwww.hawkesburyhouseboats.com.au), or Ripples Houseboats, 87 Brooklyn Rd, Brooklyn (Ⓣ02/9985 5534, Ⓦwww.ripples.com.au).

Accommodation and eating

The settlement of Wisemans Ferry was based around Wiseman's home, Cobham Hall, built in 1826. Much of the original building still exists in the blue-painted *Wisemans Ferry Inn* on the Old Great North Road (Ⓣ02/4566 4301, Ⓕ4566 4780; pub $60, motel $88), with characterful **rooms** upstairs sharing bathrooms, and en-suite motel-style rooms outside at the back. Bistro meals are served daily and there's entertainment on Sunday afternoons. Just across the road, with extensive grounds fronting onto the river, is the contrastingly modern *The Retreat at Wisemans* (Ⓣ02/4566 4422, Ⓦwww.wisemans.com.au; B&B $220 mid-week, $450 weekend), a 54-room resort. The upmarket motel rooms can't compete with the inn's colonial charm, but the location is superbly scenic and facilities include a restaurant, golf course, tennis courts, swimming pool, in-house masseuse and bike hire. Other accommodation in the area includes the *Del Rio Riverside Resort* (Ⓣ02/4566 4330, Ⓦwww.delrioresort.com.au; en-suite cabins $93–140), a **campsite** in Webbs Creek across the Webbs Creek car ferry, 3km south of Wisemans Ferry; facilities include a Chinese restaurant, swimming pool, tennis court and golf course.

Rosevale Farm Resort, 3km along Wisemans Ferry Road en route to Gosford (Ⓣ & Ⓕ02/4566 4207; on-site vans $45, riverfront $55, motel units $75), has more inexpensive camping and cabins in extensive bushland close to Dharug National Park.

The Upper Hawkesbury: Windsor and beyond

About 50km inland from Sydney and just a few kilometres apart, Windsor and Richmond are two of five towns founded by Governor Macquarie in the early nineteenth century to capitalize on the fertile, well-watered soil of the Upper Hawkesbury River area. Both are reached easily by train from Central Station via Blacktown.

WINDSOR is probably the best preserved of all the historic Hawkesbury towns, with a lively centre of narrow streets, spacious old pubs and numerous historic colonial buildings. It's terrifically popular on Sundays, when a market takes over the shady, tree-lined mall end of the main drag, George Street, and the *Macquarie Arms Hotel*, which claims to be the oldest pub in Australia, puts on live music – raucous rock'n'roll to befit the crowd of bikers and assorted cliques crowding the front verandah – on Thompson Square, the grassy village green opposite. Next door to the pub, the **Hawkesbury River Museum and Tourist Information Centre** (daily 10am–4pm; museum $2.50; Ⓣ02/4577 2310, Ⓦwww.hawkesburyweb.com) doles out local info. There are picnic tables along the river and a Sunday cruise leaves from the jetty across the road from the tourist office (see box opposite).

Just 7km northwest of Windsor, **Richmond**'s attractions include its unspoilt riverside setting, an old graveyard and settlers' dwellings. Cinema buffs could take in a bargain-priced film at the beautifully preserved Regent Twin Cinema, on the main road through town at 149 Windsor St (Ⓣ02/4578 1800, Ⓦwww.richmondregent.com.au).

Scenic drives from Windsor and Richmond

Driving via the Hawkesbury River area from Sydney is a very scenic way to get to the Blue Mountains via the Bells Line of Road or Hawkesbury Road, and to the Hunter Valley via Putty Road.

From Windsor, **Putty Road** (Route 69) heads north through beautiful forest country, along the eastern edge of the Wollemi National Park, to Singleton in the Hunter Valley.

From Richmond, the **Bells Line of Road** (Route 40), goes to Lithgow (see p.325) via Kurrajong, and is a great scenic drive; all along the way are fruit stalls stacked with produce from the valley. There's a wonderful view of the Upper Hawkesbury Valley from the lookout point at **Kurrajong Heights**, on the edge of the Blue Mountains.

Another scenic drive from Richmond to the Blue Mountains, emerging near Springwood (see p.314), is south along the **Hawkesbury Road**, with the **Hawkesbury Heights Lookout** halfway along providing panoramic views. Not far from the lookout is the modern solar-powered *Hawkesbury Heights YHA* (Ⓣ02/4754 5621; beds $20), with more views from its secluded bush setting, and no chance of overcrowding with only six twin rooms.

The Central Coast

The shoreline between Broken Bay and Newcastle, known as the **Central Coast**, is characterized by large **coastal lakes** – saltwater lagoons almost entirely enclosed, but connected to the ocean by small waterways. To travel anywhere on the Central Coast, you need to go through **GOSFORD**, perched on the north shore of Brisbane Water and just about within commuting distance of Sydney. Its proximity to the city has resulted in uncontrolled residential sprawl which has put a great strain on the once-unspoilt lakes. Around Gosford are two excellent **national parks** – Brisbane Water and Bouddi – and a couple of wildlife attractions: **Calga Springs Sanctuary** and the nearby **Australian Reptile Park**. Beyond the national parks, **Pearl Beach** and nearby **Patonga** are idyllic bay beach retreats, while, on the ocean, **Terrigal**, **Avoca** and **The Entrance** are all enjoyable holiday resorts.

For tourist information on the whole region, and accommodation bookings, contact **Central Coast Tourism** (ⓣ1800/806 258, ⓦwww.cctourism.com.au).

Gosford and around

Although there's plenty of accommodation in and around Gosford – details from **Central Coast Tourism**, near the train station at 200 Mann St (Mon–Fri 10am–4pm, Sat 10am–12.30pm; ⓣ02/4385 4074, ⓦwww.cctourism.com.au) – there's not much incentive to stay. Gosford's main appeal is as a gateway to a couple of excellent wildlife reserves, two wonderful national parks and beyond them a pair of idyllic beach retreats.

Transport on the coast

If you're **driving**, and want to enjoy the coastal scenery and lakes, follow the older Pacific Highway which heads to Newcastle via Gosford and Wyong, rather than the speedier Sydney–Newcastle Freeway which runs some way inland. The frequent **train** service from Central Station (Country Trains) to Gosford or Woy Woy also follows a very picturesque route. Bennetts Airport Shuttle (see "Airport Buses" box on p.33) gets you to the area direct from Sydney airport.

The fit and intrepid can get here by **bike**: from Manly, head up the northern beaches and hop on a ferry service from Palm Beach (see p.151) to **Ettalong** (departs Palm Beach daily 6.30am, 7.30am, 9am, 10.30am, noon, 2pm, 3.30pm & 5pm, except Sat from 7.30am, Sun from 9am; departs Ettalong daily 6am, 7am, 8am, 9.40am, 11.10am, 12.40pm, 4.10pm & 5.40pm, except Sat from 8am, Sun from 9.40am; $8 one-way; ⓣ02/9918 2747, ⓦwww.palmbeachferry.com.au), then continue up through Woy Woy and Gosford to the coast.

You can also reach **Patonga** by **ferry** with Palm Beach and Hawkesbury River Ferries (ⓣ02/9997 4815, ⓦwww.sydneysceniccruises.com), departing from Palm Beach daily at 11am (also 9am & 3.45pm hols & weekends; $6.50 one-way) and returning from Patonga at 4.15pm (also 9.30am & 3pm hols & weekends); Hawkesbury River Ferries (see box on p.290) also run a service from Brooklyn. Walkers can alight from the ferry and hike to Pearl Beach (see p.294).

Within the Central Coast area, a well-developed **bus service** is run by a collection of operators: Busways Central Coast (ⓣ02/4368 2277), Busways Peninsula (ⓣ02/4392 6666), Gosford Bus Service (ⓣ02/4325 1781) and The Entrance Red Bus Services (ⓣ02/4332 8655). For **taxis**, call Central Coast Taxis ⓣ13 10 08.

▲ Avoca Beach

Calga Springs Sanctuary

Fifteen minutes' drive west of Gosford, **Calga Springs Sanctuary**, just off the F3 freeway, at Peats Ridge Road, Calga (daily 9am–5pm; $15; ⓦwww.calgasanctuary.com), was set up by the former Federal Minister for the Environment, Barry Cohen, and his son in an attempt to save Australian wildlife from introduced species; entry fees to the 170-acre site, with its huge variety of native plants, birds and animals, include a knowledgeable guided tour along the 2km of walking trails past Aboriginal rock engravings.

Australian Reptile Park

A similar distance west of Gosford, just off the Pacific Highway, the **Australian Reptile Park** (daily 9am–5pm; $18; ⓦwww.reptilepark.com.au) has a long history of providing snake and funnel web spider venom for the Commonwealth Serum Laboratories, and you can watch both kinds of creatures being milked. The park has a good selection of native reptiles, many of which you would be lucky to spot in the wild. Eric, the largest saltwater crocodile in NSW, a hefty turtle found in a Sydney sewer and the Perentie lizard of central Australia are highlights. There are regular reptile shows and talks throughout the day. Kangaroos wander the grounds freely and are happy to be hand fed and patted. There are also displays of other native mammals including Tasmanian Devils, koalas and wombats.

Brisbane Waters and Bouddi national parks

Brisbane Waters National Park ($7 cars), immediately south of Gosford, is the site of the **Bulgandry Aboriginal engravings**, which are of a style unique to the Sydney region, with figurative outlines scratched boldly into sandstone. The site, no longer frequented by the Guringgai people – whose territory ranged south as far as Sydney Harbour and north to Lake Macquarie – is 7km southwest of Gosford off the Woy Woy Road.

Tiny **Bouddi National Park** ($7 cars) is 20km southeast along the coast, at the mouth of Broken Bay, and is a great spot for bushwalking, with **camping** facilities at Putty Beach, Little Beach and Tallow Beach: book through the NPWS office at 207 Albury St, Gosford (ⓣ02/4320 4203), which also has information on both parks.

Pearl Beach and Patonga

Surrounded by Brisbane Waters National Park, friendly, undeveloped **PEARL BEACH**, just over a 25-kilometre drive from Gosford via Woy Woy and Umina, is a small community which expands at weekends. There are holiday houses to rent, but no other accommodation. Besides the popular *Sit 'n' Chats Beach Cafe* (live jazz Sun noon–4pm) and a restaurant, *Pearls on the Beach* (licensed and BYO; bookings ⓣ02/4342 4400; closed Mon–Wed, no dinner Sun), there's a general store (daily 8am–6pm) also selling petrol, a real estate agent which can arrange holiday lets (ⓣ02/4341 7555, ⓦwww.pearlbeachrealestate.com.au; from $700 per week in peak season), and some tennis courts. The very pretty, sheltered beach, popular with families, has a relaxing open-access saltwater pool at one end.

You can walk from the end of Crystal Avenue to the neighbouring beach settlement of **PATONGA**, visiting Mount Ettalong lookout for excellent views and the **Crommelin Native Arboretum** en route (by road from Pearl Beach, Patonga is 2km southwest). The 45-minute walk is best undertaken on the last Sunday of the month when the **Patonga Beach market** is held (8am–4pm). Ocean Planet, 25 Broken Bay Rd, Ettalong Beach (ⓣ02/4342 2222, ⓦwww.oceanplanet.com.au; kayak hire from $30 half-day), offers **kayaking trips** on Patonga Creek (8km; 7hr; $92.50), with pick-ups from Woy Woy station.

To get to Pearl Beach or Patonga, take the Busways Peninsula **bus #50–53** (ⓣ02/4392 6666) from Woy Woy station or the **ferry** to Patonga from Palm Beach or Brooklyn (see box on p.290).

Terrigal

Twelve kilometres southeast of Gosford, beautiful **TERRIGAL**, backed by bush-covered hills, is one of the liveliest spots on the Central Coast, a thriving beach resort with a strong café culture. The big curve of beach has a picturesque sandstone headland, and the sheltered eastern end, The Haven, where the boats moor, is popular with families. With rocketing house prices all along the Central Coast, Terrigal's main street has been invaded by real estate agents and the town has taken a decidedly upmarket turn. Much of the social life revolves around the five-star *Crowne Plaza Hotel*, with its grand marble lobby and pricey boutiques, which dominates one end of **The Esplanade**.

Central Coast Tourism at Rotary Park, Terrigal Drive (daily 9am–5pm, May–Sept closed Sun; ⓣ02/4385 4430, ⓦwww.cctourism.com.au) is a good source of information on the whole region, and can make free accommodation bookings. Terrigal is a popular spot for **water-based activities**, and operators include Erina Sail 'n' Ski (ⓣ02/4365 2355; sailboarding lessons and hire); Sea Surf School (ⓣ02/4325 1870; private lesson $44 per hr); Central Coast Charters (ⓣ0427 665 544; ⓦwww.centralcoastcharters.net; ocean and river cruises, deep sea and game fishing); Kincumber Water-ski School (ⓣ0414 685 005; first-timer sessions $50); and the long-running, well-respected Terrigal Dive School (ⓣ02/4384 1219; five-day diving courses $385, shore or boat dives $45 own gear, $85 gear supplied).

To get to Terrigal, take Busways #67–69 from Gosford; #69 also links Terrigal to Avoca Beach (see opposite).

Accommodation and eating

Crowne Plaza Hotel Terrigal, the swanky resort **hotel** on the corner of Pine Tree Lane (☎02/4384 9111, ⓦwww.crowneplaza.com), has three restaurants, two bars, a nightclub, a pool, gym and tennis courts; all this costs from $210 per night, including buffet breakfast and champagne. The pleasant YHA-affiliated *Terrigal Beach Backpackers Lodge*, 12 Campbell Crescent (☎02/4385 3330, ⓦwww.terrigalbeachlodge.com.au; rooms $60, dorms $25), is only one minute's walk from the beach; boogie-boards are provided free. The upmarket motel *Tiarri Terrigal Beach* (☎02/4385 9654, ⓦwww.accommodationterrigal.com; all rooms with own courtyard $89 mid-week, $148 weekend) provides quality accomodation, and rents out apartments ($350–895). If you're after a holiday unit (from around $400 weekly), contact Hunters Real Estate, 104 Terrigal Esplanade (☎02/4384 1444, ⓔhunters@ozemail.com.au).

Terrigal has a great **café** scene: *Louvres*, 60 The Esplanade, is beachy but sophisticated with a lovely plant-filled courtyard, and serves all the café favourites (daily 8am–9pm); *Aromas on Sea* has the best café position (and great coffee, or drinks from the hotel bar with your food), on the breezy terrace of the *Crowne Plaza* looking right over the beach (daily 8am–5pm); while the local favourite is the tiny *Patcinos*, a block back from the beach at 17 Church St, near the hostel. The best fish and chips comes from *Fish Bonez,* 90 The Esplanade (takeaway or eat-in), while *The Break*, on Pinetree Lane behind the *Crowne Plaza*, specializes in gourmet pizzas; its fun, intimate **bar** is a good alternative to the *Crowne*'s packed beer garden – the *Florida Beach Bar* – or its posh *Lord Ashley Lounge* upstairs. The **restaurant** scene is dominated by Thai eateries: two of the best are the stylish *A-Oi Thai*, near the *Crowne Plaza* at 3 Kurrawyba Ave (☎02/4385 6611), and the cheap and cheerful *N Thai Sing*, 84 The Esplanade (☎02/4385 9700).

Avoca Beach

Six kilometres to the south of Terrigal, and altogether quieter, **AVOCA BEACH** is especially popular with surfers. A large, crescent-shaped and sandy beach between two headlands, it has its own surf life-saving club and a safe children's rock pool. West of the beach are the still waters of **Avoca Lake**. Avoca's pleasant small-town atmosphere is enhanced by the Avoca Beach Theatre (☎02/4382 2156), a little-changed early-1950s cinema near the beach on Avoca Drive. You can **learn to surf** with Central Coast Surf School (☎02/4382 1020; 1hr lesson $25); Aquamuse (☎02/4368 4172), by the bridge in Heazlett Park, hires out pedal-boats, pedal-bikes, kayaks and surf skis to use on the lake.

To **get to Avoca**, take Busways #65–67 from Gosford or #69 from Terrigal.

Accommodation and eating

Limited overnight **accommodation** in Avoca includes the self-contained cabins and villas of *The Palms*, Carolina Park, off The Round Drive (☎02/4382 1227, ⓦwww.palmsavoca.com.au; $160–215), an upmarket, garden-set holiday resort which has swimming pools, spa, and games room. Otherwise, the best bet is to rent a holiday unit (from $450 per week) – call George Brand Real Estate (☎02/4382 1311) for listings.

For **eating**, grab fish and chips, gourmet and veggie burgers and Turkish bread sandwiches from the groovy, colourful *Burger Girls*, at the end of the main set of shops at 168 Avoca Drive (8.30am–9.30pm, closed Tues & Wed, except school hols), or there's fine dining at the expensive French-run *Feast* at Shop 3, 85 Avoca Drive (☎02/4381 0707), at the end of the beach near the Surf Life Saving

Club, with an open deck right over the beach; adjacent *Aspex & Seafood Spot* is a great place for a coffee or a cheaper meal with its own beachfront terrace.

The Entrance

Further north, Tuggerah and Munmorah lakes meet the sea at **THE ENTRANCE**, a beautiful place with water extending as far as the eye can see. It's a favourite fishing spot with anglers – and with swarms of **pelicans**, which turn up for the afternoon fish-feeds (daily 3.30pm; free) at Memorial Park, near the visitor centre (see below).

The beaches and lakes along the coast from here to Newcastle are crowded with caravan parks, motels and outfits offering the opportunity to fish, windsurf, sail or waterski; although less attractive than places further north, they make a great day-trip or weekend escape from Sydney. Pro Dive Central Coast, 96 The Entrance Rd (T02/4334 1559), arranges **scuba-diving** lessons and daily boat dives, and rents out snorkelling and dive gear.

The **Entrance Visitors Centre**, on Marine Parade (daily 9am–5pm; T02/4385 4430 or 1800 806 258, Wwww.cctourism.com.au), has a free **accommodation** booking service. Get to The Entrance **by bus**, with The Entrance Red Bus Services: #21, #22, #23 from Gosford station; #24, #25, #26 from Tuggerah or Wyong train stations.

23

The Hunter Valley

New South Wales' most well-known wine region is the **Hunter Valley**, an area long synonymous with fine **wine** – in particular its golden, citrusy **semillon** and soft and earthy **shiraz**. While South Australian wines dominate the nation in terms of volume and popularity, the wineries of the Hunter Valley are mainly boutique operations where many of the wines offered for tasting can only be bought at the cellar door or through wine clubs. The first vines were planted in 1828, and some of the area's current wine-making families, such as the Draytons, date back to the 1850s. In what seems a bizarre juxtaposition, this is also a very important **coal-mining region**: in the **Upper Hunter Valley**, especially, the two often go hand-in-hand, but there is a big cultural divide between "the mineries and the wineries", as the locals put it. By far the best-known wine area is the **Lower Hunter Valley**, nestled under the picturesque **Brokenback Range** around the main town of **Cessnock** – even the town's jail and high school have their own vineyards – and the nearby wine-tasting area of **Pokolbin**.

However, the Pokolbin area can seem a little like an exhausting winery theme park. To experience the real appeal of the Hunter Valley wine country, with its charming bush and farming feel and its vast vineyards seemingly lost among forested ridges, red-soiled dirt tracks and paddocks with grazing cattle, take the Lovedale/Wilderness Road area north of Cessnock, or visit towns such as Wollombi, 28km southwest; Broke, 35km northwest; Branxton, 22km north; and the still unspoilt Upper Hunter, west of Muswellbrook, with its marvellous ridges and rocky outcrops.

The Lower Hunter

CESSNOCK, two hours' drive north of Sydney, is uninteresting in itself, and surprisingly unsophisticated given the wine culture surrounding it. Its big old country pubs are probably its best feature and staying in one provides a taste of Australian rural life. Most of the **wine-tasting** is around the area called **Pokolbin**, spread over three kilometres at the centre of the vineyards, 12–15km northwest of Cessnock, with some very salubrious accommodation and a fine-dining scene – all well enjoyed by weekending Sydneysiders out to pamper themselves. However, with its hot-air balloon trips, horse-and-carriage rides, overabundance of B&Bs, resorts packed with cafés, restaurants and shops, and a huge range of wineries offering tours, tastings and courses, the area can be less than relaxing. The focus of the area is the **Hunter Valley Gardens Village**

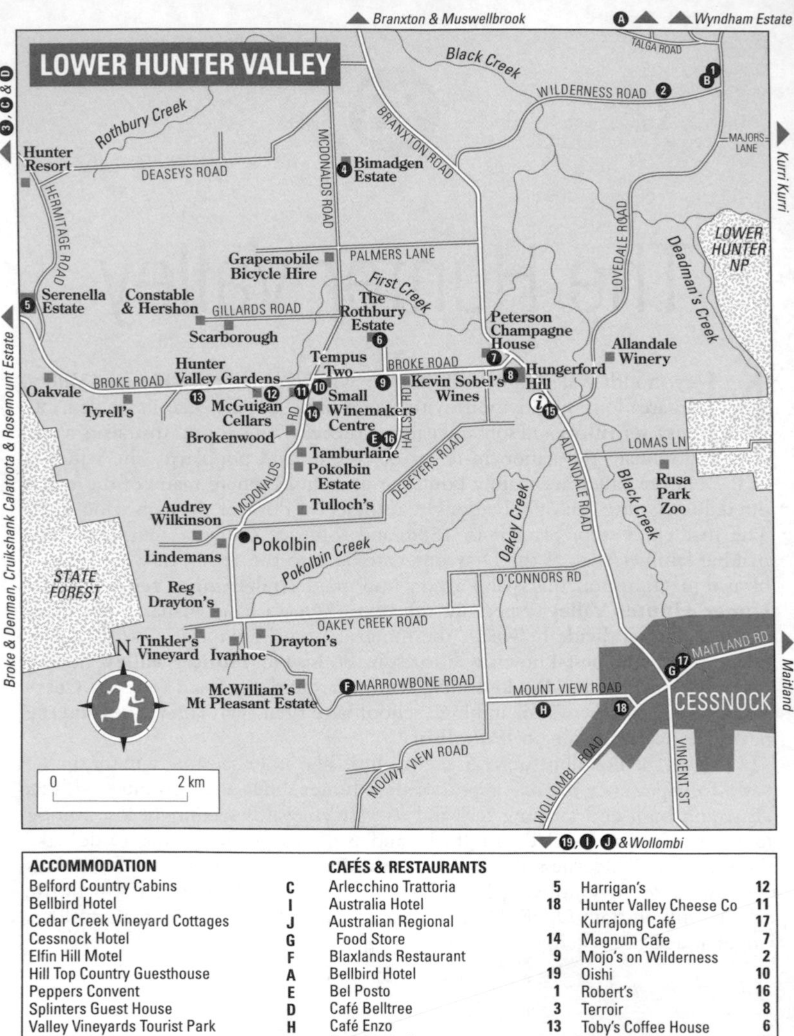

ACCOMMODATION		CAFÉS & RESTAURANTS			
Belford Country Cabins	C	Arlecchino Trattoria	5	Harrigan's	12
Bellbird Hotel	I	Australia Hotel	18	Hunter Valley Cheese Co	11
Cedar Creek Vineyard Cottages	J	Australian Regional Food Store	14	Kurrajong Café	17
Cessnock Hotel	G	Blaxlands Restaurant	9	Magnum Cafe	7
Elfin Hill Motel	F	Bellbird Hotel	19	Mojo's on Wilderness	2
Hill Top Country Guesthouse	A	Bel Posto	1	Oishi	10
Peppers Convent	E	Café Belltree	3	Robert's	16
Splinters Guest House	D	Café Enzo	13	Terroir	8
Valley Vineyards Tourist Park	H	Esca Bimbadgen	4	Toby's Coffee House	6
Wandin Valley Estate	B			Wine Country Cafe	15

a resort, shopping and dining complex set on extensive lakeside lawns against a backdrop of hills. The gardens include picnic grounds with coin-operated BBQs and a playground, and there's a handy general store plus specialist outlets for books, gifts, homewares, art, fashion and antiques.

Information and events

Pick up the excellent free *Hunter Valley Wine Country* guide with a handy pull-out map from the **Hunter Valley Wine Country Visitor Information Centre** (Mon–Thurs 9am–5.30pm, Fri & Sat 9am–6pm, Sun 9am–4pm; ⓣ02/4990 4477, ⓦwww.winecountry.com.au), Main Road, Pokolbin, scenically sited among vineyards with the pleasant, affordable *Wine Country Café*. If it's closed you can still pick up the free guides from a rack outside. Try to tour the wineries during the week; at weekends both the number of visitors and accommodation prices go up, and it can get booked out completely when there's a concert on in the valley. In late October Wyndham Estate (see box on pp.300–301) hosts the night-time **Opera in the Vineyards** (bookings via Ticketek ⓣ02/9266 4800; tickets $72–112; ⓦwww.wyndhamestate.com) on the banks of the Hunter River, followed a week later by a day of fine food, wine and music at **Jazz in the Vines** (ⓣ02/4933 2439, ⓦwww.jazzinthevines.com.au; tickets $35–70) based at Tyrell's vineyard (box on pp.300–301). In late November (and in early March), Bimbadgen Estate (p.304) hosts **A Day on the Green**, a sunset concert in their amphitheatre, featuring the likes of Elvis Costello and Bryan Adams (tickets through Ticketek; $75–100; ⓦwww.adayonthegreen.com.au).

Other Hunter Valley activities include **hot air ballooning** – Balloon Aloft Australia offers sunrise champagne flights ($280, standbys $220; ⓣ02/4938 1955 or 1800 028 568, ⓦwww.balloonaloft.com). *Hill Top Country Guesthouse* (see p.303) offers cross-country **horseriding** on its 300-acre property ($45; 1hr 30min) and a 4WD wildlife-spotting tour ($30; 1hr), which leaves at dusk, when you're likely to see kangaroos, wallabies and wombats.

Getting there and tours

By car, the Lower Hunter Valley is two hours north of Sydney along the National Highway 1 (the F3), or for a more scenic route turn off the F3 towards Peats Ridge and drive via the **Wollombi Valley**, stopping off at the the pretty village of Wollombi, with its nineteenth-century sandstone architecture and popular pub. A meandering route from the Blue Mountains via **Putty Road** is popular with motorcyclists. Rover Coaches (ⓣ02/4990 1699, ⓦwww.rover-coaches.com.au) leaves daily from Sydney Airport, Central Station and Circular Quay via Newcastle and Maitland to Cessnock and on to Pokolbin resorts. Keans (ⓣ02/6543 1322) goes from Central Station to Scone via the Hunter Valley (once daily except Sat); stops include Kurri Kurri, Neath, Cessnock, Pokolbin and Muswellbrook. For the Upper Hunter, take a train to Newcastle and then Sid Fogg's Coachlines (ⓣ02/4928 1088).

Getting around has been made easier with the introduction of Rover Coaches daily **hop-on, hop-off** Wine Rover service; stops include the tourist office, around eighteen wineries plus eating places (Mon–Fri $35, Sat & Sun $40). **Vineyard tours** are also an option, with a big range on offer. Many are exhausting return trips from Sydney (see box on pp.300–301), but several local operators offer day-trips from within the valley. The excellent, long-established Hunter Valley Day Tours (ⓣ02/4938 5031, ⓦwww.huntertourism.com/daytours) offers a wine-and-cheese tasting tour ($80 for Cessnock, Pokolbin and Maitland pick-ups; $95 from Newcastle; restaurant lunch included), with very informative commentary. The long-established, family-run, Hunter Vineyard Tours (ⓣ02/4991 1659, ⓦwww.huntervineyardtours.com.au) visits five wineries (Cessnock pick-up $50, Newcastle or Maitland $55; restaurant lunch $25 extra). Also recommended are Trek About 4WD Tours (ⓣ02/4990 8277, ⓦwww.hunterweb.com.au/trekabout; $44) and Aussie Wine Tours (ⓣ02/4991 1074, ⓦwww.aussiewinetours.com.au; $45 weekend, $40 mid-week), both supportive of small local wineries and flexible. Otherwise, you can **rent bikes** from Grapemobile, on the corner of McDonalds Road and Palmers Lane, Pokolbin (ⓣ0500 804 039, ⓦwww.grapemobile.com.au; $22 per day), or hire a **taxi** (Cessnock RadioCabs ⓣ02/4990 1111).

Hunter Valley wineries

Nearly 150 wineries cluster around the Lower Hunter Valley and fewer than twenty in the Upper Hunter; almost all offer **free wine tastings**. Virtually all wineries are open daily, at least between 10am and 4pm, and many offer **guided tours**. These include: McWilliams Mt Pleasant Estate, Marrowbone Rd, Pokolbin (daily 11am; 45min; $2.20; no bookings required); Hunter Resort, Hermitage Rd, Pokolbin (daily 11am & 2pm; 45min; $5, refunded on wine purchase; bookings ⊕02/4998 7777); and at Drayton's, Tyrell's, Wandin Valley and Wyndham Estate, all detailed below.

The Hunter Resort also runs an excellent **wine course** (daily 9–11am; $25; bookings essential) including a tour followed by a tasting instruction tutorial; and Ivanhoe, Marrowbone Rd, Pokolbin, conducts free wine appreciation classes (daily 10.30am & 1pm; 45min; no bookings required) with hillside vineyard views from the balcony. There are **museums** at the famous Lindeman's, McDonalds Rd, Pokolbin (daily 10am–5pm), where Dr Lindeman first planted his vines in 1842; the swish Tulloch's (Debeyers Rd, Pokolbin), whose display includes early twentieth-century photos by Australian photographer and family friend, Max Dupain; Reg Drayton Wines (cnr McDonalds and Pokolbin Mountains roads, Pokolbin); and a nineteenth-century "shop" museum at Oakvale (Broke Rd, Pokolbin), whose tasting area also sells a great selection of **wine-related books**. Some impressive new **state-of-the art wineries** are worth checking out, too, including the space-station-like Hungerford Hill (Broke Rd, Pokolbin ⊕02/4990 0711), with its fine-dining restaurant *Terroir* (mains $15–32) and smart café. Enjoy fine panoramic **views** at Audrey Wilkinson (Debeyers Rd, Pokolbin) and Tinklers Vineyard (see p.304), from where you can continue to the Pokolbin Mountains Lookout. The award-winning Pepper Tree Wines, Halls Rd, Pokolbin, with its French-rustic feel, has beautiful **gardens**. Below are a few more of our favourites, but by meandering you'll inevitably discover your own gems.

Allandale Lovedale Rd, Pokolbin. Picturesque, medium-sized winery established in 1978. Set on a hill, with great views overlooking the vineyard and the Brokenback Range. All their wines are highly recommended but make sure you try the prize-winning chardonnay. Mon–Sat 9am–5pm, Sun 10am–5pm.

Constable & Hershon Gillards Rd, Pokolbin. Established in 1981 by two best friends, this small establishment feels like a personal dream come true (wine is made by contract winemaker Neil McGuigan; the owners visit on annual holiday from England). The vineyard under the Brokenback Ranges has five formal gardens – Sculpture, Camellia, Rose, Herb and Secret – and you're encouraged to wander around with a glass of semillon; or on weekdays at 10.30am the gardener leads a tour. Unhurried sit-down tastings. Daily 10am–5pm.

Cruikshank Callatoota Estate Wybong Rd, Wybong, Upper Hunter Valley, 18km north of Denman. Owner John Cruikshank has been making red wine here since 1974. All grapes are estate-grown and everything is done in-house, including the bottling. The slow pace – only the well-regarded rosé is rushed off the shelves – and unpretentious cellar door suits the remote feel of the place whose vineyards nestle below bush-covered ridges. BBQ and picnic facilities, or light lunch available. Daily 9am–5pm.

Drayton's Family Wines Oakey Creek Rd, Pokolbin. Friendly, down-to-earth winery, established in 1853. Everything is still done here and the excellent free tours (Mon–Fri

Accommodation

Since the Hunter Valley is a popular weekend trip for Sydneysiders, accommodation **prices** rise on Friday and Saturday nights and most places only offer two-night deals; the price ranges below indicate the substantial mid-week to

11am; 40min) show the whole process. A pretty picnic area with wood-fired BBQ overlooks a small dam and vineyards. Mon–Fri 8am–5pm, Sat & Sun 10am–5pm.

Peterson Champagne House Cnr Broke and Branxton roads, Pokolbin. The only Hunter Valley winery to specialize in sparkling wines, who also use their *methode champenoise* expertise to produce for other wineries. The pretty duck-pond-set stone building makes a pleasant tasting and eating spot: the *Magnum Café*'s fantastic, well-priced cooked breakfast (daily 9am–11am) can be teamed with some champers. For more indulgence, the Hunter Valley Chocolate Factory is right next door. Daily 9am–5pm.

Rosemount Estate Rosemount Rd, 8km west of Denman, Upper Hunter ⓣ02/6549 6400. Producer of some of Australia's best-known, award-winning wines. Its excellent brasserie with pub-food prices (lunch Wed–Sun, dinner Thurs–Sat) is a relaxing spot, with marvellous vineyard views. Also picnic tables and BBQs. Daily 10am–4pm.

Scarborough Gilliards Rd, Pokolbin. Small, friendly winery with a reputation for outstanding wines; specializes in chardonnay and pinot noir. Pleasantly relaxed sit-down tastings are held in a small cottage on Hungerford Hill with wonderful valley views. Daily 9am–5pm.

Tamburlaine McDonalds Rd, Pokolbin. The jasmine-scented garden outside offers a hint of the flowery, elegant wines within. Tastings are well orchestrated and delivered with heaps of experience. Daily 9.30am–5pm.

Tempus Two Broke Rd, Pokolbin. This huge, spectacular winery – all steel, glass and stone – looks worth every cent of the $7 million it cost. A high-tech urban chic exterior – terrace, fountains and ampitheatre – meets a rural landscape of vineyards and dam; its contemporary interior continues down even to the sinuous bottles with their distinctive pewter labels. Owned by Lisa McGuigan, of the well-known winemaking family, whose unique-tasting wines are the result of using lesser-known varieties such as pinot gris, viognier and marsanne. The attached Japanese-Thai *Oishi* (ⓣ02/4993 3999) restaurant has surprisingly moderate prices (noodle soups $8, mains $16.50), or there's a lounge area where you can relax over an espresso. Daily 9am–5pm.

Tyrrell's Broke Rd, Pokolbin. The oldest independent family vineyards, producing consistently fine wines. The tiny ironbark slab hut, where Edward Tyrrell lived when he began the winery in 1858, is still in the grounds, and the old winery with its cool earth floor is much as it was. Beautiful setting against the Brokenback Range. One of the best. Mon–Sat 8am–5pm, with free tour 1.30pm.

Wandin Valley Estate Cnr Wilderness and Lovedale roads. Picturesquely sited on a hundred acres of vineyard with magnificent views across the Wategos and the Brokenback Ranges, especially from the balcony of the European-style *Bel Posto* café/restaurant (ⓣ02/4930 7317; mains $17–20; cellar-door priced wine). Free tours Sat & Sun 11am. Daily 10am–5pm.

Wyndham Estate, Dalwood Rd, Dalwood. A scenic drive through the Dalwood Hills leads to the Lower Hunter's northern extent, where Englishman George Wyndham first planted shiraz in 1828. Now owned by multinational Pernod Ricard, there's an excellent guided tour (daily 11am; free) which covers the vines and winemaking techniques and equipment, including the original basket press. The idyllic riverside setting – grassy lawns, free BBQs – makes a great spot for picnics and the annual opera concert. Restaurant (ⓣ02/4938 3444) and outdoor café. Daily 10am–4.30pm.

weekend variable. Advance **booking** is essential for weekends, or during the October–November events.

Belford Country Cabins 659 Hermitage Rd, Pokolbin ⓣ02/6574 7100, ⓦwww.belfordcabins.com.au. Family-run, fully equipped self-catering two- and four-bedroom wooden bungalows set in bushland. Comfy, spacious and clean cabins – renovated

▲ Pepper Tree cellar door

ones are quite stylish – each with its own barbecue. Games room with pool table, table tennis and TV, outdoor pool and playground. $100–120.

Bellbird Hotel 388 Wollombi Rd, Bellbird, 5km southwest of Cessnock ⓣ02/4990 1094, ⓕ4991 5475. Classic country pub, circa 1908, with wide iron-lace verandah and a bar full of rustic charm. Eat inexpensive no-frills bistro food in the pleasant beer garden, which has an adjacent playground. All rooms share bathrooms. Mid-week light breakfast included ($69), and weekend cooked breakfast ($85–105).

Cedar Creek Vineyard Cottages Wollombi Rd, Cedar Creek, 10km northwest of Wollombi ⓣ02/4998 1576, ⓦwww.cedarcreekcottages.com.au. An idyllic choice away from the busy Pokolbin area on a 550-acre deer- and cattle-stocked farm. Run by Stonehurst Wines, the tiny chapel-like tasting room, constructed from recycled materials, stocked with wine from insecticide-free, handpicked, estate-grown grapes, well illustrates the owner's philosophy. Self-catering cottages are made from recycled timber. Expect queen-sized beds, wood combustion stoves, ceiling fans, CD-players, stylish decor, breakfast hampers and a BBQ; civilized noon check-out. $129–179.

Cessnock Hotel 234 Wollombi Rd, Cessnock ⓣ02/4990 1002, ⓦwww.huntervalleyhotels.com.au. Renovated pub with a great bistro-cum-bar, the *Kurrajong Café*. Rooms all share bathrooms but they're huge with high ceilings, fans and really comfy beds. Big verandah to hang out on and cooked breakfasts served in the café. B&B $65–105.

Elfin Hill Motel Marrowbone Rd, Pokolbin ⓣ02/4998 7543, eelfinhill@hunterlink.com

.au. Friendly, family-run hilltop motel with comfortable timber-cabin-style air-con units and extensive views – particularly good value mid-week. Facilities include a pool and BBQ area and there are plans for a common room and guest kitchen. Mon–Thurs $98, includes breakfast. Fri & Sat $159, Sun $120.

Hill Top Country Guest House 288 Talga Rd, Rothbury ⓣ02/4930 7111, ⓦwww.hilltopguesthouse.com.au. Rural retreat on three hundred acres with fantastic views. Explore the property on foot, by horse (see p.299), two-seater bush buggy ($60 per hour), mountain bike ($16.50 half-day), 4WD tour (see p.299), or take a canoe on the dam ($35 per hour). The modern brick building has the feel of an old-fashioned guesthouse, with a piano, billiard table and wood fires. Mock-antique-style bedrooms have TV ($110–160); cheaper ones share bathroom ($88–140). Also a large unit with a spa (mid-week $154, weekend $220). Light breakfast included (lunch and dinner available).

Hunter Valley Gardens Broke Rd, Pokolbin ⓣ02/4998 7854, ⓦwww.hvg.com.au. Set in extensive lakeside gardens, this resort has a handy upmarket shopping mall complete with cafés – including the recommended *Bliss Coffee Roasters* – and restaurants. The modern combined motel and hotel complex overlooks the vineyards, and has a popular Irish pub and bistro, *Harrigan's*, an Italian restaurant, a heated pool, spa, sauna, tennis courts and three standards of accommodation: pricey four-and-a-half-star in the 72-room *Tallawanta Lodge* ($300 B&B mid-week, weekend $330); smart four-star motel-style in *Harrigan's* ($225–250); or in self-contained one- and two-bedroom cabins at *Grapeview Villas* ($79–145).

Peppers Convent Halls Rd, Pokolbin ⓣ02/4998 7764, ⓦwww.peppers.com.au. The swankiest place to stay in the Hunter Valley, with a price to match (from $360 per night). The guesthouse, converted from an old nunnery, is very cosy, with fireplaces and low beams, and is part of the Pepper Tree Winery (see box on pp.300–301), with fine-dining at *Robert's at Peppertree* (see p.304), just a stroll away.

Splinters Guest House 617 Hermitage Rd, Pokolbin ⓣ02/6574 7118, ⓦwww.splinters.com.au. Built and run by an affable former woodwork teacher, the mezzanine-bedroomed cottages on this 25-acre property come with slate floors, wood-combustion stoves, leather armchairs and kitchens with coffee machines (cook-your-own breakfast supplied). En-suite rooms have mini espresso machines and egg cookers (light breakfast included); port and chocolate in every room. There's a covered BBQ area with a telescope, a practice golf green and walking tracks. Wineries and restaurant within wandering distance. Best value around, especially mid-week. Cottages $150–240 weekend; rooms $115–165.

Valley Vineyards Tourist Park Mount View Rd, 2km northwest of Cessnock ⓣ02/4990 2573, ⓦwww.valleyvineyard.com.au. High-standard camping site with camp kitchen, BBQ area, pool and on-site Thai restaurant. Cabins (BYO linen) have external en suites, cottages (linen included) internal. Cabins $60–85; cottages $85–120.

Wandin Valley Estate Wilderness Rd, Lovedale ⓣ02/4930 7317, ⓦwww.wandinvalley.com.au. Two- to four-bedroom cathedral-ceilinged, two-level Tuscan-style villas situated on a wonderful winery estate (see box on pp.300–301). You can wander from your villa through vineyards, where grazing kangaroos are a common sight. Comfortable and stylish (though some bathrooms are disappointing), with everything from woodfires to wine books. Expect two bottles of wine and generous cook-your-own breakfast provisions. Portable BBQ, swimming pool and tennis court. Rates include up to four people: mid-week $200 (three nights for $400), weekends $300–400.

Eating and drinking

Many of the Hunter's excellent (and pricey) restaurants are attached to wineries or are among vineyards rather than in the towns (see box on pp.300–301), while the large old pubs dish out less fancy but more affordable grub; see the "Accommodation" section above for bistro options. Every year over a mid-May weekend around eight wineries along and around the scenic Lovedale and Wilderness roads team up with local restaurants to host the **Lovedale Long Lunch** (ⓣ02/4930 7611, ⓦwww.lovedalelonglunch.com.au). The Hunter olive-growing industry has also taken off: check out the Hunter Olive Centre (Pokolbin Estate Vineyard, McDonalds Rd, Pokolbin; ☎02/4998 7524), where you can enquire about the weekend-long **Feast of the Olive Festival** in late September. Other places where you can taste the local wares include The Hunter Valley Cheese Company at the McGuigan Cellars, Broke Road; the newer Binnorie Dairy, just across the road from the Hunter Resort (p.303), which specializes in soft fresh cheeses; and fresh farm produce at Tinkler's Vineyard, Pokolbin Mountain Road. Just about every winery and accommodation place in the valley has a BBQ, – for picnic or self-catering supplies there's the large Coles **supermarket** in Cessnock, at 1 North Ave (Mon–Sat 6am–midnight, Sun 8am–8pm), or the small supermarket in the Hunter Valley Gardens Village. You can also get deli supplies from the Australian Regional Food Store at the Small Winemakers Centre on McDonalds Rd and try local-brewed beer at the Blue Tongue Brewery at the Hunter Resort (daily 7.30am–midnight).

Arlecchino Trattoria Serenella Estate, Hermitage Rd, Pokolbin ☎02/4998 7120. Stylish interpretation of a trattoria, attached to the Cecchini-family-established winery. The wood-fired pizza ($10.50–18) is worth the drive out here; a small but delicious menu includes pasta and risotto ($17), a few meaty mains ($24) and *gelato*. The dining room, with cool stone floors and crisp white tablecloths, overlooks a dam and vineyards from windows on three sides. Lunch Wed–Sun, dinner Wed–Sat.

Australia Hotel 136 Wollombi Rd, Cessnock. The excellent bistro here is popular with the locals, and the pub showcases the Hunter's coal-mining roots with mining paraphernalia and related art. Though some steaks hit the $25 mark, mains average $15–19, and the menu encompasses stir-fries, gourmet salads and vegetarian dishes.

Café Belltree Margan Family Winegrowers, 266 Hermitage Rd, Pokolbin ☎02/6574 7216. Winemaker Andrew Margan turns out some tasty wines, and the attached Mediterranean-influenced eatery is pretty good too. Dishes use seasonal local produce, and a changing blackboard menu of shared platters (around $20) adds to the convivial atmosphere. You'll need to book, despite the café appellation. The deck is a great spot to hang out with a slice of cake and a coffee and soak up the isolated bush feel in the quiet mornings or late afternoons. Daily 10am–5pm.

Café Enzo Peppers Creek Antiques, Broke Rd, Pokolbin. Relaxing courtyard café which feels like it's been lifted from the south of France; light Mediterranean menu ($14–25) and excellent Italian-style coffee, or start the day here with a cooked breakfast. It's pricey but the spot is worth it. Mon & Tues 10am–4pm, Wed–Sun 9am–5pm.

Esca Bimbadgen Lot 21, McDonalds Rd, Pokolbin ☎02/4998 4666. With a squint this winery, complete with fountain and bell tower, could be in Europe. Its modern restaurant, however, is all timber and glass, reached via the working winery (make sure you taste the wines before dining), and with wonderful vineyard and mountain views from the balcony. Food, with mains around the $32 mark, is contemporary European, with veal, spatchcock and roast duck all on the menu. Lunch daily, dinner Wed–Sat.

Mojo's on Wilderness Wilderness Rd, Lovedale ☎02/4930 7244. A British Michelin-rated chef and his Australian chef-wife create the divine modern British/Australian food at this bush-set restaurant. Warm, local-art decorated interior, flowery courtyard with hillside views, cheerful staff and a laidback vibe. Set dinner menu (2-courses $48, 3-courses $60) has suggested wines for each course, many from the immediate area and all available by the glass (lunch mains $17–27). Popular all-day Sunday brunch (10am–3pm) with outstanding Eggs Benedict. Lunch & dinner Thurs–Mon.

Robert's at Peppertree Peppertree Winery, Halls Rd, Pokolbin ☎02/4998 7330. Robert's is a long-established Hunter Valley fine-dining institution, as much for the setting in a charming 1876 wooden farmhouse filled with flowers and antiques, and shaded by a huge peppertree, as for the French rustic-style food cooked in a wood-fired oven. Mains average $38.

Toby's Coffee House The Rothbury Estate, Broke Rd, Pokolbin. Upstairs, above the Rothbury Estate cellar door, this contemporary-style café's huge windows provide views over vineyards and bush to far-off hills. Focus is on the smooth, rich Toby's Estate Coffee to enjoy with a selection of great cakes and cookies. A simple all-day menu – shareable cheese plates from Binnorie Dairy ($20), antipasto plates ($17) or mugs of soup with a baguette ($6.50) – can be enjoyed with a glass of Rothbury Estate wine ($5.50). Daily 10.30am–3.30pm.

The Upper Hunter

If you plan to tour the **Upper Hunter**, ask the tourist office at Pokolbin for the useful fold-out brochure and map, *Discover the Wineries of the Upper Hunter Valley*, produced by the Upper Hunter Winemakers Association; the little settlement of **SANDY HOLLOW** on the Golden Highway (Route 84), in the Goulburn River Valley and close to the Goulburn River National Park and Wollemi National Park, makes a good base; try the excellent *Sandy Hollow Tourist Park*, set in twenty grassy acres backed by bush-covered outcrops, with a large swimming pool, camp kitchen and open fires (Ⓣ02/6547 4575, en-suite cottages and cabins with linen $68–140, plus camping). There are good meals at the country pub, the *Tourist Hotel*, and excellent coffee at *David Mahoney Art Gallery and Coffee House* on the edge of town.

24

The Blue Mountains region

The section of the Great Dividing Range nearest Sydney gets its name from the blue mist that rises from millions of eucalyptus trees and hangs in the mountain air, tinting the sky and the range alike. In the early days of the colony, the **Blue Mountains** were believed to be an insurmountable barrier to the west. The first expeditions followed the streams in the valleys until they were defeated by cliff faces rising vertically above them. Only

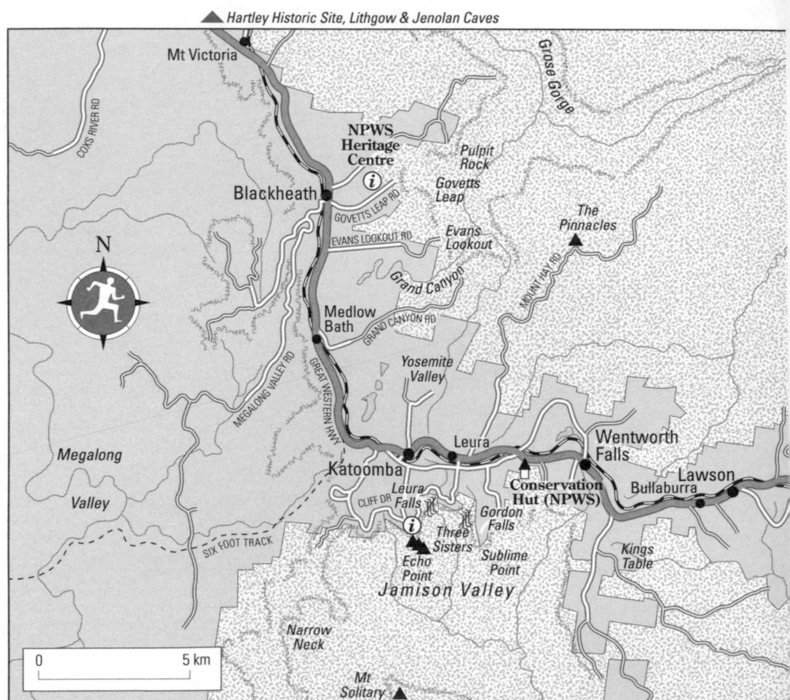

in 1813, when the explorers Wentworth, Blaxland and Lawson followed the ridges instead of the valleys, were the mountains finally conquered, allowing the western plains to be opened up for settlement. The range is surmounted by a plateau at an altitude of more than 1000m where, over millions of years, rivers have carved deep valleys into the sandstone, and winds and driving rain have helped to deepen the ravines, creating spectacular scenery of sheer precipices and walled canyons. Before white settlement, the Daruk Aborigines lived here, dressed in animal-skin cloaks to ward off the cold. An early coal-mining industry, based in Katoomba, was followed by tourism which snowballed after the arrival of the railway in 1868; by 1900 the first three mountain stations of Wentworth Falls, Katoomba and Mount Victoria had been established as fashionable resorts, extolling the health-giving benefits of eucalyptus-tinged mountain air. In 2000 the Blue Mountains became a **World Heritage Listed** site, joining the Great Barrier Reef; the listing came after abseiling was finally banned on the mountains' most famous scenic wonder, the **Three Sisters**, after forty years of clambering had caused significant erosion. The Blue Mountains stand out from other Australian forests, in particular for the recently discovered **Wollemi Pine** (see p.321), a "living fossil", which dates back to the dinosaur era.

All the villages and towns of the romantically dubbed "**City of the Blue Mountains**" – the main ones being Glenbrook, Springwood, Wentworth Falls, Leura, Katoomba and Blackheath – lie on a ridge, connected by the Great Western Highway. Around them is the **Blue Mountains National Park**, the fourth-largest national park in the state and to many minds the best. The region

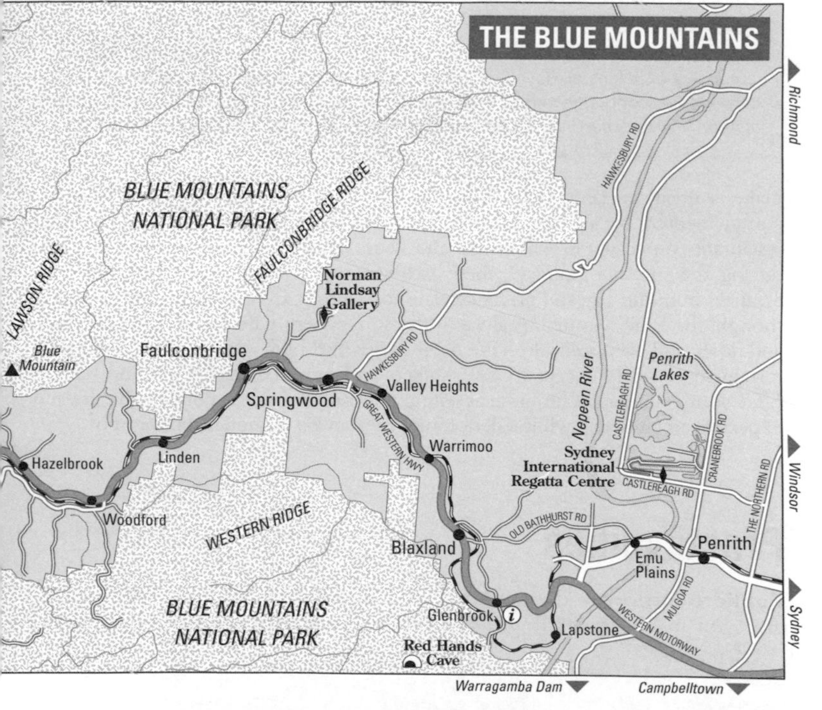

Blue Mountains tours

From Sydney

Several operators run day-tours from Sydney; we've listed a range of recommended outfits below. Some operators also package up accommodation and activity deals.

Oz Experience 761–763 George St, near Central Station (ⓣ02/9213 1766 or 1300 300 028, ⓦwww.ozexperience.com). Their active one-day tour ($85) includes a 3-hour mountain bike trip along a bush track, a day and an evening bush walk, and a ride on the Scenic Railway. You can go back the same day, or opt to stay overnight at Katoomba YHA (for an extra charge).

Oz Trek (ⓣ02/9666 4662 or 1300 661 234, ⓦwww.oztrek.com.au). Active full-day tours ($54), with a choice of three bushwalks (30min–1hr 30min) in small groups (max 21). The trips can be extended to overnight packages with either horse riding ($209), abseiling ($209) or a Jenolan Caves visit ($179–199). City, Glebe, Kings Cross, Coogee and Bondi pick-ups.

Wildframe Ecotours (ⓣ02/9440 9915, ⓦwww.wildframe.com). Two full-day tours are available (both $82). The Grand Canyon Eco-tour, for fit walkers, includes a small-group bushwalk (max 16) through the Grand Canyon (5km; 3hr); BYO lunch in Katoomba. The Blue Mountains Bush Tour is more relaxed with several short bushwalks and BYO lunch in Blackheath. Kangaroo-spotting promised on both trips. Kings Cross and city pick-ups.

Wildspirit Adventure Company (ⓣ02/9371 5859, ⓦwww.wildspirit.com.au). Exploring the Blue Mountains' deep canyons requires a thrilling mixture of abseiling down waterfalls, swimming through cave slots, bushwalking and rock-climbing. Wet canyoning is offered Oct–April; dry canyoning is available all year. Depending on the area or the number of abseils, trips range from $160 to $210. The most popular wet-canyoning trip is to Fortress Creek (grade 2; $160), near Leura, picking up in central Sydney 7am, returning 7pm.

From the Blue Mountains

Blue Mountains Walkabout (ⓣ0408 443 822, ⓦwww.bluemountainswalkabout.com). An excellent all-day (8hr), off-the-beaten-track bush roam (around 10km) between Faulconbridge and Springwood led by an Aboriginal guide. Expect to look at Aboriginal rock carvings, taste bushtucker and swim in waterholes in summer ($95,

makes a great weekend break from the city, with stunning views and clean air complemented by a wide range of accommodation, cafés and well-regarded restaurants, especially in Katoomba and Leura. But be warned: at weekends, and during the summer holidays, these two spots in particular are thronged with escapees from the city, and prices escalate accordingly. Even at their most crowded, though, the Blue Mountains always offer somewhere where you can find peace and quiet, and even solitude – the deep gorges and high rocks make much of the terrain inaccessible except to bushwalkers and mountaineers. Climbing schools offer courses in rock-climbing, abseiling and canyoning for both beginners and experienced climbers, while Glenbrook is a popular mountain-biking spot.

Practicalities

Public transport to the mountains is quite good but your own vehicle will give you much greater flexibility once you've arrived, allowing you to take

BYO lunch; own train journey to Faulconbridge and back from Springwood). You can also plan to camp overnight in the bush with your own gear.

Fantastic Aussie Tours Main St, by Katoomba station (ⓣ02/4782 1866 or 1300 300 915, ⓦwww.fantastic-aussie-tours.com.au). Operate the **Blue Mountains Explorer Bus**, red double-decker ex-London buses which link Katoomba and Leura taking in all attractions with over thirty stops (departs Katoomba hourly 9.30am–4.30pm, last return 5.15pm, with a half-hourly shuttle service between Katoomba, Echo Point and Scenic World; $25 all-day pass can be used for up to seven days; includes discounts to attractions. There's no commentary but the pass comes with a useful 29-page guidebook with several maps and details of bushwalk and sightseeing options on the route. Also included (once only) is the one-hour Cliff Tops and Valleys Tour in an open-topped bus which takes in the scenic delights of lookouts such as Narrow Neck and the Landslide (departs from Scenic World hourly 11.45am–2.45pm), and a once-daily shuttle bus to the national park at Wentworth Falls (depart Katoomba St 9.15am, returning 5.25pm), where walks of one, two or three hours will get you to other Explorer Bus stops. Fantastic Aussie Tours also do large-group coach tours: there's a day-tour to the Jenolan Caves (daily; $85–92 with one cave entry) and a combined bushwalk and cave visit ($105), plus adventure caving ($150). A small-group half-day 4WD tour takes in the Blue Mountains National Park ($92).

Tread Lightly Eco Tours (ⓣ02/4788 1229, ⓦwww.treadlightly.com.au). Offering small-group expert-guided off-the-beaten-track half-day and full-day bushwalk and 4WD tours, picking up from Katoomba accommodation; their two-hour morning Wilderness Walk ($25) takes in some of the Six Foot Track (see box on p.319).

Trolley Tours Main St, by train station (ⓣ02/4782 7999 or 1800 801 577, ⓦwww.trolleytours.com.au). A minibus decked out like a tram, which does a scenic circuit with commentary from Katoomba (outside the Carrington Hotel) to Leura around Cliff Drive to the Three Sisters and back, taking in attractions along the way (8 daily, hourly to coincide with train arrivals, roughly 9.30am–5pm, plus shuttle buses every 30min between Katoomba, Echo Point and Scenic World; $12 all-day pass includes local Blue Mountains Bus Co services (see below) and discounts to attractions; wheelchair accessible.

detours to old mansions, cottage gardens and the lookout points scattered along the ridge. **Trains** leave from Central Station to Mount Victoria and/or Lithgow and follow the highway, stopping at all the towns and villages en route (frequent departures – roughly every hour, more frequently at rush hour – until about midnight; 2hr; $11.40 one-way to Katoomba, $14 off-peak day return). If you're dependent on public transport, Katoomba makes the best base: facilities and services are concentrated here, and there are **local buses** to attractions in the vicinity and to other centres. Blue Mountains Bus Co (ⓣ02/4751 3333, ⓦwww.mountainlink.com.au) has several commuter routes from Katoomba: to Blackheath via Medlow Bath; to Mount Victoria via Medlow Bath (no service weekends); to Echo Point and the Scenic World complex; to Leura and Gordon Falls; to Leura and Wentworth Falls via the Valley of the Waters; to North Katoomba via Minni Ha Ha Falls; to the Katoomba Aquatic Centre and Narrow Neck Rd; and to Springwood. Buses run daily between about 7am and 6pm, roughly half-hourly, and it costs $2.60, for example, to get to Echo Point, while an all-day bus pass, valid on all routes, including the Trolley Tour minibus detailed in the box above, costs $12. All buses leave from Katoomba Street outside the Carrington Hotel.

Information

The **Blue Mountains Information Centre** (Mon–Fri 9am–5pm, Sat & Sun 8.30am–4.30pm; ⓣ1300 653 408, ⓦwww.bluemts.com.au) is on the Great Western Highway at Glenbrook (see p.313), the gateway to the Blue Mountains. The centre has a huge amount of information on the area, including two of the most useful free publications: the quarterly *Blue Mountains Wonderland Visitors Guide*, which has several detailed colour maps and bushwalking notes (see the handy web version at ⓦwww.bluemountainswonderland.com), and an events guide, *Imag Monthly*. The other official tourist information centre is at **Echo Point**, near Katoomba (see p.316); both offices offer a **free accommodation booking** service. The Blue Mountains Online website (ⓦwww.bluemountainsonline.com.au) has a useful **weather report** worth consulting in advance: rain, mist and fog will mean no or very restricted views from lookout points; temperatures in winter are much lower than in Sydney, and nights are cool even in summer.

The huge **Blue Mountains National Park** has its main ranger station at Blackheath (p.323), where you can get comprehensive walking and camping information – there are NPWS camping and picnic sites reached by car near Glenbrook, Woodford, Wentworth Falls, Blackheath and Oberon and bush camping is allowed in most areas. The only point where vehicle entry must be paid to the national park is at Glenbrook ($7).

Accommodation

Katoomba has the greatest concentration of accommodation in the mountains. Bear in mind that **accommodation rates** rise on Friday and Saturday nights, so you might choose to visit on weekdays when it's quieter and cheaper. The prices given are for double rooms available in high season and the price range indicates midweek to weekend rates. Several real estate agents also rent out charming **holiday homes**: weekend rates, which average $300, are only $75 to $100 less than the weekly rate (linen extra), so consider staying longer: contact Soper Bros, 173 The Mall, Leura (ⓣ02/4784 1633, ⓦwww.soperbros.com.au), or Raine & Horne, 66 Katoomba St (ⓣ02/4782 2822, ⓦwww.bluemts.com.au/raineandhorne/holiday.asp). You can also **camp** at the NPWS sites (or there are two council-run **caravan parks**: on Katoomba Falls Rd, Katoomba (ⓣ02/4782 1835; en-suite cabins $72), and at Prince Edward St, Blackheath (ⓣ02/4787 8101; cabins $41, en suite $59).

Festivals

The **Blue Mountains Music Festival** (ⓦwww.bmff.org.au) is a three-day mid-March bash featuring folk, roots and blues from Australian and international musicians on several indoor and outdoor stages in Katoomba; it includes food and craft stalls and kids' entertainment (weekend ticket $135; $90 full-day ticket; $70 night ticket). **Winter Magic** (ⓦwww.wintermagic.com.au) is a day-long, pagan-feeling fancy dress celebration of the Southern Hemisphere winter solstice on a Saturday in mid-June. Katoomba Street is closed to traffic and lined with market and food stalls; there's a morning street parade, music stages dotted around town, and a firework display from the roof of the *Carrington Hotel*. On Sunday, the gardens at Everglades (see p.315) are the scene for a marvellous kids' treasure hunt and live entertainment.

Blue Mountains directory

Bookshops There are several interesting secondhand bookshops on Katoomba Street, and in Blackheath and Mount Victoria. The best place to buy new books, and great for browsing, is the very literary Megalong Books, 183 The Mall, Leura ⓣ02/4784 1302.

Bus services Blue Mountains Bus Co ⓣ02/4751 3333. See p.309 for details.

Camping equipment *Flying Fox Backpackers* (p.318) rents out camping equipment to guests. Otherwise, rent it in Sydney (see "Directory", p.281). Paddy Pallin, 166 Katoomba St (ⓣ02/4782 4466), sells camping gear and a good range of topographic maps and bushwalking guides, as does nearby Mountain Designs, at no. 190 (ⓣ02/4782 5999). For cheap gear try K-Mart (next door to Coles supermarket, see below).

Car rental Redicar, 80 Megalong St, Leura ⓣ02/4784 3443, ⓦwww.redicar.com.au.

Hospital Blue Mountains District Anzac Memorial, Great Western Highway, Katoomba ⓣ02/4784 6500.

Internet access Katoomba Book Exchange, 34 Katoomba St, has several terminals ($2.60 15min, $8 1hr); access over 15min includes a free coffee or tea; Mon & Tues 10.30am–5pm; Wed–Sun 10am–6pm.

Laundry The Washing Well, Shop 4, Pioneer Place (opposite K-Mart), Katoomba. Daily 7am–7pm.

Pharmacies, late-night Blooms Springwood Pharmacy, 161 Macquarie Rd, Springwood ⓣ02/4751 2963; Mon–Fri 8.30am–9pm, Sat 8.30am–7pm, Sun 9am–7pm. Greenwell & Thomas, 145 Katoomba St ⓣ02/4782 1066; Mon–Fri 8.30am–7pm, Sat & Sun 8.30am–6pm. Deliveries available from both Mon–Fri.

Post office Katoomba Post Office, Pioneer Place opposite Coles supermarket, off Katoomba St, Katoomba, NSW 2780.

Supermarket Coles, Pioneer Place off Katoomba St, Katoomba (daily 6am–midnight).

Taxis Taxis wait outside the main Blue Mountains train stations to meet arrivals; otherwise for Katoomba to Mt Victoria call Katoomba Radio Cabs ⓣ02/4782 1311, for the lower mountains call Blue Mountains Taxi Cab ⓣ02/4759 3000.

Trains Katoomba Station general enquiries ⓣ02/4782 1902. Transport Infoline ⓣ13 15 00.

Travel Agents Backpackers Travel Centre, 283 Main St, Katoomba ⓣ02/4782 5342, ⓦwww.backpackerstravel.net.au. Bookings for domestic buses, trains, flights and tours.

The foothills: Penrith

At the foot of the Blue Mountains in a curve of the Nepean River, **PENRITH** is the most westerly of Sydney's satellite towns. Penrith has an old-fashioned Aussie feel about it – a tight community that is immensely proud of the Panthers, its boisterous rugby league team. The huge *Panthers Leagues Club* on Mulgoa Road (ⓣ02/4720 5555) is the town's eating, drinking, entertainment and gambling hub

From Penrith Station, you can't miss the huge lettering announcing the **Museum of Fire** on Castlereagh Road in a former power station (daily 10am–4.30pm, closed last fortnight Dec; $8; ⓦwww.museumoffire.com.au), which focuses on one of Australia's greatest and most widespread perils, with a serious message about fire safety. The museum has around fifty fire-fighting vehicles – which kids especially love – and memorabilia.

Penrith is also the home to the extensive International Regatta Centre on Penrith Lakes, between Castlereagh and Cranebrook roads north of the town centre. **Penrith Whitewater Stadium** here was the 2000 Olympics competition venue for the canoe/kayak-slalom events. You can take part in a thrilling, ninety-minute **white-water rafting** session, completing five to eight circuits of the 320-metre-long, grade-three course ($66; bookings ⓣ02/4730 4333, ⓦwww.penrithwhitewater.com.au).

You can also experience the splendour of the spectacular **Nepean Gorge** from the decks of the paddle steamer *Nepean Belle* (range of cruises from $15 for 1hr 30min, morning or afternoon tea extra; bookings ⓣ02/4733 1274, ⓦwww.nepeanbelle.com.au) or head 24km south to the **Warragamba Dam**, the source of Sydney's water supply. The dam has created the huge reservoir of **Lake Burragorang**, a popular picnic spot with barbecues and a kiosk, and some easy walking trails through the bush.

Mountain activities

There's heaps to do in the mountains, from bushwalking to canyoning, meditation and yoga. The free **local newspaper**, *Blue Mountains Gazette*, comes out every Wednesday and has good entertainment and activities listings (80¢ from newsagents but usually floating around cafés).

Adventure activities

There are loads of outdoor adventure companies on Main and Katoomba streets in Katoomba offering activities. The **Australian School of Mountaineering** at Paddy Pallin, 166 Katoomba St (ⓣ02/4782 2014, ⓦwww.asmguides.com), is Katoomba's original abseiling outfit, offering daily day-long courses ($125), plus canyoning trips to Grand Canyon, Empress Canyon or Fortress Canyon (daily Oct–May, 9am; $135; trips to a range of other canyons offered less frequently), rock-climbing and bush-survival courses. Another long-established operator, **High 'n' Wild Mountain Adventures** 3/5 Katoomba St (ⓣ02/4782 6224, ⓦwww.high-n-wild.com.au), has a consistently good reputation for its beginners' courses in abseiling (full day $135, half-day $85), canyoning (from $145), rock-climbing (full-day $159, half-day $109) and mountain biking (full-day $149, half-day $109), plus guided bushwalking and bushcraft courses. Both companies include lunch on the full-day courses. If the weather is bad, you can train at the **climbing wall** at Village Fitness in Leura, 185 The Mall (ⓣ02/4784 2163; Mon & Wed 6.30am–9pm, Tues & Thurs 9am–9pm, Fri 6.30am–8pm, Sat 8am–6pm, Sun 9.30am–6pm; climbing wall $10 plus $4 harness hire).

Bike rental

The friendly **Vélo Nova**, 182 Katoomba St, Katoomba (ⓣ02/4782 2800), has mountain bikes from $28 half-day, $50 full day; ask in-store about the weekly free guided bike rides. There's cheaper bike hire at the YHA for guests.

Cinemas

The **Edge Maxvision Cinema**, 225–237 Great Western Highway, Katoomba (ⓣ02/4782 8928, ⓦwww.edgecinema.com.au), shows *The Edge – The Movie* (see p.321), as well as new-release feature films on a giant screen ($12.50; cheap tickets $8.50 all day Tues). **Mount Vic Flicks**, Harley Ave, off Station St, Mount Victoria (ⓣ02/4787 1577, ⓦwww.bluemts.com.au/mountvic/), is a quaint local cinema in an old hall with an old-fashioned candy bar; it shows a fine programme of prestige new releases and independent films (Thurs–Sun, daily during school holidays; good-value $9 tickets, cheaper $6 tickets Thurs). **Glenbrook Cinema**, cnr Ross Street and Great

Glenbrook to Faulconbridge

Once you're off the busy highway and away from the information centre, **GLENBROOK**, 10km on from Penrith, is a pleasant village arranged around the train station, with a great cinema (see p.321), lots of cafés and an outdoor shop on Ross Street. The section of the **Blue Mountains National Park** here is popular for **mountain biking** along the **Oaks Fire Trail** (it's best to start the thirty-kilometre trail higher up the mountain in **WOODFORD** and head downhill, ending up at Glenbrook; bike rental is only available at Katoomba). The park entrance (cars $7) is just over a kilometre from the train station following Burfitt Parade then Bruce Road alongside the railway line. There's a part-time NPWS office at the end of Bruce Rd (Sat & Sun, public and school hols 8.30am–4.30pm; ⓣ02/4739 2950), where several bushwalks can be commenced. In summer, head for the swimmable **Blue Pool** and **Jellybean Pool** (2km return; easy). But one of the best walks from the NPWS office is to see the Aboriginal hand stencils on

Western Highway, Glenbrook, is a quality, family-run cinema with cheap tickets for all sessions (ⓣ02/4739 4433, ⓦwww.glenbrookcinema.com.au).

Horse riding

Below Blackheath, there are horse-riding opportunities in the scenic Megalong Valley. **Blue Mountains Horse Riding Adventures** (ⓣ02/4787 8688, ⓦwww.megalong.cc) offers a variety of escorted trail rides in the valley and along the Coxs River, from a beginners' one-hour Wilderness Ride ($40) to an experienced riders' all-day adventure ride along the river ($135). Pick-ups from Blackheath are included. **Werriberri Trail Rides** (ⓣ02/4787 9171) offers horse riding for all abilities and pony rides for children (from $5.50 for 5min); their two-hour ride, including pick-up from Katoomba, costs $70.

Massage

Crystal Lodge, 19 Abbotsford Rd, Katoomba (ⓣ02/4782 5122, ⓦwww.crystallodge.com.au), offers a wide range of holistic therapies, including aromatherapy massage (1hr 30min; $90), therapeutic massage (1hr; $65) and foot reflexology (1hr; $65). Health-resort-style accommodation and therapy packages available.

Meditation

Australian Buddhist Vihara, 43 Cliff Drive, Katoomba (ⓣ02/4782 2704), hosts free meditation sessions Sunday 8–11am and one-hour sessions daily 8am & 6pm.

Swimming

Katoomba Aquatic Centre, Gates Ave, Katoomba (Mon–Fri 6am–8pm, Sat & Sun 8am–8pm, winter weekends closes 6pm; ⓣ02/4782 1748), has outdoor pools, with a heated Olympic-sized and children's pools, plus an attached complex which is open all year with heated 25m indoor pool, toddlers' pool, sauna, spa and gym. Entry is $4.20 (plus sauna and spa $7.50; plus gym, sauna and spa $12.50; gym only $9). For details of pools at Glenbrook, Springwood, Lawson and Blackheath, contact the Blue Mountains City Council (ⓣ02/4780 5000, ⓦwww.bmcc.nsw.gov.au). You can swim at waterholes at Glenbrook (see above) and in the Megalong Valley (see p.323).

Yoga

The **Blue Mountains Yoga Studio**, 4/118 Main St, Katoomba (ⓣ02/4782 6718), is a highly regarded Iyengar Yoga school where you can join in casual yoga classes for beginners to advanced (around $15 per class).

the walls of **Red Hands Cave** (3hr return; medium difficulty). You can also drive or cycle to the cave and on to the grassy creekside Eoroka picnic ground (camping available), where there are usually lots of eastern grey kangaroos.

Eleven kilometres northwest of Glenbrook, **SPRINGWOOD**, the Blue Mountains' second largest town, with express train links to Sydney, has the feel of a commuter suburb, but with several cafés, and bushwalks in **Sassafras Gully** (8km circuit; easy). You can turn off here onto Hawkesbury Road to take a scenic drive down to Richmond (see p.291). Three kilometres further west is **FAULCONBRIDGE**, where many artists and writers were first drawn to the mountains in the footsteps of Norman Lindsay, the controversial artist and poet (1879–1969), whose nude studies scandalized Australia in the 1930s and whose story was told in the 1994 film *Sirens* (with Elle McPherson as one of the life models). From 1912, Lindsay spent a great part of his life at the 42-acre bush property "Springwood", now owned by the National Trust as the **Norman Lindsay Gallery**, set among extensive gardens at 14 Norman Lindsay Crescent (daily 10am–4pm; $9). The exhibition of paintings and drawings, many of them erotic, and some from his famous, enduring and very funny children's tale, *The Magic Pudding* (itself made into a film in 2001), is well worth visiting.

Wentworth Falls

The small town of **WENTWORTH FALLS**, 23km further west, was named after William Wentworth, one of the famous trio who conquered the mountains in 1813. A signposted road leads from the Great Western Highway to the **Wentworth Falls Reserve**, with superb views of the waterfall tumbling down into the Jamison Valley. You can reach this picnic area from Wentworth train station by following the easy creekside 2.5-kilometre **Darwin's Walk** – tracing the route followed by the famous naturalist in 1836 where he described the view from the great precipice as "magnificent". Most of the other bushwalks in the area start from the national park's **Valley of the Waters Conservation Hut** (daily 9am–5pm; ☎02/4757 3827), about 3km from the station at the end of Fletcher Street. Blue Mountains Bus Co services run from Wentworth Falls train station (Mon–Fri 2 daily, Sat & Sun 4 daily), with more frequent services from the highway, outside the *Grand View Hotel* (Mon–Fri 7 daily, Sat & Sun 4 daily), and from Katoomba (Mon–Fri 10 daily, Sat 8 daily, Sun 4 daily). Blue Mountains Explorer Bus offers a once-daily shuttle bus to the national park at Wentworth Falls (Katoomba 9.15am, returning 5.25pm) as part of their daypass. The hut is in a fantastic location overlooking the Jamison Valley, and from its wonderful *Conservation Hut Cafe* you can take full advantage of the views through the big windows or from the deck outside; in winter an open fire crackles in the grate. Bushwalks, detailed on boards outside, range from the two-hour **Valley of the Waters track** to one of the most rewarding, along the strenuous **National Pass**, a 5.4 kilometre, four-hour circuit walk.

A great place to **eat** in Wentworth Falls is the relaxed BYO café *Il Postino*, at 13 Station St, opposite the train station. Housed in the original post office, this relaxed café is light and airy, with outside tables on a street-facing courtyard. The menu is Mediterranean- and Thai-slanted, with plenty for vegetarians and nothing over $14. Also opposite the station is the wonderful *Patisserie Schwartz* – divine German-style pastries to eat in or take away are the perfect reward after a long bushwalk.

Leura

Just 2km west of Wentworth Falls, and 2km east of Katoomba, the wealthy **LEURA**, packed with cafés, antique stores, elegant boutiques and a hugely popular old-fashioned sweet shop, retains its own distinct identity and a village atmosphere. It's a very scenic spot: arriving by train, there are stunning views across the Jamison Valley to the imposing plateau that is **Mount Solitary**. The main shopping strip, **Leura Mall**, has a wide area lined with cherry trees and makes a popular picnicking spot. In fact, Leura is renowned for its beautiful **gardens**, nine of which can be visited during the **Leura Gardens Festival** (early to mid-Oct; $16 all gardens, or $5 per garden; ⓦwww.leuragardensfestival.com.au). Open all year round, though, is the beautiful National Trust-listed **Everglades Gardens** (daily 9am–sunset; $6) at 37 Everglades Ave, 2km southeast of the Mall. There are wonderful Jamison Valley views from its formal terraces, a colourful display of azaleas and rhododendrons, an aboretum, and a simple tearoom.

Just over a kilometre south of the Mall, the privately run **NSW Toy and Railway Museum** (daily 10am–5pm; $10, $6 garden only) is located at 36 Olympian Parade, within an Art Deco mansion set in twelve acres of gardens; inside there's a huge collection of dolls, teddies and push-button model trains, while in the grounds, a miniature railway tracks its way around a six-metre Matterhorn replica ($2 extra). Opposite, a separate $2 entry fee gets you into **Olympian Park**, where a natural ampitheatre gives more stunning Jamison valley views. From the nearby **Gordon Falls** picnic area on Lone Pine Ave, Leura's mansions and gardens give way to the bush of the **Blue Mountains National Park**; it's an easy ten-minute return walk to the lookout over the falls or there's a canyon walk (two-hour circuit; medium difficulty) via Lyre Bird Dell and the Pool of Siloam which takes in some of the Blue Mountains' distinctive hanging swamps, an Aboriginal rock shelter and cooling rainforest. From Gordon Falls, a 45-minute bushwalk partway along the Prince Henry Cliff Walk (see p.322) heads to **Leura Cascades** picnic area off **Cliff Drive** (the scenic route around the cliffs which extends from Leura to beyond Katoomba) where several bushwalks include a two- to three-hour circuit walk to the base of the much-photographed **Bridal Veil Falls**. To the east of Gordon Falls, Sublime Point Road leads to the aptly named **Sublime Point** lookout, with panoramic views of the Jamison Valley.

Accommodation and eating

You can **stay** near the village at the impressive *Peppers Fairmont Resort*, 1 Sublime Point Rd (ⓣ02/4782 5222, ⓦwww.peppers.com.au). This huge four-and-a-half-star resort (with over 200 rooms) has peaceful grounds with Jamison Valley views and fantastic recreational facilities. There's a large indoor pool and spa, but a swim in the heated outdoor pool on a cold day and a dip in the steaming spa is a magical experience. There's also a gym, squash and tennis courts, two restaurants (*Jamison's* offers a buffet and dramatic views), a café and a bar. Prices start from $280 a night, though special deals are available.

There are a number of options if you're looking for something to **eat**. In a street of overpriced and noisy cafés, lunching at the smart *Silk's Brasserie*, 128 The Mall, with its white tablecloths, Parisian-style bar and excellent service is the best value. A veal and mushroom saffron ravioli with puttanesca sauce ($17) costs the price of a sandwich elsewhere and lunch mains peak at $22. At dinner the sophisticated European-style dishes, from confit of duck to Tasmanian salmon, cost $26–33 and there are divine desserts on offer for around $18. In contrast, *Bakehouse on Wentworth*, at the southern end of the Mall next to th fire station, is a spacious, sophisticated bakery-café away from the tourist traps, selling organic bread, plus yummy pies, pastries and excellent coffee.

Katoomba and around

KATOOMBA, 103km west of Sydney, is the biggest town in the Blue Mountains and the area's commercial heart; it's also the best located for the major sights of Echo Point and the Three Sisters. There's a lively café culture on the main drag, **Katoomba Street**, which runs downhill from the train station; the street is also full of vintage and retro clothes shops, secondhand bookstores, antique dealers and gift shops. When the town was first discovered by fashionable city dwellers in the late nineteenth century, the grandiose **Carrington**

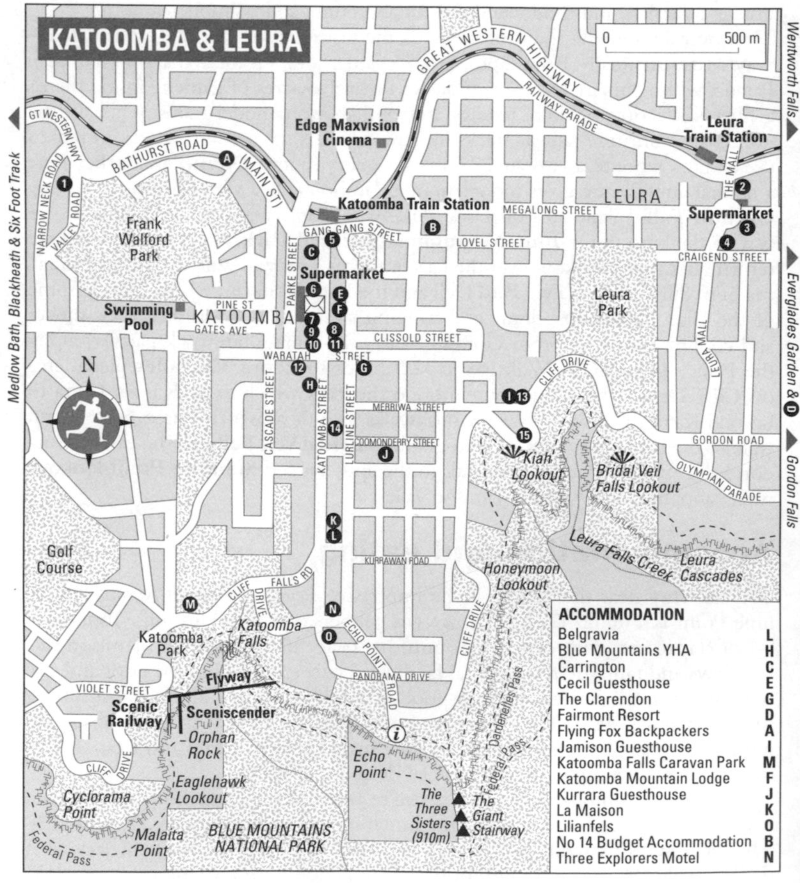

CAFÉS & RESTAURANTS

Arjuna	1	Café 123	6	Elephant Bean	7	Mes Amis	11	Siam Cuisine	8
Avalon	5	Café Bon Ton	3	Fresh	9	Mountain Japanese	12	Silk's Brasserie	2
Bakehouse	4	Canton Palace	14	Hominy	10	The Rooster	13	Solitary	15

Specialist guides to the Blue Mountains

Of the many guides to the area, the best is the sturdy paperback *Exploring the Blue Mountains* (Leonard Cronin et al), one of the immaculately researched Key Guides series. It's aimed at bushwalkers, cyclists and adventure sports enthusiasts as well as visitors on a driving tour. There are full-colour maps, photographs and illustrations – the nature section's illustrated plants and mammals provides a useful field guide. The Pocket Pals series is small bushwalking guides to specific mountain walks, including *Federal Pass*, *The Giant Stairway* and *Prince Henry Cliff Walk*. The NPWS also publishes a series of walking track guides for the Blue Mountains National Park and the Wollemi National Park, including *Glenbrook and the Eastern Blue Mountains*, *Bushwalking in the Wentworth Falls Area* and the most popular *Bushwalking in the Katoomba and Leura Area*. All the above are available at Megalong Books, Leura (see p.311).

Hotel, prominently located at the top of Katoomba Street, was the height of elegance, with its lead lighting and wood panelling (an historian gives 1hr tours of the hotel; $8; bookings ⓣ02/4754 5726). It's recently been returned to its former glory, with elegant sloping lawns running down to the new **town square**. Katoomba also boomed during the **Art Deco** era and many of its cafés and restaurants feature the style, notably the **Paragon Cafe** at 65 Katoomba St (closed Mon), also known for its handmade chocolates and sweets.

Accommodation

Hotels and guesthouses

Carrington Hotel 15–47 Katoomba St, Katoomba ⓣ02/4782 1111, ⓦwww.thecarrington.com.au. When it opened in 1882, the *Carrington Hotel* was one of the region's finest hotels. Now fully restored, original features include stained-glass windows, open fireplaces, a splendid dining room and ballroom, a cocktail bar, a library and snooker and games rooms. The spacious, well-aired rooms are beautifully decorated in rich heritage colours. Budget rooms, which share bathrooms, are very good value and there are masses of very private bathrooms (with baths) to use. Buffet breakfast included. Also see p.319 and p.320. $119–139, en suite $170–190, de luxe $245–275.

The Clarendon Cnr Lurline and Waratah streets, Katoomba ⓣ02/4782 1322, ⓦwww.clarendonguesthouse.com.au. Classic 1920s guesthouse on three levels, with its own cocktail bar and restaurant, and a music and cabaret programme (see p.320). Also heated pool, sauna, gym, open fires, games room and garden. The guesthouse rooms aren't flashy but atmospheric in an old-fashioned way. Mostly en suite ($65–88), but budget rooms without bathroom (but with TV) are available ($65) and exude a faded charm. There are also modern motel rooms along the front ($65–88).

Jamison Guesthouse 48 Merriwa St, cnr Cliff Drive ⓣ02/4782 1206, ⓦwww.jamisonhouse.com.au. Built as a guesthouse in 1903 and still going strong, this is a charming place in a great spot with amazing, unimpeded views across the Jamison Valley. The feel is very much that of a small European hotel, enhanced by the French restaurant *The Rooster* downstairs (dinner daily, lunch Sat & Sun; set price two- and three-course menus $56–68), with big picture windows. Upstairs, a breakfast room has splendid views – provisions (including an egg cooker) are supplied – and there's a sitting room with a fireplace. All rooms en suite ($140–170).

Kurrara Guesthouse 17 Coomonderry St ⓣ02/4782 6058, ⓦwww.kurrara.com. Kurrara is the ultimate in cosy old-fashioned mountains' atmosphere – the eight characterful guestrooms, each different, are filled with antique or four-poster beds, huge armchairs, books and bric a brac, all with an eclectic charm. Rooms are en suite, and some even have spa baths. The two-storey 1903 building has original features including working fireplaces (plus central heating).

Evening drinks are offered in the parlour, and a buffet breakfast in the dining room ($10, or $15 cooked). A loyal Sydney-escapee following means you should in advance. Rooms $90–140 midweek, $140–160 weekend, suites $160–180.

La Maison Guesthouse **175–177 Lurline St ⓣ02/4782 4996, ⓦwww.lamaison.com.au.** This modern place with large foyer and Asian-style conservatory-style dining room (where the included buffet breakfast is served) feels more like a small hotel than a guesthouse. With a four-star level of comfort in the spacious, conservatively decorated, well-furnished rooms (all en suite, some with bathtubs; $110–120), and very obliging management, it's one of the best-value places in Katoomba, and in a good spot in between the town centre and Echo Point. There's also a garden and deck, guest spa and sauna. The same management runs the more inexpensive *Belgravia Mountain Guesthouse* in a cosy bungalow next door at no. 179 ($86–98, light breakfast included).

Lilianfels **Lilianfels Ave ⓣ02/4780 1200, ⓦwww.lilianfels.com.au.** Spectacularly sited on the edge of the cliffs near Echo Point with stunning Jamison Valley views, the luxurious Lilianfels consists of the original 1889 mansion and a 1992 country house – with two restaurants (Darley's, with its top chef, seasonal menu and cottage setting is a fine-dining experience) and bars – set on two acres of landscaped gardens. Rooms are romantic but in contemporary style. There's a guest lounge with open fires, a reading room, billiards room, indoor and outdoor pools, a gym, spa treatments, tennis court and mountain bikes. From $298 per night.

Three Explorers Motel **197 Lurline St ⓣ02/4782 1733, ⓦwww.3explorersmotel.com.au.** In a great spot near Echo Point, this well-run place is a cut above the usual charmless motel, It's set over two levels, with tastefully decorated units ($96–136) as well as spa rooms ($170–220) and large family suites ($116–156).

▾ Zig Zag Railway

Hostels

No 14 Budget Accommodation **14 Lovel St ⓣ02/4782 7104, ⓦwww.bluemts.com.au/No14.** This relaxed hostel in a charming restored former guesthouse – polished floors, cosy fire and original features – is like a home away from home, run by an informative, friendly and enthusiastic young couple. Mostly twin and double rooms, some en suite, plus four-share dorms with comfy beds instead of bunks; all centrally heated. Peaceful verandah surrounded by pretty plants and valley views. Dorms $22, rooms $59, en suite $65.

Blue Mountains YHA **207 Katoomba St ⓣ02/4782 1416, ⓔbluemountains@yhansw.org.au.** Huge 200-bed YHA hostel right in the town centre with helpful staff on reception. The former 1930s guesthouse has been modernized but retains its charming leaded windows, Art Deco decor, huge ballroom and an old-fashioned ambience. There's an open fire in the reading room, a separate games room (with pool table), Internet access and a very pleasant courtyard. Most rooms and some of the four-bed dorms are en suite; eight-share dorms are also available. Mountain-bike rental for guests and abseiling and Jenolan Caves trips are offered. A dedicated information room comes complete with topographic maps. Dorms $22–28, rooms $68–76.

The Flying Fox Backpackers **190 Bathurst Rd ⓣ02/4782 4226 or 1800 624 226, ⓦwww.theflyingfox.com.au.** Colourfully painted, homely and comfortable bungalow near

The Six Foot Track

Along the Great Western Highway, about 2.5km west of Katoomba train station, is the **Explorers Tree**, initialized by Blaxland, Lawson and Wentworth during their famous 1813 expedition and now sadly covered due to vandalism. From Nellies Glen Road here is the start of the 42km **Six Foot Track**, – a two to three day walk – and shorter walks to Pulpit Rock and Bonnie Doon Falls. There are four basic **campsites** along the way, plus well-equipped cabins at Binda Flats (see p.326). Blackheath NPWS information centre (see p.323) can provide more bushwalking and camping information. Blue Mountains Guides (ⓣ02/4782 6109, ⓦwww.bluemountainsguides.com.au) offers a three-day, two-night fully catered and supported **guided walk** along the track ($550; tent camping). Otherwise, Fantastic Aussie Tours (see box on pp.308–309) provides a daily transfer service for bushwalkers from Katoomba to the start of the track and then a return service a few days later from the Jenolan Caves (2hr; $50); you can leave cars in their depot. A more unusual way to do the Six Foot is to enter the annual Six Foot Track Marathon held in March (for more details see ⓦwww.coolrunning.com.au).

the station, with spacious dorms (6- to 10-bed; linen $1 extra) and lovely laidback doubles, decked out with cushions and lamps (no en suites). Separate TV/video room, board games, Internet access, a small kitchen with free tea and coffee. Outside, there's a courtyard and a popular "chillout" hut with a fire, and a camping site ($12 per person). Camping gear is rented out at reasonable rates and the knowledgeable managers offer info on bushwalks and camping, and free transport to walks. Dorms $21, rooms $58.

Katoomba Mountain Lodge 31 Lurline St ⓣ02/4782 3933, ⓦwww.bluemts.com.au/kmtlodge. Friendly, family-run, central budget accommodation on three floors with great views from the verandah, TV room and some bedrooms. Dorms (4- to 6-bed), and cute doubles with window seats (one en suite; most with TV), all heated with electric blankets. Small kitchen, large dining room, free tea and coffee, pleasant sundeck and BBQ area. Free broadband Internet access. Cheap breakfast and dinner available. Dorms $16–20, rooms $52–58, en suite $68.

Eating

A huge number of cafés line thriving **Katoomba Street**; several cafés at the top of the street are open and lively at night, including the *Savoy*, *Isobar* and *Zuppa*, but those that are most popular with locals, and open by day (daily from 9am to 5pm), cluster at the bottom of the hill. There are some great bakeries too: top of the list is *Hominy* at 185 Katoomba Street, with public picnic tables just outside. At the *Carrington Hotel*, the splendid "Grand Dining Room", all columns and decorative inlaid ceilings, offers a high tea buffet on Sundays (3–5pm; $16.50), or for a full dinner mains are around $33; there's also a regular Friday night seafood and carvery buffet ($55).

Cafés and light meals

Cafe 123 123 Katoomba St, Katoomba. White, bright modern place with just a counter and a couple of outside tables. Healthy cleansing juices, organic wheat-grass shots, sushi, sandwiches, focaccia and muffins. Coffee is freshly roasted.

The Elephant Bean 159 Katoomba St. Tiny café known for its great all-day breakfasts. Eggs every which way or there's even a big vegan breakfast ($10.95). Other choices include the popular burgers for veggies or carnivores and gourmet sandwiches (all $10.95) and salads ($8.95).

Fresh 181 Katoomba St. Spacious, goldfish-bowl-sized café at the bottom of the street, by the busy lane heading up to the post office and supermarket. With sunny outside tables. It's a popular place with locals, who are lured by the gourmet pies (Thai, vegetable, Rogan Josh), Turkish bread sandwiches (from $7), changing blackboard lunch (around $12), big fruit muffins, good music, magazine stash and the best coffee in town.

Mountain Japanese Food 43 Waratah St. Popular Japanese sushi joint: get there early to snap up the sushi. Also noodle soups and dumplings. Mainly take away, with a few tables inside and out. Tues–Sat 11.30am–4pm.

Restaurants

There's also French provincial cuisine available at the *Jamison Guesthouse* restaurant *The Rooster* (see p.317), and meals on offer at the *Carrington Hotel* (see p.317).

Arjuna 16 Valley Rd, just off the Great Western Highway ⓣ02/4782 4662. Excellent, authentic Indian restaurant. A bit off the beaten track but positioned for spectacular sunset views, so get there early. Good veggie choices too. BYO. Evenings from 6pm; closed Tues & Wed.

Avalon Restaurant 18 Katoomba St ⓣ02/4782 5532. Stylish restaurant with the ambience of a quirky café, located in the dress circle of the old Savoy Theatre, with Art Deco features intact. Beautiful views down the valley too – come here for lunch, or an early dinner in summer. Moderately expensive menu, but generous servings and to-die-for desserts. Separate bar, so you can come just for a drink and soak up the atmosphere. BYO & licensed. Lunch & dinner Wed–Sun.

Canton Palace 246 Katoomba St ⓣ02/4782 2868. Not fantastic, but the best Chinese in the mountains, and the one most frequented by Asian tourists. With dinner from 5pm, it's popular with families too; come later to avoid the kids. Mains from $10.80. Licensed.

Mes Amis Cnr Waratah and Lurline streets ⓣ02/4782 1558. French-owned and run *Mes Amis* offers classic and delicious fare in the ambient setting of a high-ceilinged, candle-lit old stone church. Mains range from $26 to $31 but there's a two-course (or $40 per person) minimum on Sat nights. Alternatively, go for the *dégustation* menu, at $87 for six courses ($120 with matching wine). Licensed, with French wines available. Dinner Wed–Sun.

Siam Cuisine 172 Katoomba St ⓣ02/4782 5671. Popular, inexpensive and long-running Thai place. Cheap lunch-time specials. BYO. Closed Mon.

Solitary 90 Cliff Drive ⓣ02/4782 1164. Perched on a hairpin bend on the mountains' scenic cliff-hugging road, the views of the Jamison Valley and Mount Solitary from this Modern Australian restaurant are sublime. Expect beautifully laid tables, eager service, a well-chosen and reasonably priced wine list, fine moderate to expensive mains, and a fireplace in the back room. The café section, *Solitary Kiosk*, allows you to enjoy the views and ambience without the expense, and picnic tables outside are popular for weekend breakfast. Opposite the Kiah Lookout on the Prince Henry Cliff Walk, it makes a perfect bushwalking break. Restaurant: lunch Sat & Sun, dinner Tues–Sat; café: Mon–Fri 10am–4pm, Sat & Sun 9am–4pm.

Drinking and nightlife

There are several **nightlife** options in Katoomba. The salubrious cocktail bar and cabaret room at *The Clarendon* (see p.317) hosts eclectic folk, blues, jazz, and world music (bar 6pm, dinner 7pm, show 8.30pm, Thurs–Sat, sometimes Sun; $10–45; dinner plus show extra $20–25). *Tris Elies Nightclub* beside the train station at 287 Bathurst Rd (ⓣ02/4782 4026; Wed 9pm–midnight, Thurs–Sat 9pm–3am) puts on karaoke (Wed), jamming sessions (Thurs; $5), world, blues, rock music (Fri; $10) and eclectic club nights (Sat; $10–15), plus grill-style meals. On the other side of the tracks, opposite the station, the huge and now rather hip *Gearin Hotel* (ⓣ02/4782 4395) is a hive of activity, with several bars where you can play pool, see touring bands (Fri and Sat nights) or boogie at the club nights ($10). There's more mainstream action at *The*

Carrington, on Katoomba Street (☎02/4782 1111), which has a host of bars in and around its grand old building. In the old hotel, *Champagne Charlies Cocktail Bar* has a decorative glass ceiling and chandeliers where you can order a pricey drink and wander through to one of the classic palm filled lounges or out to the wonderful front verandah overlooking the lawns. Cheaper drinks and a more lively atmosphere are found in the modern annexe next door, the *Carrington Bar* (live music Wed–Fri includes a piano player on Thurs night), and the more down-to-earth public bar, which has a separate entrance on Main Street opposite the train station; there's a nightclub above it, *The Attic* (Fri & Sat 10.30pm–3am).

The Edge Maxvision Cinema

Across the railway line (use the foot-tunnel under the station), a stunning introduction to the ecology of the Blue Mountains can be explored at the **Edge Maxvision Cinema**, at 225–237 Great Western Highway (☎02/4782 8928, Ⓦwww.edgecinema.com.au), a huge six-storey cinema screen created as a venue to show *The Edge – The Movie* (daily 10.20am, 11.05am, 12.10pm, 1.30pm, 2.15pm & 5.30pm; $14.50). The highlight of the forty-minute film is the segment about the "dinosaur trees", a stand of thirty-metre-high **Wollemi Pine**, previously known only from fossil material over sixty million years old. The trees – miraculously still existing – survive deep within a sheltered rainforest gully in the **Wollemi National Park** north of Katoomba, and made headlines when they were first discovered in 1994 by a group of canyoners. To film the pines, whose exact location is kept secret, it was necessary to work closely with the NPWS; there is an informative NPWS display in the cinema lobby. After the discovery, the first cultivated Wollemi Pine was planted in 1998 at Sydney's Royal Botanical Gardens, and you can see a Wollemi Pine sapling in the Blue Mountains at the Mount Tomah Botanic Garden (see p.324).

Echo Point

A 25-minute walk south from the train station or a tour or regular bus from the top of Katoomba Street will bring you to **Echo Point**. From the projecting lookout platform between the **information centre** (daily 9am–5pm; ☎1300 653 408, Ⓦwww.bluemts.com.au) and souvenir shops and eateries at the Three Sisters Heritage Plaza, breathtaking vistas take in the Kedumba and Jamison valleys, Mount Solitary, the Ruined Castle, Kings Tableland and the Blue Mountains' most famous landmark, the **Three Sisters** (910m). These three gnarled rocky points take their name from a – possibly apocryphal – Aboriginal Dreamtime story which relates how the Kedumba people were losing a battle against the rival Nepean people: the Kedumba leader, fearing that his three beautiful daughters would be carried off by the enemy, turned them to stone, but was tragically killed before he could reverse his spell. An easy half-hour return stroll from the information centre will get you closer to the Sisters at Spooners Lookout.

The Three Sisters are at the top of the **Giant Stairway** (1hr 45min one-way), a very steep 800-step stairway leading into the three-hundred-metre-deep **Jamison Valley** below, passing Katoomba Falls en route. There's a popular walking route, taking about two hours and graded medium, down the stairway and part way along the **Federal Pass** to the **Landslide**, and then on to the Scenic Railway or Flyway (see below), either of which you can take back up to the ridge.

Scenic World and beyond

If you want to spare yourself the trek down into the Jamison Valley – or the walk back up – head for the very touristy **Scenic World complex** (daily 9am–5pm) at the end of Violet Street off Cliff Drive, where you can choose between two modes of transport, the original Scenic Railway and the modern Flyway; there's also a thrilling return gondola ride, Skyway ($25 combined ticket for Scenic Railway, Flyway and Skyway; $14 for railway down, Flyway up or vice versa; $7 one-way railway or Skyway; Skyway only $14; ⓦwww.scenicworld.com.au). To satisfy visitors who have missed the fabulous views on wet and misty days, the **Scenic Cinema** (entry included with ticket purchase) shows a seventeen-minute film of the mountain sights. There are more views at the complex's **revolving restaurant**, the *Skyway Brasserie*, and from the terrace at *Harry's Cafe-Bar* where you need only grab a take-away ice cream or coffee to enjoy them.

The **Scenic Railway** (every 10min; last train up leaves at 4.50pm), originally built in the 1880s to carry coal, is a funicular that glides down an impossibly steep gorge to the valley floor. Even more vertiginous, but not as nail-bitingly thrilling, is **Flyway** (same times), an A$8-million, high-tech cable car (wheelchair accessible), with floor-to-ceiling windows – the views of the Three Sisters as the car drops 545m are really spectacular. At the base, there's a 330-metre elevated boardwalk (also wheelchair accessible) through forest – en route you can drink clean rainwater from a spring – to the base of the Scenic Railway via the entrance to the old coal mine, where an audiovisual display tells the story of the mine at the time when the railway still hauled coal. A further 1.5km of boardwalk on various levels, with interpretative boards detailing natural features, is worth exploring, and there's access to longer bushwalks in the national park, including a 12km return walk (medium difficulty) to the Ruined Castle (see below).

Back up on the ridge, you can get your legs trembling again with the state-of-the-art **Skyway** (daily 9am-5pm), the 2005 replacement for the rickety-looking cable-car contraption that had been plying its way 350m across to the other side of the gorge and straight back again since 1958. As if the bird's-eye view of **Orphan Rock**, the Three Sisters and Katoomba Falls weren't exhilarating enough, the new gondala has a glass floor which starts out opaque then becomes crystal clear, revealing the 270-metre drop to the ravines and waterfalls below. Though the price for a few minutes is high, the thrill is worth it. A short walk from the Scenic World complex along Cliff Drive is the **Katoomba Falls picnic area** where there's a kiosk and several bushwalking options. The **Prince Henry Cliff Walk** (9km one way; 1hr 30min; easy) is a long but pleasant stroll along the plateau clifftop via Echo Point all the way to **Gordon Falls** (see p.315) with glorious lookouts along the way; a great refreshment/lunch stop en route is *Solitary* (see p.320) across Cliff Drive from the Kiah Lookout. A scenic drive following Cliff Drive southwest of Katoomba Falls leads to several spectacular lookouts: Eaglehawk, the Landslide, and Narrow Neck – a great sunset spot, with views into both the Jamison and Megalong valleys. To get to Narrow Neck peninsula itself, a popular mountain biking spot, take the unsealed, winding Glen Raphael Road. From here, the top of the **Golden Stairs** provide access down to a difficult 14km-return, eight- to ten-hour walking route to **Mount Solitary**, where you can bush camp overnight (but take NPWS advice first). The track to Mount Solitary goes past the turn-off to the **Ruined Castle**, which is a six-hour medium to hard return walk from the Golden Stairs (or it can be reached via the base of Scenic World).

Medlow Bath and Blackheath

One train stop beyond Katoomba, and 6km further northwest along the Great Western Highway, the quiet village of **MEDLOW BATH** is based around the distinctively domed **Hydro Majestic Hotel**, built as an exclusive health resort in 1904 on an escarpment overlooking the **Megalong Valley**. The hotel was given a meticulous make-over by the Mercure chain in 2000, and it's worth a stop-off to gaze at the interiors and the stunning bush views from the balcony beer garden – walk through the Megalong Room to get outside. The Megalong Room has the same view from its windows, but the buffet-style café is overpriced.

Five kilometres north of Medlow Bath along the Great Western Highway, there are more lookout points at **BLACKHEATH** – just as impressive as Echo Point and much less busy. One of the best is **Govetts Leap**, at the end of Govetts Leap Road (just over 2km east of the highway through the village centre), near the **Blue Mountains National Park** headquarters, the **Blackheath Heritage Centre** (daily 9am–4.30pm; ⓣ02/4787 8877). The two-kilometre **Fairfax Heritage Track** from the NPWS Centre is wheelchair- and pram-accessible and takes in the Govetts Leap Lookout with its marvellous panorama of the **Grose Valley** and Bridal Veil Falls. Many walks start from the centre, but one of the most popular, **The Grand Canyon** (5km; 3hr 30min; medium difficulty), begins from **Evans Lookout Road** at the south end of town, west of the Great Western Highway.

Govetts Leap Road and its shady cross-street, Wentworth Street, have lots of antique and craft shops, an antiquarian bookshop, and great cafés and restaurants (see p.324). Ten kilometres southwest of Blackheath, across the railway line, the beautiful unspoilt **Megalong Valley** is reached via winding Megalong Road; it's popular for **horse riding** (see "Mountain activities" box, pp.312–313) and there are creeks with swimmable waterholes.

Accommodation

Blackheath has some great **accommodation** including *Glenella* on Govett's Leap Rd (ⓣ02/4787 8352), a guesthouse in a charming 1905 homestead with its own licensed restaurant (dinner Fri & Sat) and antique-furnished rooms, mostly en suite, and a few cheaper share-bathroom options ($110, en suite $180). If you have your own transport you can easily indulge in some of the more unusual and characterful guesthouses in Blackheath, where you will find pricier bush set cabins and retreats all along Evans Lookout Road, backing onto the national park. One highly recommended place is *Jemby-Rinjah Lodge*, 336 Evans Lookout Rd (ⓣ02/4787 7622, ⓦwww.jembyrinjahlodge.com.au; $150–199), where accommodation is in distinctive one- and two-bedroom timber cabins with wood fires, sleeping two to six people. There's a licensed common area where the focal point is a huge circular "fire pit"; a restaurant operates here most Friday and Saturday nights.

Eating

Govett's Leap Road and Wentworth Street have the pick of places to **eat**. *Bakehouse on Wentworth*, 105 Wentworth St, is the original outlet of a cottage-like bakery selling European-style and organic bread and yummy pies and pastries, along with excellent coffee. Phenomenally popular with locals, and offering seating in a shady front courtyard, the *Bakehouse* has recently expanded wit branches in Leura (by the fire station) and Springwood (opposite the train station). The *Victory Café*, 17 Govetts Leap Rd (☎02/4787 6777), is a very pleasant space at the front of an old Art Deco theatre now converted into an antiques centre. Gourmet sandwiches are around $8.60, there's an all-day breakfast, and plenty of choice for vegetarians. The Malaysian and Thai curry nights (Fri & Sat from 6pm; bookings essential) are very popular. Bookings are also essential at the raved-about and recommended **restaurant** *Vulcan's*, at 33 Govetts Leap Rd (☎02/4787 6899; lunch & dinner Fri–Sun). Housed in an early twentieth-century bakery, the wood-fired oven is used to produce sensational, seasonal food and there are fantastic desserts, such as the trademark chequerboard liquorice and pineapple ice cream. It's expensive, with mains around the $30 mark, though BYO makes it more affordable.

Mount Victoria and around

At the top of the Blue Mountains, secluded and leafy **MOUNT VICTORIA**, 6km northwest of Blackheath along the Great Western Highway and the last mountain settlement proper, is the only one with an authentic village feel. The great old pub, the *Imperial*, is good for a drink or **meal**, and there are old-fashioned scones on offer at the *Bay Tree Tea Shop* opposite. Mount Victoria is also fondly regarded for its tiny **cinema**, Mount Vic Flicks, in the public hall (see box on pp.312–313). Also worth a browse are several antique and secondhand bookshops. Some short **walks** start from the Fairy Bower Picnic area, a ten-minute walk from the Great Western Highway via Mount Piddington Road.

Beyond Mount Victoria, drivers can circle back towards Sydney via the scenic **Bells Line of Road**, which heads east through the fruit- and vegetable-growing areas of Bilpin and Kurrajong to Richmond, with growers selling their produce at roadside stalls. **Mount Tomah Botanic Garden** is on the way (daily: Oct–March 10am–5pm; April–Sept 10am–4pm; $4.40; ⓦwww.rbgsyd.gov.au; no public transport), where the collection of southern hemisphere cool-climate species includes Wollemi Pine. The popular *Garden Restaurant* (lunch daily; ☎02/4567 2060; mains $30; licensed) with a pricey contemporary Australian menu has fantastic north-facing views over the gardens, Wollemi National Park and Bilbin orchards. Cheaper light lunches are also available and there's a kiosk, plus free electric barbecues and picnic tables in the grounds. By car, you can continue west along the Bells Line of Road to the Zig Zag Railway at Clarence, just over 35km away (see below).

The **Hartley Historic Site** (daily 10am–1pm & 2–4.30pm; ⓦwww.npws.nsw.gov.au; no public transport), a well-preserved but deserted nineteenth-century village, lies at the foot of the scenic Victoria Pass, 11km from Mount Victoria on the Great Western Highway. As settlers headed west and forged roads through the mountains, the need for a police centre led to the building of a courthouse here in 1837, but Hartley was eventually bypassed by the Great Western Highway in 1887. It's free to look at the site, and a map is provided in the NPWS information centre and shop (daily 10am–4.30pm) but to enter the buildings – only the courthouse is currently visitable – you have to take a guided tour (10am, 11am, noon, 2pm & 3pm; 30min; $4.40).

The Zig Zag Railway

LITHGOW, 21km northwest of Mount Victoria on the Great Western Highway, is a coal-mining town nestled under bush-clad hills, with wide leafy streets, quaint mining cottages and some imposing old buildings. About 13km east of the town on the Bells Line of Road, by the small settlement of **Clarence**, is the **Zig Zag Railway**. In the 1860s engineers were faced with the problem of how to get the main western railway line from the top of the Blue Mountains down the steep drop to the Lithgow Valley, so they came up with a series of zigzag ramps. These fell into disuse in the early twentieth century, but tracks were relaid by rail enthusiasts in the 1970s. Served by old steam trains, the picturesque line passes through two tunnels and over three viaducts. You can stop at points along the way and rejoin a later train.

The Zig Zag Railway can be reached by ordinary State Rail train on the regular service between Sydney and Lithgow, by requesting the guard in advance to stop at the Zig Zag platform; you then walk across the line to Bottom Point platform at the base of the Lithgow Valley. To catch the Zig Zag Railway from Clarence, at the top of the valley, you'll need to have your own transport. Zig Zag trains depart from Clarence daily (11am, 1pm & 3pm; from the Zig Zag platform add 40min to these times; $20; no bookings required; ⓣ02/6353 1795, ⓦwww.zigzagrailway.com.au).

Being en route to Bathurst and the Central West, there are plenty of **motels** in and around Lithgow, especially on the Great Western Highway; the **Lithgow Visitor Information Centre**, 1 Cooerwull Rd (daily 9am–5pm; ⓣ02/6353 1859, ⓦwww.tourism.lithgow.com), can advise on accommodation options.

The Jenolan Caves and Kanangra Boyd National Park

Kanangra Boyd National Park shares a boundary with the Blue Mountains National Park. Further south than the latter, much of it is inaccessible but you can explore the rugged beauty of **Kanangra Walls**, where the Boyd Plateau falls away to reveal a wilderness area of creeks, deep gorges and rivers below. Reached by driving via the **Jenolan Caves**, three **walks** leave from the car park at Kanangra Walls: a short lookout walk, a waterfall stroll and a longer plateau walk – contact the NPWS in Oberon for details (38 Ross St, ⓣ02/6336 1972; $7 car entry). Boyd River and Dingo Dell camping grounds, both off Kanangra Walls Road, have **free bush camping** (pit toilets; no drinking water at Dingo Dell). You can get to **Oberon**, a timber-milling town and the closest settlement to Kanangra, by Countrylink bus from Mount Victoria (3 weekly).

The Jenolan Caves

The **Jenolan Caves** lie 30km southwest across the mountains from Katoomba on the far edge of the Kanangra Boyd National Park – over 80km by road – and contain New South Wales' most spectacular limestone formations. There are nine "show" caves, with prices for a guided tour of each cave ranging from $15 to $27.50 depending on the cave (guided tours various times daily

▲ Jenolan Caves Resort

10am–5pm; 1hr 30min–2hr). If you're coming for just a day, plan to see one or two caves; the best general cave is the Lucas Cave ($15; 1hr 30min), with lots of features, and a more spectacular one is the Temple of Baal ($22; 1hr 30min), while the extensive River Cave, with its tranquil Pool of Reflection, is the longest and priciest ($27.50; 2hr). Buying a ticket for two more caves works out to be a better deal; for example, the Lucas combined with the Temple of Baal is $29.50. The system of caves is surrounded by the **Jenolan Karst Conservation Reserve**, a fauna and flora sanctuary with picnic facilities and walking trails to small waterfalls and lookout points. It and the caves are looked after by the **Jenolan Caves Trust** (☎02/6359 3311, ⓦwww.jenolancaves.org.au), who also offer **adventure caving** in various other caves (2hr "Plughole" tour $55; 7hr Central River Adventure Cave tour $187.50).

There's no public **transport** to Jenolan Caves but you can get here with Fantastic Aussie Tours (see box on pp.308–309; 2hr; departs Katoomba 10.30am, departs Jenolan Caves 3.45pm; $50), designed as an overnight rather than a day-return service; otherwise the same company offers day-tours from Katoomba, as do several other operators (see "Listings" p.282), or for tours from Sydney see box on pp.308–309. You can actually **walk** from Katoomba to the Jenolan Caves along the 42-kilometre-long **Six Foot Track** (see box on p.319).

Accommodation

The focus for the area, apart from the caves themselves, is a rather romantic, charming old **hotel** which found fame as a honeymoon destination in the 1920s and is now part of the *Jenolan Caves Resort*. In the old hotel, which also has a good restaurant, you'll find *Chisholm's Grand Dining Room* (3-course dinner $45), plus a bar and a more casual bistro; there are recently refurbished en-suite rooms ($190–290), and cheaper shared-bathroom versions ($110–160). The newer annexe, the *Mountain Lodge*, has motel-style rooms and two- to three-bedroom units without the character ($130–210); family rooms sleep four to six in the *Gatehouse* ($60–80; BYO linen), which has shared communal areas, including a kitchen. The Jenolan Karst Conservation Park has well-equipped cabins, *Jenolan Cottages*, at Binda Flats, reached by car from Jenolan Caves Road (sleep 6–8; $89–121; BYO linen) as well as a spacious, simple, unpowered

campsite, in a rural and secluded spot 1.6km from the caves along the Jenolan River. Another place to stay, 4km west of Jenolan Caves on Porcupine Hill, is *Jenolan Cabins*, 42 Edith Road (Ⓣ02/6335 6239, Ⓦwww.jenolanccabins.com.au; $98–105). The very reasonably priced, well-equipped, modern, two-bedroom timber cabins with wood fires accommodate six (BYO linen) and offer magnificent bush views; 4WD tours of the area are also offered (from $80 half-day, including lunch).

25

The Royal National Park and beyond

The Princes Highway and the Illawarra railway – the two main transport arteries out of bustling Sydney's southern reaches to the unspoiled NSW south coast – hug the edge of the **Royal National Park**, a huge nature reserve right on Sydney's doorstep, for more than 20km. The park is only 32km from the city, just over an hour's drive on a good day, but marks Sydney's southern extent, separating it from the gradual suburban sprawl of Wollongong, a working-class industrial centre 85km south of Sydney. A stunning **coastal route** heads through the Royal National Park to **Thirroul**, outside Wollongong, where D.H. Lawrence famously wrote most of his novel *Kangaroo*. Eight kilometres south of Wollongong, Australia's largest **Buddhist temple, Nan Tien**, rewards a visit for its peaceful atmosphere.

The Royal National Park

In 1879, the **Royal National Park** was established as only the second national park in the world, after Yellowstone in the USA. On the eastern side, from Jibbon Head to Garie Beach, the park falls away abruptly to the ocean, creating a spectacular coastline of steep cliffs broken here and there by creeks cascading into the sea and little coves with fine sandy beaches; the remains of **Aboriginal rock carvings** are the only traces of the original Dharawal people.

Practicalities

The railway between Sydney and Wollongong marks the Royal National Park's western border, and from the train the scenery is fantastic – streams, waterfalls, rock formations and rainforest flora fly past the window. If you want to explore further, get off at one of the **train stations** along the way: Loftus, Engadine, Heathcote, Waterfall or Otford – all starting points for walking trails into the park. The Sydney Tramway Museum at Loftus (see p.332) provides a Parklink service on an old Sydney **tram** (Sun & public holidays hourly 9.15am–4.15pm, Wed on demand 10.15am–2.15pm; 30min; $4 one-way, $6 return) to the NPWS Visitor Centre (see p.330).

A more interesting way to get to the park is by **ferry** from the southern beach-

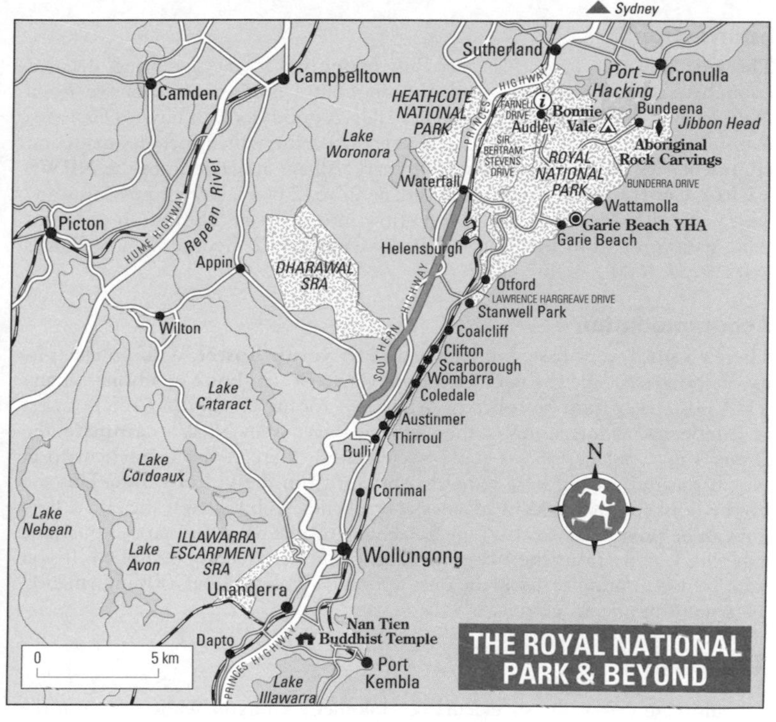

side suburb of Cronulla (see p.156) at the Tonkin Street wharf just below Cronulla's train station: Cronulla and National Park Ferries take 25 minutes to cross Port Hacking to the small town of **Bundeena** (see p.331) at the park's northeast tip (Mon–Fri hourly 5.30am–6.30pm except 12.30pm, continuous during school hols; Sat & Sun Sept–March 8.30am–6.30pm, April–Oct to 5.30pm; returns from Bundeena hourly: Mon–Fri 6am–7pm except 1pm; Sat & Sun Sept–March 9am–7pm, April–Oct to 6pm; $4.50. Narrated cruises: Sept–May daily 10.30am; June–Sept Mon, Wed, Fri & Sun 10.30am; 3hr; $17.50; cruise bookings ⓣ02/9523 2990, ⓦwww.cronullaandnationalparkferrycruises.com).

Finally, you can **drive** into the park at various points ($11 car entry; gates open 24hr except the Garie Beach gates which close at 8.30pm). Cars are allowed to pass right through the park, exiting at **Waterfall** on the Princes Highway or **Stanwell Park** on Lawrence Hargrave Drive; if you aren't planning to stop off, tell the National Parks officer in the pay-booth and the entry fee will be waived.

Surfing trips to the park

Waves Surf School offers a different way to get to and see the Royal National Park on their one-day "Learn To Surf" trip (ⓣ02/9369 3010 or 1800 851 101, ⓦwww.wavessurfschool.com.au). The trip includes transport, surfing gear, tuition and lunch ($69); they also run a two-day version to Seal Rocks on the north coast, which includes meals, guided bushwalking and cabin accommodation ($189). There are pick-ups at Bondi, Coogee and from the city YHA.

Information

The free fold-out *Royal National Park* **brochure** is excellent, and detailed enough to use for bushwalks and camping, but a more comprehensive *Royal National Park Tourist Map* ($6) is also available. A good book to buy is *Discovering Royal National Park on Foot* by Alan Fairley ($10.95), which includes maps and commentaries on the best walks in the park. All are available from the **NPWS Visitor Centre** (daily 8.30am–4.30pm; ⓣ02/9542 0648, ⓦwww.npws.nsw.gov.au), which lies on the Audley Road entry into the park, 2km south of Loftus train station, or from the National Parks Centre, 102 George St, The Rocks (ⓣ02/9253 4600).

Accommodation

There's a small, very basic but secluded YHA **youth hostel,** with no electricity or showers, inside the park 1km from Garie Beach (book in advance at any YHA hostel; key must be collected in advance; rooms $30, dorms $13). Just west of Bundeena on the shores of the Hacking River is an NPWS **campsite**, the *Bonnie Vale Camping Ground* (no powered sites); there is also a **bushcamp** at North Era but staying here requires a permit from the visitor centre. This site can be booked out weeks in advance at weekends, so book well ahead; the permit can be posted out to you (which takes up to five days), or you can purchase it before leaving from the National Parks Centre in Sydney (see p.28). If you want to stay in more comfort the only option is a holiday rental, for information see ⓦwww.bundeena.com.

The park

The ultimate trek is the spectacular 26-kilometre **Coastal Walk**, taking in the entire coastal length of the park, but the walk can be gruelling, as you need to carry your own water supplies. Give yourself two days to complete it, beginning at either Bundeena (see below) or Otford, and camping overnight at the officially designated bushcamp at North Era (several other campsites were closed at the time of writing). En route you'll pass Wattamolla and Garie beaches, both with kiosks and good surfing. An easier but still satisfying option is to hike just part of the route, such as the popular trail from **Otford** down to beachfront **Burning Palms** (2hr one-way; no camping). Some of the best **rainforest** in the Sydney area can be seen along the Bola Creek trail, rich in wildlife with many butterflies, lizards, water dragons, snakes and birdlife to be seen if you take your time and walk quietly.

In the north of the park, via Farnell Ave, the **Royal National Park Visitor Centre** is a picturesque picnic ground (with kiosk), at Audley, on the Hacking River, where you can rent a boat or canoe for a leisurely paddle. From the visitor centre an easy, one-kilometre wheelchair-accessible track heads to the **Bungoona Lookout**, which boasts panoramic views north and east across the park.

Escape Sydney Ecotours operates unhurried **guided tours** in small groups. A one-day tour explores the diverse track to Burning Palms Beach, while a two-day trip covers the entire coastal walk including overnight cabin accommodation. **Whale-watching** walks are available from May to August (ⓣ02/9664 3047, ⓦwww.escapecotours.com.au; 1-day tour $85; 2 days $240; whale watching $40; prices include food and pick up).

▲ Royal National Park

Bundeena

To begin the coastal walk from Bundeena, follow The Avenue and Lambeth Walk for 1km to the national park gate. Other less strenuous options are the pleasant half-day walk to pretty sheltered **Little Marley Beach** for a swim and a picnic (2hr one-way) – or head down a signposted pathway to **Jibbons Beach**, a thirty-minute stroll which will take you past some Dharawal rock engravings, where faint outlines of a kangaroo, stingrays, whales and a six-fingered man can be seen (pick up the *Jibbon Aboriginal Rock Engravings Walk* map and leaflet from the café near the wharf). There are a couple of great cafés and a sheltered little beach immediately by the ferry wharf.

Sydney Tramway Museum

Trams operated in Sydney for a century until 1961, and examples of the old fleet, including a Bondi tram, as well as trams from around the world, are on display at the **Sydney Tramway Museum** (Wed 10am–3pm, Sun & public holidays 10am–5pm; last entry 1hr before closing; $15, includes Parklink and unlimited tram rides; ⓦwww.sydneytramwaymuseum.com.au), right next to Loftus train station. You can ride a tram on the 3.5-kilometre line which heads via bushland towards the suburb of Sutherland, or take the two-kilometre Parklink track to the NPWS Visitor Centre at Audley (see p.330). There's a kiosk and picnic facilities at the museum.

Heathcote National Park

Heathcote National Park is much smaller and quieter than the Royal National Park across the Princes Highway. It is possible to walk the length of the park in the morning and see no one else along the way. This is a serious bushwalkers' park with no roads and a ban on trail bikes. The best **train** station for the park is Waterfall, from where you can follow a twelve-kilometre trail through the park, before catching a train back from Heathcote. On the way you pass through a variety of vegetation, including Scribbly Gums with their intriguing bark patterns, and spectacular Gymea Lilies with bright red flowers atop tall flowering spears in the spring. Along the path are several swimmable pools fed by Heathcote Creek – the carved sandstone of the **Kingfisher Pool** is the largest and most picturesque. There is a small, very basic six-site **camping ground** here (no drinking water; $3 per adult), and another one at Mirang Pool. **Camping permits** are available from the Royal National Park NPWS Visitor Centre or the Rocks NPWS office (see p.62). By car, you can reach the picnic area at Woronora Dam on the western edge of the park: turn east off the Princes Highway onto Woronora Road (free entry); parking available.

South of the parks

The **coastal drive** from the Royal National Park to **Thirroul**, just outside Wollongong, is stunning. The route runs between rugged sandstone coastal cliffs on one side and bush-covered escarpment on the other, with some beautiful beaches and great pubs and cafés en route.

Follow the Princes Highway south out of Sydney, exiting into the Royal National Park after Loftus onto Farnell Drive; the entry fee at the gate is waived if you are just driving through without stopping. The road through the park emerges above the cliffs at **Otford**, beyond which runs **Lawrence Hargreave Drive** (Route 68) to Thirroul. Unfortunately, due to some dangerous rockfalls, the stunning section between Coalcliff and Clifton has been closed for upgrading until early 2006. To access the picturesque coast and small towns between

Thirroul and Clifton in the meantime it's necessary to drive to Helensburgh from **Stanwell Park**, take the F6 freeway south to precipitous Bulli Pass and then come back up the coast.

A few kilometres from Otford is the impressive clifftop lookout on **Bald Hill** above Stanwell Park, where you're likely to see the breathtaking sight of hang-gliders taking off and soaring down. You can join in with the Sydney Hang Gliding Centre (Ⓣ02/4294 4294, Ⓦwww.hanggliding.com.au), which offers tandem flights with an instructor for around $180 during the week, $195 at weekends (available daily depending on the weather); the centre also runs courses from $195 per day. At **Clifton**, 5km south of Stanwell Park, the *Imperial Hotel*, sitting right on the cliff's edge and with great views of the ocean, is a must for a drink en route. There's more impressive cliff scenery as you pass through **Scarborough** (best seen from the historic *Scarborough Hotel*), just over 2km south, and nearby **Wombarra**, another kilometre on.

Austinmer

By the time you get to **AUSTINMER**, 4km on from Wombarra, you've come to a break in the stunning cliffs and into some heavy surf territory. The down-to-earth former coal-mining town is typical of small coastal settlements in the area, with the Pacific to the east and the soaring Illawarra escarpment looming over the town, it's easy to see why it has attracted an influx of "downsizers", who lend the place its relaxed atmosphere. It has a popular, very clean, patrolled surf beach that gets packed out on summer weekends. Across the road from the beach, there's delicious fish and chips at *Anne's Takeaway and Coffee Shop* (but expect long weekend waits), or seek out locals' secret the *Fireworks Gallery Café*, just back from the beach at 40 Moore Street, for an impressive slice of home-baked sticky date pudding in artistic surroundings.

Thirroul

Just 2km south of Austinmer, **THIRROUL** is the spot where D.H. Lawrence wrote *Kangaroo* during his short Australian interlude in 1922. The bungalow he stayed in at 3 Craig Street, the town and the surrounding area are described in some depth in the novel, though he renamed the then-sleepy village Mullumbimby. Today, Thirroul is gradually being swallowed up by the suburban sprawl of Wollongong but makes a lively alternative spot to stay.

At the southern end of Thirroul's beach, **Sandford Point** (labelled Bulli Point on maps) is a famous surfing break. A sixty-kilometre cycle track runs from Thirroul south along the coast through Wollongong to Lake Illawarra.

Thirroul is busy, with plenty of shops and cafés, including the excellent and appropriately literary *Oskar's Wild Bookstore & Coffee Bar* at 289 Lawrence Hargrave Drive. A good **place to stay**, *The Beaches Hotel*, 272 Lawrence Hargrave Drive (Ⓣ02/4267 2288, Ⓕ4268 2255; rooms $55, apartment $120), a modern, stylish pub complex that has one good-value and spacious two-bedroom apartment, plus cheaper shared-bathroom rooms. You can barbecue your own steaks in the popular beer garden or eat in the bistro; weekend bands and pool tables provide entertainment, though the former can make staying here noisy.

The Illawarra Escarpment

A kilometre south of Thirroul, Lawrence Hargrave Drive joins the Princes Highway, which heads south to Wollongong (Route 60) or northwest, up to a section of the forested Illawarra Escarpment and the **Bulli Pass**. There are fantastic views from the Bulli Lookout, which has its own café, and a couple of kilometres further north heading back towards Sydney at the appropriately named **Sublime Point Lookout**. You can explore the escarpment using the various **walking tracks** which start from the lookouts.

The Nan Tien Temple

Eight kilometres south of Wollongong the vast **Nan Tien Temple**, on Berkeley Road, is the largest Buddhist temple in Australia. Entry is through a traditional Chinese style roofed triple gate to a truly impressive complex of shrines, a museum, meditation hall and seven tier pagoda, erected to house the cremated remains of up to seven thousand devotees. It's reached by car via the F6 Expressway, turning left at the Five Islands Road exit then following the signs, or by train from Central Station to Unanderra station, followed by a twenty-minute walk. Buses are also available from Wollongong station with J.Hill Bus Co. (Ⓣ024229 4911, or Rutty's #34 or 43 from Crown Gateway in the centre of town.

The Fo Guang Shan Buddhists welcome visitors to the temple (Tues–Sun & all public holidays Mon 9am–5pm) and offer a good-value $7 vegetarian lunch, weekend meditation and Buddhist retreats in conjunction with peaceful and surprisingly upmarket **guesthouse** accommodation (Ⓣ02/4272 0500, Ⓦwww.nantien.org.au; $90; all activities included in accommodation price). Their weekend-long annual cultural festival in December, which includes food stalls, dance performances, traditional craft demonstrations and workshops, provides a good antidote to the commercial frenzy of Christmas; check the website for details.

26

The Southern Highlands and around

The **Southern Highlands**, about an hour's drive down the South Western Freeway from Sydney, have been popular as a weekend retreat for Sydneysiders since the 1920s. The area's main appeal is its beautiful countryside – rolling hills, pasture and forest – and pretty, historic towns, which are crammed with cafés, restaurants, antique shops and second-hand book stalls. It's also home to a young, yet increasingly important **wine industry**, and provides a good alternative to the Hunter Valley.

The Southern Highlands and surrounding area are well serviced by public transport. A frequent **train** service runs from Central Station in Sydney, stopping at Mittagong, Bowral, Moss Vale, Exeter and Bundanoon, or the South Coast line can take you to Kiama, Gerringong, Berry and Bomaderry ($12.80–15 one-way depending on your destination; better deals on return and off peak tickets). Priors Scenic Express (☎02/4472 4040 or 1800 816 234) from Campbelltown train station on Sydney's western fringes operate a **coach** service (3.30pm daily except Sat) to Mittagong, Bowral and Kangaroo Valley, which stops for half an hour at Fitzroy Falls and terminates in Nowra. The Premier Motor Service runs from Pitt Street outside Central Station to Kiama, Bomaderry and Nowra (daily 7.30am, 9.15am & 3.15pm). Once you are here there are plenty of **local bus services** to get you around, including Berrima Coaches (☎02/4871 3211).

Accommodation is generally more expensive at weekends and public holiday, but there are some good deals on rooms if you can visit during the week. There are also plenty of self-catering character cottages and campsites in the area.

If you're **driving** to the Southern Highlands, a good scenic route back to Sydney passes through **Kangaroo Valley**, and on to the **Shoalhaven district** of the south coast, before heading north on the Princes Highway, taking in rich pastures, rainforest, and miles of beaches.

Mittagong

Just over 100km south of Sydney, the small agricultural and tourist town of **MITTAGONG** is mostly visited en route to the limestone **Wombeyan Caves** (daily 8.30am–5pm; guided tours: one cave $15; two caves $21; all caves $26; 1hr 30min for each cave) in the nearby hills. The route to the five caves begins 4km south of the town off the highway and winds upwards for 65km on a partly unsealed road.

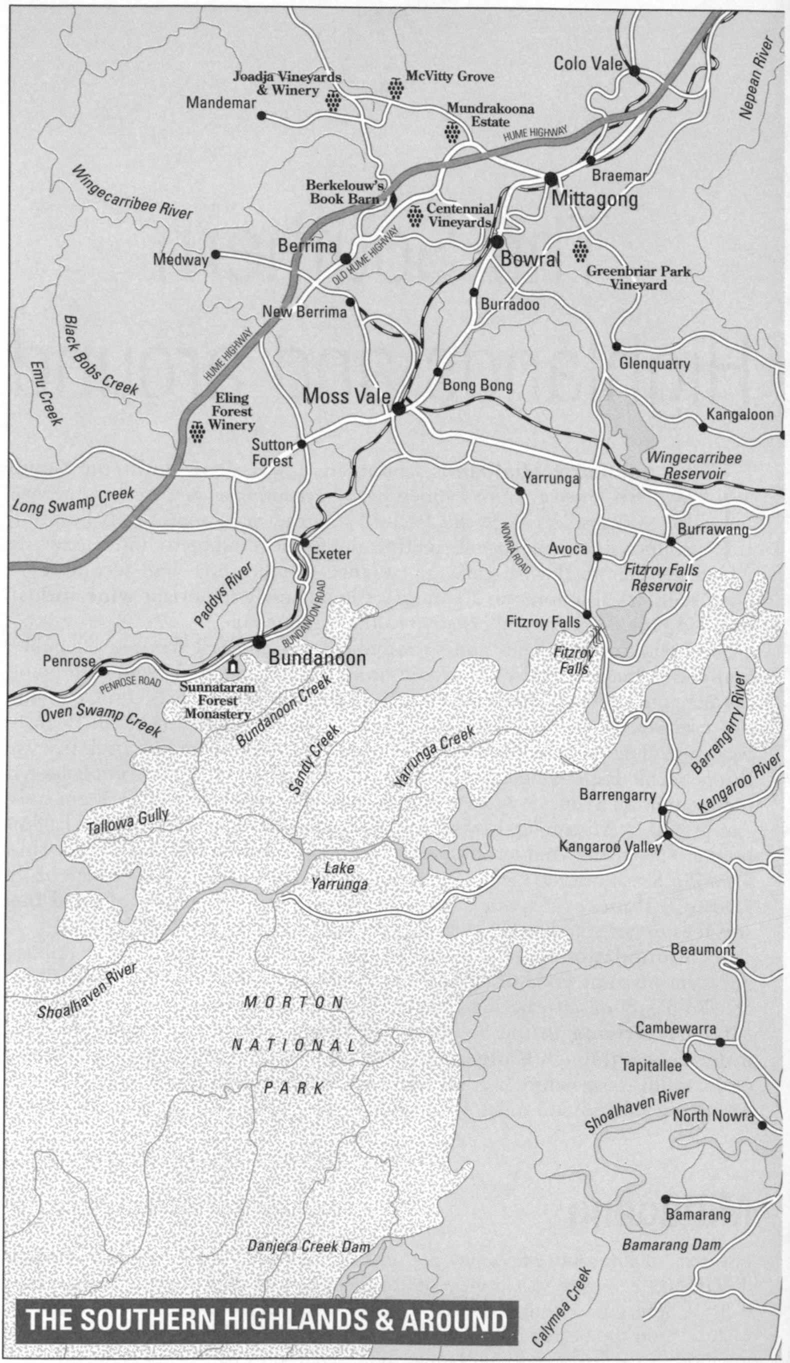
THE SOUTHERN HIGHLANDS & AROUND
Colo Vale
Nepean River
Joadja Vineyards & Winery
McVitty Grove
Mandemar
Mundrakoona Estate
HUME HIGHWAY
Braemar
Mittagong
Wingecarribee River
Berkelouw's Book Barn
Centennial Vineyards
Berrima
Bowral
Medway
OLD HUME HIGHWAY
Greenbriar Park Vineyard
Burradoo
New Berrima
Black Bobs Creek
Glenquarry
Emu Creek
HUME HIGHWAY
Bong Bong
Moss Vale
Eling Forest Winery
Kangaloon
Sutton Forest
Wingecarribee Reservoir
Yarrunga
Long Swamp Creek
NOWRA ROAD
Burrawang
Exeter
Avoca
Fitzroy Falls Reservoir
Paddys River
BUNDANOON ROAD
Fitzroy Falls
Fitzroy Falls
Penrose
Bundanoon
PENROSE ROAD
Sunnataram Forest Monastery
Oven Swamp Creek
Bundanoon Creek
Sandy Creek
Yarrunga Creek
Barrengarry River
Kangaroo River
Barrengarry
Tallowa Gully
Kangaroo Valley
Lake Yarrunga
Beaumont
Shoalhaven River
MORTON NATIONAL PARK
Cambewarra
Tapitallee
Shoalhaven River
North Nowra
Bamarang
Danjera Creek Dam
Bamarang Dam
Calymea Creek

Lake Avon
Little Burke River
Explorers Creek
Burke River
Wongawilli Creek
Lake Cordeaux
Corrimal
Keiraville
Wollongong
Mount Kembla
Unanderra
Wongawilli
Kembla Grange
Port Kembla
Dapto
SOUTHERN FREEWAY
Avondale
Lake Illawarra
Yallah
Windang
Warilla
East Kangaloon
MACQUARIE PASS NATIONAL PARK
Albion Park
ILLAWARRA HIGHWAY
PRINCES HIGHWAY
Shellharbour
Robertson
Carrington Falls
Curramore
Minnamurra
Minnamurra River
Minnamurra Rainforest Centre
JAMBEROO MOUNTAIN ROAD
Kiama Downs
Jamberoo
Bombo
BUDDEROO NATIONAL PARK
Jerrara
The Blowhole & Kiama Tourist Centre
Kiama
Upper Kangaroo Valley
Mount Saddleback Lookout
Kiama Heights
Brogers Creek
Foxground
Rose Valley
Woodhill
Wattamolla
Willow Vale
Werri Beach
Bellawongarah
Broughton Village
Gerringong
Berry
Gerroa
The Silos Winery & Restaurant
PRINCES HIGHWAY
TASMAN SEA
Meroo Meadow
SEVEN MILE BEACH NATIONAL PARK
Broughton Creek
Bomaderry
Shoalhaven Heads
Shoalhaven Tourist Centre
N
Nowra
Brundee
Comerong Island
Greenwell Point
Pyree
Orient Point
Culburra
0
10 km
Wollumboola Lake

The **visitor information centre** in Mittagong (daily 8am–5.30pm; ⓣ02/4871 2888, bookings on ⓣ1300 657 559, ⓦwww.highlandsnsw.com.au) provides a free accommodation booking service for the area, and has masses of information on bushwalks of varying lengths. The characterful *Fitzroy Inn*, 26 Ferguson Crescent (ⓣ02/4872 3457, ⓦwww.fitzroyinn.com.au; rooms $190 mid-week, $240 weekend), is a great **place to stay**; once used to house prisoners, it has been restored with a surprising touch of European chic and still retains its old stone cells. It also has a very highly regarded **restaurant**, offering interesting takes on traditional favourites like pork and rabbit (lunch Thurs–Sun noon–3pm, dinner Wed–Sat 6–10pm; mains $25–29; licensed and BYO). For a light snack, the *Tick Tock European Bakery Café* on Main Street offers a wide range of cakes and pastries cooked on the premises and live music at weekends.

Up at the caves, 65km west of Mittagong, the well-run Wombeyan Caves **campsite** (Jenolan Caves Reserve Trust, Wombeyan Caves Road; ⓣ02/4843 5976, ⓦwww.jenolancaves.org.au) offers cabin and cottage accommodation (en-suite cabins $68, cottage $100) and pitches along the pretty Wombeyan Creek; good amenities include hot showers, a communal kitchen and campfire facilities. You'll need your own linen for the cabins and cottage.

Bowral

Six kilometres southwest of Mittagong, the busy, well-to-do town of **BOWRAL** hums with activity at weekends, when the upper echelon of Sydney society pitch up to cruise the streets in flash cars, sip on cappuccinos and catch up on gossip before retiring to their country hideaways. The main strip, Bong Bong Street, is full of upmarket clothes and homeware shops, and there's also a good bookstore, Bong Bong Books, and a cinema. Bowral was the birthplace of cricket legend Don Bradman, and cricket fans will want to head straight for the **Bradman Museum** on Jude Street (daily 10am–5pm; $8.50; ⓦwww.bradman.org.au), set in an idyllic spot between a leafy park and the well-used cricket oval and club. The museum also has a pleasant café with a garden terrace.

▲ Bowral cricket oval

Southern Highlands wineries

With most producers little more than a decade old, the wine industry in the Southern Highlands is still emerging, but the financial investment in some of the larger labels is significant, and awards are rolling in. The climate here is cooler than most other Australian wine regions and the harvest later, resulting in more varietal flavours, an enhanced fruity character and increased complexity.

Centennial Vineyards Centennial Road, Bowral ⓣ02/4861 8700, ⓦwww.centennial.net.au. A larger set up, with an extensive range of wines for tasting, plus its own restaurant, which gets busy at weekends. Cellar door daily 10am–5pm.

Eling Forest Winery Hume Highway, Sutton Forest (between Berrima & Bundanoon) ⓣ02/4878 9499. Boutique winery established thirteen years ago in the area's original schoolhouse, set on two hundred acres of grounds which visitors are free to roam. It's a very friendly place, producing some excellent wines, and it also hosts the area's wine and food festival at the end of February each year. The prize-winning restaurant (lunch Fri–Sun noon–3.30pm; dinner Fri & Sat from 6pm; mains $17–30) couples modern Italian food with wines produced on site. Cellar door daily 10am–5pm.

Greenbriar Park Vineyard Old South Road, Mittagong ⓣ02/4862 2028. Drive up through grazing sheep to the cellar door set in an award-winning eucalyptus surrounded garden. There's a $5.50 entry fee to the garden, but $4.50 of this is refunded if you buy a bottle of wine, and a portion of the entry fee goes to charity. The vineyard uses only its own handpicked grapes in production, and its Sauvignon Blanc has won awards. Cellar door April–Oct Fri–Sun & public holidays 10am–3pm.

Joadja Vineyards and Winery Joadja Road, Berrima ⓣ02/4878 5236, ⓦwww.joadja.com. The first boutique winery in the area offers you the chance to walk through the working winery. Look out for "Brambelini", a fruit liqueur made from grape spirit, grape juice and seasonal berries. Cellar door daily 10am–5pm.

McVitty Grove Wombeyan Caves Rd, Mittagong ⓣ02/4878 5044, ⓦwww.mcvittygrove.com.au. Beautifully situated winery, with stunning views over the valley from the cellar door. The restaurant serves dishes (mains $18–32) made from the winery's home-produced olives and trout – you're advised to book in advance. Cellar door daily 10am–5pm.

Mundrakoona Estate Sir Charles Moses Lane, off Old Hume Highway, 5km west of Mittagong ⓣ02/4872 1311, ⓦwww.mundrakoona.com.au. Small family-run winery with its own working blacksmith shop, where you can buy ironwork bookstands, rocking chairs or even full sets of gates. Cellar door Mon–Fri 10am–5pm, Sat, Sun and public holidays 10am–6pm.

There are a couple of good **eating** options. *Coffee Culture* at the Empire Cinema Complex on Bong Bong Street, hidden at the end of a lane behind the cinema, is a slick city-style café with the best coffee in town and outstanding food. It opens on Friday and Saturday evenings for dinner too. Alternatively, *That Noodle Place*, 279 Bong Bong St (lunch Fri–Sun noon–2.30pm, dinner Tues–Sun 5.30–9pm), is a funky retro-styled place serving tasty Vietnamese, Thai and Chinese food (including yum cha) with some really interesting dishes from the specials board and mains from $17.

Berrima

The picturesque village of **BERRIMA**, 7km west of Bowral on the Old Hume Highway, is set around an English-style village green and is considered to be one of the country's best examples of an 1830s town, rich in well-preserved and restored old buildings. Of particular note is the *Surveyor General Inn*, which has been serving beer since 1835, making it the oldest continually licensed hotel in Australia. The **visitor centre** (daily 10am–4pm; ⓣ02/48771505) can be found inside the 1838 sandstone **courthouse museum** (same hours; $6), on the corner of Argyle and Wiltshire streets, while across the road is the still operational **Berrima Gaol**, which once held the infamous bushranger Thunderbolt, and acted as an internment camp for POWs and immigrants in wartime; it also has the dubious distinction of being the first place in Australia to execute a woman, in 1841. Continue up Wiltshire Street to reach the **River Walk**, a short walk ending at a nature reserve with **picnic tables** and **camping**.

If you're looking for somewhere to **stay**, the *White Horse Inn* in the Market Place (ⓣ02/4877 1204, ⓦwww.whitehorseinn.com.au; rooms mid-week $80, Fri $90, Sat $135) is a large old 1832 sandstone hotel with accommodation in modern motel units in the garden. Three kilometres north of Berrima on the Old Hume Highway, a vast converted barn houses *Berkelouw's Book Barn & Café*, which sells second-hand and rare books alongside its good **food** and coffee. *Café Fraiche*, also on the Old Hume Highway, is a good alternative coffee stop, with alfresco seating, friendly staff, and a varied and good-value menu.

Bundanoon and the Morton National Park

Five kilometres beyond Berrima on the Old Hume Highway is the turn-off south to **BUNDANOON**, famous for its annual celebration of its Scottish heritage. Exploiting the autumnal atmosphere of mist and turning leaves, Bundanoon becomes Brigadoon for one Saturday in April, overtaken by **Highland Games** – Aussie-style. It's only a small place, but its charm and easy atmosphere make it a good place to break a journey or relax for a few day's bushwalking or cycling.

The town is in an attractive spot set in hilly countryside scarred by deep gullies and with splendid views over the gorges and mountains of the huge **MORTON NATIONAL PARK** (car parking fee $7), which extends from Bundanoon to near Kangaroo Valley. You can start your explorations by setting off at sunset armed with a torch on an evening stroll to **Glow Worm Glen**; after dark the small sandstone grotto is transformed by the naturally flickering lights of these insects, and you may be lucky enough to see wombats along the way. It's a 25-minute walk from town via the end of William Street, or an easy forty-minute signposted trek from Riverview Road in the national park. At the northeast edge of the national park, 17km from Kangaroo Valley, **Fitzroy Falls** is a must-see. A short boardwalk from the car park takes you to the falls, which plunge 80m into the valley below, with glorious views of the Yarrunga Valley beyond. The **NPWS visitor centre** at the falls (daily 9am–5.30pm) has a buffet-style café with a very pleasant outside deck, and can provide detailed information about the many walking tracks and scenic drives in the park; it also issues **camping permits** for the nearby bushcamp at Yarrunga Creek and the Gambells Rest camping ground near Bundanoon, which has flush toilets and hot showers, but no drinking water. Bookings are essential (ⓣ02/4887 7270; $17.50 first night, $10 per night thereafter).

Just out of town is the **Sunnataram Forest Monastery** (visitors welcome; ⓣ02/4884 4262, ⓦwww.sunnataram.org for details and directions), where a community of Thai Buddhist Monks provide meditation retreats and teaching programs; accommodation is available.

The national park, and Bundanoon, are a **cycling** mecca, with the long established Ye Olde Bicycle Shop in Church Street, near the railway station in

Bundanoon, renting out bikes at very reasonable rates (Mon–Fri 9am–4.30pm, Sat & Sun 9am–5pm; $12.50 per hour, $18.50 half-day, $30 full day; ☎02/4883 60430). Opposite the station, the cosy *Bundanoon Hotel* is a good place to recover with a pint of stout and a filling meal after a cycling adventure, with plain, affordable **food** on offer in its *Thistle* bistro (lunch Wed–Sun, dinner Wed–Sat); you'll need to book ahead at weekends.

Accommodation options in Bundanoon include the *Bundanoon Country Inn*, Anzac Parade (☎02/4883 606, Ⓦwww.highlandsnsw.com.au/bundanooncountryinn; rooms mid-week $85, weekend $110), a good-value, centrally positioned motel with great facilities including a pool, tennis court and barbecue; the *Bundanoon YHA* on Railway Avenue (☎02/48836010; dorms $22, rooms $52; book ahead), a spacious Edwardian-era guesthouse complete with open fireplaces and an outdoor spa, set in extensive grounds where you can also camp; and, at the other end of the scale, the stylish *Tree Tops Country Guesthouse*, 101 Railway Avenue (☎02/4883 6372, Ⓦwww.treetopsguesthouse.com.au; rooms mid-week $150, weekend $270), an elegant guesthouse dating from 1910 and furnished from top to bottom with antiques – prices here include breakfast and a gourmet dinner at the weekends, and nice touches like hors d'oeuvres and sherry in the afternoon.

Kangaroo Valley

Leaving the Highlands via Moss Vale en route to Nowra and the coast, the road rises over the ridge of Barrengarry Mountain and then winds down steeply to **KANGAROO VALLEY**. Hidden between the lush dairy country of Nowra and the Highlands, the town is a popular base for walkers and canoe enthusiasts, and is brimming with cafés, craft and gift shops, plus an imposing old character pub, *The Friendly Inn*.

Before entering the main street, the road into town crosses the Kangaroo River on the picturesque nineteenth-century **Hampden Suspension Bridge**. Lying to one side of the bridge, the **Pioneer Settlement Museum** (daily 10am–4.30pm; $4) provides an insight into the origins of the area, and hosts a market in its grounds on the last Sunday of the month. Kangaroo Valley Safaris are based here, and can arrange self-guided overnight **canoe safaris** along the Kangaroo River and the Shoalhaven Gorge with a pickup service at the end (☎02/4465 1502, Ⓦwww.kangaroovalleycanoes.com.au); they also offer canoe hire from $30.

There is a very pleasant **campsite**, *Kangaroo Valley Escapes*, on Moss Vale Road (☎1300 559 977, Ⓦwww.kangaroovalleyescapes.com.au), with a bunkhouse ($25 per person) and en-suite timber cabins equipped with video recorders and air-con, sleeping from two to seven people ($110–180). Mountain bikes, canoes and kayaks can all be rented. A kilometre east of Kangaroo Village, *Tall Trees Bed & Breakfast*, 8 Nugents Creek Rd (☎02/4465 1208, Ⓦwww.talltreesbandb.com.au; rooms mid-week $100, weekend $155), is a home from home, with log fires, great views across the valley and hearty breakfasts served each morning. Self-contained accommodation in a studio or treehouse is also available (studio mid-week $150, weekend $375; treehouse mid-week $160, weekend $395).

Of the many **cafés** in Kangaroo Valley, *Café Bella* at 151 Main Rd stands out from the crowd with its relaxed, friendly feel and good-value breakfast. It's also opens on Friday and Saturday evenings with a small and similarly affordable menu. Alternatively, you can sit beneath a vine-covered verandah and enjoy a cup of tea at the *Source Café* by the Hampden Suspension Bridge. A service station near the bridge sells **groceries**.

If you aren't driving, a **coach** runs daily to Kangaroo Valley at 3.30pm from Campbelltown train station on the outskirts of Sydney with Priors Scenic Express (☎02/4472 4040 or 1800 816 2340); a half-hour stop is scheduled at Fitzroy Falls.

The Shoalhaven District

From Kangaroo Valley it's 22km to the twin town of **NOWRA-BOMADERRY** which straddles the wide **Shoalhaven River** – Bomaderry to the north of the river and Nowra to the south. The river is great for sailing, windsurfing and boating, while the nearby coast is dotted with popular holiday settlements and numerous beaches. **SHOALHAVEN HEADS**, a sleepy resort on **Seven Mile Beach**, a stunning sweep of sandy beach with its own small oceanfront national park, lies north of the river mouth, while **GREENWELL POINT** fishing village lies to the south; both are within 15km of Nowra. **JERVIS BAY** and **SUSSEX INLET** lie further down the coast within easy striking distance by car.

The Shoalhaven Tourist Centre, at the corner of the Princes Highway and Pleasant Way, just after the road bridge between the two towns (daily 9am–5pm; ☎02/4421 0778 or 1800 024 267, ⓦwww.shoalhaven.nsw.gov.au), has plenty of **information** on local accommodation and watersports. There's not a huge amount of choice when it comes to eating or nightlife in Nowra, but it does have one alternative hangout, the *Tea Club* at 46 Berry St (☎02/4422 0900; closed Sun & Mon), a vegetarian **café** with a bohemian feel, exhibitions and artworks for sale, and various artistic, musical and literary activities.

There is no public transport around the region (the rail line running south from Sydney terminates at Bomaderry), so you will need your own vehicle to explore the area, unless you opt for a **tour**: several tour companies including Southcoast Scenic Bus Tours (☎02/4455 1862) run short tours, while Down Under Close Up Tours (☎02/4454 3226) runs two-to four-day guided tours to more remote parts of the south coast.

Berry

Sixteen kilometres north of Nowra along the Princes Highway, the charming, if touristy, town of **BERRY** is set in verdant dairy country backed by the Illawarra Escarpment. The main thoroughfare, Queen Street, is packed with antique and second-hand shops, cafés and restaurants, and is rounded off by a couple of lively country pubs, while the beach lies just 6km away at **Gerringong**. All this combined with characterful places to stay within town and in the surrounding countryside, makes Berry a favourite weekend getaway for Sydneysiders. Indeed, it can be almost unbearably crowded on fine weekends, especially when the monthly **market** is on in the showgrounds on the first Sunday of the month.

Accommodation

In town, accommodation at the well-furnished *Berry Hotel*, 120 Queen St (☎02/4464 1011, ⓦwww.berryhotel.com.au; rooms mid-week $60, weekend $100; full breakfast included at weekends), includes a huge four-bedroom flat upstairs and a two-bedroom house (with kitchen) to the rear; standard rooms share bathrooms. The *Bunyip Inn*, also on Queen Street (☎02/4464 2064; rooms from $70), is an elegant, upmarket bed and breakfast in an imposing two-storey, National Trust classified former bank. Every room is different (nearly all are en suite) and the lovely hedged garden encloses a swimming pool; the stables accommodation includes a wheelchair-accessible unit and another with a kitchen. At the other extreme, the *Great Southern Hotel* (see "Eating and drinking", below; ⓣ02/4464 1009; rooms $60), has wackily decorated and hand-painted attached hotel units which are fun and cheap, and you don't have to stumble back far after a night at the pub.

In **Gerringong**, *Nestor House* YHA on Fern Street (ⓣ02/4234 1249) provides budget accommodation (dorms $20, rooms $60) just 250m from Werri Beach. It's clean, relaxed and friendly, with a communal kitchen and sitting room. Also in Gerringong, *Werri Beach Holiday Park* on Pacific Avenue (ⓣ02/4234 1285 or 1800 655 819, ⓦwww.kiama.net/holiday/werri) has a great location at the northern end of Seven Mile Beach, with en-suite cabins costing $175–220.

Eating and drinking

Berry's two **pubs**, at opposite ends of Queen Street, are attractions in themselves. You can't miss the *Great Southern Hotel*, an Outback-style bungalow pub with two rowing boats on its tin roof. The wrap-around verandah, hung with pretty flower baskets, is a great place to relax, and the beer garden is a dream if you have kids, with a fantastic enclosed playground. Inside, the pub is quirkier still, and there's a pool room, live music on Friday nights, and DJs on Saturday. The typical pub bistro fare is moderately priced. The *Old Berry Hotel* is more traditional, and also popular; its pleasant covered courtyard is a good choice for an affordable tasty meal, from chargrilled steaks to *meze* plates, and there's a tapas bar out front.

Other food options in Berry include the *Cavese Trattoria*, 65 Queen St (ⓣ02/4464 3909; Wed–Sun 10am–9pm; BYO), an authentic Italian place offering wood-fired pizzas and operating as a **café** between meal times. Also on Queen Street, at no. 127, the *Emporium Food Co.* is a deli-café serving affordable gourmet sandwiches, savoury pies, pastries, and excellent coffee. Just off Queen Street on Prince Alfred Street, the *Berry Woodfired Sourdough Bakery* is a great alternative to the more touristy cafés on the main street, with outdoor seating and wholesome treats including sourdough pasties. For something a bit special, head to *The Silos* restaurant at the Silos Winery, which lies in a beautiful rural setting just off the Princes Highway (ⓣ02/4448 6160, ⓦwww.thesilos.com.au). You can **taste wine** here from 9am to 5pm, and follow this with fine dining in the restaurant, where the Australian menu has a Mediterranean and Asian influence (lunch & dinner Wed–Sat, lunch Sun; mains $29–36).

Over in **Gerringong**, *Gerringong Gourmet Deli* on Fern Street is the best **café** in town, with divine fish and chips and gourmet burgers, or try *Perfect Break Vegetarian Café*, just along the street, for outstanding veggie food such as nachos and lentil burgers, washed down with a freshly squeezed fruit juice.

Kiama

From Berry, a 25-kilometre drive up the coast on Princes Highway sees you in **KIAMA**, one of the most attractive coastal resorts south of Sydney. Kiama is famous for its star attraction, the **Blowhole**, which you can drive right up to, or walk to in five minutes from the train station. Lying beneath the lighthouse at Blowhole point, and stemming from a natural fault in the cliffs, the blowhole explodes into a water spout and booms loudly when a wave hits with sufficient force. It's impressive when the sea is right, but also potentially dangerous as freak waves can be thrown over 60m into the air, and have swept several over-curious bystanders to their deaths – so stand well back behind the safety rails. The **Kiama Visitor Centre** nearby on Blowhole Point Road (daily 9am–5pm; ⓣ02/4232 3322 or 1300 652 262, ⓦwww.kiama.com.au), has plenty of information on other local attractions, including **Cathedral Rocks**, a few kilometres to the north, where dramatic rocky outcrops drop abruptly to the ocean.

There's budget priced, shared-bathroom **pub accommodation** at the *Grand Hotel* on the corner of Manning and Bong Bong streets (ⓣ02/4232 1037; rooms $60), one of Kiama's oldest hotels. The closest **hostel** to the train station is *Kiama Backpackers*, 31 Bong Bong St (ⓣ02/4233 1881; dorms $22, rooms $49); accommodation in the stark Seventies building is rather basic, and management perhaps a little too laid back, but the good location near the beach makes up for it. The hostel sometimes closes in winter – ring ahead. *Blowhole Point Holiday Park* on Blowhole Point Road (ⓣ02/4232 2707 or 1800 823 824, ⓦwww.kiama.net/holiday/blowhole; en-suite cabins $150) is the closest **campsite** to the centre of town, in a great spot overlooking a little harbour where you can buy fresh seafood for the barbecue. Alternatively, *East's Beach Caravan Park* on Ocean Street (ⓣ02/4232 2124 or 1800 674 444, ⓦwww.kiama.com.au/eastpark; en-suite cabins mid-week $90, weekend $120) lies a few kilometres south of Kiama on a beach with safe, sheltered swimming; the grassy park has a camp kitchen, playground and tennis courts.

The pub **restaurant** at the *Grand Hotel* serves decent filling meals (lunch and dinner daily). Alternatively, *Zumo Restaurant* at 127 Terralong St offers adventurous and globally eclectic food served up in an old building with lots of greenery (ⓣ02/4232 2222; lunch Sun only, dinner Wed–Sun; mains $22–34; licensed and BYO); outdoor seating ensures its popularity at Sunday lunchtimes.

Macquarie Pass and Budderoo national parks

One of the southernmost stands of Australia's subtropical rainforest can be found at **MACQUARIE PASS NATIONAL PARK**, which is accessed easily from the Southern Highlands via Robertson, or by taking the Illawarra Highway from Albion Park on the coast. The car park on the highway is the start point for the **Cascades Walk**, which takes you on a two-kilometre loop through the forest to Cascades Waterfall.

To the south lies **BUDDEROO NATIONAL PARK**, reached via Jamberoo Mountain Pass Road. The focal point of the park is the **Minnamurra Rainforest Centre** (daily 9am–4pm; ⓣ02/4236 0469; car entry to Minnamurra $11), from where a wheelchair-accessible elevated loop boardwalk (1.6km return; 30min–1hr; boardwalk closes 4pm) winds through subtropical rainforest to a platform with views to **Minnamurra Falls**. Halfway along, a paved walk with some steep sections leads to the upper falls (2.6km return; track closes 3pm). On both walks you'll see cabbage tree palms, staghorn ferns and impressive Illawarra fig trees. The impressive **Carrington Falls**, also within the park, are 8km east of Robertson by road, and worth the detour: a turn-off from the Jamberoo Mountain Pass Road leads to lookout points over the waterfalls.

Free **bushcamping** is possible in both Macquarie Pass and Budderoo national parks.

Contexts

Contexts

History

The first European settlers who arrived at Botany Bay in 1788 saw Australia as **terra nullius** – empty land – on the principle that Aborigines didn't "use" the country in an agricultural sense. However, decades of archeological work, the reports of early settlers and oral tradition have established a minimum date of forty thousand years for human occupation, and evidence that Aboriginal peoples shaped and controlled their land as surely as any farmer.

The early history of Sydney is very much that of white Australia, right from its founding as a **penal colony** amid brutality, deprivation and despair. The first **free settlers** began to arrive in 1793 and were able to avail themselves of convict labour, as prisoners worked as bonded domestics and labourers. Despite living under a harsh system of punishment, the convicts' good behaviour was rewarded with the opportunity to become self-employed and own their own land. Indeed, those with total pardons or whose sentences had expired, the "emancipists", eventually became some of the most influential citizens, such as architect Francis Greenway.

The opening up of the western plains to development after a trio of **explorers** successfully traversed the Blue Mountains saw more white settlers arrive, and the long era of transportation to the colony of New South Wales ended in the 1840s. Soon the **goldrushes** of the 1850s brought many more free settlers from all corners of the world, some of them **Chinese**, whose descendants still operate businesses in Haymarket today. However, the notorious **White Australia policy** was developed after a goldrush-induced xenophobia, and it wasn't until the period after World War II, when Australia desperately needed workers and a larger population, that waves of culturally varied migrants began to arrive, transforming Sydney into the cosmopolitan city it is today.

Prehistory and Aboriginal occupation

In the area around Sydney, there were about three thousand Aboriginal inhabitants at the time of colonization, divided into two tribes organized and related according to complex kinship systems, and with two different languages and several dialects: the **Eora**, whom settlers called the "coast tribe", and the **Dharug**, who lived further inland. Common to the two tribes was a belief that land, wildlife and people were an interdependent whole, engendering a sympathy for the natural processes, and maintaining a balance between population and natural resources. Legends about the mythical **Dreamtime**, when creative forces roamed the land, provided **verbal maps** of tribal territory and linked natural features to the actions of these Dreamtime ancestors.

The early records of the colony mainly describe the lifestyle and habits of the **Eora people**, who, because their staple diet was fish and seafood, made temporary camps close to the shore, usually sleeping in the open by fires. Even in the winter they went naked. Shaping canoes from a single piece of bark, they would fish on the harbour using fish-hooks made from shells attached to fishing lines of bark fibre or spear fish from rocks with multipronged wooden spears

▲ Aboriginal rock carving of a shark, Royal National Park

spiked with kangaroo teeth. The fish diet was supplemented by the hunting of kangaroo and other game and gathering plants such as yams. Besides storytelling and ceremonial dancing, other cultural expression was through **rock engraving**, usually of outlines of creatures such as kangaroo and fish.

The first Europeans

Although earlier attempts had been made to locate and map the continent by the Dutch, Spanish and French, it was only with the *Endeavour* expedition headed by Captain **James Cook** that a concerted effort was made. Cook had headed to Tahiti (where scientists observed the movements of the planet Venus), then mapped New Zealand's coastline before sailing west in 1770 to search for the Great Southern Land.

The British arrived at **Botany Bay** in April 1770; Cook commented on the Aborigines' initial indifference to seeing the *Endeavour* but when a party of forty sailors attempted to land, two Aborigines attacked them with spears and were driven off by musket fire. The party set up camp for eight days, while botanist **Sir Joseph Banks** studied, collected and recorded specimens of the unique plant and animal life. They continued up the Queensland coast, entered the treacherous passages of the Great Barrier Reef, ran aground and stopped for six weeks to repair the *Endeavour*. When they set off again Cook successfully managed to navigate the rest of the reef, and claimed Australia's eastern seaboard – which he named **New South Wales** – on August 21, 1770.

Founding of the colony of New South Wales

The outcome of the American War of Independence in 1783 saw Britain deprived of anywhere to transport convicted criminals; they were temporarily housed in prison ships or "hulks", moored on the Thames in London, while the government tried to solve the problem. Sir Joseph Banks advocated Botany Bay as an ideal location for a **penal colony** that could soon become self-sufficient. The government agreed and on May 13, 1787, the **First Fleet**, carrying over a thousand people, 736 of them convicts, set sail on eleven ships – two of them navy vessels, the *Sirius* and the *Supply* – under the command of Captain **Arthur Phillip**. Reaching Botany Bay on January 18, 1788, they expected the "fine meadows" that Captain Cook had described. What greeted them was mostly swamp, scrub and sand dunes, which Phillip deemed unsuitable for his purposes, moving the fleet north, to the well-wooded **Port Jackson** on **January 26**, a date marked nationwide as Australia Day (see p.264).

Camp was set up on what was named **Sydney Cove** (after Viscount Sydney, then secretary of state in Great Britain) beside the all-important freshwater source, the **Tank Stream**, which now runs under the city streets. Government officials camped on the eastern side of the stream while the marines and convicts were relegated to the west. The **convicts** ranged from a boy of 9 to a woman of 82 and were a multicultural bunch, including English, Scots, black and white Americans, Germans and Norwegians; 188 of them were female. (Convict ships from Ireland began arriving in 1791; ninety percent of those on board were Catholic, many of them were political prisoners and the Irish went on to have an important influence on the city.)

Once Phillip had read the Act of Parliament founding the new colony of New South Wales and was commissioned as **governor**, he gave a speech enjoining the assembled convicts to be industrious, decent and righteous. Directed by the marines, they were used as labour to build the city or became bonded servants, but unless they were found guilty of further crimes, they were not imprisoned or shackled and were free to marry (fourteen convict marriages occurred in the first weeks of settlement alone). Aged mostly between 15 and 25, the convicts had youth on their side. Phillip's method of "the gallows and the lash" and chain-gang justice deterred most from committing more crime, and there was also nowhere really to escape to; the lure of a "ticket of leave", which rewarded good behaviour and meant self-employment and the opportunity to own land, proved a strong incentive to reforming, though not necessarily refining, this former underclass of people.

In the first three years of settlement, the colonists and convicts suffered erratic weather and **starvation**, soil which appeared to be agriculturally worthless, and Aboriginal hostility. The Eora's land had been invaded, half of their numbers wiped out by smallpox, and they were also starving as the settlers shot at their game. When supply ships did arrive, they usually came with hundreds more convicts to further burden the colony.

It was not until 1790, when land was successfully farmed further west at **Parramatta**, that the hunger began to abate. Phillip returned to Britain in 1792 and the first **free settlers** arrived in 1793, while war with France reduced the numbers of convicts being transported to the colony.

The rum corps and Governor Macquarie

After Phillip's departure, the military, known as the **New South Wales Corps** (or more familiarly as the "rum corps"), soon became the supreme political force in the colony. Headed by **John Macarthur**, the 500-strong corps soon manipulated the temporary governor, Major Francis Grose, into serving their interests. Grose gave out land grants and allowed the officers liberal use of convict labour to develop their holdings. Exploiting their access to free land and cheap labour, the corrupt corps' members became rich farm-owners and virtually established a currency based on their monopoly, rum. Events culminated in the **Rum Rebellion** of 1808, when merchant and pastoral factions, supported by the military, ousted mutiny-plagued Governor **William Bligh**, formerly of the *Bounty*, who had attempted to restore order. Britain finally took notice of the colony's anarchic state, and resolved matters by appointing the firm-handed Colonel **Lachlan Macquarie**, backed by the 73rd Regiment, as Bligh's replacement in 1810. Macquarie settled the various disputes – Macarthur had already fled to Britain – and brought the colony eleven years of disciplined progress.

Macquarie has been labelled the "Father of Australia" for his vision of a country that could rise above its convict origins; he implemented enlightened policies towards former convicts or **emancipists**, enrolling them in public offices. The most famous of these was **Francis Greenway**, the convicted forger who he appointed civil architect, and with whom Macquarie set about an ambitious programme of public buildings and parks. But he offended those who regarded the colony's prime purpose as a place of punishment.

In 1813, the **explorers** Wentworth, Blaxland and Lawson were the first white men to successfully cross the Blue Mountains, opening up the western plains to agricultural development (the mountains' original Aboriginal inhabitants had been familiar with the area's seemingly insurmountable streams, forested valleys and cliff faces for thousands of years). More white settlers arrived with the opening up of the west, and in 1821 Macquarie's successor Sir Thomas Brisbane was instructed to segregate, not integrate, convicts. To this end, New South Wales officially graduated from being a penal settlement to a new **British colony** in 1823, and convicts were used to colonize newly explored regions – Western Australia, Tasmania and Queensland – as far away from Sydney's free settlers as possible. By the 1840s the transportation of convicts to New South Wales had ended (the last shipment of convicts arrived in Van Dieman's Land in 1853).

The Victorian era

Australia's first **goldrush** occurred in 1851 near Bathurst, west of Sydney. Between 1850 and 1890 Sydney's population jumped from 60,000 to 400,000, terraced houses were jammed together, and with their decorative cast-iron railings and balconies, they remain one of Sydney's most distinctive heritage features. The first railway line, to Granville near Parramatta, was built in 1855. However, until the 1880s tramway system most people preferred living in the city centre within walking distance of work.

During the Victorian era, Sydney's population became even more starkly divided into the haves and the have-nots: self-consciously replicating life in the mother country, the genteel classes took tea on their verandahs and erected grandiloquent monuments such as the Town Hall, the Strand Arcade and the Queen Victoria Building in homage to English architecture of the time. Meanwhile, the poor lived in slums where disease, crime, prostitution and alcoholism were rife. An outbreak of the plague in The Rocks in 1900 made wholesale **slum clearances** unavoidable, and with the demolitions came a change in attitudes. Strict new vice laws meant the end of the bad old days of drunken taverns and rowdy brothels.

Federation, World War I and World War II

With **federation** in 1901, the separate colonies came under one central government and a nation was created. Unhappily for Sydney, Melbourne was the capital of the **Commonwealth of Australia** until Canberra was built in 1927 – exactly halfway between the two rival cities. The **Immigration Act** was the first piece of legislation to be passed by the new parliament, reflecting the nationalist drive behind federation. The act heralded the **White Australia policy** – greatly restricting non-European immigration right up until 1958.

With the outbreak of **World War I** in 1914, Australia promised to support Britain to "the last man and the last shilling", and there was a patriotic rush to enlist in the army. This enthusiasm tapered with the slaughter at **Gallipolli** – when 11,000 **Anzacs** (Australian and New Zealand Army Corps) died in the eight-month battle in Turkey – and began the first serious questioning of Anglo-Australian relationships. The aftermath of Gallipolli is considered to be the true birth of Australian national identity.

As the **Great Depression** set in, in 1929, Australia faced collapsing economic and political systems; pressed for a loan, the Bank of England forced a restructuring of the Australian economy. This scenario, of Australia still financially dependent on Britain but clearly regarded as an upstart nation, came to a head as a result of the 1932 controversy over England's "**Bodyline**" bowling technique at an international cricket series at the **Sydney Cricket Ground**. The loan was virtually made conditional on Australian cricket authorities dropping their allegations that British bowlers were deliberately trying to injure Australian batsmen during the tour. In the midst of this troubled scenario, it was a miracle that construction continued on the **Sydney Harbour Bridge**, which opened in 1932.

During **World War II**, Labor Prime Minister **John Curtin**, concerned about Australia's vulnerability after the Japanese attack on Pearl Harbor, made the radical decision of shifting the country's commitment in the war from defending Britain and Europe to fighting off an invasion of Australia from Asia. In February the Japanese unexpectedly bombed Darwin, launched **submarine raids** against Sydney and Newcastle, and invaded New Guinea. Feeling abandoned by Britain, Curtin appealed to the USA, who quickly adopted Australia as a base for coordinating Pacific operations under **General Douglas MacArthur**, who made his headquarters in Sydney at the Grace Building, on York Street (now the *Grace Hotel*).

The postwar generation

Australia came out of World War II realizing that the country was closer to Asia than Europe, and it began to look to the USA and the Pacific, as well as Britain, for direction. **Immigration** was speeded up, fuelled by Australia's recent vulnerability. Under the slogan "Populate or Perish", the government reintroduced assisted passages from Britain – the "ten-pound-poms" – also accepting substantial numbers of European refugees. The new European migrant populations ("New Australian"), a substantial number of Italians, Greeks and Eastern Europeans among them, colonized the inner city, giving it a more cosmopolitan face.

Anglo-Australians took on board postwar prosperity during the conservative **Menzies era** – Robert Menzies remained prime minister from 1949 until 1966 – and headed for the suburbs and the now affordable dream of their own home on a plot of land. Over the next few decades, Sydney settled into comfortable suburban living as the redbrick, fibro and weatherboard bungalows sprawled west and southwards into the new suburbs, while the comfy parochialism of the Menzies years saw Australian writers, artists and intellectuals leave the country in droves.

Modern Sydney

Immigration continued in waves, with a large influx of people from postwar Vietnam and Southeast Asia aided by Gough Whitlam's tolerant Labor government (before it was famously sacked by the governor general in 1975). Concentrated ethnic enclaves include a vibrant Vietnamese community at Cabramatta, a Filippino focus in Blacktown and an emerging Chinese community in Ashfield, resulting from the thousands of Chinese students whom the prime minister **Bob Hawke** allowed to remain in Australia on humanitarian grounds after the Tian'anmen Square massacre in 1989.

Other developments were more concrete. When the restrictions limiting the height of buildings was lifted in 1957, the development of Sydney's high-rise skyline really took off. Notably tall office blocks include the 183-metre Australia Square Tower (1961–67) and the 244-metre MLC Centre (1975–78), designed by Sydney's most prominent architect, **Harry Seidler**. The Sydney Tower (1981) is – at 259m – the tallest and most recognizable structure on the skyline. But it's the **Sydney Opera House** which can claim to be both the most striking and controversial of Sydney's postwar buildings, originally designed by the Danish architect Jørn Utzon in 1957 and finally opening in 1973.

This building boom saw many Heritage buildings unthinkingly demolished. The New South Wales premier, Robin Askin (1965–74), was keen for many residential areas of the inner city to make way for new office blocks and hotels. People began protesting against developments and a radical union, the Builders' Labourers Federation (BLF), put might behind the dissent. The BLF secretary, Jack Mundey, coined the term **Green Ban**, meaning the withdrawal of union labour for projects opposed by the community and potentially damaging to the environment. In November 1971 a Green Ban was placed on demolition of The Rocks: two-thirds of the city's most historic area would have been redeveloped if the Sydney Cove Redevelopment Authority had had its way. In October 1973, non-union workers poised for demolition were stopped by eighty members of the Rocks Resident Action Group. A compromise in 1975 saw some development but the residential areas were extended and historic buildings restored.

Askin's development schemes were set aside by Labor Premier **Neville Wran** in 1976, but pressure for a bicentennial project saw a fortune spent on the controversial **Darling Harbour redevelopment**, which opened in 1988, a commercial extravaganza of shops, restaurants, a casino and tourist attractions. Environmentalists were particularly opposed to the ugly monorail trundling above the city streets and providing little more than a tourist link.

When Sydney beat Beijing in 1993 for the 2000 Olympics, the city rejoiced. But in January 1994 the world watched stunned as the future Olympic city went up in flames: front-page images of the two icons of Australia, the Opera House and the Harbour Bridge, were silhouetted against an orange, smoke-filled sky during the Black Friday **bushfires**, which destroyed 250 homes and cost four lives. Bushfires continue to endanger Sydney's bushland – dry conditions due to the long-running **drought**, which began to break with heavy rains at the end of June 2005, have provided a perfect bushfire environment. Sydney's main water source, Warragamba Dam, is still at an all-time low, and water restrictions continue with the beloved surburban garden hose now mostly out of action.

In 1995 a New South Wales Labor government was elected under the leadership of the outspoken ex-journalist **Premier Bob Carr**. Labor was re-elected for a third term in the 2003 state elections, with Carr seemingly intent on staying in office indefinitely, however he suddenly retired in July 2005 shocking everyone. High profile contenders in the battle for the state's top job included former Lord Mayor of Sydney Frank Sartor, but the surprise winner was media-shy **Morris Iemma**. Carr's own decade at the helm saw him increase the size and number of national parks, improve educational standards and, in preparation for the Olympics, undertake the unenviable task of coordinating the city's biggest infrastructure project since the construction of the Sydney Harbour Bridge. More than $2.5 billion of public money was spent on major road and rail projects, including a $630 million rail link from the airport to the city, and a $93 million rail link to Olympic venues at the $470 million Homebush Bay site.

The 2000 Sydney Olympics (see p.269) turned out to be a big success, sending the city's confidence in itself skyrocketing and the city **post-Olympics** is still exuberant. Real-estate prices are at record highs, with a generation now effectively priced out of the market, and more and more luxury apartments overtaking characterful old waterfront wharves. Apartment living has finally come to the Central Business District, too, with an injection of residential life and everyday facilities such as supermarkets into an area that used to be quiet at weekends once the workers had cleared out. Developers are closing on Sydney's deprived inner-city area, Redfern, where riots in mid-February 2004 were provoked by the death of 17-year-old T.J. Hickey, impaled on a fence while riding his bike after believing he was being pursued by the police. Around a hundred Aboriginal youths battled two hundred police with bottles, bricks and molotov cocktails; over forty police were injured and Redfern train station was set alight. The gap between rich and poor in Sydney continues to increase and as the upwardly mobile move closer to the centre and remain in the eastern suburbs and by the North Shore, the less affluent renters are forced towards the increasingly troubled, poorly serviced western suburbs, such as socially disadvantaged Macquarie Fields, which has double the Sydney average of unemployment, a high youth population and a big stock of public housing. In February 2005, after a stolen car police chase caused the death of two teenage passengers, four nights of riots in Macquarie Fields ensued. Villawood, also in the western suburbs, is a controversial immigration detention centre which is Sydney's focus for the heated and emotional national debate over Australia's mandatory immigration detention policy, particularly the incarceration of children, introduced in 1992 after over four hundred "boat people" arrived on Australia's shores between 1989 and 1992.

Books

Many of the best books by Australian writers or about Australia are not available overseas, so you may be surprised at the range of local titles available in Australian **bookshops**; we have reviewed several favourite Sydney stores on pp.249–250 and have included websites where available for online sales. A good website to check is www.gleebooks.com.au, one of Australia's best literary booksellers, with a whole host of recent reviews; you can order books online, to be posted overseas. Titles marked are especially recommended.

History and politics

John Birmingham *Leviathan: the Unauthorised Biography of Sydney*. Birmingham's 1999 tome casts a contemporary eye on the dark side of Sydney's history, from nauseating accounts of Rocks' slum life and the 1900 plague outbreak, through the 1970s traumas of Vietnamese boat people, to scandals of police corruption.

Manning Clark *A Short History of Australia*. A condensed version of this leading historian's multivolumed tome, focusing on dreary successions of political administrations over two centuries, and cynically concluding with the "Age of Ruins".

Ann Coombs *Sex and Anarchy: The Life and Death of the Sydney Push*. The legendary Sydney Push, a network of anarchists and bohemians who met at pubs through the conservative 1950s and 1960s, experienced the sexual revolution a generation before mainstream society and influenced everyone from Germaine Greer to Robert Hughes.

David Day *Claiming A Continent: A New History of Australia*. Award-winning, general and easily readable history, concluding in 2000. The possession, dispossession and ownership of the land – and thus issues of race – are central to Day's narrative. Excellent recommended reading of recent texts at the end of each chapter will take you further.

Colin Dyer *The French Explorers and the Aboriginal Australians*. From Bruny d'Entrecasteaux's (1793) to Nicolas Baudin's (1802) expeditions, the French explorers and on-board scientists kept detailed journals providing a wealth of information on Aboriginal Australians. Dyer provides engaging access to much recently translated material.

Jack Egan *Buried Alive, Sydney 1788–92: Eyewitness Accounts of the Making of a Nation*. A fascinatingly detailed, almost day-by-day view of the first five years of the city's settlement, culled from diaries and letters, and connected by Egan's narrative.

Bruce Elder *Blood on the Wattle: Massacres and Maltreatment of Aboriginal Australians Since 1788*. A heart-rending account of the horrors inflicted on the continent's indigenous peoples, covering infamous nineteenth-century massacres as well as more recent mid-twentieth-century scandals of the "Stolen Generation" children.

Tim Flannery (ed) *Watkin Trench 1788*. A reissue of two accounts – "A Narrative of the Expedition to Botany Bay" and "A Complete Account of the Settlement of Port Jackson" – written by Trench, a captain of the marines who came ashore with the First Fleet. Trench, a natural storyteller and fine writer, was a young man in his 20s, and the accounts brim with youthful curiosity. *The Birth of Sydney* (ed),

Australian writing and writers

Australian writing came into its own in the **1890s**, when a strong nationalistic movement, leading up to eventual federation in 1901, produced writers such as Henry Lawson and the balladeer A.B. "Banjo" Paterson, who romanticized the bush and glorified the mateship ethos. Outstanding women writers, such as Miles Franklin and Barbara Baynton, gave a feminine slant to the bush tale and set the trend for a strong female authorship.

In the **twentieth and twenty-first centuries**, Australian novelists came to be recognized in the international arena: Patrick White was awarded a Nobel Prize in 1973, Peter Carey won the Booker Prize in 1988 and again in 2001, and Kate Grenville scored the 2001 Orange Prize for Fiction. Other writers who have made a name for themselves within Australia include David Malouf, Julia Leigh, Tim Winton, Thomas Keneally, Richard Flanagan, Chloe Hooper and Robyn Davidson. Literary journals such as *Meanjin*, *Southerly*, *Westerly* and *Heat* provide a forum and exposure for short fiction, essays, reviews and new and established writers. The big prizes in Australian fiction include the **Vogel Prize** for the best unpublished novel written by an author under the age of 35, and the country's most coveted literary prize, the **Miles Franklin Award**.

Many British and multinational **publishers** have setups in Australia, publishing an Australian list which is never seen overseas, and the same goes for Australian publishers. As booksellers usually have separate Australian fiction and non-fiction sections you can easily zero in on the local stuff. Gleebooks (p.250), Ariel (p.249) and Dymocks (p.250) hold readings and literary events, but the best chance to see a host of Australian (and international) writers read and talk about their work is at the Sydney Writers Festival in May (see p.265). Also check out the Writers' Walk at Circular Quay (p.66).

an anthology of writings from the 1770s to the 1850s, includes accounts by Captain Cook, Charles Darwin, Anthony Trollope and Mark Twain, as well as Flannery's essay, "The Sandstone City", which draws connections between ecology, Aboriginal history and present-day Sydney.

Alan Frost *Botany Bay Mirages: Illusions of Australia's Convict Beginnings*. Historian Frost's well-argued attempt to overturn many long-cherished notions about European settlement.

Robert Hughes *The Fatal Shore*. A minutely detailed epic of the origins of transportation and the brutal beginnings of white Australia in this popular history.

Grace Karskens *The Rocks: Life in Early Sydney*. Karskens' social history draws a vivid picture of Australia's earliest neighbourhood from 1788 until the 1830s.

Mark McKenna *Looking For Blackfellas Point: An Australian History of Place*. McKenna uncovers the uneasy history of Aboriginals and European settlers on the south coast of NSW and widens his scope to the enduring meaning of land to both Aboriginal and white Australians.

Geoffrey Moorhouse *Sydney*. All the latest developments – from the Gay Mardi Gras to police corruption and inner-city Aboriginal poverty – are analysed by internationally renowned British historian and travel writer Moorhouse, with their roots traced back to the city's beginnings.

Maria Nugent *Botany Bay: Where Histories Meet*. Botany Bay was where Captain Cook famously first landed in 1770, and in 1788 was the British choice for an Antipodean convict colony. A substantial and enduring Aboriginal settlement at La Perouse is the focus of Nugent's cultural history.

Portia Robinson *The Women of Botany Bay*. Uses painstaking research into the records of every woman transported from Britain between

1787 and 1828, and the wives of convicts who settled in Australia.

Gavin Souter *Times & Tides: A Middle Harbour Memoir*. Esteemed historian Souter weaves his intimate knowledge of Middle Harbour's bush-covered suburban shores – so close to the city yet so idyllic – into the cultural and natural history of the area, from Aboriginal to European occupation.

Peter Spearitt *Sydney's Century: A History*. A very readable academic history, following Sydney's social and physical development in the twentieth century. Archival photographs, maps, cartoons, advertisements and snippets from novels and magazines help flesh out a fascinating portrait.

Martin Thomas *The Artificial Horizon: Imagining the Blue Mountains*. Taking a thought-provoking cultural studies approach to the Blue Mountains, Thomas focuses his lens on explorers, Aboriginal people, the tourism industry and even the long tradition of suicidal cliff-leapers, supported by maps and photographs.

Larry Writer *Razor*. A satisfyingly lurid account of the mean streets of inner-city Sydney of the 1930s, with its vicious gang wars and rule by two blood-enemy vice queens, Tilly Devine and Kate Leigh. Engrossing photos and crims' mugshots accompany the text.

Ecology and environment

Meredith and Verity Burgmann *Green Bans, Red Union*. The full political ins and outs of the Green Bans of the 1970s – when the radical New South Wales Builders' Labourers union, led by Jack Mundey, resisted developers' plans for The Rocks and other areas of Sydney.

Tim Flannery *The Future Eaters*. Palaeontologist Flannery here explains how as the first human beings migrated down to Australasia, Aborigines, Maoris and other Polynesian peoples changed the region's flora and fauna in startling ways, consuming the resources needed for their own future; Europeans made an even greater impact on the environment, of course, continuing the "future eating" of natural resources.

Tim Low *Bush Tucker: Australia's Wild Food Harvest* and *Wild Food Plants of Australia*. Guides to the bountiful supply of bushtucker that was once the mainstay of the Aboriginal diet; the latter is pocket-sized and contains clear photographs of over 180 plants, describing their uses.

Mary White *The Greening of Gondwana*. Classic work on the evolution of Australia's flora and geography.

James Woodford *The Wollemi Pine: The Incredible Discovery of a Living Fossil from the Age of the Dinosaurs*. The award-winning environment writer at the *Sydney Morning Herald* tells the story of the 1994 discovery in Wollemi wilderness near Sydney (see p.321).

Biography and autobiography

John Dale *Huckstepp: A Dangerous Life*. The still-unsolved 1986 murder of Sallie-Anne Huckstepp, herself steeped in Sydney's criminal underworld of drugs and prostitution, continues to capture the public imagination. When her drug-dealing boyfriend, Lanfranchi, was shot dead in 1981 by detective Roger Rogerson (later proved to be one of New South Wales' most corrupt officers), the young, beautiful and articulate Huckstepp went to the national media to accuse the police force of cold-blooded murder.

Robin Dalton *Aunts Up the Cross*. Dalton, a prominent London literary agent, spent her childhood in the 1920s and 1930s in Kings Cross, in a huge mansion peopled by the eccentric aunts (and uncles) of the title.

Robert Holden *Crackpots, Ratbags & Rebels: A Swag of Aussie Eccentrics*. From *Eternity* graffiti-guy Arthur Stace to Shakespeare-spouting bag-lady Bea Miles and the "Witch of the Cross" Rosaleen Norton, the majority of the famous eccentrics here hail from Sydney.

Clive James *Unreliable Memoirs*. The expat satirist humorously recalls his postwar childhood and adolescence in Sydney's southern suburbs.

Jill Ker Conway *The Road from Coorain*. Conway's childhood, on a drought-stricken Outback station during the 1940s, is movingly told, as is her battle to establish herself as a young historian in sexist, provincial 1950s Sydney.

Hazel Rowley *Christina Stead: A Biography*. Stead (1902–83) has been acclaimed as Australia's greatest novelist. After spending years in Paris, London and New York with her American husband, she returned to her native Sydney in her old age.

Bernard Smith *The Boy Adeodatus: The Portrait of a Lucky Young Bastard*. Art historian Smith is author of several books including *Australian Painting*, but his best writing is in this prize-winning memoir. Writing honestly about growing up as a state ward in Sydney, Smith beautifully captures the atmosphere of the city from the first World War to the 1930s.

Shane Weaver *Blacktown*. This working-class survival autobiography provides a harsh but compelling account of life in Sydney's socio-economically deprived outer west. From a difficult childhood in the 1950s and 1960s involving a violently abusive stepfather, and immersion in a culture of drugs and alcohol as a young adult, the late Weaver went on to become a champion boxer, a psychiatric nurse and finally creative director of a multinational advertising agency.

Travel writing

Bill Bryson *Down Under* (published in the US as *In a Sunburnt Country*). Famously funny travel writer Bill Bryson devotes a chapter of his Australia book to "the frappaccino heaven that is modern Sydney".

Peter Carey *30 Days in Sydney*. Based in New York, famous Australian writer Carey set himself a thirty-day time frame and subtitled his book "A wildly distorted account", to defuse ideas that it might be a comprehensive guide. As he hangs out with old friends, it is their lives, the tales they tell and the often nostalgic trips around Sydney that form the basis of this vivid city portrait.

Michael Duffy, David Foster et al *Crossing the Blue Mountains: Journeys Through Two Centuries*. Eleven personal Blue Mountains' journey accounts including Gregory Blaxland's famous expedition with Wentworth and Lawson in 1813 when they found a route across; Charles Darwin's visit in 1836 as part of his world trip on the *Beagle*; and contemporary novelist David Foster's reflections on wilderness and solitude as he walks from Mittagong to Katoomba.

Richard Hall (ed) *The Oxford Book of Sydney*. This wide-ranging collection of writing – including journalism, letters, poems and novel excerpts – spans 1788 to 1997.

Jan Morris *Sydney*. An insightful and informative account of Australia's favourite city by one

of the world's most respected travel writers, written in the early 1990s.
Ruth Park *Ruth Park's Sydney*. By one of Australia's most loved storytellers (see p.360), Park's impressionistic and personal look takes the form of a walking guide full of anecdotes and literary quotations; written in 1973, and long out of print, it was revised and expanded in 1999.

Sydney and around in fiction

Murray Bail *Eucalyptus*. A beautifully written novel with a fairy-tale-like plot. A NSW farmer has planted nearly every type of eucalyptus tree on his land. When his extraordinarily beautiful daughter is old enough to marry, he sets up a challenge for her legion of potential suitors to name each tree.
Peter Corris *The Coast Road*. Australia's answer to Raymond Chandler, former academic Corris brings a glittering but seedy Sydney alive in all his detective novels. Private eye Cliff Hardy, chucked out of his Paddington terrace office, operates from his Glebe home. His clients include a Sydney University linguistics professor, and his investigations take him down the coast south of Sydney. Corpses, bikie gangs and undercover cops all feature.
Eleanor Dark *The Timeless Land*. Classic historical novel, written in the 1940s, which recounts the settlement of Sydney in 1788.
Tom Gilling *Miles McGinty*. Nineteenth-century Sydney comes alive in this colouful historical fable. The riotous, entertaining love story of Miles, who becomes a levitator's assistant and begins to float on air, and Isabel, who wants to fly.
Kate Grenville *The Secret River*. Inspired by research into the author's convict ancestry, and her troubled imaginings of her forebears interaction with indigenous people. Grenville's latest novel vividly evokes the landscape of the Hawkesbury River, where emancipated convict William Thornhill takes up a land grant, but also the London where he worked as a Thames waterman, using transcripts of his Old Bailey trail to great effect.
Linda Jaivin *Eat Me*. Billed as an "erotic feast", the story opens with a memorable fruit-squeezing scene. Three trendy women (fashion editor, academic and writer) hang out in Darlinghurst cafés and swap stories of sexual exploits.
Malcolm Knox *Summerland*. Narrator Richard has been coming to Palm Beach, Sydney's summer playground for the wealthy, every year to stay with friend and golden boy Hugh Bowman, and now, in adulthood, with their partners. Richard's telling of the disintegration of a friendship and the downfall of Hugh gives a critical insight into an exclusive, less-than-perfect social milieu.
Gabrielle Lord *Baby Did a Bad, Bad Thing*. One of Australia's best crime-fiction writers bases her immaculately researched novels in hometown Sydney. Former police officer and private investigator Gemma Lincoln's policeman boyfriend has gone undercover to investigate the city's biggest crime boss. Meanwhile Gemma deals with her own investigation into the rape and murder of local prostitutes and an insurance case involving the death of a millionaire.
Roger McDonald *Mr Darwin's Shooter*. The shooter of the title is Syms Covington, Charles Darwin's servant on the famous *Beagle* expedition. He eventually settled in Sydney's Watsons Bay, and is captured here in the 1850s as, now middle-aged and troubled by the theory of evolution he helped to evolve, he awaits with trepidation the publication of *The Origin of the Species*. Finely written

and immaculately researched.
Ruth Park *The Harp in the South*. First published in 1948, this first book of the trilogy is a well-loved tale of inner-Sydney slum life in 1940s Surry Hills. The spirited Darcy family's battle against poverty provides memorable characters, not least the Darcy grandmother with her fierce Irish humour.
Christina Stead *For Love Alone*. Set largely around Sydney Harbour in the 1920s, where the late author grew up, this novel follows the obsessive Teresa Hawkins, a poor but artistic girl from an unconventional family, who scrounges and saves to head for London and love.
Kylie Tennant *Ride on Stranger*. First published in 1943, this is a humorous portrait of Sydney between the two world wars, seen through the eyes of a newcomer.

Sydney in children's fiction

Gabrielle Carey and Kathy Lette *Puberty Blues*. This hard-hitting novel for teenagers explores the sexist underworld of Sydney's surf culture. Set at Cronulla Beach in the late 1970s, the reality of peer pressure and the temptations of sex and drugs are examined with frankness and gritty honesty. A 1981 film brought this story to the big screen.
Jean Chapman *Opera House Mouse* and **Lindy Batchelor** *ZOOming in on Taronga*. These delightful picture books give the very young a glimpse behind the scenes at two of Sydney's best loved attractions, Sydney Opera House and Taronga Zoo, and are suitable as either a pre-visit introduction or a post-visit souvenir.
Jean Chapman *A Day with May Gibbs at Nutcote*. This picture book introduces the 1930s world of May Gibbs, Australia's much loved children's book author and illustrator, during the time she lived at Nutcote, in the harbour-side suburb of Neutral Bay. May Gibbs is best remembered as the creator of the gumnut babies and the big bad banksia men, found most famously in the classic of Australian Children's literature, *Snugglepot and Cuddlepie*.
Deirdre Hill *Bridge of Dreams*. This novel is a detailed retelling of the story of one of Sydney's best known icons, the Sydney Harbour Bridge. The construction, associated accidents and controversial opening, together paint a complex picture of not only the bridge but Sydney itself in the first third of the twentieth century.
Victor Kelleher *Taronga* and **John Heffernan** *CBD*. These novels for older readers are set in a future, post-apocalyptic Sydney and present bleak but compelling visions of the city's possible destiny.
Melina Marchetta *Looking for Alibrandi*. A passionate and gently humorous novel that tells the story of Josie, a teenager in her last year at a strict Sydney Catholic high school in the late 1990s, whose world is thrown into turmoil by the revelation of family secrets and the suicide of a friend. Made into a highly successful film in 2000, this story presents the complex, multicultural face of contemporary Sydney.
Lilith Norman *A Dream of Seas*. In this novel for young readers, a boy and his mother move to Bondi Beach in Sydney's east after the drowning death of the boy's father. A misfit at his new school, the boy finds peace and solace through the affinity he feels with the sea and its resident seals.
Ruth Park *Playing Beatie Bow*. Set in the historic Rocks district, this novel takes older readers on an exciting

adventure as they follow troubled teen Abigail Kirk back through time to Sydney's colonial era. Park vividly re-creates the sights, sounds and smells of the area's slums in 1873, as Abigail uses her experiences in a Sydney of old to put her twentieth-century problems into perspective. In 1985 this novel stepped off the pages of the book to become a film, beautifully shot on location in The Rocks.

John Pye *Ferryboat Fred: The Big Race*. Sydney's answer to *Thomas the Tank Engine* is a little ferryboat called Fred. This picture book takes the pre-school set along on Fred's adventures, as he plies the waters of Sydney Harbour accompanied by his trusty friends.

Ethel Turner *Seven Little Australians*. The lives of the seven Woolcot children take readers around late nineteenth-century Sydney, from the rambling family home, Misrule, by the Parramatta River, to their father's job as Captain at Victoria Barracks. The misadventures of the bright and precocious Judy and her brothers and sisters are charming young readers as much today as they did when the book was first published more than a hundred years ago. The story was made into a successful television series in 1974, which has recently been released on DVD.

Nadia Wheatley *My Place*. This fascinating picture book depicts the multi-layered evolution of a Sydney street through time, up until the present day. A lovely way to introduce the very young to Sydney's history.

Food and wine

Ben Canaider and Greg Duncan Powell *Drink Drank Drunk*. Fun, no-nonsense guide to Australian wine by an irreverent duo.

Bill Granger *Sydney Food*. Self-taught chef Granger – his cooking style is based on using the freshest ingredients in simple combinations – runs three very popular *bills* restaurants (see p.187) in his adopted city. A great souvenir, with gorgeous photographs of city settings.

James Halliday *Australian Wine Companion*. Released every year, the venerable Halliday provides an authoritative guide not only to the best wines but also to the wineries themselves, with over 1800 wineries covered. A great accompaniment to a Hunter Valley visit.

Huon Hooke and Ralph Kyte-Powell *The Penguin Good Australian Wine Guide*. Released every year, this is a handy book for a wine buff to buy on the ground, with the best wines and prices detailed to help navigate you around the bottle shop.

Kylie Kwong *Kylie Kwong: Recipes and Stories*. Sydney chef Kylie Kwong cooks contemporary Chinese at her stylish restaurant *Billy Kwong* (see p.197). Her cookbook not only provides some great recipes but also gives an insight into Chinese-Australian culture, from shopping in Chinatown to memorable family meals.

R. Ian Lloyd *Australian Wine Regions: Hunter Valley*. With informative text by Lloyd and beautiful photographs by Steve Elias, this glossy coffee-table tome, published in 2001, is one of a series introducing Australia's premier wine-producing areas.

Joanna Savill *The SBS Eating Guide to Sydney*. This annual guide to the best of ethnic food in Sydney will help you hunt down authentic cuisines. Researchers work at Australia's multicultural TV station, SBS.

Art and architecture

Wally Caruana *Aboriginal Art.* An excellent illustrated paperback introduction to all styles of Aboriginal art.

Philip Drewe and Jørn Utzon *Sydney Opera House.* A study of one of the world's most striking pieces of contemporary architecture, designed by Jørn Utzon, with detailed photographs and notes.

Robert Hughes *The Art of Australia.* The internationally acclaimed art historian, author of *The Shock of the New*, cut his teeth on this seminal dissection of Australian art up to the 1960s.

Sylvia Kleinert & Margo Neale (eds) *The Oxford Companion to Aboriginal Art and Culture.* Weighty 644-page tome, illustrated in colour, emphasizes visual art – photography to rock art and body painting – but also covers Aboriginal music, writing and even theatre.

Alice Spigelman *Almost Full Circle: Harry Seidler.* Biography of Australia's most notable architect, the Viennese-born Seidler, who migrated to Australia in 1948 after a wartime internment in Canada. He went on to build Sydney's first skyscraper, the fifty-storey Australia Square on George Street, in 1963, and has continued to revolutionize Sydney's skyline.

Specialist guides

Bruce Ashley *Sydney: The Complete Guide to Sydney's Best Rides.* Published in 2005 by cycling advocacy group Bicycle NSW: 25 cycling routes take in the city, the suburbs, the beach and the bush.

Peter and Gibson Dunbar-Hall *Deadly Sounds Deadly Places.* Comprehensive guide to contemporary Aboriginal music in Australia, from Archie Roach to Yothu Yindi; includes a handy discography.

Alan Fairley *Sydney's Best Bushland Walks.* The "Top 30" walks detailed – which include nature notes and maps – are all accessible by public transport.

Wendy Preston *The Choice Guide to Sydney For Kids.* The updated 2004 edition features over 300 fun activities, plus practical detail from transport to baby-changing facilities. Categories include cycling, swimming, animals and "freebies and cheapies". Preston also manages a useful website www.sydneyforkids.com.au.

Greg Pritchard *Climbing Australia: The Essential Guide.* Recent, comprehensive guide for rock-climbers, with a section on the Blue Mountains.

Seana Smith *Sydney For Under Fives: The Best of Sydney For Babies, toddlers and Preschoolers.* A bible for locals with small children, with over 450 pages in the updated 2004 edition. Smith makes sure that parents enjoy themselves, too, including information on kid-friendly cafés and restaurants, baby-friendly cinemas and childcare contacts.

Tyrone Thomas *100 Walks in NSW.* Forty-six of the walks cover the area detailed in this book, with tracks on the Central Coast, in the Royal National Park and the Blue Mountains.

Mark Thornley and Veda Dante *Surfing Australia: A Guide to the Best Surfing Down Under.* One of the *Periplus Guides* series, with loads of full-colour photos and maps, and over thirty pages on the Sydney area, including the Central and South coasts.

Jeff Toghill *Walking Sydney: Over 20 Original Walks In and Around Sydney.* Published in 2004, this wide-ranging walking guide covers city, harbour, suburban and coastal walks. Includes maps.

Travel store

UK & Ireland
Britain
Devon & Cornwall
Dublin DIRECTIONS
Edinburgh DIRECTIONS
England
Ireland
The Lake District
London
London DIRECTIONS
London Mini Guide
Scotland
Scottish Highlands & Islands
Wales

Europe
Algarve DIRECTIONS
Amsterdam
Amsterdam DIRECTIONS
Andalucía
Athens DIRECTIONS
Austria
Baltic States
Barcelona
Barcelona DIRECTIONS
Belgium & Luxembourg
Berlin
Brittany & Normandy
Bruges DIRECTIONS
Brussels
Budapest
Bulgaria
Copenhagen
Corfu
Corsica
Costa Brava DIRECTIONS
Crete
Croatia
Cyprus
Czech & Slovak Republics
Dodecanese & East Aegean
Dordogne & The Lot
Europe
Florence & Siena
Florence DIRECTIONS
France
French Hotels & Restaurants
Germany
Greece
Greek Islands
Hungary
Ibiza & Formentera DIRECTIONS
Iceland
Ionian Islands
Italy
The Italian Lakes
Languedoc & Roussillon
Lisbon
Lisbon DIRECTIONS
The Loire
Madeira DIRECTIONS
Madrid DIRECTIONS
Mallorca DIRECTIONS
Mallorca & Menorca
Malta & Gozo DIRECTIONS
Menorca
Moscow
The Netherlands
Norway
Paris
Paris DIRECTIONS
Paris Mini Guide
Poland
Portugal
Prague
Prague DIRECTIONS
Provence & the Côte d'Azur
Pyrenees
Romania
Rome
Rome DIRECTIONS
Sardinia
Scandinavia
Sicily
Slovenia
Spain
St Petersburg
Sweden
Switzerland
Tenerife & La Gomera DIRECTIONS
Turkey
Tuscany & Umbria
Venice & The Veneto
Venice DIRECTIONS
Vienna

Asia
Bali & Lombok
Bangkok
Beijing
Cambodia
China
Goa
Hong Kong & Macau
India
Indonesia
Japan
Laos
Malaysia, Singapore & Brunei
Nepal
The Philippines
Singapore
South India
Southeast Asia
Sri Lanka
Taiwan
Thailand
Thailand's Beaches & Islands
Tokyo
Vietnam

Australasia
Australia
Melbourne
New Zealand
Sydney

North America
Alaska
Boston
California
Canada
Chicago
Florida
The Grand Canyon
Hawaii
Honolulu
Las Vegas DIRECTIONS
Los Angeles
Maui DIRECTIONS
Miami & South Florida
Montréal
New England
New Orleans DIRECTIONS
New York City
New York City DIRECTIONS
New York City Mini Guide
Orlando & Walt Disney World DIRECTIONS
Pacific Northwest
The Rocky Mountains
San Francisco
San Francisco DIRECTIONS
Seattle
Southwest USA
Toronto
USA
Vancouver
Washington DC
Washington DC DIRECTIONS
Yosemite

Caribbean & Latin America
Antigua & Barbuda DIRECTIONS
Argentina
Bahamas
Barbados DIRECTIONS
Belize
Bolivia
Brazil
Cancùn & Cozumel DIRECTIONS
Caribbean
Central America
Chile
Costa Rica
Cuba
Dominican Republic
Dominican Republic DIRECTIONS
Ecuador
Guatemala
Jamaica
Mexico
Peru
St Lucia
South America
Trinidad & Tobago
Yúcatan

TRAVEL

Africa & Middle East
Cape Town & the Garden Route
Egypt
The Gambia
Jordan
Kenya
Marrakesh DIRECTIONS
Morocco
South Africa, Lesotho & Swaziland
Syria
Tanzania
Tunisia
West Africa
Zanzibar

Travel Theme guides
First-Time Around the World
First-Time Asia
First-Time Europe
First-Time Latin America
Travel Online
Travel Health
Travel Survival
Walks in London & SE England
Women Travel

Maps
Algarve
Amsterdam
Andalucia & Costa del Sol
Argentina
Athens
Australia
Baja California
Barcelona
Berlin
Boston
Brittany
Brussels
California
Chicago
Corsica
Costa Rica & Panama
Crete
Croatia
Cuba
Cyprus
Czech Republic
Dominican Republic
Dubai & UAE
Dublin
Egypt
Florence & Siena
Florida
France
Frankfurt
Germany
Greece
Guatemala & Belize
Hong Kong
Iceland
Ireland
Kenya
Lisbon
London
Los Angeles
Madrid
Mallorca
Marrakesh
Mexico
Miami & Key West
Morocco
New England
New York City
New Zealand
Northern Spain
Paris
Peru
Portugal
Prague
Rome
San Francisco
Sicily
South Africa
South India
Spain & Portugal
Sri Lanka
Tenerife
Thailand
Toronto
Trinidad & Tobago
Tuscany
Venice
Washington DC
Yucatán Peninsula

Dictionary Phrasebooks
Croatian
Czech
Dutch
Egyptian Arabic
French
German
Greek
Hindi & Urdu
Italian
Japanese
Latin American Spanish
Mandarin Chinese
Mexican Spanish
Polish
Portuguese
Russian
Spanish
Swahili
Thai
Turkish
Vietnamese

Computers
Blogging
iPods, iTunes & Music Online
The Internet
Macs & OS X
Music Playlists
PCs and Windows
Website Directory

Film & TV
Comedy Movies
Cult Movies
Cult TV
Gangster Movies
Horror Movies
James Bond
Kids' Movies
Sci–Fi Movies

Lifestyle
Ethical Shopping
Babies
Pregnancy & Birth

Music Guides
The Beatles
Bob Dylan
Cult Pop
Classical Music
Elvis
Frank Sinatra
Heavy Metal
Hip-Hop
Jazz
Opera
Reggae
Rock
World Music (2 vols)

Popular Culture
Books for Teenagers
Children's Books, 0-5
Children's Books, 5-11
Conspiracy Theories
Cult Fiction
The Da Vinci Code
Lord of the Rings
Shakespeare
Superheroes
Unexplained Phenomena

Sport
Arsenal 11s
Celtic 11s
Chelsea 11s
Liverpool 11s
Man United 11s
Newcastle 11s
Rangers 11s
Tottenham 11s
Cult Football
Muhammad Ali
Poker

Science
The Universe
Weather

stay in touch!

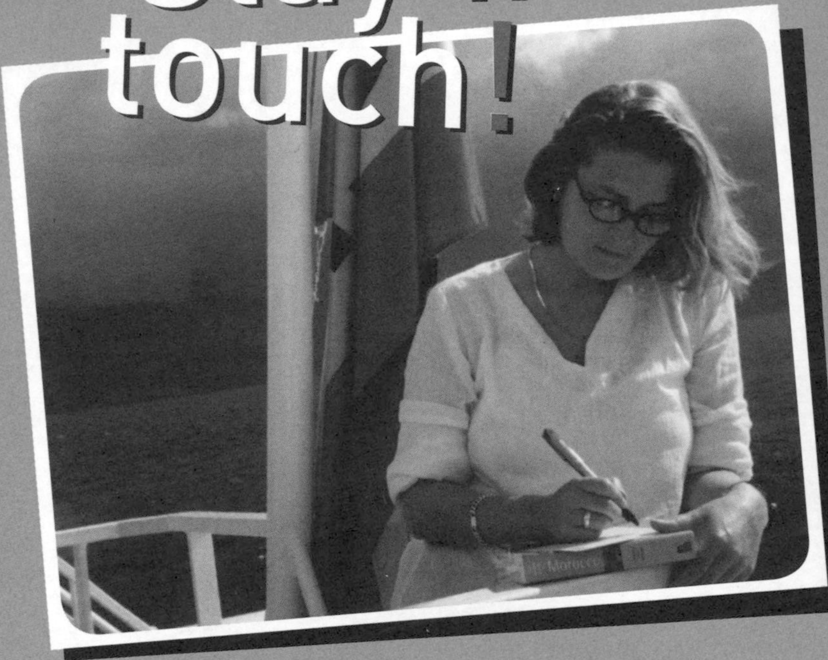

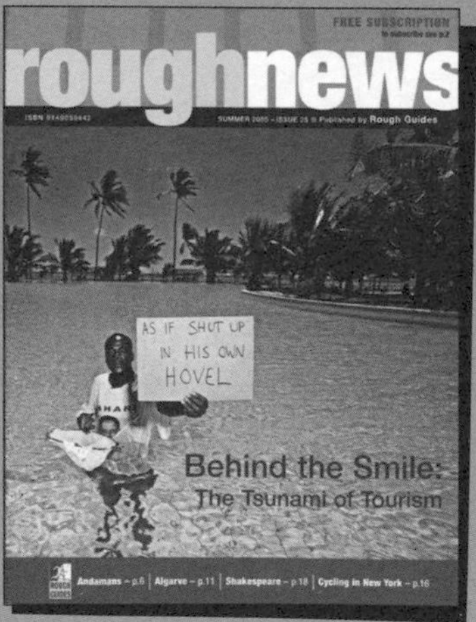

Rough Guides' FREE full-colour newsletter

News, travel issues, music reviews, readers' letters and the latest dispatches from authors on the road

If you would like to receive roughnews, please send us your name and address:

Rough Guides, 80 Strand
London, WC2R 0RL, UK

Rough Guides, 4th Floor, 345 Hudson St
New York NY10014, USA

newslettersubs@roughguides.co.uk

ROUGHNEWS

Small print and Index

A Rough Guide to Rough Guides

Published in 1982, the first Rough Guide – to Greece – was a student scheme that became a publishing phenomenon. Mark Ellingham, a recent graduate in English from Bristol University, had been travelling in Greece the previous summer and couldn't find the right guidebook. With a small group of friends he wrote his own guide, combining a highly contemporary, journalistic style with a thoroughly practical approach to travellers' needs.

The immediate success of the book spawned a series that rapidly covered dozens of destinations. And, in addition to impecunious backpackers, Rough Guides soon acquired a much broader and older readership that relished the guides' wit and inquisitiveness as much as their enthusiastic, critical approach and value-for-money ethos.

These days, Rough Guides include recommendations from shoestring to luxury and cover more than 200 destinations around the globe, including almost every country in the Americas and Europe, more than half of Africa and most of Asia and Australasia. Our ever-growing team of authors and photographers is spread all over the world, particularly in Europe, the USA and Australia.

In the early 1990s, Rough Guides branched out of travel, with the publication of Rough Guides to World Music, Classical Music and the Internet. All three have become benchmark titles in their fields, spearheading the publication of a wide range of books under the Rough Guide name.

Including the travel series, Rough Guides now number more than 350 titles, covering: phrasebooks, waterproof maps, music guides from Opera to Heavy Metal, reference works as diverse as Conspiracy Theories and Shakespeare, and popular culture books from iPods to Poker. Rough Guides also produce a series of more than 120 World Music CDs in partnership with World Music Network.

Visit www.roughguides.com to see our latest publications.

Rough Guide travel images are available for commercial licensing at www.roughguidespictures.com

Rough Guide credits

Text editor: Ella O'Donnell
Layout: Diana Jarvis, Link Hall, Tanya Hall
Cartography: Jasbir Sandhu
Picture editor: Jj Luck
Production: Aimee Hampson
Proofreader: Susannah Wight
Cover design: Chloë Roberts
Photographer: Helena Smith

Editorial: **London** Kate Berens, Claire Saunders, Geoff Howard, Ruth Blackmore, Polly Thomas, Richard Lim, Clifton Wilkinson, Alison Murchie, Karoline Densley, Andy Turner, Keith Drew, Edward Aves, Nikki Birrell, Helen Marsden, Alice Park, Sarah Eno, Joe Staines, Duncan Clark, Peter Buckley, Matthew Milton, Tracy Hopkins, David Paul, Lucy White, Ruth Tidball; **New York** Andrew Rosenberg, Richard Koss, Steven Horak, AnneLise Sorensen, Amy Hegarty, Hunter Slaton, April Isaacs, Sean Mahoney
Design & Pictures: **London** Simon Bracken, Dan May, Diana Jarvis, Mark Thomas, Jj Luck, Harriet Mills, Chloë Roberts; **Delhi** Madhulita Mohapatra, Umesh Aggarwal, Ajay Verma, Jessica Subramanian, Amit Verma, Ankur Guha, Pradeep Thapliyal
Production: Sophie Hewat, Katherine Owers, Aimee Hampson
Cartography: **London** Maxine Repath, Ed Wright, Katie Lloyd-Jones; **Delhi** Manish Chandra, Rajesh Chhibber, Jai Prakash Mishra, Ashutosh Bharti, Rajesh Mishra, Animesh Pathak, Jasbir Sandhu, Karobi Gogoi, Pradeep Thapliyal
Online: **New York** Jennifer Gold, Suzanne Welles, Kristin Mingrone; **Delhi** Manik Chauhan, Narender Kumar, Shekhar Jha, Rakesh Kumar, Chhandita Chakravarty
Marketing & Publicity: **London** Richard Trillo, Niki Hanmer, David Wearn, Demelza Dallow, Louise Maher; **New York** Geoff Colquitt, Megan Kennedy, Katy Ball; **Delhi** Reem Khokhar
Custom publishing and foreign rights: Philippa Hopkins
Manager India: Punita Singh
Series Editor: Mark Ellingham
Reference Director: Andrew Lockett
PA to Managing and Publishing Directors: Megan McIntyre
Publishing Director: Martin Dunford
Managing Director: Kevin Fitzgerald

Publishing information

This 4th edition published June 2006 by **Rough Guides Ltd**,
80 Strand, London WC2R 0RL
345 Hudson St, 4th Floor,
New York, NY 10014, USA
14 Local Shopping Centre, Panchsheel Park,
New Delhi 110017, India
Distributed by the Penguin Group
Penguin Books Ltd,
80 Strand, London WC2R 0RL
Penguin Putnam, Inc.
375 Hudson Street, NY 10014, USA
Penguin Group (Australia)
250 Camberwell Road, Camberwell,
Victoria 3124, Australia
Penguin Books Canada Ltd,
10 Alcorn Avenue, Toronto, Ontario,
Canada M4V 1E4
Penguin Group (New Zealand)
Cnr Rosedale and Airborne Roads
Albany, Auckland, New Zealand
Cover design by Peter Dyer.

Typeset in Bembo and Helvetica to an original design by Henry Iles.

Printed and bound in China

384pp includes index

A catalogue record for this book is available from the British Library

ISBN 1-84353-508-4

ISBN 13: 9781843535089

The publishers and authors have done their best to ensure the accuracy and currency of all the information in **The Rough Guide to Sydney**, however, they can accept no responsibility for any loss, injury, or inconvenience sustained by any traveller as a result of information or advice contained in the guide.

1 3 5 7 9 8 6 4 2

Help us update

We've gone to a lot of effort to ensure that the 4th edition of **The Rough Guide to Sydney** is accurate and up to date. However, things change – places get "discovered", opening hours are notoriously fickle, restaurants and rooms raise prices or lower standards. If you feel we've got it wrong or left something out, we'd like to know, and if you can remember the address, the price, the time, the phone number, so much the better. We'll credit all contributions, and send a copy of the next edition (or any other Rough Guide if you prefer) for the best letters. Everyone who writes to us and isn't already a subscriber will receive a copy of our full-colour thrice-yearly newsletter. Please mark letters: "**Rough Guide Sydney Update**" and send to: Rough Guides, 80 Strand, London WC2R 0RL, or Rough Guides, 4th Floor, 345 Hudson St, New York, NY 10014. Or send an email to **mail@roughguides.com**
Have your questions answered and tell others about your trip at
www.roughguides.atinfopop.com

Acknowledgements

Margo Daly: Special thanks to Linden Hyatt for so much kindness and support at home and in the Hunter Valley; also thanks to Margaret and Arthur Daly, Mahalya Middlemist, Janine Daly and Naomi Parry. Thanks to enthusiastic Sydney updaters Michael Schofield, Tania Paschen, Ann Mercer and Neal Drinnan, and tireless editor Ella O'Donnell and also Claire Saunders. I'm grateful for the assistance provided by Nicole Bradshaw, Jo Banning, Marie Blackmore, Rob McLauglin, Annie and Peter Sullivan, Silke Kerwick of YHA NSW, and the staff of Megalong Books, Leura.

Tania Paschen: Many thanks to Graham Dadd and the truck, for all those runs up the coast, and to Paul Keating, who always knows what's hot and what's not!

Michael Schofield: Thanks to Janine for her map reading and reviews of toilet facilities.

Readers' letters

Thanks to all those readers of the third edition who took the trouble to write in with their amendments and additions. Apologies for any misspellings or omissions.

Marie Barbieri, Catherine Berry, Lisa Brown, Kip Feytag, Max Greenhalgh, Suzanne Genever, Lesley Hustinx, Susan Jackson, Tamara Jungwirth, Ian Knowlson, Robyn Ludwig, Joanna Lynch, Tracy Lynch, Orlaith Mannon, Lorraine Mikhail, Ragnhild P. Sandvik, Andrew Savvides, Frieder Schurr, Leila Shabankarch, David Snowden, Gary Spinks, Fay & Boyd Thompson, Alan Tyrer, Kalie Zervos.

Photo credits

All photos © Rough Guides except the following:

Cover
Front image: North Bondi junior surf lifesaver © Wildlight images
Back image: Sydney Opera House and Harbour Bridge © Getty
Inside cover image: Koala, Sydney © David Wall/Alamy

Title page
Bondi Beach Surfer Mural © Neil Setchfield/ Alamy

Full page
Opera House in Harbour Bridge © Grant Faint/Getty Images

Introduction
Luna Park fun fair © Rob Walls/Alamy

Things not to miss
03 Courtesy sass and bide
04 Cliffs by Settlers Road, Hawkesbury © Abbie Enock; Travel Ink/Corbis
06 Sydney house © DK Images
08 Rocks area at night © Varner Holdings/ Photolibrary
10 Courtesy bills restaurant
13 Vineyard with the Brokenback Ranges in the background courtesy Tourism NSW
14 *The Golden Fleece*, 1894 (oil on canvas) by Roberts, Tom (1856–1931) © Art Gallery of New South Wales, Sydney, Australia
18 Mardi Gras © Network Photographers/ Alamy

Black and whites
p.155 Whale watching © David Wall/Alamy
p.159 Sydney Olympic Park © S.T. Yiap/ Alamy
p.207 Courtesy Blu Horizon
p.222 Homebake Music Festival © Patrick Riviere/Getty Images
p.226 Historic State Theatre © David Wall/ Alamy
p.234 Mardi Gras Parade © Chris McGrath/ Getty Images
p.260 Paddington Market © Network Photographers/Alamy
p.264 Courtesy Sony Tropfest
p.293 Avoca Beach © Photolibrary
p.302 Courtesy of Pepper Tree
p.318 Steam train on Zig Zag Railway viaduct © Robin Smith/Photolibrary
p.326 Jenolan Caves Hotel © Robin Smith/ Photolibrary
p.331 Royal National Park © AustraliaPhotography.com/Alamy
p.338 Bradman Oval, Bowral © Photolibrary
p.348 Aboriginal rock carving of shark © David Hancok/Alamy

Festivals insert
Fireworks over the Sydney Opera House and Harbour Bridge © nagelestock.com/Alamy
"Of Angels and Light" show held at Sydney Festival © Chris McGrath/Getty Images
Australia Day boat parade on Sydney Harbour during Australia Day © Chris McGrath/Getty Images
Tropfest Short Film Festival © Patrick Riviere/ Getty Images
Gay and Lesbian Mardi Gras © Chris McGrath/Getty Images
Saddle Bronc Riding at Royal Easter Show © Jeff Albertson/Corbis
Manly International Jazz Festival courtesy of The Manly International Jazz Festival
Sydney Food and Wine Fair courtesy of Sydney Food and Wine Fair
Seton's Facial Reconstructing, part of the annual "Sculpture by the Sea" exhibition © Greg Wood/AFP/Getty Images
Sydney to Hobart yacht race © Forster/AFP/ Getty Images

Index

Map entries are in colour.

INDEX

N

O

P

Q

R

S

INDEX

INDEX

Map symbols

maps are listed in the full index using coloured text

Expressway
Main road
Minor road
Pedestrianized street
Steps
Path
Railway
Metro Monorail
Metro Light Rail
Ferry route
Waterway
Mountains
Peak
Rocks
Waterfall
Cave
Wine/vineyard
Airport
Place of interest
Museum
Lighthouse
Lookout
Temple
Buddist temple
Monastery
Hut
Campsite
Accommodation
Restaurant
Post office
Information office
Hospital
Statue
CityRail station
Monorail station
Metro Light Rail station
Sydney ferries
Parking
Gate
Fountain
Golf course
Building
Church
Stadium
Park
Christian cemetery
Beach

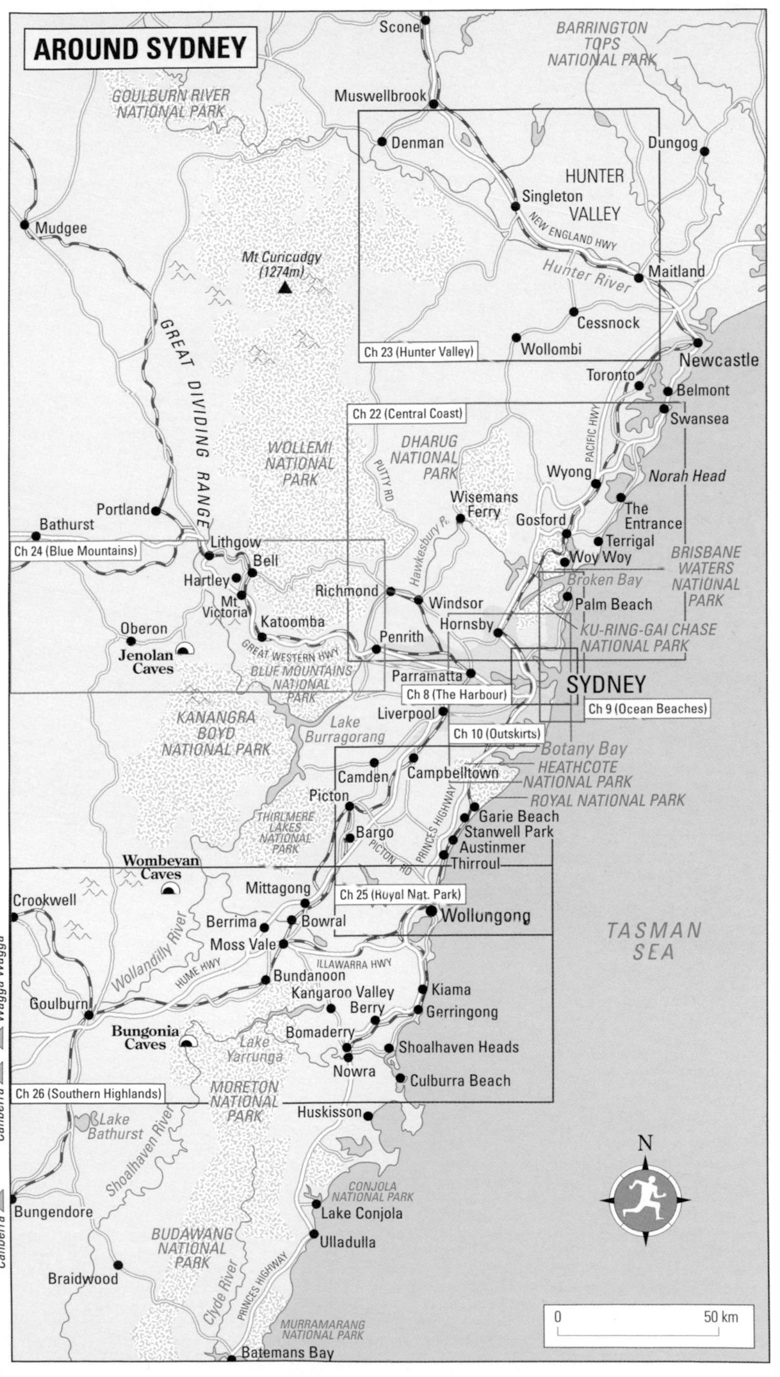

AROUND SYDNEY
Scone
BARRINGTON TOPS NATIONAL PARK
GOULBURN RIVER NATIONAL PARK
Muswellbrook
Denman
Dungog
HUNTER VALLEY
Singleton
Mudgee
NEW ENGLAND HWY
Mt Curicudgy (1274m)
Maitland
Hunter River
Cessnock
Wollombi
Ch 23 (Hunter Valley)
Newcastle
GREAT DIVIDING RANGE
Toronto
Belmont
Swansea
Ch 22 (Central Coast)
WOLLEMI NATIONAL PARK
DHARUG NATIONAL PARK
PUTTY RD
PACIFIC HWY
Wyong
Norah Head
The Entrance
Wisemans Ferry
Portland
Gosford
Bathurst
Terrigal
Lithgow
Ch 24 (Blue Mountains)
Bell
Woy Woy
BRISBANE WATERS NATIONAL PARK
Hawkesbury R.
Hartley
Broken Bay
Richmond
Mt Victoria
Windsor
Palm Beach
Katoomba
Hornsby
Oberon
KU-RING-GAI CHASE NATIONAL PARK
Jenolan Caves
Penrith
GREAT WESTERN HWY
BLUE MOUNTAINS NATIONAL PARK
Parramatta
SYDNEY
Ch 8 (The Harbour)
Ch 9 (Ocean Beaches)
Liverpool
KANANGRA BOYD NATIONAL PARK
Lake Burragorang
Ch 10 (Outskirts)
Botany Bay
HEATHCOTE NATIONAL PARK
Camden
Campbelltown
Picton
ROYAL NATIONAL PARK
PRINCES HIGHWAY
THIRLMERE LAKES NATIONAL PARK
Garie Beach
Bargo
Stanwell Park
Austinmer
PICTON RD
Thirroul
Wombeyan Caves
Mittagong
Ch 25 (Royal Nat. Park)
Crookwell
Wollongong
Berrima
Bowral
TASMAN SEA
Wollandilly River
Moss Vale
ILLAWARRA HWY
HUME HWY
Bundanoon
Kiama
Kangaroo Valley
Goulburn
Berry
Gerringong
Wagga Wagga
Bungonia Caves
Bomaderry
Lake Yarrunga
Shoalhaven Heads
Nowra
Culburra Beach
Ch 26 (Southern Highlands)
MORETON NATIONAL PARK
Huskisson
Canberra
Lake Bathurst
Shoalhaven River
N
CONJOLA NATIONAL PARK
Bungendore
Lake Conjola
Canberra
BUDAWANG NATIONAL PARK
Ulladulla
Braidwood
Clyde River
PRINCES HIGHWAY
0
50 km
MURRAMARANG NATIONAL PARK
Batemans Bay

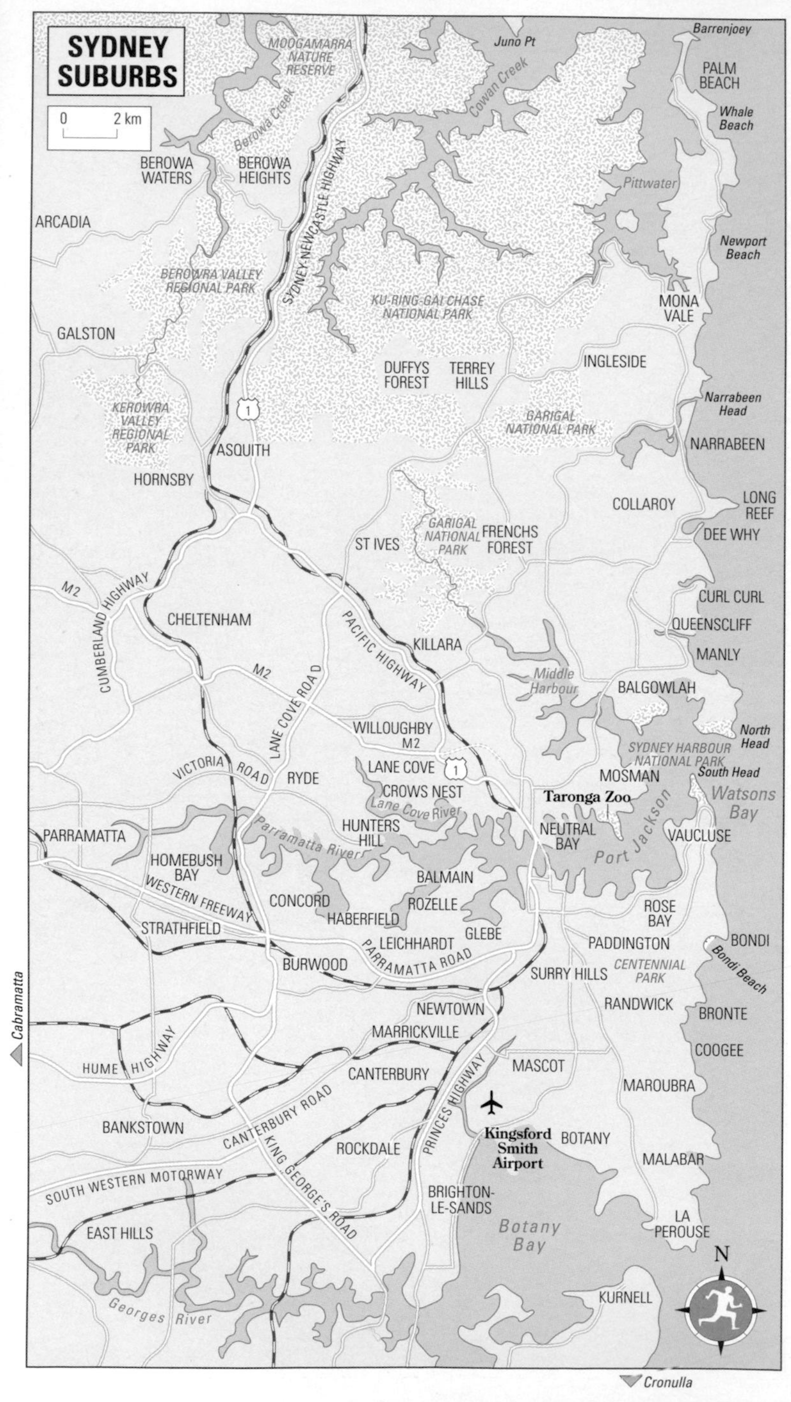
SYDNEY SUBURBS
0
2 km
Moogamarra Nature Reserve
Juno Pt
Barrenjoey
Palm Beach
Whale Beach
Cowan Creek
Berowa Creek
Berowa Waters
Berowa Heights
Sydney-Newcastle Highway
Pittwater
Arcadia
Newport Beach
Berowra Valley Regional Park
Ku-Ring-Gai Chase National Park
Mona Vale
Galston
Duffys Forest
Terrey Hills
Ingleside
Narrabeen Head
Kerowra Valley Regional Park
Garigal National Park
1
Asquith
Narrabeen
Hornsby
Collaroy
Long Reef
Garigal National Park
Frenchs Forest
Dee Why
St Ives
M2
Cumberland Highway
Curl Curl
Cheltenham
Pacific Highway
Queenscliff
Killara
Manly
M2
Lane Cove Road
Middle Harbour
Balgowlah
Willoughby
North Head
M2
Sydney Harbour National Park
Victoria Road
Lane Cove
1
Mosman
South Head
Ryde
Crows Nest
Taronga Zoo
Watsons Bay
Lane Cove River
Port Jackson
Hunters Hill
Neutral Bay
Vaucluse
Parramatta
Parramatta River
Homebush Bay
Balmain
Western Freeway
Concord
Rozelle
Rose Bay
Haberfield
Strathfield
Glebe
Leichhardt
Paddington
Bondi
Parramatta Road
Burwood
Surry Hills
Centennial Park
Bondi Beach
Cabramatta
Randwick
Newtown
Bronte
Marrickville
Hume Highway
Coogee
Mascot
Canterbury
Princes Highway
Maroubra
Canterbury Road
Bankstown
Kingsford Smith Airport
Botany
King George's Road
Rockdale
Malabar
South Western Motorway
Brighton-Le-Sands
East Hills
La Perouse
Botany Bay
N
Kurnell
Georges River
Cronulla

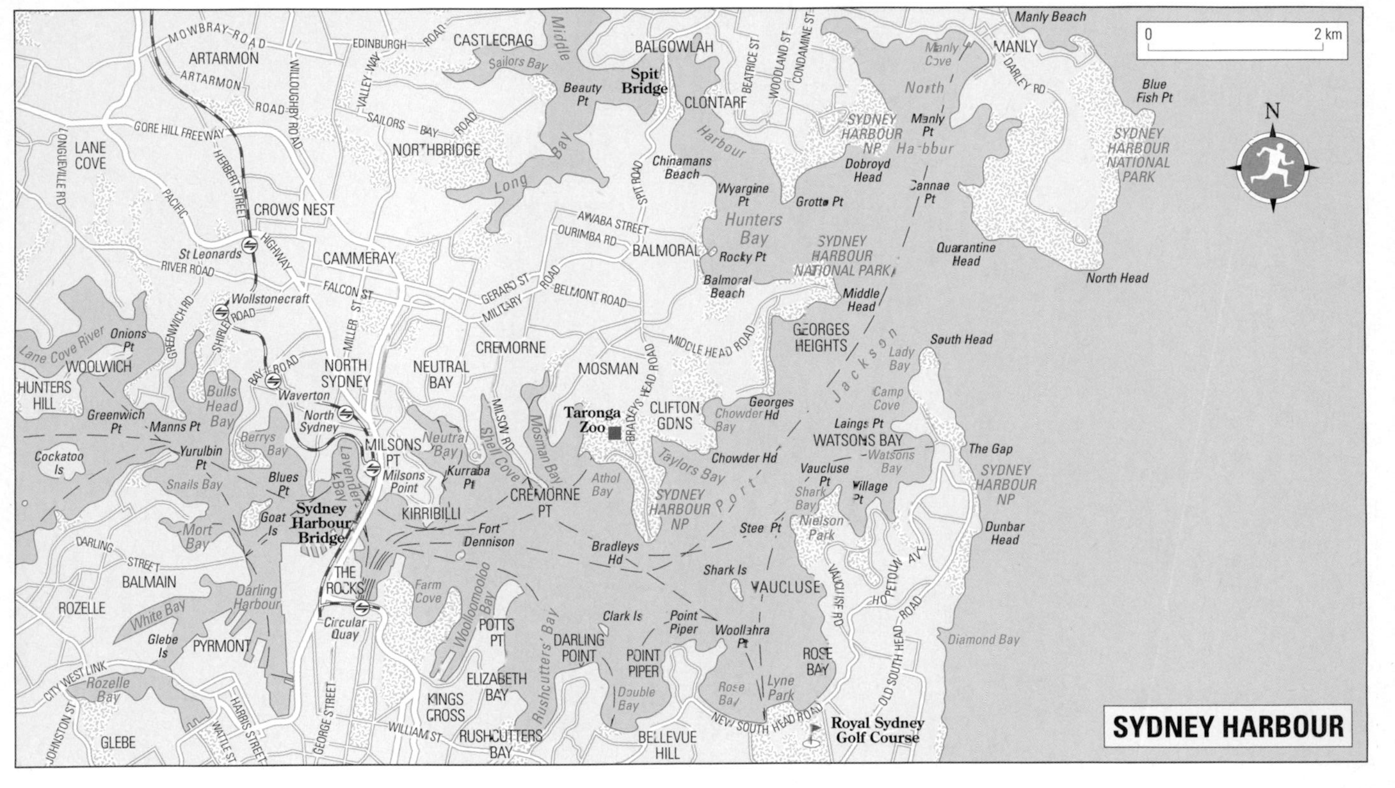
SYDNEY HARBOUR
0
2 km
N
Manly Beach
MANLY
Manly Cove
North Harbour
DARLEY RD
Blue Fish Pt
SYDNEY HARBOUR NATIONAL PARK
North Head
Quarantine Head
Cannae Pt
Manly Pt
SYDNEY HARBOUR NP
Dobroyd Head
Grotto Pt
BALGOWLAH
CLONTARF
Spit Bridge
Beauty Pt
Middle Harbour
CASTLECRAG
Sailors Bay
Long Bay
NORTHBRIDGE
Chinamans Beach
Wyargine Pt
Hunters Bay
Rocky Pt
Balmoral Beach
BALMORAL
SYDNEY HARBOUR NATIONAL PARK
Middle Head
GEORGES HEIGHTS
South Head
Lady Bay
Camp Cove
Port Jackson
Laings Pt
WATSONS BAY
Watsons Bay
The Gap
SYDNEY HARBOUR NP
Dunbar Head
Diamond Bay
Vaucluse Pt
Village Pt
Shark Bay
Nielson Park
Stee Pt
Shark Is
VAUCLUSE
VAUCLUSE RD
HOPETOUN AVE
OLD SOUTH HEAD ROAD
NEW SOUTH HEAD ROAD
Royal Sydney Golf Course
ROSE BAY
Rose Bay
Lyne Park
Woollahra Pt
Point Piper
POINT PIPER
Clark Is
Double Bay
BELLEVUE HILL
DARLING POINT
Rushcutters' Bay
RUSHCUTTERS BAY
ELIZABETH BAY
POTTS PT
KINGS CROSS
WILLIAM ST
Woolloomooloo Bay
Farm Cove
Bradleys Hd
Fort Dennison
Georges Hd
Chowder Bay
Chowder Hd
Taylors Bay
SYDNEY HARBOUR NP
CLIFTON GDNS
Taronga Zoo
Athol Bay
MOSMAN
BRADLEYS HEAD ROAD
MIDDLE HEAD ROAD
CREMORNE
CREMORNE PT
Mosman Bay
Shell Cove
MILSON RD
NEUTRAL BAY
Neutral Bay
Kurraba Pt
KIRRIBILLI
MILSONS PT
Milsons Point
Lavender Bay
Sydney Harbour Bridge
THE ROCKS
Circular Quay
GEORGE STREET
NORTH SYDNEY
North Sydney
Waverton
Wollstonecraft
CAMMERAY
CROWS NEST
St Leonards
AWABA STREET
OURIMBA RD
SPIT ROAD
GERARD ST
MILITARY ROAD
BELMONT ROAD
FALCON ST
MILLER ST
HIGHWAY
PACIFIC
RIVER ROAD
HERBERT STREET
GORE HILL FREEWAY
ARTARMON
MOWBRAY ROAD
ARTARMON ROAD
WILLOUGHBY ROAD
EDINBURGH ROAD
VALLEY WAY
SAILORS BAY ROAD
BEATRICE ST
WOODLAND ST
CONDAMINE ST
LANE COVE
LONGUEVILLE RD
GREENWICH RD
SHIRLEY ROAD
BAY ROAD
Berrys Bay
Bulls Head Bay
Blues Pt
Goat Is
Lane Cove River
WOOLWICH
Onions Pt
HUNTERS HILL
Greenwich Pt
Manns Pt
Yurulbin Pt
Cockatoo Is
Snails Bay
Mort Bay
DARLING STREET
BALMAIN
Darling Harbour
ROZELLE
White Bay
Glebe Is
PYRMONT
HARRIS STREET
WATTLE ST
CITY WEST LINK
Rozelle Bay
JOHNSTON ST
GLEBE

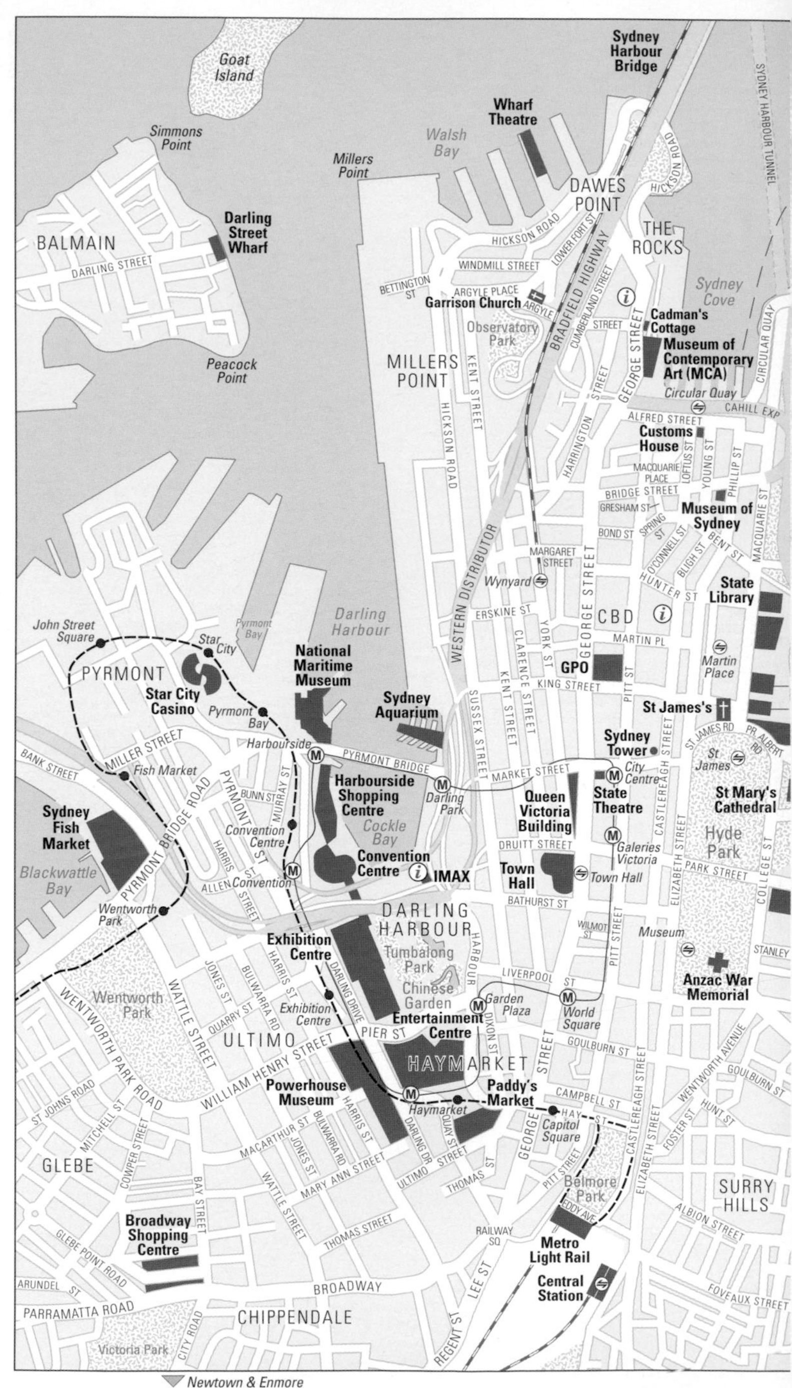

Goat Island
Sydney Harbour Bridge
SYDNEY HARBOUR TUNNEL
Wharf Theatre
Simmons Point
Walsh Bay
Millers Point
DAWES POINT
HICKSON ROAD
BALMAIN
Darling Street Wharf
DARLING STREET
THE ROCKS
LOWER FORT ST
WINDMILL STREET
BRADFIELD HIGHWAY
CUMBERLAND STREET
Sydney Cove
BETTINGTON ST
ARGYLE PLACE
ARGYLE
Garrison Church
Observatory Park
Cadman's Cottage
Museum of Contemporary Art (MCA)
CIRCULAR QUAY
Peacock Point
MILLERS POINT
KENT STREET
GEORGE STREET
HARRINGTON STREET
Circular Quay
CAHILL EXP
ALFRED STREET
Customs House
LOFTUS ST
YOUNG ST
PHILLIP ST
MACQUARIE PLACE
BRIDGE STREET
GRESHAM ST
Museum of Sydney
MACQUARIE ST
SPRING ST
BOND ST
O'CONNELL ST
BLIGH ST
BENT ST
WESTERN DISTRIBUTOR
MARGARET STREET
Wynyard
HUNTER ST
State Library
Darling Harbour
Pyrmont Bay
ERSKINE ST
YORK ST
CBD
John Street Square
Star City
CLARENCE STREET
MARTIN PL
PYRMONT
National Maritime Museum
GPO
Martin Place
Star City Casino
Sydney Aquarium
KING STREET
PITT ST
Pyrmont Bay
SUSSEX STREET
St James's
ST JAMES RD
PRINCE ALBERT RD
Harbourside
Sydney Tower
MILLER STREET
PYRMONT BRIDGE
BANK STREET
Fish Market
MARKET STREET
City Centre
St James
PYRMONT STREET
MURRAY ST
Harbourside Shopping Centre
Darling Park
Queen Victoria Building
State Theatre
St Mary's Cathedral
PYRMONT BRIDGE ROAD
BUNN ST
CASTLEREAGH STREET
Sydney Fish Market
Convention Centre
Cockle Bay
Galeries Victoria
Hyde Park
HARRIS ST
DRUITT STREET
Convention Centre
IMAX
Town Hall
Town Hall
Blackwattle Bay
ALLEN
Convention
ELIZABETH STREET
PARK STREET
COLLEGE ST
BATHURST ST
DARLING HARBOUR
Wentworth Park
WILMOT ST
PITT STREET
Museum
Exhibition Centre
Tumbalong Park
HARBOUR
STANLEY
LIVERPOOL ST
Chinese Garden
Anzac War Memorial
Wentworth Park
JONES ST
BULWARRA RD
HARRIS ST
DARLING DRIVE
Garden Plaza
World Square
WENTWORTH PARK ROAD
WATTLE STREET
QUARRY ST
Exhibition Centre
Entertainment Centre
DIXON ST
WENTWORTH AVENUE
ULTIMO
PIER ST
GOULBURN ST
WILLIAM HENRY STREET
HAYMARKET
GOULBURN ST
Powerhouse Museum
Paddy's Market
CAMPBELL ST
Haymarket
HAY ST
HUNT ST
ST JOHNS ROAD
Capitol Square
FOSTER ST
MITCHELL ST
GEORGE ST
COWPER STREET
MACARTHUR ST
DARLING DR
QUAY ST
GLEBE
ULTIMO STREET
THOMAS ST
WATTLE STREET
MARY ANN STREET
PITT STREET
Belmore Park
SURRY HILLS
BAY STREET
EDDY AVE
ALBION STREET
Broadway Shopping Centre
THOMAS STREET
RAILWAY SQ
Metro Light Rail
GLEBE POINT ROAD
LEE ST
Central Station
ARUNDEL ST
BROADWAY
FOVEAUX STREET
PARRAMATTA ROAD
CHIPPENDALE
CITY ROAD
Victoria Park
REGENT ST
Newtown & Enmore

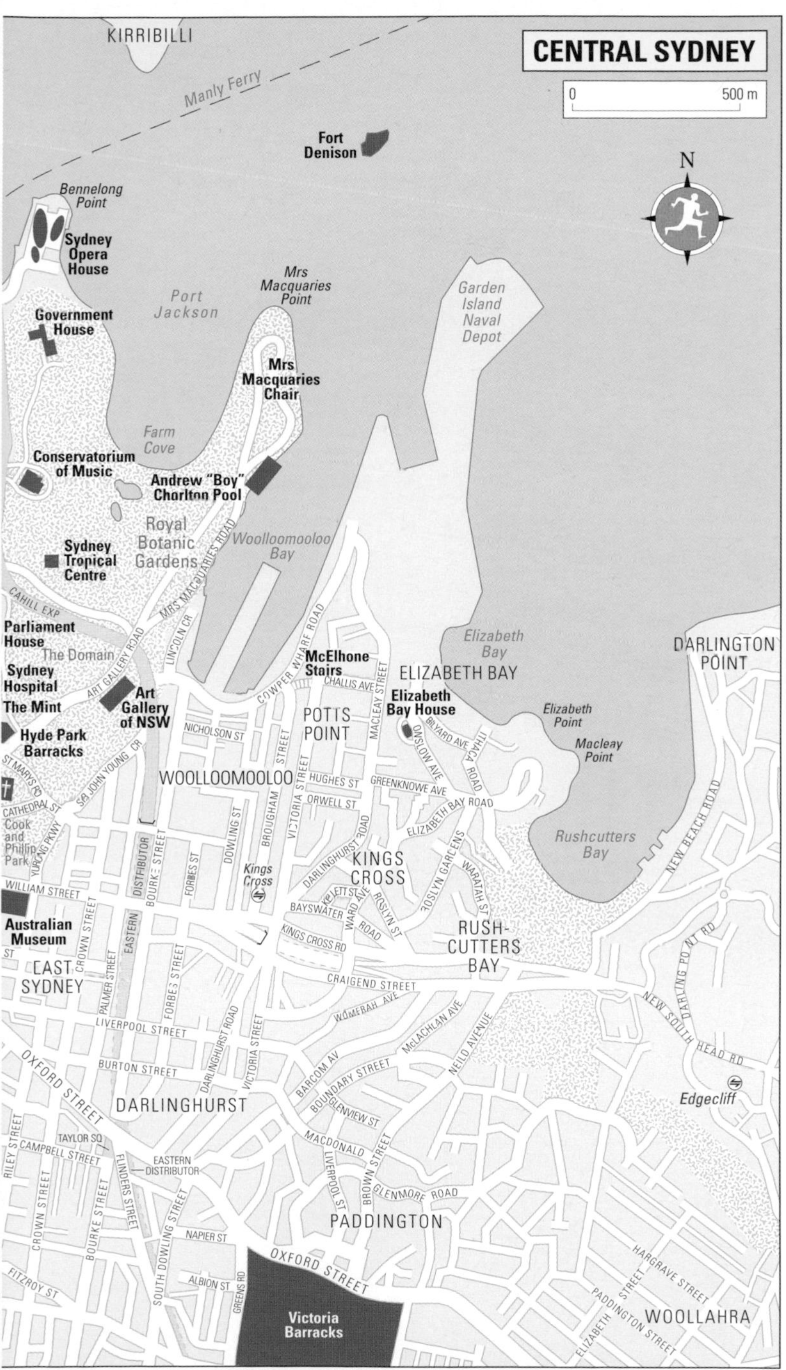
CENTRAL SYDNEY
0
500 m
N
KIRRIBILLI
Manly Ferry
Fort Denison
Bennelong Point
Sydney Opera House
Port Jackson
Mrs Macquaries Point
Garden Island Naval Depot
Government House
Mrs Macquaries Chair
Farm Cove
Conservatorium of Music
Andrew "Boy" Charlton Pool
Royal Botanic Gardens
Woolloomooloo Bay
Sydney Tropical Centre
MRS MACQUARIES ROAD
CAHILL EXP
Parliament House
The Domain
Sydney Hospital
The Mint
Hyde Park Barracks
ART GALLERY ROAD
Art Gallery of NSW
LINCOLN CR
COWPER WHARF ROAD
McElhone Stairs
CHALLIS AVE
MACLEAY STREET
Elizabeth Bay
ELIZABETH BAY
Elizabeth Bay House
DARLINGTON POINT
Elizabeth Point
Macleay Point
POTTS POINT
NICHOLSON ST
ST MARYS RD
SIR JOHN YOUNG CR
WOOLLOOMOOLOO
HUGHES ST
GREENKNOWE AVE
ORWELL ST
ONSLOW AVE
BILYARD AVE
ITHACA ROAD
ELIZABETH BAY ROAD
Rushcutters Bay
NEW BEACH ROAD
CATHEDRAL ST
Cook and Phillip Park
YURONG PKWY
DISTRIBUTOR
BOURKE STREET
FORBES ST
DOWLING ST
BROUGHAM STREET
VICTORIA STREET
DARLINGHURST ROAD
KINGS CROSS
Kings Cross
WILLIAM STREET
KELLETT ST
WARD AVE
ROSLYN ST
ROSLYN GARDENS
WARATAH ST
BAYSWATER ROAD
KINGS CROSS RD
Australian Museum
CROWN STREET
EASTERN
RUSH-CUTTERS BAY
EAST SYDNEY
PALMER STREET
FORBES STREET
CRAIGEND STREET
DARLING PO NT RD
WOMERAH AVE
McLACHLAN AVE
NEW SOUTH HEAD RD
LIVERPOOL STREET
DARLINGHURST ROAD
VICTORIA STREET
NEILD AVENUE
BURTON STREET
BARCOM AV
BOUNDARY STREET
OXFORD STREET
Edgecliff
DARLINGHURST
GLENVIEW ST
RILEY STREET
TAYLOR SQ
CAMPBELL STREET
MACDONALD
BROWN STREET
EASTERN DISTRIBUTOR
FLINDERS STREET
LIVERPOOL ST
GLENMORE ROAD
CROWN STREET
BOURKE STREET
SOUTH DOWLING STREET
PADDINGTON
NAPIER ST
OXFORD STREET
HARGRAVE STREET
FITZROY ST
ALBION ST
GREENS RD
PADDINGTON STREET
ELIZABETH STREET
WOOLLAHRA
Victoria Barracks
SCG
Bondi, Paddington Market & Centennial Parklands

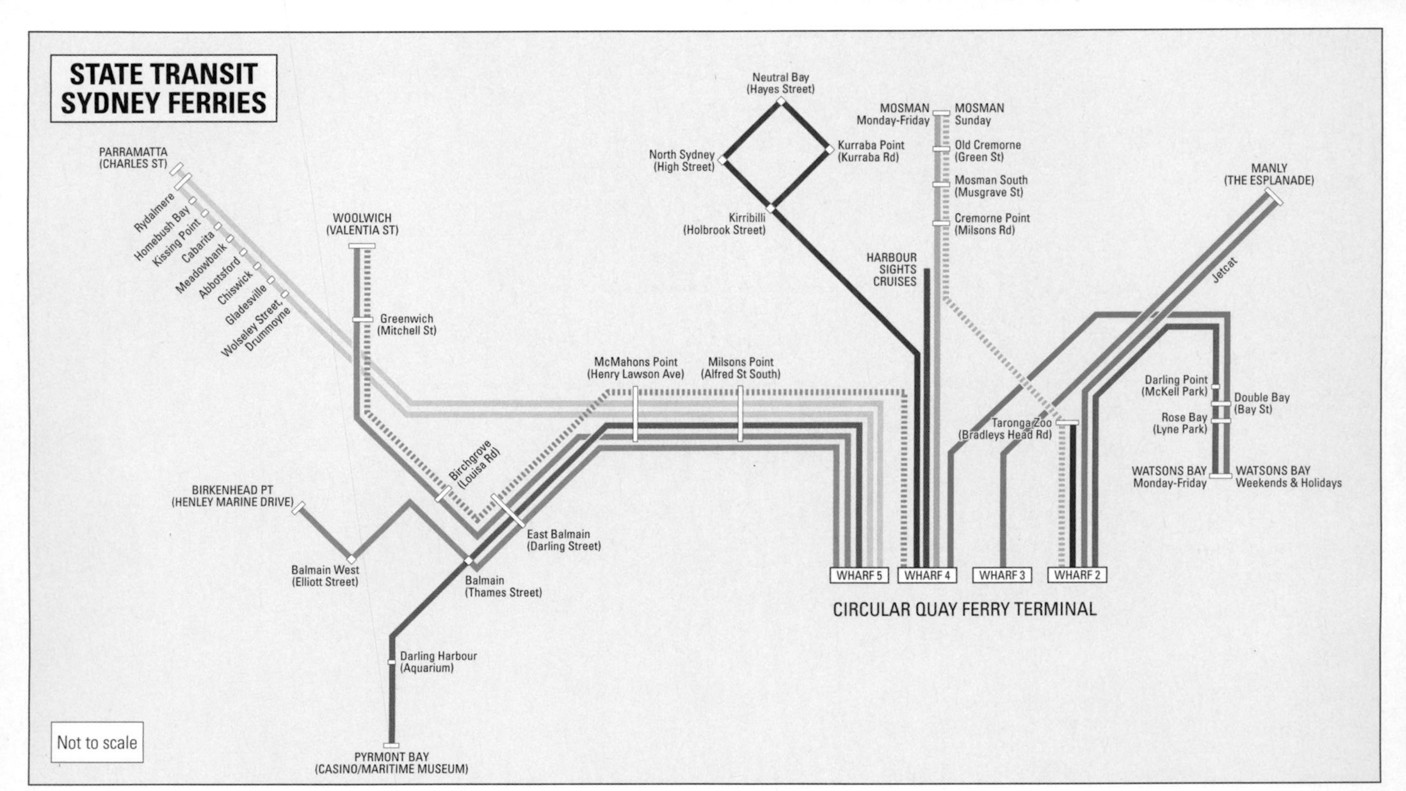
STATE TRANSIT
SYDNEY FERRIES
PARRAMATTA (CHARLES ST)
Rydalmere
Homebush Bay
Kissing Point
Cabarita
Meadowbank
Abbotsford
Chiswick
Gladesville
Wolseley Street, Drummoyne
WOOLWICH (VALENTIA ST)
Greenwich (Mitchell St)
Neutral Bay (Hayes Street)
North Sydney (High Street)
Kurraba Point (Kurraba Rd)
Kirribilli (Holbrook Street)
MOSMAN Monday-Friday
MOSMAN Sunday
Old Cremorne (Green St)
Mosman South (Musgrave St)
Cremorne Point (Milsons Rd)
HARBOUR SIGHTS CRUISES
MANLY (THE ESPLANADE)
Jetcat
McMahons Point (Henry Lawson Ave)
Milsons Point (Alfred St South)
Birchgrove (Louisa Rd)
BIRKENHEAD PT (HENLEY MARINE DRIVE)
East Balmain (Darling Street)
Balmain West (Elliott Street)
Balmain (Thames Street)
Darling Harbour (Aquarium)
PYRMONT BAY (CASINO/MARITIME MUSEUM)
Taronga Zoo (Bradleys Head Rd)
Darling Point (McKell Park)
Double Bay (Bay St)
Rose Bay (Lyne Park)
WATSONS BAY Monday-Friday
WATSONS BAY Weekends & Holidays
WHARF 5
WHARF 4
WHARF 3
WHARF 2
CIRCULAR QUAY FERRY TERMINAL
Not to scale

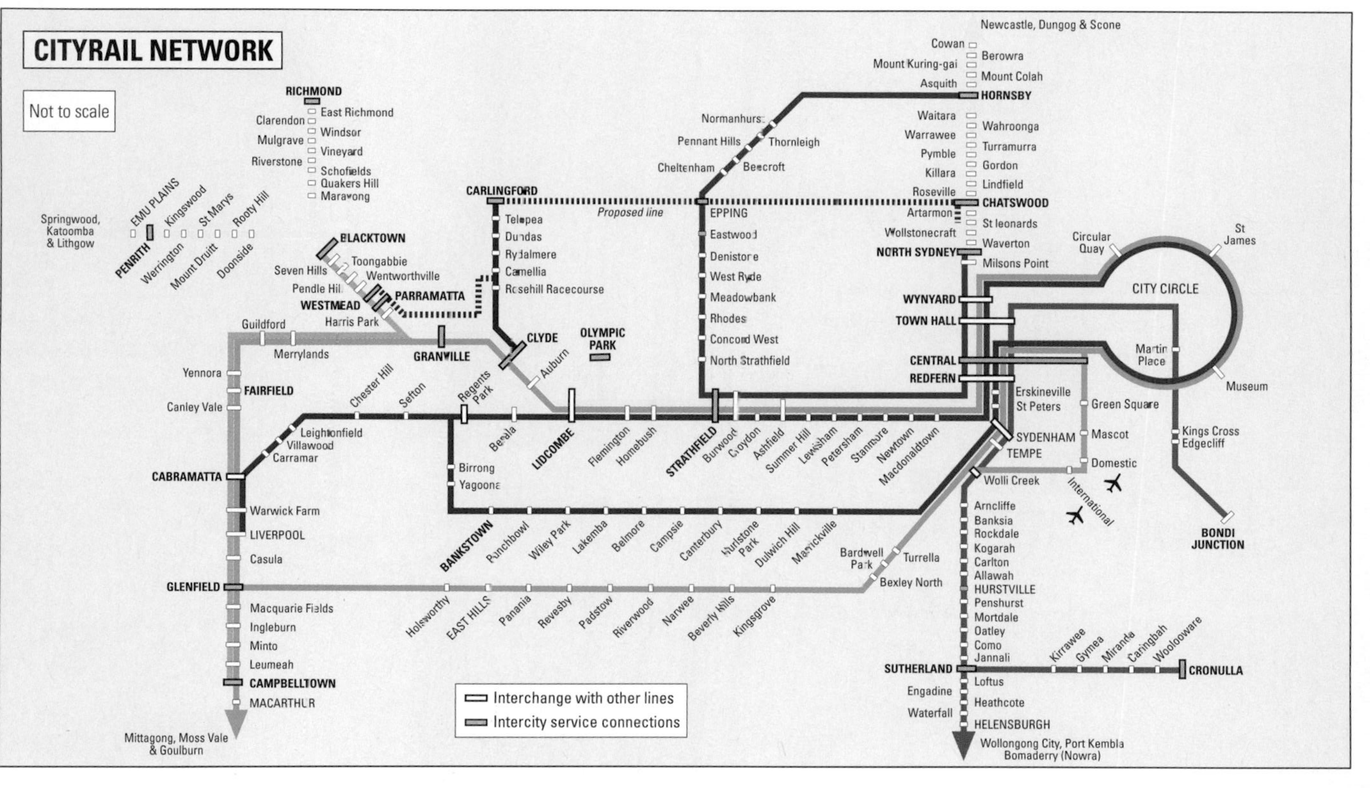

CITYRAIL NETWORK
Not to scale
Newcastle, Dungog & Scone
Cowan
Berowra
Mount Kuring-gai
Mount Colah
Asquith
HORNSBY
Waitara
Wahroonga
Warrawee
Turramurra
Pymble
Gordon
Killara
Lindfield
Roseville
CHATSWOOD
Artarmon
St leonards
Wollstonecraft
Waverton
NORTH SYDNEY
Milsons Point
Circular Quay
St James
CITY CIRCLE
Martin Place
Museum
Kings Cross
Edgecliff
BONDI JUNCTION
WYNYARD
TOWN HALL
CENTRAL
REDFERN
Erskineville
St Peters
SYDENHAM
TEMPE
Green Square
Mascot
Domestic
International
Wolli Creek
Arncliffe
Banksia
Rockdale
Kogarah
Carlton
Allawah
HURSTVILLE
Penshurst
Mortdale
Oatley
Como
Jannali
SUTHERLAND
Kirrawee
Gymea
Miranda
Caringbah
Woolooware
CRONULLA
Loftus
Engadine
Heathcote
Waterfall
HELENSBURGH
Wollongong City, Port Kembla
Bomaderry (Nowra)
RICHMOND
East Richmond
Clarendon
Windsor
Mulgrave
Vineyard
Riverstone
Schofields
Quakers Hill
Marayong
Springwood, Katoomba & Lithgow
EMU PLAINS
PENRITH
Kingswood
Werrington
St Marys
Mount Druitt
Rooty Hill
Doonside
BLACKTOWN
Toongabbie
Seven Hills
Wentworthville
Pendle Hill
PARRAMATTA
WESTMEAD
Harris Park
CARLINGFORD
Telopea
Dundas
Rydalmere
Camellia
Rosehill Racecourse
Proposed line
Normanhurst
Thornleigh
Pennant Hills
Cheltenham
Beecroft
EPPING
Eastwood
Denistone
West Ryde
Meadowbank
Rhodes
Concord West
North Strathfield
CLYDE
OLYMPIC PARK
Auburn
GRANVILLE
Guildford
Merrylands
Yennora
FAIRFIELD
Canley Vale
Chester Hill
Sefton
Regents Park
Berala
LIDCOMBE
Flemington
Homebush
STRATHFIELD
Burwood
Croydon
Ashfield
Summer Hill
Lewisham
Petersham
Stanmore
Newtown
Macdonaldtown
Leightonfield
Villawood
Carramar
CABRAMATTA
Birrong
Yagoona
Warwick Farm
LIVERPOOL
Casula
BANKSTOWN
Punchbowl
Wiley Park
Lakemba
Belmore
Campsie
Canterbury
Hurlstone Park
Dulwich Hill
Marrickville
Bardwell Park
Turrella
Bexley North
GLENFIELD
Holsworthy
EAST HILLS
Panania
Revesby
Padstow
Riverwood
Narwee
Beverly Hills
Kingsgrove
Macquarie Fields
Ingleburn
Minto
Leumeah
CAMPBELLTOWN
MACARTHUR
Mittagong, Moss Vale & Goulburn
Interchange with other lines
Intercity service connections

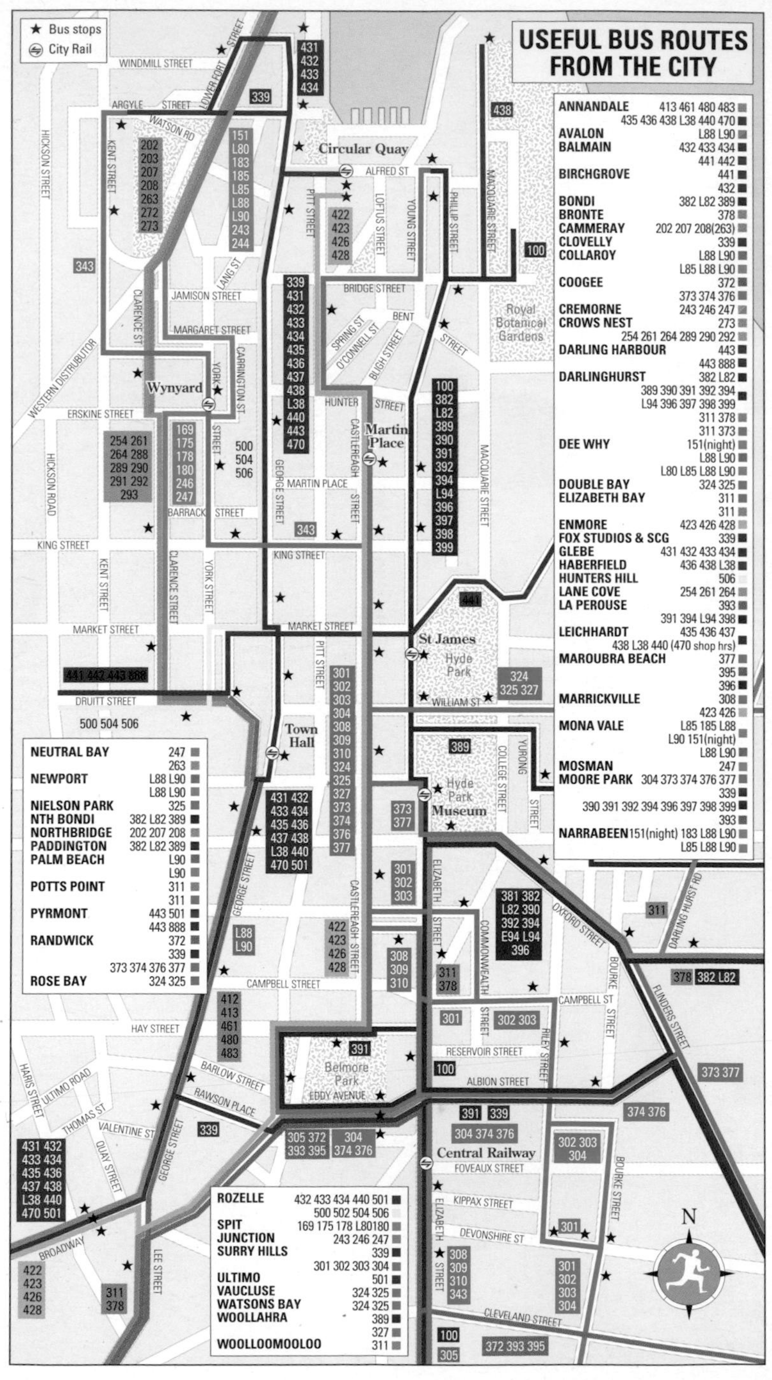

USEFUL BUS ROUTES FROM THE CITY
★ Bus stops
City Rail
ANNANDALE 413 461 480 483
435 436 438 L38 440 470
AVALON L88 L90
BALMAIN 432 433 434
441 442
BIRCHGROVE 441
432
BONDI 382 L82 389
BRONTE 378
CAMMERAY 202 207 208(263)
CLOVELLY 339
COLLAROY L88 L90
L85 L88 L90
COOGEE 372
373 374 376
CREMORNE 243 246 247
CROWS NEST 273
254 261 264 289 290 292
DARLING HARBOUR 443
443 888
DARLINGHURST 382 L82
389 390 391 392 394
L94 396 397 398 399
311 378
311 373
DEE WHY 151(night)
L88 L90
L80 L85 L88 L90
DOUBLE BAY 324 325
ELIZABETH BAY 311
311
ENMORE 423 426 428
FOX STUDIOS & SCG 339
GLEBE 431 432 433 434
HABERFIELD 436 438 L38
HUNTERS HILL 506
LANE COVE 254 261 264
LA PEROUSE 393
391 394 L94 398
LEICHHARDT 435 436 437
438 L38 440 (470 shop hrs)
MAROUBRA BEACH 377
395
396
MARRICKVILLE 308
423 426
MONA VALE L85 185 L88
L90 151(night)
L88 L90
MOSMAN 247
MOORE PARK 304 373 374 376 377
339
390 391 392 394 396 397 398 399
393
NARRABEEN 151(night) 183 L88 L90
L85 L88 L90
NEUTRAL BAY 247
263
NEWPORT L88 L90
L88 L90
NIELSON PARK 325
NTH BONDI 382 L82 389
NORTHBRIDGE 202 207 208
PADDINGTON 382 L82 389
PALM BEACH L90
L90
POTTS POINT 311
311
PYRMONT 443 501
443 888
RANDWICK 372
339
373 374 376 377
ROSE BAY 324 325
ROZELLE 432 433 434 440 501
500 502 504 506
SPIT JUNCTION 169 175 178 L80180
243 246 247
SURRY HILLS 339
301 302 303 304
ULTIMO 501
VAUCLUSE 324 325
WATSONS BAY 324 325
WOOLLAHRA 389
327
WOOLLOOMOOLOO 311
Circular Quay
Wynyard
Martin Place
St James
Town Hall
Museum
Central Railway
Hyde Park
Royal Botanical Gardens
Belmore Park
WINDMILL STREET
ARGYLE STREET
LOWER FORT STREET
WATSON RD
HICKSON STREET
KENT STREET
CLARENCE ST
JAMISON STREET
LANG ST
MARGARET STREET
YORK STREET
CARRINGTON ST
WESTERN DISTRIBUTOR
ERSKINE STREET
HICKSON ROAD
BARRACK STREET
KING STREET
MARKET STREET
DRUITT STREET
GEORGE STREET
PITT STREET
ALFRED ST
LOFTUS STREET
YOUNG STREET
PHILLIP STREET
MACQUARIE STREET
BRIDGE STREET
SPRING ST
O'CONNELL ST
BENT STREET
BLIGH STREET
HUNTER STREET
CASTLEREAGH STREET
MARTIN PLACE
WILLIAM ST
COLLEGE STREET
YURONG STREET
ELIZABETH STREET
COMMONWEALTH STREET
OXFORD STREET
DARLINGHURST RD
BOURKE STREET
FLINDERS STREET
CAMPBELL STREET
CAMPBELL ST
HAY STREET
RESERVOIR STREET
RILEY STREET
ALBION STREET
BARLOW STREET
RAWSON PLACE
EDDY AVENUE
HARIS STREET
ULTIMO ROAD
THOMAS ST
VALENTINE ST
QUAY STREET
BROADWAY
LEE STREET
FOVEAUX STREET
KIPPAX STREET
DEVONSHIRE ST
CLEVELAND STREET
N